P9-AOS-368

Management Accounting: A Decision Emphasis

Management Accounting:

A Decision Emphasis

Second Edition

DON T. DECOSTER
University of Washington,
Seattle

ELDON L. SCHAFER
Pacific Lutheran University,
Tacoma

JOHN WILEY & SONS, INC.
New York Chichester Brisbane Toronto

Library of Congress Cataloging in Publication Data

DeCoster, Don T
  Management accounting

  Includes bibliographies and index.
  1. Managerial accounting. 2. Decision-making.
  I. Schafer, Eldon L., joint author. II. Title.

HF5635.D3 1979   658.1'51   78-16488
ISBN 0-471-04356-7

Printed in the United States of America

10 9 8 7 6 5 4 3 2 1

About the Authors

DON T. DECOSTER, Ph.D., C.P.A. is Professor of Accounting at the University of Washington in Seattle. He holds a Ph.D. in Business Administration from The Universiry of Texas and a Ph.D. in Counseling Psychology from The University of Oregon. He wrote, with William J. Bruns, Jr., *Accounting and Its Behavioral Implications* and with Kavasseri V. Ramanthan and Gary L. Sundem, *Accounting for Managerial Decision Making.* He has published articles in *The Accounting Review, The Journal of Accounting Research, Cost and Management, The Journal of Accountancy, Business Budgeting, The Journal of Vocational Behavior,* and other professional journals. Teaching interests include management accounting at both the graduate and undergraduate level, as well as executive development programs. He has served as both Editor of the Educational Research Section of *The Accounting Review* and Editor of *The Accounting Review.* Research interests focus on the interactions of human beings with the accounting function.

ELDON L. SCHAFER, Ph.D., C.P.A. is Professor of Accounting at Pacific Lutheran University in Tacoma, Washington. He holds a Ph.D. in Business Organization and Management from the University of Nebraska. He taught previously at the University of Washington, Syracuse University, San José State University, and the University of Nebraska. A member of the American Accounting Association, the Washington Society of Certified Public Accountants, and the National Association of Accountants, he has been active in professional development programs in management accounting throughout the United States. He has been engaged in research and writing on financial management of ambulatory health care organizations under a grant from the Center for Research in Ambulatory Health Care Administration.

Preface to Second Edition

This book is an introductory text in management accounting. It is intended to meet the needs of students in a second or third course in accounting. The authors assume that students have had a rudimentary introduction to the basic accounting process of measuring and summarizing business transactions. However, it is not necessary that previous exposures to accounting theory and practice be extremely rigorous.

The authors intend that this book accomplish more than one pedagogical goal. First, the basic framework of the text recognizes that management accounting has moved from the more classical role of accumulating and reporting data to the more complicated role of communicating relevant data for decision making. The purposes of data collection must necessarily converge at that crucial point when a decision is to be made. The organization of this book focuses the student's attention upon the primary purpose of data—decisions by management.

Second, the authors have stayed within the bounds of current management accounting techniques and theories. Since this book is intended for students studying management accounting for the first time, it would be inappropriate to cover advanced topics. The organization and the focus are unique, not the theory and practice covered. Although a few mathematical techniques and current findings from the behavioral sciences are included, they are not emphasized.

Finally, the authors intended to keep the content and explanations clear and understandable to undergraduate or MBA students who may or may not major in accounting. The topics in this book are important to any person who must make business decisions. The authors believe that an understanding of the subject must rest upon active practice by the student. Numerous problems, both simple and complex, are presented at the end of each chapter. The authors hope that the student is challenged and his ability to use management accounting skills enhanced through solving these problems.

CONTENT OF SECOND EDITION

This edition represents a significant revision of the first edition. The revisions include a reorganization of the material to present a new pedagogical approach, chapter rewrites to simplify and increase clarity, and substantial revision of the problem materials. Approximately two-thirds of the problems are new or rewritten. Problem revisions included reducing the number of "questions" from fifteen to ten, adding from five to ten new numerical problems, and an ordering of the problems by level of difficulty. Most chapters have 10 questions, 15 exercises, and 10 or more problems. We have also added a short description to each problem in the text to facilitate homework problem selection. The solutions manual rates the problems by difficulty and provides estimated solution times, just as it did for the first edition.

In the following paragraphs we will discuss the contents of the chapters in the second edition and show how this edition differs from the first edition. In the second edition there are 16 chapters organized into five broad sections. The first section is entitled "Accounting Data for Decision Making." The three chapters in this section introduce the student to the decision process by discussing the planning and control process and the role of fixed and variable costs in decision making.

Chapter 1, "The Planning and Control Process for Decision Making," sets the stage by providing a planning and control framework through a review of the nature of the decision process and the types of decisions that business management must make. This chapter, substantially revised by elimination of the microeconomic theory that appeared in the first edition, is much simpler and easier for the student to follow than it was earlier.

Chapter 2, "Determining Cost Behavior Patterns," includes definitions of fixed and variable costs and a detailed discussion of the methods accountants use to measure and evaluate cost behavior patterns. This revised chapter is essentially the first half of the original Chapter 2.

Chapter 3, "Cost-Volume-Profit Interaction for Operating Decisions," which is primarily the last half of the old Chapter 2, discusses the role of fixed and variable costs in decision making by focusing upon the breakeven point and the contribution margin.

The second section is entitled "Systems for Product Costing." The four chapters in this section introduce the student to the current accounting methodologies of data gathering and selection with a minimum of bookkeeping. These four chapters represent a departure from the more traditional textbook presentation. Since it is generally accepted among management accountants that variable costing is preferred for management decision making, these chapters emphasize variable costing for data collection. Then, for external financial reports, the variable costing systems are converted to absorption costing systems. Our experience is that this approach is considerably more logical to the student and enables him to acquire a thorough understanding of both absorption and variable costing. The teacher is spared the embarrassing position of first teaching absorption costing and then having to say "this is a less valuable system for decision making than variable costing, which we haven't emphasized."

Chapter 4, "Cost Flows for Product Costing," is a discussion of the differences between variable and absorption costing, their strengths and weaknesses, and the position of the various accounting organizations toward these cost flow systems. Essentially, this is Chapter 5 from the first edition.

Chapter 5, "Variable Historical Costing for Recording Past Costs," concentrates on how historical accounting creates the flow of costs necessary for measuring production costs. Both job order and process costing are illustrated using variable costing. The conversion from variable to absorption costing is also illustrated. This revision simplifies the process costing while adding FIFO cost flow to the weighted average discussion in the first edition.

Chapter 6, "Variable Standard Costing for Cost Efficiency," introduces standard cost systems. Emphasis is placed upon setting standards, operating a standard cost system, and understanding variable standard cost variances. This is a simplification of Chapter 11 in the first edition since it covers only variable standard costing.

Chapter 7, "Overhead and Absorption Costing," deals with the problems of indirect overhead costs. Special emphasis is placed upon predetermined overhead rates for absorption costing and the analysis of overhead variances. The illustration of standard costs from Chapter 6 is carried forward to this chapter to contrast variable and absorption costing. This is a substantial revision of Chapter 4 in the first edition.

The third section is entitled "Planning and Control Systems for Decision Implementation." The focus in this section is upon integrating decision data into a meaningful, coordinated package via the budgetary process.

Chapter 8, "Budgeting: A Systematic Approach to Planning," develops the master budget using a single company as an example. The focus of this chapter is budgeting through responsibility centers, as contrasted with most books which develop budgets by product line. This approach is consistent with the overall focus of this book. This chapter represents a substantial rewrite and condensation of Chapters 10, 12, and 13 in the first edition.

Chapter 9, "Budgetary Control, Responsibility Accounting, and Their Behavioral Implications," is a new chapter (based upon Chapter 14 in the first edition), which relates the budgetary process to the budgetary reporting system. Throughout the budgetary reporting system, responsibility accounting is stressed. The organizational and human sides of the budget are also discussed.

Chapter 10, "Measurement of Divisional Performance," deals with problems that are unique to larger, decentralized organizations. Problems discussed include divisional profits, intercompany transfer pricing, and divisional rates of return. This is essentially Chapter 15 from the first edition.

Part Four is entitled "The Use of Data in Making Operating Decisions." The three chapters in this section focus upon the data needed for specific types of short-range decisions.

Chapter 11, "Revenue and Pricing Decisions," contains a discussion of both economic and accounting approaches to pricing decisions. This chapter is an expansion of Chapter 6 from the first edition.

Chapter 12, "Production Decisions," covers a number of short-range decisions that affect production output and costs including make-or-buy, sell-or-process, and linear programming. This is Chapter 7 from the first edition with minimum rewriting and shortening.

Chapter 13, "Decisions Concerning Resource Levels," is substantially a new chapter written for this edition. The focus is upon working capital management. Topics included are cash budgeting, inventory control, and ratio analysis.

The fifth section, "The Use of Data in Making Capacity Decisions," concentrates upon long-range decisions involving productive capacity and long-lived assets. The present-value model of project assessment is taken as normative.

Chapter 14, "Information for Long-Run Decisions," introduces long-range decisions and discusses the measurement of benefits and costs for long-range decisions, determination of an acceptable rate of return, the effect of income taxes, and an introduction of present-value techniques. This chapter is a rewrite of Chapter 8 in the first edition.

Chapter 15, "Techniques of Investment Analysis," presents the techniques of investment analysis. Various methods are compared and evaluated with emphasis upon those that consider the time value of money. A new section on capital rationing has been added. This chapter is a rewrite of Chapter 9 in the first edition.

Chapter 16, "Planning and Control Systems in Not-for-Profit Organizations," is a new chapter. In the first edition these subjects were located in three chapters; in this edition they have been consolidated into a separate chapter.

Overall, the revisions should provide for a more systematic and logical coverage of management accounting. The ability to focus upon the contribution margin and responsibility accounting throughout the 16 chapters provides a unifying, central theme. At the same time, the requirements for external reporting are adequately covered.

Throughout the text the masculine pronoun is used generally to refer to accountants, economists, and other members of the financial community, simply to avoid the burdensome repetition of *he or she* and *him or her.* Unfortunately, no neuter pronoun has yet been formed. Although we use the traditional masculine reference, we fully acknowledge and respect the involvement of women in the business world—those currently employed and those preparing to enter.

We have been encouraged and supported in our writing by many people. We would like to offer a special word of thanks to many of our colleagues and friends who have read and commented upon the manuscript. First, we would like to thank the formal reviewers: Mohammed Onsi of Syracuse University, Lyle Jacobsen of the University of Hawaii, Eric Noreen of the University of Washington, Michael J. Piasecki of Marquette University, M. E. Moustafa of California State College at Long Beach, W. Thomas Lin of the University of Southern California, and Grant W. Newton of the California State University at Los Angeles. Second, we would like to thank our colleagues who informally assisted us. Among these are Mary T. Soulier of Seattle University, Dwight Zulauf of Pacific Lutheran University, Gary L. Sundem of the University of Washington, and John Waterhouse of the University of Alberta. Third, we would like to add a special thanks to the students and teachers who used the first edition and made many valuable suggestions.

Each of these reviewers made valuable comments and suggestions. We have given serious consideration to each suggestion. Beyond doubt, they had a positive influence on our thinking and we believe their efforts strengthened the manuscript. Of course, we must take full responsibility for the text.

We are also indebted to the American Institute of Certified Public Accountants, the National Association of Accountants, the Institute of Management Accounting, the Society of Industrial Accountants of Canada, and many publishers and companies for their permission to quote from their publications and examinations. Problems from the Uniform CPA Examinations are designated *CPA adapted;* problems from the examinations administered by the Society of Industrial Accountants are designated *Canada SIA adapted;* and problems from the Certificate in Management Accountant examination given by the Institute of Management Accounting are designated *CMA adapted.*

The authors and the publisher welcome comments from users.

Don T. DeCoster
Eldon L. Schafer

Contents

Management Accounting: A Decision Emphasis

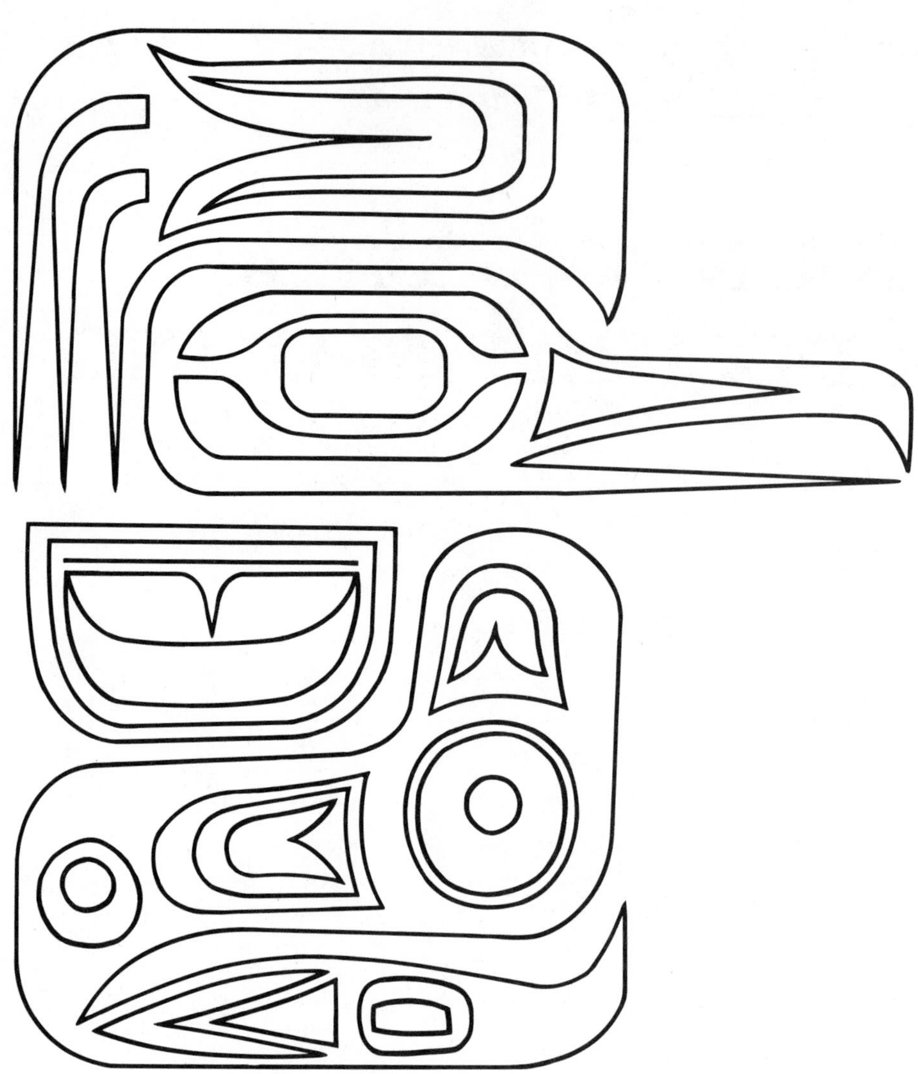

PART 1

ACCOUNTING DATA FOR DECISION MAKING

The Planning and Control Process for Decision Making

ACCOUNTING FOR BUSINESS DECISIONS
- *Interfirm Allocation Decisions*
- *Intrafirm Allocation Decisions*

THE PLANNING STAGE
- *Organizational Goals*
- *Resource Utilization Decisions*
- *Types of Decisions*
- *Benefits and Costs Relevant to Decisions*
    - *Relevant Benefits and Costs for Operating Decisions*
    - *Relevant Benefits and Costs for Capacity Decisions*
- *Decisions Expressed through Budgets*

POST-DECISIONAL CONTROL STAGE
- *Performance Data*
- *Nonfinancial Controls*

THE MANAGEMENT ACCOUNTANT'S RESPONSIBILITIES

SUMMARY

The primary purpose of an economic system is to satisfy the wants and needs of its members by allocating the resources available to meet these needs. In the not-for-profit segment of the economy, particularly governmental entities, the plans for resource allocation are made through the budgetary process. The legislative and executive branches, through their agencies, decide what resources will be used for national defense, maintenance of law and order, recreational and park activities, welfare benefits, and resource reclamation, among others. Once these needs have been determined and budgeted, taxes are levied to support them. It is through the collection of taxes and subsequent governmental expenditures that economic resources are allocated in the public sector.

The decisions of business managers allocate resources in the profit-oriented segment of the economy. Business resource allocations take place at two levels. First, and most visible, are interfirm decisions made in the capital markets, such as the stock and bond exchanges. The flow of resources between firms is determined in part by these markets. Investors commit their resources (funds) to those firms where they believe they can earn an acceptable rate of return on their investment.[1] As the rate of return declines in one economic activity, its capital tends to flow to another that has a higher rate of return. Second, and less visible, are intrafirm decisions. Once resources have been invested in a firm, its managers must make decisions about how best to use them. Efficient use of a firm's resources is necessary if the firm is to earn a satisfactory rate of return and maintain its capital investment.

The role of accounting is to provide meaningful information for both of these resource-allocation decisions. In the broadest sense, accounting is a vehicle for communicating the data necessary for making intelligent decisions. Its task is not the making of decisions. This job is the responsibility of the operating managers within a firm and the investors outside the firm.

ACCOUNTING FOR BUSINESS DECISIONS

Because accounting provides a data base for both types of economic decisions, interfirm and intrafirm, it is logical to assume that accounting data must be multipurpose. The focus of accounting data for *interfirm* resource allocations is termed **financial accounting.** The focus of accounting data for *intrafirm* allocations through the planning and control process is termed **management accounting.** There is much common ground between financial and management accounting. The development of a single system for both financial and management accounting involves overlapping data and common terminology. There are, however, important differences in both data requirements and philosophical approaches to these data.

[1]Rate of return on investment is measured by; Income ÷ Investment. A discussion of rate of return for performance evaluation will be found in Chapter 10; the role of the rate of return on asset additions is discussed in Chapter 14.

Interfirm Allocation Decisions

For interfirm decisions, where the focus is upon the flow of resources between firms, data needs are more general than for intrafirm decisions. Financial accounting directs its attention to the problems of generating and allocating the resources of industry through the capital markets. This application requires that accounting data be useful to people beyond the firm's management structure. Financial accounting data are used by people who do not have access to the data resources or to the accounting system that accumulates, transposes, and reports the data. Thus, data published in the accounting reports must communicate to persons outside the firm. These people include past, present, and future stockholders, bondholders, bankers and creditors, labor unions, governmental agencies, and any others interested in the firm's operations. When the stock of a corporation is publicly held, this information becomes available to anyone seeking it.

Financial accounting data serve two distinct purposes. First, these data serve as an information source for investors and creditors making their investing and lending decisions. Financial reports (statement of financial position, income statement, statement of retained earnings, and statement of changes in financial position) are used by the prudent investor in selecting his investments. They provide clues to the financial security and stability of a firm and point toward the possible result of future operations. Second, for society at large, financial data are used to ensure that a firm has complied with societal regulations and laws.

Examples of the compliance function of accounting data are myriad. To the absentee owner it is important to know that management has acted to protect and conserve the firm's resources. The data should be fair and reliable and show that management is not misusing the firm's assets. Compliance focuses upon the implicit and explicit duties corporate management owes to the owners. Compliance reporting also focuses on general societal needs. For example, financial accounting data are used to meet the legal requirements of federal, state, and city tax-collecting agencies; for registration with stock exchanges and the Securities and Exchange Commission; for reports to the Interstate Commerce Commission and the Department of Commerce; and, more recently, for compliance with Environmental Protection Agency regulations.

When financial accounting data are made available to the public, certain requirements are imposed. First, the users, whether they are stockholders, bondholders, or governmental agencies, typically use these data in their decision-making activities without access to the detailed transactions that are the basis of the summary reports. They must have assurance of a fair and objective presentation of facts. The independent auditor (Certified Public Accountant) serves the function of attesting to the general fairness of the data.

Second, because the financial data serve many diverse interests and people, there is a need for uniformity and standardization. Accounting data would resemble the Tower of Babel without some commonality of terms and language, measurement systems, and methods of presentation. This need for standardization and uniformity has generated many accounting activities seeking to develop a common base of knowledge and, hence, communication. For example, the Financial Accounting Standards Board seeks to develop a common theory of identifying, measuring, and reporting financial and economic events to the public.

Intrafirm Allocation Decisions

Intrafirm operating decisions begin when resources have been committed to the firm. The goal of management accounting is to optimize the use of these financial resources. Typically, the focus of management accounting is specific rather than general. The data demands of the manager are more specific than the data demands of the investor. There must be allocations between products, asset structures, territories, departments, and management responsibility centers.[2] The nature of a specific decision is often well defined so that the data can be pinpointed and decision rules developed. It should be pointed out that it may be relatively simple to determine what data are needed for a decision. This does not mean, however, that the gathering of this information is simple or easy. It may be difficult, and at times impossible, to isolate the data necessary for a particular decision. But management has one advantage that people outside the firm may not have. With access to the sources of events, management can modify the accounting system and reports to meet its unique specifications. This accessibility makes the data flexible and allows the development of specific data for specific decisions.

This text emphasizes management accounting, that is, information that management needs to make specific intrafirm resource allocations. Such emphasis assumes that accounting must perform the two separate, distinct functions of financial and management reporting and that the data needs for each are often different. However, there are common threads that run through both financial and management accounting. Moreover, the societal and legal requirements of financial accounting often act to limit the flexibility of management accounting.

THE PLANNING STAGE

As a philospher once said, "To make no decision at all is to make a decision." Businessmen cannot avoid making decisions, even if the decision is to do nothing. They must choose whether to focus their decision making toward specific goals or merely to react to events as they take place. Without goals, and without data about these goals, decisions will lack purpose. A good management decision will be both effective and efficient. An **effective** decision

---

[2]We will use the term *responsibility center* a few times in a general sense before we give a detailed definition. A responsibility center is an organizational unit where there is specific managerial responsibility for a specific activity and, therefore, for the related costs, revenues, and/or resources.

accomplishes the goals management seeks. An **efficient** decision consumes the minimum amount of resources necessary to achieve the goal.

The following section discusses the nature of business decisions. Three assumptions are implicit in this discussion. First, it is assumed that the firm has scarce, but unallocated, resouces at its disposal. These resources may be financial, such as cash; physical, such as material, equipment, and buildings; or human, such as the time, skill, and energy of people. Second, it is assumed that management desires to make decisions about how to use these resources in an effective and efficient way. Third, it is assumed that the planning process can be generalized and applied to all types of economic entities. Each firm or organization will approach the steps in the process somewhat differently, but we can isolate and study the common thread running through the planning process. Exhibit 1–1 provides a generalized overview of the planning and decision process.

The first step in making a decision is **planning,** which involves the selection of enterprise goals and the development of programs to allocate resources to achieve these goals. Planning is the backbone of effective decision making. The total firm, including the principal segments that comprise it, must have a plan. It is through the planning process that management formulates courses of action that reduce uncertainty about the future and assimilate the many pressures that bear on the firm.

The planning process may be formal or informal. Formal planning is generally superior to informal planning, but informal planning is better than none at all. Formal planning should begin with the development of the firm's goals and a recognition of the individual and societal limitations the firm faces in accomplishing its goals.

Organizational Goals

During her adventures in Wonderland, Alice was walking down a path when she came to a fork in the road. There appeared before her a Cheshire Cat of whom Alice asked:

> "Would you tell me, please, which way I ought to go from here?"
> "That depends a good deal on where you want to get to," said the Cat.
> "I don't much care where—" said Alice.
> "Then it doesn't matter which way you go," said the Cat.
> "—so long as I get *somewhere,*" Alice added as an explanation.
> "Oh, you're sure to do that," said the Cat, "if you only walk long enough."[3]

Without a definite destination any decision will lack purpose—it makes no difference which path you take. Even the energy used in gathering data, such as the energy used by Alice in asking questions, is wasted if it provides no useful information.

[3]Lewis Carroll, *Alice's Adventures in Wonderland,* New Junior Classics, Ed. Mabel Williams and Marcia Dalphin (New York: P. F. Collier and Son Corporation, 1949), V, p. 51.

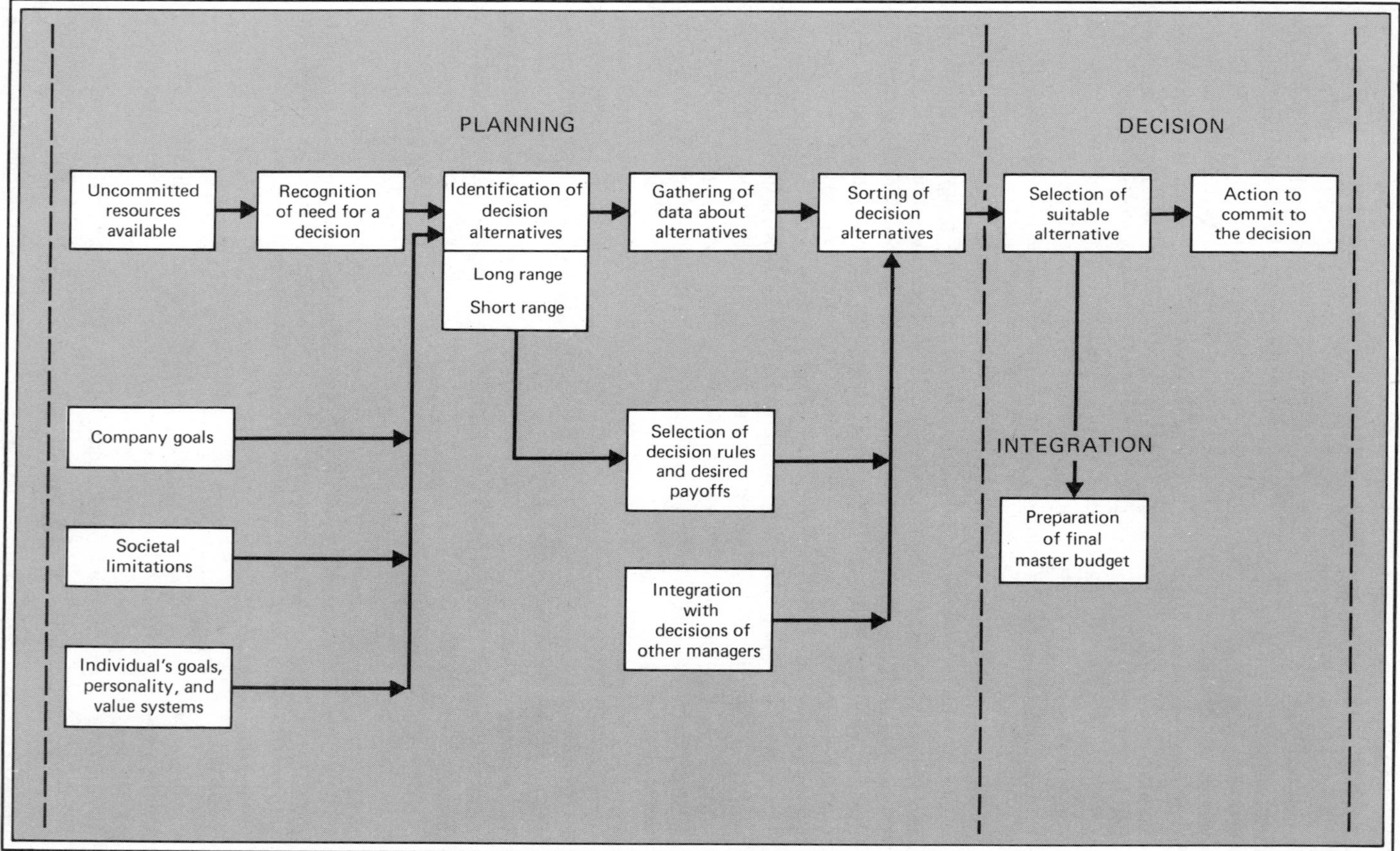

EXHIBIT 1–1
The planning and decision process

Before there can be purposeful decisions, there must be a goal—a direction. The goal is the basic aim of the decision maker. It is the direction toward which all decisions and activities are focused. In capitalistic countries such as the United States and Canada, it is generally held that business activity has the common goal of making a profit. Springing from traditional economic theory, this fundamental goal is often stated directly. At other times the profit goal is implied within broader statements such as "providing a public service" or "providing for the long-run existence of the firm." The assumption is that if a firm provides a useful, sought-after service, it will receive a fair price and profits will result. Similarly, the long-run existence of a firm is assured if it can continue to provide a desired service with an acceptable profit. Certainly, the common element that links all business firms, from the smallest to the largest, is the profit motive.

It would be too simplistic to say that the *only* goal of a business firm is to *maximize* profits, however. There are many goals other than profit. Some managers seek to establish a power base and build an empire. Others seek social prestige and peer-group or public approval. Another goal is security. The removal of uncertainty or ambiguity about the future can often override the pure profit motive. Finally, many individuals and firms have humanitarian goals. Hiring disabled workers, maintaining a clean environment, and providing an enjoyable place to work are examples of humanitarian goals.

For a particular firm many goals must be combined. Absentee stockholders commit their funds to the firm so they can earn dividends and capital gains. Management people, as representatives of the stockholders, also desire a profit. At the same time each manager and worker will have a unique set of personal goals. Within the overriding requirement that the firm earn a satisfactory profit to maintain its existence, managers and workers strive to meet their own goals. These owners', managers', and workers' goals must be combined within the framework of the legal, political, and economic objectives of society.

The problems of combining many diverse yet separate goals into a unified whole should be apparent. Unless management is successful in blending the majority of goals, the firm will operate at cross purposes with society or the workers or the owners. The firm must find a way to achieve adequate **goal congruence.** This need is complicated by the fact that most goals are subjective and unspoken. Further, they are broad and rarely capable of being quantified. Perhaps it is because of the vagueness of many goals that decision makers emphasize the most quantifiable objective—the profit motive.

Resource Utilization Decisions

When a firm has uncommitted resources, or resources that may be shifted from one use to another, a decision in regard to their utilization is necessary. The goals of the firm, as well as any external limitations, act as guides for the managers' decisions. Beginning with these goals there are several planning steps that management should take to ensure an effective and efficient decision.

The first step shown in Exhibit 1–1, once the need for a decision has been recognized, is to define the problem and list decision alternatives. J. Maurice Clark, in his classic, *Studies in the Economics of Overhead Costs,* succinctly summarized the types of resource utilization decisions faced by a firm:

> 1. The plant is not yet built, and the problem is whether the building of a new plant is economically justified or not. . . .
> 2. The plant is not yet built, and the problem is how large to build it. . . .
> 3. The plant is built and in operation, and the problem is whether it is economical to change the methods of production. . . .
> 4. The plant is built and in operation, and the problem is: What income is available for dividends? . . .
> 5. It is estimated that a reduced price will make possible increased sales, and the problem is how cheaply it will pay to sell goods. . . .
> 6. Competition becomes increasingly keen and threatens to cut into the existing sales of the concern. The problem is how low the concern can afford to cut prices in order to hold its business. . . .
> 7. A depression occurs, and the problem arises whether the plant should be shut down temporarily, pending revival. . . .
> 8. It is proposed to develop a side line which can keep the plant and working force occupied during seasons when experience shows that the main product is in slack demand. The problem here is: What are the costs attributable to this side line for purposes of determining whether it is worth undertaking? . . .
> 9. Finally we come to the stage at which the question arises whether this plant is no longer needed, and should be permanently abandoned.[4]

Written more than fifty years ago, this list of possible economic decisions remains provocative and surprisingly complete.

Types of Decisions

The first four decisions listed by Clark call for the generation and commitment of company resources to plant and equipment, whereas the last decision concerns disposing of plant and equipment. Usually these decisions are termed **long-range** or **capacity decisions.** Long-range decisions have two unique characteristics. First, they involve changes in the productive or service potential of the firm. Second, and equally important, they cover a relatively long time span, so their effect on the firm is best measured in terms of cash flow, adjusted for the time value of money. The **time value of money** is a formal recognition of the simple fact that a dollar invested today will earn interest and be worth more later. Conversely, a dollar to be received in the future is worth less today.

---

[4] J. Maurice Clark, *Studies in the Economics of Overhead Costs* (Chicago: University of Chicago Press, 1923), pp. 177–180.

The decisions involving production output, competitive pricing, additions to the product line, and temporary shutdown are **short-range** or **operating decisions.** Each of these decisions spans a short enough time period so the time value of money is not considered significant, although it is present. Further, none involves adding to or reducing production facilities; rather, they involve obtaining the best results possible from existing facilities or resources.

Benefits and Costs Relevant to Decisions

As shown in Exhibit 1–1, after the decision alternatives have been identified, the next step in the planning process is the development of data on benefits and costs of the alternatives. The accounting system is a valuable source of data about the possible alternatives, although it is not the only source. The accounting system accumulates financial data resulting from past decisions. Such data are useful for subsequent decisions if, management is interested in data measured in dollars and believes that past results are useful in predicting the future.

To make an effective and efficient decision, management requires estimates of all benefits and costs relevant to the alternatives being considered. A **relevant benefit** or **cost** is one affected by the decision. A benefit or cost not affected by the decision is **nonrelevant.** A nonrelevant benefit or cost can be ignored in making a decision because it will not change as a result of that decision. The ability to distinguish between which benefits and costs are relevant and which are nonrelevant underlies any effective decision.

To illustrate the concept of relevant benefits and costs, let's take a simple example. John is currently working in a lumber yard. He is considering returning to college. What data are relevant to his decision? Obviously, the added costs of tuition, books, and school fees are relevant. How about his room and board? Since he is self-supporting, he would incur room and board costs whether he went to school or continued working at the lumber yard. Only the difference, if any, in room and board between the two alternatives would be relevant. If he could continue to live in the same boardinghouse, his costs of room and board would be nonrelevant. More difficult to estimate are the benefits of the two alternatives. If he goes to college, he must forego the revenue he would earn at the lumber yard. Economists and accountants call this foregone revenue an **opportunity cost.** However, if he continues to work at the lumber yard, he might earn less in later years than he would if he were a college graduate. It is the difference in income across time that is relevant to his decision.

To illustrate relevant and nonrelevant benefits and costs in a business setting, let's assume that the Bradford Company recently spent $100,000 to purchase a building with an estimated useful life of 10 years. The firm has two alternative uses for the building. One alternative is to lease it to another company for a flat monthly rental fee. The second alternative is to store inventory in the building. In this illustration, the depreciation charges are nonrelevant since they will not be affected by either choice. Only the differences in maintenance and operating costs are relevant costs to compare with the alternative benefits of a monthly rental fee or the value of the warehouse as storage space.

Another way of thinking about benefits and costs that is useful for decision making is that of differential benefit or differential cost. A **differential benefit** is the difference in benefits between any two available, acceptable alternatives. A **differential cost** is the difference in cost between any two available, acceptable alternatives. This approach compares the two alternatives directly by looking at the differences between them. The difference in benefits between receiving a commission as opposed to a fixed salary is a differential benefit. The difference in cost between operating a Cadillac and a Pinto is a differential cost. The difference in cost between leasing and purchasing a car is a differential cost. Many accountants also call this process **incremental analysis,** since they are measuring the total "additional" benefits or costs of one alternative over another.

As shown in Exhibit 1–1, the next step in the planning process, after scanning the decision alternatives, is the sorting of alternatives by determining which benefits and costs are relevant. This sorting requires the development of decision criteria or rules. Because long-range decisions are conceptually different from short-range decisions, accountants have developed different decision rules for each. In the next two sections we will develop an overview of these two decision rules. Then, in later chapters, we will look at them in even more detail.

RELEVANT BENEFITS AND COSTS FOR OPERATING DECISIONS

Operating decisions involve choosing alternatives that best use the existing capacity to maximize net income. These short-run choices revolve around two types of decisions: what quantity to produce and what price to charge. If the firm can optimize the selling price per unit and the quantity of units sold, while simultaneously controlling costs, it will maximize net income.

Experience and study have shown that one of the best methods accountants have for determining which costs are relevant and which costs are nonrelevant in operating decisions is to view costs from a perspective of how they change as output changes. Some costs change with output changes; others do not change. Costs that change with variations in output (**variable costs**) are relevant to output decisions; costs that do not change (**fixed costs**) are not relevant.

The understanding of a firm's fixed and variable costs facilitates the measurement of differential costs in operating decisions. In most differential production decisions involving volume output the variable costs are relevant and the fixed costs are nonrelevant. The identification and reporting of fixed and variable cost behavior patterns is a major contribution that the management accountant can make to management decision making.

To measure benefits from operating decisions, the accountant uses the selling price of the items being produced. He assumes that the items can be sold at the average selling price per unit. The difference between the average revenue per unit and the average variable cost per unit is the **contribution**

margin per unit. To illustrate the concept of the contribution margin, let's assume that the Terry Company produces 10,000 units of a single product that sells for an average of $5.00 per unit. Variable cost to produce the product is $2.50 per unit, and variable cost to sell the product is $.50 per unit. Total fixed costs for production and selling are $15,000 per year. The selling price of $5.00 less the total variable cost of $3.00 gives a contribution margin of $2.00 per unit. The **total contribution margin** is 10,000 units × $2.00 per unit, or $20,000. The **contribution margin ratio** is $2.00 ÷ $5.00, or 40%.

The contribution margin approach assumes that the selling price per unit is constant over a relevant range of activity and, therefore, that total revenue is proportional to volume. Total variable costs will also increase in proportion to volume. Thus, the total contribution margin is also proportional to volume. This relationship makes the contribution margin useful in differential production decisions. The accountant's rule for operating decisions is to produce and sell so as to maximize the *total* contribution margin of the firm. This will maximize profits. The greater the total contribution margin, the greater the amount to cover fixed costs and, after the fixed costs are recovered, to contribute to profits.

We can see the effect of the contribution margin approach by examining the comparative income statements of the Terry Company at 10,000 units and 15,000 units presented in Exhibit 1–2. The net income at 10,000 units is $5,000; at 15,000 units net income is $15,000. This $10,000 increase in net income with a 5,000-unit increase in sales volume is the result of 5,000 units of differential sales at $2.00 contribution margin per unit. The fixed costs are not relevant since they do not change with volume. The use of the contribution margin recognizes that both sales revenue and variable costs change in linear proportion to volume. This is also shown in Exhibit 1–3.

TERRY COMPANY
COMPARATIVE INCOME STATEMENTS

	10,000 Units		*15,000 Units*	
Sales Revenue ($5 per unit)	$50,000	100%	$75,000	100%
Variable Costs ($3 per unit)	30,000	60%	45,000	60%
Contribution Margin ($2 per unit)	$20,000	40%	$30,000	40%
Fixed Costs ($15,000 per year)	15,000		15,000	
Net Income	$ 5,000		$15,000	

EXHIBIT 1–2
Comparative contribution margin income statements

In Exhibit 1–3 the total fixed costs do not change with volume. This is shown by the horizontal fixed cost line. Both the total revenue and variable cost lines increase in direct relationship to volume increases. If the quantity sold is zero, the loss is the amount of the fixed costs. As long as the contribution margin per unit is positive, there will be a quantity level where the firm's total revenue will equal total costs. At this point the firm will break even. Beyond the breakeven point the firm will earn a profit. The maximum profit that the firm can earn is at the quantity (volume) available at maximum capacity.

The contribution margin approach, whether in income statement or graphic format, assumes that the revenue and variable costs *per unit* are constant and that the *total* fixed costs are constant. In order to make this statement, the accountant assumes a **relevant range of activity.** This is the volume level over which these simplifying assumptions are considered valid. We will look at this concept in more detail in Chapter 3.

Much of this text is concerned with short-run, or operating, decisions. Chapters 2 and 3 deal specifically with defining and using fixed and variable costs in decisions. Chapters 4 through 10 focus upon accounting systems that generate decision-making information—both historical and planned. In Chapters 11 to 15 we focus directly upon pricing, production, and resource-level decisions.

RELEVANT BENEFITS AND COSTS FOR CAPACITY DECISIONS

As noted earlier, long-range decisions involve adding to or decreasing the productive capacity of the firm. Typically, long periods of time must elapse before the benefits of the decision are fully realized by the firm.

This time element makes the time value of money a significant factor in long-range decisions. Money, like any other resource, has a cost. In long-range decisions this cost is significant. As noted earlier, in short-range decisions the time value of money, while present, does not have a significant impact.

The benefits and costs relevant to a capacity decision are different from the benefits and costs relevant to an operating decision. In the long run, all costs and all cost behavior patterns can be changed because the firm can adjust its productive facilities. Since fixed and variable cost concepts are not meaningful in the long run, accountants use the more basic view of cash inflow and cash outflow to measure benefits and costs. In long-run decisions benefits and costs are measured in terms of their impact on cash, not on accounting net income.

From this perspective, out-of-pocket and sunk costs are meaningful. An **out-of-pocket cost** is one that requires an expenditure of cash as a result of a decision. The expenditure of cash has already been made for a **sunk cost**[5] and

---

[5]The economist often uses the terms *fixed costs* and *sunk costs* interchangeably. In this text they have different meanings.

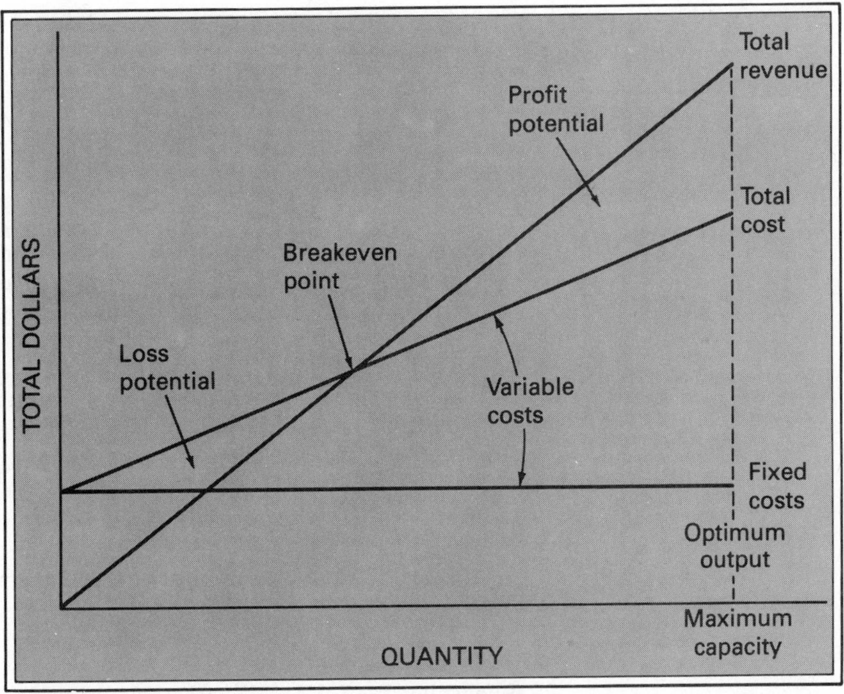

EXHIBIT 1–3
Accountant's total cost and revenue curves

a current cash expenditure is not required. Out-of-pocket and sunk costs are opposites. A sunk cost is a prior investment of cash resources; an out-of-pocket cost is a current or near-future cash expenditure.

Some decision makers assume that all variable costs are out-of-pocket costs and that all fixed costs are sunk costs. This is not so. The president's salary may be fixed, but it is still an out-of-pocket cost. The cost of petroleum to an oil company may be sunk since it has already expended cash resources in obtaining the oil, but it will be a variable cost per gallon of product produced. However, in most instances the costs of depreciation, depletion, and the amortization of intangibles are sunk costs. Likewise, in most instances the costs of material and labor are out-of-pocket costs and are also variable. It is imperative that the decision maker keep in mind that the perspective of fixed and variable costs is different from the perspective of out-of-pocket and sunk costs. While at times they may overlap and appear synonymous, they are not the same view of cost.

A long-range decision must consider both the time value of money and the timing of the investment and recovery of cash. The accountant's long-range decision rule is that an investment decision is favorable if incremental benefits, measured by cash inflows directly attributable to the decision and adjusted for the time value of money, are at least equal to incremental costs, measured by cash outflows directly attributable to the decision and adjusted for the time value of money. The specific techniques of this analysis will be covered in detail in Chapters 14 and 15.

Decisions Expressed through Budgets

As managers begin to select possible alternatives and collect data to facilitate their decisions, they are preparing a **tentative budget.** While they sort the decision alternatives (see Exhibit 1–4) leading to an ultimate selection, they rely upon a forecast of what they believe would happen if they made a certain decision. These forecasts are not final until there is a commitment to a specific decision. They are tentative budgets.

Budgets express management's plans in quantitative terms. Budgets show the probable impact upon the responsibility centers and the firm if plans are committed to action. A budget may be limited to a particular activity, as is an advertising budget or a capital additions budget. It may deal with total operations including expected income, expenses, and assets, or it may be in terms of anticipated cash flow, as in a cash budget.

The planning process begins to take final shape when all tentative budgets for the responsibility centers are integrated. Budgets for each individual decision ultimately must be combined into a coordinated whole called the **master budget.** The master budget expresses the anticipated total impact of all the responsibility centers' decisions upon revenues, expenses, assets, liabilities, and owners' equity. In this function the master budget is the principal coordinating vehicle for the firm's plans. The master budget is shown in Chapter 8.

The master budget also serves another important role. By requiring a formal, written commitment to coordinated decisions, it serves as a benchmark against which actual performance can be compared. This control function acts to ensure that plans and performance are congruent.

POST-DECISIONAL CONTROL STAGE

Control is the process of measuring and correcting actual performance to ensure that the firm's goals and plans are accomplished. Control presupposes the existence of plans. There is no way to know whether the firm is meeting its goals without a previous statement of what is desirable and some feedback on operating results.

Performance Data

The old adage, it's too late to shut the barn door after the horse has run away, is particularly applicable to the control process. A manager cannot control what is past. He may study the effects of past actions, but his focus should be to find ways to avoid unwanted actions in the future. The best control process a manager can install is one that forestalls deviations. The next best control process is one that detects deviations as they happen. The later the report of a need for correction is received after the actual event, the weaker the control system.

Exhibit 1–4 shows the sequence of the control process, which begins with selection of suitable alternatives, and expression of these plans in the form of a final budget. Comparing Exhibit 1–4 with Exhibit 1–1, we can see that the control process begins with the completion of the planning process. Once the desired alternatives have been chosen, there must be definitive action to commit the firm to the decision. Contracts are signed, employees hired, production scheduled, and raw materials purchased.

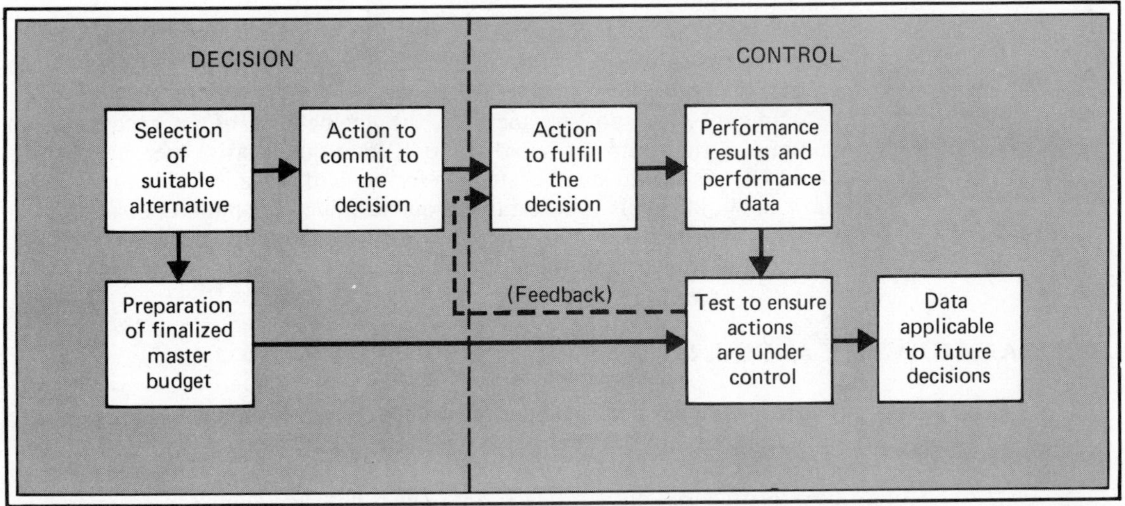

EXHIBIT 1–4
The control process

As these actions are taken, the firm begins to build performance data. Accounting, as a data base, is a major source of performance data. The control process evaluates actual performance by comparing it with the plans. This comparison ensures that actions are under control. Any deviations are communicated to management for corrective action. Simultaneously, a comparison of planned and actual performance serves as the beginning of the next planning process, and the cycle starts again. The control function of budgeting is shown in Chapter 9.

NONFINANCIAL CONTROLS

The preceding discussion may be misleading since it focuses on quantified plans and controls. It is dangerous to assume that *all* plans are quantifiable into a master budget and that *all* performance data are financial in nature. Many activities are planned and controlled through nonfinancial data. The planning process (Exhibit 1–1) and the control process (Exhibit 1–4) are general statements applicable to both quantifiable and nonquantifiable control systems, although our discussion has concentrated upon the financial aspect.

One broad class of nonfinancial planning and control data is comprised of physical measures. These are particularly applicable at the lower organizational levels where materials are used, labor and services are consumed, machine hours are operated, ton-miles of freight are carried, kilowatt hours are consumed, units are produced per direct labor hour, customers are served, or employee turnover exists. The number of possible physical measures is almost infinite.

Many other aspects of crucial importance to the firm's long-run existence cannot be expressed in financial terms. How do you measure, in dollars, an employee's morale or the value of a "team" attitude within a department? How do you measure the competence of an accountant in minimizing the company's tax liability? What quantitative measures can be used to assess the goodwill customers feel toward salesmen? These questions show how difficult it is to establish quantitative plans and controls for *all* phases of busines activities. In many places nonfinancial plans and controls are more useful than financial measures.

THE MANAGEMENT ACCOUNTANT'S RESPONSIBILITIES

The management accountant, often called the **controller,** is the manager of the data base used in decision planning and in the subsequent control of operations. As the manager of the data base, the management accountant must bear in mind that different decisions require different data. Short-run production decisions require different data than long-run decisions do, and external reports require different data than do internal reports. Decisions affecting the total company, such as product lines to be produced, require more aggregate data than do decisions affecting the optimum use of a particular machine. The generation of different data for different decisions requires a high degree of flexibility.

The management accountant is a decision maker himself. He must gather data applicable to others' decisions and data for his own use as well. He must decide how best to structure the accounting system to meet both financial and management accounting requirements. The development of the data base consumes resources of the firm that could be used in other ways. Accounting is an economic activity requiring economic resources. As such, a good accounting system is one where the benefits of having the data exceed the cost of gathering it. Unless data generated by the accounting system are relevant, no effort should be expended in gathering them. Unfortunately, the determination of benefits from accounting data are vague and difficult to measure. An emerging area called **information economics** deals with this difficult topic of benefits and costs of accounting data.

SUMMARY

Management's role is to make decisions about how to use the firm's resources effectively and efficiently so the firm will have a satisfactory rate of return on its investment. These decisions can be classified as either long-range or short-range. Long-range decisions involve adding to or deducting from the firm's service potential. Because long-range decisions span a long period of time, the time value of money is important. The manager's long-range decision rule is to add to productive capacity whenever the cash inflows resulting from the decision, adjusted for the time value of money, are at least equal to the cash outflows resulting from the decision, adjusted for the time value of money.

Short-range decisions are concerned with how best to use existing capacity. They span a short time period, so the time value of money need not be considered. The accountant assumes that within the relevant range of activity both the revenue and variable cost curves are linear and that revenue minus variable costs is the contribution margin.

The process of planning focuses management's attention on needed decisions. Planning involves the determination of the firm's goals and the selection of specific courses of action to achieve these goals. The summary of management's plans is the master budget. The master budget serves as a way of coordinating the firm's plans and as a benchmark to control the effectiveness and efficiency of actual performance.

SUPPLEMENTARY READING

Alex, Marcus, and Charles Z. Wilson. *Organization Decision Making.* Englewood Cliffs, NJ: Prentice-Hall, Inc., 1967.

*Anthony, Robert N. "Framework for Analysis." *Management Sciences,* March/April, 1964.

Anthony, Robert N. *Planning and Control Systems: A Framework for Analysis.* Cambridge, Mass.: Harvard Business School, 1965.

Archer, Stephen H. "The Structure of Management Decision Theory." *Academy of Management Journal,* December, 1964.

*Bruns, William J., Jr. "Accounting Information and Decision-Making: Some Behavioral Hypotheses." *The Accounting Review,* July, 1968.

Ijiri, Yuji, Robert K. Jaedicke, and Kenneth E. Knight. "The Effects of Accounting Alternatives on Management Decisions." *Research in Accounting Measurement,* Ed. Robert Jaedicke, Yuji Ijiri, and Oswald Nielson. Evanston, Ill.: American Accounting Association, 1966.

Kemp, Patrick S. "Accounting Data for Planning, Motivation, and Control." *The Accounting Review,* January, 1962.

Killough, Larry N. "Does Management Accounting Have a Theoretical Structure?" *Management Accounting,* April, 1972.

Steiner, George A. "Strategic Planning in a Changing Environment." *Cost and Management,* January/February, 1971.

Note: All readings listed at the end of the chapters that are preceded by a star (*) can be found in DeCoster, Don T., Kavasseri V. Ramanathan, and Gary L. Sundem. *Accounting for Managerial Decision Making.* Santa Barbara: Wiley/Hamilton Publishing Company, 1978

QUESTIONS

1-1 What purpose should a statement of goals serve in an organization? Does the purpose differ between a profit-seeking organization and a not-for-profit organization?

1-2 What is meant by goal congruence within a firm? Why is goal congruence essential to a successful, prospering organization?

1-3 Although maximizing profit is the most commonly stated objective of business firms, there are other motivations. Discuss the more important nonprofit motivations.

1-4 Making an optimal decision requires careful planning. Outline the steps necessary to make a business decision.

1-5 Define both *long-range* and *short-range decisions,* distinguish between them, and discuss how the data needs between the two differ.

1-6 "While historical data may be suitable for external reporting, they are not suitable for management decisions." Do you agree or disagree? Why?

1-7 "Planning and control are interrelated." Discuss this statement.

1-8 Discuss how the master budget provides flexibility and how it restricts flexibility in the planning and control process.

1-9 "The role of planning is to reduce uncertainty about the future." Discuss this statement. How does a budget help reduce uncertainty?

1-10 Distinguish between financial accounting activities and management accounting activities. Would it be correct to say that the financial accountant is primarily concerned with the control process, whereas the management accountant is primarily concerned with the planning process? Discuss.

EXERCISES

1-11 *(Matching).* Match the following terms and definitions.

1. Goal congruence
2. Financial accounting
3. Responsibility center
4. Operating decisions
5. Management accounting
6. Master budget
7. Contribution margin approach
8. Capacity decisions
9. Goals

A. Statements that provide broad direction for the decision makers.
B. Focus of accounting upon intrafirm resource allocations and optimizing use of firm's resources.
C. The matching and combining of diverse, separate goals into a unified whole.

10. Interfirm decisions

D. Decisions involving productive capacity and spanning a period of time over which the time value of money is important.
E. Decisions involving allocation of resources in the capital markets.
F. Decisions concerning production volume and selling prices of the product.
G. Focus of accounting data necessary for interfirm allocations and for maintenance of capital markets.
H. Result of combining budgets of individual responsibility centers into a coordinated plan.
I. Analysis based upon fixed and variable costs.
J. The organization structure for the classification of costs and revenues to the department responsible for them.

1-12 *(Matching).* Match the following terms and definitions.

1. Relevant range of activity
2. Planning
3. Fixed cost
4. Variable cost
5. Sunk cost
6. Time value of money
7. Out-of-pocket cost
8. Control
9. Information economics
10. Contribution margin

A. Costs that do not change with volume changes.
B. Ensuring that actions agree with plans.
C. Costs that increase proportionally as output increases.
D. The process of deciding upon future actions.
E. Costs that require a cash outflow now or in the immediate future.
F. The process of analyzing the value of data to management.
G. Range of output over which fixed costs are assumed to remain constant.
H. A dollar to be received in the future is worth less than a dollar received today.
I. Net profit plus fixed costs.
J. Costs that do not require a current cash outflow because of past actions.

1-13 *(Long- and Short-run Decisions).* Indicate whether the following are long-range or short-range decisions. Give the reasons for your choice.

1. A manufacturing company is trying to decide whether or not plant expansion is economically justifiable.

2. A wholesaler is considering a decrease in selling price to regain lost markets. Competitors have increased their share of the market.

3. The unemployment rate has increased substantially. The state legislature is trying to decide whether to create jobs through a park-renovation project.

4. Technological advancements in new equipment will drastically decrease production costs. A factory manager is trying to decide whether to purchase the new equipment and change production methods.

5. An analysis of last period's sales shows that some products are declining in sales volume while others are showing growth. The marketing manager is trying to decide which products should be advertised.

6. The price of feed grain has tripled in the past year. A chicken farmer is trying to decide whether to sell his flock or continue to produce eggs.

7. The profit picture looks good for the year. Sales have risen and costs have remained stable, but the increased production has caused a drain on cash. The board of directors is trying to decide how much in cash dividends can be paid without placing the firm in a dangerously low cash position.

8. Demand for the company's product has fallen almost to zero. The president is trying to decide whether to shut down the plant until demand increases or another product is developed.

9. A research institute has found a cure for a disease. The board of trustees is now considering new goals and challenges.

10. The city council of a small town is attempting to decide whether to grant a permit for a new regional shopping center.

1-14 *(Long- and Short-run Goals).* You have just accepted a position as assistant manager of the Eastside Neighborhood Health Center. You will be responsible for nonmedical administration and financial management. The center was organized four months ago to serve the health needs of a low-income neighborhood including a public health project. About 75% of the family heads in the housing project are employed, but many have low incomes.

The center was started with a federal grant and has provided health care for slightly more than two months. The grant will reimburse the center for service provided to low-income families not covered by Medicaid or Medicare.

On your first day of work you are notified by the bank that the center's account is overdrawn. You find that the financial records are limited to a desk drawer full of documents supporting the transactions and a checkbook that has not been reconciled. The federal grant requires a financial report in two months, including cost and utilization data to support the billing rate.

REQUIRED:

A. What should you do? Your answer should cover actions aimed at both the short-range and long-range concerns of the center.

B. State the primary goal of the center as completely as you can.

1-15 *(Data for Planning and Control).* Each division manager of the Brickbat Salvage Company prepares a report on the division for the corporate office. The report must include data on the past year's accomplishments as well as problems facing the division.

Agnes Hummer included the following items in her report for the scrap rubber division.

Division net income forecast for the next year.
Division sales for the past year.
Five-year sales forecast.
Operating expenses for the past year.
Progress report on the new milling plant under construction.
Efficiency study of processing facilities.
Proposed labor contract for the division.
Description of a campaign to reduce the use of paper and other supplies.
Proposal for installation of computer facilities.
Reevaluation of credit policies.

REQUIRED:

Indicate how each of the items selected by Agnes Hummer would be useful in planning, decision making, and control.

1-16 *(Goals and Performance Assessment).* The Mayor of Swamp City formed a Citizens' Task Force to study the operations of the city and make suggestions for better service to the people. He was particularly interested in being able to improve services.

The Citizens' Task Force suggested the following measures of accomplishment for the fire department.

Reduction of fires in the city.
Reduction of losses from fires.
Reduction of fire-related injuries or deaths.
Modernization of fire equipment.
Reduction of fire insurance rates in the city.
Improvement in fire-prevention programs in the area.
Presentation of fire-prevention programs through the schools.
Development of a first-aid unit for the district.
Reduction of number of fund-raising events needed to supplement funding from taxes.
Intensification of training for fire-combat units.
Expansion of fire permit and inspection service.

The fire chief feels that the list is confusing, conflicting, and excessive. He has asked your help in ranking these performance measures and preparing a statement of objectives for the fire department.

REQUIRED:

A. Rank these performance measures in *your* order of priority.
B. State each performance measure as an objective that will provide specific targets for the fire department. (You will not be able to provide specific quantities or dates; therefore use "x" amount, etc.)

1–17 *(Planning Data).* Billy and Bobby recently graduated from Skyking Vocational and Technical College. Billy studied diesel mechanics, and Bobby studied commercial truck driving. They are considering forming a partnership to buy a large sleeper tractor. They plan on hauling the trailers of two moving companies on a contract basis. The dispatcher of one of the companies told them that both he and the other moving company need tractors and drivers.

REQUIRED:

A. What specific data should the two men obtain to assist them in their decisions. Where would you go to get this data?
B. What governmental agencies would likely affect their planning and decisions?
C. What are Billy and Bobby's opportunity costs?

1–18 *(Control Data).* John graduated from high school last year. To earn money for his college education, he took a job with a local bakery, delivering bread. When he took the job, he thought that his salary of $600 per month would allow him to save from $150 to $200 per month, particularly if he lived frugally. After nine months of working, he had been able to save only $300. He was quite disappointed and came to you for help. He had his checkbook, which showed all of his earnings and expenditures. The checkbook was in agreement with the bank and very complete.

REQUIRED:

A. Explain to John why he is "out of control."
B. What specific steps would you recommend to John to ensure that he saves as much as possible?
C. What use will you make of John's excellent historical records in bringing his activities "under control?"

PROBLEMS

1-19 *(Pricing Strategy).* The Bunny Corporation has the following sales volume at each of three selling prices.

Selling Price	Sales in Units
$7	50,000
$6	140,000
$5	260,000

In addition, variable costs are $4 per unit and fixed costs are $125,000.

REQUIRED:

A. What price should be charged to maximize sales?
B. What price should be charged to maximize profits?
C. Why do the answers for Parts A and B differ?

1-20 *(Differential and Incremental Revenues and Costs).* The Sandstorm Corporation prepared the following schedule.

Units	Variable Costs	Fixed Costs	Total Costs	Total Revenue
300	$300	$200	$ 500	$ 900
301	$301	$200	$ 501	$ 903
400	$400	$200	$ 600	$1,200
800	$800	$500	$1,300	$1,600

All units produced are sold.

REQUIRED:

A. At 300 units, what is the differential revenue from selling one more unit? What is the differential cost?
B. What is the difference in costs of a change from producing and selling 300 units to producing and selling 800 units? What is the difference in revenue? Is this an advantageous move to the firm? Explain.
C. As production increases to 800 units, the fixed costs rise and the revenue per unit decreases. What might be the causes for each of these occurrences? If these fixed costs rise, are they really fixed costs?

1-21 *(Decision Making Using Differential Revenues and Costs).* The Spencer Company has an idle production line after discontinuing a losing product. After careful study, the company has narrowed potential new products to two: Zeon and Trion. Only one of the two products may be manufactured on the production line. Revenue and cost estimates for the two products are presented below. In addition to the variable costs for each product, fixed costs associated with the production line are $500.

Zeon			Trion		
Output in Units	*Total Revenue*	*Total Variable Costs*	*Output in Units*	*Total Revenue*	*Total Variable Costs*
50	$ 7,500	$ 6,000	2,000	$4,000	$3,000
60	$ 8,400	$ 6,600	2,100	$4,200	$2,520
70	$ 9,100	$ 7,000	2,200	$4,400	$2,200
80	$ 9,600	$ 7,200	2,300	$4,600	$2,990
90	$ 9,900	$ 9,000	2,400	$4,800	$3,840
100	$10,000	$11,000	2,500	$5,000	$4,750

REQUIRED:
Prepare a schedule that shows management the most profitable product and the optimum quantity of that product it should produce and sell.

1-22 *(Determination of Unit Costs).* The Nipper Company manufactures a barking toy dog. Their income statement for 19X7, when they sold 90,000 units, was:

THE NIPPER COMPANY
INCOME STATEMENT
For the Year 19X7

Sales		$360,000
Variable costs:		
Materials	$54,000	
Labor	90,000	
Sales commissions	36,000	
Total variable costs		180,000
Contribution margin		$180,000
Fixed costs:		
Rent on building	$30,000	
Depreciation of machinery	45,000	
Administrative salaries	65,000	
Total fixed costs		140,000
Net income		$ 40,000

During the planning cycle for 19X8, management forecasted sales volume of 110,000 units.

REQUIRED:
A. Prepare a profit plan (budgeted income statement) for 19X8.
B. Calculate:
  1. The contribution margin per unit.
  2. The differential cost per unit.
  3. The differential revenue per unit.

4. The average cost per unit at a sales volume of 90,000 units.
5. The average cost per unit at a sales volume of 110,000 units.
6. Explain why the average cost per unit in (4) above and (5) above differ.

1-23 *(Long- and Short-run Goals)*. Samuel Johnson founded his business many years ago and through hard work has expanded it to include a manufacturing plant, three retail outlets, and a consulting branch. He now owns 75% of the outstanding stock and acts as general manager. Because of his many years of experience, Sam has a "feel" for the business. He knows approximately how the firm is doing throughout the year. When he feels production is not acceptable, he goes down to the manufacturing department and applies pressure on the employees. Sam believes that each time he purchases a new piece of equipment production should become more efficient and monthly output should increase. Unfortunately, these gains have not occurred.

As the firm has grown, Sam has found it increasingly difficult to keep track of what everyone is doing and where everything is kept. Errors have begun to increase. To make matters worse, the lease on his main retail outlet is about to expire and it cannot be renewed. As a final straw, an economic slump has reduced sales by 20%. Sam obviously has several problems and is faced with some decisions, both long-run and short-run.

REQUIRED:

A. Discuss Sam's methods of managing the firm up to this point.
B. Discuss some decisions, both long-run and short-run, that Sam should be concerned about.
C. What steps would you recommend that Sam take to ensure that his decisions are made wisely?

1-24 *(Long-run Decisions and Company Goals)*. The Smog Flats Foundry is faced with the choice of installing pollution-control equipment or terminating operations. Two pollution-control processes are available and each will meet the clean-air requirements. Economic feasibility studies of the two processes provided the information that follows. (Assume that all data are adjusted for the time value of money.)

Scrubbing unit: A scrubbing unit would be installed in two stages. Stage 1 would be installed immediately, at a cost of $500,000; Stage 2 would be installed in three years, at a cost of $1,500,000. Disposal of the sludge will cost an average of $50,000 per year.

Bag plant: A bag plant would be installed immediately, at a cost of $5,000,000. This process would capture the material previously passed through the smokestack. Approximately 100,000 tons of material per year could be recovered. By processing the emission material, at a cost of $5.00 per ton, it could be sold for $8.00 per ton as a soil conditioner. Assume the life of each process to be 10 years.

REQUIRED:

A. Which process should be installed? Explain.

B. How will the installation of the pollution-control equipment affect the goals of the company?

1-25 *(Financial Statements and Decisions by Financing Agencies).* The Steppen On Sales Company had the financial statements shown here.

BALANCE SHEET
December 31, 19X6

Assets:		Liabilities:	
Cash	$ 5,000	Accounts payable	$10,000
Accounts receivable	20,000	Notes payable	15,000
Inventory	10,000		$25,000
Equipment (net)	15,000	Owners' equity:	
Building (net)	35,000	Common stock	$40,000
		Retained earnings	20,000
			$60,000
		Total liabilities	
Total assets	$85,000	and owners' equity	$85,000

INCOME STATEMENT
Year Ending December 31, 19X6

Sales		$80,000
Cost of sales		20,000
Gross margin		$60,000
Operating expense:		
Administrative expense	$20,000	
Selling expense	5,000	
Depreciation	5,000	
Other	10,000	
Total operating expenses		40,000
Income before taxes		$20,000
Income tax (25%)		5,000
Net income after taxes		$15,000

Management is anticipating a 100% expansion of sales activity which would require an additional $30,000 in capital. This capital could be raised either through increased borrowing or through the sale of capital stock.

REQUIRED:

A. What data included in the financial statements might a bank loan officer use? What additional data would he be likely to want?

B. What data included in the financial statements might be used by an investor in the company's stock? What additional data would he be likely to want?

1-26 *(Data Needs for Decision Making).* The Black Manufacturing Company achieved a technological breakthrough in one of its products. With a limited capital investment, it could double the productive capacity of the main plant while reducing production costs by about one-fourth. The implementation of this breakthrough will require that the plant be closed for about three months. Since Black Manufacturing Company exists in a highly competitive market, the sooner it starts this new process, the bigger the jump it will have on its competitors, who are also working to perfect the same technique.

At this time it is impossible to determine the long-run environmental impact, but there is some evidence to suggest that it may be substantial. To complicate matters further, if Black's competitors implement this new process and Black does not, many of Black's sales will be lost and it will have to lay off 350 to 400 workers. Because unemployment is already high in this area, the city fathers are pressuring Mr. Jason Fleece, Black's owner, to proceed with the new process and worry about the societal consequences later.

REQUIRED:

A. What quantitative and nonquantitative factors should Mr. Fleece consider in his decision?

B. Discuss what accounting data he might need to help him in his decision.

C. How would you go about helping Mr. Fleece in the selection of an alternative from among his possible courses of action?

1-27 *(Individual and Company Goal Congruence).* Duval, Inc. is a large publicly held corporation that is well known throughout the United States for its products. The corporation has always had good profit margins and excellent earnings. However, Duval has experienced a leveling of sales and a reduced market share in the past two years which has resulted in a stabilization of profits rather than growth. Despite these trends, the firm has maintained an excellent cash and short-term investment position. The president has called a meeting of the treasurer and the vice-presidents for sales and production to develop alternative strategies for improving Duval's performance. The four individuals form the nucleus of a well-organized management team that has worked together for several years to bring success to Duval, Inc.

The sales vice-president suggests that sales levels can be improved by presenting the company's product in a more attractive and appealing package. He also recommends that advertising be increased, and that the current price be maintained. This latter step would have the effect of a price decrease because the prices of most other competing products are rising.

The treasurer is skeptical of maintaining the present price when others are increasing prices because it will curtail revenues, unless this policy provides a competitive advantage. He also points out that the repackaging will increase costs in the near future, at least, because of the start-up costs of a new packing process. He does not favor increasing advertising outright because he is doubtful of the short-run benefit.

The sales vice-president replies that increased, or at least redirected, advertising is necessary to promote the price stability and to take advantage of the new packaging; the combination would provide the company with a competitive advantage. The president adds that the advertising should be studied closely to determine the type of advertising to be used—television, radio, newspaper, magazine. In addition, if television is used, attention must be directed to the type of programs to be sponsored—children's, family, sporting events, news specials, etc.

The production vice-president suggests several possible production improvements, such as a systems study of the manufacturing process to identify changes in the work flow which would cut costs. He suggests that operating costs could be further reduced by the purchase of new equipment. The product could be improved by employing a better grade of raw materials and by engineering changes in the fabrication of the product. When queried by the president on the impact of the proposed changes, the production vice-president indicated that the primary benefit would be product performance, but that appearance and safety would also be improved. The sales vice-president and treasurer commented that this would result in increased sales.

The treasurer notes that all the production proposals would increase immediate costs, and this could result in lower profits. If profit performance is going to be improved, the price structure should be examined closely. He recommends that the current level of capital expenditures be maintained unless substantial cost savings can be obtained.

The treasurer further believes that expenditures for research and development should be decreased since previous outlays have not prevented a decrease in Duval's share of the market. The production vice-president agrees that the research and development activities have not proven profitable, but thinks that this is because the research effort was applied in the wrong area. The sales vice-president cautions against any drastic reductions because the packaging change will provide only a temporary advantage in the market; consequently, more effort will have to be devoted to product development.

Focusing on the use of liquid assets and the present high yields on securities, the treasurer suggests that the firm's profitability can be improved by shifting funds from the currently held short-term marketable securities to longer-term, higher-yield securities. He further states that cost reductions would provide more funds for investments. He recognizes that the restructuring of the investments from short-term to long-term would hamper flexibility.

In his summarizing comments, the president observes that they have a good start and the ideas provide some excellent alternatives. He states, "I think we ought to develop these ideas further and consider other ramifications. For instance, what effect would new equipment and the systems study have on the labor force? Shouldn't we also consider the environmental impact of any plant and product change? We want to appear as a leader in our industry—not a follower.

"I note that none of you considered increased community involvement through such groups as the Chamber of Commerce and the United Fund.

"The factors you mentioned plus those additional points all should be considered as we reach a decision on the final course of action we will follow."

REQUIRED:

A. State explicitly the implied corporate goals being expressed by each of the following:
   1. Treasurer.
   2. Sales vice-president.
   3. Production vice-president.
   4. President.

B. Compare the type of goals discussed above with the corporate goal(s) postulated by the economic theory of the firm. *(CMA adapted)*

2 Determining Cost Behavior Patterns

Many factors cause changes in costs and hence in profits. Costs change because of inflationary trends in the economy, changes in the labor market, technological advances, or changes in size or quality of production facilities. Each of these represents a unique, sporadic change. Regular, recurring events also cause costs to change. One of the most significant causes of variations in costs is a change in the volume of activity. In this chapter we will study how the accountant defines and determines which costs are variable and therefore change with volume, and which costs are fixed and therefore remain constant over volume changes. Then in the next chapter we will study how knowledge of fixed and variable costs helps in understanding cost-volume-profit interrelationships and how the contribution margin can be used in making operating decisions.

DEFINITIONS OF COST BEHAVIOR PATTERNS

Variable costs

Variable costs are those that vary in total dollar amount in direct proportion to changes in volume. Increases in production output result in proportionate increases in variable costs. Raw materials used in production typically represent variable costs. If raw materials cost $1.00 per unit of product, it would take a total cost of $1.00 to produce one unit, $2.00 to produce two units, $6.00 to produce six units, and $12 to produce twelve units.

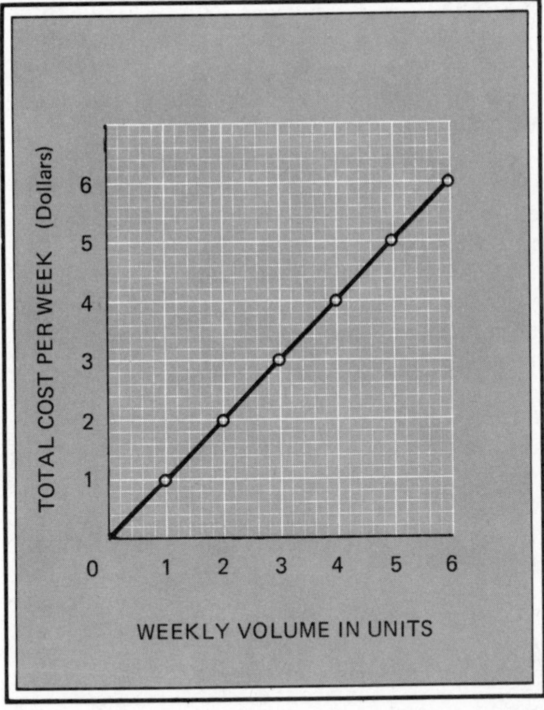

EXHIBIT 2-1
Total variable cost

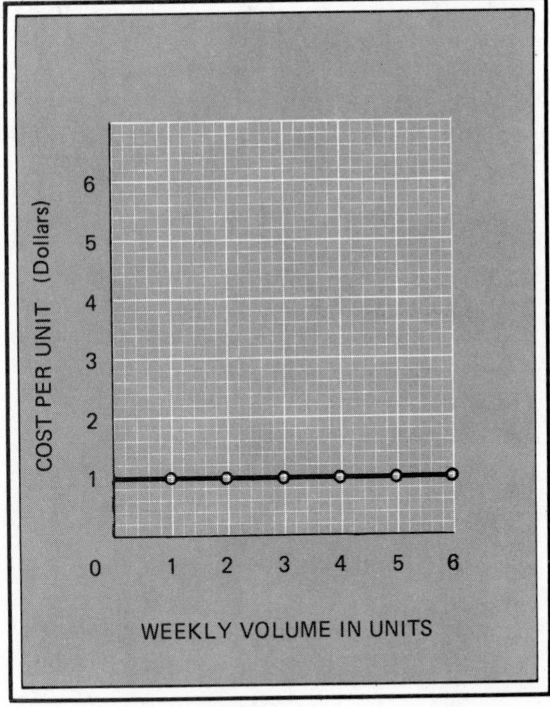

EXHIBIT 2-2
Variable cost per unit

One trait of a variable cost is that while the total variable cost increases proportionately to volume, the variable cost per unit of output is constant. Exhibit 2–1 is a graphic presentation of a completely variable cost that increases at the rate of $1.00 per unit of output. Exhibit 2–2 shows this same cost from a different perspective—that of cost per unit. If the total dollar amount of a cost varies in direct proportion to changes in volume, then it must be constant per unit of production.

Fixed costs

Fixed costs are costs that are unaffected by changes in volume. In the short run they remain the same regardless of changes in production output. For example, assume that plant maintenance is contracted with an outside firm at $600 per week, or $31,200 per year. Regardless of the plant output, this cost will not change. The greater the plant output, the lower the maintenance cost *per unit* of output. If the firm produces 600 units per week, maintenance cost will be $1.00 per unit. If the firm produces only 200 units per week, the cost per unit will be $3.00. Thus, fixed costs are constant in total as volume levels change, but vary per unit inversely with changes in volume. This effect is shown graphically in Exhibits 2–3 and 2–4. Exhibit 2–3 shows a fixed cost of $600 per week. Exhibit 2–4 shows the same fixed cost from a cost-per-unit perspective.

When looking at costs in terms of their behavior patterns (how they change with changes in volume), the time period is held constant. Ordinarily this time span is one year, although it could be any time period selected by management. This consideration puts definite limits on the interpretations of fixed and variable costs. Let's assume that a firm has a machine with a depreciable cost of $1,000 and a useful life of five years. We can see the effect of the assumption of a constant time period when considering cost variability. Management is considering the two alternative depreciation methods of straight-line and sum-of-the-years' digits in accounting for the machine. Exhibit 2–5 shows the annual depreciation charge for each of these assumptions.

In Year 1 the *fixed cost* would be $200 under the straight-line depreciation method, whereas under the sum-of-the-years'-digits method the fixed cost would be $333. Since the amount of depreciation is not related to the volume of production, the costs from either schedule would be fixed although they change from year to year. Thus, costs are fixed or variable only in relationship to volume changes within a given time period.

Semivariable costs

Of course, not all costs are perfectly fixed or perfectly variable. Many costs change with changes in volume, but not in direct proportion. These costs are called **semivariable costs.** They have both fixed and variable cost attributes. Some people call them **semifixed** although *semivariable* is more commonly used.

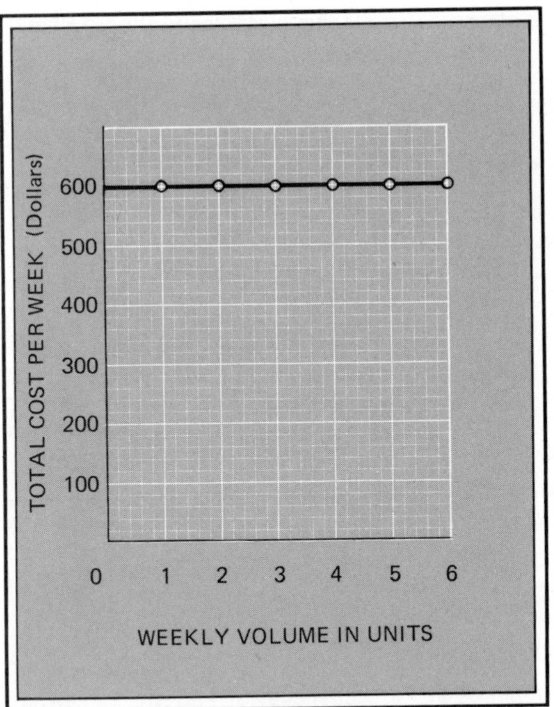

EXHIBIT 2–3
Total fixed cost

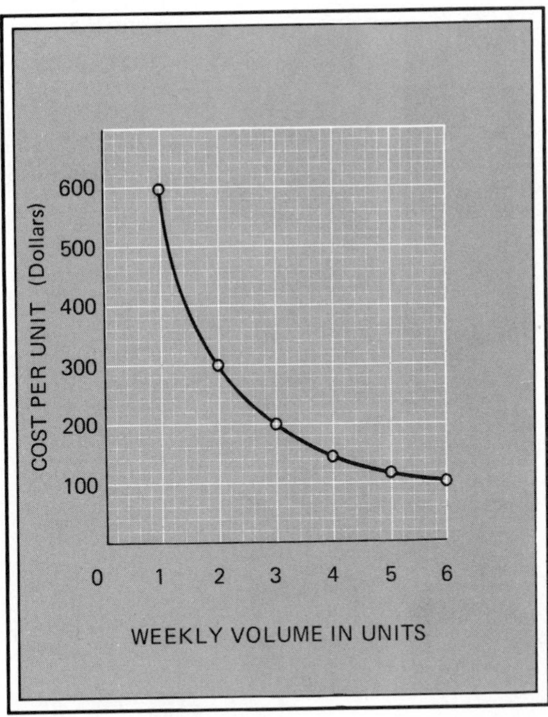

EXHIBIT 2–4
Fixed cost per unit

	STRAIGHT-LINE DEPRECIATION		SUM-OF-THE-YEARS' DIGITS DEPRECIATION	
Year	Annual Proportion of Total Cost	Annual Depreciation	Annual Proportion of Total Cost	Annual Depreciation
1	1/5	$200	5/15	$333
2	1/5	$200	4/15	$267
3	1/5	$200	3/15	$200
4	1/5	$200	2/15	$133
5	1/5	$200	1/15	$ 67

EXHIBIT 2–5
Comparative depreciation schedules

Among the factors that can make costs semivariable are the following:

1. It is frequently necessary to have a minimum organizational structure or to consume a minimum quantity of supplies or services in order to maintain productive readiness. Beyond this minimum cost, which is fixed, additional costs may vary with changes in volume.
2. The accounting classification system may group fixed and variable costs together. For example, by accumulating all insurance premiums into an account entitled "Insurance Expense," the accounting system may group together various types of policy premium costs having different behavior patterns.
3. Often production factors are not divisible into infinitely small units. For example, moving from a single-shift to a double-shift production schedule will cause some costs to change in stairstep fashion.

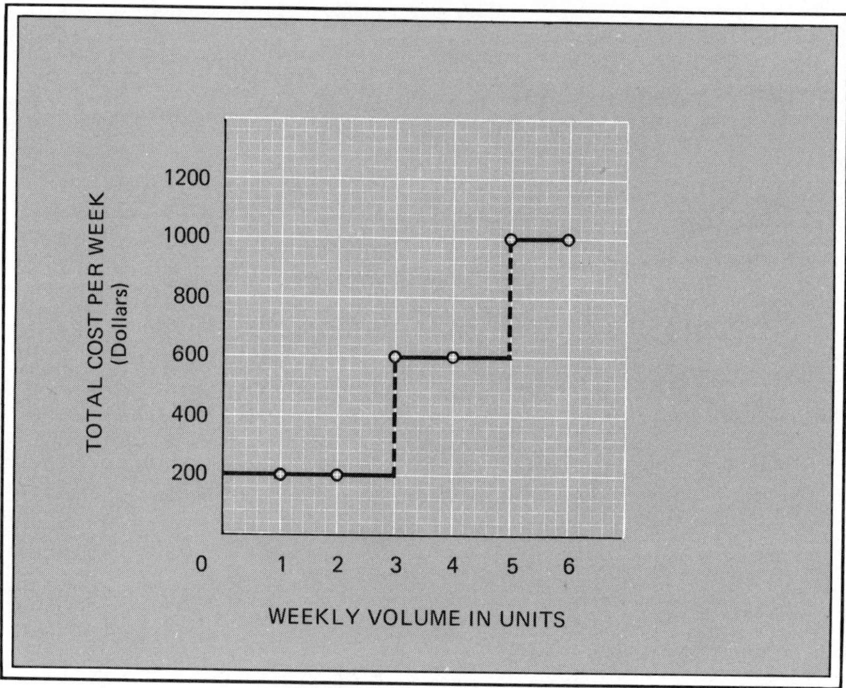

EXHIBIT 2–6
A stairstep cost

In general, there are three broad classes of semivariable costs. Perhaps the easiest to visualize is the **stairstep cost** shown in Exhibit 2–6. Supervisory salaries often behave in this way. One supervisor may supervise ten production line workers. As the number of workers increases because of increased production volume, another supervisor is added.

Stairstep semivariable costs further illustrate the nature of fixed costs and how they differ from other cost behavior patterns. One way to think about fixed costs is that they are stairstepped costs. For example, assume that a company has a machine with a maximum capacity of 1,000 units per year. The firm will have to buy a new machine to increase production to 1,001 units per year. In this sense, all fixed costs are stairstepped.

Exhibit 2–7 shows two different cost patterns. Both Costs *A* and *B* vary with changes in volume. Cost *B*, however, varies over smaller incremental changes in volume than does Cost *A*. If during the coming year the company plans to produce between 2,000 and 6,000 units, Cost *A* would be considered fixed and Cost *B* would be semivariable. If the company's volume ranges between 2,000 and 10,000 units, both costs would be semivariable. Both costs would be fixed if the production plans were between 3,001 and 5,000 units. This illustration shows that costs are fixed only in relationship to volume within the relevant range.

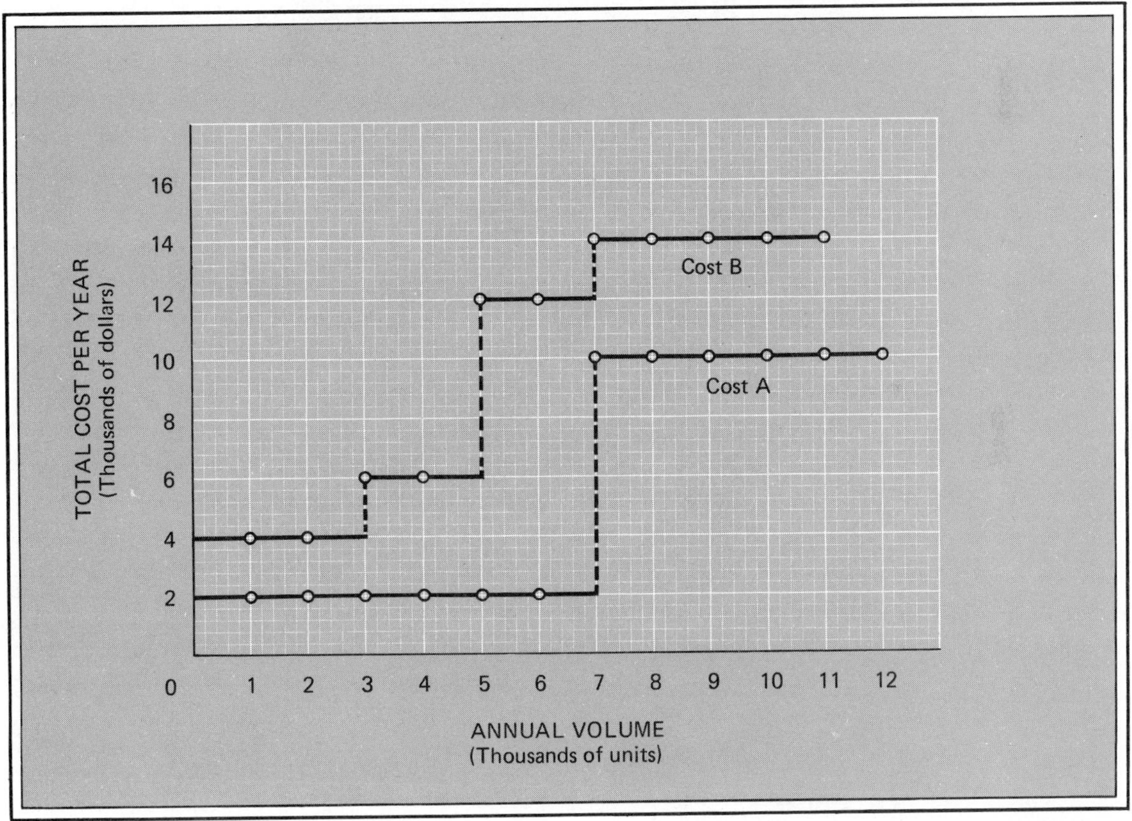

EXHIBIT 2–7
Comparison of two stairstepped costs

Another type of semivariable cost is that which includes both a fixed and a variable component. Maintenance is an example of such a cost. If the company produces nothing, maintenance will still be required. As the volume of production increases, the amount of required maintenance will increase. The common name of a cost with both fixed and variable cost attributes is **mixed cost.** A mixed cost is shown in Exhibit 2–8. In this illustration the fixed component is $200 and the variable costs increase at the rate of $.20 per unit of volume.

Other costs change with production volume, but in a nonlinear way. Costs such as utilities often increase at a decreasing rate. For example, assume that a manufacturing process requires one gallon of water per unit of output, and that the cost per gallon of water is $.03 for consumption between 1,000 and 3,000 gallons; $.02 for consumption between 3,001 and 5,000 gallons; $.01 for consumption between 5,001 and 10,000 gallons; and $.005 per gallon for consumption over 10,000 gallons. This cost is shown graphically in Exhibit 2–9.

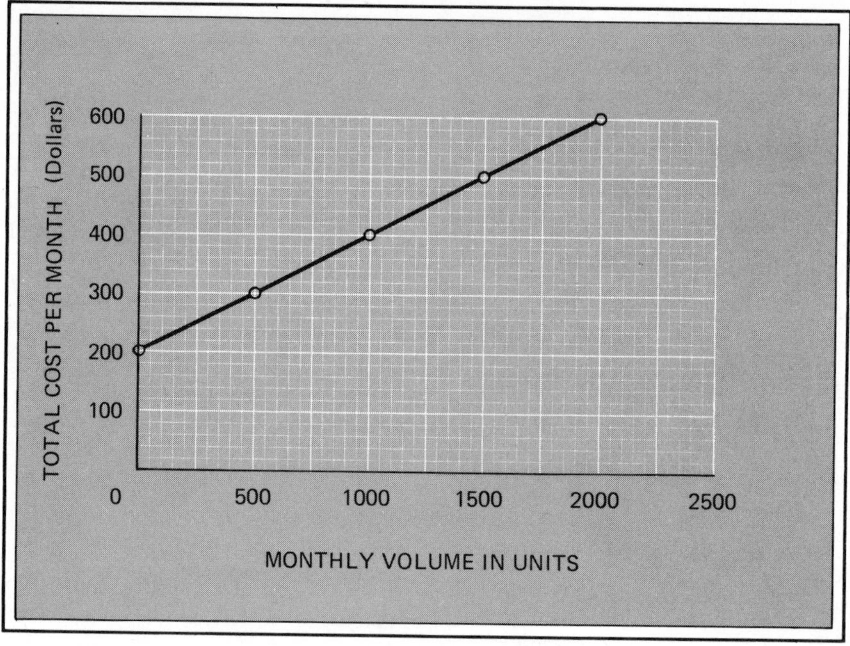

EXHIBIT 2–8
A mixed cost

A few costs increase at an increasing rate. These costs are really fines and penalties. Examples include demurrage charges on rail cars, pollution fines, and in some instances, the costs of labor. One effect of the energy crisis may be to shift the semivariable costs of energy from costs that decrease per

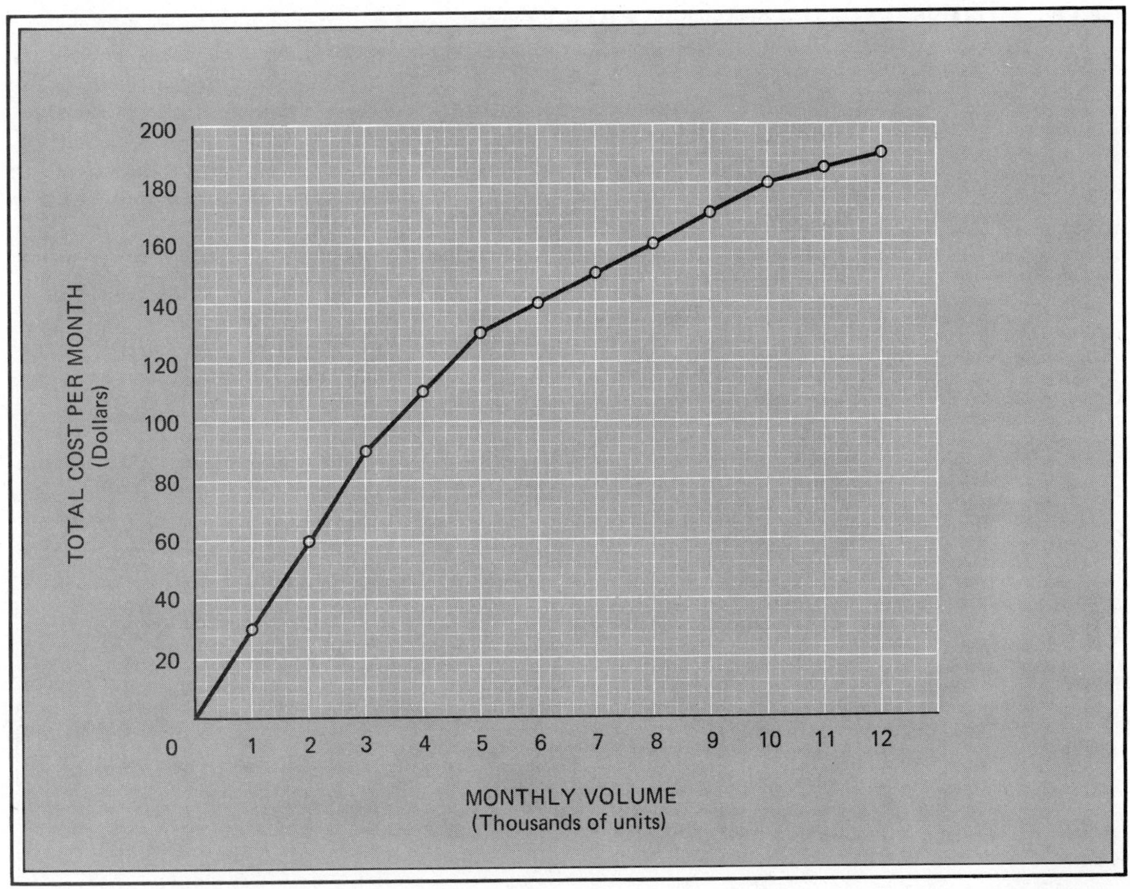

EXHIBIT 2–9
Curvilinear semivariable cost

unit with increased usage to costs that increase per unit as usage increases.

Accountants, through their measuring tools, normally convert semivariable costs into their fixed and variable components by using a straight-line assumption. We will examine these tools and their effects on semivariable costs later in this chapter.

When costs are identified by the accountant as fixed or variable, he is also implying another important concept—the relevant range of activity. The **relevant range** is the span of volume over which the cost behavior can reasonably be expected to remain valid. If raw material is a variable cost of $3.00 per unit under normal operating conditions, it is likely, because of quantity discounts, that it would increase as volume declines sharply, or decrease if production doubles or triples. Thus, costs are fixed or variable only over a relevant range of output.

DETERMINING FIXED AND VARIABLE COSTS

Fixed and variable are specific ways of viewing costs. However, the typical accounting system does not record or classify costs as fixed or variable. Traditionally, accounting summarizes costs by the nature of the expenditure. For example, when an invoice for the purchase of insurance on the factory is received, the amount is recorded in overhead as factory insurance not as a fixed or variable cost. In a very real sense the classification of costs into their fixed and variable components requires a special study above and beyond routine accounting procedures. It is a different perspective of costs that requires different measuring tools.

Choosing a Volume Measure

The first step in measuring the variability of costs is to find a suitable measure of volume or activity. When only one type of product is produced, it is possible to express volume in terms of physical units. However, when a company produces many different products, it may be difficult to find a single measure of volume. The following considerations are important when selecting a volume measure.

1. The unit of measurement must measure fluctuations in the activity level, or volume, which cause costs to vary. There must be a definite, positive relationship between the incurrence of costs and the activity measure.
2. The volume measure should be simple and easy to understand. Thus, measures such as sales dollars, labor hours, labor dollars, units of product, and machine hours are particularly attractive.
3. The activity figures should be attainable without undue additional clerical expense. The cost of gathering accounting information must be kept in mind.

Measuring Variations of Cost with Volume

There are three widely practiced ways of determining cost behavior patterns: inspection of contracts, engineering cost estimates, and inspection of past cost behavior patterns. The methods differ in the sources of data used. The first two are prospective in that they consider what cost patterns will be in the future. The last is retrospective in that it deals with past cost patterns.

INSPECTION OF CONTRACTS

The most intuitive method of determining whether a cost is fixed or variable is to examine the production activities and existing contracts. Some costs are fixed or variable by their nature, and their behavior patterns are readily determined. For example, depreciation by any method except the units-of-output basis would be fixed for any one year. Many salaries, such as the president's, are fixed. At the same time, there are many costs that are inherently variable. Costs such as raw materials and production labor paid on a piecework wage plan are variable. For those situations where the subsequent analysis is not very sensitive to errors in classification of fixed and variable costs, this method may provide a quick and inexpensive measure of cost behavior. A special warning is necessary. The examination must cut beneath the surface and seek the basic contract. *All* depreciation charges are *not* necessarily fixed, and *all* workers' salaries are *not* necessarily variable.

ENGINEERING COST ESTIMATES

Where the contracts are unclear or where there is no past experience to use in estimating cost variability, there is no recourse but to make direct estimates. The technical expertise of industrial engineers can be drawn upon to estimate the quantities of materials, labor, and production facilities needed to produce a new product or to estimate the behavior patterns of many costs. Work measurement techniques can provide reliable estimates of some fixed and variable costs. As actual production takes place and a base of experience is developed, refinements can be made and more objective methods used to examine the cost behavior patterns. This process not only increases the reliability of the cost behavior patterns, but also allows an after-the-fact measure of the accuracy of engineering cost estimates. Estimates that have proven accurate in the past may provide a greater feeling of certainty about estimates that will be necessary in the future.

INSPECTION OF PAST COST BEHAVIOR PATTERNS

Past data can provide empirical evidence of cost behavior patterns. While past experience may not always be the best guide, it can be useful. The analysis of experience inherently assumes that future cost behavior will be like past cost behavior. Where this assumption seems justified, there are systematic ways of determing how costs have varied with volume.

Earlier, variable costs were defined as costs that vary proportionately with volume. Underlying this definition is a linear, or straight-line, assumption of the relationship between cost and volume. As long as this simplifying assumption is realistic, the relationship will apply to any volume level.

In order to measure the cost-volume relationship from past data, the accountant fits a straight line to the data. We may fit a straight line to any set of two or more points. The mathematical statement of a straight line is the equation $y_c = a + b(x)$ *where:*

y_c = Total cost at a specified volume

a = Amount of cost where the straight line intercepts the cost axis at the zero activity level (total fixed cost)

b = Amount of change in cost with a change in volume or the rate of slope in a straight line (average variable cost per unit of activity)

x = Measure of activity level (volume)

This equation may be illustrated as follows:

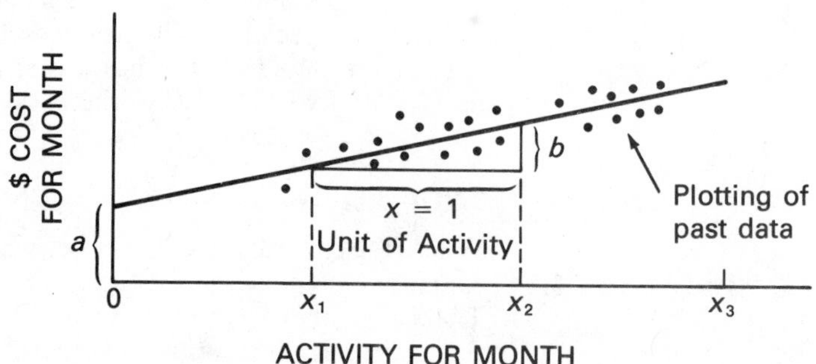

The equation allows us to describe the behavior of individual costs and sum them into one pattern of total costs. For example, a variable cost of $1.00 per direct labor hour would be expressed by the formula $y_c = \$0 + \$1.00\,(x)$, and graphed as:

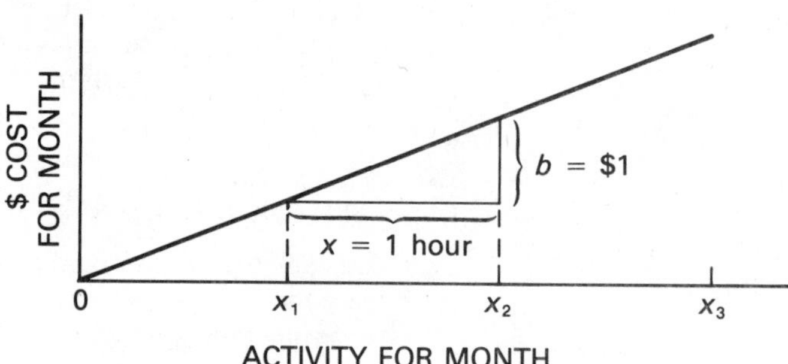

A fixed cost of $100 per month would be expressed as $y_c = \$100 + \$0(x)$, and graphed as:

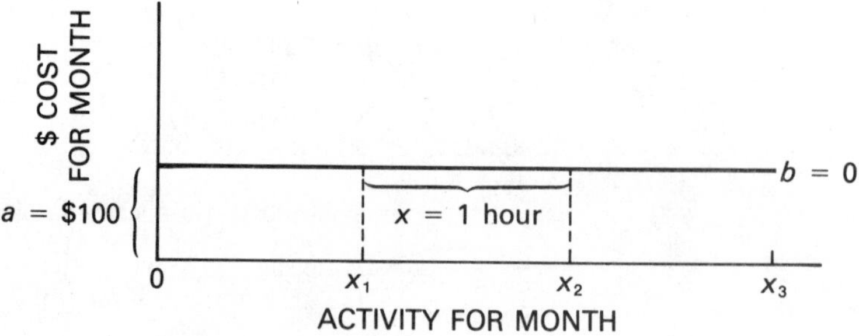

A mixed cost that includes both a fixed and a variable cost component, such as $2,500 per month fixed cost and a variable cost of $.20 per direct labor hour, would be expressed as $y_c = \$2{,}500 + \$.20(x)$ and graphed as:

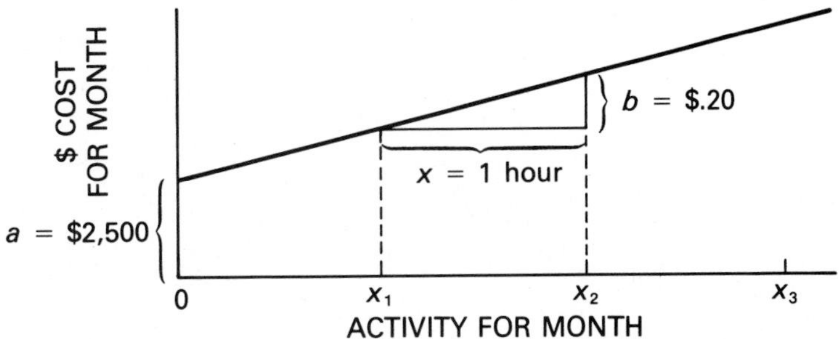

Since the volume measure on each of the three costs is direct labor hours, it is possible to add them together. The formula for the total of the individual costs is $y_c = \$2{,}600 + \$1.20(x)$. This can be used to estimate total costs at any volume level inside the relevant range of activity, that range over which the relationship expressed in the equation is assumed to be valid.

To illustrate the separation of past cost data into fixed and variable costs, let's assume that an examination of the accounting records for the past year's maintenance costs of the Clark Manufacturing Company provides cost and volume information as shown in the accompanying tabulation.

	Hours of Activity	*Total Cost of Maintenance*
January	100	$185
February	150	$255
March	300	$258
April	400	$300
May	600	$350
June	700	$390
July	800	$430
August	500	$344
September	300	$251
October	300	$265
November	200	$233
December	600	$362

From this data we can see that maintenance costs increase as activity increases and fall as activity decreases. However, it is extremely difficult to draw an accurate mental image of this relationship when the data are presented in this form.

There are three general methods of fitting a straight line to this past data: the scattergraph, which relies upon a visual fitting; the high-low point method, which fits a line to two points of data; and regression analysis, which statistically fits a line to all the observations.

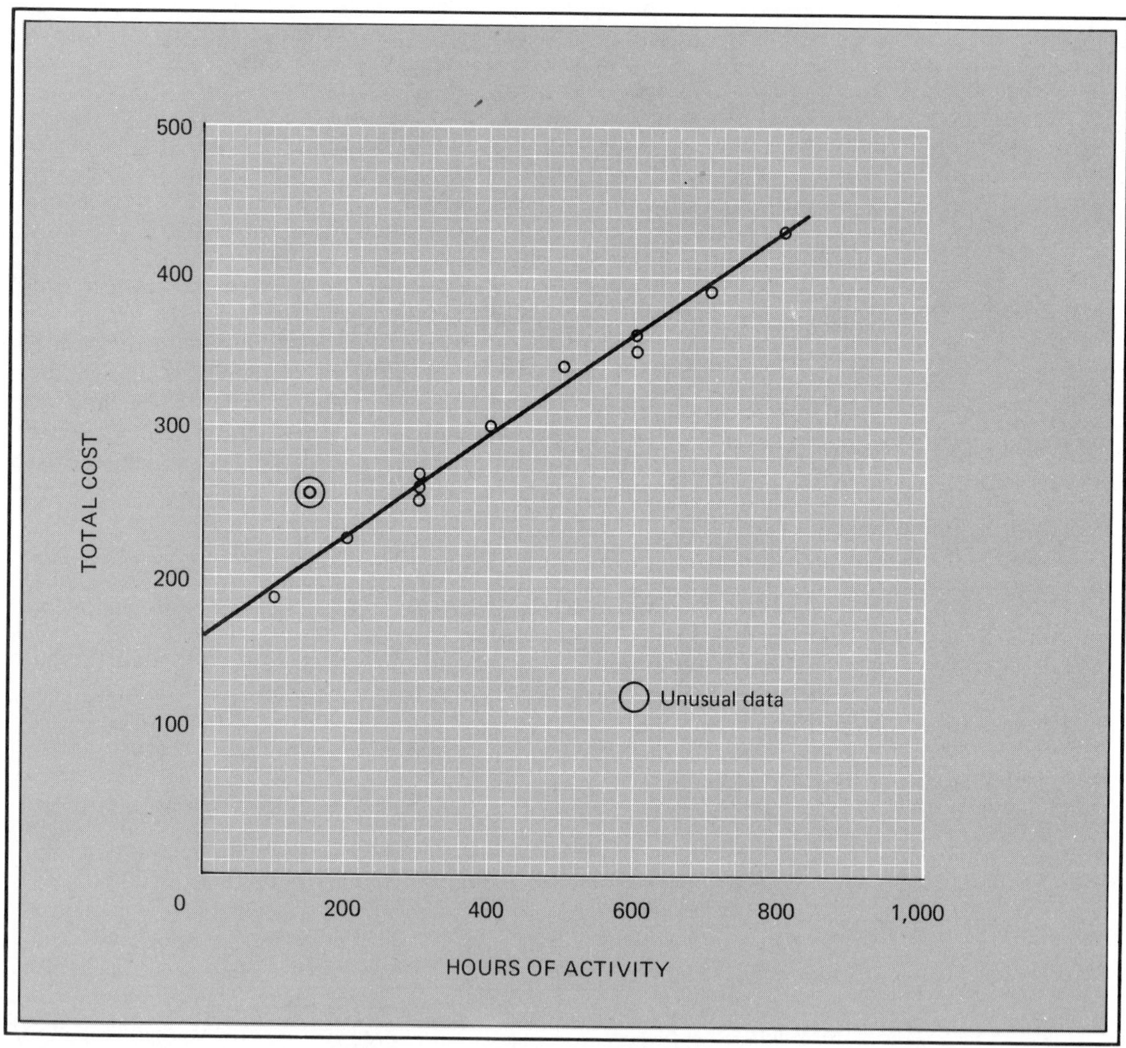

EXHIBIT 2–10
Scattergraph to determine fixed and variable cost components

SCATTERGRAPH ESTIMATES

Scattergraph estimates are made by plotting actual cost experiences at the various volume levels on graph paper and then fitting a line by visual inspection. The scattergraph allows the drawing of a mental image of the relationship. Exhibit 2–10 shows the data for the Clark Manufacturing Company plotted on graph paper. The horizontal axis (x axis) represents the volume, measured by hours of activity, and the vertical axis (y axis) represents the total cost of maintenance. The graph shows the general relationship of the total cost of maintenance to the hours of activity and allows visual examination to reveal unusual observations as well as nonlinear patterns.

The simplest way to fit a line to the scattergraph plot is to draw a line from visual inspection so that about half the dots lie above the line and half lie below the line. The point where the "fitted" line intersects the cost axis (vertical axis) is the estimate of the fixed costs designated by a. In this case fixed costs are estimated at approximately \$160. Variable costs may be determined at any given activity level by subtracting fixed costs from total costs on the line at that activity level. The variable cost per unit (b) of activity (x) is determined by dividing the total variable cost by the measure of activity at the selected level. For example, at 560 hours of activity the total cost estimate on the line is \$350. Subtracting the fixed cost estimate of \$160 from the \$350 total cost provides a variable cost of \$190. Dividing this \$190 by the activity measure (\$190 ÷ 560 hours) provides the variable cost of \$.339 per hour.

A closer examination of the data on the scattergraph reveals that the February costs of \$255 at the activity level of 150 hours seem out of line with the other costs. Something unusual may have happened that month. Perhaps extraordinary repairs were incurred, or the company made major repairs before the activity increase during summer months. Certainly, the unusually high cost calls for further analysis. If the \$255 is considered abnormal, it could be excluded from the analysis of cost variability. Then, when the company forecasts February costs, it can consider the "abnormality" as a separate issue.

A mistake in drawing the line could result in a large error. However, the error may not be significant in the relevant range of activity. For example, the following illustration shows an "estimated" pattern of cost behavior and a "correct" pattern of cost behavior. As long as the relationship is used to estimate costs *within the relevant range,* where the error in estimating costs may not be significant, the cost estimate should be useful in management decision making. However, most firms prefer the objectivity of the high-low point method or the least-squares regression analysis.

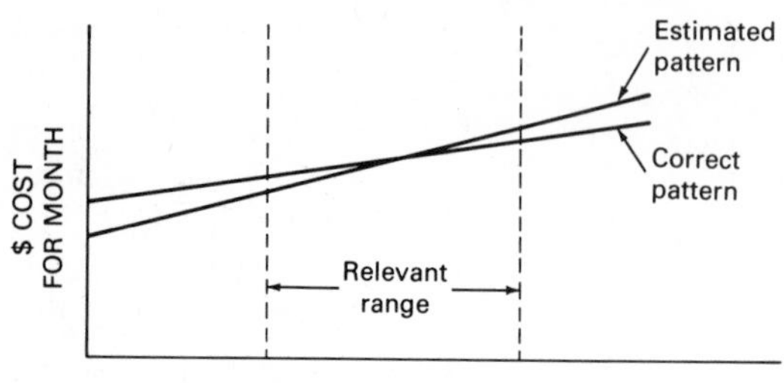

HIGH-LOW POINT ESTIMATES

The **high-low point** method of segregating fixed and variable costs uses only the highest and lowest volumes and their related costs to determine a straight-line relationship between costs and volume. It is the easiest way to objectively relate past cost patterns. The highest and lowest activity levels are isolated, along with their related costs. The change between the high and low levels of activity is divided into the change in cost to provide the measure of variable cost per unit of activity. The variable rate is then used to determine the total variable costs at either the high or low activity level. Finally, the variable costs are subtracted from the total costs to arrive at fixed costs. For example, for the Clark Manufacturing Company the lowest activity level was 100 hours when the cost was $185; the highest activity level was 800 hours when the cost was $430. The differences in costs and volume for the high-low point method would be:

	Costs	*Activity*
Highest (July)	$430	800 hours
Lowest (January)	$185	100 hours
Difference	$245	700 hours

The variable cost per hour is the change in costs divided by the change in volume ($245 ÷ 700 hours) or $.35 per hour. The fixed costs are then estimated by multiplying either the high or low activity, expressed in hours, by the variable rate ($.35 per hour) and subtracting this product from the total cost at that level. For example, multiplying the high level of 800 hours by $.35 variable cost per hour gives a total variable cost of $280. Subtracting this variable cost from the total cost of $430 provides a fixed cost estimate of $150. At the 100-hour level the variable costs are $35 (100 × $.35), and the fixed costs are again $150 ($185 − $35). Notice that fixed costs are determined by substituting the variable rate and activity level in the equation for the straight line and solving for fixed costs. For example:

$$\begin{aligned} y_c &= a + b(x) \\ \$430 &= a + \$.35(800) \\ a &= \$430 - \$280 \\ a &= \$150 \end{aligned}$$

The high-low point method of segregating fixed and variable costs is simple and easy to use, but it does have some weaknesses. It assumes that the cost patterns at the highest and lowest points of activity are typical of other cost-volume experiences. In our example, the answer would differ considerably if the costs at the 150-hour activity level had been used in lieu of those at the 100-hour level. Judgment should be exercised to select a representative low and a representative high point.

STATISTICAL REGRESSION ANALYSIS

Statistical regression analysis is a more sophisticated and reliable method of estimating fixed and variable costs than either the scattergraph or the high-low method. **Regression analysis** is a systematic way of determining whether the y values (costs) are related to the x values (volume measures).[1] The method of regression analysis using the least-squares approach provides two mathematical properties that are missing in the lines drawn by inspection or high-low methods. First, the algebraic sums of the positive and negative deviations from the fitted line equal zero. Second, the sum of the squares of these deviations is less than the sum of the squared vertical deviations from any other line.

The method of least squares uses two equations to determine the a value (fixed cost) and the b value (variable rate). These equations are:[2]

$$b = \frac{\Sigma xy - (\Sigma x\, \Sigma y/n)}{\Sigma x^2 - [(\Sigma x)^2/n]}$$

where:

Σy = Total costs	a = Total fixed costs
Σx = Total volume	b = Variable cost per unit of volume
n = Number of time periods	Σxy = Costs times volume summed

[1]It should be pointed out that the accountant assigns a cause and effect relationship to regression analysis. He says, in essence, that the cost is the "effect" resulting from the "cause" of volume. The pure statistician, on the other hand, is not willing to assign cause and effect to regression analysis. He speaks only in terms of whether the x and y values are related.

[2]It is beyond the scope of this book to show the mathematical proof of the equations. Students who are interested in the mathematical aspects of the least squares method should consult an introductory statistics book. For our purposes we can accept the mathematical validity of the equations. Many statistical texts calculate a and b with a set of normal equations that are solved simultaneously. These equations are:

I. $\Sigma y = na + b\Sigma x$
II. $\Sigma xy = a\Sigma x + b\Sigma x^2$

The equations in the text above are these normal equations recast so that it is possible to go to a direct solution thereby avoiding the mathematical complexities of simultaneous equations.

Once b is determined, then a can be found by:

$$a = \frac{\Sigma y - b\Sigma x}{n}$$

Using the data for the Clark Manufacturing Company, let's develop the cost estimates for the regression line. The first step is the development of the factors found in the formulas, as shown in the worksheet in Exhibit 2–11. Substituting these data in the formula for b provides:

$$b = \frac{1{,}671{,}750 - \dfrac{(4{,}950)(3{,}623)}{12}}{2{,}602{,}500 - \dfrac{(4{,}950)^2}{12}}$$

$$b = \$.316$$

Using the cost estimate of \$.316 for b, a is:

$$a = \frac{3{,}623 - .316\,(4{,}950)}{12}$$

$$a = \$171.56; \text{ rounded to } \$172.00$$

Month	Hours x	Costs y	xy	x^2
January	100	185	18,500	10,000
February	150	255	38,250	22,500
March	300	258	77,400	90,000
April	400	300	120,000	160,000
May	600	350	210,000	360,000
June	700	390	273,000	490,000
July	800	430	344,000	640,000
August	500	344	172,000	250,000
September	300	251	75,300	90,000
October	300	265	79,500	90,000
November	200	233	46,600	40,000
December	600	362	217,200	360,000
Total	4,950	3,623	1,671,750	2,602,500

$\Sigma x = 4{,}950$
$\Sigma y = 3{,}623$
$\Sigma xy = 1{,}671{,}750$
$\Sigma x^2 = 2{,}602{,}500$

EXHIBIT 2–11
Least-squares regression line worksheet

Using the 12-months data for the Clark Manufacturing Company, the least-squares regression line used for cost estimation would be $y_c = \$172 + \$.316(x)$. This solution differs from the high-low point method, which estimated the fixed costs at $150 and the variable costs at $.35 per hour. One reason for these differences is the effect of the month of February. The high-low point method excluded all months except January and July; the regression line method used all twelve months. Inclusion of the unusual month of February acted to increase the fixed cost estimate and reduce the slope of the line (variable rate). A regression line excluding February, to test for the effect of that month, provides a regression equation of $y_c = \$159 + \$.337(x)$. These values are much closer to the scattergraph estimate from Exhibit 2–10 and the high-low method.

Accountants use a special name, the **flexible budget,** for the cost estimation equation of $y_c = a + b(x)$. The flexible budget equation is the concise statement of how costs (y_c) change with volume (x). In a later section of the chapter, we will look at this term again.

STANDARD ERROR OF THE ESTIMATE

When the relationship between cost and volume is perfect, each point representing actual cost will fall exactly on the estimation line and there will be no unexplained variations. Exhibit 2–12 shows a scattergraph where there is a perfect relationship. Each set of data in Exhibit 2–12 falls right on the flexible budget's predicted line.

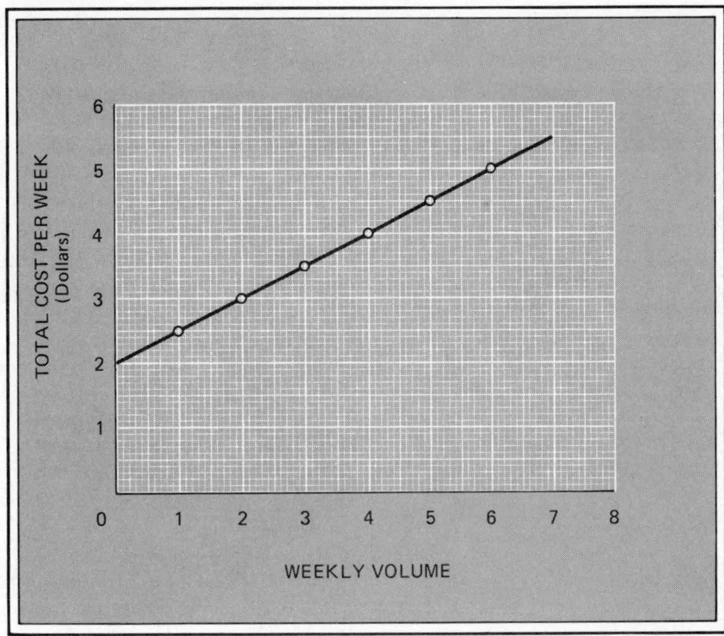

EXHIBIT 2–12
Scattergraph of a perfect cost-volume relationship

The statistician would describe this perfect relationship by saying there is no residual sum of squares. The residual sum of squares measures the remaining variation in y (cost) that cannot be accounted for by its relationship to x (volume). Where all actual costs fall directly on the flexible budget equation line, there is no remaining variation in y (cost). The calculation of the residual sum of squares is made by measuring the variation of each y value from the corresponding predicted value given by the flexible budget equation. In formula form the residual sum of squares is $\Sigma(y - \tilde{y})^2$ where:

y = Observed value of cost (actual cost)
$\tilde{y}$ = Predicted value of cost obtained from the flexible budget equation

If we divide the residual sum of squares by $n - 2$ (number of observations $- 2$), we obtain a measure known as the **residual variance.** The square root of the residual variance is called the **standard error of the estimate.** The complete formula for the standard error of the estimate is:

$$SE_{y \cdot z} = \sqrt{\frac{\Sigma(y - \tilde{y})^2}{n - 2}}$$

The standard error of the estimate measures how far the actual observations are from the flexible budget equation line. The farther the actual observations from the flexible budget predictions, the larger will be the standard error. For example, including the month of February in the regression analysis will increase the standard error of the estimate for the Clark Manufacturing Company. Conversely, the closer the actual data are to the estimates of the flexible budget line, the smaller the standard error of the estimate. The standard error permits the decision maker to determine the usefulness of the estimates. If the standard error is relatively large, the value of the equation in estimating costs may be limited.

The standard error of the estimate may be determined with any flexible budget equation, regardless of the method used to determine it. In the example that follows we will show the calcuation of the standard error with the flexible budget equation determined by least-squares regression. The same technique would be used if the flexible budget had been estimated from the scattergraph or high-low methods.

The determination of the standard error of the estimate is shown in Exhibit 2–13. Using this standard error as a test, how accurate is our 12-month regression line for the Clark Manufacturing Company? Our regression line was \$172 + \$.316(x) and the standard error of the estimate was \$15. If we can make four assumptions, we can use a table of normal probabilities[3] to evaluate the flexible budget equation. First, we have assumed that the relationship between costs and volume is linear. When this is not true, a straight line will not fit the actual data. (The assumption of nonlinearity and methods of coping with it will be discussed later in this chapter.) Second, it is assumed that the actual data are normally distributed (that is, bell-shaped) around the estimated line; that is to say, all the differences between the actual

Month	Hours of Activity x	Total Cost y	Line Estimate* $\tilde{y}$	$y - \tilde{y}$**	$(y - \tilde{y})^2$
January	100	185	204	−19	361
February	150	255	219	36	1,296
March	300	258	267	− 9	81
April	400	300	298	2	4
May	600	350	362	−12	144
June	700	390	393	− 3	9
July	800	430	425	5	25
August	500	344	330	14	196
September	300	251	267	−16	256
October	300	265	267	− 2	4
November	200	233	235	− 2	4
December	600	362	362	0	0
Total					2,380

Then: $SE_{y.x} = \sqrt{\dfrac{\Sigma(y - \tilde{y})^2}{n - 2}} = \sqrt{\dfrac{2,380}{12 - 2}}$ = \$15.43; rounded to \$15

*For example, for 100 hours the regression line would predict a cost of \$172 + \$.316 (100), or \$203.6; rounded to \$204.

**Sums of the deviations do not exactly equal zero because of rounding error.

EXHIBIT 2–13
Standard error of the estimate worksheet

[3]In statistics the normal distribution is the familiar bell-shaped curve. This curve has the property that 68.27% of all observations fall between the mean ($\bar{x}$) plus or minus one standard deviation; within the range of $\bar{x} \pm 2$ standard deviations, 95.45% are included; and with $\bar{x} \pm 3$ standard deviations, 99.73% or nearly all of the items are included. It is beyond the scope of this text to discuss the normal distribution in depth. It is sufficient that the student know that it allows the manager to assess how well the regression line fits the observed data and to make probability statements about the fit to the data.

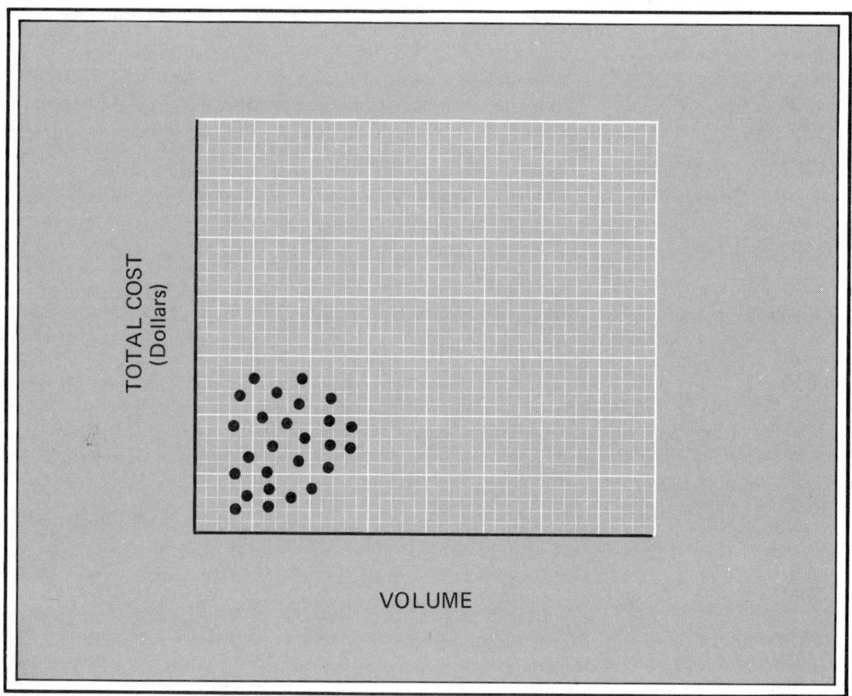

EXHIBIT 2–14
Scattergraph where no cost-volume relationship exists

costs at a given volume level and the estimates made by the flexible budget at the same volume level would create a normal, bell-shaped curve. Third, it is assumed that there is a uniform dispersion of actual costs around the estimated line. At a high volume level the actual data are distributed around the estimated line in the same way they are at lower volumes. Finally, it is assumed that the cost measures are independent of each other. For example, the costs reported in April are not dependent upon those reported in May.

If we were to use the flexible budget equation to estimate costs at the 400-hour level, we would estimate maintenance costs at $298 [$172 + $.316(400)]. If a table of normal probabilities is used, 68.27% of all observations should fall between $y_c \pm$ $15. Thus, 68.27% of the time the actual cost should fall between $283 ($298 − $15) and $313 ($298 + $15). The smaller the standard error, the more confidence the decision maker can have in the flexible budget equation for prediction.

On the 11-month basis, i.e., excluding February, the regression line was $159 + $.337(x). The standard error of the estimate for this regression line is $11. At the 400-hour level the company's estimate of maintenance cost would be $159 + $.337 (400), or $294. The actual cost should fall between $283 and $305, 68.27% of the time. This interval is tighter than that of the

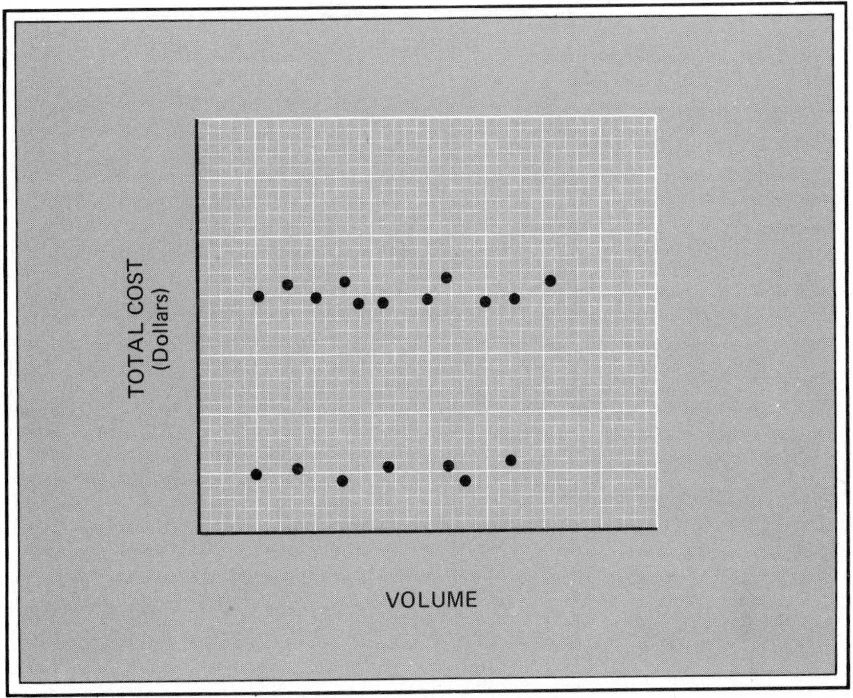

EXHIBIT 2–15
Scattergraph where cost-volume relationship is unclear

regression line based on the 12 months of data, but it is biased because it excludes an independent observation from the population.

A special warning seems appropriate here. Statistical decision-making methods are objective, yet they carry an aura of accuracy that must be approached with caution. Statistical methods do *not* remove the necessity for the decision maker to form his own judgments about the usefulness of the data. Even though the regression line and the standard error of the estimate for the Clark Manufacturing Company are known, subjective judgment is still required to determine whether or not we want to use the data. One way to give the manager a basis for subjective judgment is to prepare a scattergraph on each cost, regardless of the statistical methods of analysis. As a matter of fact most computer programs do this automatically.

There are occasions when it is impossible to fit a satisfactory estimation line. Exhibits 2–14 and 2–15 illustrate two scattergraphs which defy a segregation of the cost into its fixed and variable components. In both cases the standard error of the estimate would be so large as to negate the meaning of the flexible budget equation. In those cases where cost patterns do not lend themselves to fixed and variable cost analysis because of a high standard error of the estimate, management has no recourse but to use its judgment in planning future costs. Usually the direct establishment of the levels of these costs will result in treating them as fixed.

There are other costs that are not susceptible to fixed and variable cost analysis. Research and development costs (R & D) and advertising costs are two excellent examples. These costs cannot be directly related to either production or sales volume. The proper amount that should be incurred for these costs depends upon factors other than volume. Among these factors are the marketplace and its structure, the projected need for new products, the probability of success in developing product innovations, the projected cash flow patterns of the firm, and the competitors' behavior. As a result, these costs are established by management choice, or discretion. Accountants call them **discretionary costs.** Typically, control of discretionary costs depends more upon measuring the results of the cost expenditure than upon cost reduction.

ADVANCED STATISTICAL TECHNIQUES

The straight-line measure of cost variability is the method most widely used by accountants. It is not universally applicable, however. In some instances a linear regression line will result in an unsatisfactory standard error of the estimate. In other instances the relationship may be curvilinear. As discussed earlier in the chapter, some of the semivariable costs behave this way. To estimate this cost behavior pattern, a second-degree curve, expressed by the following formula, might be appropriate:

$$y_c = a + bx + cx^2$$

The solution of this formula requires three normal equations. With this and other higher-order curves that might be useful the mathematics become complex. Without a computer these studies may not be feasible.

The decision maker may find that the cost being studied is related to one or more factors in addition to volume, or that there are two or more different measures of volume. For some cost predictions there may be two or three independent measures, such as machine hours, labor hours, product dimensions, and labor skills. In this case the decision maker may find the techniques of multiple regression useful. Multiple regression measures the change in cost (y) for one of these variables, while holding all of the other variables constant. The formula to express the relationships among many variables is:

$$y_c = a + bx_1 + cx_2 + dx_3 \ldots$$

where: y_c is the cost to be predicted; x_1, x_2, and x_3 are the different volume measures; and a, b, and c are constants.

A detailed study of these two techniques is beyond the scope of this book. However, it is important that the student recognize some of the possible weaknesses in the single-volume, straight-line model of cost variability. The search for a single-volume base and the use of straight lines can limit the scope of inferences to be made by the decision maker about fixed and variable costs.

Expressing Cost Behavior Patterns: The Flexible Budget

Up to this point we have taken the view that management is studying each cost factor separately and individually. To make decisions involving the volume of production for the company as a whole, it must combine the behavior patterns of individual costs into a total cost picture whether on an individual cost-by-cost basis or a total cost basis. Accountants call the statement of fixed and variable costs the **flexible budget.**

Assume that a company has only three costs: a fixed cost, a variable cost, and a mixed cost. The flexible budget for each individual cost and for total costs follows.

	Flexible Budget ($y_c = a + bx$)
Cost	a b
Fixed	\$500 + \$ 0 (x)
Variable	\$ 0 + \$.25(x)
Semivariable	\$ .50 + \$.10(x)
Total cost	\$550 + \$.35(x)

For estimating and controlling individual costs, the company would use the flexible budget for each type of cost. For making decisions regarding the company as a whole the flexible budget of \$550 + \$.35(x) would be used. In order to combine the individual cost elements, it is important to seek a single measure of volume that fits all costs. The volume measures must be the same if the individual flexible budget formulas are to be additive.

When we think about the activities of a manufacturing company, we can visualize two distinct types of activities. First, the firm must manufacture the products to be sold. Second, they must undertake the sales and distribution of the products. For manufacturing costs the volume measure (x) would relate to manufacturing; possible measures of volume would be units produced, direct-labor hours, or machine hours. For selling costs the volume measure (x) would relate to selling; possible volume measures would be units sold, units shipped, or dollars of sales. When the firm uses two flexible budgets, one for manufacturing costs and another for selling and distribution costs, the two budgets will not be additive if they used different volume measures (x).

The Relevant Range of Activity

The purpose of determining cost behavior patterns and specifying costs as fixed and variable is to sharpen the decision data. Unless the concepts of cost variability allow the decision maker to be more precise and flexible in his decisions, the effort and money spent in developing fixed and variable cost patterns are wasted. The range of volume over which the cost behavior patterns can reasonably be expected to hold true is termed the **relevant range.** No analysis of fixed and variable costs should be made without specifying the relevant range of activity.

It would be a mistake to believe that the relevant range of activity extends from zero activity to maximum volume capacity. In the event of a drastic decrease in volume, management would take a different set of actions than it would if production continued at a normal pace. As volume declined, past policies and decisions would be reexamined. Perhaps executive salaries would be lowered, production lines closed, insurance policies cancelled or reduced, or products dropped from the production schedule. On the other end of the scale, as production increased to reach maximum capability, there would be "diminishing returns." Storerooms would become crowded and inefficient, machines would require additional maintenance, workers in the second shift or on overtime would be less productive, and production facilities would become overworked.

SUMMARY

Basic to profit planning and control is the knowledge of how costs change with changes in volume. Fixed costs are costs that do not change with changes in volume; variable costs vary in direct proportion to changes in volume. Costs that change with changes in volume, but not in direct proportion, are semivariable costs. There are three types of semivariable costs: stair-stepped, mixed, and curvilinear. The flexible budget is the formal statement of how costs vary with volume.

The simplest and most straightforward way of determining fixed and variable costs is to examine the firm's contracts. Where there are no contracts, fixed and variable costs can be estimated directly through special studies. Historical costs, when available, can be used to estimate fixed and variable costs. One way to separate historical costs into their fixed and variable components is to plot the data on a scattergraph; volume is shown on the horizontal axis and costs are shown on the vertical axis. A line is then drawn which bisects this plotted history. Fixed costs are determined where the line intersects the vertical axis; the variable cost rate is determined by measuring the slope of the line. Similar to the scattergraph approach is the high-low point method, which measures the variable cost rate between costs at the highest and lowest activity levels. A third method of analyzing historical costs is regression analysis. It is similar in effect to the scattergraph, but is more objective in separating costs into their fixed and variable components. The standard error of the estimate can assess the degree to which the flexible budget estimates fit the actual data.

SUPPLEMENTARY READING

Gynther, R. S. "Improving Separation of Fixed and Variable Expenses." *N.A.A. Bulletin,* June, 1963.

*Koehler, Robert W., and Charles A. Neyhart, Jr. "Difficulties in Flexible Budgeting." *Managerial Planning*, May–June, 1972.

*Mullis, Elbert N., Jr. "Variable Budgeting for Financial Planning and Control." *Management Accounting*, February, 1975.

National Association of Accountants. *Separating and Using Costs as Fixed and Variable*. New York: National Association of Accountants, 1960.

National Association of Accountants. *Analysis of Cost-Volume-Profit Relationships*. New York: National Association of Accountants, 1953.

QUESTIONS

2-1 Three important constraints in relating cost variability to volume are: constant production methods, constant management policies, and constant price level. Explain and discuss the importance of these contraints.

2-2 Define and explain the following concepts: cost behavior patterns, variable cost, fixed cost, mixed cost, and relevant range.

2-3 Define the term "flexible budget." Why is the concept of the relevant range critical to flexible budget analysis?

2-4 Choosing an appropriate volume measure is essential to measuring the variability of costs. It becomes more critical in a multiproduct situation. Discuss. What are some of the factors that should be considered in selecting a volume base?

2-5 "Fixed and variable cost analysis is not relevant in the long run." Explain what is meant by this statement.

2-6 Some costs are fixed or variable because of management decisions, while others are fixed or variable because of accounting techniques. Explain why and give example of each.

2-7 "One of the effects of the energy crisis is to shift the nature of any semivariable costs of energy that a firm incurs." Do you agree or disagree? Defend your position.

2-8 The inspection of contracts, engineering cost estimates, and past cost behavior patterns are different ways of separating costs into fixed and variable components. Explain how each method is used.

2-9 Explain how the scattergraph, the high-low method, and least-squares regression analysis are used to separate costs into fixed and variable patterns. Give examples where the use of each method would be appropriate.

2-10 In measuring cost behavior patterns by using the equation for a straight line, $y_c = a + b(x)$, what do the a and b terms represent? If $a = 0$ and b is constant, what effect will changes in x have upon y_c? What effect will changes in a have upon b?

EXERCISES

2-11 *(Identification of Cost Behaviors).* State whether the following costs are probably fixed, variable, or semivariable during a given accounting period.

A. Wages of assembly-line worker in a factory.

B. Cost of electrical power in a factory.

C. Advertising costs of purchasing a weekly ad in a newspaper.

D. Insurance or bonding fee required to practice as a CPA.

E. Depreciation on factory machinery computed upon an hours of production basis.

F. Disposable uniforms in a hospital surgery room.

G. Supervisory salaries.

H. Depreciation on factory machinery determined by the sum-of-the-years'-digits method.

I. Annual rental cost of raw material warehouse determined by a rate per square foot.

J. Rent of raw material warehouse based on an annual rate.

2-12 *(True or False).* Indiate whether the following statements are *true* or *false.*

1. Discretionary costs are best determined with regression analysis.
2. Cost are fixed or variable only in relationship to volume changes within a given time period.
3. Fixed costs per unit vary with changes in volume.
4. Total variable costs remain constant with changes in volume.
5. The use of a scattergraph in determining fixed and variable costs is more objective than the use of regression analysis.
6. Depreciation computed on the sum-of-the-years'-digits basis is a good example of a semivariable cost.
7. Total variable costs increase proportionately with changes in volume but are constant per unit of output when viewed from a per-unit basis.
8. Linear regression analysis provides a more accurate and useful method of estimating fixed and variable costs than any other method.

9. In the formula form of the flexible budget, x is the volume measure.

10. The higher the standard error of the estimate, the more reliable the cost estimate.

2-13 *(Matching).* Match the following terms and definitions.

1. Fixed cost
2. Variable cost
3. Semivariable cost
4. Discretionary cost
5. Mixed cost
6. Relevant range
7. Engineering cost estimates
8. Flexible budget
9. Regression analysis
10. Activity level

A. Measured on the x axis when studying the variability of costs.
B. Formal statement of the effect that volume changes have on costs.
C. Cost that varies in direct proportion to changes in volume.
D. Cost defined as fixed because of a specific management decision.
E. One projective method for determining cost behavior patterns.
F. Cost that varies with production, but not proportionately.
G. Cost with fixed and variable components.
H. The most objective method of separating fixed and variable costs.
I. Span of volume or activity over which cost behavior patterns are useful in predicting future costs.
J. A capacity cost that is not affected by volume changes.

2-14 *(Scattergraph and High-Low Methods).*

A. From the following data prepare a scattergraph and estimate the amount of total fixed costs and the variable cost per unit which best fits the points.

Activity Hours	*Cost*
7	$100
12	$140
15	$150
18	$190
20	$180
23	$210

B. Using the data above, determine the amount of total fixed costs and the variable cost per unit using the high-low method.

2-15 *(Determining Flexible Budgets).* Quicktest Laboratories, Inc. performs a laboratory test for hospitals and medical clinics. Their flexible budget for operating costs are $24,000 per month plus $3.00 per test. Industry data show average unit costs for tests in other similar labs of $6.50 per test when 12,000 tests are performed per month and $5.25 per test when 24,000 tests are performed. How does Quicktest's flexible budget compare with the flexible budget for similar firms?

2-16 *(Least-squares Regression).* From the following data determine the variable cost per unit, total fixed costs, and the standard error of the estimate using least-squares regression.

$$\begin{aligned} \Sigma x &= 150 \\ \Sigma y &= 1{,}625 \\ \Sigma x^2 &= 5{,}900 \\ \Sigma xy &= 53{,}000 \\ \Sigma(y-\tilde{y})^2 &= 6{,}102 \\ n &= 6 \end{aligned}$$

2-17 *(Planning and Control with Flexible Budget).* The Puget Foundry has prepared flexible budget equations for each cost. For maintenance the flexible budget is:

$$y_c = \$5{,}600 + \$.25(x)$$

where:

y_c is the estimate of total maintenance costs
x is direct machine-hours

REQUIRED:

A. Prepare a cost estimate for 6,000 machine hours; for 9,000 hours.

B. Management believes that there will be a general 10% price increase for maintenance costs that will affect both fixed and variable costs. Prepare a new flexible budget equation.

C. Prepare cost estimates for 6,000 and 9,000 machine-hours using the revised budget equation obtained in Part B.

D. Using the original equation of $\$5{,}600 + \$.25(x)$, can you tell if management controlled costs effectively if actual costs of maintenance were $7,000 last year when the actual activity level was 4,000 machine-hours?

E. Discuss the statement: "Fixed costs don't change with changes in volume, so it is impossible for management to control them." Do you agree or disagree? Why?

F. What would be the budget allowance if the department was in a "stand-by" position (zero activity but ready to produce if asked to do so)? Do you feel this allowance is realistic? Why?

2-18 *(Planning and Control with Flexible Budget)*. The Long Tail Kite Company obtained the following data from the use of least-squares regression analysis to study the relationship of production costs to direct labor hours.

$$y_c = \$20{,}000 + \$1.50\ (x)$$

Standard error = \$500

REQUIRED:

A. Explain what each part of the flexible budget equation represents.
B. Explain what the standard error represents.
C. Using the following cases, explain how the information above may be used to plan and control costs.
   (1) Management is planning an activity level for the coming accounting period of 24,000 direct labor hours. What cost level should management plan?
   (2) Actual activity was 22,000 direct labor hours, and actual costs were \$52,500. Did management control actual cost expenditures?
   (3) Management is planning an activity level of 20,000 direct labor hours the coming accounting period. Because of cash management difficulties, management would like a possible cost range. What estimate should encompass the high- and low-cost experiences 68% of the time?

2-19 *(Cost Determination)*. Total average unit costs for the Sigma Company at output levels of 400 and 500 units are shown below:

	Total Average Unit Cost	
Cost	*400 units produced*	*500 units produced*
A	\$3.75	\$3.00
B	\$2.90	\$2.60
C	\$1.75	\$1.75
D	\$ .50	\$ .40
E	\$4.15	\$4.07

REQUIRED:

Prepare a table to show:
1. Per-unit variable cost
2. Total fixed cost
3. Type of cost (i.e., variable, fixed, semivariable, mixed)

2-20 *(Selection of Volume Base).* The Snoqualmie Corp., a manufacturer of high-quality fishing reels, gathered the following historical data concerning their manufacturing process:

Total Costs	*Direct-Labor Hours*	*Machine-Hours*
$20,000	2,000	2,000
$23,000	3,100	2,500
$34,000	2,650	3,250
$35,000	3,600	3,900
$37,000	4,100	3,650
$43,000	3,300	4,350
$43,000	4,200	4,900
$46,000	5,000	4,900
$48,000	4,000	4,600
$50,000	4,600	5,100
$53,500	3,950	4,700
$54,000	4,550	5,600
$54,500	3,000	5,250
$55,000	5,350	6,000
$61,000	5,250	6,300

Management was attempting to develop this data for future cost-estimation purposes. They could not decide between direct labor hours and machine-hours for the activity base and asked your help in determining which base would be most appropriate.

REQUIRED:
Choose the appropriate activity base and support your decision.

2-21 *(High-Low Method and Standard error of the estimate).* The Dynamic Duo Company had the following cost and volume experiences for employee fringe benefit costs:

	Direct-Labor Hours	*Actual Costs*
January	8,000	$18,000
February	7,000	$17,000
March	10,000	$22,000
April	12,000	$27,000
May	8,000	$17,000
June	9,000	$20,000

REQUIRED:

A. Determine the flexible budget equation using the high-low method.

B. Calculate the standard error of the estimate using the flexible budget equation determined in A above. Comment upon the validity of the flexible budget formula.

2-22 *(High-Low Method).* The Charter Distributing Company is in the process of analyzing its cost structure. The company has determined that the following mixed cost exists at various levels of production:

Month	*Units Produced*	*Total Costs*
January	25	$45
February	18	$22
March	21	$40
April	15	$36
May	12	$32
June	19	$40

The company is anxious to break the mixed cost into the basic variable and fixed cost elements to assist in planning and control of operations. They have asked you to assist in this task.

REQUIRED:

A. By the means of the high-low method break the total costs into their fixed and variable elements. Express the answer as a linear equation.

B. Assuming that the least-squares regression technique resulted in the cost equation of $y_c = \$17.50 + \$1.00\ (x)$, compare this equation with the answer you obtained in A above. Which cost analysis would you choose for this cost? Explain. Would this hold true for all other variable and fixed cost separations? Explain.

2-23 *(Flexible Budgets and Cost Control).* The Flying Bird Badminton Manufacturing Company experienced seasonal variation in its production and sales, from a low in January of 8,500 sets to a high in July of 23,000 sets. Production costs at the lowest activity level were $39,250 and at the highest level were $63,900.

REQUIRED:

A. Using the high-low method, determine the variable cost per unit and the total fixed costs per month. Express the flexible budget for production costs in formula form.

B. Using the flexible budget determined in Part A above, calculate the budgeted costs at 10,000 units; at 28,000 units. How reliable do you believe these estimates are?

C. During the first month of the next year, 9,000 sets were produced at a cost of $42,000. How well did the firm control its costs?

2–24 *(Flexible Budgets and Cost Planning).* The following are flexible budget equations for the Sundance Corporation.

Rent	$4,700 + $ 0 (x)
Indirect labor	$ 0 + $.40($x$)
Repairs	$1,800 + $.25($x$)

REQUIRED:

A. Develop flexible budget cost estimates for 7,000, 8,000, and 9,000 units (Assume that the volume measure x is units.)

B. Calculate the per-unit cost for each level of activity. Why does the per-unit cost change as volume increases?

C. Explain why it is desirable to find a single volume measure for all production costs.

2–25 *(Identification of Cost Patterns).* Select the graph that matches the numbered factory cost or expense data.

The vertical axes of the graphs represent *total* dollars of expense, and the horizontal axes represent production. In each case the zero point is at the intersection of the two axes. The graphs may be used more than once.

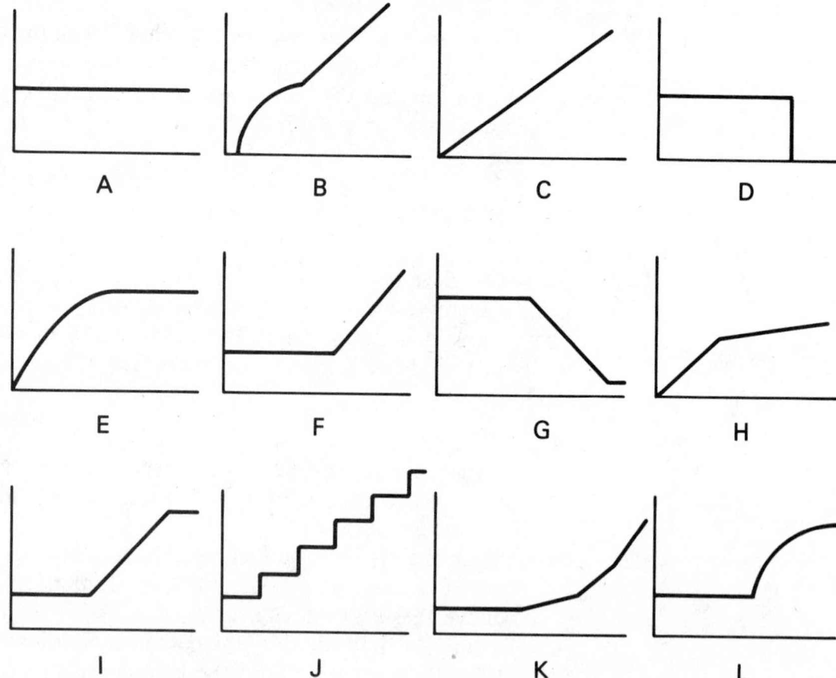

1. Depreciation of equipment, where the amount of depreciation charged is computed by the machine-hours method.

2. Electricity bill—a flat fixed charge, plus a variable cost after a certain number of kilowatt hours are used.

3. City water bill, which is computed as follows:

First 1,000,000 gallons or less	$1,000 flat fee
Next 10,000 gallons	$.003 per gallon used
Next 10,000 gallons	$.006 per gallon used
Next 10,000 gallons	$.009 per gallon used
etc., etc., etc.	

4. Cost of lubricant for machines, where cost per unit decreases with each pound of lubricant used (for example, if one pound is used, the cost is $10.00; if two pounds are used, the cost is $19.98; if three pounds are used, the cost is $29.94; with a minimum cost per pound of $9.25).

5. Depreciation of equipment, where the amount is computed by the straight-line method. When the depreciation rate was established, it was anticipated that the obsolescence factor would be greater than the wear and tear factor.

6. Rent on a factory building donated by the city, where the agreement calls for a fixed fee payment unless 200,000 man-hours are worked, in which case no rent need be paid.

7. Salaries of repairmen, where one repairman is needed for every 1,000 hours of machine-hours or less (i.e., 0 to 1,000 hours requires one repairman, 1,001 to 2,000 hours requires two repairmen, etc.).

8. Federal unemployment compensation taxes for the year, where labor force is constant in number throughout year. Federal unemployment taxes are computed at .5% of the first $4,200 earned. Average annual salary is $6,000 per worker.

9. Cost of raw material used.

10. Rent on a factory building donated by county, where agreement calls for rent of $100,000 less $1.00 for each direct labor hour worked in excess of 200,000 hours, but minimum rental payment of $20,000 must be paid.

(CPA adapted)

PROBLEMS

2-26 *(Determination of Flexible Budget; Multiple Choice).*

A. Maintenance expenses of a company are to be anlyzed for purposes of constructing a flexible budget. Examination of past records disclosed the following costs and volume measures:

	Highest	*Lowest*
Cost per month	$39,200	$32,000
Machine hours	24,000	15,000

1. Using the high-low point method of analysis, the estimated variable cost per machine hour is
a. $1.25
b. $12.50
c. $0.80
d. $0.08

2. Using the high-low technique, the estimated annual fixed cost for maintenance expenditures is
a. $447,360
b. $240,000
c. $230,400
d. $384,000

B. Adams Corporation has developed the following flexible budget formula for annual indirect labor cost:

Total cost = $4,800 + $0.50 per machine hour

1. Operating budgets for the current month are based upon 20,000 hours of planned machine time. Indirect labor costs included in this planning budget are
a. $14,800
b. $10,000
c. $14,400
d. $10,400

C. Labor hours and production costs for four months, which you believe are representative for the year, were as follows:

Month	*Labor Hours*	*Total Production Costs*
September	2,500	$ 20,000
October	3,500	25,000
November	4,500	30,000
December	3,500	25,000
	14,000	$100,000

On the basis of the information above and using the least-squares method of computation with the letters listed below, select the best answers for each of Questions 1 through 5.

Let a = Fixed production costs per month
b = Variable production costs per labor hour
n = Number of months
x = Labor hours per month
y = Total monthly production costs
Σ = Summation

1. The equation(s) required for applying the least-squares method of computation of fixed and variable production costs could be expressed
a. $\Sigma xy = a\Sigma x + bx^2$
b. $\Sigma y = na + b\Sigma x$
c. $y = a + bx^2$
$\Sigma y = na + b\Sigma x$
d. $\Sigma xy = a\Sigma x + b\Sigma x^2$
$\Sigma y = na + b\Sigma x$

2. The cost function derived by the least-squares method
a. Would be linear
b. Must be tested for minima and maxima
c. Would be parabolic
d. Would indicate maximum costs at the point of the function's point of inflection

3. Monthly production costs could be expressed
a. $y = ax + b$
b. $y = a + bx$
c. $y = b + ax$
d. $y = \Sigma a + bx$

4. Using the least-squares method of computation, the fixed monthly production cost is approximately
a. $10,000
b. $9,500
c. $7,500
d. $5,000

5. Using the least-squares method of computation, the variable production cost per labor hour is
a. $6.00
b. $5.00
c. $3.00
d. $2.00 *(CPA adapted)*

2-27 *(Determining Flexible Budgets from Scattergraphs).* The McLaine Company's cost accountant, in his study of four costs, made the following scattergraphs:

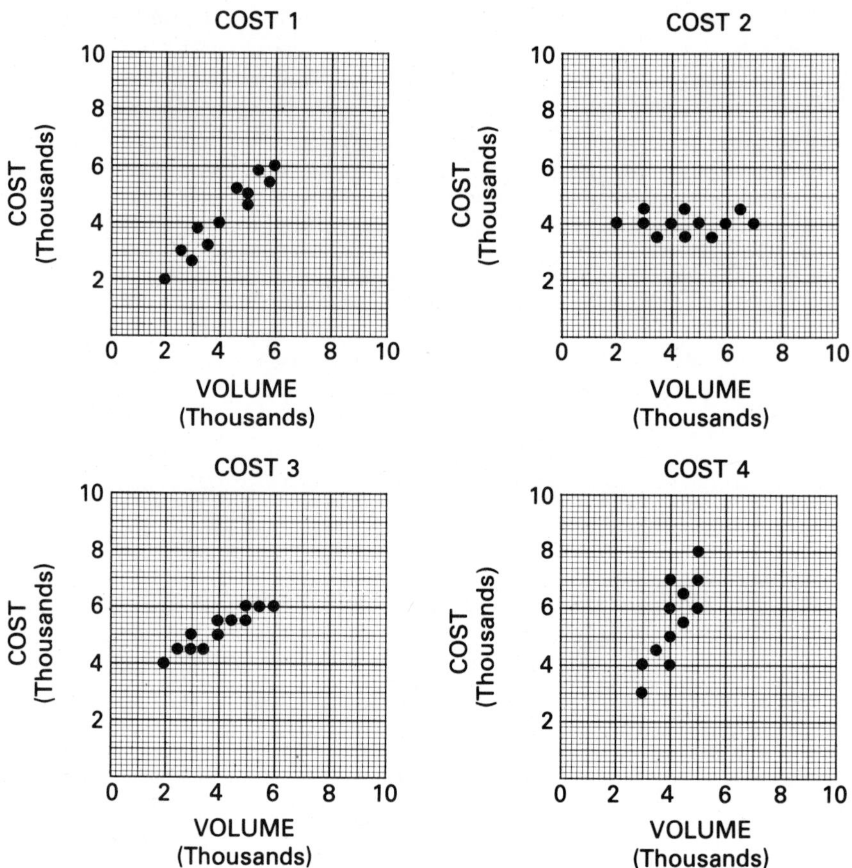

REQUIRED:

A. From the scattergraphs prepare flexible budget formulas for each individual cost.

B. Comment upon the reliability of your estimates. Which costs are the least reliable? Why?

2-28 *(Flexible Budget and High-Low Method).* The Sunny Jim Company produces lawn games. Last year, production varied from a high of 25,500 games in June to a low of 9,000 in January. Production costs were $77,100 and $40,800, respectively.

REQUIRED:

A. Determine the flexible budget using the high-low method.

B. Using the flexible budget determined in Part A above, calculate the budgeted costs at 10,000 and 30,000 units. How reliable do you believe those estimates are?

C. In other months the costs were:

Units of production	*Cost*
8,000	$42,100
9,000	$44,100
25,000	$76,100
25,000	$77,100

Determine a new flexible budget using the high-low method. Would a scattergraph aid in improving accuracy? Explain.

D. Assume that 8,500 games are produced during January of the next year at a cost of $42,000. How well did the firm control its costs? (Assume that the flexible budget in Part C above was accepted by management.)

E. What are the shortcomings of using the high-low method for determining cost behavior? How can they be remedied?

2-29 *(Regression Analysis and Standard Error of Estimate).* The Alene Company, in its annual review of the flexible budget, determined the following data about machinery repair costs.

Costs	*Volume in Hours*
$1,800	100
$5,010	320
$3,450	210
$1,790	130
$1,810	180
$5,020	340
$1,850	150
$3,380	200
$3,500	270
$5,000	350
$4,900	310
$3,050	280

Sum of hours (Σx) = 2,840
Sum of costs (Σy) = 40,560
Sum of hours times costs (Σxy) = 10,794,500
Sum of hours squared (Σx^2) = 753,800

REQUIRED:

A. From the given data determine the total fixed costs and variable costs per hour using the regression method.

B. Calculate the standard error of the estimate.

C. Your management, while appreciating your effort, does not understand the least-squares method. You are asked to plot the original data on a scattergraph. Does this scattergraph give you any insights into the cost behavior pattern of repair costs? Discuss.

2–30 *(Determination of Flexible Budgets from Financial Statements).* The Nothing-for-Everyone Company manufactures an adjustable television antenna. Since the company was founded in 19X1, sales and profits have had an upward trend, as shown in the following income statements.

	19X1	19X2	19X3	19X4	19X5
Sales					
Units	10,000	15,000	12,000	14,000	16,000
Dollars	$100,000	$150,000	$144,000	$168,000	$192,000
Costs					
Materials	$ 20,000	$ 30,000	$ 24,000	$ 28,000	$ 32,000
Labor	30,000	45,000	42,000	49,000	56,000
Maintenance	11,000	16,000	13,000	15,000	17,000
Building Rent	7,000	8,000	8,000	8,000	8,000
Administration	15,000	20,000	25,000	30,000	35,000
Depreciation	5,000	5,000	6,000	6,000	6,000
Sales Commissions	10,000	15,000	14,400	16,800	19,200
Total	98,000	139,000	132,400	152,800	173,200
Net Income	$ 2,000	$ 11,000	$ 11,600	$ 15,200	$ 18,800

Management has just started a formal planning system and has asked you to assist them. The president, N. Minnow Gray, has heard of the flexible budget and the master budget from his accountant but is not certain of their meaning. He has also heard of fixed and variable costs but, when he examined the income statements, he was uncertain as to which costs were fixed and which were variable.

One of the things that confused Mr. Gray was whether a cost is fixed or variable when there have been management policy or economic changes. For example, Mr. Gray had raised the sales price in 19X3 when the new union contract called for an across-the-board pay raise. In the same year management had purchased new equipment, which caused depreciation expense to increase. Further, while mangement had been able to keep material prices the same for the past 5 years through careful purchasing policies, there was an announced price increase for 19X6 of 10% that Mr. Gray could not avoid.

REQUIRED:

A. Using only the information in the income statements, prepare a flexible budget for each cost item using the high-low method.

B. How would you modify the flexible budget equations from Part A above using all of the information available. Explain your choices.

C. Using the flexible budget prepared in Part B above, prepare a budgeted income statement for 19X6 assuming that the planned sales volume is 18,000 units.

2-31 *(Regression Analysis).* The controller of the Sellers Corporation is studying the cost behavior patterns of indirect labor in relationship to units produced. He believes that a knowledge of fixed and variable costs will help him budget future costs as well as control actual expenditures. Past cost and production data show the following:

Units Produced	*Cost*
10	$ 5,400
20	$ 7,500
50	$13,300
80	$20,000
60	$15,400
10	$ 5,600
30	$ 9,300
50	$14,000
60	$15,500

Sum of units (Σx) = 370
Sum of costs (Σy) = 106,000
Sum of units times costs (Σxy) = 5,358,000
Sum of units squared (Σx^2) = 20,100
Sum of variance from regression line $\Sigma(y-\bar{y})^2 = 479{,}185$

REQUIRED:

A. Using the least-squares regression technique, determine the flexible budget showing total fixed costs and the variable rate per unit.

B. Calculate and evaluate the standard error of the estimate.

C. Compare the flexible budget from the regression method with a cost estimate using the high-low method.

2-32 *(Determination of Flexible Budget; Three Methods).* The Purple Cab Company had the following maintenance costs for the past six years.

	Total Maintenance Costs	*Hours of Activity*
Year 1	$122,500	65,000
Year 2	$157,500	90,000
Year 3	$159,000	165,000
Year 4	$180,000	215,000
Year 5	$205,000	315,000
Year 6	$225,000	365,000

REQUIRED:

A. Determine the fixed and variable maintenance costs using the scattergraph approach.

B. Determine the fixed and variable maintenance costs using the high-low method.

C. Determine the fixed and variable maintenance costs using the least-squares regression method. Calculate the standard error of the estimate.

D. Which method do you feel is most accurate? Why?

E. What are some disadvantages in using the least-squares regression method? Explain.

2-33 *(Determination of Flexible Budget).* The Ramon Co. manufactures a wide range of products at several different plant locations. The Franklin Plant, which manufactures electrical components, has been experiencing some difficulties with fluctuating monthly overhead costs. The fluctuations have

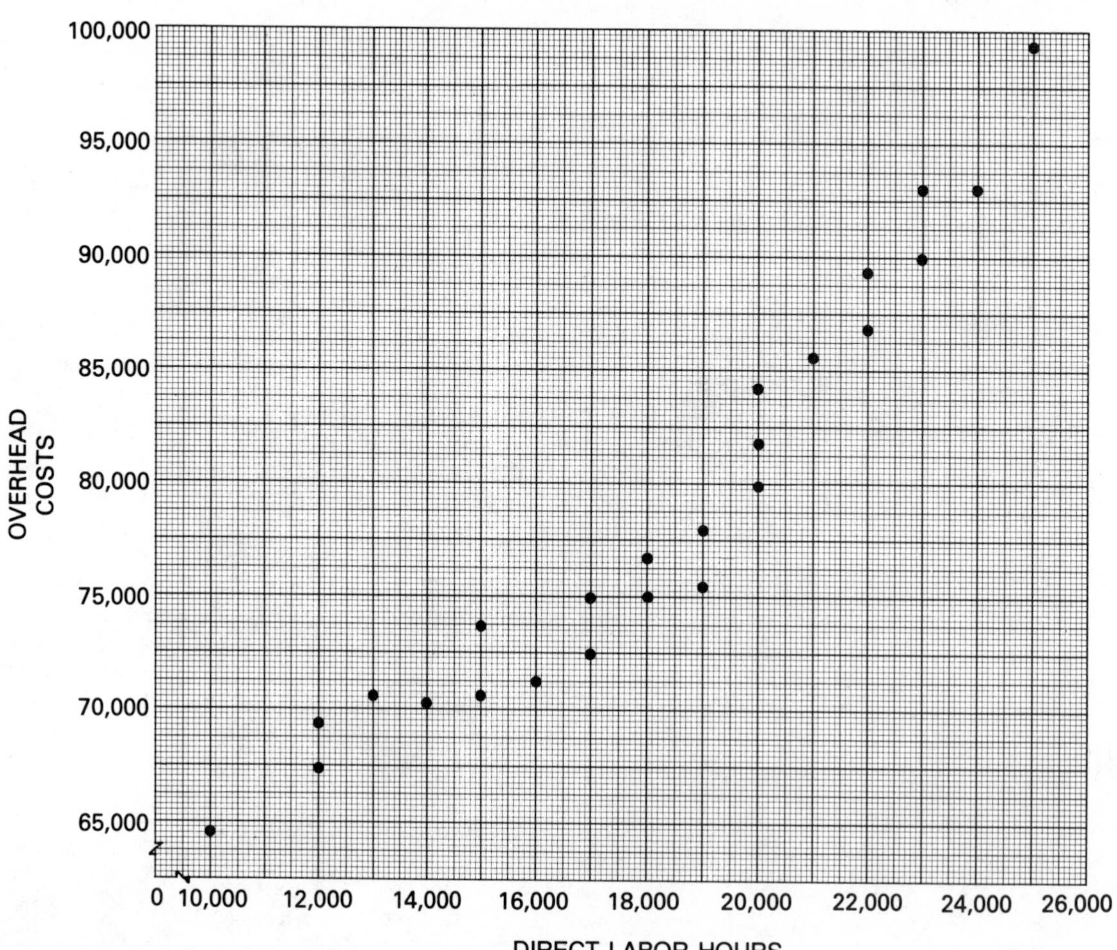

made it difficult to estimate the level of overhead that will be incurred for any one month.

Management wants to be able to estimate overhead costs accurately in order to plan its operation and financial needs better. A trade association publication to which Ramon Co. subscribes indicates that, for companies manufacturing electrical components, overhead tends to vary with direct-labor hours.

One member of the accounting staff has proposed that the cost behavior pattern of the overhead costs be determined. Then overhead costs could be predicted from the budgeted direct-labor hours.

Another member of the accounting staff suggested that a good starting place for determining the cost behavior pattern of overhead costs would be an analysis of historical data. The historical cost behavior pattern would provide a basis for estimating future overhead costs. The methods proposed for determining the cost behavior pattern included the high-low method, the scattergraph method, and simple linear regression. Data on direct-labor hours and the respective overhead costs incurred were collected for the past two years. The raw data and the scattergraph prepared from the data are as follows:

19X3	*Direct-Labor Hours*	*Overhead Costs*
January	20,000	$84,000
February	25,000	$99,000
March	22,000	$89,500
April	23,000	$90,000
May	20,000	$81,500
June	19,000	$75,500
July	14,000	$70,500
August	10,000	$64,500
September	12,000	$69,000
October	17,000	$75,000
November	16,000	$71,500
December	19,000	$78,000
19X4		
January	21,000	$86,000
February	24,000	$93,000
March	23,000	$93,000
April	22,000	$87,000
May	20,000	$80,000
June	18,000	$76,500
July	12,000	$67,500
August	13,000	$71,000
September	15,000	$73,500
October	17,000	$72,500
November	15,000	$71,000
December	18,000	$75,000

Using linear regression, the following data were obtained:

Coefficients of regression equation	
Constant	39,859
Independent variable	2.1549
Standard error of the estimate	2,840

REQUIRED:

A. Using the high-low method, determine the cost behavior pattern of the overhead costs for the Franklin Plant.

B. Using the results of the regression analysis, calculate the estimate of overhead costs for 22,500 direct labor hours.

C. Of the three proposed methods (high-low, scattergraph, linear regression), which one should Ramon Co. employ to determine the historical cost behavior pattern of Franklin Plant's overhead costs? Explain your answer completely, indicating the reasons why the other methods should not be used. *(CMA adapted)*

2-34 *(Scattergraph Approach to Flexible Budget).* The Molly Manufacturing Company has decided to make a study of its manufacturing overhead to see if it can determine what portion of overhead is variable and what portion is fixed. To begin this study, the accountant gathered the following cost and production data.

	Total Costs of Overhead	*Total Labor Hours of Production*
January	$1,950	500
February	$1,900	450
March	$2,150	600
April	$3,100	800
May	$3,450	900
June	$4,600	1,350
July	$3,750	1,100
August	$3,550	750
September	$2,300	550
October	$1,950	400
November	$2,400	3,000
December	$3,000	950

REQUIRED:

A. Prepare a scattergraph of this data. From this scattergraph develop an estimate of the flexible budget showing total fixed costs and the variable cost rate per hour of production.

B. Which month(s) might bear closer examination? Why? Could this be a normal occurrence? Why?

C. What are some of the assumptions made when this cost behavior pattern is used to forecast the future?

D. When using the scattergraph for forecasting, is there any way to remove the effects of unusual occurrences? Should this be done? Discuss some of the consequences.

2–35 *(Continuation of 2–34; High-Low Approach to Flexible Budget).*

REQUIRED:

A. Using the data of the Molly Manufacturing Company shown in Problem 2–34, determine the fixed and variable cost estimates using the high-low method.

B. Discuss some of the weaknesses in using this method of determining fixed and variable costs.

C. Using your estimates of fixed and variable costs prepared in Part A above, what is your estimate of the overhead costs at 2,750 hours?

2–36 *(Continuation of 2–34; Regression Approach to Flexible Budget).*

REQUIRED:

A. Using the data of the Molly Manufacturing Company shown in Problem 2–34, determine the fixed and variable costs using the least-squares regression method.

B. Calculate the standard error of the estimate for this regression line.

C. Discuss why this method could be considered superior to the scattergraph or high-low method.

Cost-Volume-Profit Interactions for Operating Decisions

In this chapter we explore the ways in which fixed and variable cost information can be used by the manager to assist in making operating decisions. These decisions involve the interaction of cost behavior patterns, production volume, and sales volume and revenue.

FIXED AND VARIABLE COSTS AND REVENUE

The study of cost-volume-profit relationships is most commonly called **break-even analysis.** This term can be misleading. Firms do not seek to break even. They seek an acceptable rate of return on their investment. However, breakeven analysis need not be limited merely to seeking the point at which the firm's revenue equals its costs. It can span all volumes within the relevant range of activity. Central to cost-volume-profit studies is an understanding of which costs are fixed and which are variable, as developed in the previous chapter.

Cost-Volume-Profit Analysis through Graphs

The easiest way to see breakeven analysis is graphically. Exhibit 3–1 is a graphic presentation of cost-volume-profit relationships with the breakeven point indicated. This breakeven analysis of the Gordon Company was built upon a study of its cost behavior and revenue patterns. The Gordon Manufacturing Company produces a single product, a teak-handled can opener, which it sells to souvenir stores for $1.25 each. The firm's flexible budget shows that total fixed costs are estimated to be $30,000 per year and that variable costs per unit are estimated to be $.75. Management believes that the relevant range of activity is between 40,000 and 100,000 units per year. In constructing the graph, the fixed costs were plotted as a straight horizontal line at the $30,000 level. Variable costs were plotted at the rate of $.75 per unit of volume, providing the total cost line. The sales line was plotted at the rate of $1.25 per unit of volume. As a reminder of the constraints of the relevant range, two vertical lines were added to the graph. Beyond these lines the decision maker has little assurance that the cost-volume-profit relationships are valid.

The **breakeven point** is where the sales revenue line intersects the total cost line. At this volume, total revenues equal total expenses. When operations are at the breakeven point the firm will make neither a profit nor a loss. For the Gordon Manufacturing Company the breakeven point, determined from the vertical axis of the graph, is $75,000 in sales. This point occurs at a volume of 60,000 units, which is found on the horizontal axis. The area between the sales revenue line and the total cost line at a volume below the breakeven point represents the loss potential of the firm. If the company operates at a volume beyond the breakeven point, the area between the sales revenue line and the total cost line represents the profit potential of the firm.

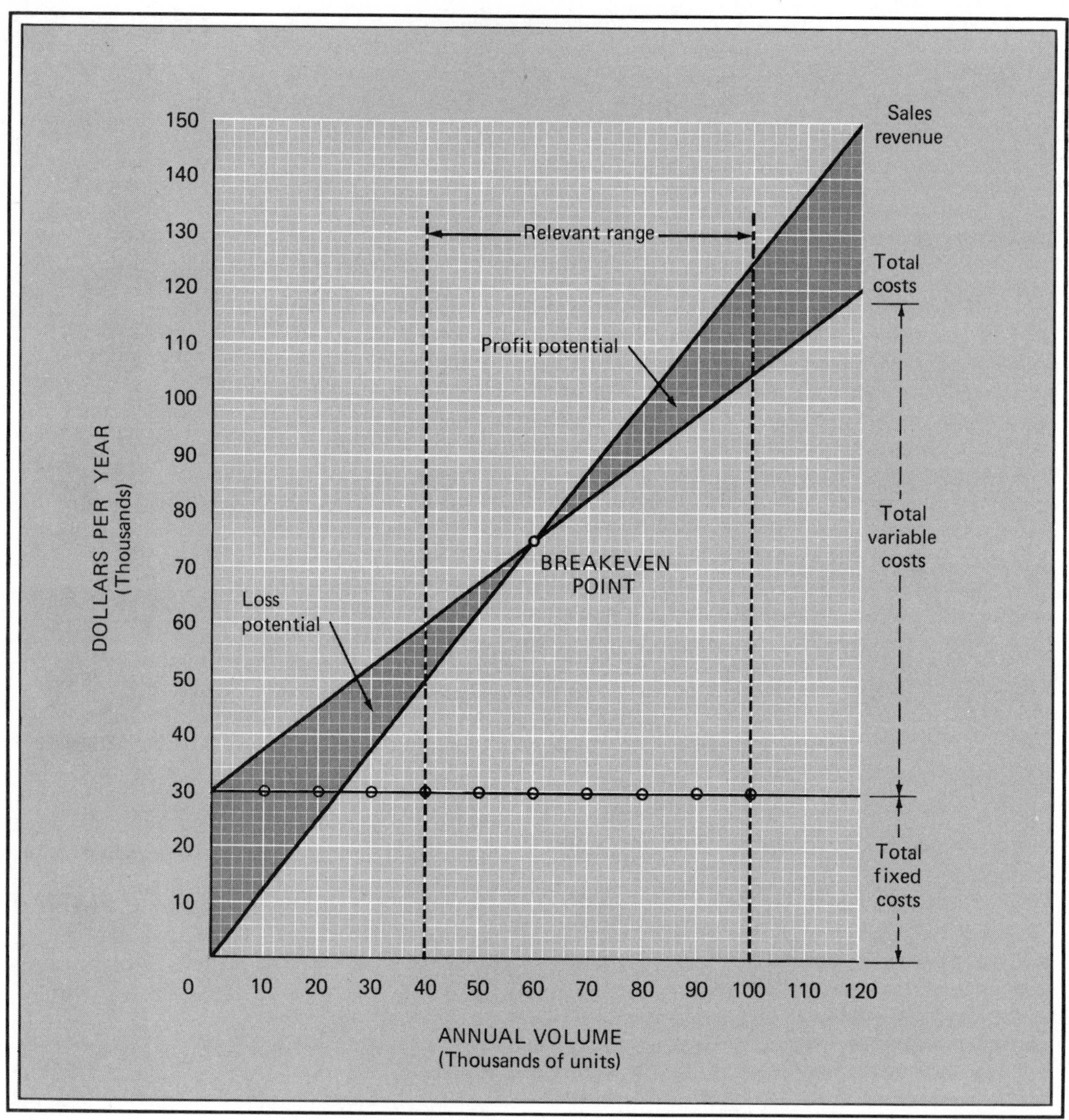

EXHIBIT 3-1
Breakeven graph for the Gordon Manufacturing Company

If the company sells 40,000 units, what will be their loss? Sales will be 40,000 units × $1.25 per unit, or $50,000. Variable costs will be 40,000 units × $.75, or $30,000. Fixed costs will be $30,000. Combining these figures into an income statement, we can see that the loss will be $10,000.

Sales (40,000 × $1.25)	$ 50,000
Variable costs (40,000 × $.75)	30,000
Contribution margin (40,000 × $.50)	$ 20,000
Fixed costs	30,000
Net loss	$(10,000)

The loss could also be found directly on the breakeven graph. Moving out the volume axis to 40,000 units, the loss of $10,000 may be determined by taking the difference between the total cost line ($60,000) and the total revenue line ($50,000).

Cost-Volume-Profit Analysis Through Equations

The graphic method is an easy way to see the implications of a cost-volume-profit relationship, but it is not the easiest way to calculate the breakeven point. Expressing the relationships in equation form is much more precise and rapid. A general form of expressing cost-volume-profit relationships that can be adapted to any situation is:

Sales − Fixed costs − Variable costs = Net income

or

Sales = Fixed costs + Variable costs + Net income

Since the amount of sales and variable costs are at the same level of activity, the equation must be restated as follows:

$$SP(x) = FC + VC(x) + NI$$

where:

SP = Selling price per unit
x = Number of units sold
FC = Total fixed costs
VC = Variable cost per unit
NI = Total net income

The Gordon Manufacturing Company's breakeven point, in number of units sold, may now be computed.

(1) $SP(x) = FC + VC(x) + NI$
(2) $\$1.25(x) = \$30{,}000 + \$.75(x) + 0$
(3) $\$.50x = \$30{,}000$
(4) $x = \$30{,}000 \div \$.50$
(5) x = 60,000 units needed to break even

Notice that Step (4) is the fixed costs ($30,000) divided by the contribution margin[1] per unit ($1.25–$.75). The breakeven equation could be stated as:

$$\text{Breakeven point in units} = \frac{\text{Total fixed costs}}{\text{Contribution margin per unit}}$$

This equation underlies the contribution margin approach to breakeven.

Cost-Volume-Profit Analysis Through the Contribution Margin

Many decision makers prefer to think in terms of an income statement for cost-volume-profit analysis. An income statement showing the contribution margin is well suited for this approach. If the selling price per unit is assumed to be constant, total revenue will be proportional to volume. We have already seen that the definition of variable costs is that total variable costs vary proportionally with volume. Since the revenue per unit is constant and the variable cost per unit is constant, the contribution margin per unit is constant. Thus, the difference between total revenue and total variable costs—the total contribution margin—will also be proportional to volume. For the Gordon Manufacturing Company the contribution margin per unit is:

	Dollars	*Percentage*
Unit sales price	$1.25	100%
Unit variable cost	.75	60%
Unit contribution margin	$ .50	40%

Each unit generates a contribution margin which is available to cover fixed costs and, after they are covered, to contribute to profit. (It should be apparent that if there is a negative contribution margin, the firm will *never* break even, since the variable costs will always exceed the sales revenue. In this case the more the company sells, the more it loses.) As shown earlier, dividing the fixed costs by the contribution margin per unit ($30,000 ÷ $.50) gives the breakeven point in units.

Alongside the income statement in dollars is a percentage analysis. If sales are considered 100%, then variable costs are 60% of each sales dollar. This relationship is called the **variable cost ratio.** The sales percentage minus the variable cost percentage is the **contribution margin ratio,** sometimes referred to as the **variable profit ratio.** For the Gordon Manufacturing Company this ratio is 40% (100% − 60%). The fixed costs divided by the

[1]Remember that in Chapter 1 the contribution margin was defined as selling price minus variable costs.

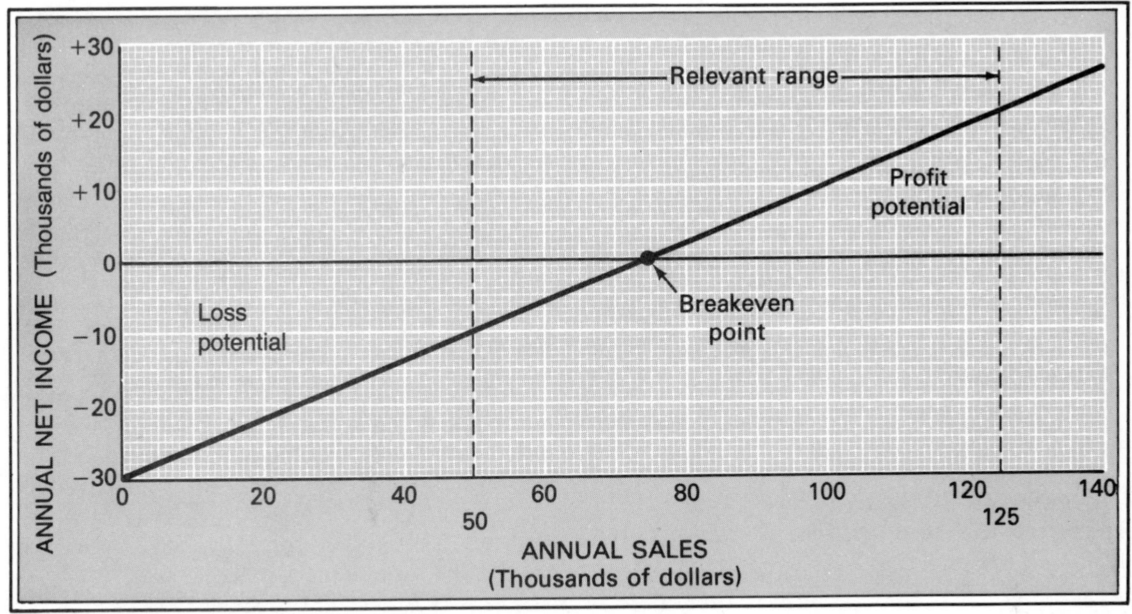

EXHIBIT 3–2
Profit-volume chart for the Gordon Manufacturing Company

contribution margin ratio ($30,000 ÷ 40%) is the breakeven point in dollars of sales ($75,000). This is the same as the formula:

$$\text{Breakeven in dollars} = \cfrac{\text{Fixed costs}}{1 - \cfrac{\text{Variable costs}}{\text{Sales}}}$$

The denominator, $1 - \dfrac{\text{Variable costs}}{\text{Sales}}$, is the contribution margin ratio.

In summary, the breakeven point is:

$$\text{Breakeven in units} = \frac{\text{Fixed costs}}{\text{Contribution margin per unit}}$$

or

$$\text{Breakeven in dollars} = \frac{\text{Fixed costs}}{\text{Contribution margin ratio}}$$

The contribution margin and the contribution margin ratio allow another useful graphic technique called the **profit-volume chart** (PV chart). Exhibit 3–2 shows the PV chart for the Gordon Manufacturing Company. On this graph the vertical axis represents the annual income. The horizontal line at zero income level is that point where there are no profits or losses. The diagonal line is the total contribution margin of the firm. The breakeven point occurs where the total contribution margin line crosses the zero income line.

Remember the question asked earlier about the amount of net loss if the company sold 40,000 units at $1.25? At sales of $50,000 (40,000 × $1.25), the net loss of $10,000 can be read directly from the PV chart. Note also that the PV chart shows that the loss at zero sales activity is equal to fixed costs. This relationship is also shown on the breakeven graph. In this illustration a sales level of 40,000 units is at the lower limit of the relevant range. In practice, most firms would aggressively reduce fixed costs as the volume began decreasing toward zero activity.

Contribution Margin Approach in Nonmanufacturing Activities

The majority of the discussion in this text assumes a manufacturing setting. However, the contribution margin approach is valid in any setting. In fact, the contribution margin is easy to apply in a nonmanufacturing setting, where inventory consists of purchased goods—all of which are variable costs. There are no fixed costs associated with inventory in nonmanufacturing activities.

To illustrate the contribution approach for a retail firm, let's assume the following traditional income statement for a florist's shop.

ROSIE'S FLOWER SHOP
INCOME STATEMENT

Sales		$200,000
Cost of goods sold		120,000
Gross margin		$ 80,000
Operating expenses:		
Salaries	$30,000	
Supplies	10,000	
Utilities	5,000	
Depreciation	13,000	
Other	2,000	60,000
Net income		$ 20,000

Assume that a study of the cost-volume relationships supplied the following cost behavior patterns for the shop.

Variable costs		*Fixed costs*	
Cost of goods sold	$120,000	Salaries	$10,000
Salaries	$ 20,000	Utilities	$ 5,000
Supplies	$ 10,000	Depreciation	$13,000
Other	$ 2,000		

The income statement that follows uses the contribution margin format.

ROSIE'S FLOWER SHOP
INCOME STATEMENT

Sales		$200,000	100%
Cost of goods sold		120,000	60%
Contribution margin from trading		$ 80,000	40%
Variable operating costs:			
Salaries	$20,000		
Supplies	10,000		
Other	2,000	32,000	16%
Contribution margin from operations		$ 48,000	24%
Fixed operating costs:			
Salaries	$10,000		
Utilities	5,000		
Depreciation	13,000	28,000	
Net income		$ 20,000	

By identifying the contribution margin, questions that concern change in volume, such as the following, may be answered.

1. How much additional income will result from a 10% increase in volume? Revenue and variable costs will each increase by 10%. Since fixed costs will remain unchanged, the increased contribution margin of $4,800 ($48,000 × 10%) will increase income by $4,800. This question cannot be answered from the traditional income statement.

2. What is the volume of sales at breakeven?

$$\text{Sales at breakeven} = \frac{\text{Fixed costs}}{\text{Contribution margin ratio}}$$

$$= \frac{\$28{,}000}{24\%}$$

$$= \$116{,}667$$

Sales would have to decrease by 42% before the breakeven point is reached.

The contribution margin approach is not limited to the private, profit-seeking sector of the economy. There are many situations where not-for-profit organizations will find the contribution margin approach useful. For example, consider the following income statement for the Eastside Community Health Center, a not-for-profit health center.

EASTSIDE COMMUNITY HEALTH CENTER
INCOME STATEMENT

	August	*September*
Revenue from patients	$20,000	$24,000
Operating costs:		
Personnel costs:		
Consulting physicians	$10,000	$12,000
Nurses and lab technicians	6,500	6,500
Administration	3,200	3,200
Medical supplies	2,000	2,400
Rent and occupancy costs	1,800	1,800
Service bureau (medical records)	600	700
Total operating costs	$24,100	$26,600
Loss from operations	$ (4,100)	$ (2,600)

The following study of cost behavior patterns assumes 2,000 patient visits in August and 2,400 visits in September.

Variable cost per visit		*Fixed costs per month*	
Consulting physicians	$5.00	Nurses and lab technicians	$ 6,500
Medical supplies	1.00	Administrative salaries	3,200
Service bureau (records)	.25	Occupancy costs	1,800
		Service bureau (records)	100
Total	$6.25	Total	$11,600

The service bureau fee for maintenance of medical records is a mixed cost that includes a fixed monthly charge of $100 plus a variable charge of $.25 per patient visit.

The monthly income statements may now be recast to a contribution margin approach. The amount of loss does not change, but the income statements are much more useful. Contribution margin approach income statements are presented in Exhibit 3–3. The director of the health center now has the financial information to answer a number of questions.

EASTSIDE COMMUNITY HEALTH CENTER
INCOME STATEMENT

	August		*September*	
	Amount	*Per Patient Visit*	*Amount*	*Per Patient Visit*
Revenue from patients	$20,000	$10.00	$24,000	$10.00
Variable operating costs:				
Consulting physicians	$10,000	$ 5.00	$12,000	$ 5.00
Medical supplies	2,000	1.00	2,400	1.00
Medical records	500	.25	600	.25
Total variable costs	12,500	6.25	15,000	6.25
Contribution margin	$ 7,500	$ 3.75	$ 9,000	$ 3.75
Fixed costs:				
Nurses and lab technicians	$ 6,500		$ 6,500	
Administration	3,200		3,200	
Occupancy costs	1,800		1,800	
Medical records	100		100	
Total fixed costs	11,600		11,600	
Loss from operations	$ (4,100)		$ (2,600)	

EXHIBIT 3–3
Contribution margin income statement of the Eastside Community Health Center

1. One of the goals of the health center is to become financially self-sufficient. Assuming that the cost-volume relationships do not change, how many patients must the center serve in order to break even?

$$\text{Breakeven in number of patients} = \frac{\text{Fixed costs}}{\text{Contribution margin per patient}}$$

$$= \frac{\$11{,}600}{\$3.75}$$

$$= 3{,}094 \text{ patient visits}$$

2. Assuming that the health center considers a volume of 2,500 patient visits per month to be a normal level that can be served within the present cost structure, what billing rate per patient visit must be charged to break even?

$$\text{Revenue} = \text{Fixed costs} + \text{Variable costs}$$
$$2{,}500(x) = \$11{,}600 + \$6.25\ (2{,}500)$$

where: x is the desired billing rate to break even.

$$2{,}500(x) = \$11{,}600 + \$15{,}625$$
$$2{,}500(x) = \$27{,}225$$
$$(x) = \$10.89$$

If the health center is to break even at a level of 2,500 patients with the present cost structure, the billing rate must be raised to $10.89 per patient visit.

The contribution margin approach can be useful in any setting where the impact of volume change on revenue and costs is needed for management decisions. Although most of our applications in this text relate to manufacturing settings, the contribution margin approach will provide useful information for decisions in other cases as well.

EFFECTS OF CHANGING FACTORS

A breakeven graph shows the relationship between four variables: sales price, fixed costs, variable costs, and volume. The study of these variables allows management to assess the potential profitability of the firm. In this section we will look at how changes in the three variables of sales revenue, fixed costs, and variable costs interact with volume to create a profit.

Effects of Changes in Selling Price

Let's assume that the management of the Gordon Manufacturing Company (an earlier example) has the opportunity to increase the unit selling price of its can opener from $1.25 to $1.50. It believes that no other factor will change by a significant amount. The immediate effect on the breakeven point is that it will be reached sooner. In this case the breakeven point in units would be:

$$\frac{\text{Fixed costs}}{\text{Contribution margin per unit}} = \frac{\$30{,}000}{\$1.50 - \$.75} = 40{,}000 \text{ units}$$

At the old selling price of $1.25 the breakeven point was 60,000 units. It is apparent that an increase in the selling price will raise the contribution margin if the variable costs are unchanged, and that an increase in the per-unit contribution margin will decrease the sales volume necessary to reach a desired goal.

What happens if the company has to lower the selling price to $1.00 per unit because of increased competition? The breakeven point will be increased to 120,000 units [$30,000 ÷ ($1.00 − $.75)]. At this output level the company will have to completely reassess its cost and revenue patterns since 120,000 units is beyond the relevant range of activity.

Effects of Changes in Variable Costs

Assume there have been changes in variable costs. The teak used in the product has increased in price by \$.05 per unit. Teak has been in short supply; due to increased demand around the world, the price increased. Also, because of inflationary pressures, the wages of the production workers increased an average of \$.20 per unit. These changes increased the total variable costs from \$.75 per unit to \$1.00 per unit. The new contribution margin becomes \$.25 (\$1.25 − \$1.00), and the breakeven point in units would be:

$$\frac{\text{Fixed costs}}{\text{Contribution margin per unit}} = \frac{\$30{,}000}{\$.25} = 120{,}000 \text{ units}$$

Again, 120,000 units is beyond the relevant range.

Any time the selling price per unit decreases or the variable cost per unit increases, the contribution margin per unit will decline and the volume necessary to achieve breakeven will increase. Of course, increases in the selling prices or decreases in the variable costs will reduce the volume necessary to achieve the breakeven point.

Effects of Changes in Fixed Costs

Assume that the original fixed costs of \$30,000 included only \$3,000 for advertising, and that it is becoming clear to management that it will be necessary to add \$6,000 for advertising if the company is to maintain its selling price of \$1.25 per unit. The new breakeven point would be:

$$\frac{\text{Fixed costs} + \text{Additional fixed cost}}{\text{Contribution margin per unit}} = \frac{\$30{,}000 + \$6{,}000}{\$1.25 - \$.75}$$

$$= 72{,}000 \text{ units}$$

Notice that the one-fifth increase in fixed costs (from \$30,000 to \$36,000) resulted in a one-fifth increase in the breakeven point (from 60,000 to 72,000 units). Changes in fixed costs will always result in proportional changes in the breakeven point.

Volume Necessary to Achieve Desired Net Income

The examples so far have stressed the effect of changes in costs upon the breakeven point. Of course, management seeks a net income. What volume must the Gordon Manufacturing Company achieve to obtain a net income of \$12,000 if it sells its can openers for \$1.25 each, incurs \$.75 per unit for variable costs, and has fixed costs of \$30,000? The desired sales volume would be:

$$\text{Sales necessary for desired net income} = \frac{\text{Fixed costs} + \text{Desired net income}}{\text{Contribution margin per unit}}$$

$$= \frac{\$30{,}000 + \$12{,}000}{\$1.25 - \$.75} = 84{,}000 \text{ units}$$

There is another way to approach the same question. If management has already calculated the breakeven point, it can approach the volume needed to earn a desired income by determining the increment in sales beyond the breakeven point. In the Gordon Manufacturing Company the breakeven point is 60,000 units, or $75,000 of sales, assuming $30,000 of fixed costs and a contribution margin of $.50 per unit. At this level all fixed costs would be recovered. Beyond the breakeven point, the entire contribution margin per unit adds to the income. For each unit sold beyond 60,000, the net income would be increased by $.50, the contribution margin per unit. Thus, to achieve a net income of $12,000, the company would have to sell 24,000 units ($12,000 ÷ $.50) beyond breakeven, or a total of 84,000 units (60,000 + 24,000).

The net income in the previous illustrations has been the net income *before* income taxes. Management may want to state its net income objectives *after* income taxes. In this case the analysis must be expanded slightly. Assume that the company wants a net income after taxes of $14,000 and that its current tax rate is 30%. In this example the net income after taxes is 70% of the net income before taxes. The formula to calculate the sales *volume* necessary to earn $14,000 after taxes is:

$$\frac{\text{Fixed costs} + \dfrac{\text{Desired income after taxes}}{1 - \text{Tax rate}}}{\text{Contribution margin per unit}} = \frac{\$30{,}000 + \dfrac{\$14{,}000}{1 - .30}}{\$1.25 - \$.75}$$

$$= \frac{\$30{,}000 + \$20{,}000}{\$.50}$$

$$= 100{,}000 \text{ units}$$

To find the sales *dollars* needed to achieve an after-tax income of $14,000, the formula would be adjusted to divide by the contribution margin ratio (.40). This calculation is:

$$\frac{\$30{,}000 + \$20{,}000}{.40} = \$125{,}000$$

Effects of Multiple Changes

Let's assume that the management of the Gordon Manufacturing Company is bombarded by changes in its environment. It believes that by lowering the selling price from $1.25 to $1.00 per unit, it could increase the current sales volume by 30%. At the same time, some changes in production methods are planned. A new machine that would automate part of the production process has just come on the market. This machine would reduce the variable costs by \$.25 per unit and would increase the fixed costs from \$30,000 to \$35,000 per year. What sales must the Gordon Manufacturing Company achieve for an after-tax net income of \$7,500 if the current tax rate is 25%? A good way to bring these changes together simultaneously is with the formula:

$$\text{Needed sales volume} = \frac{\text{Fixed costs} + \dfrac{\text{Desired net income after taxes}}{1 - \text{Tax rate}}}{1 - \dfrac{\text{Variable costs per unit}}{\text{Sales price per unit}}}$$

Taking into account the proposed changes, the data expressed in the formula would be:

$$\text{Needed sales volume} = \frac{\$30{,}000 + \$5{,}000 + \dfrac{\$7{,}500}{1. - .25}}{1 - \dfrac{\$.75 \times 130\% \times 66\tfrac{2}{3}\%}{\$1.25 \times 130\% \times 80\%}}$$

$$= \frac{\$45{,}000}{.5}$$

$$= \$90{,}000 \text{ of sales, or } 90{,}000 \text{ units}$$

This formula shows the effect of the four proposed changes. First, the fixed costs have increased by \$5,000. Second, the original price of \$1.25 was lowered to \$1.00. The new selling price is 80% of the original selling price. When the \$1.25 is multiplied by 80%, the formula reflects the new selling price of \$1.00. (If this were the only change, the contribution margin ratio would decrease.) Third, the increase in sales volume will increase both total sales and total variable costs to 130% of their original level. Thus, changes in volume do not affect the contribution margin ratio since both sales and variable costs have been multiplied by 130%. Fourth, the decrease in the variable costs by \$.25 per unit puts the variable costs at 66⅔% of their previous level (\$.50 ÷ \$.75). This decrease acts to increase the contribution margin ratio.

By thinking about the interaction of volume, selling price, variable costs, and fixed costs, the relevant variables and their effect upon income are considered simultaneously. Perhaps in this context a name for the breakeven graph that more clearly describes its function would be **profit planning chart.**

UNDERLYING ASSUMPTIONS OF COST-VOLUME-PROFIT RELATIONSHIPS

A thoughtful look at the breakeven graph provides insight into the underlying assumptions of cost-volume-profit analysis. Among them are the following.

1. The breakeven graph shows costs separated into fixed and variable components. This classification implies that the decision maker has been successful in finding and using a method of segregating fixed and variable costs. Within this assumption lie the problems and limitations of cost-volume analysis discussed in Chapter 2.
2. The fixed costs are constant across the changes in volume, and the variable costs change in direct proportion to volume. Inherent in this assumption is the concept of the relevant range. It is apparent that fixed costs will stairstep at some volume. Some variable costs are not linear. Labor will meet with diminishing returns at some activity level and raw materials may involve quantity discounts if used in large amounts. All these issues, and others like them, have been resolved via a linear relationship within the assumption of a relevant range.
3. The revenue line is also linear. Throughout the relevant range it assumes that management is not granting price concessions to obtain higher sales volume. This is the economist's definition of pure competition.
4. When both costs and revenues are plotted on the same volume (x) axis, the assumption of a single volume measure is made. It is assumed that all production was sold or that there were no significant changes in the inventory levels.
5. Since the time implied by such a cost-volume-profit graph is an accounting period, for example, the fiscal year, the cost-volume-profit graph assumes no price-level changes and no significant changes in production methods, products, or managerial policies during the accounting period.
6. Since the chart assumes a constant contribution margin per unit, it implies that there is only one product or, if more than one, that the combination of products sold provides a constant average contribution margin per unit.

A Curvilinear Approach to Cost-Volume-Profit Analysis

A contribution margin approach leads to producing and selling at the maximum plant capacity as long as the contribution margin per unit is positive. (With a negative contribution margin per unit the variable costs will exceed the sales price and the firm will lose money on each unit sold.) This assumption is valid only as long as the firm does not find it necessary to reduce the selling price per unit to increase sales volume or the variable costs per unit do not increase because of diminishing returns.

The economist, in developing a theoretical model for decisions about pricing of products and the level of production output, takes into account the possibility of decreasing sales price per unit and increasing costs per unit. In this sense the economist's model is more generalizable than the accountant's approach.

To illustrate the economist's approach to output and pricing decisions, let's examine cost and revenue structure as the economist views a business. The total costs of the firm are the sum of all fixed and variable costs needed to produce each level of output. Fixed costs are unaffected by production output decisions and are incurred even when the output is quite small. Variable costs are zero when output is zero and increase as output increases. In economic theory total costs increase at a declining *rate* per unit, then at a constant *rate* per unit, and finally at an increasing *rate* per unit. This behavior pattern of total costs recognizes that gains in operating efficiencies act to reduce costs per unit to a certain point (**economies of scale**) and that as the level of production continues to increase, operating inefficiencies take effect (**diminishing returns**). The effect of diminishing returns is to cause the total costs to increase rapidly.

Total revenue is the quantity sold times the price per unit. Economics assumes that the price per unit must be reduced to sell more units. The firm must offer price concessions to obtain increased sales volume.[2]

Total revenue minus total cost is total income. The effect of the decreasing price per unit, caused by price reductions necessary to increase demand, and the increasing cost per unit, caused by diminishing returns on the production facilities, is to have an income figure that increases to a point and then decreases until it becomes a loss. Thus, the optimum production level is where the total revenue line exceeds the total cost line by the largest amount. The total revenue and cost curves, with the optimum volume level, are shown in Exhibit 3–4.

Economists also state this decision rule on a per-unit basis. Using a per-unit analysis the optimum output by the economist's rule is the point at which the added cost of producing the next unit (marginal cost) equals the added revenue from the next unit sold (marginal revenue). These are concepts that relate the changes in cost and revenue effected by adding *one* unit. It is beyond the scope of this book to demonstrate that this economic principle is true. For our purposes we will use total revenue and cost, which provides the same results, rather than marginal revenue and cost analysis.

If we make one important assumption, then the accountant's and the economist's decision approach can result in similar solutions. The accountant assumes that there is a **relevant range of activity** over which the linear assumptions are valid. The effect of the relevant range of activity can be seen in Exhibit 3–5, which shows the economist's total cost and revenue curves. The heavy dashed lines show the accountant's cost and revenue lines. The two vertical lines show the relevant range of activity; over this volume range the economist's and the accountant's models will give similar solutions. If production falls or rises outside the relevant range of activity, the entire cost and revenue patterns of the accountant must be reassessed. The economist, on the other hand, has developed a descriptive model for wide ranges of activity.

---

[2]This statement is true in all cases except pure competition. In pure competition the selling price per unit is assumed to be constant over the output range since the individual producer cannot offer a large enough amount to influence the price. Further discussion of this point is contained in Chapter 11 where pricing decisions are discussed.

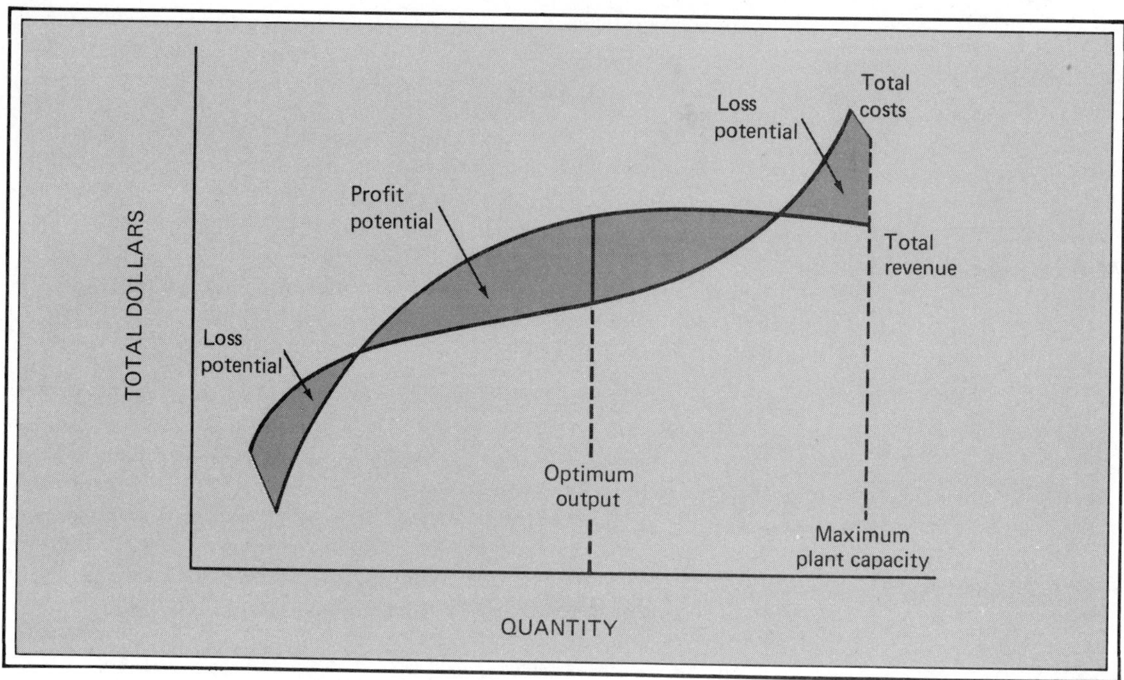

EXHIBIT 3–4
Economist's total revenue and cost curves

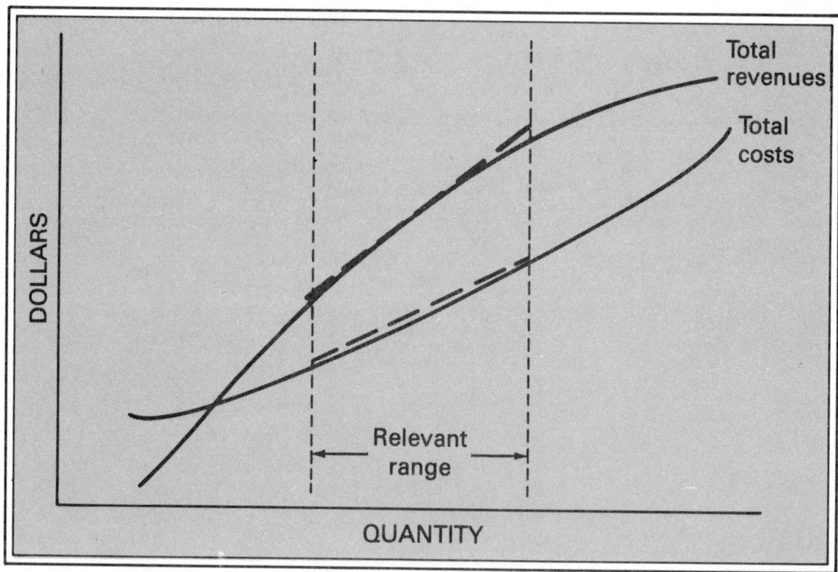

EXHIBIT 3–5
Comparison of accountant's and economist's total cost and revenue curves within the relevant range

From this short discussion we can see that within the relevant range the accountant's model can be a sound approach, consistent with economic analysis. Thus, when we say that the decision rule for operating (short-run) decisions is to maximize the total contribution margin of the firm we are consistent with economic theory, assuming the constraints of the relevant range of activity.

Multiproduct Situations

The previous illustrations assumed that the Gordon Manufacturing Company produced only one product. However, many manufacturers make more than one type of product. The relative combination of the quantities of each product sold is called the **sales mix.** If each product has an identical contribution margin, changes in the product mix will not affect the breakeven point or the profit from operations. However, when the products have different contribution margins, changes in the product mix will affect the breakeven point and the results from operations.

To explore the effect of sales mix, let's assume that the management of the Gordon Manufacturing Company added two new items to its product line. In addition to the can opener, it decided to produce and sell a bottle opener and a corkscrew. Projected selling prices, cost patterns, and volume of sales are shown in Exhibit 3–6. Exhibit 3–7 shows the projected income statements for each product and for the company as a whole.

	Can opener	*Bottle opener*	*Corkscrew*
Sales price per unit	$1.25	$2.00	$2.50
Variable cost per unit	.75	1.30	1.75
Contribution margin per unit	$ .50	$ .70	$ .75
Contribution margin ratio	40%	35%	30%
Fixed costs for total operations $36,000			
Projected units to be produced and sold	50,000	25,000	15,000

EXHIBIT 3–6
Projected cost and revenue data for the Gordon Manufacturing Company

The breakeven point for the Gordon Manufacturing Company, given the sales mix of 50,000 can openers, 25,000 bottle openers, and 15,000 corkscrews, is \$36,000 ÷ 35.8%, or \$100,559. The 35.8% is the aggregate contribution margin ratio based upon the specific sales mix. At the bottom of Exhibit 3–7 the sales for each product are shown as a percent of total sales. Given the sales mix in Exhibit 3–7, the can openers account for 41.67% of the total sales of \$150,000; the bottle openers, 33⅓%; and the corkscrews, 25%. Multiplying each product's percentage share of total sales by the contribution

THE GORDON MANUFACTURING COMPANY
PROJECTED INCOME STATEMENT
For the Year Ended December 31, 19X6

	Can opener	Bottle opener	Corkscrew	Total	
Units sold	50,000	25,000	15,000		
Sales	\$62,500	\$50,000	\$37,500	\$150,000	100.00%
Variable cost	37,500	32,500	26,250	96,250	64.17%
Total contribution margin	\$25,000	\$17,500	\$11,250	\$ 53,750	35.83%
Fixed costs				36,000	
Net income before taxes				\$ 17,750	
Sales as percentage of total sales	41.67%	33.33%	25.00%	100.00%	
times					
Contribution margin ratio	40.00%	35.00%	30.00%	35.83%	
equals					
Contribution margin of each product per dollar of revenue	16.67%	11.66%	7.50%	35.83%	

EXHIBIT 3–7
Projected income statements by product line for the Gordon Manufacturing Company

THE GORDON MANUFACTURING COMPANY
ACTUAL INCOME STATEMENT
For the Year Ended December 31, 19X6

	Can opener	Bottle opener	Corkscrew	Total	
Units sold	25,000	50,000	15,000		
Sales	$31,250	$100,000	$37,500	$168,750	100.00%
Variable cost	18,750	65,000	26,250	110,000	65.19%
Total contribution margin	$12,500	$35,000	$11,250	$ 58,750	34.81%
Fixed costs				36,000	
Net income before taxes				$ 22,750	
Sales as percentage of total sales	18.52%	59.26%	22.22%	100.00%	
times					
Contribution margin ratio	40.00%	35.00%	30.00%	34.81%	
equals					
Contribution margin of each product per dollar of revenue	7.40%	20.74%	6.67%	34.81%	

EXHIBIT 3–8
Actual income statements by product line for the Gordon Manufacturing Company

margin ratio for that product gives the total contribution margin *per sales dollar* for each product. Thus, the 16.67% for the can opener is its contribution margin per dollar of revenue.

Given this setting, and other things being equal, management should stress those products with the greatest contribution margins. Assume that during the year management actually sold 25,000 additional bottle openers in place of 25,000 can openers. The income statement for the year would be as shown in Exhibit 3–8. Based upon the sales of 25,000 can openers, 50,000 bottle openers, and 15,000 corkscrews, the breakeven point would be $36,000 ÷ 34.81%, or $103,419. The shift from selling 50,000 can openers and 25,000 bottle openers to selling 25,000 can openers and 50,000 bottle openers had a curious effect. It lowered the aggregate contribution margin ratio from 35.8% (Exhibit 3–7) to 34.81% (Exhibit 3–8) while simultaneously increasing the net profit by $5,000 ($22,750 − $17,750). The can opener has a higher contribution margin ratio (40%) than the bottle opener (35%), but the contribution margin per unit of the bottle opener is higher ($.70) than that of the can opener ($.50). The firm should move toward those products that provide the greatest *total contribution margin,* considering the product mix, rather than automatically choosing the product with the highest contribution margin ratio.

Exhibits 3–7 and 3–8 present income statements shown by product line. This arrangement presents problems in the handling of fixed costs. In these two exhibits the fixed costs are shown as a lump-sum amount deducted from the total column. Fixed costs have not been allocated or apportioned to the individual product line income statements. It is not necessary to do so because for management decisions the question of which products to emphasize and the effect of cost-volume-revenue interactions on profits and breakeven points do not depend upon allocation of fixed costs.

Multidepartmental Comparisons

The operating characteristics of different departments within a company, or of two different companies, can be examined through a closer study of their cost structures. Assume that a company has two decentralized departments with cost and revenue characteristics shown in the accompanying tabulation.

	Department A		*Department B*	
Sales	$50,000	100%	$50,000	100%
Variable costs	35,000	70%	10,000	20%
Contribution margin	$15,000	30%	$40,000	80%
Fixed costs	10,000		35,000	
Net income	$ 5,000		$ 5,000	
Breakeven points in sales dollars	$33,333		$43,750	

These two departments have the same net profit, although they have very different underlying economic characteristics. One way to examine these differences is through the **margin of safety,** which shows the difference between the actual (or budgeted) sales and the breakeven point. The two margins of safety are as follows:

	Department A	*Department B*
1. Margin of safety expressed in dollars		
($50,000 − $33,333)	$16,667	
($50,000 − $43,750)		$6,250
2. Margin of safety expressed as a percent of sales		
($16,667 ÷ $50,000)	33.33%	
($6,250 ÷ $50,000)		12.50%

Department B is operating closer to the breakeven point than is Department A. Department B has a narrower margin of safety. If the volume of Department B drops more than 12.50%, it will operate at a loss; Department A will not operate at a loss unless its volume drops 33.33%. In one sense the margin of safety is an inexact measure of the risks of investing in fixed costs rather than variable costs. A rise in the breakeven point reduces the margin of safety and increases managerial pressure to sustain a high sales volume.

SUMMARY

The breakeven graph is a pictorial presentation of cost-volume-profit interactions. It clearly shows the point where total revenue equals total cost. More importantly, it shows how managerial decisions regarding revenues and volume affect the firm's profit. Inherent in cost-volume-profit analysis is the relevant range of activity. The relevant range is that volume over which the relationships can be assumed valid.

The breakeven point in dollars is the fixed costs divided by the contribution margin ratio. The breakeven point in units is the fixed costs divided by the contribution margin per unit. For firms with multiple products, the breakeven point must be built upon a specific product mix. Where there are separate departments within the firm, the effect of cost-volume changes can be seen in the margin of safety (budgeted or actual sales minus breakeven sales) and the margin of safety ratio (the difference between actual sales and breakeven sales divided by actual sales).

SUPPLEMENTARY READING

*Bell, Albert L. "Break-Even Charts Versus Marginal Graphs." *Management Accounting,* February, 1969.

Dow, Alice S., and Orace Johnson. "The Break-Even Point Concept: Its Development and Expanding Implications." *Management Accounting,* February, 1969.

Jenkins, David O. "Cost-Volume-Profit Analysis." *Management Services,* March–April, 1970.

Soldosky, Robert M. "Accountant's Versus Economist's Concepts of Break-even Analysis." *N.A.A. Bulletin,* December, 1959.

Vickers, D. "On the Economics of Break-even." *The Accounting Review,* July, 1960.

Weiser, Herbert J. "Break-even Analysis: A Re-evaluation." *Management Accounting,* February, 1969.

QUESTIONS

3-1 Explain the meaning of contribution margin and how it is used in cost-volume-profit analysis. What is a negative contribution margin and what is its significance in cost-volume-profit analysis?

3-2 How are breakeven graphs and profit-volume graphs similar? How are they different?

3-3 In an accountant's breakeven graph there is only one breakeven point. Why is this so?

3-4 How do the breakeven graphs of accountants differ from the breakeven graphs of economists?

3-5 If more than one product is sold, can a breakeven graph be prepared for the company? Explain.

3-6 Define and explain the following concepts: sales mix, variable cost ratio, contribution margin ratio, breakeven point, and margin of safety.

3-7 If a firm is currently earning a profit, which would have the largest impact on profit—a 10% increase in selling price, a 10% decrease in variable costs, or a 10% decrease in fixed costs?

3-8 Explain the difference in the computations to determine the breakeven point in number of units and the dollar amount of sales.

3-9 When the contribution margin ratio is increased, does the slope of the profit line on the profit-volume graph become steeper or flatter? Explain.

3-10 Cost-volume-profit analysis indicates that only sales and variable costs are relevant and that the fixed costs are not relevant in the short run. Do you agree? Discuss.

EXERCISES

3-11 *(True or False)*. Indicate whether the following statements are *true* or *false*.

1. If the selling price per unit is assumed to be constant, total revenue will be proportionate to number of units sold.

2. Decreasing the selling price decreases the breakeven point.

3. Fixed costs do not change with changes in production volume.

4. The contribution margin per unit is proportional to volume.

5. It is impossible to obtain a breakeven point with a negative contribution margin.

6. To obtain the breakeven point in units, the total fixed costs should be divided by the contribution margin ratio.
7. The margin of safety is found by subtracting fixed costs from sales.
8. If the variable costs per unit increase, the contribution margin ratio will increase.
9. As production volume increases, the contribution margin ratio increases.
10. Accountants usually assume that variable costs are linear.

3–12 *(Matching).* Match the following terms and descriptions.

1. Variable costs
2. Fixed costs
3. Contribution margin
4. Contribution margin ratio
5. Breakeven graph
6. Profit-volume graph
7. Breakeven point
8. Margin of safety
9. Sales mix
10. Relevant range

A. The point where total contribution margin and fixed costs are equal.
B. The amount that must be divided into fixed costs to determine dollars of sales at breakeven.
C. The amount of decline in sales before a loss is incurred.
D. The difference between sales and fixed costs at breakeven.
E. The volume over which the accountant's linear assumptions are valid.
F. A graphic presentation of cost-volume-profit relationships that does not present the amount of sales.
G. A cost, when stated as a cost per unit, that will change as the activity level changes.
H. The combination of products sold during a particular period of time.
I. Net income plus fixed costs.
J. A graphic presentation of total costs and revenue.

3–13 *(Breakeven Point).*

A. Calculate the breakeven point in units and in dollars of sales from the following data:

Selling price per unit	$2.50
Variable cost per unit	$1.00
Total fixed costs	$6,000

B. What sales are necessary to earn a before-tax net income of $1,500?

C. What sales are necessary to earn an after-tax net income of $2,100 if the tax rate is 30%?

3–14 *(Breakeven Point).*

A. Compute the breakeven point in units and dollars from the following data.

Contribution margin per unit	$1.25
Contribution margin ratio	25%
Fixed costs per month	$75

B. If net income is $105, what is the dollar amount of sales?

3–15 *(Breakeven Graph).* The Sharpe Tack Company had the following income statement when 10,000 units were sold:

SHARPE TACK COMPANY
INCOME STATEMENT

Sales		$20,000
Expenses:		
Variable expenses	$12,000	
Fixed expenses	6,000	18,000
Net income		$ 2,000

REQUIRED:
A. Prepare a breakeven graph for the company.
B. From the graph, how many units must be sold to break even?
C. What is the margin of safety in dollars?

3–16 *(Profit-Volume Graph).* The Eight Penny Nail Company had the following revenue and cost data when 2,000 units were sold.

Selling price per unit	$12.00
Variable cost per unit	$ 6.00
Fixed cost per unit	$ 4.50

REQUIRED:
A. Prepare a profit-volume graph for the company.
B. Determine the breakeven point from the graph.
C. From the graph, determine how many units must be sold to generate a net income of $3,000.

3–17 *(Breakeven Analysis in Hospital Setting).* A hospital has an average revenue of $100 per patient day. Variable costs are $20 per patient day, and fixed costs are $3,200,000 per year.

REQUIRED:

A. How many patient days does the hospital need to break even?

B. How many dollars in revenues are needed to earn $320,000 per year?

C. If variable costs drop to $18, what increase in fixed costs can be tolerated without changing the breakeven point determined in Part A above?

3-18 *(Breakeven Graph).*

REQUIRED:

A. List the assumptions that were made when the accompanying breakeven graph was prepared.

B. Determine the flexible budget formula for total costs.

C. Calculate total costs, revenue, and net income from the graph, assuming a production and sales level of 150 units.

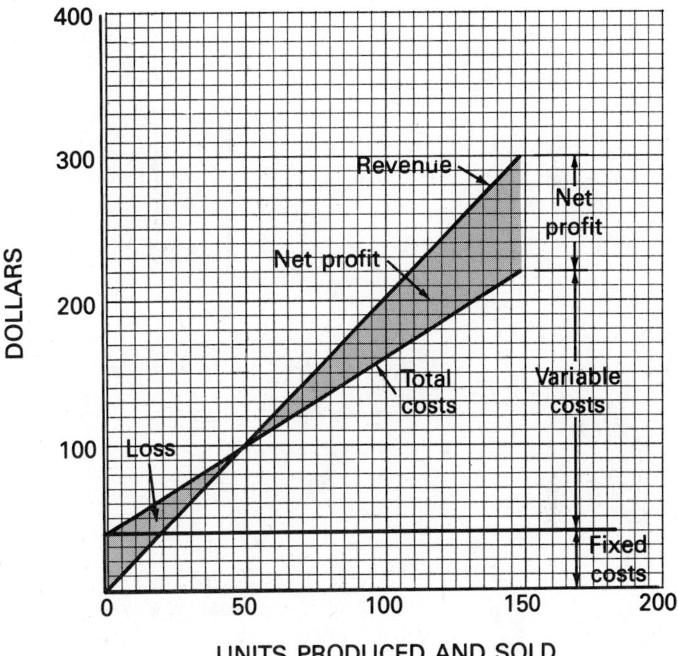

3-19 *(Profit-Volume Graph).*

REQUIRED:

A. List the assumptions that were made when the accompanying profit-volume graph was prepared.

B. Calculate the contribution margin per unit and total net income from the graph, assuming a production and sales level of 150 units.

C. Are you able to determine total costs and revenue from the profit-volume graph? Why or why not?

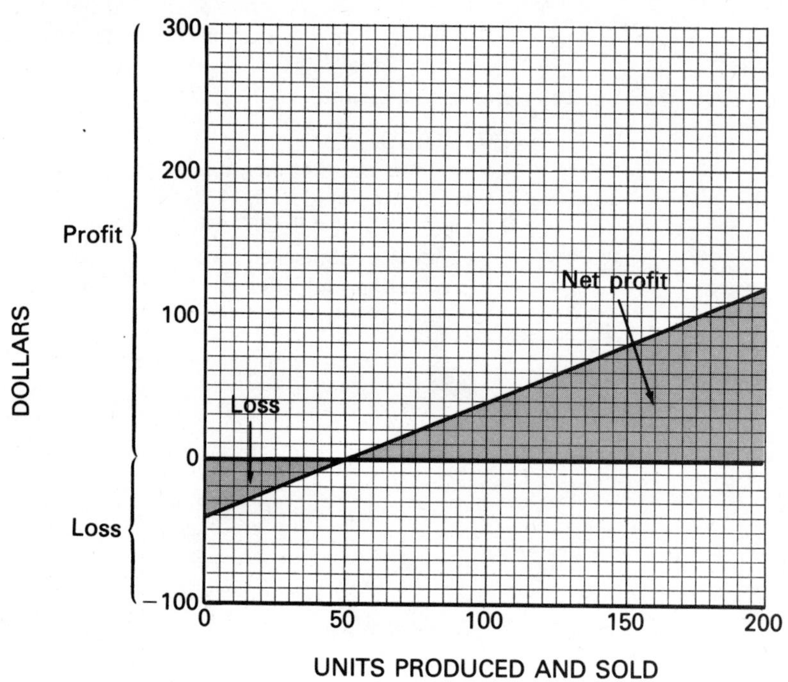

3-20 *(Cost-Volume-Profit Decision).* Sherri Brown operates a frozen yogurt stand. In an average week she will sell 500 yogurt cones at \$.75 each. Her cost structure is:

Yogurt mix	\$0 + \$.32 (per cone)
Cone	\$0 + \$.08 (per cone)
Rent	\$50 per week
Utilities	\$20 per week
Napkins and Supplies	\$15 per week + \$.10 (per cone)

REQUIRED:

A. Prepare a contribution margin income statement.

B. Determine the breakeven point in cones per week.

C. How many cones must Sherri sell to make the same profit if her rent increases $12.50 per week to a total rent of $62.50?

3-21 *(Cost-Volume-Profit Analysis under Different Assumptions).* The Roaring Blaze Manufacturing Company produces a line of fireplace logs that are packaged and sold in a container of 20 logs. During the past month it had the following revenue and cost patterns:

Selling price per unit	$ 4.00
Variable costs per unit	$ 2.00
Nonvariable costs	$1,000
Volume in units	1,000

REQUIRED: (Consider each case separately.)

A. Assume a 20% increase in production volume; what is the increase in profits?

B. Assume a decrease of 20% in the nonvariable costs; what is the new nonvariable cost and the impact on profit?

C. Assume a 20% decrease in variable costs; what is the new variable cost and the new profit figure?

D. Assume a 20% increase in the selling price; what is the total revenue and the new profit figure?

E. Assume a 10% decrease in the selling price and a resultant 20% increase in production volume; what is the new profit figure?

3-22 *(Cost-Volume-Profit Decisions).* The Popular Paper Company produces a line of quality napkins and paper tablecloths. One particular product, a 72-inch round tablecloth, is causing disagreement between the sales department and the cost accounting department. The sales department believes that the product is selling well and contributing greatly to the profitability of the firm, stressing the fact that the product has a variable cost ratio of 55%. The cost accounting department, on the other hand, says that the yearly sales of 250,000 units at $1.00 per unit did not produce sufficient volume to cover the fixed costs of $130,000 per year.

REQUIRED:

A. What is the volume of sales necessary to break even?

B. What selling price per unit is necessary to break even at the present volume level?

C. Prepare a contribution margin income statement based upon the original data in the problem.

3-23 *(Cost-Volume-Profit Analysis; Fill in Blanks).* Three independent situations involving cost-volume-profit situations follow. In each case you are to determine the amount where the question mark appears.

	Case A	Case B	Case C
Selling price per unit	$?	$ 2.00	$ 8.00
Variable costs per unit	$ 2.10	$?	$?
Fixed costs per unit	$ .60	$?	$ 3.00
Contribution margin ratio	?	100%	25%
Total fixed costs	$180,000	$?	$?
Breakeven point in units	200,000	?	6,000
Breakeven point in sales	$600,000	$?	$?
Contribution margin per unit	$ .90	$?	$ 2.00
Margin of safety in units	?	8,000	?
Net income (loss)	$ 90,000	$16,000	$?
Number of units sold	?	12,000	4,000

3-24 *(Cost-Volume-Profit Analysis Under Different Assumptions).* Ceramics Productions produces, among other products, a line of four-inch clay pots. Breakeven is currently at a sales volume of $18,000, or 36,000 clay pots. Each pot generates a contribution margin of $.20. The company desires a profit of $4,000 on the sale of these pots and is willing to increase advertising by $2,000 to obtain the needed volume increase.

REQUIRED: (Consider each case separately.)

A. How many pots beyond the breakeven point would the company have to sell to earn their desired profit without the advertising?

B. If fixed costs were to increase 10%, what volume of sales would be necessary to earn the desired profit of $4,000?

C. If the company decided to spend the $2,000 for advertising, what volume would be necessary to earn the $4,000 profit?

D. The company believes it can double sales by lowering the selling price to $.28 per unit. Would you advise doing this? Why or why not? Would your answer differ if the selling price were lowered to $.35 to achieve this volume increase?

3-25 *(Breakeven with Multiple Products).* The Blackbeard Company, a manufacturer of old pirate treasure chests for the modern collector, has two product sizes: a 48-inch chest and a 36-inch chest. Planned costs, revenue, and production data for the coming year are as follows:

	48-inch	*36-inch*
Selling price	$ 50	$ 36
Variable cost per unit	$ 30	$ 27
Sales volume in units	500	2,000
Fixed costs traceable to each product	$2,000	$6,000

REQUIRED:

A. Calculate the breakeven point for each product and for the company as a whole. What is the combined contribution margin ratio?

B. Calculate the margin of safety for each product.

PROBLEMS

3-26 *(Breakeven Graph; Identification of Components).* After reading an article you recommended on cost behavior, a friend asks you to explain the following excerpts from it:

1. "*Fixed costs* are variable per unit of output and *variable costs* are fixed per unit of output (though in the long run all costs are variable)."
2. "*Depreciation* may be either a fixed cost or a variable cost, depending on the method used to compute it."

REQUIRED:

For each excerpt:

A. Define the italicized terms. Give examples where appropriate.

B. Explain the meaning of the excerpts to your friend.

A breakeven graph as illustrated below, is a useful technique for showing relationships between costs, volume, and profits.

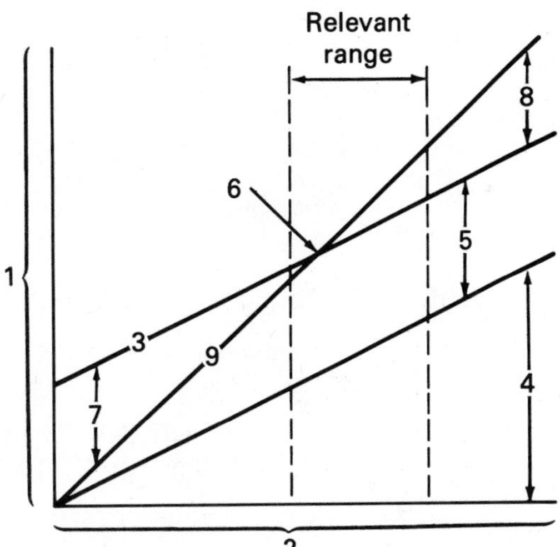

REQUIRED:

C. Identify the numbered components of the breakeven graph.

D. Discuss the significance of the concept of the "relevant range" to breakeven analyses. *(CPA adapted)*

3-27 *(Identification of Terms and Cost-Volume-Profit Decisions).* Cost-volume-earnings analysis (breakeven analysis) is used to determine and express the interrelationships of different volumes of activity (sales), costs, sales prices, and sales mix to earnings. More specifically, the analysis is concerned with the effect on earnings of changes in sales volume, sales prices, sales mix, and costs.

REQUIRED:

A. Certain terms are fundamental to cost-volume-earnings analysis. Explain the meaning of each of the following terms:

1. Fixed costs
2. Variable costs
3. Relevant range
4. Breakeven point
5. Margin of safety
6. Sales mix

B. Several assumptions are implicit in cost-volume-earnings analysis. What are these assumptions?

C. In a recent period Zero Company had the following experience:

Sales (10,000 units @ $200)			$2,000,000
	Fixed	*Variable*	
Costs:			
Direct material	$ 0	$ 200,000	
Direct labor	0	400,000	
Factory overhead	160,000	600,000	
Administrative expenses	180,000	80,000	
Other expenses	200,000	120,000	
Total costs	$540,000	$1,400,000	1,940,000
Net income			$ 60,000

Each item below is independent.

1. Calculate the breakeven point for Zero in terms of units and sales dollars. Show your calculations.
2. What sales volume would be required to generate a net income of $96,000? Show your calculations.
3. What is the breakeven point if management makes a decision which increases fixed costs by $18,000? Show your calculations. *(CPA adapted)*

3-28 *(Cost-Volume-Profit Decisions under Different Assumptions).* The Prairie Manufacturing Company has the following revenue and cost characteristics on their only product.

Selling price per unit	$6.00
Variable costs per unit	$4.20
Annual fixed costs	$360,000
Annual volume	270,000 units

REQUIRED:

A. Determine the following:

1. Variable cost ratio
2. Contribution margin ratio
3. Contribution margin per unit
4. Breakeven point in units and in dollars
5. Net profit at current operating level

B. For each of the following *independent* cases, determine the new contribution margin ratio, breakeven point in dollars, and net profit.

1. 5% increase in selling price
2. 20% increase in variable costs
3. 50% increase in fixed costs
4. 5% increase in sales and production volume
5. Decrease of $30,000 in fixed costs
6. Decrease in variable costs of $.20
7. Decrease in variable costs of $.60 and 20% increase in selling price
8. 20% decrease in fixed costs and 20% increase in variable costs

3-29 *(Cost-Volume-Profit Decisions in Small Business).* Peggy formed Rent-A-Student Company. She advertises for temporary jobs and sends students out to do the work.

Financial data for first two months of operation are:

	November	*December*
Revenue	$160	$240
Student help salaries	$120	$180
Office and supplies expenses	28	32
Advertising	40	40
Total costs	188	252
Net income (loss)	$(28)	$(12)
Student hours worked	40	60

REQUIRED:

A. Develop the flexible budget equation for Peggy's costs.
B. What is the contribution margin per hour?
C. How many hours and revenue dollars need to be earned to break even?
D. Peggy wants to earn $100 per month from this venture. What volume of business must be achieved to earn the target of $100 of net income per month?

E. Peggy has the opportunity to expand her advertising by an additional $20 per month. How many additional hours of service are needed to cover the advertising cost?

F. If the hourly rate charged to customers is changed to $4.20, what is the new breakeven point in hours? How many hours are needed at the new rate to earn $100 per month?

3-30 *(Margin of Safety and Breakeven Point with Multiple Products).* The Oaken Cask Company produces two main product lines made of oak: an old-fashioned bucket, which sells for $6.00, and a five-gallon decorative wine cask, which sells for $7.50. The variable cost for the bucket is $4.50 per unit; for the wine cask it is $5.00. The bucket department had sales of 50,000 units, while the wine cask department had sales of 30,000 units. Identifiable fixed costs are $50,000 and $55,000 for the bucket and cask departments, respectively.

REQUIRED:

A. Prepare contribution margin income statements for each product line and for the company as a whole.

B. Calculate the breakeven point for each product and for the company as a whole.

C. Calculate the contribution margin ratio for the company as a whole.

D. For each product, and for the company as a whole, determine:

1. The margin of safety in dollars

2. The margin of safety expressed as a percent of sales

E. Which line offers the least risk? Why?

3-31 *(Cost-Volume-Profit Decisions and Flexible Budget Determination).* Cider Press Co. was organized at the beginning of the year to process apples grown on Vashon Island into apple cider.

The firm has three employees: a clerk, a crushing machine operator, and a bottling machine operator. All employees are paid $3.00 per hour plus $1.50 per hour for any time worked over the regular working hours of 40 hours in one week. The clerk must be on hand during regular working hours to purchase any apples brought into the plant by orchard operators. The other two employees work only if there are apples ready to be crushed. (They are not guaranteed any specific number of hours of work in a week.)

About 50 gallons of cider are processed in an hour if sufficient apples are on hand. If apples are always on hand, 2,000 gallons may be processed in a week during normal working hours.

Cider Press Co. leases the machinery and building for $340 per week.

The firm purchases apples for $2.40 per bushel. About six gallons of cider can be produced from one bushel.

The cider is bottled in glass jugs that cost $.29 each (including the cap).

Maintenance costs and power costs are $2.00 for each hour the machinery is run. (The machinery is run only when apples are available.)

Summary of costs (assuming 2,000 gallons produced in a week):

Clerk's wages	$.06 per gallon
Crushing machine operator	$.06 per gallon
Bottling machine operator	$.06 per gallon
Leasing costs	$.17 per gallon
Apples	$.40 per gallon
Jugs and caps	$.29 per gallon
Maintenance and power	$80.00 per week

The cider is immediately sold to a distributor for $1.21 per gallon.

REQUIRED:

A. What is the breakeven point (in gallons per week)?

B. If sufficient apples are available, should the machines be run more than 40 hours in a week? (All the apples can be purchased by the clerk during regular working hours.)

C. How many gallons would have to be processed and sold to realize a net income of $300 in a week?

D. What is the contribution margin per gallon if the cost of apples falls to $1.80 per bushel due to an unusually large harvest?

(Prepared by Eric Noreen)

3-32 *(Flexible Budgets and Breakeven Point in a Retail Setting).* Hank Rugger operates a lumberjack equipment store specializing in axes and chain saws. His income statement for 19X8 was as follows.

HANK RUGGER
INCOME STATEMENT
For the Year 19X8

Sales:		
Axes	$30,000	
Saws	80,000	$110,000
Cost of goods sold:		
Axes	$20,000	
Saws	60,000	80,000
Gross profit		$ 30,000
Operating expenses:		
Rent	$ 2,400	
Utilities	1,500	
Bookkeeping service	3,900	
Advertising	1,800	
Sales commissions	9,500	19,100
Net income		$ 10,900

Hank asked the bookkeeper to perform a fixed and variable cost study. The bookkeeper's report was as follows.

Dear Hank:

As you requested I studied the contracts of your firm. As you know, your lease agreement calls for an annual lease payment of $2,400. Over the years your utilities have averaged $125 per month.

The bookkeeping service fee is as we agreed. I receive $50 per month for the basic work plus 3% of gross sales since the greater your sales the larger the number of sales and purchase invoices I must process.

The advertising costs result from the ads you run in the weekly newspaper. Typically you run ads 50 weeks per year at an average cost of $36 per week.

The sales commissions are a direct percentage of sales. You pay a commission of 5% on all gross sales of axes and 10% on all gross sales of saws.

The cost of goods sold percentage is a result of your pricing policy. Over the years you have used the industry-wide markup on both axes and saws. For axes the markup was 50% of cost. For example, if an axe cost $10, the sales price was $15. For saws the markup was 33⅓% of cost. For example, if a saw cost $12, the selling price was $16.

Hope this helps you Hank. Cheers.

Casper M.

REQUIRED:

A. Recast the income statement for 19X8 using the contribution margin approach. Show both total and product line data.

B. What is Hank's breakeven point in dollars of sales. How would the breakeven point change if sales of saws increased while sales of axes decreased?

C. Prepare a profit plan (budgeted income statement) for 19X9 assuming that sales are budgeted at $48,000 for axes and $120,000 for saws.

D. Do you approve of Hank's policy on sales commissions? Explain.

3-33 *(Cost-Volume-Profit Decisions in Manufacturing Setting).* R. A. Ro and Company, maker of quality handmade pipes, has experienced a steady growth in sales for the past five years. However, increased competition has led Mr. Ro, the president, to believe that an aggressive advertising campaign will be necessary next year to maintain the company's present growth.

To prepare for next year's advertising campaign, the company's accountant has prepared and presented Mr. Ro with the following data for the current year, 19X2:

Cost Schedule	
Variable costs:	
Direct labor	$ 8.00/pipe
Direct materials	3.25/pipe
Variable overhead	2.50/pipe
Total variable costs	$13.75/pipe
Fixed costs:	
Manufacturing	$ 25,000
Selling	40,000
Administrative	70,000
Total fixed costs	$135,000
Selling price, per pipe:	$ 25.00
Expected sales, 19X2 (20,000 units):	$500,000
Tax rate: 40%	

Mr. Ro has set the sales target for 19X3 at a level of $550,000 (or 22,000 pipes).

REQUIRED:

A. What is the projected after-tax net income for 19X2? 19X3?

B. What is the breakeven point in units for 19X2? 19X3?

C. Mr. Ro believes that an additional selling expense of $11,250 for advertising in 19X3, with all other costs remaining constant, will be necessary to attain the sales target. What will be the after-tax net income for 19X3 if the additional $11,250 is spent?

D. What will be the breakeven point in dollar sales for 19X3 if the additional $11,250 is spent for advertising?

E. If the additional $11,250 is spent for advertising in 19X3, what is the required sales level in dollar sales to equal 19X2's after-tax net income?

F. At a sales level of 22,000 units, what is the maximum amount that can be spent on advertising if an after-tax net income of $60,000 is desired?

(CMA adapted)

3-34 *(Cost-Volume-Profit Decisions in Animal Husbandry Setting).* Ahmul and Ashmir raise and sell camels. They acquire the camels they sell by two methods. Half they buy from other breeders at an average price of $100. The other half is taken from their own herd. They try to maintain a stable breeding herd of 500 camels by selling their one-year old camels. It costs them an average of $50 per camel per year to feed, watch, and maintain their herd. They have a reputation for fair dealing and quality merchandise so there is no problem selling their supply. They sell an average of 600 camels every year, at an average price of $175 each.

This year, however, due to unexpected circumstances, the slightly larger than normal crop of 340 calves consisted of 80% white camels—a most unfortunate occurrence. White camels cannot be bartered or sold as beasts of burden because of local taboos. They must keep the white camels until they are two years old and then transport them, at a cost of $72 per head, to another country. There they can receive only $27 for each camel.

To add to their troubles, their principal customer insists that they deliver their normal quantity. If they do not meet his demands, their sales will fall to 250 camels this year. The other camel raisers, knowing Ahmul and Ashmir cannot afford to lower their breding herd below 500, are taking advantage of the supply and demand situation by increasing their prices from $100 to $150 per head.

REQUIRED:

A. Prepare a contribution margin income statement for a normal year for Ahmul and Ashmir.

B. Prepare a contribution margin income statement for the current year, assuming they decide to supply their normal sales volume of 600 camels.

C. Would it be better to buy the extra camels they need at current prices or allow their sales to fall to 250 camels? Support your decision.

D. Calculate the breakeven point under normal conditions. Calculate the new breakeven point, assuming they decide to buy the needed camels.

E. Assume that several zoos are interested in the white camels. They have no money to buy the camels but have offered to take the camels at the end of the first year if Ahmul and Ashmir deliver them to the town of Abdul. They estimate it will cost $120 per head for delivery. Should Ahmul and Ashmir keep the camels for two years and then sell them in another country, or should they ship them to the zoos at the end of the first year? Support your conclusions. *(Prepared by Mary T. Soulier)*

3-35 *(Cost-Volume-Profit Decisions in a Restaurant Setting).* Mr. Calderone started a pizza restaurant in 19X0. A building was rented for $400 per month. Two ladies were hired to work full time at the restaurant and six college boys were hired to work 30 hours per week delivering pizza. An outside accountant was hired for tax and bookkeeping purposes. For this service Mr. Calderone pays $300 per month. The necessary restaurant equipment and delivery cars were purchased with cash. Mr. Calderone has noticed that expenses for utilities and supplies have been rather constant.

Mr. Calderone increased his business between 19X0 and 19X3. Profits have more than doubled since 19X0. Mr. Calderone does not understand why his profits have increased faster than his volume.

A projected income statement for 19X4 prepared by the accountant is shown below:

CALDERONE COMPANY
PROJECTED INCOME STATEMENT
For the Year Ended December 31, 19X4

Sales		$95,000
Cost of food sold	$28,500	
Wages & fringe benefits of restaurant help	8,150	
Wages & fringe benefits of delivery boys	17,300	
Rent	4,800	
Accounting services	3,600	
Depreciation of delivery equipment	5,000	
Depreciation of restaurant equipment	3,000	
Utilities	2,325	
Supplies (soap, floor wax, etc.)	1,200	73,875
Net income before taxes		$21,125
Income taxes		6,338
Net income		$14,787

Note: The average pizza sells for $2.50. Assume that Mr. Calderone pays out 30% of his income in income taxes.

REQUIRED:

A. What is the breakeven point in number of pizzas that must be sold?

B. What is the cash flow breakeven point in number of pizzas that must be sold?

C. Mr. Calderone would like an after-tax net income of $20,000. What volume must be reached in number of pizzas in order to obtain the desired income?

D. Briefly explain to Mr. Calderone why his profits have increased at a faster rate than his sales. *(CMA adapted)*

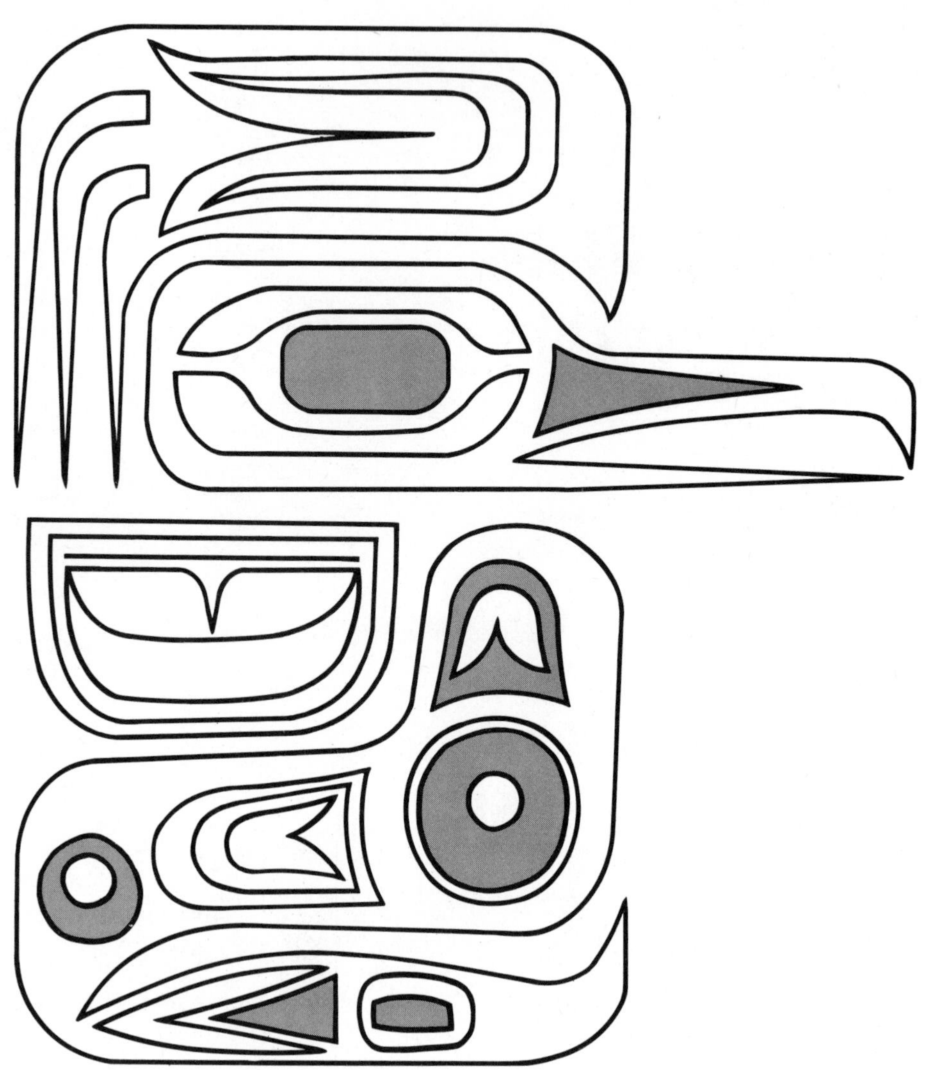

PART 2

SYSTEMS FOR PRODUCT COSTING

4 Cost Flows for Product Costing

In the first three chapters we examined ways in which the decision maker can view costs relevant to decisions. In this and the next three chapters we will look at the cost accumulation systems accountants use to gather data for both financial reporting and management planning and control. If the decision maker is to select relevant costs, he must understand the way historical costs are actually measured and reported in practice.

Our emphasis will be upon a manufacturing concern. This emphasis is based on the premise that the physical flow, and hence the cost flow, of a manufacturing concern is more involved than that of a retailing or service concern. With an understanding of the more involved system, the student should be able to transfer his knowledge to less complicated situations.

COSTS FROM A FINANCIAL REPORTING PERSPECTIVE

Financial accounting entails the measurement and reporting of financial position and its changes due to operations. Central to measurement of financial position and net income are the concepts of expired and unexpired costs. As resources are acquired, they are considered as **unexpired costs** (assets) on the statement of financial position. These costs are carried forward to future periods where they are expected to contribute to future revenues. When they have been consumed in the generation of revenue and have no future revenue-producing potential, they are considered as **expired costs** (expenses) on the income statement. For example, as a firm produces goods for resale, the costs incurred in production are carried in the inventory as unexpired costs on the statement of financial position. When the goods are sold, the inventory cost is matched with revenue as expired costs.

Expired costs have already produced their share of revenue, or they have been consumed without providing a benefit to the firm. A cost that has been consumed in the production of revenue is called an **expense.** A cost that has been consumed without providing a benefit or revenue is termed a **loss.** The problem of measuring expired and unexpired costs is important in financial accounting practice since they directly affect the reported net income and statement of financial position.

In a manufacturing concern, materials flow through the factory where labor and other factory costs are expended to convert them into a finished, salable product. Production costs can be thought of as adhering or attaching to the unit of product so that cost flow in the books of account parallels physical flow in the factory. Costs incurred in one form, such as materials, workers' wages, heat, light, and power, are converted and transformed into the product. **Product costs** are costs that accountants attach to the unit of product and hold as an asset in the inventory until the goods to which they are attached are sold. They are matched with revenue when the sale is measured. Costs that are not inventoried and, as a result, are treated as expenses in the period they are considered consumed, are called **period costs.**

Historically, accountants have used the following logic in deciding which costs are product costs and which costs are period costs. In service concerns there are no inventoriable product costs since there are no tangible products; all costs are period costs. In retailing concerns there are inventoriable costs of the merchandise purchased and held for resale. All costs, other than the costs of the purchased merchandise, are related to the current period and therefore, treated as period costs. In a manufacturing firm the cost flow structure is more complex. First, the firm must produce the goods that it sells. The costs incurred in producing these goods are called **production costs** (also called **manufacturing costs**). The firm also incurs the **nonproduction costs** of selling and distributing the products, administering the operations, and financing the company.

By classifying costs as production and nonproduction the definition of product and period costs in a manufacturing concern may be seen to parallel that of the product and period costs of a retailing concern. Product costs are those costs necessary to have a tangible product available for sale; period costs are the costs associated with the sales and administration activities of the period. Product costs are matched with revenue as cost of goods sold in the period of the sale. Period costs are matched with revenue on a time-period basis.

In a manufacturing concern raw materials are purchased and then converted into a new product. Iron is converted into steel, aluminum into airplanes, logs into lumber, and lumber into boat hulls. The complexity of the manufacturing activity is best accounted for by using three inventory accounts. The **raw materials inventory** contains the cost of the raw materials on hand but not yet processed. The **work-in-process inventory** contains the costs of the raw materials, labor, and other production costs of the uncompleted goods in the process of being manufactured. The **finished goods inventory** contains the costs of the completed goods awaiting sale. Each of the three inventory accounts is an unexpired cost; an asset. Thus, when raw materials are issued to Work-in-Process and combined with labor and other factory costs, the cost of manufacturing is treated as a product cost and, therefore, an unexpired cost until the product is sold. At the point of sale these product costs move from an asset account, Finished Goods, to the expired cost account, Cost of Goods Sold.

It is sometimes difficult to know whether a cost should be treated as a production or a nonproduction cost. Two examples should highlight this problem. The president, in his daily activities, supervises both production and distribution activities. Should his salary be allocated between the two activities, and if so, what basis of allocation should be used? To solve this dilemma most firms simply assign his salary to nonproduction costs. Another example is that of packaging the final product. Some firms wait until the item is sold and treat the packaging costs as selling costs; others assign packaging costs to production costs. Typically, cost assignment depends on *when* the packaging is done. If the packaging is done in the warehouse, it will usually be treated as a selling expense; if it is done in the factory, it will probably be considered a production expense.

Production Costs

Production costs can be separated into three cost elements: raw materials, labor, and overhead. In this section we will look at each of these elements.

DIRECT AND INDIRECT MATERIALS

Raw materials include the physical commodities that are consumed in making the final product. Two views of materials seem prevalent. One view takes a physical approach. **Materials** are defined as all physical commodities that become a part of the final product. This approach is useful in the engineering design of the product but poses distinct accounting problems for commodities that are either physically small or of low cost. The other view is less physical and is oriented more toward the ease of accounting for costs. Only the major materials in terms of cost per unit or the materials that involve large physical quantities justify the record keeping necessary to trace them directly to the product. These are called **direct materials.** Minor materials are not traced to the product, although they may be vital to its production. Rather, these **indirect materials** are included in overhead. While the latter view is more practical, it does not completely describe the physical phenomenon.

Production materials, particularly direct materials, are variable costs. As more finished units are produced, more materials are used. Some of the indirect materials not physically incorporated in the finished product may behave as semivariable costs; generally however, it would be reasonable to say production material costs are variable costs.

DIRECT AND INDIRECT LABOR

Labor costs include the wages paid to factory workers who directly or indirectly aid in converting the raw materials into a finished product. **Direct labor** costs represent labor that is expended directly on the final product and traced directly to it. For example, through accounting records, the time of the machine operators, welders, grinders, and assemblers may be traced directly to the product they produce. Other employees, such as foremen, janitors, material handlers, and maintenance employees, do not work directly with the product. Their wages are considered **indirect labor** costs since there is no reasonable way to trace their activities directly to specific units of output. These costs are regarded as a part of overhead.

Direct labor generally behaves as a variable cost. This is obvious when the workers are paid on a piecework wage plan. Where direct labor is paid on an hourly basis, direct labor can be variable if a constant productivity per labor hour can be assumed. If direct labor is paid on a salaried basis, the costs will be stairstep semivariable costs; the appropriateness of treating labor as a variable cost will depend upon the size of the stairstep.

OVERHEAD

Overhead includes all costs of operating the factory except those costs that have been designated as direct materials and direct labor. Included in overhead are indirect materials, indirect labor, and other factory costs such as depreciation of factory buildings and machinery, factory supplies, factory maintenance and repairs, insurance, property taxes, factory employees' fringe benefits, heat, light, and power. A variety of terms is used to describe these costs, including: **factory overhead, factory burden, manufacturing expenses, indirect factory costs, manufacturing overhead, indirect expenses,** and **indirect manufacturing costs.** Each firm seems to select a title that communicates best to its management. We use the simple term **overhead.**

Overhead is a potpourri of costs. It includes some material costs, some labor costs, and the costs of providing and maintaining productive capacity. The one thing these costs have in common is that they are difficult, if not impossible, to trace directly to the units of product. For this reason, accountants typically use an averaging technique called an *overhead rate* to apply overhead to the product. We will explain this technique in a later chapter.

Unlike direct material and direct labor, which are variable costs, overhead is a mixture of variable costs, semivariable costs, and fixed costs. Rent, depreciation of the factory building and machinery, insurance, and property taxes are normally fixed costs. Repairs, maintenance, and many fringe benefits of labor are mixed costs. Some indirect labor costs are variable; others, such as supervisors' salaries, are fixed or stairstepped costs.

Nonproduction Costs

Accountants have emphasized production costs in their cost studies. One reason for this emphasis has been the ability to find reliable cause and effect relationships between production costs and production volume. This relationship is more difficult to find in the nonproduction cost area. Another reason has been the rapid growth of industrialization and mechanization in the past century. This growth has forced management to scrutinize production cost patterns. As a practical matter, the concentration upon production activities has resulted in too little time and effort being spent studying nonproduction costs. In many firms the nonproduction costs are equal to or greater than production costs.

The elements of nonproduction costs are not as well defined as those of production costs. However, for our purposes they can be separated into four distinct categories: selling, distribution, general and administrative, and financial.

SELLING COSTS

Often called **order-getting costs,** selling costs are the result of marketing activities. They include, for example, the salespeople's salaries, commissions, and travel costs; advertising, catalog costs; and promotional costs. Selling costs can be both fixed and variable. However, unlike production costs, which vary with production output, selling costs vary with sales volume.

DISTRIBUTION COSTS

At times called **order-filling costs,** distribution costs arise from ensuring that the proper goods are in the proper location, ready to sell. Distribution costs include outbound freight and transportation, warehousing, insurance, finished goods materials handling, packing, and shipping costs. As with selling costs, distribution costs are both fixed and variable. Distribution costs vary with the volume shipped. In most firms the volume sold and the volume shipped are the same; therefore, many firms relate distribution costs to sales volume.

GENERAL AND ADMINISTRATIVE COSTS

There are a large number of costs that are not directly associated with production, selling, or distribution. Executive and clerical salaries, home office or headquarters costs, corporate legal costs, board of directors' fees, general accounting costs, and corporate public relation costs are all examples of general and administrative costs. Most firms find that their general and administrative costs do not vary with either production or sales volume. Because the amount of these costs depends upon top management discretion rather than production or sales volume, they are often treated as discretionary fixed costs.

FINANCIAL COSTS

The costs of financing the organization's capital requirements often require special attention and are separated from administrative costs. Bank service charges, interest expense on both long-term and short-term borrowing, and the costs of underwriting stock issues comprise some of the financial costs. As with general and administrative costs, financial costs do not vary with either production or sales volume; most firms treat them as discretionary fixed costs.

PRODUCT COSTING WITH ABSORPTION AND VARIABLE COSTING

Before the advent of industrialization, with its concurrent heavy equipment investments, production costs consisted primarily of material and labor costs. These **prime costs,** the sum of direct materials and direct labor, were the only production costs of any significance to be inventoried. When industrialization began requiring large investments in capacity, the growth of overhead costs was rapid. For the first time the differences between fixed and variable costs became relevant, because many of the costs of providing the productive capacity were fixed. Accountants have long measured the cost of an asset as the amount expended to bring it to a proper condition and location to use. It made intuitive sense to include in the unit cost of inventory *all* the costs necessary to make it salable, including the costs of capacity. Until recently, accountants did not think of costs as fixed and variable, only as production and nonproduction costs.

By the turn of the twentieth century, accounting in the United States was solidified in the use of absorption product costing. **Absorption product costing** related the accounting cost flow system to physical activity in the plant. With absorption costing, *all production* costs are treated as product costs; all nonproduction costs are treated as period costs. Until recently most accounting activity focused upon stewardship reporting via income measurement; little attention was paid to the specific problems of information for management decision making. Absorption costing became generally accepted practice in external, financial reporting.

Independently of accounting, however, economists were using the nature of fixed and variable cost behavior patterns in their marginal analysis. In the 1930s, economic theory became more widely integrated with accounting thought, and an alternative to absorption costing was proposed. This alternative, which we call **variable costing,**[1] revolved around cost analysis from a fixed and variable viewpoint, rather than from a production and nonproduction viewpoint. With variable costing *all variable production* costs are treated as product costs. Fixed production costs and all nonproduction costs are treated as period costs.

The 1940s and World War II added impetus to the study of fixed and variable costs in accounting. The need to make efficient economic allocation decisions was urgent, and many of our current scientific decision-making theories and models were born during this period. By the 1950s considerable discussion was going on among accountants regarding alternative methods of presenting cost data for both internal and external purposes. In this chapter we will look at the two alternatives most widely proposed for reporting inventory values: absorption costing and variable costing.

Important differences exist between absorption and variable costing methods. One way to see these differences is to compare the way in which the systems affect inventory values and income determination. From this financial reporting view, product and period costs are relevant because they are defined differently by the two costing methods.

Absorption costing defines product costs as including *all* costs of production, and period costs as *all* nonproduction costs. The product "absorbs" all costs necessary to produce it and have it in salable form. Exhibit 4–1 shows the flow of costs in an absorption costing system. The white boxes represent product costs; the dark boxes are period costs. The production cost flow with absorption costing results in a unit cost that can be described as the *average unit cost to produce.*

---

[1]It is also called **direct costing** by many accountants in the United States, although this term is a misnomer. In England it is called **marginal costing.** We will use the more descriptive term, *variable costing,* in this text.

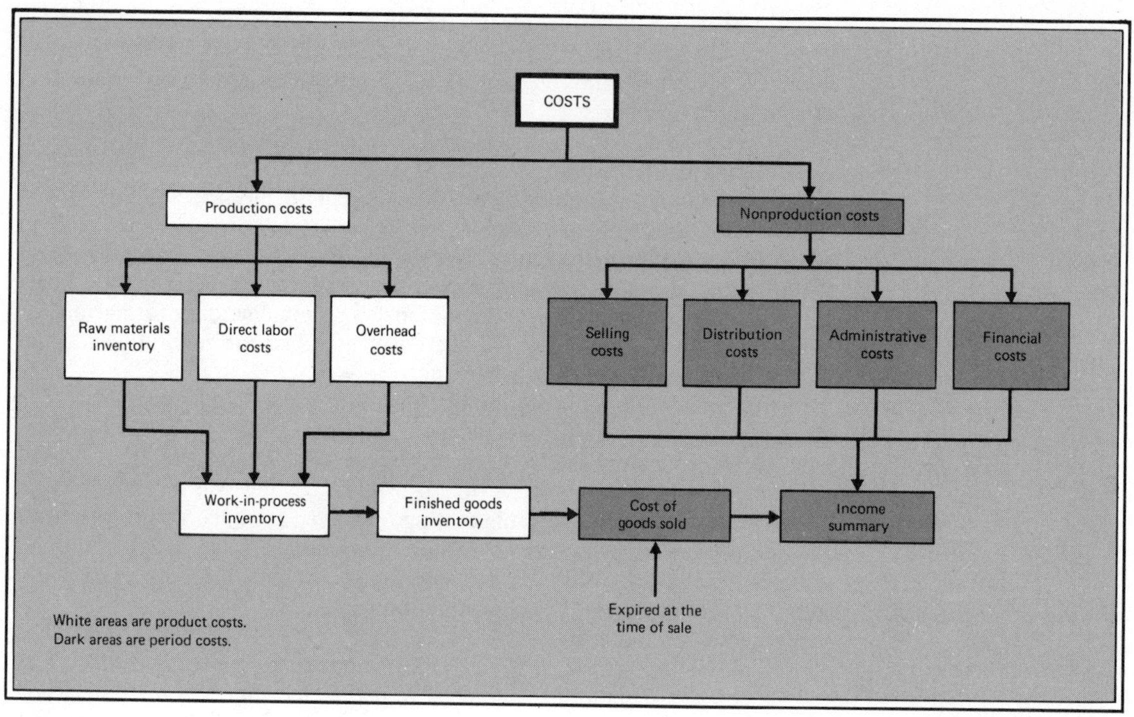

EXHIBIT 4–1
Cost flow with absorption costing

Variable costing stems from an entirely different premise than absorption costing. Beginning with the idea that the separation of costs into their fixed and variable components provides management with information relevant for differential pricing and production decisions, variable costers redefine product and period costs. Variable costing defines the product costs as the variable costs to produce the product. Fixed production costs and all nonproduction costs are treated as period costs. The cost flow pattern for variable costing is shown in Exhibit 4–2. The white boxes represent product costs under the variable costing method; the dark boxes are period costs. A close examination of this diagram shows that the unit cost of the Work-in-Process Inventory and the Finished Goods Inventory include only the *variable cost to produce.*

VARIABLE AND ABSORPTION COSTING ILLUSTRATED

To illustrate the differences between variable and absorption costing in measuring inventory values and net income, let's assume that the McKay

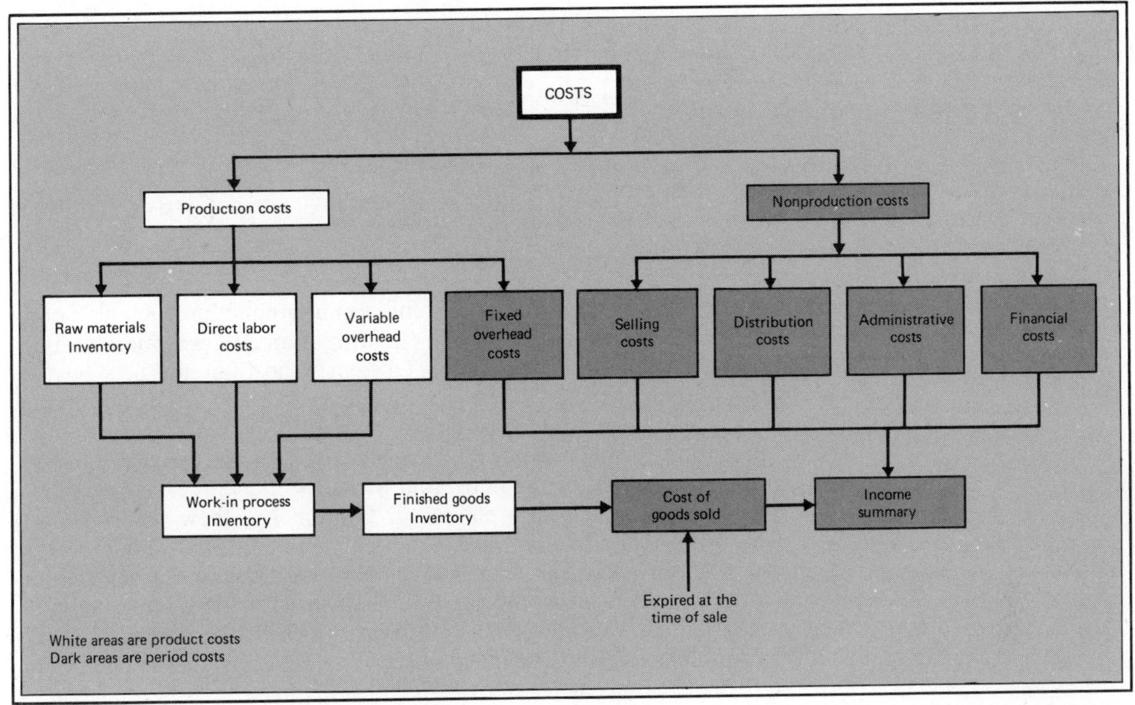

EXHIBIT 4–2
Cost flow with variable costing

Manufacturing Company manufactures toy rocking horses. During the past year it manufactured 200,000 horses, but sold only 190,000 of them. The final inventory was 10,000 horses, since the period was started with no beginning inventory. The 190,000 horses were sold for $25 each, and the following production costs were incurred: direct materials $1,000,000; direct labor $1,200,000; variable overhead $800,000; and fixed overhead $600,000. The nonproduction costs were $700,000, of which $320,000 were fixed costs. Production costs per unit included: direct materials $5.00 ($1,000,000 ÷ 200,000 units); direct labor $6.00 ($1,200,000 ÷ 200,000 units); variable overhead $4.00 ($800,000 ÷ 200,000 units); and fixed overhead $3.00 ($600,000 ÷ 200,000 units).

The product costs per unit to be inventoried under the two costing systems are as follows:

	Absorption Costing	*Variable Costing*
Direct material	$ 5	$ 5
Direct labor	6	6
Variable overhead	4	4
Fixed overhead	3	0
Total product cost	$18	$15

If the firm adopted variable costing, the unit cost of production, including only variable product costs,would be $15. If the firm adopted absorption costing, the unit cost of production would be $18. Obviously the difference between the two costing systems is the inclusion of the $3.00 per unit of fixed overhead in the product under absorption costing. Fixed overhead is treated as a product cost in absorption costing, whereas in variable costing it is treated as a period cost and is not allocated to the individual products.

Comparative income statements in Exhibit 4–3 show the effects of these two costing systems upon net income. The net income shown on the absorption costing income statement is $30,000 larger than the net income shown on the variable costing income statement. In variable costing the total fixed production costs of $600,000 were treated as a period cost; that is, all $600,000 was deducted in the current accounting period when the costs were incurred. In absorption costing only $570,000 of the fixed costs are included in the cost of goods sold, which was matched with revenue; the other $30,000 was retained in the final inventory of horses. The company produced 200,000 horses, but it sold only 190,000. Thus, the final inventory increased by 10,000 units. Under variable costing the final inventory is $150,000 (10,000 units × $15); under absorption costing the final inventory is $180,000 (10,000 units × $18). If the beginning and ending inventories of unsold horses had been zero, the net income under both systems would have been the same.

VARIABLE AND ABSORPTION COSTING ACROSS TIME PERIODS

Some accountants have argued that variable costing should be used in external reporting in lieu of absorption costing. One argument used to support this view is that fixed costs are the result of providing capacity in general, and that this productive capacity does not relate to any one specific unit. Another argument for variable costing is that fixed costs are more closely related to the passage of time than to production and thus are properly treated as period costs. A third argument for the adoption of variable costing for income measurement is that the profits increase or decrease in direct relationship to increases or decreases in sales. With absorption costing the effects upon net

ABSORPTION COSTING

McKAY MANUFACTURING COMPANY
INCOME STATEMENT
For the Year Ended December 31, 19X5

Sales (190,000 × $25)		$4,750,000	100%
Less cost of goods sold:			
Production costs (200,000 × $18)	$3,600,000		
Less: Cost of units in ending inventory (10,000 × $18)	180,000	3,420,000	72%
Gross margin		$1,330,000	28%
Less: Nonproduction costs		700,000	
Net income		$ 630,000	

VARIABLE COSTING

McKAY MANUFACTURING COMPANY
INCOME STATEMENT
For the Year Ended December 31, 19X5

Sales (190,000 × $25)		$4,750,000	100%
Less variable costs:			
Production costs (200,000 × $15)	$3,000,000		
Less: Cost of units in ending inventory (10,000 × $15)	150,000		
Variable production costs of units sold (190,000 × $15)	$2,850,000		
Variable nonproduction costs (190,000 × $2)	380,000	3,230,000	68%
Contribution margin (190,000 × $8)		$1,520,000	32%
Less fixed costs:			
Fixed production costs	$ 600,000		
Fixed nonproduction costs	320,000	920,000	
Net income		$ 600,000	

EXHIBIT 4–3
Comparative income statements of the McKay Manufacturing Company

income of increases or decreases in sales are intermingled with the effects of increases or decreases in production output.

Exhibit 4–4 compares the net income under variable and absorption costing for the same company over a four-year time span. In the first year more units are produced than sold. In the second and fourth years more units are sold than produced. In the third year production and sales are equal. The selling price and cost structure remain unchanged throughout the example. For simplicity, the only costs are production costs.

Selling price	\$ 10 per unit
Variable production costs	\$ 6 per unit
Fixed production costs	\$270 per year

In this illustration we have assumed a LIFO (last-in, first-out), flow of inventory costs. Other methods, such as FIFO or average, would also illustrate the difference between absorption and variable costing, but income and inventory values would differ. LIFO was chosen because it presents a clearer flow of costs. With LIFO, cost of goods sold includes costs from the previous year only when the inventory level is decreased.

We have assumed that the cost behavior patterns remain unchanged throughout the four years. Under variable costing all units are costed at \$6.00 per unit throughout the illustration. The unit cost under absorption costing will depend upon the number of units produced. When 100 units are produced, the unit cost under absorption costing is \$8.70 [\$6.00 variable + \$2.70 fixed (\$270 ÷ 100 units)]. When production is 90 units, the unit cost will increase to \$9.00 [\$6.00 variable + \$3.00 fixed (\$270 ÷ 90 units)].

In the first year, production exceeded sales and the finished goods inventory increased by 20 units. The income under variable costing is lower than under absorption costing because all fixed costs are treated as period costs. Under absorption costing each of the 20 units in inventory includes \$2.70 of fixed costs.

In the second year, sales exceeded production. In addition to current fixed costs for that year, the income statement for absorption costing includes the additional fixed costs applicable to the 10 units produced in the first year. Therefore, income under variable costing in the second year exceeds income under absorption costing by \$27 (10 × \$2.70).

During the third year, income is the same under the two costing systems. Since production and sales were equal, only current costs were included in the income statements.

The last year is comparable to the second year. Sales exceeded production, and the income statement for absorption costing included extra fixed costs from the beginning inventory.

Let's look at the differences in income determination for these four years.

1. In years where production exceeds sales, the net income reported by absorption costing is greater than that reported by variable costing. This is true because some of the fixed costs remain in inventory under absorption costing.

2. In years where sales exceed production, variable costing reports a higher net income than absorption costing. This is true because

	FIRST YEAR		SECOND YEAR		THIRD YEAR		FOURTH YEAR		TOTAL FOR FOUR YEARS	
	Variable	Absorption	Variable	Absorption	Variable	Absorption	Variable	Absorption	Variable	Absorption
Units sold	80	80	100	100	100	100	110	110	390	390
Units produced	100	100	90	90	100	100	100	100	390	390
Sales	$800	$800	$1,000	$1,000	$1,000	$1,000	$1,100	$1,100	$3,900	$3,900
Current production costs:										
Variable costs	$600	$600	$ 540	$ 540	$ 600	$ 600	$ 600	$ 600	$2,340	$2,340
Fixed costs	270	270	270	270	270	270	270	270	1,080	1,080
Total costs	$870	$870	$ 810	$ 810	$ 870	$ 870	$ 870	870	$3,420	$3,420
Change in inventory										
(Increase)	(120)	(174)							(120)	(174)
Decrease			60	87	–	–	60	87	120	174
Costs matched with revenue	750	696	870	897	870	870	930	957	3,420	3,420
Net income	$ 50	$104	$ 130	$ 103	$ 130	$ 130	$ 170	$ 143	$ 480	$ 480
Beginning inventory:										
Units	0	0	20	20	10	10	10	10	0	0
Cost	–	–	$ 120	$ 174	$ 60	$ 87	$ 60	$ 87	–	–
Ending inventory:										
Units	20	20	10	10	10	10	0	0	0	0
Cost	$120	$174	$ 60	$ 87	$ 60	$ 87	–	–	–	–

EXHIBIT 4–4
Comparative income statements across four time periods

absorption costing matches both current, and some previously deferred fixed costs against revenue, whereas variable costing matches only current fixed costs against revenue.

3. In years where sales and production are equal, the two methods produce the same net income.
4. Comparing the second and third years, we can see that in years where sales volume is constant but production fluctuates, variable costing gives identical net incomes. This is so because net income under variable costing is not affected by inventory changes. In absorption costing, net income fluctuates with changes in the inventories, as well as with changes in sales, because fixed costs are spread over a different number of units.
5. When the total production output over the years equals total sales, the total net income will be the same under either costing method.

In most industries, production tends to equal sales over time. Therefore, over the long run the two procedures produce similar results. Any controversy between the advocates of absorption costing and those who favor variable costing, in terms of income determination, is a matter of timing in the matching of fixed costs with revenue.

EXTERNAL REPORTING AND VARIABLE COSTING

The controversy over the proper reporting of cost data can be examined from two perspectives: external financial statements for investors and internal reports for management. A particular reporting method may be generally accepted for one purpose and rejected as nonrelevant in another. In this and the following section we will look at the use of variable costing for external reports and internal reports, respectively.

For external reporting purposes, generally accepted accounting principles view absorption costing as the proper way to account for production costs. Professional and governmental accounting groups have approved absorption costing and rejected variable costing as a generally acceptable method of inventory valuation for external reports. The American Institute of Certified Public Accountants (AICPA), the professional organization primarily concerned with attesting to published financial data, stated its opinion in *Accounting Research Bulletin No. 43,* issued in 1953:

> The primary basis of accounting for inventories is cost, which has been defined generally as the price paid or consideration given to acquire the asset. As applied to inventories, cost means in principle the sum of the applicable expenditures and charges directly or indirectly incurred in bringing an article to its existing condition and location. . . . Although principles for the determination of inventory costs may be easily stated, the application, particularly to such inventory items as work in process and finished goods, is difficult because of the variety of problems

> encountered in the allocation of costs and charges. For example, under some circumstances, items such as idle facility expense, excessive spoilage, double freight, and rehandling costs may be so abnormal as to require treatment as current period charges rather than as a portion of the inventory cost. Also, general and administrative expenses should be included as period charges, except for the portion of such expenses that may be clearly related to production and thus constitute a part of inventory costs (product charges). Selling expenses constitute no part of inventory costs. It should also be recognized that the exclusion of all overheads from inventory costs does not constitute an accepted accounting procedure.[2]

A careful reading of the AICPA's statement can be confusing. It says that *all* overhead costs may not be excluded, but it does not say that *all* overhead costs must be included. This is a moot point, however. Accountants in public practice have interpreted the statement to support absorption costing and reject variable costing for costing of inventories.

An American Accounting Association (AAA) committee took a firm position against variable costing in 1957. The committee report stated:

> Thus the cost of a manufactured product is the sum of the acquisition costs reasonably traceable to the product and should include both direct and indirect factors. The omission of any element of manufacturing cost is not acceptable.[3]

Unlike *Research Bulletin No. 43* of the AICPA, the AAA committee report does not constitute binding, generally accepted accounting principles and does not represent an official position of the association. Committee members who dissented to the committee report stated:

> . . . Direct costing (variable costing) is at least as acceptable in accounting theory as is the conventional "full costing" concept. Moreover, they believe that use of direct costing (variable costing) procedures will, in many cases, yield results more useful to investors as well as management.[4]

Another accounting organization, the National Association of Accountants (NAA), does not issue *official* pronouncements upon accounting practice, but has issued a number of research reports and published a number of journal articles in support of variable costing for external, as well as internal, reports. The NAA actively advocates variable costing. Since the members of this organization are primarily management accountants, their position is not too surprising.

In the governmental sphere there are three organizations concerned with costing of inventories for external reports. The most dominant has been the Securities and Exchange Commission (SEC). With responsibility for

---

[2]Committee on Accounting Procedure, *Accounting Research Bulletin No. 43* (New York: American Institute of Certified Public Accountants, 1953), pp. 28–29.

[3]*The Accounting Review* (October, 1957), p. 539.

[4]Ibid.

administering the federal securities acts, the SEC requires, among other reports, financial statements. The commission has refused to accept variable costing unless it is permitted by generally accepted accounting principles. Thus, any firms that use variable costing for internal purposes must adjust their inventory values and net income to absorption costing when filing with the SEC.

The Internal Revenue Service (IRS) has also refused to sanction variable costing until the method is a generally accepted accounting procedure. Overall, the IRS has held that any inventory accounting method must conform as nearly as possible to the best accounting practice in the trade or business and that the cost of inventory produced should include the cost of raw materials and supplies consumed, expenditures for direct labor, and indirect expenses as a reasonable proportion of management expenses. Recently the IRS specifically prohibited the use of variable costing, although some firms had reported this way for many years.

The newest governmental agency concerned with the costing of manufactured inventories is the Cost Accounting Standards Board (CASB). Established in 1970 as an agent of Congress, the CASB is responsible for establishing uniform cost accounting standards for contractors that sell to the federal government. It has been common practice in cost accounting for negotiated government contracts to use a full allocation of costs. The CASB indicated in its first standards that it intends to adhere to the concept of full costing.

From this discussion we can see that variable costing has not been accepted by the accounting profession *for external reporting*. Determination of acceptable reporting practice revolves around the question: "What is a product cost?" Inherent in this question is another: "What is the proper timing in matching fixed costs with revenue?" Absorption costers hold that fixed costs are necessary to produce the product and cannot be excluded from inventories. As a consequence, they believe that fixed costs should be matched with revenue on a sales basis. For external reports they hold that the users of the financial statements are taking a more global, long-range view and that for this view the "averaging" of all costs is relevant to their decisions. Absorption costing meets these criteria and thus is considered the appropriate method for external reports.

INTERNAL REPORTING AND THE CONTRIBUTION MARGIN APPROACH

There is no question among accountants that the separation of costs into their fixed and variable components is useful in management decision making. This knowledge can help management decide which products to emphasize or de-emphasize, what prices to charge on special orders, the effects of price-cost-volume changes, and when to increase or decrease output. It can also serve as input to other decision models.

Variable Costing and the Contribution Margin Approach

At the heart of variable costing is the contribution margin, which, as noted earlier, may be measured simply as revenue minus variable costs. However, there are two ways of viewing variable costing and the contribution margin.

The first view is from the standpoint of what costs are considered product costs and thus are included in the inventory, and what costs are considered period costs. This is essentially a question of income measurement. We will call this view **variable costing.** With both variable and absorption costing methods, accountants exclude all nonproduction costs from inventory. Under variable costing, fixed production costs are also excluded from the inventory; the contribution margin is sales revenue less variable production costs. This format is relevant when management is concerned with cost-volume relationships from production activities only.

The second view of contribution margin is much broader. Here the contribution margin is the amount of net revenue remaining after deducting *all* variable costs, both production and selling. It must cover fixed costs and provide a satisfactory profit. We will call this perspective the **contribution margin approach.** When management is concerned with the firm's total cost-volume relationships, the variable nonproduction costs become relevant, as well as the variable production costs.

Actually, variable costing should be considered a subset of the contribution margin approach. In this text, when we are dealing with only the production area and therefore variable costing, the contribution margin will be called **contribution margin from production,** to exclude nonproduction variable costs. However, when we are concerned with cost-volume-profit relationships for the entire firm, we will use the term **contribution margin from total operations** or simply **contribution margin.**

Let's return to the McKay Manufacturing Company illustration to examine these two views of the contribution margin. Remember that the McKay Company manufactured 200,000 rocking horses during the past accounting period. It sold 190,000 horses at $25 each and incurred the following variable production costs per unit: direct materials $5.00; direct labor $6.00; and variable overhead $4.00. The fixed production costs totaled $600,000; the nonproduction costs were $700,000, of which $320,000 were fixed.

To arrive at an inventory cost for income determination purposes, the product cost with variable costing flow would be:

Direct materials	$ 5
Direct labor	6
Variable overhead	4
Total inventoriable cost	$15

Using the inventoriable cost, the **unit contribution margin from production** is $10 (the selling price of $25 less the variable production cost per unit of $15). The **total contribution margin from production** is the excess of total sales revenue over total variable production costs, which in our case is \$1,900,000 (190,000 units × \$10), and the **contribution margin ratio from production** is 40% (\$10 ÷ \$25). These contribution margins from production do not include the variable nonproduction costs.

The broader view of contribution margin includes the total variable costs of the company. Total variable costs per unit of product for the McKay Company are:

Direct materials	\$ 5
Direct labor	6
Variable overhead	4
Variable nonproduction costs	2
Total variable costs	\$17

The variable nonproduction costs per unit were determined by dividing the variable nonproduction costs of \$380,000 (\$700,000 − \$320,000) by the number of units sold, 190,000. No variable nonproduction costs were incurred for the units produced but not sold.

Using the total variable costs of the firm, not just the variable production costs, the **unit contribution margin from total operations** is the selling price of \$25 less the variable cost per unit of \$17, or \$8.00. The **total contribution margin from total operations** is \$1,520,000 (190,000 units × \$8.00) and the **contribution margin ratio from total operations** is 32% (\$8.00 ÷ \$25).

The variable costing approach is useful in making incremental production decisions. The contribution margin approach is useful in making both incremental production *and* incremental selling decisions, in addition to its value in the study of cost-volume-profit relationships for the firm as a whole.

Contribution Margin Approach and Cost-Volume-Profit Analysis

Underlying the contribution margin's relevance to management decisions are two assumptions. First, the contribution margin approach assumes that the sales revenue per unit is constant. Second, it assumes that the variable costs per unit are also constant. These assumptions of a linear relationship of revenue and variable costs with volume imply that the total contribution margin will also change linearly with changes in volume. Because the assumptions of linearity may not be valid over the full range of production and sales volume levels, the accountant specifies a relevant range of activity.

The breakeven graph, which was shown in Chapter 3, has been described as a graphic contribution margin income statement. To see the implications of this statement, let's use the McKay Manufacturing Company illustration again. An income statement based upon the contribution margin approach is shown in Exhibit 4–5. Using that information, let's determine the breakeven point by both formula and graph to show how the contribution

MCKAY MANUFACTURING COMPANY INCOME STATEMENT For the Year Ended December 31, 19X5			
Sales (190,000 × $25)		$4,750,000	100%
Less variable costs:			
Direct material (190,000 × $5)	$ 950,000		
Direct labor (190,000 × $6)	1,140,000		
Variable overhead (190,000 × $4)	760,000		
Nonproduction costs (190,000 × $2)	380,000		
Total variable costs (190,000 × $17)		3,230,000	68%
Contribution margin (190,000 × $8)		$1,520,000	32%
Less fixed costs:			
Fixed overhead	$ 600,000		
Nonproduction costs	320,000		
Total fixed costs		920,000	
Net income		$ 600,000	

EXHIBIT 4-5
Contribution margin income statement of the McKay Manufacturing Company

margin approach facilitates cost-volume-profit decisions. The following calculations show the breakeven point for the McKay Company, in dollars and in units.

$$\text{Breakeven point in dollars} = \frac{\text{Fixed costs}}{\text{Contribution margin ratio}} = \frac{\$920{,}000}{.32}$$

$$= \$2{,}875{,}000$$

$$\text{Breakeven point in units} = \frac{\text{Fixed costs}}{\text{Unit contribution margin}} = \frac{\$920{,}000}{\$8}$$

$$= 115{,}000 \text{ units}$$

For a net income of $600,000, which was the firm's actual net income, the following sales would be needed.

$$\text{Dollars of sales needed for desired profit} = \frac{\text{Fixed costs} + \text{Desired net income}}{\text{Contribution margin ratio}}$$

$$= \frac{\$920{,}000 + \$600{,}000}{.32}$$

$$= \$4{,}750{,}000$$

The needed sales volume could also be expressed in units.

$$\text{Units of sales needed for desired profit} = \frac{\$920{,}000 + \$600{,}000}{\$8}$$

$$= 190{,}000 \text{ units}$$

Exhibit 4–6 shows the same data plotted on a breakeven graph. From this graph we can read directly the breakeven point and the net income earned under actual operations. The contribution margin income statement is, in fact, another mode of presenting cost-volume-profit relationships. It lends itself directly, without reinterpretation, to cost-volume-profit analysis.

A second graphic representation of breakeven analysis discussed in Chapter 3 is the profit-volume (PV) chart. Only the contribution margin is plotted on the chart. At zero activity there is no contribution margin and the loss is equal to the fixed costs. A profit-volume chart for the McKay Manufacturing Company is presented in Exhibit 4–7. Note that the same breakeven point and amount of profit are determined from the two graphs.

Returning to Exhibit 4–4 for a moment, we can see that the gross margin using absorption costing does not lend itself to cost-volume-profit analysis. The gross profit percentage of 28% was predicted on the fact that the McKay Manufacturing Company allocated the fixed costs of production over 200,000 units ($600,000 ÷ 200,000 units = $3.00 per unit). What would have happened if the volume had increased to 250,000 units? With the same sales of 190,000 units, the inventory would have increased by 60,000 units instead of 10,000. The fixed costs of production would have been apportioned to the units at $2.40 per unit ($600,000 ÷ 250,000 units), and the total inventoriable cost per unit would have been $17.40 ($5.00 + $6.00 + $4.00 + $2.40). The new gross margin, as follows, uses absorption costing.

Sales (190,000 × $25)	$4,750,000	100.0%
Cost of goods sold (190,000 × $17.40)	3,306,000	69.6%
Gross margin (190,000 × $7.60)	$1,444,000	30.4%

The gross margin does not fulfill the same information role as does the contribution margin. Under absorption costing, the per-unit cost changes with changes in volume because the fixed production costs must be spread over the production volume. In variable costing, changes in volume do not affect the contribution margin ratio or the unit contribution margin because both sales and variable costs are assumed to be linear over a relevant range.

Limitations of the Contribution Margin Approach

The contribution margin approach is useful in making incremental production and distribution decisions, but it has limitations. First, it is based upon the

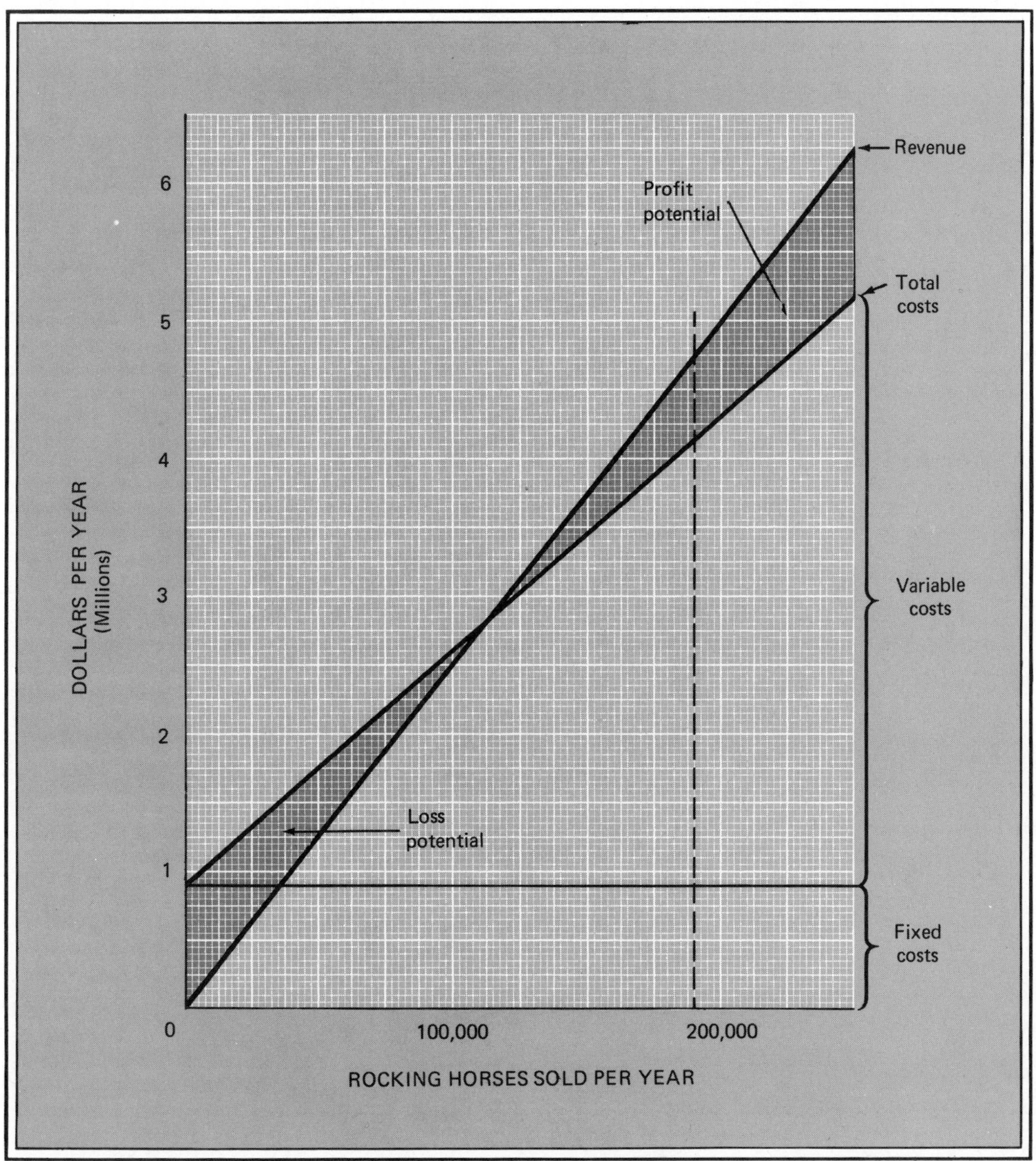

EXHIBIT 4–6
Breakeven chart of the McKay Manufacturing Company

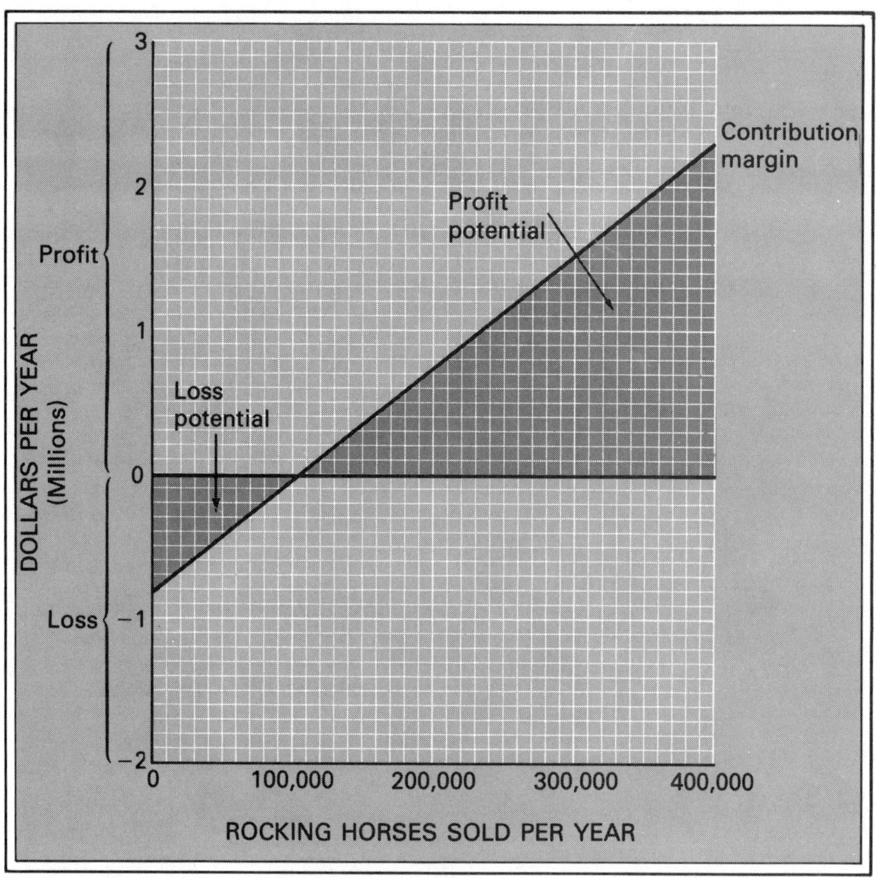

EXHIBIT 4–7
Profit-volume chart of the McKay Manufacturing Company

cost-volume analysis used in determining fixed and variable costs. It assumes that the accountant has determined which costs are fixed and which are variable. As we discussed in Chapter 2, this analysis requires special tools which are based on certain underlying assumptions.

Second, many accountants have felt that an overemphasis on the contribution margin may mislead the decision maker into assuming *only* a short-range decision attitude. They argue that the contribution margin approach may underemphasize the importance of the fixed costs. Proponents of the contribution margin approach counter that it actually highlights the fixed costs, since it does not "lose" them in the unit cost but keeps them intact instead.

Third, opponents of the contribution margin approach argue that heavy reliance upon variable costing may lead management to mistakenly overlook the need to maintain an adequate production volume. If the total contribution margin is allowed to fall too low, it will not cover the fixed costs, even though the unit contribution margin is good. That is to say, the contribution margin approach may lead management to adopt only a short-range viewpoint. In the long run the firm may go broke with a good unit contribution margin. Proponents of the contribution margin approach argue that it reports profits and operating data in a way easily understood by management, and that this understanding leads to better short- and long-range decisions.

Fourth, even the best kept records of *past* costs are not useful in decision making unless they help predict future costs. This point applies to absorption costing as well as to the contribution margin approach. Since decisions are future-oriented, past data are useful only if it is believed that the future will be similar to the past. Changes in operations, cost behavior classifications, and organizational structures cause the exact fixed and variable costs to change from year to year. If there are significant changes, neither absorption costing nor the contribution margin approach will be relevant. Decision data would have to come from special studies, not from the accounting records.

Allowing for these limitations, most accountants concerned with decision making believe that the knowledge of fixed and variable costs and the resultant contribution margin are of significant value to management, although they might advocate the use of absorption costing in external reports.

ALTERNATIVE PROPOSALS

We cannot solve the controversy over variable costing versus absorption costing for external reporting. Neither can we ignore the value that the contribution margin provides to management. An acceptable alternative is to provide each group with its data needs. Internally, the firm can use the contribution margin approach. When external reports are prepared, the accountant can make a simple adjustment to convert the financial statements to absorption costing. This is the approach we will take in the next two chapters. We will illustrate in Chapters 5 and 6 how the accountant can develop variable costing systems for management. Also, we will show how this variable costing data can be converted to absorption costing for external financial reports. Finally, in Chapter 7 we will explore overhead costing for absorption costing more fully.

SUMMARY

There are two major costing systems for determining product and period costs. Absorption costing classifies all production costs as product costs and all nonproduction costs as period costs. Variable costing treats the variable costs to produce the product as product costs; fixed production costs and nonproduction costs are treated as period costs. It is generally accepted accounting practice to use absorption costing for external reports. This practice has the support of most major accounting and governmental agencies.

There is wide agreement that the contribution margin is useful for management decision making. The contribution margin is sales revenue less variable costs; the contribution margin ratio is the contribution margin divided by the sales revenue. The contribution margin is particularly useful in cost-volume-profit analysis. As a matter of fact, the breakeven graph has been called a graphic variable costing income statement. The contribution margin from the variable cost flow system used in income determination can be different from that of the contribution margin approach; a contribution margin approach will include variable nonproduction costs.

To compromise between the two data needs of internal and external reports, it is possible to use the contribution margin approach within the firm, but to use absorption costing in external reports. The accountant has the opportunity to present different costs for different purposes.

SUPPLEMENTARY READING

Broster, E. J. "The Dynamics of Marginal Costing." *The Accountant,* March 26, 1970.

Fremgen, James H. "The Direct Costing Controversy—An Identification of Issues." *The Accounting Review,* January, 1964.

Frye, Delbert J. "Combined Costing Method: Absorption and Direct." *Management Accounting,* January, 1971.

Largay, James A., III. "Microeconomic Foundations of Variable Costing." *The Accounting Review,* January, 1973.

Marple, Raymond P. (Ed.) *National Association of Accountants on Direct Costing: Selected Papers.* New York: The Ronald Press Company, 1965.

Moss, Morton F., and Wilber C. Haseman. "Some Comments on the Applicability of Direct Costing to Decision Making." *The Accounting Review,* April, 1957.

National Association of Accountants. *Current Application of Direct Costing.* New York: National Association of Accountants, 1961.

National Association of Accountants. *Direct Costing.* New York: National Association of Accountants, 1953.

Swalley, Richard W. "The Benefits of Direct Costing." *Management Accounting,* September, 1974.

QUESTIONS

4-1 Variable costing begins with an entirely different premise than does absorption costing. What is this basic difference and why is it important?

4-2 How does an increase in Work-in-Process or Finished Goods Inventories affect the measurement of income when variable costing is used?

4-3 When a company sells the same number of units it produces, the net income under variable costing and absorption costing tends to be the same. Explain.

4-4 Some accountants consider variable costing as a short-run view of costs and absorption costing as a long-run view of costs. Do you agree? Explain.

4-5 When will an income statement under the contribution margin approach provide the same net income as shown on a breakeven chart? When will it not?

4-6 When will the income statement under absorption costing provide the same net income as shown on a breakeven chart? When will it not?

4-7 Is variable costing acceptable for reporting to stockholders? Explain the position of the following organizations concerning the use of variable costing for external reporting.
A. Financial Accounting Standards Board
B. Securities and Exchange Commission
C. Internal Revenue Service
D. American Institute of Certified Public Accountants
E. National Association of Accountants

4-8 How can the manager of a profit center increase reported net income without changing price or cost structure or selling more units? Explain.

4-9 Variable costing is a subset of the contribution margin approach. Contrast the two concepts and illustrate their relationship.

4-10 What are the significant limitations of the contribution margin approach?

EXERCISES

4-11 *(True or False).* Indicate whether the following statements are true or false.

1. The contribution margin approach is useful in a manufacturing setting but cannot be used for other types of firms, such as retailing.

2. Using a contribution margin approach is the same as using variable costing.

3. The contribution margin approach is not acceptable for external reporting in a manufacturing concern.

4. When sales are greater than production, net income is less under variable costing than under full absorption costing.
5. When sales are less than production, net income is greater under absorption costing than under variable costing.
6. Using absorption costing for income tax returns and variable costing for internal use is illegal.
7. Sales less product costs equals fixed administrative expenses.
8. Variable costs less product costs equals zero.
9. The contribution margin approach is useful for long-range decisions because it defines costs as fixed or variable.
10. Differences in income between absorption and variable costing are only timing differences.

4-12 *(Cost Classification).* Classify the following costs as (1) product or period cost; and (2) as primarily variable or fixed.

	Product	*Period*	*Fixed*	*Variable*
A. Direct material				
B. Salesperson's commission				
C. Factory manager's salary under absorption costing				
D. President's salary				
E. Factory rent under variable costing				
F. Prime costs				
G. Cost of TV ads for a new product				
H. Interest on loan to finance the new product				
I. Depreciation of factory equipment by the units of production method				
J. Wages of a grape stomper in a winery.				

4-13 *(Variable and Absorption Costing).* Bomber Electronics manufactures a special electronic component used in calculators. The company sold 100,000 units at $2.00 each during 19X3. Unit costs for 19X3 follows:

	Fixed	Variable
Material and labor	$.60	
Overhead	$.30	$.10
Selling and administrative	$.20	$.30

REQUIRED:

A. What is the unit cost for inventory purposes:

1. under absorption costing?
2. under variable costing?

B. What is the net income per unit:

1. under absorption costing?
2. under variable costing?

C. How many units must be sold to break even?

4-14 *(Definitions; Multiple Choice)*. Slipping Gear Company produces a special gear used in automatic transmissions. Each gear sells for $28. The company sells approximately 500,000 gears each year. Unit cost data for 19X3 follow.

	Variable	Fixed
Direct material	$6.00	
Direct labor	$5.00	
Other costs		
Manufacturing	$2.00	$7.00
Distribution	$4.00	$3.00

A. The unit cost of gears for inventory purposes with variable costing is
a. $13
b. $20
c. $17
d. $27
e. $11
f. None of the above

B. Gear has received an offer from a foreign manufacturer to purchase 25,000 gears. Domestic sales would be unaffected by this transaction. If the offer is accepted, variable distribution costs will increase $1.50 per gear for insurance, shipping, and import duties. The unit cost that is relevant to a pricing decision on this offer is
a. $17.00
b. $14.50
c. $28.50
d. $18.50
e. $12.50
f. None of the above

C. The unit cost of gears for inventory purposes with absorption costing is
 a. $13
 b. $20
 c. $17
 d. $27
 e. $11
 f. None of the above

D. The prime cost of the gears is
 a. $13
 b. $20
 c. $17
 d. $27
 e. $11
 f. None of the above

E. The average total cost of the gears under absorption costing is
 a. $11
 b. $27
 c. $13
 d. $17
 e. $20
 f. None of the above

F. The average total cost of the gears under variable costing is
 a. $11
 b. $27
 c. $13
 d. $17
 e. $20
 f. None of the above

(CPA adapted)

4-15 *(Effects of Absorption and Variable Costing).* The Cook Island Company was recently formed and is about to start production. The directors are trying to decide whether to use variable or absorption costing. The following projections were made for the first year of operations.

Production	10,000 units
Sales	8,000 units
Direct materials	$30,000
Direct labor	$20,000
Variable overhead	$10,000
Fixed overhead	$40,000
Variable selling	$16,000

REQUIRED:

A. Compute the cost to be assigned to the inventory under variable costing and under absorption costing.

B. What is the difference between net income determined under variable costing and under absorption costing during the first year?

C. What considerations are important in deciding which method of inventory costing to use?

4-16 *(Absorption Costing).* The Tejas Company produced 36,000 units of its product during 19X6. There were no beginning inventories. Ending inventories consisted of 6,000 units in Finished Goods Inventory. The selling price is $10 per unit.

Costs for the year were as follows:

	Fixed Costs	*Variable Costs*
Direct materials		$72,000
Direct labor		$54,000
Overhead	$36,000	$36,000
Selling expenses	$39,000	10% of sales
Administrative expenses	$31,600	$12,000

REQUIRED:

Compute the following:

A. Sales for the year.
B. Gross margin.
C. Gross margin ratio.
D. Net income under absorption costing.
E. Breakeven point in units.
F. Cost of ending inventory under absorption costing.

4-17 *(Variable Costing).* The Utah Company produced 36,000 units of its product during 19X6. There were no beginning inventories. Ending inventories consisted of 6,000 units in Finished Goods Inventory. The selling price is $10 per unit.

Costs for the year were as follows:

	Fixed Costs	*Variable Costs*
Direct materials		$72,000
Direct labor		$54,000
Overhead	$36,000	$36,000
Selling expenses	$39,000	10% of sales
Administrative expenses	$31,600	$12,000

REQUIRED:

Compute the following:

A. Sales for the year.
B. Contribution margin from production.
C. Contribution margin from total operations.
D. Contribution margin ratio.
E. Net income under variable costing.
F. Breakeven point in dollars of sales.
G. Cost of ending inventory under variable costing.

4-18 *(Contribution Margin Approach in Wholesale Setting).* The president of Wholesale Products Company is not satisfied with the following income statement that was prepared by his bookkeeper. Net income is lower than he thinks it should be. He doubts that all product lines are generating the income they should but does not have the information to evaluate individual product lines.

WHOLESALE PRODUCTS COMPANY
INCOME STATEMENT
For the Year 19X7

Sales		$600,000
Cost of goods sold	$365,000	
Sales commissions	49,000	
Delivery costs	20,000	
Salaries	70,000	
Advertising	40,000	
Rent	24,000	
Other	6,000	574,000
Net income		$ 26,000

The president asks you to prepare an income statement that shows "how well he is doing" on each of his three product lines.

Additional information:

Sales for the three product lines:

Product A	$100,000
Product B	$300,000
Product C	$200,000

Cost of goods sold by product line:

Product A	60% of sales
Product B	55% of sales
Product C	70% of sales

Commissions by product line: Product A, 10% of sales; Product B, 5% of sales; Product C, 12% of sales.

Salesmen's salaries: $20,000 for Product A and $30,000 for Product B.

Delivery expense: 5% of sales for Products A and B.

Advertising: Product A $10,000; Product B $20,000; Product C $10,000.

The balance of the salaries are sales management and administration.

Rent and other expenses cannot be traced to product lines.

REQUIRED:

A. Prepare an income statement by product line using the contribution margin approach.

B. What can you tell from the contribution margin income statement that you could not tell from the income statement prepared by the bookkeeper?

C. Other firms in the industry have a return on sales of 8%. Were the president's suspicions correct? Explain.

4–19 *(Contribution Margin Approach in Educational Setting).* The voters of Happy Hollow rejected the $50,000 supplemental operating levy for the city's school system. As a result, the school board must reduce budgeted expenses by $50,000. The budget proposed to the voters was:

CITY OF HAPPY HOLLOW
PROPOSED BUDGET
For the Year 19X7–19X8

Revenues:	
Property taxes (regular levy)	$454,000
Property taxes (special levy)	50,000
Admission to athletic events	40,000
School lunch revenue	48,000
Total budgeted revenues	$592,000
Expenses:	
Salaries	$432,000
Material and supplies	76,000
Building repairs and utilities	36,000
Other	48,000
Total budgeted expenses	$592,000

An examination of expenses shows the following:

Salaries:		
Classroom teachers	(fixed)	$363,000
Coaching staff	(fixed)	10,000
School administration	(fixed)	40,000
Cafeteria personnel	(fixed)	15,000
Ticket takers for athletic events	(10% of revenue)	4,000
		$432,000

Material and supplies:		
Classroom materials	(variable)	$ 24,000
Athletic supplies	(variable)	10,000
Food	(variable)	42,000
		$ 76,000
Building repairs and utilities	(fixed)	$ 36,000
Other	($12,000 fixed; balance variable)	$ 48,000

Some members of the school board want to eliminate the athletic program and school lunch program because "they are a financial drain on the basic education resources."

REQUIRED:

A. The chairman of the school board wants you to recast the original budget into a contribution margin approach and show the identifiable revenues and expenses for (1) basic education, (2) athletics, and (3) school lunch program.

B. How does your revised budget in Part A assist the school board in its decisions? Explain.

4-20 *(Absorption versus Variable Costing).* The Frosty Manufacturing Company produces a line of small portable refrigerators. During the past year the following costs were incurred.

Direct materials	$270,000
Direct labor	$540,000
Compensation insurance (7% of direct and indirect labor)	$ 60,900
Power (variable)	$ 8,700
Factory supplies (variable)	$ 2,400
Indirect factory labor (variable)	$330,000
Repairs and maintenance (variable)	$ 39,000
Light and heat (variable)	$ 4,800
Property taxes (fixed)	$ 4,200
Rent (fixed)	$ 7,200
Depreciation on factory (fixed)	$ 8,400
Insurance on factory (fixed)	$ 2,400
Selling expenses (fixed)	$120,000
Administrative expenses (fixed)	$340,000

There were no beginning inventories in Raw Materials, Work-in-Process, or Finished Goods. There were no ending inventories in Raw Materials or Work-in-Process. The firm manufactured 4,500 units during the year and sold 4,100 units.

REQUIRED:

A. What is the cost of the Finished Goods Inventory under absorption costing? Under variable costing?

B. Assuming that sales were $1,700,000 for the year, how would the net income differ under the two systems? Why?

4-21 *(Absorption versus Variable Costing Using Flexible Budgets).* The Jonesville Company accountant developed the following flexible budget equations for the year 19X6:

Materials	\$0 + \$4 per unit
Labor	\$0 + \$6 per unit
Overhead:	
Depreciation of machinery	\$0 + \$3 per unit
Utilities	\$2,400 + \$1 per unit
Supervisory salaries	\$18,000 + \$0 per unit
Repairs and maintenance	\$4,600 + \$2 per unit
Depreciation of factory building	\$5,000 + \$0 per unit
Selling Expenses:	
Sales salaries	\$4,000 + 10% of sales
Advertising	\$6,000 + \$0
Administrative salaries	\$20,000 + \$0

During 19X6, production was 30,000 units; sales were 28,000 units at an average sales price of $20 per unit.

REQUIRED:

A. Prepare a contribution margin income statement.
B. Prepare an absorption costing income statement.
C. Determine the final inventory values under (1) variable costing, and (2) absorption costing. What accounts for the difference in inventory values?
D. Why was depreciation of machinery a variable cost and depreciation of factory building a fixed cost?

4-22 *(Strengths and Weaknesses of Variable Costing).* Supporters of variable costing contend that it provides management with more useful accounting information. Critics of variable costing believe that its negative features outweigh its contributions.

REQUIRED:

A. Describe variable costing. How does it differ from conventional absorption costing?
B. List the arguments for and against the use of variable costing.
C. Indicate how each of the following conditions would affect the amounts of net income reported under conventional absorption costing and variable costing.

1. Sales and production are in balance at normal volume.
2. Sales exceed production.
3. Production exceeds sales.

(CPA adapted)

4-23 *(Income Differences Between Absorption and Variable Costing).* The following cost structure was developed for the Allen Company, a producer of a single product.

Direct materials	$ 5.00 per unit
Direct labor	$ 10.00 per unit
Variable overhead	$ 2.00 per unit
Fixed overhead	$20,000 per year
Selling expenses	$12,000 per year

The product sells for $25 per unit. In an average year 10,000 units are produced and sold.

REQUIRED:

A. What is the net income under absorption costing, assuming that 10,000 units are produced and sold? What is the cost per unit?

B. What is the net income under variable costing, assuming that 10,000 units are produced and sold? What is the cost per unit?

C. Assuming that production dropped to 8,000 units and that sales dropped to 7,000 units, what would be the net income under absorption costing? What would be the net income under variable costing?

D. What factors affect the cost per unit under absorption costing between the two production levels?

4-24 *(Identifying Absorption and Variable Costing).* Two income statements are prepared from the same data for the Benz Manufacturing Company.

	Case A		*Case B*	
Sales		$10,000		$10,000
Cost of goods sold	$7,000		$5,000	
Operating expenses (all of which are fixed)	1,000	8,000	3,000	8,000
Net income		$ 2,000		$ 2,000

REQUIRED:

A. Which of the two cases is prepared under absorption costing? Which under variable costing? How did you tell?

B. Was the number of units produced larger than, equal to, or smaller than the number of units sold?

C. What is the amount of selling and administrative costs? Are they fixed or variable?

D. What is the amount of fixed overhead?

4-25 *(Contribution Margin Approach in a Compensation Plan).* The president of Taylor School Supply Company, a wholesaler, presents you with a comparison of distribution costs for two salesmen and wants to know if you think the salesmen's compensation plan is working to the detriment of the company. He supplies you with the following data.

	Salesmen	
	McKinney	*Sim*
Gross sales	$247,000	$142,000
Sales returns	$ 17,000	$ 2,000
Cost of goods sold	$180,000	$ 85,000
Reimbursed expenses (e.g., entertainment)	$ 5,500	$ 2,100
Other direct charges (e.g., samples distributed)	$ 4,000	$ 450
Commission rate on gross sales dollars	5%	5%

REQUIRED:

A. The salesmen's compensation plan encourages a salesman to work to increase the measure of performance to which his compensation is related. List the questionable sales practices by a salesman that might be encouraged by basing commissions on gross sales.

B. What evidence that the compensation plan may be working to the detriment of the company can be found in the data?

C. What other information should the president obtain before reaching definite conclusions about this particular situation? Why?

(CPA adapted)

PROBLEMS

4-26 *(Contribution Margin Approach in a Service Concern).* The accounting firm of Coe, Roe, and Low is considering a number of changes including expansion and an increase of billing rates to clients. The following income statement does not provide the information needed by the partners.

COE, ROE, AND LOW
INCOME STATEMENT
For the Year 19X7

Revenue		$200,000
Operating expenses:		
Salaries of employees	$64,000	
Salaries of partners	75,000	
Supplies	6,000	
Equipment depreciation	2,000	
Rent and utilities	12,000	
Travel	20,000	
Other	16,000	195,000
Net income		$ 5,000

A study of operating expenses revealed the following cost behavior patterns.

Salaries of employees	\$2,000 per month plus 20% of revenue
Salaries of partners	\$25,000 per year for each of three partners
Supplies	3% of revenue
Equipment depreciation	\$2,000 per year
Rent and utilities	\$1,000 per month
Travel	10% of revenue
Other	\$1,000 per month plus 2% of revenue

REQUIRED:

A. Prepare an income statement using the contribution margin approach showing revenue and costs when revenue is \$200,000, \$220,000, and \$250,000.

B. Prepare a profit-volume chart.

C. Does the income statement in Part A and the profit-volume chart in Part B show the same income at each of the three levels of revenue? Why or why not?

D. What kind of decisions will the income statement in Part A and profit-volume chart in Part B help the partners answer?

4-27 *(Variable and Absorption Costing Across Time Periods).* The Johnson Company had the following production and sales quantities during the past year.

	1st Quarter	*2nd Quarter*	*3rd Quarter*	*4th Quarter*
Units produced	50	45	50	50
Units sold	40	50	50	55

During the year the selling price was constant at \$10 per unit, variable production costs were \$6.00 per unit, and fixed production costs were \$135 per quarter. Assume a LIFO inventory flow.

REQUIRED:

A. Prepare income statements that set forth sales, variable and fixed costs, and net income for each quarter under both absorption and variable costing approaches.

B. Calculate the ending inventory values for each quarter under both absorption and variable costing.

C. Prepare a schedule that compares the ending inventory values and net incomes showing how they differ under absorption and variable costing.

4-28 *(Contribution Margin Income Statements).* The Nelson Company manufactures three principal products. During the past year it had the following cost, revenue, and production experiences.

	Product A	Product B	Product C
Units produced	5,000	10,000	1,000
Units sold	5,000	9,000	900
Unit sales price	$ 20	$ 15	$ 50
Direct material per unit	$ 5	$ 5	$ 20
Direct labor per unit	$ 6	$ 4	$ 10
Variable overhead per unit	$ 2	$ 1	$ 5
Fixed overhead per year	$2,500	$10,000	$5,000
Fixed selling expenses	$5,000	$10,000	$1,000

REQUIRED:

A. Prepare income statements for each product using the contribution margin approach.

B. Calculate for each product the contribution margin per unit and the contribution margin ratio per unit.

C. Prepare a schedule showing the ending inventory values for each product under both absorption costing and variable costing.

D. Discuss the value of the contribution margin in making incremental production decisions.

4–29 *(Contrast of Income Statements Under Variable and Absorption Costing).* The Elite Pottery Company manufactures a line of pottery dishes. During 19X2 it produced 10,000 sets of dishes, but sold only 9,500 sets. The selling price of the sets was $50. Production and distribution costs for the year were:

Materials	$100,000
Labor	$120,000
Variable overhead	$ 80,000
Fixed overhead	$ 60,000
Selling costs	$ 70,000

REQUIRED:

A. Develop the cost per unit under (1) absorption costing, and (2) variable costing.

B. Develop income statements under (1) absorption costing, and (2) variable costing.

C. Prepare a schedule showing the inventory values at the end of the year under both absorption and variable costing. What is the total difference in the ending inventory values? What causes this difference?

D. What would be the effect upon net income under both absorption and variable costing if the sales volume decreased to 6,000 units, assuming that the cost structures and production level remained unchanged?

4–30 *(Contrast of Income Statements Under Variable and Absorption Costing).* The controller of the newly formed Cain Company was asked to prepare a recommendation to the board of directors concerning the inventory costing method to be adopted by the company. One member of the board is also a director of another company that uses the contribution margin approach for internal reporting. He thinks the Cain Company should prepare reports for the board of directors using the contribution margin approach. Another member of the board thinks it is wrong for the company "to keep two sets of books."

Data for the first year of operations follow.

Units produced	100,000, of which 80,000 were sold at $11 per unit.
Direct materials	$240,000
Direct labor	$320,000
Overhead:	
Variable costs	$ 80,000
Fixed costs	$160,000
Selling and administrative expenses:	
Variable costs	$ 48,000
Fixed costs	$180,000

REQUIRED:

A. Indicate the cost to be assigned to the inventory using:
  1. Variable costing
  2. Absorption costing

B. Prepare an income statement for the member of the board of directors who wants the company to use the contribution margin approach.

C. Prepare an income statement that will meet the requirements for reporting to the stockholders.

D. Prepare a recommendation to the board of directors concerning the costing method to be used for inventory costing. Your recommendation should consider the concerns of both directors.

4–31 *(Cost-Volume-Profit Analysis and Pricing Policy).* The president of Easy Listening Corporation, which manufactures tape decks and sells them to producers of sound reproduction systems, anticipates a 10% wage increase on January 1 of next year to the manufacturing employees (variable labor). He expects no other changes in costs. Overhead will not change as a result of the wage increase. The president has asked you to assist him in developing the information he needs to formulate a reasonable product strategy for next year.

You are satisfied by regression analysis that volume is the primary factor affecting costs and have separated the semivariable costs into their fixed and variable segments by means of the least-squares criterion. You also observe that the beginning and ending inventories are never materially different.

The following data for the current year are assembled for your analysis.

Current selling price per unit	$80
Variable cost per unit:	
Material	$30
Labor	12
Overhead	6
Total	$48
Annual volume of sales	5,000 units
Fixed costs	$51,000

REQUIRED:

Provide the following information for the president, using cost-volume-profit analysis.

A. What increase in the selling price is necessary to cover the 10% wage increase and still maintain the current contribution margin ratio?

B. How many tape decks must be sold to maintain the current net income if the sales price remains at $80 and the 10% wage increase goes into effect?

C. The president believes that an additional $190,000 of machinery (to be depreciated at 10% annually) will increase present capacity (5,300 units) by 30%. If all tape decks produced can be sold at the present price, and the wage increase goes into effect, how would the estimated net income before capacity is increased compare with the estimated net income after capacity is increased? Prepare income statements under the contribution margin approach *before* and *after* the expansion.

(CPA adapted)

4-32 *(Contrast of Variable and Absorption Costing Across Time Periods).* The Komfy Quilt Company manufactures a line of fine-quality patchwork quilts. Due to increased demand, the manager is faced with the decision of adding productive capacity. During the analysis of past costs, revenues, and net incomes, a question was raised in staff meeting about the definition of product cost. The company is currently using absorption costing, but the manager has heard that a variable costing system might prove more informative to management. The following information was developed to facilitate a comparison between the two systems.

	19X1	*19X2*	*19X3*	*19X4*
Units produced	1,200	1,500	1,200	1,200
Units sold	1,000	1,200	1,300	1,600

Cost and revenue information:

Variable costs:		
Raw materials	$30	
Direct labor	40	
Variable overhead	20	
Total variable costs	$90	
Other costs:		
Fixed production costs		$18,000 per year
Administrative costs		$14,000 per year
Selling costs		5% of sales revenue
Sales price		$150 per unit

Assume no beginning inventory and a LIFO inventory flow.

REQUIRED:

A. Prepare a schedule that shows net income for each year using both variable and absorption costing.

B. For each year reconcile the differences in net income between variable and absorption costing. As a part of your reconciliation show the ending Finished Goods Inventory under both variable and absorption costing.

4-33 *(Variable Costing and Breakeven Analysis).* At the end of the Bond Company's first year of business the following income statement was prepared by a Certified Public Accountant.

BOND COMPANY
INCOME STATEMENT
For the Year 19X7

Sales	(20,000 units × $12)		$240,000
Cost of goods sold:			
Production costs	(25,000 units × $ 8)	$200,000	
Ending inventory	(5,000 units × $ 8)	40,000	160,000
Gross margin			$ 80,000
Selling and administrative expenses			76,000
Net income			$ 4,000

Mr. Bond showed the income statement to his daughter, Wendy, who was home from college during the semester break. He was pleased that the company had shown a profit for the first year.

Wendy had just completed a course in management accounting and eagerly set about to apply the concepts from the course. From the accountant's report and other information about the company, Wendy found that the unit product cost of $8.00 included fixed costs of $2.00, and that of the $76,000 selling and administrative expenses $16,000 were fixed.

After preparing a breakeven chart, Wendy said, "Sorry pops, but my breakeven chart shows that you lost about $6,000."

REQUIRED:

A. Prepare a breakeven chart for the Bond Company. What income or loss do you show at the 20,000-unit sales level?

B. Mr. Bond is confused about whether or not his company earned a profit last year. Is either his income statement or the breakeven chart wrong? Explain.

C. Prepare an income statement using variable costing and the contribution margin approach. Does your income or loss agree with the income statement or breakeven chart? Why?

D. What is the breakeven point in units? In sales dollars?

4-34 *(Cost Flow Systems and Management Performance Assessment).* The Leaky Tank Company presents a Plant Manager of the Month Award to the plant manager with the highest monthly income. The award is very important to the plant managers; it carries peer-group approval. Because of the high freight costs of the finished tanks, the company has several plants in strategic locations. The plants are of approximately the same size and have about the same cost structures, so top management believes that net income is a fair measure to use in presenting the monthly incentive award.

The plant manager of the Mud Flats Plant distrusts the accounting system because the manager of the Green River Plant has won the award for the past two months. The Green River Plant has sold fewer units in the past month and has had labor problems. Income statements follow for the two plants.

MUD FLATS PLANT
INCOME STATEMENT

	June	*July*
Sales (@ $400)	$40,000	$40,000
Cost of goods sold	30,000	30,000
Gross margin	$10,000	$10,000
Operating expense	5,000	5,000
Net income	$ 5,000	$ 5,000

GREEN RIVER PLANT
INCOME STATEMENT

	June	*July*
Sales (@ $400)	$40,000	$36,000
Cost of goods sold	25,000	22,950
Gross margin	$15,000	$13,050
Operating expense	5,000	5,000
Net income	$10,000	$ 8,050

You were asked to study the income statements of the two plants. The entire company uses a full-absorption costing system to measure unit cost and a LIFO cost flow method to match inventory cost with revenue. In the process of your investigation you discover the following additional information.

MUD FLATS PLANT

	June	*July*
Variable production costs (per unit)	$ 150	$ 150
Fixed production costs (per month)	$15,000	$15,000
Beginning inventory	0	0
Units sold	100	100
Units produced	100	100

GREEN RIVER PLANT

	June	*July*
Variable production costs (per unit)	$ 150	$ 180
Fixed production costs (per month)	$15,000	$15,000
Beginning inventory	0	50
Units sold	100	90
Units produced	150	200

REQUIRED:

A. Explain to the Mud Flats Plant manager why the award was won by the Green River Plant manager.
B. Prepare revised income statements under variable costing.
C. To whom would you give the award? Why?

4-35 *(Variable Costing and Decision Making).* Joe Bottler was a successful farmer who had, on his farm, a spring that was famous throughout the state. It had an ever-flowing supply of mineral water that tasted like sparkling burgundy and was reported to cure all manner of ailments. Joe's friends had often urged him to bottle and sell this water as a beverage. One year, when his crops were poor, Joe decided to look into the matter.

Joe checked with the general store and found that he could buy jugs for $.25 each. Joe talked about his project with a neighbor named Sally Fuller, who was an amateur artist. She offered to fill the jugs at the spring and paint labels on them for $.25 each. He then approached Oscar Deal, the soda fountain operator. Oscar said he could sell this drink for $1.50 a jug and that he was willing to pay Joe $1.00 a jug and pick them up at the farm. This looked like a sound venture, so Joe decided to start operations.

After a short time, Joe had a nice little business. Sally was bottling, and Deal was selling, 40 jugs a day. Joe was receiving $1.00 each, or $40 a day. He was paying Sally $.25 each, or $10 a day. His jugs were costing him $.25 each, or another $10 a day. He was making a profit of $.50 each, or $20 a day.

Joe soon found, however, that the soft drink business was not so simple as it seemed. One morning the local board of health ordered Joe to stop bottling and selling his beverage because the jugs were not being sterilized. He finally found a washer that could be rented for $10 a day. Steam could be piped from a geyser close to his spring. The board inspected this arrangement and gave Joe permission to resume operations.

Joe's business was getting more complex. He now could figure his profit in two ways. If he continued to sell 40 jugs a day, his additional cost per jug would be: $10 ÷ 40 = $.25 per jug. Thus, his profit would be reduced $.25 per jug, or $10 a day. This is the conventional accounting method.

However, Joe was not an accountant and he preferred to figure it in a simpler way. His basic profit (or profit contribution) was still $.50 a jug. That is, the difference between his sales price of $1.00 and his variable expense per unit for jugs and labor was still $.50 each, no matter how many jugs he sold. The first 20 jugs he sold paid the rent on his washer and he made a profit of $.50 each on all over 20 he sold. In other words, his breakeven point was 20 jugs per day. If he should sell less than that, he would fail to cover his constant washer rent and would lose money. If he continued to sell 40 jugs a day he would make his profit of $.50 each on the second 20 jugs, or $10 a day. By figuring it this way, Joe could easily see just how he was coming out on any volume of business.

But Joe was not satisfied with $10 a day. He talked to Deal about increasing the sales. Deal told Joe that if he could supply 7-oz. bottles for his cooler, he could sell 1,000 bottles a day at $.10 a bottle. He was willing to pay $.06 a bottle. Joe could buy bottles for $.03 each and Sally's sister, Suzie, was willing to wash and fill the bottles for $.01 each. No labels were needed, but Sally was to furnish a new hand-painted poster to Deal each day to put over his cooler. Sally was willing to paint these posters for $2.00 each. Joe looked at this proposition in the following way.

Income per bottle		$ .06
Cost of bottle	$.03	
Labor cost	.01	
Total		.04
Basic profit per bottle		$ .02
Added constant cost		$2.00 per day

Thus Joe figured that he only needed to sell 100 bottles a day to cover his added constant cost. It sounded like a good proposition so he decided to go ahead with it. His overall situation was now as follows:

Washer rent	$10.00 per day
Posters	2.00 per day
Total constant cost	$12.00 per day
Basic profit per jug = $.50	
Basic profit per bottle = $.02	

Now the value of Joe's simple method of figuring his profit by thinking of total constant cost per day and basic profit or "profit contribution" per unit rather than allocating fixed charges to each product on a unit basis really began to show up. He could easily figure his profit on any combination of sales. If he continued to sell 40 jugs a day and also sold 1,000 7-oz. bottles, his profit would be as follows:

Basic profit on jugs	40 × $.50 =	$20.00
Basic profit on bottles	1,000 × $.02 =	20.00
Total basic profit		$40.00
Total constant cost		12.00
Net profit		$28.00

However, after a short time he found that he was selling 30 jugs and 1,500 bottles per day.

Basic profit on jugs	30 × $.50 =	$15.00
Basic profit on bottles	1,500 × $.02 =	30.00
Total basic profit		$45.00
Total constant cost		12.00
Net profit		$33.00

If Joe had been trained in accounting, he no doubt would have figured his costs by allocating the washer rental to each product on an estimate of the portion of washer time used by each. He then would have divided this allocated amount by his assumed quantities. When his actual sales differed from his assumed sales, he would have had an overabsorbed or underabsorbed burden. All very complex. But since Joe kept his constant costs separate, and thought in terms of basic profit per unit, he could figure his profit picture for any assortment or volume by simple arithmetic.

The beverage business went along smoothly for some time. Joe was making a profit of $33 a day, Sally was making $9.50 a day and Suzie was making $15 a day. One day Sally came to Joe and told him she was tired of getting the short end of the deal while Joe and Suzie were making big money. She demanded $.50 per jug and $3.00 per poster, or she would quit painting labels and posters. Joe blustered and squirmed, but since Sally was the only capable artist in the community he was forced to agree to her demands. Joe figured his profit under the new circumstances.

Income per jug		$ 1.00
Cost of jug	$.25	
Labor cost	.50	.75
Basic profit per jug		$ .25
Basic profit on jugs	30 × $.25 =	$ 7.50
Basic profit on bottles	1,500 × $.02 =	30.00
Total basic profit or *profit contribution*		$37.50
Constant cost of washer	$10.00	
Constant cost of posters	3.00	
Total constant cost		13.00
Net profit per day		$24.50

Again, Joe was dissatisfied with his profit. He told Deal he would have to get $.25 more per jug because of his increased labor cost. Deal agreed to pay $1.25 per jug, but said he would raise the retail price to $1.75 and this might reduce the volume of sales to as low as 20 a day. He checked with a number of Deal's customers and convinced himself that this was a good estimate of the maximum loss of volume he could expect. Joe figured his profit picture this way.

Basic profit on $1.00 jugs = 30 × $.25 = $ 7.50
Basic profit on $1.25 jugs = 20 × $.50 = $10.00
Increased net profit per day = $2.50

He decided to take the gamble and make the change.

REQUIRED:
Comment upon Joe's use of accounting data in making his decisions.

5 Variable Historical Costing for Recording Past Costs

In the previous chapter we illustrated the differences between absorption costing and variable costing. We summarized our discussion by saying that most management accountants believe that variable costing is valuable because it provides contribution margin data for decision making. At the same time, generally accepted accounting principles require absorption costing for external reports. In this and the following chapter we will present product costing with variable costing. In this chapter we will present variable historical costing; in the following chapter we will show the benefits of variable standard costing over historical costing in creating efficient operations. However, in the light of external reporting requirements, we will convert the results from variable costing to absorption costing. In this way the management accountant can meet both reporting requirements.

METHODS OF CALCULATING UNIT COST OF PRODUCTION

Two systems have been developed to trace production costs to the product: job and process costing. Both systems have the same ultimate objective of determining the unit cost of the products produced. It is through this unit cost that the accountant determines the cost to hold in the inventory or the cost to match with revenue. Job and process costing are two methods of keeping the detailed records supporting the Work-in-Process Inventory and of determining the unit cost of production. Job order and process costing may be used with either variable or absorption costing. Variable or absorption costing concerns the problem of which costs are product costs and which costs are period costs. Job order or process costing concerns the question of how product costs, regardless of their definition, are combined to determine the unit cost of manufacture.

Job costing is used in factories where the products are manufactured in a series of identifiable and separate jobs, lots, or batches. Often the company has a firm sales order before it begins work on a job. Examples of industries where job costing is suitable include building construction, shipbuilding, printing, and aircraft manufacturing. In these plants each product unit is identifiable from the beginning of production. Costs are accumulated for each job, and the unit cost is the sum of all costs identified with the particular job. It is as if the product is sticky, like flypaper, and the costs cling to it. In these plants the **job cost sheet** serves as the focal point of costs. There is one job cost sheet for each unit or batch produced, and the sum of the costs on the job cost sheets must equal the dollars charged to the Work-in-Process Inventory.

In plants where the production is a continuous flow, or where one unit of product is indistinguishable from another, costs are assigned to the products through **process costing.** In a process cost system the costs are traced to departments during a specified time period on a *departmental cost sheet,* and the cost per unit of product is determined by:

$$\text{Unit cost} = \frac{\text{Production costs of department during time period}}{\text{Output produced by department during time period}}$$

The result is an average unit cost for all items produced. Industries that use process costing include steel mills, petroleum refineries, meat-packing plants, lumber mills, and aluminum manufacturers.

JOB COSTING ILLUSTRATED

In a job costing system the detailed record (subsidiary ledger) supporting the Work-in-Process Inventory is the **job cost sheet.** With a large product, such as an airplane or ship, there is usually one job cost sheet for each unit. With small units there could be a job cost sheet for a number of units; the cost of a single unit of product would be determined by dividing the total cost for the lot by the number of units in the lot.

Each job cost sheet is numbered so that each cost can be traced accurately. All product costs incurred must be traced to job cost sheets, either directly, through material requisitions and labor-time tickets, or indirectly, through an overhead rate. The total costs charged to Work-in-Process Inventory during any specific time period will be equal to the charges on the job cost sheets. When a product is completed, the job cost sheet for that product is totaled. The total of charges on the job cost sheet is the amount transferred to Finished Goods Inventory. Any jobs started but not completed represent the ending Work-in-Process Inventory. In a job costing system, accumulation of costs for a particular product is important. It may take two or more accounting periods before a particular job is finished and the unit cost determined.

To illustrate the flow of costs in a job costing system, let's examine the cost system for the Roving Jack Company, a manufacturer of mobile camper units. The journal entries illustrating the flow of costs for the Roving Jack Company are keyed to the cost flow diagram shown in Exhibit 5–1. Transactions will not always be in numerical sequence. Refer to Exhibit 5–1 occasionally to maintain an overall perspective of the flow of costs through the system.

At the beginning of October the Roving Jack Company had three units in the process of construction. Inventories at the beginning of the month included \$2,500 of materials in the Raw Materials Inventory, \$5,182 in the Work-in-Process Inventory for the three partially completed units, and no units in the Finished Goods Inventory. The job cost sheets in Exhibit 5–2 show the following detail for the three units in process.

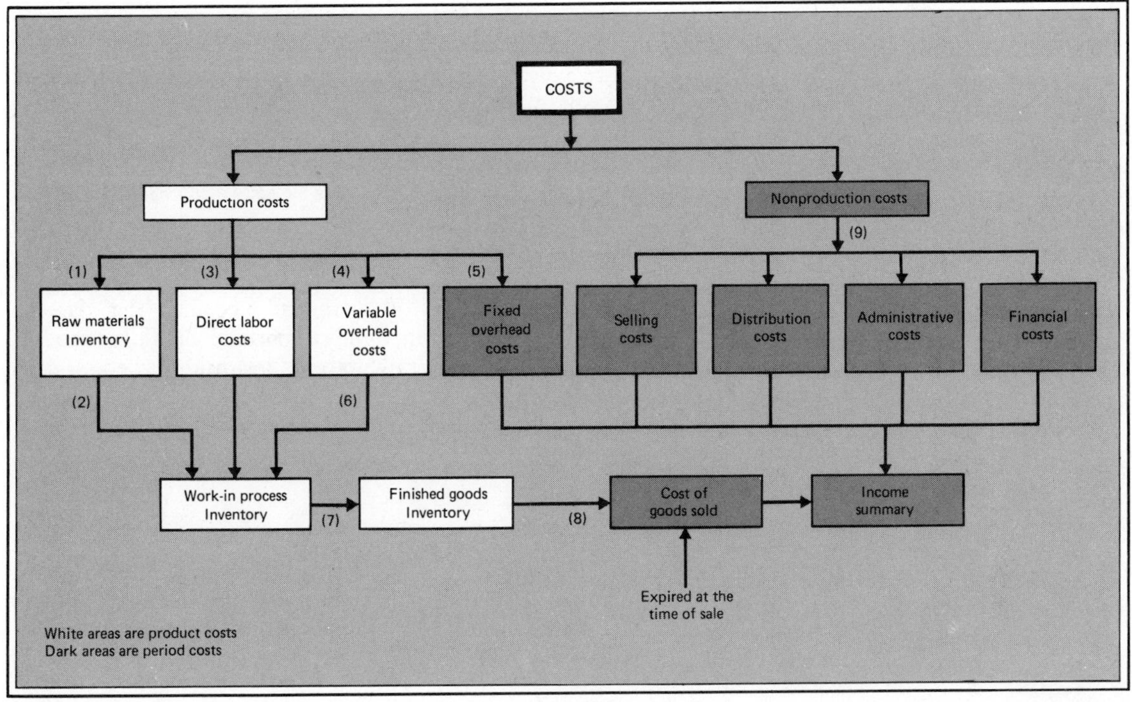

EXHIBIT 5-1
Cost flow with variable costing

	101-24'	*102-18'*	*103-20'*	*Total*
Direct materials	$1,355	$ 917	$1,080	$3,352
Direct labor	625	520	215	1,360
Variable overhead	215	180	75	470
Total cost	$2,195	$1,617	$1,370	$5,182

The transactions of the Roving Jack Company for October follow.

PURCHASE OF RAW MATERIALS

The storeroom records indicated that the company needed additional raw materials. The storekeeper sent a **purchase requisition** to the purchasing department to advise of the need for raw materials. Using the purchase requisition as authority, the purchasing agent issued a **purchase order** notifying his supplier of the material needs. No accounting entry was made for these two events, since no exchange with outside parties was completed.

When the supplier received the purchase order he shipped the materials. At the same time, he sent an **invoice** for the selling prices of the materials. After the goods were received, inspected, and accepted by the Roving Jack Company, the accountant made the following journal entry to record the purchase of raw materials.

(1) Raw Materials Inventory	$4,400	
Accounts Payable (or Cash)		$4,400
To record the purchase of raw materials.		

The Raw Materials Inventory is a control account; that is, the aggregate total is kept in the general ledger and supported by detailed records in a subsidiary ledger. For each type of raw material a subsidiary ledger card is kept to show the quantity and price of the items received, issued, and on hand. (We have not included the subsidiary ledger records for the Raw Materials Inventory account.)

ISSUE OF RAW MATERIALS

The production schedule for October called for the completion of Jobs 101–24′, 102–18′, and 103–20′ and for the start of one new job: 104–28′. On the basis of this production schedule, the production manager prepared **material requisitions** for the material necessary to perform the scheduled work.

Material requisitions serve as authority for the storeroom to release materials to the factory and as evidence to support the accounting entry. The following summation of these material requisitions for October showed direct materials issued to the jobs.

Job 101–24′	$ 500
Job 102–18′	317
Job 103–20′	820
Job 104–28′	3,350
Total direct materials	$4,987

Materials issued from the storeroom were removed from the raw materials ledger card (not shown) and were posted to the individual job cost sheets, as shown in Exhibit 5–2. The following journal entry records the issue of this direct material.

(2) Work-in-Process Inventory	$4,987	
Raw Materials Inventory		$4,987
To record the issue of direct materials.		

The material requisitions showed that in addition to the direct materials previously listed, $1,000 of indirect materials were issued to the factory. The following journal entry records this issue.

ROVING JACK COMPANY

Job Cost Sheet No. 101-24

Date	Material	Labor	Variable Overhead	Total
Bal. 9-30	$1,355	$ 625	$ 215	$2,195
October	500	2,200	750	3,450
Total	$1,855	$2,825	$965	$5,645

ROVING JACK COMPANY

Job Cost Sheet No. 102-18

Date	Material	Labor	Variable Overhead	Total
Bal. 9-30	$ 917	$ 520	$ 180	$1,617
October	317	950	300	1,567
Total	$1,234	$1,470	$ 480	$3,184

ROVING JACK COMPANY

Job Cost Sheet No. 103-20

Date	Material	Labor	Variable Overhead	Total
Bal. 9-30	$1,080	$ 215	$ 75	$1,370
October	820	1,600	550	2,970
Total	$1,900	$1,815	$ 625	$4,340

ROVING JACK COMPANY

Job Cost Sheet No. 104-28

Date	Material	Labor	Variable Overhead	Total
October	$3,350	$3,100	$1,000	$7,450
Total				

EXHIBIT 5–2
Job cost sheets for the Roving Jack Company

(4) Variable Overhead Control $1,000
    Raw Materials Inventory $1,000
To record the issue of indirect materials.

The accounts Variable Overhead Control and Fixed Overhead Control are used by accountants to record actual overhead costs. These accounts will be discussed later in this chapter.

PURCHASE AND CONSUMPTION OF LABOR

Two distinct functions are involved in labor accounting. First, the time for which the workers are to be paid is determined by their **clock cards.** From these cards the payroll department prepared their paychecks and distributed them on payday. The clock cards used in preparing the payroll show what the workers have earned but do not indicate the activities they performed while working. To determine these activities there must be a second document. At the end of each day employees or their supervisors prepare **time tickets** that list the amount of time spent on each job (treated as direct labor) and the amount of nonproduction time (treated as indirect labor). From the details of the time tickets, the Roving Jack Company's accountants found that of the $8,850 paid to the workers, $7,850 was direct labor that could be traced directly to the jobs, and $1,000 was indirect labor that was treated as fixed overhead. The direct labor was used as follows:

Job 101–24′	750 hours	$2,200
Job 102–18′	300 hours	950
Job 103–20′	550 hours	1,600
Job 104–28′	1,000 hours	3,100
Total direct labor		$7,850

The following journal entry records the labor costs.

(3) Work-in-Process Inventory	$7,850	
Cash		$7,850
To record direct labor cost.		
(5) Fixed Overhead Control	$1,000	
Cash		$1,000
To record the indirect labor cost.		

The amount of the direct labor was also posted to the individual job cost sheets shown in Exhibit 5–2.

PURCHASE OF OVERHEAD

We have already recorded indirect materials of $1,000 and indirect labor of $1,000 as overhead. Assume that the Roving Jack Company's accountant processed other overhead costs as listed below.

Heat, light, and power	$ 700
Labor-related costs	1,300
Depreciation of building	1,500
Factory insurance	200
Miscellaneous (normally detailed)	1,200
Total	$4,900

The following journal entry records these actual overhead costs incurred.

(4) Variable Overhead Control	$2,000	
(5) Fixed Overhead Control	$2,900	
Accumulated Depreciation		$1,500
Cash, or Payables, or Prepaids		$3,400

To record the incurrence of overhead.

This journal entry was based upon a study by the accountant of the overhead costs incurred in past periods. It was determined that overhead costs were fixed and variable as shown in the following tabulation. (We have simplied the problem by omitting semivariable costs.)

Variable Overhead Costs		*Fixed Overhead Costs*	
Indirect materials	$1,000	Indirect labor	$1,000
Heat, light, power	700	Depreciation	1,500
Labor-related costs	1,300	Factory insurance	200
		Miscellaneous	1,200
Total	$3,000	Total	$3,900

TRANSFER OF OVERHEAD TO WORK-IN-PROCESS INVENTORY

Overhead costs are diverse and difficult to trace directly to the individual jobs. Therefore, it is necessary to apportion or allocate them to the jobs. The **overhead rate** is the accountant's method of allocating these costs. Under variable costing, only the variable overhead costs are included in the overhead rate.

At the beginning of the year the management of the Roving Jack Company estimated that the units produced during the year would require 32,000 direct labor hours. The accountant for the Roving Jack Company had prepared an analysis of the cost behavior pattern for overhead costs and arrived at the flexible budget of:[1]

$$\text{Total Overhead costs} = \$48{,}000 + \$1.00\ (\text{direct labor hours})$$

[1]In our example we use direct labor hours as the volume measure. Other measures are discussed in Chapter 7.

This total flexible budget was based upon the following flexible budgets for the individual costs:

Cost Items		*Annual Fixed Costs*		*Variable Cost per Direct Labor Hour*
Indirect material		$ 0		$ .40
Indirect labor		13,200		0
Heat, light, power		0		.15
Labor-related costs		0		.45
Depreciation		18,000		0
Factory insurance		4,800		0
Miscellaneous		12,000		0
Total Cost	=	$48,000	+	$1.00

Total overhead for the year was predicted at $80,000 [$48,000 + $1.00 (32,000 direct labor hours)]. The variable overhead rate of $1.00 per direct labor hour was used during the previous months and will be used for the rest of the year to cost the jobs. Until the current month of October the incurrence of overhead costs and the actual direct labor hours worked for the year have been exactly as planned.

The following journal entry applies variable overhead to individual jobs in the Work-in-Process Inventory for October.

(6) Work-in-Process Inventory	$2,600	
Variable Overhead Applied		$2,600

To apply variable overhead to jobs at the rate of $1.00 per direct labor hour.

The variable overhead applied to each job is listed below and shown in Exhibit 5–2. For example, note that for Job 101–24′ $750 of variable overhead is listed for the month of October.

Job	*Direct Labor Hours*	×	*Variable Overhead Rate per Labor Hour*	=	*Total Variable Overhead Applied*
101–24′	750		$1		$ 750
102–18′	300		$1		300
103–20′	550		$1		550
104–28′	1,000		$1		1,000
Total overhead applied to jobs					$2,600

The two previous overhead entries used two accounts that require special comment. When actual overhead costs are incurred accountants accumulate the amounts in overhead control accounts: Variable Overhead

Control and Fixed Overhead Control. When variable overhead is applied to the individual jobs with an overhead rate determined at the beginning of the accounting period the amount of the overhead charged to the jobs is accumulated in the account, Variable Overhead Applied. The difference between the Variable Overhead Control account and the Variable Overhead Applied account results because the actual costs were not incurred in conformity with the flexible budget equation for the year. In our example variable overhead was underapplied by $400.

To explore the underapplied variable overhead and to see if fixed costs were controlled the management accountant prepared the report in Exhibit 5–3. In the left hand column are the actual variable and fixed costs extracted directly from the accounting system (see entry 5). The performance budget column comes from the original flexible budgets adjusted to the actual hours worked. For example, the indirect materials were budgeted at $.40 per direct labor hour. At 2,600 actual direct labor hours the company should have spent $1,040 ($.40 × 2,600 hours). Since actual expenses were $1,000 the management had a favorable[2] variance of $40 on indirect materials. The performance

THE ROVING JACK COMPANY
OVERHEAD COST REPORT
For the Month of October, 19X3

	Actual Overhead Costs	*Performance Budget*	*Spending Variance*
Variable Costs:			
Indirect Materials	$1,000	$1,040	$ 40 F
Heat, Light, Power	700	390	(310) U
Labor-related Costs	1,300	1,170	(130) U
Total Variable Costs	$3,000	$2,600	$(400) U
Fixed Costs:			
Indirect Labor	$1,000	$1,100	$ 100 F
Depreciation	1,500	1,500	-0-
Factory Insurance	200	400	200 F
Miscellaneous	1,200	1,000	(200) U
Total Fixed Costs	3,900	4,000	100 F
Total Overhead Costs	$6,900	$6,600	$(300) U

EXHIBIT 5–3
Overhead cost control report

[2]A favorable variance results when actual cost is less than the performance budget; an unfavorable variance results when the actual cost exceeds the performance budget. Throughout the book we will use **F** to show a favorable variance and **U** to show an unfavorable variance.

budget for the fixed costs was derived by assuming that the fixed costs were budgeted uniformily throughout the year ($48,000 ÷ 12 months), or $4,000 per month. For indirect labor the monthly budget was $1,100 ($13,200 ÷ 12 months). Since actual costs were $1,000 there was a $100 favorable indirect labor cost variance.

COMPLETION OF THE JOBS

The costs of production shown on the job cost sheets are transferred from Work-in-Process Inventory to Finished Goods Inventory when the jobs are completed and moved from the factory to the warehouse. Factory records for the Roving Jack Company indicate that Jobs 101–24′, 102–18′, and 103–20′ were completed during the month and transferred to the showroom. Job cost sheets for the completed mobile units showed the following completed job costs.

Job 101–24′	$ 5,645
Job 102–18′	3,184
Job 103–20′	4,340
Total cost of completed jobs	$13,169

Job 104–28′ was uncompleted and remained in the factory. The following journal entry records the completed units.

(7) Finished Goods Inventory	$13,169	
Work-in-Process Inventory		$13,169
To record the completion of Jobs 101–24′, 102–18′, and 103–20′.		

After this journal entry is posted to the Work-in-Process Inventory account, the balance will be $7,450, the accumulated costs of Job 104–28′.

SALE OF FINISHED PRODUCTS

The **sales invoices** of the Roving Jack Company indicate that the salesmen sold Job 102–18′ for $6,000 cash and Job 103–20′ for $8,500 cash. Two entries are required to recognize the sale. First, the sales revenue must be recognized.

(8a) Cash	$14,500	
Sales Revenue		$14,500
To record the sales revenue ($6,000 + $8,500).		

Second, the cost of the units sold must be transferred from Finished Goods Inventory to Cost of Goods Sold. The amounts shown on the completed job cost sheets associated with the units sold serve as the source of the amounts for this journal entry.

(8b) Cost of Goods Sold $7,524
  Finished Goods Inventory $7,524
To record the goods sold of Jobs 102–18' and 102–20' ($3,184 + $4,340).

After this entry has been posted to the Finished Goods Inventory account, the balance will be $5,645. This is the cost of Job 101–24', which is still unsold.

INCURRENCE OF NONPRODUCTION COSTS

For simplicity, we will assume that the Roving Jack Company incurred $800 of selling costs and $700 of administrative costs, and that it incurred no distribution or financial costs. The following journal entry records these costs.

(9) Selling Expense Control $800
Administrative Expense Control $700
  Cash, or Payables, or Prepaids $1,500
To record the incurrence of actual selling and administrative expenses.

In an actual setting, detailed information about the selling and administrative costs would be recorded in subsidiary ledgers to the control accounts. This subsidiary ledger would be similar to the details kept for Overhead Control. Also, if the firm had flexible budgets for these costs, a cost report similar to Exhibit 5–3 would be prepared. To simplify our example we have used only the total costs incurred and have omitted these details.

CLOSING THE OVERHEAD ACCOUNTS

At the end of the month, the Variable Overhead Control account, which shows the costs actually incurred, and the Variable Overhead Applied account, which shows the overhead charged to the jobs, are closed. The difference between the two accounts for variable costs is computed and transferred to an account called Under- or Overapplied Variable Overhead. If the overhead applied to production during the month is larger than the actual variable overhead incurred (shown in the Variable Overhead Control), overhead is *overapplied*. If the control balance is larger than the applied balance, the overhead is *underapplied*. The following journal entry closes the overhead accounts.

Variable Overhead Applied $2,600
Under- or Overapplied Variable Overhead .... $ 400
  Variable Overhead Control $3,000
To close the variable overhead accounts.

Exhibit 5–4 shows the T-accounts of the Roving Jack Company for the month of October. In Exhibit 5–5 we have presented a monthly income statement for the Roving Jack Company. This report is for management's use; it is not intended for external reporting.

RAW MATERIALS INVENTORY

Bal. 9-30	$2,500	(2)	$4,987
(1)	4,400	(4)	1,000
		Bal. 10-31	913
	$6,900		$6,900
Bal. 10-31	$ 913		

VARIABLE OVERHEAD CONTROL

(4)	$1,000	To Close	$3,000
(4)	2,000		
	$3,000		$3,000

VARIABLE OVERHEAD APPLIED

To Close	$2,600	(6)	$2,600

CASH OR PAYABLES

(8a)	$14,500	(1)	$4,400
		(3)	7,850
		(5)	1,000
			3,400
		(9)	1,500

ACCUMULATED DEPRECIATION

			$1,500

WORK-IN-PROCESS INVENTORY

Bal. 9-30	$ 5,182	(7)	$13,169
(2)	4,987		
(3)	7,850		
(6)	2,600	Bal. 10-31	7,450
	$20,169		$20,619
Bal. 10-31	$ 7,450		

FINISHED GOODS INVENTORY

Bal. 9-30	$ 0	(8b)	$ 7,524
(7)	$13,169	Bal. 10-31	5,645
	$13,169		$13,169
Bal. 10-31	$ 5,645		

UNDER- OR OVERAPPLIED VARIABLE OVERHEAD

From Closing	$400		

SALES

		(8a)	$14,500

COST OF GOODS SOLD

(8b)	$7,524		

SELLING EXPENSE CONTROL

(9)	$800		

ADMINISTRATIVE EXPENSE CONTROL

(9)	$700		

FIXED OVERHEAD CONTROL

(5)	$1,000		
(5)	2,900		
	$3,900		

EXHIBIT 5–4
General ledger accounts for the Roving Jack Company

ROVING JACK COMPANY
INCOME STATEMENT FOR MANAGEMENT
For the Month of October, 19X3

Sales		$14,500	100%
Variable cost of goods sold		7,524	52%
Contribution margin unadjusted		$ 6,976	48%
Less: Underapplied variable overhead		400	3%
Contribution margin adjusted		$ 6,576	45%
Less:			
Fixed overhead	$3,900		
Selling expenses	800		
Administrative expenses	700	5,400	37%
Net income		$ 1,176	8%

EXHIBIT 5-5
Contribution margin income statement for the Roving Jack Company

Additional Considerations of Accounting for Overhead

In the previous journal entries for overhead we separated the overhead costs into two separate accounts; one for variable overhead and another for fixed overhead. This may be a too simplistic assumption for many firms which find it impossible to separate costs into fixed and variable components at the time the costs are incurred. In this case another approach can be used. All costs, regardless of whether they are fixed or variable overhead, can be charged to a single Overhead Control account. The variable costs can be applied to the Work-in-Process Inventory as before. For the Roving Jack Company these two accounts would be:

Overhead Control	
$1,000	
700	
1,300	
1,000	
1,500	
200	
1,200	

Variable Overhead Applied	
	$2,600

Overhead underapplied is $4,300. This total is composed of the actual fixed costs ($3,900) and the variable cost spending variance ($400). Since both of these are period costs, there are no additional complications of accounting for inventories or net income. Cost control would be maintained through the preparation of the cost control report in Exhibit 5–3.

Conversion from Variable Costing to Absorption Costing

The variable costing system used by the Roving Jack Company did not include fixed overhead costs in its beginning or ending inventories; rather they were treated as period costs and expensed in the income statement. For external reporting purposes it is necessary to convert the *financial statements* to absorption costing by apportioning the fixed overhead costs to the inventories and cost of goods sold. The accounting records do not have to be changed; the ledger accounts and job cost sheets can remain on variable costing. The conversion simply involves restating the inventories and cost of goods sold amounts in the financial statements prepared for creditors, stockholders, and other external users. In this section we will take the illustration of the Roving Jack Company and show how to convert the income statement from variable costing to absorption costing.

At the beginning of the month of October, inventories were:

Raw Materials Inventory	$2,500
Work-in-Process Inventory	$5,182
Finished Goods Inventory	$ 0

Since the Raw Materials Inventory consists only of materials before they enter the factory, no fixed overhead cost will be apportioned to them and they may be ignored in the remainder of the illustrations. There were three jobs in process at the beginning of October with the following total variable costs. Also assume that the direct labor hours applicable to these jobs were as follows:

Job	*Total variable costs*	*Direct labor hours*
101–24′	$2,195	210
102–18′	1,617	170
103–20′	1,370	70
	$5,182	450

Assume that during September actual fixed overhead costs were $4,030 and that 3,100 direct labor hours were worked. A fixed overhead rate of $1.30 per hour ($4,030 ÷ 3,100 hours) is applicable to the beginning inventory under absorption costing. The beginning Work-in-Process Inventory would be increased in the financial statements by $585 (450 hours ×

$1.30). This makes the beginning inventory value for Work-in-Process Inventory $5,767 ($5,182 + $585). There were no finished units on hand so the remaining fixed overhead costs were applicable to cost of goods sold.

At the end of the current month of October the Work-in-Process and Finished Goods inventories, under variable costing consisted of:

Work-in-Process Inventory	(Job 104–28′)	$7,450
Finished Goods Inventory	(Job 101–24′)	$5,645

During October the actual fixed costs were $3,900 and the actual labor hours were 2,600. The fixed overhead rate for the month is $1.50 ($3,900 ÷ 2,600 hours). The hours of direct labor in each inventory and the overhead to be added to each inventory are:

Inventory	*Direct labor hours*	×	*Fixed overhead rate*	=	*Applicable fixed overhead*
Work-in-Process					
(Job 104–28′)	1,000 (Oct)		$1.50		$1,500
Finished Goods					
(Job 101–24′)	210 (Sept)		$1.30		$ 273
	750 (Oct)		$1.50		1,125
					1,398
Total Fixed Costs Added to Ending Inventories					$2,898

The ending inventories in the financial statements for October must be increased by $2,898.

The adjustments to the income statement would be as follows:

	Variable costing		*Increase beginning inventory*		*Increase ending inventory*		*Fixed costs*	*Absorption costing*
Sales	$14,500							$14,500
Cost of goods sold (including underapplied variable overhead)	7,924	+	$585	−	$2,898	+	$3,900	9,511
Fixed overhead	3,900					−	3,900	0
Selling expenses	800							800
Administrative expenses	700							700
Net income	$ 1,176							$ 3,489

ROVING JACK COMPANY INCOME STATEMENT FOR EXTERNAL REPORTS For the Month of October, 19X3			
Sales		$14,500	100%
Cost of goods sold (including underapplied overhead)		9,511	66
Gross profit		$ 4,989	34%
Operating expenses:			
Selling expense	$800		
Administrative expense	700	1,500	10
Net income		$ 3,489	24%

EXHIBIT 5–6
Absorption costing income statement for the Roving Jack Company

The absorption costing income statement is presented in Exhibit 5–6. Net income under absorption costing is $2,313 ($3,489 − $1,176) larger than it is under variable costing. This difference in net income resulted from increasing the beginning inventory (and therefore increasing cost of goods sold) by $585 and increasing the ending inventory (and therefore decreasing cost of goods sold) by $2,898. There is a net decrease in cost of goods sold and increase in net income of $2,313 ($2,898 − $585).

The same results would have been reached if fixed costs had been added to each job (on a worksheet, not actually in the ledger accounts or job cost sheets). The total cost of those jobs completed and sold would provide the amount of cost of goods sold; the total cost of the uncompleted jobs would be the balance of work-in-process; and the total cost of the completed but not sold jobs would be the balance of finished goods.

From these calculations we can see that it is possible for a firm to maintain its records on variable costing to provide management with useful information for decision making and then to restate the financial statements to absorption costing for external users. One large company with which the authors are familiar has many different plants and products, yet throughout the year they systematically gather the necessary data so that the actual fixed cost adjustment at the end of their fiscal year takes less than one day.

PROCESS COSTING ILLUSTRATED

Process costing differs from job costing in the way in which costs are traced to the factory and unit costs are determined. In a process costing system the costs are accumulated for departments or processes for a specified period of time, often one month. The unit cost of manufacturing the goods is found by dividing these departmental costs by the units produced during the time period. It should be apparent that process costing is used where a large quantity of similar units are produced.

To illustrate process costing, let's assume that the Supertronics Company manufactures a circuit board in two departments: A and B. In Department A the materials are issued at the beginning of the process and attached and soldered to the board. In Department B the board is coated and completed through testing. Department B uses no new raw materials. Any supplies they use are included in overhead. Labor and overhead are added uniformly throughout the production process in the factory. Exhibit 5–7 shows this diagrammatically.

The Supertronics Company follows the policy of combining direct labor and overhead in its Work-in-Process Inventory accounts. The sum of direct labor and overhead is called **conversion costs,** and treated as a package, since overhead is charged to the departments on the basis of direct labor. Treating these two cost elements as a single cost enables the accountants of the Supertronics Company to simplify their calculation of unit costs.

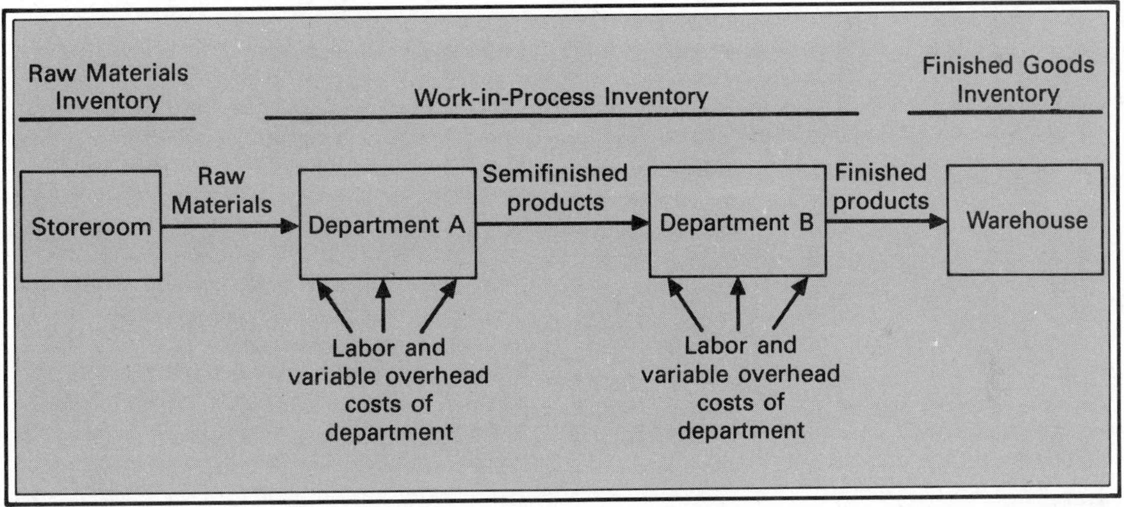

EXHIBIT 5–7
Cost and product flow diagram of Supertronics Company

Exhibit 5–8 shows the quantity and cost reports for the two departments for the month of March. These monthly production and cost reports are focused on the departments and serve as the data base for calculating the unit cost of units transferred out of the departments and of those left in the final inventories. The departmental production report shows the units and costs for which the department must account.

THE SUPERTRONICS COMPANY
DEPARTMENTAL PRODUCTION AND COST REPORT
For the Month of March, 19X2

	DEPARTMENTS	
	A	B
QUANTITY DATA;		
Units in process, March 1		
Department A	None	–
Department B (100% complete as to prior department costs; 1/4 complete as to conversion costs)	–	8,000
New units started	60,000	–
Units received from prior departments		40,000
Units completed and transferred to:		
Department B	40,000	–
Finished goods inventory	–	36,000
Units in process, March 31		
Department A (100% complete as to materials costs; 1/5 complete as to conversion costs)	20,000	–
Department B (100% complete as to prior department costs; 1/3 complete as to conversion costs)	–	12,000
COST DATA		
Beginning inventory, March 1		
Prior department costs	None	$9,600
Conversion costs	None	$4,000
New costs incurred this period		
Raw materials	$60,000	None
Prior department costs	None	?
Conversion costs	$22,000	$114,000

EXHIBIT 5-8
Departmental production and cost reports for the Supertronics Company

Recasting the units found on the production report into a quantity report, we find the following.

	Department A	Department B
Beginning units in process	0	8,000
New units started	60,000	40,000
Units available to finish	60,000	48,000
Ending units in process	20,000	12,000
Units transferred out	40,000	36,000

This schedule shows the flow of the units throughout the factory. The 40,000 units transferred from Department A become the "raw materials" for Department B. The 36,000 units leaving Department B are transferred to Finished Goods Inventory, where they await sale.

We will proceed systematically through the two departments to see how the unit cost of production is calculated and used as the basis of journal entries.

Department A

In Department A there was no beginning Work-in-Process Inventory. During the month of March, $60,000 of raw materials and $22,000 of direct labor and variable overhead were used.

In Department A there are units in the final inventory in addition to the units transferred out. To calculate the unit cost for the period, it is necessary to calculate **equivalent units of production,** the number of equivalent "whole" units of product that the department or cost center completed during the time period. For example, two half-completed units are equivalent in cost to one totally complete unit. Equivalent units of production recognizes that not all of the units in process shown on the quantity report are fully completed.

The equivalent units of production schedules for Department A for the month of March are as shown in the accompanying tabulation.

	Equivalent Units of Production	
	Raw Materials (100% Complete)	*Conversion Costs*
Transferred out to Department B (100% complete)	40,000	40,000
Ending inventory (20% of work in Department A completed)	20,000	4,000 (20,000 × 20%)
Equivalent units of production	60,000	44,000

The ending inventory in Department A is 100% complete as far as raw material costs are concerned. Conversion costs, on the other hand, are not 100% complete. Since the 20,000 units in the final inventory have progressed only one-fifth of the way through the process, and conversion costs are added uniformly throughout the process, the department "equivalently" completed only 4,000 of these 20,000 units. Next period the department will have to add sufficient conversion costs to finish the equivalent of 16,000 units. Of course, the 40,000 units transferred to Department B were 100% as to all cost factors, or they would not have been finished and suitable to transfer.

Because each cost factor can be at a separate stage of completion, most firms determine equivalent units of production and, subsequently, unit costs for each type of cost element. The total unit cost is then the sum of the unit costs for the individual cost factors. The total cost, equivalent units of production, and unit cost for each cost element in Department A are shown in the computations that follow.

Computation of Unit Cost–Department A

	Total Cost	÷	*Equivalent Units of Production*	=	*Unit Cost*
Raw material costs	$60,000		60,000		$1.00
Conversion costs	22,000		44,000		.50
Total cost	$82,000				$1.50

The following computations show the inventory values and the costs transferred out.

Computation of Costs of Inventory and Transferred Out–Department A

Ending work-in-process Inventory of Department A, March 31:	
Raw material costs (20,000 × $1.00)	$20,000
Conversion costs (4,000 × $.50)	2,000
Total ending work-in-process inventory	$22,000
Transferred to Department B (40,000 × $1.50)	60,000
Total costs of Department A accounted for	$82,000

The following journal entry records the transfer to Department B.

Work-in-Process Inventory—Department B	$60,000	
Work-in-Process Inventory—DepartmentA		$60,000

To transfer production costs from Department A to Department B.

After this entry is posted, the Work-in-Process Inventory—Department A will have a $22,000 balance, which was the amount determined in the preceding computation as the value of the ending inventory,

Department B

In Department B there was a beginning inventory of 8,000 units at a cost of $13,600. These 8,000 units had all of the prior-department costs but were only one-fourth completed with respect to conversion costs. The $9,600 and $4,000, respectively, were the inventory balances determined at the end of February. During March Department B received $60,000 of boards from Department A and added $114,000 of conversion costs.

The equivalent units of production schedules for Department B are as shown in the accompanying tabulation.

Equivalent Units of Production

	Prior-Department Costs (100% Complete)	*Conversion Costs*
Transferred out to finished goods inventory (100% complete)	36,000	36,000
Plus: Ending inventory (33 ⅓ % of work in Department B completed)	12,000	4,000 (12,000 × 33 ⅓ %)
Total	48,000	40,000
Less: Beginning Inventory (25% of work of Department B completed)	8,000	2,000 (8,000 × 25%)
Equivalent production for March	40,000	38,000

The calculation of the equivalent units in Department B was based upon the following logic. The 36,000 units transferred out had to be wholly complete with respect to both prior-department costs and conversion costs. This figure is added to the work on the final inventory that was accomplished this period. The final inventory of 12,000 units was wholly complete relative to prior-department costs. That is, the material received from Department A was fully complete as far as Department A was concerned. However, these 12,000 units had not been fully processed through Department B. They were only one-third completed in Department B; this is the equivalent of 4,000 units of conversion costs in the final inventory. The beginning inventory of 8,000 equivalent units for prior-department costs and 2,000 for conversion costs represents work accomplished in the previous accounting period and is deducted to arrive at the equivalent units of work accomplished solely within this accounting period.

The equivalent production for prior-department costs for March is 40,000 units; for conversion costs it is 38,000 units. Using these equivalent units, the unit cost computation would be as follows.

Computation of Unit Cost—Department B

	Total Costs	÷	Equivalent Units of Production	=	Unit Cost
Prior-department costs:					
Beginning inventory	$ 9,600		8,000		$1.20
Current production	60,000		40,000		$1.50
Total	$ 69,600		48,000		$1.45
Conversion costs:					
Beginning inventory	$ 4,000		2,000		$2.00
Current production	114,000		38,000		$3.00
Total	118,000		40,000		$2.95
Total	$187,600				

A close examination of the unit cost computation shows that there are two layers of equivalent units and costs. Prior-department costs consist of 8,000 equivalent units in the beginning inventory at a unit cost of $1.20, and 40,000 equivalent units added this period at a unit cost of $1.50. For conversion costs there is a beginning inventory layer of 2,000 equivalent units at a unit cost of $2.00, and 38,000 equivalent units added this period at a unit cost of $3.00. Because there are two layers of units, it is possible to create the different inventory cost flows of FIFO or weighted average.

FIFO COST FLOW

With FIFO cost flow the units in the final inventory come from the most current production. Therefore the final inventory should be valued at the most current costs; all other costs are transferred out. The following computation shows the inventory values and costs transferred out using FIFO cost flow.

FIFO Computation of Costs of Inventory and Transferred Out—Department B

Ending work-in-process inventory of Department B, March 31:	
Prior department costs (12,000 × $1.50)	$ 18,000
Conversion costs (4,000 × $3.00)	12,000
Total ending work-in-process inventory	$ 30,000
Transferred out to finished goods inventory	157,600
Total costs of Department B accounted for	$187,600

The ending inventory was costed at the unit costs of the current period. Thus, for prior-department costs the 12,000 units were costed at $1.50; for the 4,000 equivalent units of conversion costs the current cost was $3.00. The

$157,600 transferred to the finished goods inventory was determined by deducting the value of the ending inventory ($30,000) from the total costs to be accounted for of $187,600.[3]

The following journal entry transfers the 36,000 units to Finished Goods Inventory with FIFO.

Finished Goods Inventory	$157,600	
Work-in-Process Inventory—Department B		$157,600

To record the transfer of cost of completed units from Department B to Finished Goods Inventory.

After this entry is posted, the balance of Work-in-Process Inventory—Department B will be $30,000.

WEIGHTED-AVERAGE

With weighted-average costing the two layers are combined into a single, average unit cost. For prior-department cost the weighted-average unit cost is $1.45; for conversion costs it is $2.95. Both the units in the final inventory and those transferred out are costed at this average cost. The following computations show the inventory values and the costs transferred out using the weighted-average cost flows.

Weighted-Average Computation of Costs of Inventory and Transferred Out—Department B

Ending work-in-process inventory of Department B, March 31:	
Prior-department costs (12,000 × $1.45)	$ 17,400
Conversion costs (4,000 × $2.95)	11,800
Total ending work-in-process inventory	$ 29,200
Transferred out to finished goods inventory (36,000 × $4.40)	158,400
Total costs of Department B accounted for	$187,600

[3]It is possible to prove that the $157,600 was properly calculated as follows.

Transferred out (36,000 units):	
From Beginning Inventory (8,000 units):	
Prior-department costs (8,000 @ $1.20)	$ 9,600
Conversion costs from last period (2,000 @ $2.00)	4,000
Conversion costs from this period (6,000 @ $3.00)	18,000
From new units started and completed this period (36,000 units − 8,000 units):	
Prior-department costs (28,000 @ $1.50)	42,000
Conversion costs (28,000 @ $3.00)	84,000
Total Costs transferred to finished goods inventory	$157,600

The following journal entry transfers the 36,000 units to Finished Goods Inventory with weighted average.

Finished Goods Inventory	$158,400	
Work-in-Process Inventory—Department B		$158,400

To record the transfer of cost of completed units from Department B to Finished Goods Inventory.

After this entry is posted, the balance of Work-in-Process Inventory—Department B will be $29,200.

Process costing may be used with either variable or absorption costing. If variable costing is used internally, the conversion to absorption costing for external reports would be made upon the basis of the equivalent units, that is, the fixed production costs would be association with the equivalent units in work-in-process, finished goods, and cost of goods sold.

SUMMARY

There are two systems of combining the product costs to determine the inventory value. A job costing system is used in those industries where the product is large, identifiable, and often made to special order. In a job costing system the job cost sheet serves as the focal point of cost accumulation. The unit cost is determined by summing the costs that are recorded on the job cost sheets. In a process costing system the unit cost is determined by summing the costs of a department over a period of time and dividing by the number of equivalent units produced. A process costing system is used in industries where a large number of similar units are produced.

SUPPLEMENTARY READING

Anthony, Robert N., and James S. Hekimian. *Operations Cost Control.* Homewood, Ill.: Richard D. Irwin, Inc., 1967.

Benninger, L. J. "Accounting Theory and Cost Accounting." *The Accounting Review,* July, 1965.

Colbert, Bertram A. "Pathway to Profit: The Management Information System." *The Price Waterhouse Review,* Spring, 1967.

Davidson, H. Justin, and Robert M. Trueblood. "Accounting for Decision-Making." *The Accounting Review,* October, 1961.

*Haseman, Wilber C. "An Interpretative Framework for Cost." *The Accounting Review,* October, 1968.

National Association of Accountants. "Costs Included in Inventories." *N. A. (C.) A. Bulletin,* August 15, 1947.

National Association of Accountants. *Accounting for Labor Related Costs.* New York: National Association of Accountants, 1957.

QUESTIONS

5-1 "Inventory accounts are really unexpired costs." Explain and discuss.

5-2 What costs are included in the following inventory accounts? Raw Materials, Work in Process, and Finished Goods.

5-3 Describe the purpose of each of the following documents.
A. Material requisition
B. Labor-time ticket
C. Overhead subsidiary ledger
D. Labor clock card
E. Purchase order
F. Purchase requisition

5-4 Explain the purpose of a job cost sheet. How could the data on a job cost sheet be useful to management?

5-5 Distinguish between *actual* and *applied* overhead. What is meant by each?

5-6 What is the primary objective of job costing?

5-7 What is the primary objective of process costing?

5-8 If the under- or overapplied overhead account has a debit balance at the end of the year, is the overhead underapplied or overapplied? Why?

5-9 Define the term *equivalent units of production* and indicate how it is determined.

5-10 Explain how the unit cost is determined under both job costing and process costing.

EXERCISES

5-11 *(True and False)*. Indicate whether the following statements are true or false.

1. Job costing and process costing are ways of separating costs into their fixed and variable components.

2. Purchase requisitions are a source of accounting entries.

3. A lumber mill would probably use process costing.

4. All product costs are recorded in the Work-in-Process Inventory.

5. All period costs are recorded in the Cost of Goods Sold Account.

6. The Overhead Applied account is used to record the amount of overhead that is recorded on the job cost sheets.

7. Job cost sheets are subsidiary ledgers for the Finished Goods Inventory.

8. Underapplied overhead occurs when the company spends more on variable overhead than the flexible budget allows.

9. Process costing differs from job costing because in process costing the unit of production is determined by tracing costs directly to the products produced.

10. Equivalent units of production are the whole units transferred from the Work-in-Process Inventory to the Finished Goods Inventory.

5-12 *(Matching).* Match the following terms and definitions:

1. Product cost
2. Unexpired cost
3. Indirect labor
4. Material requisition
5. Equivalent production
6. Period cost
7. Direct materials
8. Job cost sheet
9. Time ticket
10. Prior-department costs

A. The wages of maintenance employees.
B. The denominator used in computing the unit cost in a process system.
C. The record of costs traced to a specific lot of goods.
D. Factory costs related to goods transferred into a department.
E. A record of how an employee spent his time.
F. An asset.
G. Costs that accountants attach to the unit of product.
H. Materials that are traced to job cost sheets in a job cost system.
I. Costs that are treated as expenses in the period incurred.
J. The document used to authorize the withdrawal of materials from the storeroom.

5-13 *(Classification as Job or Process).* For the following types of companies, indicate whether a job costing or process costing system would be used and briefly explain why.

A. Petroleum refiner
B. Student newspaper
C. Custom printing shop
D. Automobile repair shop
E. University computer center
F. Television set manufacturer
G. Soft drink bottler
H. Highway construction firm
I. Food canning plant
J. Photo processing lab

5-14 *(Determination of Job Cost).* The Marten Company uses a variable costing system and accumulates the costs for its products by jobs. Variable overhead is applied to jobs on the basis of direct labor hours. The budget for 19X2 included the following information:

Direct labor (2,000 hours)	\$8,000
Variable overhead	\$6,000
Fixed overhead	\$4,000

In March, a special order (Job #684) for 25 special parts was received and completed. Material requisitions for Job #684 amounted to \$121. Labor time tickets totaled 13 hours at a wage rate of \$5.00 per hour.

REQUIRED:

A. What was the total cost to complete Job #684?

B. If the selling price was \$14 per unit, what was the contribution margin from production per unit?

5-15 *(Journal Entries for Cost Flows).* Prepare journal entries for the Purple Kite Company. The company uses a variable costing system.

A. Purchased raw materials on account, \$250.

B. Issued materials to production, \$200.

C. Paid employees: direct labor \$180, indirect labor \$20. (Indirect labor is a variable cost.)

D. Applied variable overhead to production at the rate of 60% of direct labor cost.

E. Paid actual costs: variable overhead \$100, fixed overhead \$50, and selling and administrative expenses, \$150.

F. Sold products costing \$600 for \$950 on account.

G. Closed the variable ovehead control and variable overhead applied accounts.

5-16 *(Under- or Overapplied Overhead).* The Gross Jok Company accumulated the following data relating to labor and overhead. The company uses a variable costing system.

Flexible budget for overhead =
\$1,200 per month plus \$2.40 per direct labor hour.

Actual variable overhead for April	\$4,000
Actual fixed overhead for April	\$1,150

Actual direct labor for April: 1,600 hours @ \$5.00 per hour.

REQUIRED:

A. How much overhead was applied to products?

B. What was the amount of under- or overapplied overhead for April?

C. Prepare the entry to close the under- or overapplied overhead to cost of goods sold.

5-17 *(Conversion to Absorption Costing)*. At the end of 19X0 the ending inventory for the Jawbone Company consisted of the following partially finished job.

Job #283		
Material	*Labor*	*Variable overhead*
$132	52 hours @ $4.00 $208	52 hours @ $2.00 $104

Actual total overhead was exactly as planned for the 3,000 hours worked. The flexible budget for overhead was determined at the beginning of the year to be $12,000 per year plus $2.00 per direct labor hour.

REQUIRED:

A. What is the balance of the Work-in-Process Inventory at the end of 19X0, assuming that variable costing is followed?

B. The company wants the financial statements to conform to generally accepted accounting principles. Convert the ending inventory to absorption costing for external reporting.

5-18 *(Calculation of Equivalent Production)*. The Continuous Processing Company uses a process costing system to determine the unit cost of their product. At the beginning of February there were 100 units in process 50% complete. During the month 600 units were started, and 200 units remained in process at the end of the month, 40% complete.

REQUIRED:

A. Prepare a quantity report showing how many units were completed and transferred to Finished Goods Inventory during the month.

B. What was the number of equivalent units of production for determining the February unit cost?

5-19 *(Process Costing)*. The Eight-Up Soda Company incurred $29,600 of production costs during October. Materials costing $24,000 were added at the beginning of the process; the variable conversion costs of $5,600 were added throughout the process. During the month, 12,000 units were started, 10,000 were completed, and 2,000 were in process 60% complete. There were no beginning inventories.

REQUIRED:

A. Determine the cost of the 2,000 units in the ending inventory.

B. Determine the cost of the 10,000 units completed and transferred to the Finished Goods Inventory.

5-20 *(Calculation of Equivalent Production)*. The Six-Up Company produces a soft drink in a continuous process. All ingredients are added at the beginning of the Cooking Process; conversion costs are added uniformly. After blending and cooking the product is transferred to the Aging Process.

	Cooking Process	*Aging Process*
Beginning inventory (barrels)	300	500
% conversion costs complete	60%	40%
Barrels started in process	1,000	?
Ending inventory (barrels)	400	300
% conversion costs complete	50%	80%

REQUIRED:

A. How many barrels of Six-Up were transferred to the Aging Process during the month?

B. What was the number of equivalent units of production in the Cooking Process: for materials? for conversion? Why are they different?

C. How many barrels of Six-Up were completed and transferred to Finished Goods Inventory during the month?

D. What was the number of equivalent units of production for conversion costs in the Aging Process?

5-21 *(Journal Entries for Cost Flows).* The Harrison Publishing Company had the following information in its general ledger accounts at the beginning of the current month.

Raw Materials Inventory Balance	$ 7,500
Work-in-Process Inventory Balance	$25,000
Finished Goods Inventory Balance	$12,500

During the current month the following transactions took place.

a. Purchased raw materials of $24,000.
b. Incurred and distributed direct labor of $42,000.
c. Incurred fixed utilities costs of $6,400.
d. Recorded fixed depreciation of $12,000.
e. Incurred fixed administrative expenses of $18,000.
f. Requisitioned $22,000 of raw materials from the storeroom.
g. Purchased and used $840 of variable factory supplies.
h. Incurred miscellaneous variable overhead of $23,900.
i. Applied variable overhead to work in the factory using a variable overhead rate of 50% of direct labor cost.
j. Completed production of $94,000 of work in the factory.
k. Sold $138,000 of products that cost $102,500.
l. Closed the overhead accounts treating any under- or overapplied overhead as a product cost.

REQUIRED:

A. Prepare general journal entries assuming variable costing.

B. Determine the inventory balances at the end of the month.

C. Prepare an income statement for the month.

5-22 *(Job Cost Sheet)*. The Foxe Company uses job costing to account for its products. It applies variable overhead to the jobs on the basis of direct labor hours. The predetermined overhead rate was estimated at the beginning of the year using the following data.

Fixed overhead	$ 36,000
Variable overhead	72,000
Total estimated overhead	$108,000
Total estimated direct labor hours	12,000

Job #411 was completed during the past month. Raw materials used on Job #411 were $68, direct labor was four hours at $5.00 per hour, and total machine hours were seven hours. Job #411 was a special order for the Sheep Company consisting of 56 machine-lathed candlesticks.

REQUIRED:

A. Prepare a job cost sheet for Job #411 assuming variable costing.
B. Calculate the cost per candlestick.
C. Prepare the journal entries for Job #411.
D. Assume that during the year the company actually worked 20,000 direct labor hours instead of the planned 12,000, and that it incurred actual overhead of $142,000, of which $110,000 was variable. Prepare the journal entry to close the overhead accounts.
E. Determine the total cost and unit cost of Job #411 for external reporting. Explain how the cost was determined.

5-23 *(Process Costing: Weighted Average)*. Kleenzit Company produces an industrial cleaner. Materials are added at the beginning of the blending process. After the product is blended, it is sent to the packaging department. Conversion costs are added uniformly through the process. Cost and production records for the blending process during September show the following:

Sept. 1, 20 barrels in process, 40% complete as to conversion costs.
Sept. 30, 30 barrels in process, 70% complete as to conversion costs.
Material was added in September to start 90 barrels.
80 barrels of Kleenzit were transferred to packaging during September.
Cost of Sept. 1 inventory: Materials $1,000; Conversion costs $160.
Cost of material added during September, $4,500.
Conversion costs during September, $2,870.

REQUIRED:

A. Compute the equivalent units of production for both materials and conversion costs during September.
B. Compute the material and conversion unit costs during September assuming weighted average costing.
C. Determine the cost of the 30 barrels in the ending inventory at the end of September.

D. Determine the cost of the 80 barrels sent to packaging during September.

5-24 *(Process Costing: FIFO).* The Suma Company produces piggy banks. Materials are added at the beginning of the process in the molding department. After the product is molded, it is sent to the painting department. Conversion costs are added uniformly throughout the plant. Cost and production data for the month of December show the following.

December 1, 5,000 banks in process, 60% complete as to conversion costs.
December 31, 3,000 banks in process, 33⅓% complete as to conversion costs.
Material was added in December to start 28,000 banks.
Cost of December 1 inventory:

Material	$3,750
Conversion costs	$1,500

Costs added during December:

Material	$25,200
Conversion costs	$16,800

REQUIRED:

A. Compute the equivalent units of production.
B. Compute the material and conversion unit costs during December assuming a FIFO cost flow.
C. Determine the cost of the banks in the ending inventory at the end of December.
D. Determine the cost of the banks sent to painting during December.

5-25 *(Conversion from Variable to Absorption Costing).* The Solid State Company manufactures mini-computer components to special order. The firm uses a variable, job cost system. The variable overhead rate was based upon the following flexible budget equations where the volume measure is direct labor hours. The planned level of operations for 19X7 was 10,000 direct labor hours.

Supervision	$12,000 + $ 0 (x)
Repairs	$ 6,000 + $ .75 (x)
Utilities	$ 0 + $1.00 (x)
Depreciation of machinery	$ 0 + $1.25 (x)
Depreciation of building	$ 9,000 + $ 0 (x)
Indirect materials	$ 1,000 + $ .50 (x)
Fringe benefits	$ 2,000 + $1.50 (x)

At the beginning of May, 19X7, there were two jobs in process—#102 and #103. During May, work was begun on four jobs—#104, #105, #106, and #107. Jobs #102, #103, #104, and #105 were finished in May and sent to the Finished Goods warehouse. Jobs #102, #103, and #105 were delivered to the customers for $26,000. The cost data on all jobs were as follows.

	102	*103*	*104*	*105*	*106*	*107*
Beginning Inventory:						
Materials	$1,450	$ 850				
Labor	1,295	700				
Overhead	925	500				
Current Period:						
Materials	305	1,150	$1,475	$2,800	$ 200	$ 400
Labor	210	665	1,750	1,680	1,960	1,190
Overhead	150	475	1,250	1,200	1,400	850
Total	$4,335	$4,340	$4,475	$5,680	$3,560	$2,440

REQUIRED:

A. Determine the ending balances of Work-in-Process, Finished Goods, and Cost of Goods Sold for May using variable costing.

B. Determine the ending balances of Work-in-Process, Finished Goods, and Cost of Goods Sold for their May financial statements assuming that the firm converts from variable to absorption costing using the budgeted fixed costs and budgeted production volume.

PROBLEMS

5-26 *(Reconstructing Journal Entries for Cost Flows).* The Franklin Company, a firm manufacturing gym equipment, uses variable costing in its accounting system. A schedule of various general ledger accounts and other relevant data has been prepared and presented for analysis.

Schedule of Account Balances

Account	*Beginning Jan. 2, 19X1*	*Ending Dec. 31, 19X1*
Raw Materials Inventory	$ 8,000	$ 10,000
Variable Overhead Control	$ 0	$ 0
Variable Overhead Applied	$ 0	$ 0
Work-in-Process Inventory	$ 25,000	$ 33,000
Finished Goods Inventory	$ 15,000	$ 35,000
Cost of Sales	$ 0	$155,000
Other Data:		
Raw materials purchased	$ 62,000	
Raw materials issued to production	$?	
Direct labor cost incurred	$ 75,000	
Variable overhead incurred	$ 48,000	
Fixed overhead incurred	$ 25,000	
General and administrative expenses	$ 12,000	
Variable selling expenses	$ 13,000	
Sales	$225,000	

Variable Overhead is applied at a rate of two-thirds of direct labor cost. The firm's policy is to charge under- or overapplied overhead against cost of sales at the end of each year.

REQUIRED:

A. Make journal entries to summarize activities for year 19X1 that were recorded in the accounts shown.
B. Show T-accounts for the inventories, overhead accounts, and cost of sales.
C. Prepare an income statement for the year.

5-27 *(Reclassifying Product and Period Costs).* The Jeff Smith Company was formed on January 2 and has operated for a year. The owner's wife ran the office and kept the books. Because her experience was limited, she set up a Work-in-Process account and recorded all "expenses" as debits and sales as a credit. The balance of the account was closed to Retained Earnings as income or loss for the month. The owner of the company was surprised that a loss was sustained. The company had received many orders, and goods were shipped the day they were finished. The owner asked you for help. The Work-in-Process account follows:

WORK-IN-PROCESS INVENTORY

Materials purchased	$120,000		
Payroll for year	250,000	Sales (50,000 @ $8.00)	$400,000
Depreciation expense	30,000		
Selling expense	50,000	Loss to Retained	
Other factory costs	60,000	Earnings	130,000
Advertising	20,000		
	$530,000		$530,000

An analysis of the items in Work-in-Process revealed the following:

1. There were $40,000 of raw materials in the storeroom at the end of the year.
2. Payroll included:

Owner's salary	$ 20,000
Direct labor payroll	$120,000
Other factory labor	$ 60,000
Selling and administrative payroll	$ 50,000

3. One-third of the fixed assets are used in selling and administrative activities. Depreciation is computed on the straight-line basis.
4. During the year 100,000 units were started, 60,000 were finished, of which 50,000 were sold, and 40,000 were in process one-half complete.
5. The selling expense and other factory costs are variable. All other overhead and nonproduction costs are fixed.

REQUIRED:

A. For each "expense" item recorded in Work-in-Process, indicate if it is properly recorded. If it is not properly recorded, determine the correct amount. Assume that the company uses variable costing.

B. Determine the equivalent production and cost per unit for the year.

C. Determine the proper balances at the end of the year for:

   1. Raw Materials Inventory
   2. Work-in-Process Inventory
   3. Finished Goods Inventory

D. Prepare a contribution margin income statement for the Jeff Smith Company.

5-28 *(Reconstructing T-accounts for Cost Flows).* The following are partially completed T-accounts and additional information for the Marc Burley Company for the month of November.

RAW MATERIALS INVENTORY

	Debit	Credit
Bal. Nov. 1	$ 200	
	$1,000	

FINISHED GOODS INVENTORY

	Debit	Credit
Bal. Nov. 1	$ 400	

VARIABLE OVERHEAD APPLIED

Debit	Credit

WORK-IN-PROCESS INVENTORY

	Debit	Credit
Bal. Nov. 1	$ 300	$2,100
Material requisition	$ 700	

COST OF GOODS SOLD

Debit	Credit
$2,500	

VARIABLE OVERHEAD CONTROL

Debit	Credit

Additional information:

1. Labor-time tickets totaled 200 direct labor hours. Employees are paid at the rate of $5.00 per hour.

2. Variable overhead is applied at the rate of $3.00 per direct labor hour.

3. Actual variable overhead incurred during November amounted to $500.

4. Sales during the month were $4,000.

REQUIRED:

Determine the following amounts:

A. The balance of Raw Materials Inventory at November 30.
B. Direct labor cost for the month.
C. The amount of variable overhead applied to products during November.
D. The balance of Finished Goods Inventory on November 30.
E. The total of the job cost sheets at the beginning of November.
F. The total of the job cost sheets at the end of November.
G. The total of the costs added to the job cost sheets during November.
H. The amount of under- or overapplied variable overhead for November.
I. Contribution margin for November before closing under- or overapplied overhead.
J. Assuming that fixed overhead and fixed selling and administrative expenses totaled $1,100, what was the net income for November?

5-29 *(Job Cost Sheets; Journal Entries).* The Loggerwell Company had three orders in its Work-in-Process inventory at the beginning of April. The following costs were assigned to these jobs during March.

	Jobs		
	A	*B*	*C*
Direct materials	$42.00	$118.00	$64.00
Direct labor	$32.50	$ 42.00	$32.00
Variable overhead*	$16.25	$ 21.00	$16.00

*Variable overhead is applied to Work-in-Process at the rate of 50% of direct labor cost.

At the beginning of April the Raw Materials inventory had a balance of $1,890, and there was no Finished Goods Inventory. During the month the company purchased $5,300 of raw materials. The following is a summary of the material requisitions and labor time tickets for the month.

	Jobs				
	A	*B*	*C*	*D*	*E*
Direct materials	$320.00	$256.00	$480.00	$124.00	$150.00
Direct labor	$266.00	$496.00	$790.00	$200.00	$ 75.00

The variable overhead rate remained the same in April as in the previous month. Jobs A, B, and D were completed and transferred to Finished Goods Inventory during April. The company uses variable costing and computes unit costs through a job costing system.

REQUIRED:

A. Develop job cost sheets for each job.
B. Make appropriate journal entries using totals for April.

C. Determine the cost of the ending Work-in-Process Inventory.
D. What was the contribution margin for April, assuming the following sales were made?

Job A	$1,250
Job B	$1,600
Job D	$ 600

5-30 *(Process Costing—FIFO)*. Cost and production data for two departments are presented below for the Mexico Instruments Company. The company uses FIFO costing in its process costing system.

	DEPARTMENTS	
QUANTITY DATA	*Mixing*	*Cooking*
Units in process, Feb. 1:		
Mixing department	None	
Cooking department (100% complete as to prior department cost, 50% as to conversion costs)		4,000
New units started	10,000	None
Units completed and transferred to:		
Cooking department	5,000	
Finished goods inventory		6,000
Units in process, Feb. 28:		
Mixing department (100% complete as to material, 80% complete as to conversion)	5,000	
Cooking department (100% complete as to prior department costs, ⅓ as to conversion costs)		3,000
COST DATA		
Costs in beginning inventory:		
Prior department costs	None	$11,600
Conversion costs	None	$ 7,800
New costs incurred this period:		
Raw materials	$10,000	None
Prior-department costs	None	?
Conversion costs	$18,000	$20,000

REQUIRED:
Assuming that 3,000 units were sold for $10 each, prepare all journal entries for February, including the transfer of costs within the factory.

5-31 *(Process Costing—Weighted-Average)*. The Packhard Company produces a product called Hewletts in a process costing system. The following cost and production data were accumulated by the company's bookkeeper. Material for Hewletts is added only at the beginning of the process.

	Units	COSTS Material	Variable Conversion
Beginning inventory of work-in-process (conversion costs 60% complete)	300	$ 575	$ 585
Costs and production data for October:			
Additional units started	600		
Material costs incurred		$1,225	
Variable conversion costs			$1,755
Ending inventory of work-in-process (conversion costs 40% complete)	200		
Units completed and sold	700		

REQUIRED:

A. Determine the equivalent production for materials and conversion costs.

B. Determine the unit cost for materials and conversion costs assuming weighted-average costing.

C. The selling price was $9.00 per unit, fixed overhead costs were $600, variable selling costs were $300, and fixed selling and administrative costs $700. Prepare an income statement for October using the contribution margin approach.

D. Determine the cost of the Work-in-Process Inventory under variable costing.

E. Determine the cost of the ending Work-in-Process Inventory under absorption costing. Assume that the beginning inventory includes $180 of fixed overhead costs under absorption costing.

5-32 *(Process Costing with Weighted Average; Journal Entries).* Hangwell Company produces a special metal hanger for the construction industry. Metal strips are cut and shaped in the Shaping Department and finished in the Finishing Department. Because production requirements are rigorous and costs are difficult to control, the company uses a weekly period of accounting. All materials are added at the beginning of the shaping process. At the beginning of Week 23 the following inventories were on hand:

Raw materials, $4,800
Work-in-process:
  Shaping Department, 600 units
    Material (100% complete), $660
    Conversion (40% complete), $430
  Finishing Department, none
Finished goods, 5,000 units @ $5.50

JOB COST SHEET #11
Product: Little Skates
Started 2-25-X7 Completed 3-20-X7

Date	Material	Labor	Overhead	Total
Bal. 2-28	$2,000	$1,000	$ 500	$ 3,500
3-1	3,000			6,500
3-2	1,500			8,000
3-20		7,000		15,000
3-20			3,500	18,500
Total	$6,500	$8,000	$4,000	$18,500

JOB COST SHEET #12
Product: Big Skates
Started 3-1-X7 Completed 3-29-X7

Date	Material	Labor	Overhead	Total
3-7	$4,000			$ 4,000
3-8	2,000			6,000
3-25	3,500			9,500
3-26		$6,200		15,700
3-29			$3,100	18,800
Total	$9,500	$6,200	$3,100	$18,800

JOB COST SHEET #13
Product: Little Skates
Started 3-15-X7 Completed

Date	Material	Labor	Overhead	Total
3-15	$2,500			$2,500
3-20		$4,250		6,750
3-31			$2,125	$8,875
Total				

VARIABLE OVERHEAD CONTROL
Subsidiary Ledger for March

Date	Indirect Material	Indirect Labor	Utilities	Repairs	Total
3-20		$5,300			$5,300
3-29	$ 500				5,800
3-29	700				6,500
3-31			$800		7,300
3-31				$1,200	8,500
Total	$1,200	$5,300	$800	$1,200	$8,500

RAW MATERIAL STOCK CARD
Material #1

Date	Receipts	Issues	Balance
2-28			$10,000
3-1		$3,000	$ 7,000
3-3	$4,000		$11,000
3-7		$4,000	$ 7,000
3-15		$2,500	$ 4,500
3-29		$ 500	$ 4,000

RAW MATERIAL STOCK CARD
Material #2

Date	Receipts	Issues	Balance
2-28			$8,000
3-2		$1,500	$6,500
3-8		$2,000	$4,500
3-25		$3,500	$1,000
3-29		$ 700	$ 300
3-29	$6,000		$6,300

FINISHED GOODS STOCK CARD
Little Skates

Date	Receipts	Issues	Balance
2-28			$ 2,000
3-5		$ 1,000	$ 1,000
3-20	$18,500		$19,500
3-22		$ 5,000	$14,500
3-25		$12,000	$ 2,500

FINISHED GOODS STOCK CARD
Big Skates

Date	Receipts	Issues	Balance
2-28			$ 4,000
3-29	$18,800		$22,800
3-30		$16,500	$ 6,300

The transactions for Week 23 follow:

1. Purchased raw materials on account, $8,600.
2. Issued materials to the Shaping Department to start 5,000 units, $6,060.
3. Paid direct labor for the week:
   Shaping Department, $6,300.
   Finishing Department, $7,420.
4. Sold 4,000 units at $9.00 each on account from beginning inventory.
5. Overhead for the week (credit Various Accounts):
   Variable overhead in Shaping Department, $2,990.
   Variable overhead in Finishing Department, $3,140.
   Fixed overhead for the company, $6,000.
6. During the week, 5,100 shaped units were transferred from the Shaping Department to the Finishing Department. This left 500 units complete as to material and 60% complete as to conversion costs in the Shaping Department.
7. During the week 4,700 units were completed in the Finishing Department and sent to finished goods. At the end of the week there were 400 units in the Finishing Department complete as to material and 25% complete as to conversion costs.

REQUIRED:

A. Prepare journal entries for the transactions assuming variable and weighted-average costing. Your entries should be supported by computations of equivalent production and unit costs in good form. (Do not compute separate unit costs for direct labor and variable overhead.)
B. Prepare T-accounts and post the transactions.
C. Prepare a contribution margin income statement.

5-33 *(Reconstruction of Journal Entries from Subsidiary Ledgers).* You are head accountant for the Rolling Roller Skate Company. Your company has the following cost system: they maintain a perpetual inventory system on all items; they maintain accounts for Raw Materials, Work-in-Process, Finished Goods, Variable Overhead Control, Variable Overhead Applied, Under- or Overapplied Variable Overhead; all inventory accounts are supported by subsidiary ledgers, as is the Variable Overhead Control; the Variable Overhead accounts are closed monthly to Under- or Overapplied Variable Overhead; and variable costing is used internally.

Listed on the facing page are the subsidiary ledgers for the month of March.

REQUIRED:

Using the subsidiary ledgers as your source of information, reconstruct all of the journal entries for the month; make your entries in summary form (do not make an entry for each entry in the subsidiary ledger). Assume that no purchases are returned to the suppliers and that no materials are returned from the factory to the Raw Material storeroom.

5-34 *(Comprehensive Cost Flow Problem—Journal Entries and Statements).* The Lotone Company has adopted a variable costing system. At the beginning of the year the following flexible budget was developed for overhead. From this budget a variable overhead rate of $1.00 per direct labor hour was developed.

	Fixed cost per month	*Variable cost per direct labor hour*
Supplies	$ 0	$ .20
Indirect labor	2,000	0
Supervision and maintenance	3,500	0
Depreciation	1,300	0
Other factory costs	0	.80
Total	$ 6,800	$1.00

Inventories at the beginning of October were as follows:

Raw Materials	$ 7,500
Work-in-Process	$ 9,800
Finished Goods	$25,000

During the month of October the following transactions occurred. (Assume that all sales and purchases are on credit.)

October 1 Purchased $6,300 of raw materials which were received, inspected, and accepted.

3 Sold finished goods costing $5,000 for $7,500.

6 Material requisitions were issued for $6,500 for raw materials.

7 Paid the weekly factory payroll:

Direct labor (1,200 hours @ $3.00)	$3,600
Indirect labor	550
Total	$4,150

10 Received a sales order for $15,000 of goods that will be completed during the month and will be shipped on October 31.

13 Purchased $1,200 of supplies that will be consumed during the month.

14 Paid the weekly factory payroll:

Direct labor (1,100 hours @ $3.00)	$3,300
Indirect labor	500
Total	$3,800

14 Paid the semimonthly supervisory and maintenance payroll in the amount of $1,750.

15 Purchased $8,500 of raw materials.

18 Received bill for other factory costs of $2,000.

19 The purchasing agent issued a purchase order in the amount of $2,300.

19 Issued raw materials in the amount of $9,000 determined from approved materials requisitions.

21 Paid the weekly factory payroll:

Direct labor (1,400 hours @ $3.00)	$4,200
Indirect labor	540
Total	$4,740

22 Received and shipped an order for sales of $12,000; the units cost $9,000.

28 Paid the weekly factory payroll:

Direct labor (1,300 hours @ $3.00)	$3,900
Indirect labor	500
Total	$4,400

28 Paid the semimonthly supervisory and maintenance payroll of $1,800.

29 Sold and delivered goods that cost $10,000 for a sales price of $14,250.

30 Recorded monthly depreciation of $1,300.

30 Applied variable overhead to Work-in-Process at $1.00 per direct labor hour.

30 Recorded completion of jobs in Work-in-Process Inventory and transferred them to Finished Goods Inventory in the amount of $40,000. Records indicate that 120 units were equivalently produced during the month.

30 Shipped the order received on October 10. The cost of the order was $10,500.

30 Received $42,000 from customers in payment of accounts receivable.

30 Paid $10,000 to creditors in payment of accounts payable.

30 Incurred selling and administrative expenses of $7,500 for the month, on account. Of this total $2,500 is variable.

REQUIRED:

A. Prepare journal entries for the month using variable costing. Post the transactions to T-accounts.

B. Compute the end of the month inventory amounts.

C. Prepare an income statement for the month. Any under- or overapplied overhead should be added to cost of goods sold.

D. Prepare a report to the factory management comparing actual overhead costs with the budget.

Variable Standard Costing for Cost Efficiency

One of the weaknesses of historical costing, presented in the previous chapter, is its failure to provide criteria for judging the results of day-to-day operating decisions. A comparison of the current period's costs with those of last period will not assure management of proper control over operations. The current period's activities could be just as inefficient as those of the previous period. Thus, management needs criteria for judging the results of operating decisions. Standard costs are one way to plan and control the costs of any repetitive task such as production, shipping, or clerical activities. If management can assume that the sales price per unit of product is relatively constant within the relevant range of activity, profits will be maximized if costs are minimized.

A **standard** is a precise measure of what *should* occur if performance is efficient. Par is a standard for the golf course; 80 words per minute is a standard for typists; and a four-minute mile is a difficult standard for runners. A **standard cost** is a measure of acceptable cost performance. Such a measure is derived from the expenditure of considerable thought and energy as to how a task should be accomplished and how many resources (costs) should be consumed. Although many different tasks and activities are performed in a business firm, standard costs are usually focused on the costs of manufacturing the product—raw materials, direct labor, and overhead costs. The focus upon manufacturing activities is deliberate. These activities are repetitive and hence susceptible to the establishment of standards. Standards can be set for any repetitive task—selling and administrative duties as well as production tasks—but most firms concentrate on the control of their production activities through the standard-setting process.

Many benefits are associated with using standard costs. First, a standard cost system, once installed, can be cheaper to maintain than an historical cost system because it eliminates some bookkeeping and paperwork. Second, the time and energy expended in developing standards may highlight possible production inefficiencies *before* actual production begins. The potential benefits of these efforts are cost savings and, as a result, higher profits. Third, standard costs assist management in formally constructing its plans and budgets. Fourth, standards allow management to maintain operational control.

The difference between actual cost and standard cost is called a **variance.** By frequently comparing actual results with standard costs via the variances, management can determine whether actual performance is under control. If the actual exceeds the standard, the variance is unfavorable, indicating the need for management action. The variance is favorable if the actual is less than the standard, which would imply that the firm's costs are under control. It is the ability to create meaningful variances by comparing actual results with a measure of what *should* happen that makes the standard cost system a potent management tool.

TYPES OF STANDARD COSTS

There is more than one philosophical approach to the scientific determination of a performance standard. One approach is to set an **ideal standard** that estimates what should happen if all conditions are perfect—no waste, no scrap, no idle time, no rest periods, and no machine breakdowns. Over any extended period of time it would be impossible for the actual activities to equal the ideal standard.

A normal, or average, standard is a widely used philosophy in establishing standard costs. **Normal standards** are achievable, but their attainment requires that activities be efficient. Sometimes they are called **currently attainable** standards. They allow for normal workers performing in normal settings. In a production firm, allowances would be made for normal scrap and waste, normal fatigue and breaks, normal machine breakdowns and maintenance, and normal mistakes in production.

Another concept of a standard is used by some firms. The **expected standard** is based upon the most likely attainable result. Technically, this is not a standard cost because it has no inherent provision for efficiency, although many people call it a standard. It is an estimate of what *will* happen, not what *should* happen.

The difference between ideal, currently attainable, and expected standards is a philosophical one. The mental approach to the setting of standards determines the philosophy. If the standard is so tight that very few can attain it, it is an ideal standard; if it is based upon an estimate of what will happen, it is an expected standard; and if it is tight but attainable, it is a normal standard. The method of establishing the standard does *not* determine whether it is ideal, normal, or expected. All may be set by past experience, by work measurement and time-and-motion studies, by engineering estimates, or by a combination of these. It is the intent that determines the type of standard.

THE SETTING OF STANDARDS

The primary purpose of a standard cost system is to keep the unit cost of production as low as possible, given the current state of the industry. The standard cost per se does not keep the unit cost of production at a minimum. The system is made efficient by the achievements of the workers in using no more than the standard amount of materials, labor, and overhead to produce the product. Thus, the standard cost is a motivational system. Its goal is to provide a benchmark of good performance that workers will strive to achieve.

Standards for Motivation

When a standard is set at the ideal or perfect level, the worker will almost always fail to achieve the standard, and variances will be unfavorable. In the long run, this failure can frustrate the worker and create a feeling of hopelessness. When the standards are too loose, the worker has no need to perform efficiently, and his performance may or may not be satisfactory. The observation that motivational factors seem to improve with tightening standards up to a point, and then drop off, has led most standard costers to believe that a tight, but attainable, standard is most useful in motivating efficient performance. The normal, or currently attainable, standard aims for this motivational level.

The role of standards in motivating employees is a complicated subject. There are definite interactions among the tightness of the standards, employee attitudes, organizational structure, performance feedback, and employee reward systems. At this time we know far too little about these interactions. Current beliefs seem to be that standards motivate best when there is valid participation in their establishment, when they are tight but reasonable, when there is rapid performance feedback, and when the employee's rewards are tied to success in achieving the standard.

Establishing Technical Standards

At the heart of a standard cost system is the **standard cost card,** the predetermined estimate of what one unit of product should cost if produced efficiently. It includes detailed estimates of material quantities and prices, labor quantities and prices, and overhead quantities and rates. These details serve as the benchmarks of efficiency against which actual quantities and costs are compared. This focus upon the efficient cost of producing one unit requires a reemphasis of the relevant range of activity concept. When standards for material, labor, and overhead are established, there is an implicit assumption that the actual production volume will be within a relevant range of activity.

MATERIAL STANDARDS

In most companies the material quantities are determined by the industrial engineers who design the product and determine the production process. Typically, the prices paid for raw materials are the responsibility of the purchasing agent. If the quantity of raw material consumed results in price discounts, the material prices must be set through cooperation between the purchasing department and the production schedulers. For a new product, management cannot rely upon past experience; the parts list must be taken from blueprints, and the material prices obtained from suppliers' quotations and bids.

LABOR STANDARDS

Labor time standards are often established from work measurement and time-and-motion studies. Performed by the industrial engineering department, these studies are often a source of conflict between the workers and management. The industrial engineer usually observes a worker in actual working conditions and then suggests ways of increasing worker efficiency. The methods of measuring labor time standards require special training and a considerable amount of professional judgment. Based on a certain amount of subjectivity, the labor time standards are often less certain and more open to variation than material standards.

Standard wage rates are often the result of collective bargaining agreements. Where union contracts exist, they can be used as the basis for establishing wage standards. In unionized plants the responsibility for wage rate standards rests with those involved in contract negotiations. In nonunion plants this responsibility often lies with the departmental managers or the personnel department. Although the wage rate for each skill level may be determined by contract negotiations, the establishment of standard costs can be complicated if the manager is able to mix worker skill levels. The standard wage rate is usually a composite of many wage rates, assuming a specific mix of employee skills.

OVERHEAD STANDARDS

The development of standard overhead costs begins with cost-volume analysis. The separation of overhead costs into fixed and variable components allows not only the prediction of costs, but also a detailed examination of *how* costs behave relative to volume. With this understanding management can undertake a study of what costs *should* be at different volumes of output.

The flexible budget based upon past experience cannot automatically be considered a standard. It becomes a standard only when energy and thought have been applied to see if these are what costs *should* be. Only when management is satisfied that the flexible budget expresses what costs should be if operations are efficient can it serve as a standard for overhead.

Acceptance of Standards

The advocates of standard costing see it as a way to achieve efficient operations through its planning and control influences on managers and workers. The operation of a good standard cost system—with currently attainable, yet tight, standards—is not an easy task. It requires considerable thought, effort, and commitment. The value of the system may be negated if the standards are constantly under attack by the managers and workers.

Acceptance of the standards is necessary for at least two reasons. First, the workers must believe that they are reasonable. If the standards set are considered unfair, the workers may not attempt to achieve them and may try to subvert the standard cost system. The results are misdirected energy and, ultimately, misused resources—the antithesis of the goal of standard costs.

Second, the standards must be accepted if the variances are to have meaning. Standard cost minus actual cost equals variance. If the standards are open to question, then so are the variances. When the workers consider the standard cost to be "incorrect," the automatic implication is that actual cost is "correct" and the variance becomes a measure of the inaccuracy of the standard cost. Thus, there is no attitude of measuring or correcting inefficiencies. Let's look at the nature of the variance if the standard cost is accepted as "correct" by the workers. Here, the actual cost is "incorrect." (It is not necessarily incorrect in terms of its measurement. We assume the actual cost has been accounted for correctly. It is "incorrect" because it is not what it *should* be.) It is not efficient. The unfavorable variance is the measure of resources wasted through inefficiency; the favorable variance is a measure of resources saved through efficiency.

Revision of Standards

Standards must be revised whenever the conditions upon which they are based change. Most firms find that a continual program of revision is necessary. A typical policy is to revise the standards whenever quantity or prices change significantly, but at least once per year. Failure to revise them periodically can result in the standards becoming unfair for evaluating performance.

Typically, price standards are more subject to change than quantity standards. New contracts and inflation are regular occurrences in most firms. With a significant change, the price standards must be adjusted. Changes in the quantity standards are required when there are improvements in performance, new production specifications or methods, or changes in product mixes. If a long-range decision results in the purchase of new production equipment, the quantity standards may have to be modified.

Many firms trace the direction of variance details to glean information about production efficiency and about the existing standards. If the variances are continually unfavorable, employees may begin to reduce their effort, believing that the standards are unattainable. If, on the other hand, the variances are always favorable, the standards may be too loose and thus ineffective in stimulating efficient performance. The amount and the direction of the variances can point to the need for revising the standard costs.

A VARIABLE STANDARD COST SYSTEM ILLUSTRATED

The process of establishing standards is a valuable activity in itself. The strengths and weaknesses of the production system are highlighted, along with opportunities for cost reduction. Planning is improved because the standards provide managers with a statement of what costs should be and simultaneously serve as a starting place in the budgetary process. They also provide a method of projecting the amount of resources needed to meet budgeted production. In addition, the benchmarks established allow day-to-day comparison of actual results with the standards. Through this comparison, production costs can be controlled.

The standard cost system is not only a method of controlling operating efficiency by the reporting of variances, but also a system of income determination. When it is used as an inventory costing system, each unit of product in the Work-in-Process Inventory, Finished Goods Inventory, or Cost of Goods Sold is costed at standard cost. The resources actually used will be recorded at their actual cost. The differences between standard and actual—the variances—typically are treated as period costs in the income statement. Exhibit 6–1 summarizes the flow of costs for a variable standard costing system.

To explain the way standard costs are used in an ongoing accounting system, let's assume that the workers and management of the Forddon Furniture Company established the standard cost cards in Exhibit 6–2 for its two products before the beginning of the accounting period. These standards represent the best estimates of what production costs should be during the coming accounting period.

When the standards were set, management anticipated producing 575 Style 10A bookcases and 1,000 Style 11A bookcases each month. In addition to the variable standard costs per product for material and labor, management also prepared the following flexible budgets:

Total overhead = \$9,600 per month + \$1.50 per direct labor hour

Total selling expenses = \$2,400 per month + \$2.00 per unit sold

Total administrative expenses = \$3,000 per month

The standard variable overhead rate shown on the standard cost cards in Exhibit 6–2 was taken directly from the flexible budget for overhead at \$1.50 per direct labor hour. This results in variable overhead costs of \$12.00 for Bookcase 10A and \$7.50 for Bookcase 11A. Because fixed overhead, selling expenses, and administrative expenses are treated as period costs under variable costing, they are not included on the standard cost cards which show only the product costs. However, budgets would be prepared and actual costs would be controlled by comparing them with the budget at the end of the accounting period. This role of the Performance Budget was discussed in the last chapter and will be illustrated again later.

To ensure that planned activities were within the relevant range, the accountant also estimated the normal activity hours. Plans called for production of 575 Style 10A bookcases at eight hours each, for a total of 4,600 direct labor hours; and 1,000 Style 11A bookcases at five hours each, for a total of 5,000 direct labor hours. Thus, the total of 9,600 direct labor hours was planned. This level was considered by the accountant as being within the relevant range of activity.

During January, actual production was started on 550 Style 10A bookcases and 1,200 Style 11A bookcases. (Actual production differed from planned production because of unexpected shifts in sales demand.) Two batches of raw material were purchased. The first batch was 70,000 feet at a price of \$.27 per foot. The second batch was 50,000 feet at \$.32 per foot. During the month 118,000 feet of direct materials were issued to the factory. Production employees spent 10,400 direct labor hours on the bookcases, at \$4.10 per hour. Actual overhead incurred was \$24,400, of which \$9,000 was fixed and $15,400 was variable. At the end of the accounting period, 50 of the Style 10A bookcases were incomplete and remained in the factory. These 50 units had all materials issued and 40% of the direct labor and variable overhead needed to complete the 50 units (or 20 equivalent units for direct labor and variable overhead; 50 equivalent units for material). The completed bookcases (500 of 10A and 1,200 of 11A) were placed in the finished goods storeroom. Customers purchased 450 of the 10A bookcases at $125 each and 1,100 of the 11A bookcases at $60 each. Actual selling expenses were $2,000 fixed and $2,800 variable. The actual administrative expenses were $3,500. There were no beginning inventories in the Work-in-Process Inventory or Finished Goods Inventory.

MATERIALS PURCHASES

The following two journal entries record the purchases of materials.[1]

	Debit	Credit
Raw Materials Inventory	$21,000	
Material Price Variance		$ 2,100
Accounts Payable		$18,900

	Debit	Credit
Raw Materials Inventory	$15,000	
Material Price Variance	$ 1,000	
Accounts Payable		$16,000

By recording the Raw Materials Inventory at standard price (70,000 × $.30 = $21,000), there are no accounting complications such as LIFO, FIFO, or average inventory costing, because all materials will be carried at their standard cost. The credit to Accounts Payable must, of course, be recorded at the actual price suppliers are paid (70,000 × $.27 = $18,900).

The **material price variance** is the difference between the actual price and the standard price, times the actual quantity of materials purchased. Perhaps a more accurate title would be the *material purchased price variance*. The material price variance may be expressed in formula form.

$$\text{Material price variance} = \left[\text{Standard price per unit of material} - \text{Actual price per unit of material}\right] \times \text{Actual quantity of materials purchased}$$

When actual costs exceed standard costs, the variance is unfavorable. Thus, a Material Price Variance account with a debit balance is unfavorable. With a credit balance it is favorable.

[1] We will omit explanations of all journal entries in this chapter.

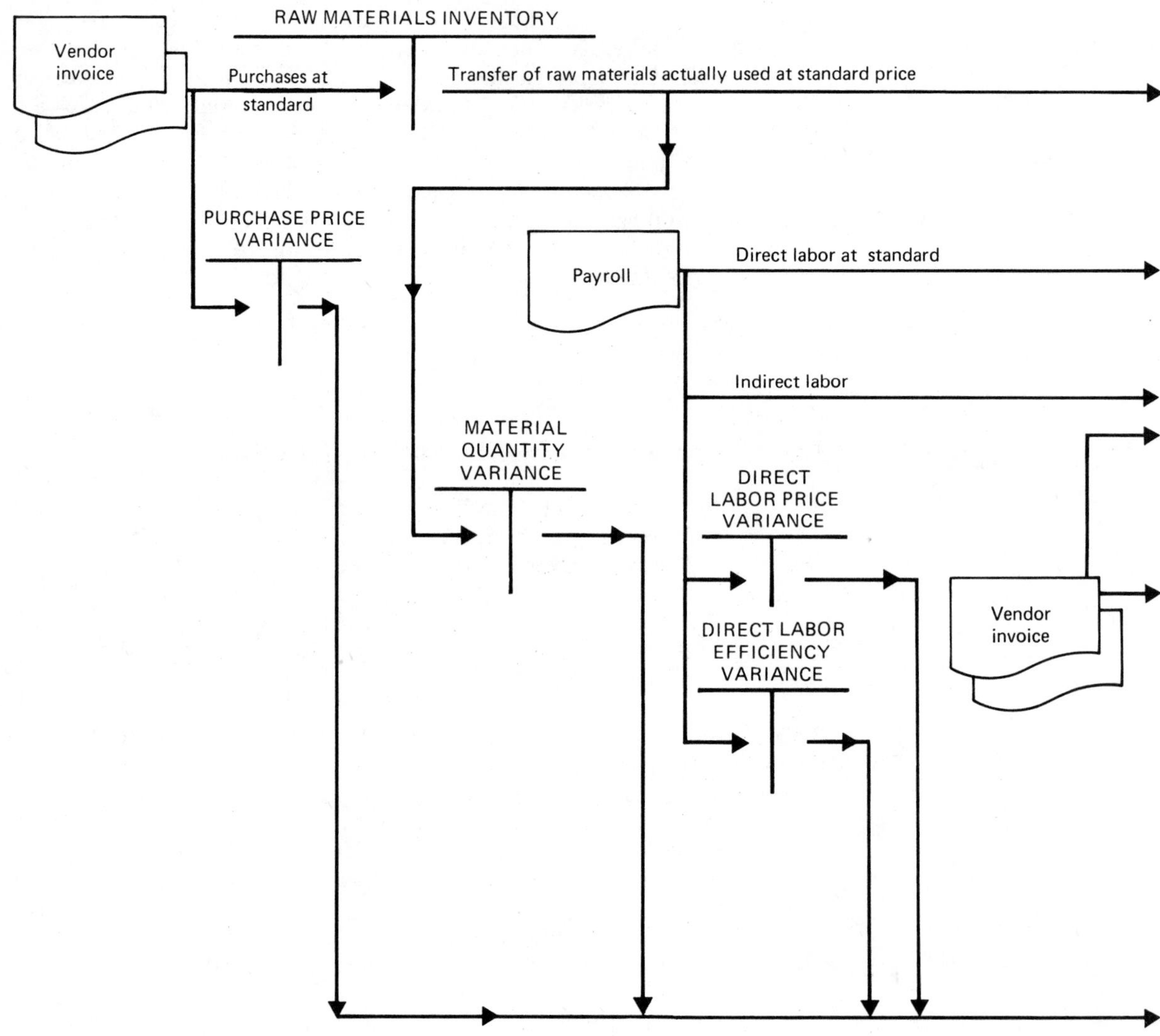

EXHIBIT 6–1
Variable standard cost system

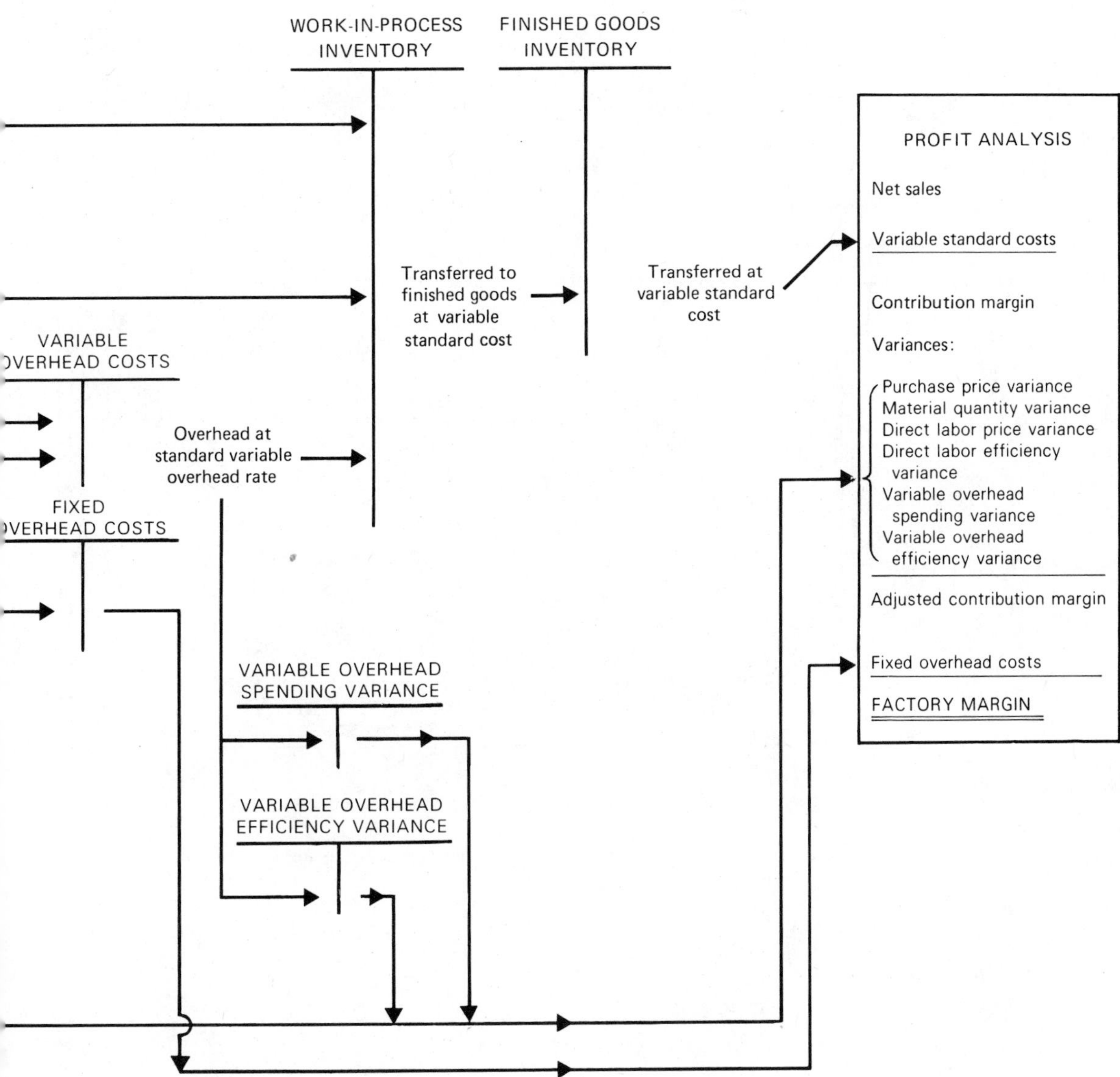
WORK-IN-PROCESS INVENTORY
FINISHED GOODS INVENTORY
PROFIT ANALYSIS
Net sales
Variable standard costs
Transferred to finished goods at variable standard cost
Transferred at variable standard cost
Contribution margin
VARIABLE
VERHEAD COSTS
Variances:
Purchase price variance
Material quantity variance
Direct labor price variance
Direct labor efficiency variance
Variable overhead spending variance
Variable overhead efficiency variance
Overhead at standard variable overhead rate
FIXED
VERHEAD COSTS
Adjusted contribution margin
Fixed overhead costs
FACTORY MARGIN
VARIABLE OVERHEAD SPENDING VARIANCE
VARIABLE OVERHEAD EFFICIENCY VARIANCE

BOOKCASE 10A—LARGE
STANDARD COST CARD

Direct materials	
100 feet @ $.30	$30.00
Direct labor	
8 hours @ $4.00	32.00
Variable overhead	
8 hours @ $1.50	12.00
Total variable standard cost	$74.00

BOOKCASE 11A—SMALL
STANDARD COST CARD

Direct materials	
50 feet @ $.30	$15.00
Direct labor	
5 hours @ $4.00	20.00
Variable overhead	
5 hours @ $1.50	7.50
Total variable standard cost	$42.50

EXHIBIT 6–2
Variable standard cost cards for Forddon Furniture Company

In the Forddon Company the material price variance is computed as:

First purchase:

Material price variance = [$.30 − $.27] × 70,000 feet

= $2,100 Favorable

Second purchase:

Material price variance = [$.30 − $.32] × 50,000 feet

= $(1,000) Unfavorable

The total material price variance is favorable in the amount of $1,100.

Ideally, the material price variance should be isolated at the time the purchase invoice is recorded. It is then possible to sum all the invoices on a particular day by raw material class, by supplier, or by purchasing agent. Purchasing management can receive daily reports on the price variance for the previous day's purchases.

Responsibility for analyzing the price variance lies with the purchasing officers. Because purchases are made continuously, it is important to report the variances regularly. There may be many causal factors for the price variance. A sudden change in the production volume can force the purchasing agent to buy uneconomic quantities, inflation can force the prices upward, material shortages can modify the supplier's pricing structure, or the purchasing department may simply fail to find the most desirable supplier. Obviously, the responsibility for some of these factors, such as the sudden change in production schedule, rests with someone other than the purchasing agent. It would be naive to automatically assign all results directly to the purchasing officer without a detailed analysis. It is generally true, however, that the causes rest with the purchasing agent and that it is his or her responsibility to explain unusual circumstances.

ISSUE OF MATERIALS

The following journal entry records the issue of raw materials to the factory.

Work-in-Process Inventory	$34,500	
Material Quantity Variance ...	$ 900	
Raw Materials Inventory		$35,400

Each unit of product in the Work-in-Process Inventory is costed at the cost shown on the standard cost card. Because materials for 550 large bookcases and 1,200 small bookcases were issued to production, the Work-in-Process Inventory should be charged for (550 × $30) + (1,200 × $15), or $34,500. The Raw Materials Inventory must be credited for the actual quantity issued, costed at the standard material price. Since 118,000 feet were actually used and the Raw Materials Inventory is costed at standard cost ($.30), the credit to the inventory is $35,400.

The **material quantity variance,** or as sometimes called the **material usage variance,** measures how well the physical resources were utilized. It is computed by multiplying the standard cost per unit by the difference between the actual materials used and the amount of materials that should have been used to produce the actual units. In formula form the material quantity variance is:

$$\text{Material quantity variance} = \left[\left(\begin{array}{c}\text{Actual units}\\ \text{produced}\end{array} \times \begin{array}{c}\text{Standard quantity}\\ \text{per unit}\end{array}\right) - \begin{array}{c}\text{Actual quantity of}\\ \text{materials used}\end{array}\right] \times \begin{array}{c}\text{Standard price}\\ \text{per unit of}\\ \text{raw materials}\end{array}$$

In the Forddon Company the material quantity variance is computed as:

$$\text{Material quantity variance} = [(550 \times 100) + (1{,}200 \times 50) - 118{,}000] \times \$.30$$

$$= [55{,}000 + 60{,}000 - 118{,}000] \times \$.30$$

$$= \$(900) \text{ Unfavorable}$$

The company used 3,000 feet of materials in excess of standard; the result is an unfavorable material quantity variance of $900.

The material quantity variance can be isolated any time output is measured (in some cases on an hourly or daily basis), by department, by worker, or by responsibility center. Some firms find a two-stage issue procedure works best. When a worker receives management's instructions (production releases) to produce a unit of product, he presents the work order to the raw materials storeroom. The storekeeper will issue exactly the standard quantity of materials on a materials requisition. At that time the entry would be:

Work-in-Process Inventory	$34,500	
Raw Materials Inventory		$34,500

If the worker needs more materials to finish, having failed to meet standard, the needed materials are issued on an excess materials requisition. The issue of these excess materials would be recorded as:

Material Quantity Variance	$900	
Raw Materials Inventory		$900

This method works well if the standards are tight. If the standards are too loose, more materials than are necessary for production will be issued the first time. Unless the company controls the handling of materials in the factory, the workers may try to stockpile any excess materials as a hedge against a time when the standard cannot be met. If the worker is not encouraged to return excess materials to the storeroom, there will be no favorable quantity variance. The goal of the standard cost system is negated, and the possibilities for materials theft and loss are increased.

There can be many reasons for a material quantity variance. Excess usage may be the result of carelessness by the workers using the material, improper machine adjustment, or the substitution of substandard material. Also, employees could be taking materials home or squirreling them throughout the factory. Another possible cause is a modification of quality-control standards during a period. Less-than-standard usage could result from the substitution of materials of higher quality than the standard, improvements in the production process, or extra care by the workers in performing their jobs.

Examination of some of the causal factors for the material quantity variance indicates that overall responsibility for the variance lies with the production personnel. As with all variances, however, this premise should not be accepted without further investigation. For example, assume that a close examination showed the principal cause of a favorable material quantity variance to be the substitution of above-standard materials. This higher-quality material should result in less waste than was anticipated when the standard quantity was set, and could account for a favorable quantity variance. It could also help account for an unfavorable material price variance because above-standard materials would probably cost more. Both variances would have been unavoidable if the materials specified in developing the standard costs were not available, and the purchasing agent bought what he could.

DIRECT LABOR PURCHASED AND CONSUMED

The following journal entry records the direct labor.

Work-in-Process Inventory	$40,640	
Labor Price Variance	$ 1,040	
Labor Quantity Variance	$ 960	
Wages Payable		$42,640

The debit to Work-in-Process Inventory is for the actual units produced times standard hours per unit times the standard wage rate per hour. During the month the company worked on 550 of the Style 10A bookshelves, completing the equivalent of 520 (500 units finished plus 50 units 40% complete). Material was issued for 550 units, but direct labor and variable overhead were sufficient to complete only 520 units. The production of 520 of the 10A style *should* consume 4,160 labor hours (520 units × 8 hours), and the 1,200 Style 11A bookcases should consume 6,000 hours (1,200 units × 5 hours). Thus, the debit to Work-in-Process Inventory would be 10,160 standard hours times the $4.00 standard wage rate. The credit to Wages Payable is for the actual wages paid (10,400 × $4.10).

The **labor price variance** parallels the material price variance. Often called the **wage rate variance,** it is the difference between the standard wage rate and the actual wage, multiplied by the actual hours worked. The labor price variance may be expressed as a formula.

$$\text{Labor price variance} = \left[\text{Standard wage rate per hour} - \text{Actual wage rate per hour}\right] \times \text{Actual hours worked}$$

For the Forddon Company the labor price variance is computed as:

$$\text{Labor price variance} = [\$4.00 - \$4.10] \times 10{,}400 \text{ hours}$$

$$= \$(1{,}040) \text{ Unfavorable}$$

An actual wage rate of $.10 above the standard rate, times the 10,400 hours actually worked, resulted in an unfavorable labor price variance of $1,040.

One possible cause of a favorable wage rate variance is that management was able to obtain a better worker mix than predicted when the standard was developed. By hiring more workers with lower wage rates, management can affect the wage rate variance. If these workers are less skilled than the skill level planned in the standard wage rate, their employment could have an unfavorable effect on both the material quantity variance and the labor quantity variance. Unskilled workers probably waste more material and time than do skilled workers. Also, a labor-mix problem may arise because of failures in production control to properly schedule the workers' activities.

Just as the labor price variance parallels the material price variance, the **labor quantity variance** is built upon the same theory as the material quantity variance. Also called the **labor efficiency variance,** it is the difference between the hours workers should have consumed in actual production and the actual hours worked, multiplied by the standard hourly wage rate. This variance may be expressed in formula form.

$$\text{Labor quantity variance} = \left[\left(\text{Actual units produced} \times \text{Standard hours per unit}\right) - \text{Actual hours worked}\right] \times \text{Standard wage rate}$$

For the Forddon Company the labor quantity variance is computed as:

$$\text{Labor quantity variance} = [(520 \times 8) + (1{,}200 \times 5) - 10{,}400 \text{ hours}] \times \$4.00$$

$$= [4{,}160 + 6{,}000 - 10{,}400] \times \$4.00$$

$$= \$(960) \text{ Unfavorable}$$

Bookcase 10A required 4,160 standard hours (520 × 8), and Bookcase 11A required 6,000 (1,200 × 5). The excess of actual hours (10,400) over the standard hours allowed (10,160), times the standard wage rate resulted in an unfavorable labor quantity variance of $960.

The calculation of the two variances for labor can be summarized into the following schedule.

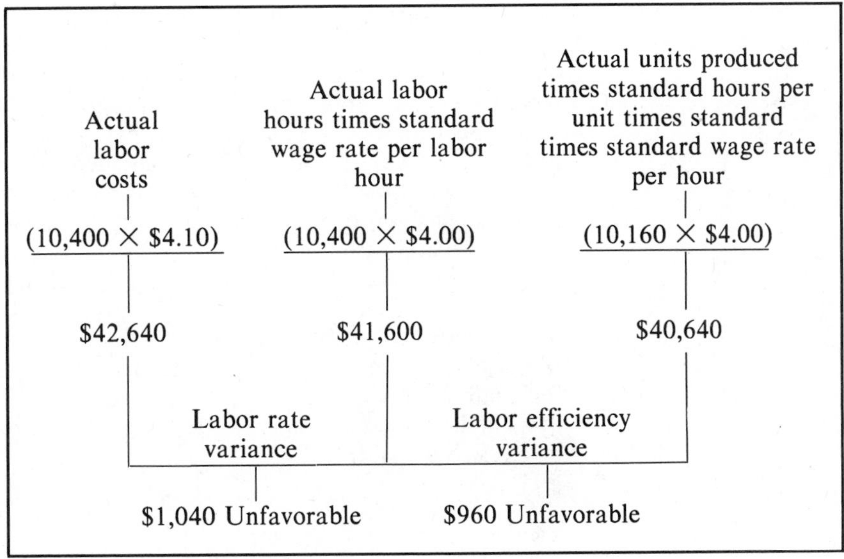

If actual hours worked had been identified by product, the labor quantity variance could be computed for each product. For example, if 4,500 of the actual labor hours were spent on Product 10A the labor quantity variance for Product 10A would be $1,360 unfavorable [(4,160 − 4,500) × $4.00]. The labor quantity variance for Product 11A would be $400 favorable [(6,000 − 5,900) × $4.00]. This would facilitate management's decisions about production plans and selling prices by product line.

This variance is of prime significance to the production managers. It measures how well they use their workers' time. Many causes of the variance stem from the work itself. Poor production planning may have created idle time, machine breakdowns could have occurred, changes in planned volumes could have affected the learning-curve estimates, blueprints and designs could have had errors, or failures to receive raw materials on time could have created worker inactivity. The individual worker and group foreman should be aware of the labor efficiency variances, in hours or units of output, on a daily basis. The *real* control takes place at this point. The statement of the variance in dollar terms at the end of the month is less valuable to the foreman than is the variance stated in hours; his actual planning and controlling activities are in hours.

INCURRENCE OF ACTUAL OVERHEAD COSTS

The following journal entry records the actual overhead costs.

Variable Overhead Control	$15,400	
Fixed Overhead Control	$ 9,000	
Various Accounts		$24,400

The Variable Overhead Control and Fixed Overhead Control accounts will have subsidiary ledgers where the details are classified. Some firms have a *natural* classification of factory overhead in their subsidiary ledgers. They record overhead detail by the nature of the invoice. Separate records are kept for indirect materials, indirect labor, maintenance, heat-light-power, insurance, depreciation of factory buildings, depreciation of factory machinery, and so forth. Other firms prefer a *functional* classification of costs in the subsidiary ledger. In these firms the costs are recorded by the function they perform. Examples of functional classifications are departments, cost centers, and factory operations such as materials handling and storage, purchasing, production engineering, and quality control.

Many accounts would be credited to record actual overhead. Raw Materials Inventory would be credited for indirect materials; Wages Payable, for indirect labor; Accumulated Depreciation, for depreciation charges; Prepaid Expenses, for such things as prepaid insurance; and Payables, for invoices to be paid.

APPLICATION OF VARIABLE OVERHEAD TO WORK-IN-PROCESS INVENTORY

The following journal entry records the application of variable overhead to the units produced.

Work-in-Process Inventory	$15,240	
Variable Overhead Applied		$15,240

Work-in-Process Inventory is charged for the units produced times the standard hours allowed per unit times the standard *variable* overhead hourly rate (10,160 hours × $1.50). The 10,160 hours are the same 10,160 hours used in the charge to Work-in-Process Inventory for standard labor. The Variable Overhead Applied account accumulates the amount of variable overhead charged to Work-in-Process Inventory.

DETERMINATION AND ISOLATION OF VARIABLE OVERHEAD VARIANCES

The difference between Variable Overhead Applied and Variable Overhead Control is Under- or Overapplied Variable Overhead, which can be separated into the variable overhead spending variance and the variable overhead efficiency variance.

When the volume base of the flexible budget is direct labor hours, it is implied that every hour the workers save or waste has a direct impact upon variable overhead expenditures. Since variable costs should change with changes in volume, and volume is measured by direct labor hours, a savings in labor hours also results in a savings of variable overhead costs. Labor hours saved means variable overhead dollars saved, and labor hours wasted means variable overhead dollars wasted. The **variable overhead efficiency variance** measures the cost impact upon variable overhead caused by the labor efficiency. This may be expressed as a formula.

$$\text{Variable overhead efficiency variance} = \left[\left(\text{Actual units produced} \times \text{Standard labor hours per unit}\right) - \text{Actual labor hours worked}\right] \times \text{Standard variable overhead rate per hour}$$

For the Forddon Company the variable overhead efficiency variance would be:

$$\text{Variable overhead efficiency variance} = (10{,}160 \text{ hours} - 10{,}400 \text{ hours}) \times \$1.50$$

$$= \$(360) \text{ Unfavorable}$$

This variance is unfavorable because the actual hours exceeded the standard hours per unit times actual production. The company wasted $360 of variable overhead because the workers were not efficient. Note that the variable overhead efficiency variance is equal to the labor efficiency variance in hours times the standard variable overhead rate (240 hours × $1.50).

The causal factors for the variable overhead efficiency variance would be identical with the causes for the labor quantity (efficiency) variance. For this reason, some firms combine the labor efficiency and the variable overhead efficiency variances in their management reports. In formula form this variance is:

$$\text{Combined labor and variable overhead efficiency variance} = \left[\left(\text{Actual units produced} \times \text{Standard labor hours per unit}\right) - \text{Actual labor hours worked}\right] \times \left[\text{Standard wage rate per hour} + \text{Standard variable overhead rate per hour}\right]$$

The variable overhead efficiency variance will not be directly related to the labor quantity (efficiency) variance if the company does not use direct labor hours as a volume base for determining the flexible budget. What if the company uses machine hours as a basis of measuring cost variability? The following formula would express the efficiency variance.

$$\text{Variable overhead efficiency variance} = \left[\left(\begin{array}{l}\text{Actual}\\\text{units}\\\text{produced}\end{array} \times \begin{array}{l}\text{Standard}\\\text{machine hours}\\\text{per unit}\end{array}\right) - \begin{array}{l}\text{Actual}\\\text{machine hours}\\\text{used}\end{array}\right] \times \begin{array}{l}\text{Standard variable}\\\text{overhead rate}\\\text{per machine hour}\end{array}$$

The theory of this variance is the same as that of the variance based upon labor hours, but the causal factors are different. Causes for an unfavorable variable overhead efficiency variance based upon machine hours could include improper maintenance schedules, unscheduled and random machine breakdowns, or human failures in the use of the machines.

As stated earlier, the best method of establishing overhead standards begins with developing a flexible budget. The flexible budget in a standard-cost setting states the cost behavior patterns for overhead that the company *should* experience if operations are efficient. It is a standard of performance. The **variable overhead spending variance** is the difference between the actual variable overhead costs incurred and the amount that the flexible budget indicates should be spent on variable overhead costs for the actual volume worked. It is the difference between actual costs and the flexible budget allowance computed for actual hours worked. In formula form the variable overhead spending variance is:

$$\text{Variable overhead spending variance} = \left(\begin{array}{l}\text{Standard variable}\\\text{rate per hour}\\\text{from flexible budget}\end{array} \times \begin{array}{l}\text{Actual}\\\text{hours}\\\text{worked}\end{array}\right) - \begin{array}{l}\text{Actual}\\\text{variable}\\\text{overhead costs}\end{array}$$

For the Forddon Furniture Company the flexible overhead budget developed before production began was

Overhead flexible budget = \$9,600 + \$1.50 per direct labor hour

The variable overhead spending variance would be:

$$\text{Variable overhead spending variance} = [\$1.50 \times 10{,}400 \text{ hours}] - \$15{,}400$$

$$= \$200 \text{ Favorable}$$

The calculation of the two variances for variable overhead can be summarized into the following schedule.

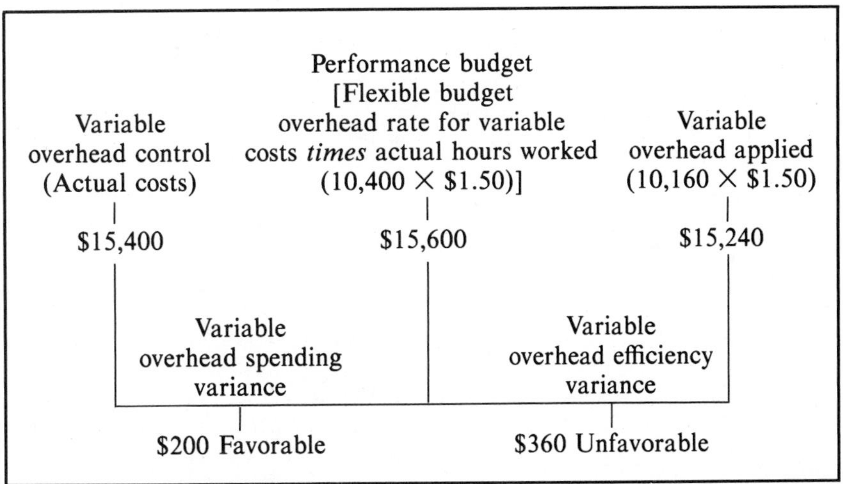

To isolate these variances within the accounting system, the following entry is made.

Variable Overhead Applied	$15,240	
Variable Overhead Efficiency Variance	$ 360	
Variable Overhead Spending Variance		$ 200
Variable Overhead Control		$15,400

This entry closes the Variable Overhead Applied and the Variable Overhead Control accounts, transferring the differences between these accounts into two variance accounts. The algebraic sum of the two variances is $160 unfavorable, which is the amount of underapplied variable overhead.

COMPLETION AND TRANSFER TO FINISHED GOODS INVENTORY

The following journal entry transfers the goods from Work-in-Process Inventory to the Finished Goods Inventory.

Finished Goods Inventory	$88,000	
Work-in-Process Inventory		$88,000

The amount of the transfer was determined as [(500 × $74) + (1,200 × $42.50)], or $88,000. The Work-in-Process Inventory account, after posting, would be as shown in the following T-account.

Work-in-Process Inventory

Beginning Inventory	$ 0	Transferred to Finished Goods	$88,000
Materials	34,500	Ending Inventory	2,380
Labor	40,640		$90,380
Variable Overhead	15,240		
	$90,380		
Inventory	$ 2,380		

The 50 units of Product 10A in the final Work-in-Process Inventory is complete as to materials (50 equivalent units of material) but only 40% complete as to direct labor and variable overhead (50 units × 40%, or 20 equivalent units of direct labor and variable overhead). The cost of the ending inventory of $2,380 is composed of the following:

Materials (50 units × $30)	$1,500
Labor (20 units × $32)	640
Variable Overhead (20 units × $12)	240
Total	$2,380

SALES AND COST OF GOODS SOLD RECOGNITION

The entry to record the sales for the period would be:

Cash or Accounts Receivable $122,250
  Sales $122,250

There were 450 Style 10A bookcases sold at $125 each and 1,100 Style 11A bookcases sold at $60 each.

The following journal entry records the transfer from Finished Goods Inventory to Cost of Goods Sold.

Cost of Goods Sold $80,050
  Finished Goods Inventory $80,050

Since the Finished Goods Inventory is carried at variable standard cost, the transfer to Cost of Goods Sold will be at variable standard cost [(450 × $74) + (1,100 × $42.50)]. The Finished Goods Inventory account, after posting, would be:

Finished Goods Inventory

Beginning Inventory	$ 0	Units Sold	$80,050
Units Completed	88,000	Ending Inventory	7,950
	$88,000		$88,000
Inventory	$ 7,950		

The final Finished Goods Inventory, based upon the physical count, can be reconciled as:

Style 10A	50 × \$74.00 =	\$3,700
Style 11A	100 × \$42.50 =	4,250
Total ending inventory		\$7,950

RECORDING SELLING AND ADMINISTRATIVE EXPENSES

The following summary entry records the selling and administrative expenses.

Fixed Selling Expense Control	\$2,000	
Variable Selling Expense Control	\$2,800	
Administrative Expense Control	\$3,500	
Various Accounts		\$8,300

At this point managerial reports for the period costs can be prepared. These reports should contrast the planned level of expenditures with the actual performance. The accompanying tabulation shows such a report for the Forddon Company.

	Performance Budget Allowances	*Actual Expenditures*	*Spending Variance*
Variable Expenses:			
Selling Expenses	\$ 3,100	\$ 2,800	\$300
Fixed Expenses:			
Overhead	\$ 9,600	\$ 9,000	\$600
Selling Expenses	2,400	2,000	400
Administrative Expenses	3,000	3,500	(500)
Total Fixed Expenses	15,000	14,500	500
Total Period Costs	\$18,100	\$17,300	\$800

Variable selling expenses should be \$2.00 times the actual units sold. The company sold 450 Style 10A bookcases and 1,100 Style 11A bookcases for a total of 1,550 units. Thus, variable selling expenses in the performance budget are (1,550 × \$2.00), or \$3,100. The performance budget for the fixed costs came from the original flexible budget equations.

DISPOSITION OF VARIANCES

The following entry closes the standard cost variances to Cost of Goods Sold.

Cost of Goods Sold (or Income Summary)	$1,960	
Variable Overhead Spending Variance	$ 200	
Material Price Variance	$1,100	
Material Quantity Variance		$ 900
Labor Price Variance		$1,040
Labor Quantity Variance		$ 960
Variable Overhead Efficiency Variance		$ 360

PREPARATION OF INCOME STATEMENT

Exhibit 6–3 shows the income statement prepared with variable standard costs. This income statement is constructed in the format of the contribution margin approach with the variances from standard costs treated as period costs.

SUMMARY OF STANDARD COST VARIANCES

The previous discussion in this chapter has shown how the standard cost variances are calculated as a part of the on-going, recording system. This approach of explanation was chosen since it parallels how the variances would be measured in an actual firm. However, there are times, particularly for management analysis, where the calculation of the variances will not be presented in journal entry form. Exhibit 6–4 shows an analysis of all of the variances of the Forddon Furniture Company without journal entries.

SELECTION OF A STANDARD COST SYSTEM

Management's selection of accounting policies is influenced by many factors. Some of these factors include the need for planning and control information within the firm, the requirements for external and compliance reporting, and the provisions of the Internal Revenue Service Tax Code.

The Forddon Furniture Company illustration in this chapter was based upon a variable standard costing system. A variable standard costing system is consistent with the planning process because it allows management to use variable costs in several decision models without adjustment. The unit cost under absorption standard costing cannot be used directly as a measure of incremental costs because it includes fixed overhead, and we know that the per-unit cost for fixed costs is a function of the volume. However, the absorption standard costing system is consistent with external reporting and income tax requirements. If the standard costs represent currently attainable performance standards, the inventory values under absorption standard costing are acceptable under generally accepted accounting principles. Typi-

THE FORDDON FURNITURE COMPANY
CONTRIBUTION MARGIN INCOME STATEMENT
For the Month of January, 19X7

Sales		$122,250	100%
Less: Standard variable cost of goods sold		80,050	65%
Standard contribution from production		$ 42,200	35%
Adjustments for variances			
Material price variance	$ 1,100		
Material quantity variance	(900)		
Labor price variance	(960)		
Labor quantity variance	(1,600)		
Variable overhead spending variance	200		
Variable overhead efficiency variance	(360)	(1,960)	
Adjusted contribution margin from production		$ 40,240	
Variable selling costs		2,800	
Contribution margin from operations		$ 37,440	
Less fixed costs			
Fixed overhead expense	$ 9,000		
Fixed selling expenses	2,000		
Administrative expenses	3,500		
Total fixed costs		14,500	
Net income		$ 22,940	

EXHIBIT 6–3
Income statement using variable standard costing

cally, the financial accountant will say, "If treating the variance as period costs does not materially distort net income in comparison with what it would have been using historical costing, then standard costing is acceptable for income determination purposes." However, the inventory values under variable standard costing are not acceptable for external reporting because they exclude fixed overhead costs.

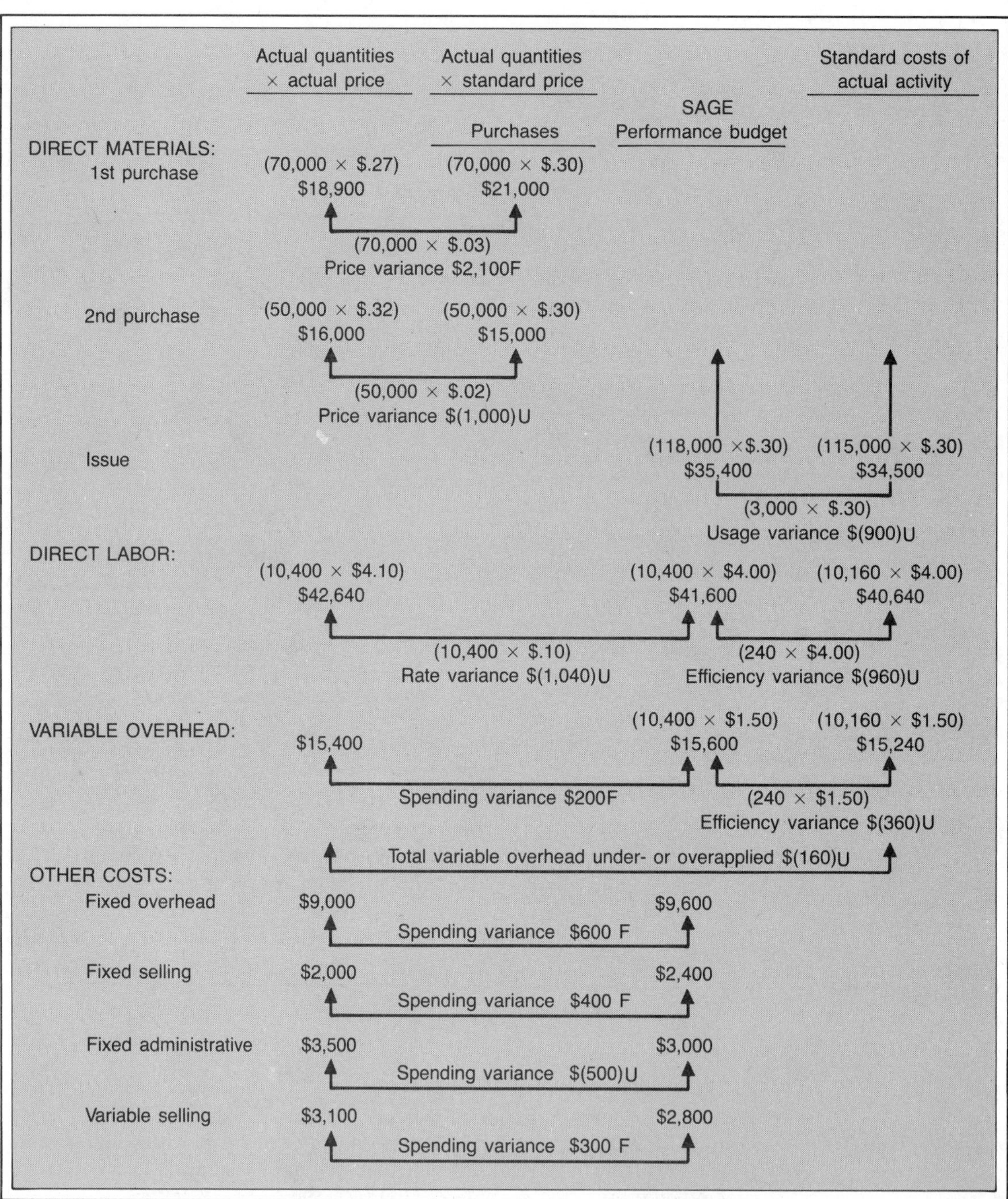

EXHIBIT 6–4
Summary of Standard Cost Variances

In the next chapter we will present an absorption standard costing system and also show how to convert a variable standard cost system, used for managerial planning and control, to an absorption standard cost system, used for external reporting.

SUMMARY

Standard cost systems are intended to aid management in the planning and control of costs. Standard costs are predeterminations of what costs *should* be if production is efficient. Standards must be established for each material, labor, and variable overhead cost. They are set by examining production processes, material usage patterns, work measurement and time studies, learning curves, and the development of a flexible budget for overhead.

There are numerous approaches to the setting of standards. The most useful in planning and controlling costs are normal standards, sometimes called *currently attainable standards.* These costs are achievable. They are useful in providing realistic benchmarks for workers' activities and represent reasonable goals for performance.

The value of a standard cost system is predicated upon the ability to extract meaningful variances by developing standard costs for one unit of product. Then, by comparing actual activity with standards, it is possible to assess performance. There are two types of variances applicable to all variable costs: the price variance and the quantity variance. The price variance is:

$$(\text{Standard price} - \text{Actual price}) \times \text{Actual quantity}$$

The quantity variance is:

$$(\text{Standard quantity} - \text{Actual quantity}) \times \text{Standard price}$$

These variances act as direction finders. They indicate when actual performance differs from standard performance but do not give the causal factors for these differences. In this sense, the variances could be looked upon as the starting point of investigation, rather than as the terminal point. Management must use the variances as attention-directing devices, and then follow up with a more detailed analysis of the causes and their effects.

To achieve the maximum benefits from standard costs, they should be blended into the accounting system. In this way standard costs become both planning and control vehicles and inventory costing values.

SUPPLEMENTARY READING

Claydon, Henry L. "Setting Standards and Evaluating Performance." *Cost and Management,* May, 1965.

Kravitz, Bernard J. "The Standard Cost Review." *Management Controls,* November, 1968.

Miles, Raymond E., and Roger C. Vergin. "Behavioral Properties of Variance Controls." *California Management Review,* Spring, 1966.

National Association of Accountants. *How Standard Costs are Used Currently.* New York: National Association of Accountants, 1948.

Rayburn, L. Gayle. "Setting Standards for Distribution Costs." *Management Services,* March–April, 1967.

Solomons, David. "Flexible Budgets and the Analysis of Overhead Variances." *Management International,* 1961.

Wright, Wilmer. *Direct Standard Costs for Decision Making and Control.* New York: McGraw-Hill Book Company, 1962.

Wright, Wilmer. "Use of Standard Direct Costing." *Management Accounting,* January, 1967.

Zannetos, Zenon S. "On the Mathematics of Variance Analysis." *The Accounting Review,* July, 1963.

QUESTIONS

6–1 Define the term *standard* as it is used in accounting.

6–2 What are some of the benefits of using standard costs? What are some of the costs?

6–3 Is a standard cost system suitable for all types of firms? Explain. What types of businesses could make the most effective use of a standard cost system? In what types of businesses would a standard cost system be least effective?

6–4 Does the method of establishing the standard determine the type of standard it is? Explain and describe three types of standards.

6–5 "A standard cost system is a motivational system." Do you agree? Why or why not? Discuss.

6–6 Explain the advantages and disadvantages of using an ideal standard, a normal standard, and an expected actual standard. Which would you recommend for most situations? Why?

6–7 What is a standard cost card? What items should be included on a standard cost card?

6–8 In using standards as a motivating tool, who should be responsible for setting:
a. Material quantities
b. Material prices
c. Labor times

d. Standard wage rate
e. Standard variable overhead rate
f. Standard total fixed overhead costs.

6-9 Explain how the establishment of standard labor costs can be complicated by the mix of labor skills used. Would a schedule of wage rates for each skill level help? Explain.

6-10 A flexible budget based upon past experience cannot automatically be considered a standard. Explain.

EXERCISES

6-11 *(True or False).* Indicate whether the following statements are true or false.

1. A standard is a precise measure of what will occur in a particular operation.
2. The method of establishing a standard does not determine whether it is ideal, normal, or expected.
3. A standard cost system is applicable only to process costing where the operation is repetitive; it cannot be used in a job costing situation.
4. If standards are realistic, the variances can be treated as period costs in the income statement for external purposes.
5. The material price variance is computed as the difference between actual price and standard price per unit of raw materials times the standard quantity of materials used.
6. When overhead is applied on the basis of direct labor hours, if the labor efficiency variance is unfavorable the variable overhead efficiency variance must also be unfavorable.
7. The sum of the variable overhead spending variance and the variable overhead efficiency variance is equal to under- or overapplied overhead in a variable costing system.
8. In a variable standard costing system the fixed overhead costs are included in the unit cost of the product.
9. A variance with a debit balance indicates favorable performance.
10. The difference between standard contribution margin and adjusted contribution margin in the income statement reflects an adjustment for out-of-date standards.

6-12 *(Matching).* Match the following terms and definitions.

1. Ideal standard
2. Normal standard
3. Expected actual standard
4. Material price variance
5. Material usage variance
6. Labor rate variance
7. Labor efficiency variance
8. Variable overhead spending variance
9. Overhead efficiency variance
10. Total variable overhead variance

A. The difference between the actual price and the standard price, times the actual quantity of materials purchased.
B. What should be achieved with normal workers in a normal setting.
C. The difference between actual hours worked and the hours that should have been worked at the level of production, times the standard wage rate.
D. The difference between actual hours worked and the hours that should have been worked at the level of production, times the standard variable overhead rate.
E. What should be achieved if all conditions are perfect.
F. The sum of the variable overhead spending variance and the variable overhead efficiency variance.
G. A measure of how well materials were utilized in the production process.
H. The difference between the actual variable overhead incurred and a performance budget for variable overhead.
I. An estimate of what will happen.
J. The difference between the actual hours worked times the standard wage rate and the actual payroll.

6-13 *(Essay on Theory of Standards).* The Ace Manufacturing Company, Ltd. is a medium-sized manufacturing concern producing a variety of regular stock items. The present accounting system is designed primarily for purposes of preparing the financial statements of the business and does not include any formal cost system. The general manager has relied upon periodic statements of profit and loss to indicate the efficiency of operations.

R. Jones, recently appointed as cost accountant, has suggested to the general manager that a standard cost system be installed, because it would provide more effective control over the operations of the various plant departments.

REQUIRED:
The general manager has had little experience with cost accounting systems and has asked you to explain briefly each of the following points.

A. The basic principles and theory of standard costing.
B. How standard costs are established.
C. The changes or additions that would have to be made to the present accounting system.
D. How standard costing could be used to effectively control the operations of the various plant departments. *(Canada SIA adapted)*

6-14 *(Material Variances)*. The Zeta Banding Company produces banding materials for industry. The following data apply to the production of wide bands in their Upland plant.

Standard material cost per roll of wide banding	100 ft. at $.60 per foot
Actual cost of materials purchased (120,000 ft.)	$84,000
Units produced	1,050 units
Inventory of raw materials:	
Beginning inventory	none
Ending inventory	10,000 ft.

REQUIRED:

A. Compute the material price variance.
B. Compute the material usage variance.
C. Prepare journal entries to record the raw material transactions for the Upland plant.

6-15 *(Labor Variances)*. The Lamda Lock Company produces a line of locks. The following data apply to labor costs for the company.

Standard direct labor hours per unit of production	.5 hours
Standard wage rate per hour	$6.00 per hour
Actual wages paid	$11,000
Actual direct labor hours	2,000 hours
Standard variable overhead application rate	$4.00 per hour
Number of units produced	4,400 units

REQUIRED:

A. Compute the labor rate variance.
B. Compute the labor efficiency variance.
C. Compute the variable overhead efficiency variance.
D. Prepare the journal entries to record the labor transactions for the month.

6-16 *(Variable Overhead Variances)*. The Alabaster Egg Company produces decorative eggs for sale at art fairs. The company uses a standard variable costing system. Data for the month of February follow:

Flexible budget on which the overhead standard is based:

$600 per month plus $1.50 per direct labor hour	
Standard direct labor hours per unit	.2 hours
Number of units produced	1,000 units
Actual overhead for the month	$1,000, of which $650 was fixed
Actual direct labor hours during February	220 hours

REQUIRED:

A. Compute the variable overhead spending variance.
B. Compute the variable overhead efficiency variance.
C. Compute the labor efficiency variance in hours.
D. Prepare the journal entries for overhead for the month.
E. Did the firm control the fixed overhead costs?

6-17 *(Causes of Variance).* For each of the following events indicate which variances would be affected and if the independent effect is favorable or unfavorable.

1. The material standard was based upon a test run of 100 units. Demand exceeded expectation and the number of units produced during June was much greater than the number planned.

2. The purchasing agent bought substandard material at a large savings. Because of the lower quality of material, more scrap will be produced and an additional employee must be hired to assist in the cutting operation.

3. Several rush orders were completed during the month within the standard time allotted; however, a large amount of overtime was required.

4. The wage rate increases with the cost of living index. The rate of inflation is lower than what was predicted at this point in time.

5. The plant supervisor hired some temporary, unskilled production line workers to substitute for skilled workers who were on temporary assignment at a new out-of-state plant.

6. Production control failed to schedule a new job and had to notify the customer that delivery would have to be postponed until next month.

7. To ensure an on-time completion of an important order, the plant manager hired an outside firm to clean the plant; the cleanup is usually done by the regular workers at the end of the day and is included in the labor standards. Because of this action, no overtime work was needed.

8. A power outage hit the plant for 3 hours during the mid-day shift.

9. The manager of Department A transferred to Department B, 100 units with a subcomponent that was inadequately tightened. The workers in Department B tightened the subcomponent as they performed their normal duties on the units.

10. A new quality-control inspector was unusually severe. His rejections required extra rework on the units.

6–18 *(Material and Labor Variances in a Hospital).* The Vista General Hospital has established standards to control costs for several repetitive operations. The standards for one X-ray are .3 hours at $10 per hour, plus one plate at $2.00 per plate. During 19X5, 8,000 X-rays were taken. Actual costs were:

Labor ($9.50 per hour)	$24,700
Plates ($2.25 per plate)	$18,765

REQUIRED:

A. How many hours were used in 19X5?

B. How many plates were used in 19X5?

C. Compute the price (rate) variance and efficiency (usage) variance for labor and plates. Indicate whether the variances were favorable or unfavorable.

6–19 *(Material and Labor Variances in a Hospital).* The Eastridge Community Health Center has established standards for some routine activities including certain lab tests. The standards for performing a particular lab test are:

Lab technician	.2 hours	@ $8.00	= $1.60
Materials	2 cc's	@ $1.00	= $2.00

During 19X7, 3,000 tests were performed. The tests used 650 hours and 5,800 cc's of material. Actual costs were:

Lab technician	$5,850
Material	$8,700

REQUIRED:

A. Compute the price (rate) variance and the efficiency (usage) variance for both the technicians and the material. Indicate whether the variances were favorable or unfavorable.

B. The lab technicians maintained the records of their time by type of tests performed. There are no independent checks on their time. Overall the tests show a small unfavorable technician efficiency variance. None of the tests shows a large favorable or large unfavorable variance for the year. The health center is trying to decide whether to hire another lab technician or contract outside for some of the tests. How useful will the technician efficiency variance by type of tests be for this decision? Explain.

6–20 *(Multiple-Choice Variance Computation).* The T. P. Dome Company has developed standards for its variable costs of manufacturing. The following data relate to February.

Direct material:
  Standard quantity allowed: 3 pounds per unit
  Standard cost allowed: $2.00 per pound

Quantity purchased: 260 pounds (Total cost: $532)
Quantity used: 230 pounds
Direct labor:
Standard hours allowed: 2 hours per unit
Standard wage allowed: $4.00 per hour
Actual direct labor: 165 hours (Total cost: $644)
Variable overhead:
Standard cost allowed: $3.00 per direct labor hour
Actual variable overhead incurred: $518

During February, 90 units were scheduled for production, but only 80 units were actually produced.

1. The material price variance was
a. $12 favorable
b. $12 unfavorable
c. $72 favorable
d. $72 unfavorable
e. None of the above

2. The material usage variance was
a. $20 favorable
b. $40 favorable
c. $40 unfavorable
d. $80 favorable
e. None of the above

3. The direct labor rate variance was
a. $4 favorable
b. $4 unfavorable
c. $16 favorable
d. $16 unfavorable
e. None of the above

4. The direct labor efficiency variance was
a. $16 unfavorable
b. $20 favorable
c. $20 unfavorable
d. $60 unfavorable
e. None of the above

5. The variable overhead spending variance was
a. $15 unfavorable
b. $23 unfavorable
c. $38 favorable
d. $38 unfavorable
e. None of the above

6. The variable overhead efficiency variance was
a. $15 unfavorable
b. $23 unfavorable

c. $38 favorable
d. $38 unfavorable
e. None of the above *(Canada SIA adapted)*

6-21 *(Working Back from Variances).* Standard costs have been developed for the Freeman Scott Company. The standard cost card shows the variable cost of producing one unit as follows:

Standard Cost Per Unit

Direct material	6 pounds	@ $3.00 per pound	= $18
Direct labor	2 hours	@ $4.00 per hour	= 8
Variable overhead	2 hours	@ $5.00 per hour	= 10
			$36

At the end of the first month of operations, the T-account balances were reported as shown below. There were no beginning or ending inventories.

	Dr.	*Cr.*
Materials price variance	$ 420	
Materials quantity variance		$600
Labor rate variance	$ 300	
Labor efficiency variance	$ 1,200	
Variable overhead spending variance		$750
Variable overhead efficiency variance	$ 1,500	
Variable cost of goods sold	$72,000	

REQUIRED:

A. How many units did the company produce?
B. How many pounds of material were used?
C. How many hours of labor were used during the month?
D. What was the actual labor cost?
E. What was the actual variable overhead?

6-22 *(Process Standard Costing).* The King Company manufactures a line of high-impact plastic cabinets for portable television sets. At the beginning of 19X9 they established the following standard cost per unit.

Material (8 pounds at $4.00 per pound)	$32.00
Labor (2 hours at $7.00 per hour)	14.00
Variable Overhead (2 hours at $5.00 per hour)	10.00
Total Standard Cost per unit	$56.00

At the beginning of May, there were 4,000 units in process; these units had 100% of the material and 40% of the conversion costs added. During May, 20,000 new units were started. At the end of May, 3,000 units were in process; these units had 100% of the material and 33⅓% of the conversion costs added.

Actual costs for May were:

Material (175,000 pounds)	$ 714,000
Labor (40,000 hours)	280,000
Variable Overhead	206,000
Total Actual Costs for May	$1,200,000

REQUIRED:

A. Calculate the equivalent production for materials, labor, and overhead.
B. Prepare a schedule of variances.
C. Which variances, if any, would you investigate further?

6–23 *(Labor and Overhead Variances).* The Clean Drip Company uses a standard variable cost system in its factory. The flexible budget, which serves as a standard for the Assembly Department, which assembles electric coffee pots, is:

	Budget Allowances	
	Fixed cost per month	*Variable cost per direct labor hour*
Direct Labor	—	$5.00
Overhead:		
Inpection	$1,800	$ .05
Rework labor	—	$ .25
Supervision	$3,000	—
Labor fringe benefits	$1,000	$ .30
Payroll taxes	$ 500	$ .40
Supplies	—	$ .50
Other	$1,700	$ .10

The standard labor hours for the assembly of one coffee pot is .5 hours. During the month of June the department assembled 14,000 coffee pots. Actual direct labor hours totaled 7,100. Actual departmental costs for the month were:

Direct labor	$36,210
Inspection	1,900
Rework labor	2,125
Supervision	3,300
Labor fringe benefits	2,970
Payroll taxes	3,900
Supplies	3,900
Other	2,100
	$56,405

REQUIRED:

A. Prepare a standard cost card for labor and variable overhead in the Assembly Department.

B. Calculate the labor rate variance, the labor efficiency variance, and the overhead efficiency variance.

C. Prepare a performance budget report that shows the total overhead spending variance, in total and by each cost item.

6–24 *(Calculation of Variances).* The B. Turner Company manufactures a linkage for automobile overdrives. The standard cost for this part is:

Material:	
Shaft (1 @ \$30.00)	\$30.00
Ballbearing unit (4 @ \$5.00 each)	20.00
Labor (3 hours @ \$10.00)	30.00
Variable overhead (4 machine hours @ \$2.00)	8.00
Total Standard Cost per Unit	\$88.00

During October actual production was 90 units, although the management had originally planned to produce 100 units. Actual data for October were:

Material:
  Purchases:
    100 shafts at \$32.00 each
    450 ballbearing units at \$4.80 each
  Issues:
    94 shafts
    380 ballbearing units
Labor:
  100 hours at \$9.00
  200 hours at \$11.00
Variable overhead incurred was \$775
Actual machine hours totaled 400

REQUIRED:

Prepare a schedule of the standard cost variances.

6–25 *(Setting Labor Standards).* The Alton Company is going to expand its punch press department. It is about to purchase three new punch presses from Equipment Manufacturers, Inc. Equipment Studies indicate that for Alton's intended use, the output rate for one press should be 1,000 pieces per hour. Alton has very similar presses now in operation. At the present time, production from these presses averages 600 pieces per hour.

A study of the Alton experience shows that the average is derived from the following individual outputs.

Worker	*Daily Output*
L. Jones	750
J. Green	750
R. Smith	600
H. Brown	500
R. Alters	550
G. Hoag	450
Total	3600
Average	600

Alton management also plans to institute a standard cost accounting system in the very near future. The company engineers are supporting a standard based upon 1,000 pieces per hour, the accounting department is arguing for 750 pieces per hour, and the department foreman is arguing for 600 pieces per hour.

REQUIRED:

A. What arguments would each proponent be likely to use to support his case?

B. Which alternative best reconciles the needs of cost control and the motivation of improved performance? Explain. *(CMA adapted)*

PROBLEMS

6–26 *(Computing Variances and Journal Entries).* The following standard and actual unit-cost data are for the G. Bernard Company.

	Standard Cost per Unit	*Actual Cost per Unit*
Direct materials	10 pounds @ $ .50 = $ 5.00	11 pounds @ $ .40 = $ 4.40
Direct labor	2 hours @ $3.00 = 6.00	1.9 hours @ $3.10 = 5.89
Variable overhead (based upon direct labor hours)	2 hours @ $2.00 = 4.00	1.9 hours @ $2.20 = 4.18
Total	$15.00	$14.47

During the month, G. Bernard Company produced 10,000 units of this product. There were no beginning or ending inventories.

REQUIRED:

A. Compute each of the following variances and indicate whether they are favorable or unfavorable.

1. Material price variance
2. Labor rate variance
3. Material usage variance
4. Labor efficiency variance
5. Variable overhead efficiency variance
6. Variable overhead spending variance

B. What additional information do you need to tell whether costs are out of control?

C. Prepare journal entries for the data above. (Assume that beginning and ending inventories of Raw Materials and Work-in-Process are zero.)

6-27 *(Reconstructing Journal Entries from Variances).* The Ground Gear Company produces only one product. During November the following production variances were shown.

Material price variance	\$5,000 Unfavorable
Material quantity variance	\$3,000 Unfavorable
Labor rate variance	\$2,000 Unfavorable
Labor efficiency variance	\$4,000 Favorable
Variable overhead spending variance	\$1,000 Unfavorable
Variable overhead efficiency variance	\$2,000 Favorable

During November, production consisted of 10,000 gears. There were no inventories at the beginning or end of the month. Selling price of the product was \$20 per unit. Fixed manufacturing costs amounted to \$30,000, and selling and administrative costs were \$40,000. The standard variable cost per gear is:

Material	\$ 4
Labor	4
Variable overhead	2
	\$10

REQUIRED:

A. Reconstruct the journal entries for the month.

B. Prepare an income statement for the month using the contribution margin approach.

6-28 *(Standard Variable Costing—Journal Entries and Income Statement).* Gemcote Company produces a single product called Gemcote and uses a standard cost system. Cost and revenue data for each unit are shown in the following schedule.

Per Unit
(Based on producing and selling 10,000 units)

Material: 3 quarts of Compound R @ \$3.20 =	\$9.60	
2 ounces of Compound C @ \$4.40 =	8.80	\$18.40
Direct labor:		
2 hours @ \$5.80		11.60
Overhead: Applied on the basis of direct labor (40% fixed)		8.00
General and Selling (75% fixed)		12.80
Total cost		\$50.80
Net profit		9.20
Selling price		\$60.00

All inventories are maintained at standard variable cost. Variances are closed to cost of goods sold.

Transactions for the month of April follow:

1. During April, purchases consisted of 7,000 gallons of Compound R for \$12 per gallon, 1,200 pounds of Compound C at a cost of \$70 per pound, and \$8,000 of factory supplies.

2. During April, 9,000 units of Gemcote were completed and sent to finished goods. Because of its highly perishable nature during production, no work-in-process inventory is carried from one day's production to the next. Sixty-eight hundred and fifty gallons of Compound R and 1,100 pounds of Compound C were used in production during April.

3. Hourly wage rates were 5% above the standard rate. Direct labor cost was \$103,530.

4. Factory overhead for the month was \$74,800, of which \$30,000 was fixed.

5. Selling and administrative expenses for the month were \$125,000, of which \$24,000 was variable.

6. During April, 8,000 units of Gemcote were sold at the standard selling price.

REQUIRED:

A. Assuming standard variable costing, prepare journal entries to record the transactions for April.

B. Prepare an income statement using the contribution margin approach.

6-29 *(Standard Process Costing).* The Strong Scent Company produces a liquid product used in perfume. A standard variable costing system is used with process costing. Standard material and variable conversion costs for a one-centigram vial are as follows:

Direct materials	(10 packets @ \$6.00) =	\$60.00
Variable labor	(2 hours @ \$5.00) =	10.00
Variable overhead	(2 hours @ \$2.50) =	5.00
Total		\$75.00

Material is added only at the beginning of the process, and conversion costs are added uniformly throughout the process. At the beginning of the month, there were 200 vials in process complete as to materials but only 60% complete as to conversion costs. During the month, material was added to start 500 vials of product; 400 vials were finished and sent to finished goods; and 300 vials were left in the ending inventory 40% finished as to conversion costs.

Actual costs for the month were:

Direct materials	5,200 packets @	\$6.20
Variable labor	750 hours @	\$4.90
Variable overhead		\$2,300

REQUIRED:

A. What is the total cost of the units in the beginning inventory of work-in-process?

B. Assuming a FIFO flow of goods, what is the number of equivalent units (vials) for material? For conversion costs?

C. What is the cost of the 300 units in ending inventory of work-in-process?

D. Prepare journal entries for the month setting forth all variances. Assume that beginning and ending inventories of Raw Materials are zero.

6-30 *(Computation of Variances).* The Dearborn Company manufactures Product X in standard batches of 100 units. A variable standard cost system is used. The standard costs for one batch of X follow.

Raw materials (60 pounds @ \$.45)	\$ 27.00
Direct labor (36 hours @ \$3.00)	108.00
Variable overhead (36 hours @ \$2.75)	99.00
	\$234.00

The overhead rate was based upon normal output of 240 batches.

The flexible budget for overhead is:

$$\text{Budgeted overhead per month} = \$15{,}120 + \$2.75 \text{ per direct labor hour}$$

Production for April amounted to 210 batches. There were no beginning or ending inventories. Actual data for April are:

Raw materials used	13,000 pounds
Cost of raw materials used	$ 6,110
Direct labor cost	$23,600
Actual overhead (of which $14,544 is fixed)	$35,344
Average actual variable overhead rate per hour	$ 2.60

REQUIRED:
Prepare a schedule that contains a detailed explanation of the variances between actual costs and standard costs. Indicate whether they are favorable or unfavorable. (The number of actual direct labor hours is not stated in the problem but can be computed from the data. Remember that variable overhead is applied on the basis of direct labor hours.)

(CPA adapted)

6–31 *(Job Order/Standard Cost System Variances).* Ross Shirts, Inc., manufactures short- and long-sleeved men's shirts for large stores. Ross produces a single quality shirt in lots to each customer's order and attaches the store's label to each. The standard variable costs for a dozen long-sleeved shirts are:

Direct materials (24 yards at $.75)	$18.00
Direct labor (3 hours at $7.45)	22.35
Variable overhead (3 hours at $6.00)	18.00
	$58.35

During October, Ross Shirts worked on three orders for long-sleeved shirts. Job cost records for the month disclose the following:

Lot	*Units in Lot*	*Material Used*	*Hours Worked*
30	1,000 dozen	24,100 yards	2,980
31	1,700 dozen	40,440 yards	5,130
32	1,200 dozen	28,825 yards	2,890

The following information is also available:

1. Ross purchased 95,000 yards of material during the month at a cost of $72,000.

2. Direct labor costs incurred amounted to $82,500 during October.

3. There was no work in process at October 1. During October, Lots 30 and 31 were completed. All material was issued for Lot 32 and it was 80% completed as to labor and overhead on October 31.

4. Actual variable overhead costs incurred were $63,684.

REQUIRED:

A. Compute the materials price variance for October and indicate whether it is favorable or unfavorable.

B. For each production lot and for the company as a whole compute the total amount of each of the following variances and indicate whether the variance is favorable or unfavorable; (1) material usage variance; (2) labor efficiency variance; (3) variable overhead efficiency variance.

C. Compute for the company as a whole the labor rate variance and variable overhead spending variance. *(CPA adapted)*

6–32 *(Journal Entries and Income Statement).* The Lazy Suzie Knitting Factory produces a line of mohair sweaters for distribution to wholesalers. Standards for their costs are:

Direct material: 5 skeins @ 4 ounces	$7.50
Direct labor: 2 hours @ $4.00	$8.00
Overhead: $24,300 + $2.10 per direct labor hour	
Selling expenses: $15,300 + $1.00 per unit sold	
Administrative expenses: $21,986 + $0 per unit sold	

Normal capacity is 9,000 units, or 18,000 direct labor hours per month. There were no beginning inventories in the Raw Materials, Work-in-Process, or Finished Goods Inventories.

Actual data for the month were:

Sales: 9,200 units at $30 per unit

Production: Materials were issued for 9,500 units; labor and overhead were added for 9,400 units; 9,300 units were completed and transferred to Finished Goods Inventory

Raw materials:

Purchases: 2,000 boxes of yarn (24 skeins per box) at $37.20 per box

Issues: 1,990 boxes of yarn

Direct labor: 19,850 actual hours at $4.10 per hour

Overhead:	
Variable	$42,985
Fixed	$26,320
Selling expenses:	
Variable	$ 9,300
Fixed	$15,345
Administrative expenses:	$23,500

REQUIRED:

A. Prepare journal entries for the Lazy Suzie Knitting Factory, assuming that the firm uses variable standard costing.

B. Prepare an income statement for the month. Treat all variances as period costs.

6–33 *(Comprehensive Variance Analysis).* The Pine Furniture Company uses a variable standard cost system in accounting for its production costs. The standard cost of a unit of furniture follows.

Lumber (100 feet at \$200 per 1,000 feet)	\$20.00
Direct labor (4 hours at \$2.50 per hour)	10.00
Variable overhead (60% of standard direct labor)	6.00
Total unit cost	\$36.00

Standard variable overhead was determined from the following overhead costs at different levels of activity.

Direct Labor Hours		*Overhead*
5,200		\$10,800
4,800		\$10,200
4,400		\$ 9,600
4,000	(normal capacity)	\$ 9,000
3,600		\$ 8,400

The actual unit costs for one month were as follows:

Lumber used (110 feet at \$180 per 1,000 feet)		\$19.80
Direct labor (4¼ hours at \$2.60 per hour)		11.05
Variable overhead (\$7,500 ÷ 1,200 units)		6.25
Total actual unit cost		\$37.10
Actual fixed overhead	\$3,060	

REQUIRED:

A. From the overhead data, develop the linear equation for the flexible budget.

B. Determine the variable overhead rate per direct labor hour.

C. Compute the following variances and indicate whether they were favorable or unfavorable. (Assume that beginning and ending inventories are zero.)

1. Material price variance
2. Material usage variance
3. Labor rate variance
4. Labor efficiency variance
5. Variable overhead efficiency variance
6. Variable overhead spending variance

D. Prepare journal entries for the data above. *(CPA adapted)*

6-34 *(Case Problem on Dual Standards).* Harden Company has experienced increased production costs. The primary area of concern identified by management is direct labor. The company is considering adopting a standard cost system to help control labor and other costs. Useful historical data are not available because detailed production records have not been maintained.

Harden Company has retained Finch & Associates, an engineering consulting firm, to establish labor standards. After a complete study of the work process, the engineers recommended a labor standard of one unit of production every 30 minutes or 16 units per day for each worker. Finch further advised that Harden's wage rates were below the prevailing rate of $3.00 per hour.

Harden's production vice-president thought that this labor standard was too tight and the employees would be unable to attain it. From his experience with the labor force, he believed a labor standard of 40 minutes per unit or 12 units per day for each worker would be more reasonable.

The president of Harden Company believed the standard should be set at a high level to motivate the workers, but he also recognized the standard should be set at a level to provide adequate information for control and reasonable cost comparisons. After much discussion, management decided to use a dual standard. The labor standard recommended by the engineering firm of one unit every 30 minutes would be employed in the plant as a motivation device, and a cost standard of 40 minutes per unit would be used in reporting. Management also concluded that the workers would not be informed of the cost standard used for reporting purposes. The production vice-president conducted several sessions prior to implementation in the plant informing the workers of the new standard cost system and answering questions. The new standards were not related to incentive pay but were introduced at the time wages were increased to $3.00 per hour.

The new standard cost system was implemented on January 1, 19X4. At the end of six months of operation, the following statistics on labor performance were presented to top management. (*U* designates an unfavorable variance; *F*, a favorable variance.)

	Jan.	*Feb.*	*Mar.*	*Apr.*	*May*	*June*
Production (units)	5,100	5,000	4,700	4,500	4,300	4,400
Direct labor hours	3,000	2,900	2,900	3,000	3,000	3,100
Variance from labor standard	$1,350 U	$1,200 U	$1,650 U	$2,250 U	$2,250 U	$2,700 U
Variance from cost standard	$1,200 F	$1,300 F	$ 700 F	$ 0	$ 400 U	$ 500 U

Raw material quality, labor mix, and plant facilities and conditions have not changed to any great extent during the six-month period.

REQUIRED:

A. Discuss the impact of different types of standards on motivation, and specifically discuss the effect on motivation in Harden Company's plant of adopting the labor standard recommended by the engineering firm.

B. Evaluate Harden Company's decision to employ dual standards in its standard cost system. *(CMA adapted)*

6-35 *(Comprehensive Standard Variable Cost Problem).* Mr. Beal, the president of Beal Boats, a producer of small, fiberglas boats, has asked you for assistance. Mr. Beal described his concern in the following conversation.

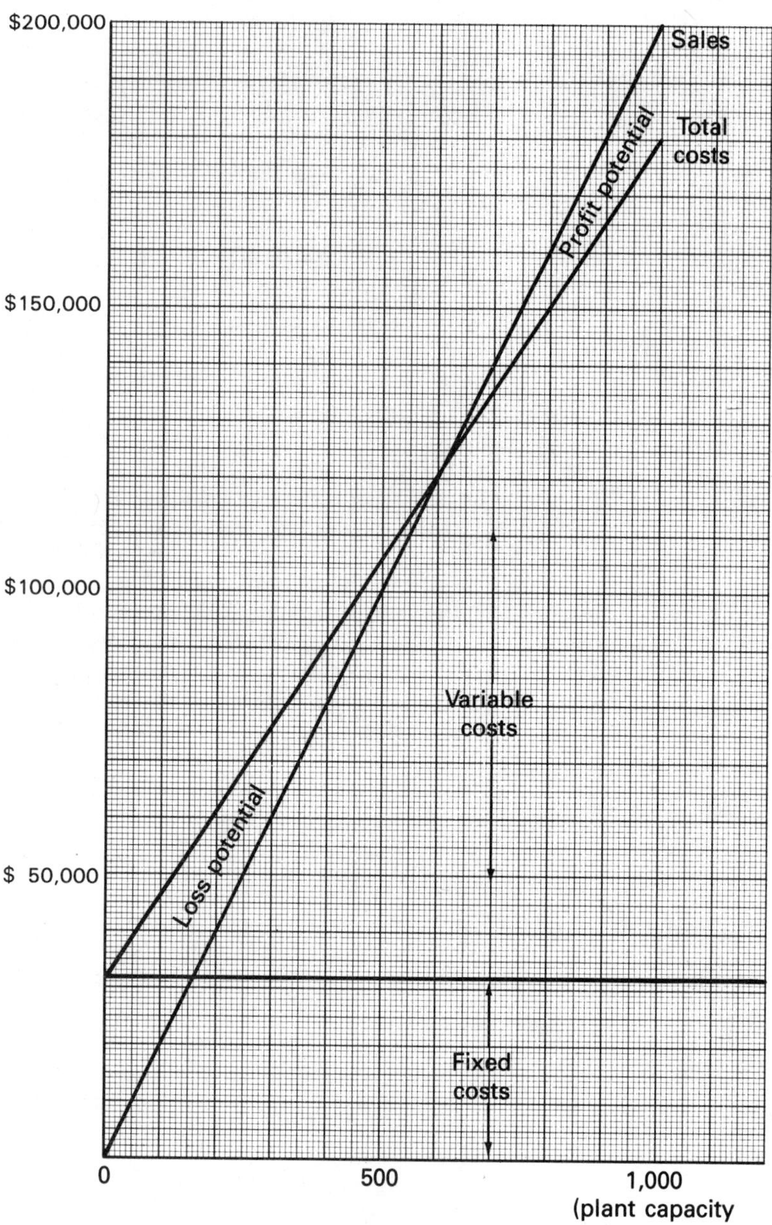
$200,000
$150,000
$100,000
$ 50,000
0
500
1,000
(plant capacity
NUMBER OF BOATS SOLD
Sales
Total
costs
Profit potential
Loss potential
Variable
costs
Fixed
costs

EXHIBIT 1

When my daughter Sally was home last month she made a study of our costs and prepared the profit-chart in Exhibit 1. She said that this chart shows what my profit should be at different levels of sales. I think she has done a great job; from this chart I can tell what my profits ought to be if we sell more boats or lose an order. She also suggested that my bookkeeper prepare a new kind of income statement that would agree with the chart. It has something to do with expensing fixed overhead costs rather than putting them in the inventory like we have been doing. Today my bookkeeper gave the new income statement for March (Exhibit 2), and the profit is about one-third of what the profit-chart says it ought to be. I know that we cut the price on one special order, but that should account for only about $2,000. We got a good buy on some substandard material but the supplier's salesperson said it would take only a little more material and a little more labor to use the substandard material. He assured me that we would save money on the deal. I haven't checked with the factory manager yet, but the sales manager assures me that he spent about what he should have."

BEAL'S BOATS
ACTUAL INCOME STATEMENT
(Variable costing format)
Month of March

Sales (1,000 boats)		$198,000
Variable costs:		
Raw material purchased	$52,640	
Less: Ending inventory	2,000	
Cost of raw materials used	$50,640	
Direct labor	61,200	
Variable overhead	24,000	
Selling commissions	19,800	155,640
Contribution margin		$ 42,360
Fixed costs:		
Overhead	$23,000	
Selling and administration	13,500	36,500
Net income		$ 5,860

Additional data:

Boats produced	1,000		
Boats sold	1,000, regular selling price $200		
Direct labor	12,000 labor hours		
Materials:	*Purchases*	*Beginning Inventory*	*Ending Inventory*
Compound R	70,000 lbs. @ $.50	0	4,000 lbs.
Finish	980 gallons @ $18	0	0

EXHIBIT 2

"Sally won't be home for a couple of months and I can't wait that long to find out what is wrong. Can you tell me if something is wrong with the income statement or the profit-chart? Here's a copy of Sally's notes on how the profit-chart was prepared. (Exhibit 3). Oh yeah, it's our policy to maintain no inventory of Work-in-Process or Finished Goods."

Dear Pop:

As you know, two materials are required to produce the boat, 60 pounds of Compound R and 1 gallon of finish. The regular market prices are $.60 per pound and $18.00 per gallon, respectively. On the average, a boat should be built and finished in ten hours of direct labor with an average wage rate of $5 per hour. Variable overhead is directly related to direct labor hours.

A sales commission of 10% of sales is paid to the sales force. A month of high activity and a month of low activity were selected to develop the cost behavior patterns in the profit-chart. The particular months were chosen because everyone agreed that costs were under control in those months. Cost data for the two months were:

	Month of Low Activity	*Month of High Activity*
Number of units sold	600	1,000
Number of units produced	600	1,000
Overhead	$34,000	$44,000
Selling and administrative expenses (excluding sales commissions)	$13,000	$13,000

Love,
Sal

EXHIBIT 3

REQUIRED:

A. Prepare a standard cost card showing the standard variable production costs for the cost of one boat.

B. State the flexible budget for each cost not included in the standard cost card.

C. Compute the variances from standard for material, labor, and variable overhead.

D. Recast the income statement into a standard variable costing format.

E. Prepare a report explaining the reason profit is not as large as it should be.

7 Overhead and Absorption Costing

In the two preceding chapters we looked at how the accountant traces variable production costs to the product to determine the variable unit cost of manufacture. In this chapter we will discuss some of the techniques the accountant uses to allocate nonvariable overhead costs to the product to satisfy the requirements of absorption costing.

DIRECT AND INDIRECT COSTS

The concepts of direct and indirect costs become important as costs are classified, segregated, and traced to specific focal points. Some costs are capable of being traced and logically associated with the unit of product. These are **direct costs.** Others, **indirect costs,** are not logically assignable to the unit of product without an allocation process. For example, in Chapter 4 we discussed direct and indirect materials. Direct materials were defined as those which the accountant could trace to a specific unit of product; indirect materials were those which the accountant could not or did not elect to trace to specific units of product.[1] The whole theory of financial accounting for external reports is predicated upon the requirement that all production costs, whether direct or indirect, must be assigned to the products and held as unexpired costs until the products are sold.

RELATING INDIRECT COSTS TO PRODUCTS AND SERVICES

When we view costs as fixed and variable, we are making a statement about the direct and indirect costing objective. Let's assume that a company has analyzed costs into fixed and variable components and developed a flexible budget for overhead costs of $y_c = \$36{,}000 + \$1.00$ (direct labor hour). This flexible budget implies that the $36,000 does not change with changes in the quantity of direct labor hours. Hence, by implication, these fixed costs are indirect in relation to the volume measure. The variable cost of $1.00 per direct labor hour varies with volume; there is an implied direct relationship between the variable cost and the volume measure.

When a firm uses variable costing, those factory costs that vary directly with production volume are assigned to product costs. In this sense the costs are directly related to the product. Fixed costs that are not directly related to the product are treated as period costs. Thus, variable costing defines direct and indirect costs in terms of product *volume.*

With absorption costing, both the variable overhead, which is directly related to the product output, and fixed overhead, which is not directly related to the product output, are assigned to the product. The fixed overhead, when it

---

[1]The unit of product is not the only possible costing objective. Management could also be concerned with tracing costs to organizational units such as departments or responsibility centers. We will discuss this tracing and how it can redefine direct and indirect costs later in this chapter and in subsequent chapters.

is included in the product cost, is an allocated indirect cost. This apportionment is made through an overhead rate that includes both fixed and variable overhead costs. In our example above the variable overhead rate is $1.00. The fixed overhead rate can be expressed by the following equation:

$$\text{Fixed Overhead Rate} = \frac{\text{Dollars of Fixed Overhead}}{\text{Measure of Production Output}}$$

As the volume measure of production output increases or decreases, the fixed overhead rate will change. To show this, let's calculate a fixed overhead rate for the firm that has a monthly flexible overhead budget of: $y_c = \$36{,}000 + \$1.00(x)$, where x represents direct labor hours. The overhead rate with absorption costing would be computed as shown in the accompanying tabulation.

	January	*February*	*March*
Production output in terms of direct labor hours	18,000	24,000	12,000
Overhead:			
Fixed costs	$36,000	$36,000	$36,000
Variable costs	18,000	24,000	12,000
Total overhead costs	$54,000	$60,000	$48,000
Overhead rate per direct labor hour			
Fixed overhead rate	$ 2.00	$ 1.50	$ 3.00
Variable overhead rate	1.00	1.00	1.00
Total overhead rate	$ 3.00	$ 2.50	$ 4.00

A close examination of this illustration shows that the total overhead rate fluctuates because of the interaction of production volume with fixed costs. The variable rate of $1.00 per hour remains constant during the three months. With variable costing the overhead rate applied to the products would always be $1.00; with absorption costing using a monthly overhead rate the overhead rate would be either $3.00, $2.50, or $4.00, depending upon the month. The $3.00, $2.50, or $4.00 could be described as an *average* total overhead cost per unit of production during the time period.

In the following sections we will look at some of the problems of determining and applying overhead rates with absorption costing. Three issues are involved in the development of overhead rates that include fixed overhead: (1) What is an acceptable measure of production volume? (2) When should the overhead rate be calculated? and (3) How many overhead rates should be used to apply the overhead costs to Work-in-Process Inventory?

Production Bases for Overhead Rates

The production base is a common denominator—a way to equate all of the units produced. If a firm produces only one product, such as a 12-ounce bottle of soft drink, the overhead rate can be determined quite simply by dividing the dollars of overhead by the number of bottles produced. This automatically results in an overhead cost per unit of product.

In firms where different items are produced, the production base must serve as a common denominator among products. Where the firm produces dissimilar products, the validity of the overhead rate rests upon the determination of a cause-and-effect relationship between the dollars spent for overhead and the base used to allocate the dollars to the product.

To clarify this point, we divide firms into two categories: those which are highly automated and those which are labor intensive. In highly automated firms the overhead costs are composed primarily of equipment costs such as power, maintenance, and depreciation charges. A measure of the time the machines are used to produce the product is a good basis for allocating overhead. These firms would typically use some form of machine-hour basis for applying overhead.

Other firms are labor intensive. The production process uses relatively few machines, and the majority of overhead dollars is composed of labor-oriented costs. In labor-oriented firms, the best common denominator among products is the amount of labor time or labor dollars spent on each product. The overhead rate in these firms is based upon direct labor hours or direct labor dollars. Of these, direct labor hours are more widely used. Most overhead costs are more closely related to the time workers spend in production than to the amount of pay workers receive. Only if labor wage rates are the same throughout the production process, or if higher-paid skills require proportionately less time, will the direct labor-hour basis and the direct labor-dollar basis of applying overhead yield approximately the same results. When this is not the case, the overhead rate based upon direct labor hours will probably describe more accurately a cause-and-effect relationship.

Where firms have dissimilar departments, they may use departmental rates. One department could use an overhead rate with a labor base while another department uses an overhead rate with a machine-hour basis. This will be discussed later in this chapter.

Timing of Overhead Rates

The second question involves the problem of *when* the overhead rate is calculated and when the overhead costs are applied to the product. An **historical overhead rate** is applied to work in process *after* the production period is completed. To illustrate the application of overhead using an historical overhead rate, let's assume that the Alene Shipbuilding Company worked on three ships during the past accounting period. Cost records indicate that total overhead of $12,000, both fixed and variable, was incurred and that

9,600 direct labor hours were consumed. These 9,600 labor hours were used as follows:

Ship 90-1A	3,000 hours
Ship 110-4A	5,000 hours
Ship 30-3B	1,600 hours

The historical overhead rate, based on actual direct labor hours for the month, is:

$$\frac{\$12{,}000}{9{,}600 \text{ hours}} = \$1.25 \text{ per direct labor hour}$$

This rate shows that, on the average, the firm spent $1.25 of overhead for each labor hour consumed. The overhead costs charged to the individual ships would be:

Ship 90-1A	3,000 hrs. × $1.25 =	$ 3,750
Ship 110-4A	5,000 hrs. × $1.25 =	6,250
Ship 30-3B	1,600 hrs. × $1.25 =	2,000
Total	9,600 hrs. × $1.25 =	$12,000

Since all actual overhead costs are charged to Work-in-Process Inventory, there will be no under- or overapplied overhead. For this reason, the Overhead Applied account is not used; Overhead Control is credited directly. At the end of each accounting period the balance of Overhead Control will be zero.

The use of an historical overhead rate has distinct drawbacks. First, the unit costs of production cannot be calculated on a timely basis because overhead cannot be charged to Work-in-Process Inventory until all production for the period has been completed and measured. Second, there are problems of seasonality. Some of the overhead costs are fixed and do not change with changes in volume. Thus, when there are seasonal fluctuations in volume, the overhead rate will fluctuate. Remember that a fixed cost is constant in total dollar amount but varies per unit as the volume changes. Third, with an historical overhead rate, there is no implicit way to ensure that overhead costs are being incurred efficiently.

To overcome the deficiencies in the historical overhead rate, many firms adopt a **predetermined overhead rate.** Before the beginning of the accounting period the firm estimates the overhead and the volume base for the year and computes a predetermined rate.

$$\text{Predetermined overhead rate} = \frac{\text{Estimated dollars of overhead for the coming accounting period}}{\text{Estimated production measurement base for the coming accounting period}}$$

The product costs via the fixed overhead rate can be affected by the choice of the predetermined activity level for the denominator. The higher the proportion of fixed costs to variable costs in overhead, the more sensitive the choice of the denominator. It is the presence of fixed costs interacting with production output that creates fluctuations in the total overhead rate.

The production output depends upon available plant volume and customer demand for the product. Using either plant volume or sales demands as their starting point, accountants typically use one of three possible volume philosophies.

1. *Practical Capacity*—This capacity is the maximum output capability of the existing plant over a long period of time. As the maximum capacity that can be achieved over an extended period of time, given the existing management policies of work week, shifts, and employee mix, the fixed overhead rate will be the minimum unit cost that the firm can achieve. In the language of the standard coster it would be an *ideal* standard.

2. *Average or Normal Volume*—This volume is that needed to meet sales expectancies over a relatively long period of time—say three to five years. This estimate allows the averaging of seasonal, cyclical variations in volume.[2] In the language of the standard coster this would be an *average* standard.

3. *Expected or Budgeted Volume*—This volume is the planned or anticipated level of activity for the coming accounting period. It corresponds to the *expected* standard.

Most firms tend to use the expected volume as the denominator base. It is easier to forecast than the others, it relates to current activities, and since it represents a volume that is likely to be achieved, the fixed overhead rate will, on the average, have fewer deviations from the historical overhead rate than the other denominator bases.

The predetermined overhead rate overcomes some of the averaging problems and lack of timeliness problems that result with use of an historical overhead rate. One additional step is necessary to make it a *standard* overhead rate. The cost estimates used in the numerator must represent what costs should be if the firm adequately controls costs. The flexible budget and the analysis that underlies it are applicable here. A "tight" flexible budget would serve as an excellent tool for estimating standard costs. For the volume estimate, the rate would be a standard rate if the base was a measure of the production activity that *should* be used to achieve the planned output.

[2]Seasonal variations are variations in output or customer demand within a fiscal or calendar year. Cyclical variations are variations in output or customer demand occurring over an economic business cycle.

Departmentalization of Overhead Costs

The third question involves departmental overhead rates. In the factory there are two broad classes of departments. **Producing departments** actually work on the product. They modify and convert the raw materials, by adding labor and overhead, into a finished product. Examples of producing departments are machining, fabricating, painting, plating, stamping, and assembly departments. Departments that support the producing departments but do not work directly on the final product are called **service departments.** Their purpose is to make the producing departments more efficient and effective. Examples of service departments include toolrooms, storerooms, timekeeping, cafeterias, maintenance, production scheduling, personnel, medical services, power generating plants, and materials handling.

In the development of an absorption costing overhead rate all overhead costs must be related to the products in the producing departments—the only departments that come in contact with the products. Therefore, service department costs must be allocated to the producing departments in order for the producing departments' overhead rates to include all production costs.

The determination of departmental overhead rates requires a multistep sequence of apportioning costs. First, all direct departmental costs are *traced* to individual producing or service departments. Then, all indirect departmental costs are *apportioned* to the individual departments. Next, the service departments must be *allocated* to the producing departments. Finally, the producing departments' fully allocated costs must be *applied* to the products via the overhead rate. Costs traced to a department, whether a producing department or a service department, are direct costs to that department. They do not require allocation. The costs that cannot be traced to a particular department, but are necessary to the department's activities, are indirect costs relative to that particular department.

For a complete illustration of the development of departmental overhead rates, let's assume that the Strident Company has two producing departments, fabrication and assembly, and two service departments, maintenance and medical services. The various parts going into the final products are machined in the fabrication department and assembled in the assembly department. Overhead costs in the overhead control subsidiary ledger are: indirect labor, employee fringe benefits, indirect materials, depreciation of machinery, depreciation of building, factory supervision, and telephone expense. Because of the nature of the production activities, management uses machine hours in the fabrication department and direct labor hours in the assembly department to apply overhead to the Work-in-Process Inventory. Statistical data necessary to allocate the indirect costs were gathered by the company and are shown in Exhibit 7–1.

Exhibit 7–2 shows the allocation of the costs to the producing departments through a worksheet. When the worksheet is completed, *all* overhead costs will be allocated to the two producing departments for the computation of departmental overhead rates. Through the departmental overhead rates, each unit of product will receive a share of overhead. In this worksheet the

Departmental Statistics	Total	SERVICE DEPARTMENTS Maintenance	Medical	PRODUCING DEPARTMENTS Fabrication	Assembly
Machine hours	6,000	None	None	4,000	2,000
Total labor hours	8,000	1,500	500	2,000	4,000
Value of equipment	$ 120,000	$ 10,000	$ 20,000	$ 50,000	$ 40,000
Square feet occupied	50,000	8,000	2,000	20,000	20,000
Number of telephones	35	7	8	10	10
Maintenance hours used	2,900	100	50	1,750	1,000
Number of employees	97	10	7	30	50

EXHIBIT 7–1
Departmental statistics of the Strident Company

four departments are shown in the column headings and the overhead costs are listed on the left. Taking the four sequential steps one at a time, let's develop the worksheet.

Step 1. All departmentally direct costs are *traced* to individual producing or service departments. Indirect labor, employee fringe benefits, and indirect materials were traced to the two service and producing departments when the costs were originally recorded by department as direct costs incurred.

Step 2. Costs that are indirect to the service or producing departments must be *apportioned* to them before service department costs are reallocated to the producing departments. The Strident Company could not trace depreciation of machinery, depreciation of building, factory supervision, and telephone expense directly to any departments. Therefore, these costs must be apportioned. This requires an allocation base. The most important criterion in choosing an allocation base is a cause-and-effect relationship. To find a cause-and-effect relationship, the accountant should ask, "Why do these costs rise and fall?" One way to ask this question is by using an analytical method such as regression analysis to test for significant relationships. In this way the cost allocation is made so that the costs are allocated relative to their causal factor.

Using the criterion of cause and effect, the following allocations were made. Depreciation of machinery was apportioned on the basis of machinery value. Since the maintenance department had $10,000 in equipment, out of a total equipment base of $120,000, it received $400 [($10,000 ÷ $120,000) × $4,800] as its share. In a similar manner, building depreciation was appor-

THE STRIDENT COMPANY
DEPARTMENTAL COST WORKSHEET
For the Year 19X4

Step	Cost	Allocation Base	Total	SERVICE DEPTS. Maintenance	SERVICE DEPTS. Medical	PRODUCING DEPTS. Fabrication	PRODUCING DEPTS. Assembly
1	Indirect labor	Direct	$28,500	$2,000	$1,500	$10,000	$15,000
1	Employee fringe benefits	Direct	12,900	500	300	5,000	7,100
1	Supplies/indirect materials	Direct	6,700	1,000	700	3,000	2,000
2	Depreciation of machinery	Value of machinery	4,800	400	800	2,000	1,600
2	Depreciation of building	Square feet occupied	6,000	960	240	2,400	2,400
2	Factory supervision	Total labor hours	3,200	600	200	800	1,600
2	Telephone expense	Number of phones	700	140	160	200	200
	Total overhead costs		$62,800	$5,600	$ 3,900	$23,400	$29,900
3	Distribute maintenance department	Maintenance hours used		($5,600)	100	3,500	2,000
	Subtotal				$4,000	$26,900	$31,900
3	Distribute medical department	Number of employees			($4,000)	1,500	2,500
	Total overhead costs					$28,400	$34,400
	Basis of overhead rate					4,000 machine hours	4,000 labor hours
4	Departmental overhead rate					$7.10 per machine hour	$8.60 per labor hour

EXHIBIT 7–2
Worksheet for the departmental allocation of costs of the Strident Company

tioned on the basis of square feet occupied, factory supervision on the basis of direct labor hours, and telephone expense on the number of instruments.

The total overhead costs of operating each of the four departments can now be determined. The sum of the direct and indirect costs of operating the maintenance department is $5,600; medical service, $3,900; fabrication, $23,400; and assembly, $29,900.

Step 3. The next step is the *allocation* of the service department costs to the producing departments. The method chosen by the Strident Company was to allocate maintenance department costs first on the basis of maintenance hours used by other departments. The maintenance department serviced the medical department as well as the two producing departments.

Thus, the medical department received an allocated share of maintenance costs. After the allocation of maintenance department costs was completed, medical department costs were allocated to the producing departments. This particular sequence was chosen because the maintenance department provided relatively more service to the medical department than the medical department provided to the maintenance department. As a general rule, the sequence should begin with the department that renders the greatest service to the greatest number of departments and continue stepwise to the departments giving the least service to other departments.[3]

The maintenance department costs in Exhibit 7–2 were allocated on the basis of maintenance hours used. The fabrication department used 1,750 hours of maintenance time, resulting in an allocation of \$3,500 [(1,750 ÷ 2,800) × \$5,600]. Notice that the allocation is based upon 2,800 hours. Excluded are the 100 hours used by the maintenance department to take care of its own equipment. If these hours were included in the allocation base, the maintenance department would be apportioned some of its own costs. These would have to be reallocated, and the reallocations would continue indefinitely.

The medical services department costs were allocated on the basis of the number of employees. The assembly department received \$2,500 of medical services costs [(50 ÷ 80) × \$4,000]. Only 80 employees were used in the allocation, not the full 97; once the costs of a service department are allocated to the producing departments, no subsequent service department costs are reallocated to it.

Step 4. The final step involves the computation of departmental overhead rates so the fully allocated costs can be *applied* to the products. The total, fully allocated costs of the fabrication department are \$28,400. Since the department used 4,000 machine hours, the overhead rate is \$7.10 per machine hour (\$28,400 ÷ 4,000 machine hours). The overhead rate for the assembly department is \$8.60 per direct labor hour (\$34,400 ÷ 4,000 direct labor hours).

The Strident Company could have chosen to use a single, **plant-wide (blanket)** overhead rate for the entire company. If a plant-wide rate had been used, the allocation of indirect costs and service department costs would not have been necessary. The single rate would have been computed by dividing total overhead by some activity base. For the Strident Company, a plant-wide rate based upon machine hours would have been \$10.47 per machine hour (\$62,800 ÷ 6,000 machine hours).

Before we leave the departmentalization of costs, one other point should be made. The worksheet in Exhibit 7–2 was motivated by the need to

[3]It should be observed that the medical department also provided services to the maintenance department, although the allocation procedure in this example does not take this into account. Our choice of allocating the maintenance department first and then allocating the medical department is not the only possibility. An alternative is to allocate the service departments directly to the producing departments without going through the sequential allocation of the service departments. Another method is to use simultaneous equations. A study of the many possible methods of allocating these costs is beyond the scope of our study in this text.

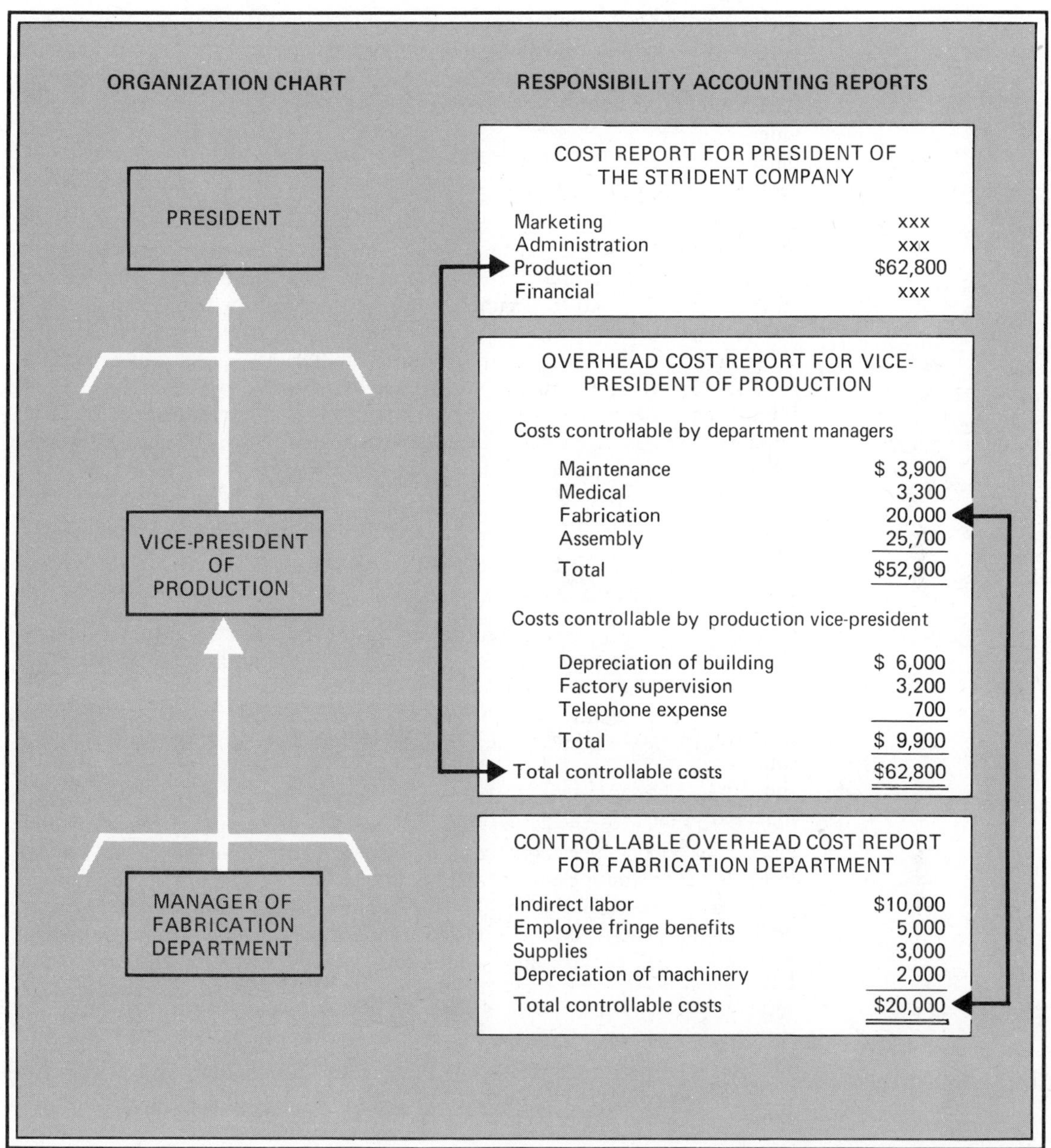

EXHIBIT 7–3
Responsibility reports of the Strident Company

have overhead rates that include *all* overhead costs. This allocation process is not useful for management planning or assessing an individual manager's performance. In responsibility accounting the individual manager should be held responsible for only those costs he can control through his own actions; certainly he cannot control the costs of other departments. For this reason a report similar to the format in Exhibit 7–3 would be used by management in the planning and control process.

STANDARD ABSORPTION COSTING ILLUSTRATED

To illustrate overhead costing under standard absorption costing and to compare it with standard variable costing, let's assume that the Forddon Company, illustrated in Chapter 6, uses standard absorption costing instead of standard variable costing. As shown by the comparative journal entries in Exhibit 7–4, the accounting for direct materials, direct labor, variable overhead, selling, and administrative expenses would not change. The only difference between the two cost flow systems is that fixed overhead has been applied to the products with absorption costing; of course, this also affects the values of the inventories and the cost of goods sold. In the sections that follow we will show how the amounts of the entries that differ between the two systems were determined.

APPLICATION OF FIXED OVERHEAD

The detailed study of overhead costs by the Forddon Furniture Company resulted in a flexible budget of y_c = \$9,600 per month + \$1.50 per direct labor hour. When the company developed their flexible budget, they also developed the volume data necessary for a fixed overhead rate. When a normal monthly forecasted output of 575 Style 10A bookcases at 8 standard direct labor hours each and 1,000 Style 11A bookshelves at 5 standard direct labor hours each was used, the normal activity level was 9,600 direct labor hours [(575 × 8 hours) + (1,000 × 5 hours)]. Using the overhead flexible budget of \$9,600 per month and \$1.50 per direct labor hour, the variable overhead rate would be \$1.50 and the fixed overhead rate would be \$1.00 per direct labor hour (\$9,600 ÷ 9,600 direct labor hours). This is a plant-wide, or blanket overhead rate. The adjusted standard cost sheets, assuming standard absorption costing, are shown in Exhibit 7–5. Except for the addition of a fixed overhead rate, they are identical to the standard cost cards in Exhibit 6–2.

During the month, 520 (equivalent) units of Style 10A and 1,200 units of Style 11A were produced. For this level of production, 10,160 standard direct labor hours are allowed [(520 × 8) + (1,200 × 5)].

APPLICATION OF OVERHEAD TO WORK-IN-PROCESS INVENTORY

In addition to the variable overhead applied to the product under variable standard costing, the Forddon Furniture Company would have applied \$10,160 of fixed overhead to the Work-in-Process Inventory. Work-in-Process Inventory is charged for the units produced, times the standard hours allowed per unit, times the standard variable overhead rate and the standard fixed overhead rate [($15,240 = 10,160 × $1.50) + ($10,160 = 10,160 × $1.00)]. The respective applied accounts accumulate the variable and fixed overhead costs charged to Work-in-Process Inventory.

DETERMINATION AND ISOLATION OF FIXED OVERHEAD VARIANCES

The actual fixed overhead costs were $9,000; fixed overhead applied was $10,160. Fixed overhead was overapplied by $1,160. The overapplied fixed overhead can be divided into two variances: a spending variance and a volume variance.

First, we can see that the Forddon Company originally planned to spend $9,600 for fixed overhead. It actually spent $9,000. The difference of $600 between the planned level of expenditure and the actual level is the **fixed overhead spending variance.** This variance was also calculated with variable costing. Expressed in formula form:

$$\text{Fixed overhead spending variance} = \left(\text{Fixed costs from standard flexible budget}\right) - \left(\text{Actual fixed overhead costs}\right)$$

For the Forddon Company this variance is:

$$\text{Fixed overhead spending variance} = (\$9{,}600 - \$9{,}000) = \$600 \text{ Favorable}$$

Second, since the Forddon Company actually produced more than the number of units planned, the fixed overhead costs were overapplied. If only the production planned for the period were produced, the Forddon Company would have had 9,600 standard direct labor hours. Instead, actual production required 10,160 standard direct labor hours, or 560 hours above plan. The 560 extra hours times the fixed overhead application rate of $1.00 per standard direct labor hour resulted in a favorable volume variance of $560 (560 × $1.00), as shown in the following computation.

$$\begin{aligned}\text{Fixed overhead volume variance} &= \left(\text{Standard fixed overhead rate} \times \text{Standard direct labor hours}\right) - \text{Fixed costs from standard flexible budget}\\ &= (\$1.00 \times 10{,}160) - \$9{,}600\\ &= \$10{,}160 - \$9{,}600\\ &= \$560 \text{ Favorable}\end{aligned}$$

The volume variance is favorable because the company applied more fixed costs than it had planned.

Type of Entry	Entries for Standard Variable Costing			Entries for Standard Absorption Costing		
Materials Purchases	Raw Materials Inventory	$ 21,000		Raw Materials Inventory	$ 21,000	
	Materials Price Variance		$ 2,100	Materials Price Variance		$ 2,100
	Accounts Payable		$ 18,900	Accounts Payable		$ 18,900
	Raw Materials Inventory	$ 15,000		Raw Materials Inventory	$ 15,000	
	Materials Price Variance	$ 1,000		Materials Price Variance	$ 1,000	
	Accounts Payable		$ 16,000	Accounts Payable		$ 16,000
Issue of Materials	Work-in-Process Inventory	$ 34,500		Work-in-Process Inventory	$ 34,500	
	Material Quantity Variance	$ 900		Material Quantity Variance	$ 900	
	Raw Materials Inventory		$ 35,400	Raw Materials Inventory		$ 35,400
Direct Labor Purchased and Consumed	Work-in-Process Inventory	$ 40,640		Work-in-Process Inventory	$ 40,640	
	Labor Price Variance	$ 1,040		Labor Price Variance	$ 1,040	
	Labor Quantity Variance	$ 960		Labor Quantity Variance	$ 960	
	Wages Payable		$ 42,640	Wages Payable		$ 42,640
Incurrence of Actual Overhead Costs	Variable Overhead Control	$ 15,400		Variable Overhead Control	$ 15,400	
	Fixed Overhead Control	$ 9,000		Fixed Overhead Control	$ 9,000	
	Various Accounts		$ 24,400	Various Accounts		$ 24,400
Application of Variable Overhead to Work-in-Process Inventory	Work-in-Process Inventory	$ 15,240		Work-in-Process Inventory	$ 15,240	
	Variable Overhead Applied		$ 15,240	Variable Overhead Applied		$ 15,240
Determination and Isolation of Variable Overhead Variances	Variable Overhead Applied	$ 15,240		Variable Overhead Applied	$ 15,240	
	Variable Overhead Efficiency Variance	$ 360		Variable Overhead Efficiency Variance	$ 360	
	Variable Overhead Spending Variance		$ 200	Variable Overhead Spending Variance		$ 200
	Variable Overhead Control		$ 15,400	Variable Overhead Control		$ 15,400
Application of Fixed Overhead to Work-in-Process Inventory	No Entry			Work-in-Process Inventory	$ 10,160	
				Fixed Overhead Applied		$ 10,160

Completion and Transfer to Finished Goods Inventory	Finished Goods Inventory	$ 88,000		Finished Goods Inventory	$ 98,000	
	Work-in-Process Inventory		$ 88,000	Work-in-Process Inventory		$ 98,000
Determination of Fixed Overhead Variances	No Entry			Fixed Overhead Applied	$ 10,160	
				Fixed Overhead Spending Variance		$ 600
				Fixed Overhead Volume Variance		$ 560
				Fixed Overhead Control		$ 9,000
Sales and Cost of Goods Sold Recognition	Cash	$122,250		Cash	$122,250	
	Sales		$122,250	Sales		$122,250
	Cost of Goods Sold	$ 80,050		Cost of Goods Sold	$ 89,150	
	Finished Goods Inventory		$ 80,050	Finished Goods Inventory		$ 89,150
Disposition of Variances	Cost of Goods Sold	$ 1,960		Cost of Goods Sold	$ 800	
	Variable Overhead Spending Variance	$ 200		Variable Overhead Spending Variance	$ 200	
	Material Price Variance	$ 1,100		Material Price Variance	$ 1,100	
	Material Quantity Variance		$ 900	Fixed Overhead Spending Variance	$ 600	
	Labor Price Variance		$ 1,040	Fixed Overhead Volume Variance	$ 560	
	Labor Quantity Variance		$ 960	Material Quantity Variance		$ 900
	Variable Overhead Efficiency Variance		$ 360	Labor Price Variance		$ 1,040
				Labor Quantity Variance		$ 960
				Variable Overhead Efficiency Variance		$ 360
Selling and Administrative Expenses	Fixed Selling Expense Control	$ 2,000		Fixed Selling Expense Control	$ 2,000	
	Variable Selling Expense Control	$ 2,800		Variable Selling Expense Control	$ 2,800	
	Administrative Expense Control	$ 3,500		Administrative Expense Control	$ 3,500	
	Various Accounts		$ 8,300	Various Accounts		$ 8,300

EXHIBIT 7–4
Comparative journal entries for standard variable costing and standard absorption costing

BOOKCASE 10A—LARGE
STANDARD COST CARD

Direct materials	
100 feet @ $.30	$30.00
Direct labor	
8 hours @ $4.00	32.00
Variable overhead	
8 hours @ $1.50	12.00
Total variable standard cost	$74.00
Fixed overhead	
8 hours @ $1.00	8.00
Total standard cost	$82.00

BOOKCASE 11A—SMALL
STANDARD COST CARD

Direct materials	
50 feet @ $.30	$15.00
Direct labor	
5 hours @ $4.00	20.00
Variable overhead	
5 hours @ $1.50	7.50
Total variable standard cost	$42.50
Fixed overhead	
5 hours @ $1.00	5.00
Total standard cost	$47.50

EXHIBIT 7–5
Absorption standard cost card for Forddon Furniture Company

The **fixed overhead volume variance** results from the application of fixed overhead costs to the products through a predetermined overhead rate. The standard fixed overhead rate is determined by dividing budgeted fixed overhead by the planned level of direct labor hours. Unless the planned number of hours is actually attained during the period, a volume variance will occur. The volume variance is favorable (overabsorbed) if more hours are worked (and therefore more fixed overhead applied) than planned. If the volume used to apply fixed overhead is less than the standard normal hours, the volume variance is unfavorable (underabsorbed).

The volume variance can be illustrated through use of a graph. The Forddon Furniture Company budgeted fixed overhead at $9,600 per month. Since production was planned at 9,600 standard normal hours for the month, the standard fixed overhead rate is $1.00 ($9,600 ÷ 9,600 hours) per standard direct labor hour. The accompanying graph shows the volume variances.

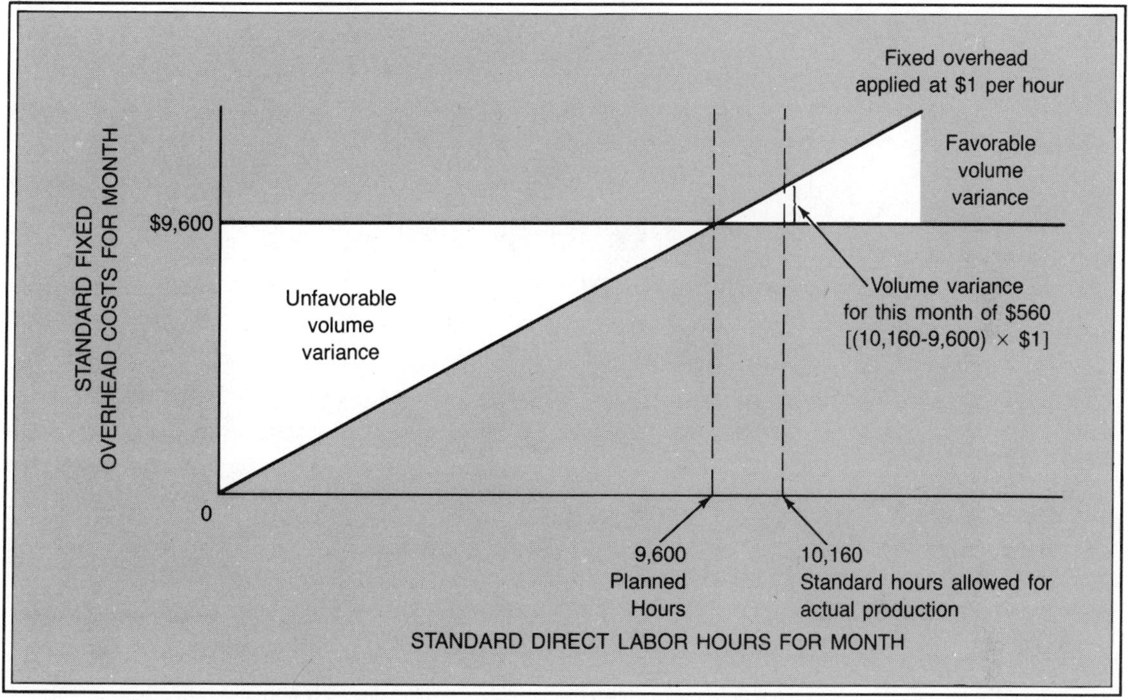

In our example the $9,600 of fixed overhead costs are assumed to remain constant over the entire production range. At the same time, the fixed overhead costs assume the characteristics of a variable cost when they are applied to work in process through the overhead rate. The application of fixed overhead is represented by a straight line from the zero cost and activity point through $9,600 of cost at the 9,600-hour level. Short of the 9,600-hour level, an unfavorable volume variance results when an insufficient amount of fixed overhead costs is applied to the products. Beyond the 9,600-hour level, more fixed overhead costs are applied than budgeted.

The calculation of the two fixed overhead variances can be summarized into the following schedule.

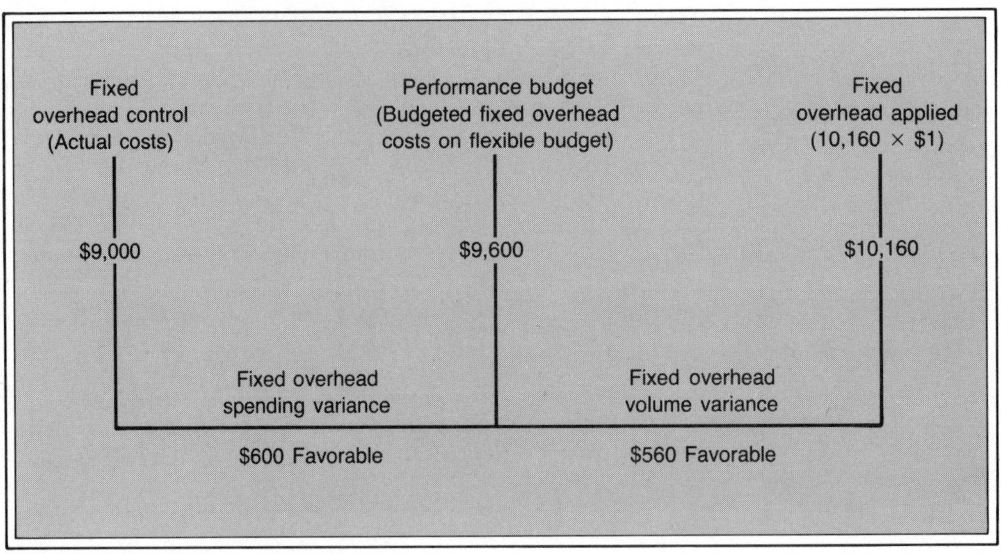

To isolate the fixed overhead variances within the accounting system, the following entry is made.

Fixed Overhead Applied	$10,160	
Fixed Overhead Spending Variance		$ 600
Fixed Overhead Volume Variance		$ 560
Fixed Overhead Control		$9,000

This entry closes the Fixed Overhead Applied and the Fixed Overhead Control accounts, transferring the differences to the two variance accounts. The variance accounts will be closed to Cost of Goods Sold in a later entry.

COMPLETION AND TRANSFER TO FINISHED GOODS INVENTORY

The journal entry under standard absorption costing transferring the goods from Work-in-Process Inventory to the Finished Goods Inventory was for $98,000. The amount of the transfer is determined by multiplying the number of units completed and transferred to Finished Goods Inventory times the standard cost from the standard cost cards, $98,000 [(500 × $82) + (1,200 × $47.50)]. The Work-in-Process account under standard absorption costing is shown in the following T-account.

Work-in-Process Inventory (Standard Absorption Costing)

Beginning Inventory	$ 0	Transferred to	
Materials	34,500	Finished Goods Inventory	$ 98,000
Direct Labor	40,640	Ending Inventory	2,540
Variable			$100,540
Overhead	15,240		
Fixed			
Overhead	10,160		
	$100,540		
Inventory	$ 2,540		

The final Work-in-Process Inventory consists of the cost of 50 units of Style 10A bookcases. They are complete as to materials but only 40% complete as to direct labor, variable overhead, and fixed overhead. The cost of the ending inventory of $2,540 is composed of the following:

Materials (50 units × $30)	$1,500
Labor (20 units × $32)	640
Variable Overhead (20 units × $12)	240
Fixed Overhead (20 units × $8)	160
Total	$2,540

The Work-in-Process Inventory under absorption costing is $160 larger than the Work-in-Process Inventory under standard variable costing (in Chapter 6) because they have absorbed $160 of fixed overhead (20 units × $8 standard fixed overhead per unit).

The cost of units transferred to Finished Goods under standard absorption costing exceeds the cost under standard variable costing by $10,000. This difference is due to the inclusion of fixed overhead under standard absorption costing [(500 × $8) + (1,200 × $5) = $10,000].

COST OF GOODS SOLD RECOGNITION

The journal entry recording the transfer of the cost of 450 units of Style 10A and 1,100 units of Style 11A from Finished Goods Inventory to Cost of Goods Sold under standard absorption costing was for $89,150. Since the Finished Goods Inventory is carried at full standard cost, the transfer to Cost of Goods Sold will be at $82 per unit for Style 10A and $47.50 per unit for Style 11A [(450 × $82) + (1,100 × $47.50)]. The cost of the units transferred under standard absorption costing will exceed the cost under standard variable costing by $9,100 [(450 × $8.00) + (1,100 × $5.00)], the amount of fixed overhead included in the standard cost. The Finished Goods Inventory account would be:

Finished Goods Inventory (Standard Absorption Costing)

Beginning Inventory	$ 0	Units Sold	$89,150
Units Completed	98,000	Ending Inventory	8,850
	$98,000		$98,000
Inventory	$ 8,850		

The cost of the final Finished Goods Inventory under standard absorption costing exceeds the cost under standard variable costing by $900 [(50 units of 10A × $8.00) + (100 units of 11A × $5.00)], owing to the inclusion of fixed overhead.

INCOME STATEMENT UNDER STANDARD ABSORPTION COSTING

There are three major differences between the income statements under standard variable costing in Exhibit 6–3 and standard absorption costing in Exhibit 7–6. First, under standard absorption costing Cost of Goods Sold is $89,150, while under standard variable costing it is $80,050. The $9,100 difference is due to the inclusion of fixed costs. Second, the additional variances computed under standard absorption costing, Fixed Overhead Spending Variance and Fixed Overhead Volume Variance, are included in the adjustments to Cost of Goods Sold. Finally, because the fixed overhead costs are included in the product costs under standard absorption costing, they are not shown separately as period costs as under standard variable costing.

The difference in net income between standard absorption costing ($24,000 in Exhibit 7–6) and standard variable costing ($22,940 in Exhibit 6–3) is $1,060. This is accounted for by the fixed overhead costs that remain in the ending inventories under standard absorption costing. This is true in this example because there were no beginning inventories. All fixed costs were matched with the revenue of the period under standard variable costing. These differences can be reconciled as follows:

Work-in-Process Inventory:		
Absorption costing	$2,540	
Variable costing	2,380	$ 160
Finished Goods Inventory:		
Absorption costing	$8,850	
Variable costing	7,950	900
		$1,060

CONVERSION FROM VARIABLE COSTING TO ABSORPTION COSTING

Rather than maintain the accounting system on standard absorption costing and lose the benefits of standard variable costing for management needs

THE FORDDON FURNITURE COMPANY
ABSORPTION COSTING INCOME STATEMENT
For the Month of January, 19X7

Sales		$122,250
Less: Standard cost of goods sold		89,150
Gross margin		$ 33,100
Adjustments for variances:		
Material price variance	$ 1,100	
Material quantity variance	(900)	
Labor price variance	(1,040)	
Labor quantity variance	(960)	
Variable overhead spending variance	200	
Variable overhead efficiency variance	(360)	
Fixed overhead spending variance	600	
Fixed overhead volume variance	560	(800)
Adjusted gross margin		$ 32,300
Less:		
Fixed selling expenses	$ 2,000	
Variable selling expenses	2,800	
Administrative expenses	3,500	8,300
Net income		$ 24,000

EXHIBIT 7-6
Income statement using standard absorption costing

during the period, the firm could merely convert the financial statements at the end of the year to what they would have been under absorption costing to satisfy external reporting requirements. This conversion requires the inclusion of an allocated share of fixed overhead in the ending Work-in-Process Inventory, Finished Goods Inventory, and Cost of Goods Sold.

Using the data from the illustration for the Forddon Furniture Company the following journal entry would be required.

Work-in-Process Inventory	$ 160	
Finished Goods Inventory	$ 900	
Cost of Goods Sold	$9,100	
Fixed Overhead Spending Variance		$ 600
Fixed Overhead Volume Variance		$ 560
Fixed Overhead Control		$9,000

This entry will convert the income statement in Exhibit 6–3 to the income statement in Exhibit 7–5. This entry would be made on a worksheet used to adjust the financial statements and *not* in the formal accounting records. The formal accounting records would be maintained under variable standard costing.

The adjusting entry must also reflect the fixed costs that should have been associated with any units in the beginning inventories of Work-in-Process and Finished Goods. For example, instead of no beginning inventories of Work-in-Process and Finished Goods, assume that the beginning inventory of Finished Goods consisted of 200 units of Style 11A bookcases. Under absorption costing the cost of the 200 units in beginning inventory should have included $1,000 (200 units × $5.00 per unit) of fixed overhead. The additional $1,000 was expensed last period (now in retained earnings) and should be in the Cost of Goods Sold of this month. The journal entry would now be:

Work-in-Process Inventory	$ 160	
Finished Goods Inventory	$ 900	
Cost of Goods Sold	$10,100	
Retained Earnings		$1,000
Fixed Overhead Spending Variance		$ 600
Fixed Overhead Volume Variance		$ 560
Fixed Overhead Control		$9,000

A SECOND ILLUSTRATION OF VARIANCE ANALYSIS UNDER ABSORPTION COSTING

As a second illustration of overhead analysis with absorption costing, let's assume that the Hang Ten Company manufactures fiberglass surfboards. Their accountant, in a cost-volume study, developed an overhead flexible budget of y_c = $18,000 per year + $2.00 (per direct labor hour). (Cost-volume studies performed for direct materials, direct labor, selling expenses, and administrative expenses are not included here.) The projected relevant range was from 450 to 625 surfboards per year. Management believed that the flexible budget represented a tight but achievable standard which could be achieved if costs and activities were well controlled.

Sales and production forecasts for the coming year were 500 surfboards. Standards for direct labor were 12 hours per surfboard. On the basis of these estimates the budgeted standard labor hours were 6,000 (500 × 12 hours). These are the hours the company *should* use to produce budgeted production. Using these estimates of labor hours, the *total* overhead rate would be:

$$\text{Total Overhead Rate} = \text{Variable Overhead Rate} + \text{Fixed Overhead Rate}$$

$$= \$2.00 + (\$18,000 \div 6,000 \text{ hours})$$

$$\$5.00 = \$2.00 + \$3.00$$

The overhead cost per surfboard would be $60.00 (12 hours × $5.00). This predetermined standard overhead rate would be used to cost all units produced during the year.

During the year the company's actual production was 520 surfboards and the actual direct labor hours consumed totaled 5,720. This represents average labor hours of 11 per unit (5,720 ÷ 520). Further, the actual overhead was $30,200, of which $18,200 was fixed costs and $12,000 was variable costs.

The following journal entry would record the incurrence of the actual overhead.

Variable Overhead Control	$12,000	
Fixed Overhead Control	18,200	
Payables, Cash,		$30,200

The following journal entry applies overhead to Work-in-Process Inventory.

Work-in-Process Inventory	$31,200	
Overhead Applied		$31,200

The overhead charged to Work-in-Process Inventory is $31,200; this was determined by multiplying the actual production of 520 units by the 12 standard hours multiplied by the overhead rate of $5.00 per hour. Notice that in this example we are using only one overhead applied account. It would be possible to use separate accounts for variable overhead applied and fixed overhead applied as we did in the previous example.

In our example the Overhead Control accounts total $30,200. This is $1,000 less than the Overhead Applied; accordingly, overhead is overapplied by $1,000. There are three reasons for this overapplied overhead. First, management anticipated spending $18,000 on fixed overhead plus $2.00 for each labor hour worked. Actual costs did not meet this budget. According to the flexible budget allowances, $18,000 for fixed costs plus $11,440 (5,720 × $2.00) for variable costs should have been spent to work 5,720 hours. Actual costs were $18,200 and $12,000, respectively.

The **spending variance,** the deviation of actual costs from a performance budget allowance, is shown in the following tabulation:

	Actual Overhead	−	*Performance Budget*	=	*Overhead Spending Variance*
Fixed Costs	$18,200		$18,000		$(200) U
Variable Costs	12,000		11,440		(560) U
Total Overhead Costs	$30,200		$29,440		$(760) U

Since the actual costs exceeded the performance budget the variances are unfavorable.

Second, the workers were efficient. According to the standards, they should have used 6,240 standard hours to produce 520 units (520 × 12); actual labor hours totaled 5,720, or 11 hours per unit. The workers, by being efficient, saved 520 hours. This would result in a favorable labor efficiency variance (not shown). It would also result in a saving of variable overhead costs of $1,040 (520 hours × $2.00 per hour), which is a favorable overhead efficiency variance.

The sum of the total overhead spending variance ($760 unfavorable) and the variable overhead efficiency variance ($1,040 favorable) is $280 favorable. This represents the **controllable variance.** Since the individual manager can control the rate of expenditure (the spending variance) and the workers activity level (the efficiency variance), these two variances are controllable by him.

Third, when management selected the capacity to determine the total overhead rate, it decided to absorb fixed costs over 6,000 direct labor hours. However, it absorbed the fixed costs over 6,240 standard direct labor hours. As a result, $18,720 of fixed costs were charged to the product, although the original plan was to charge $18,000 to the Work-in-Process Inventory. This $720 difference is called the **volume variance.** Because the fixed costs applied exceeded the budget, the volume variance is favorable.

These variances are summarized in an overhead variance analysis worksheet shown in Exhibit 7–7.

To further explore the nature of the volume variance, let's make a different assumption. Let's assume that the company based the overhead rate upon a forecasted volume of 600 units instead of 500 units. The overhead rate would be:

Total Overhead Rate	=	Variable Overhead Rate	+	Fixed Overhead Rate
	=	$2.00	+	($18,000 ÷ 7,200 hours)
$4.50	=	$2.00	+	$2.50

Also assume that the actual production and cost levels are unchanged at 520 units and $30,200, respectively. The Hang Ten Company would apply $28,080 (520 units × 12 hours × $4.50) of overhead to Work-in-Process Inventory, and overhead would be underapplied by $2,120. The spending variances and the overhead efficiency variances would be unchanged. However, the volume variance would be $2,400 ($18,000 − $15,600). The firm planned to absorb $18,000 of fixed costs over 7,200 hours, but they actually absorbed fixed costs of $15,600; the result is an unfavorable volume variance of $2,400. By comparing the two assumptions of the overhead rate, we can see that the volume variance is the result of the difference between fixed costs budgeted and fixed costs absorbed. Further, the amount of the fixed costs absorbed is dependent upon the volume measure chosen and the standard hours allowed. Because of this, the volume variance is often called the **noncontrollable variance,** since the individual manager cannot control the components used in determining the volume variance.

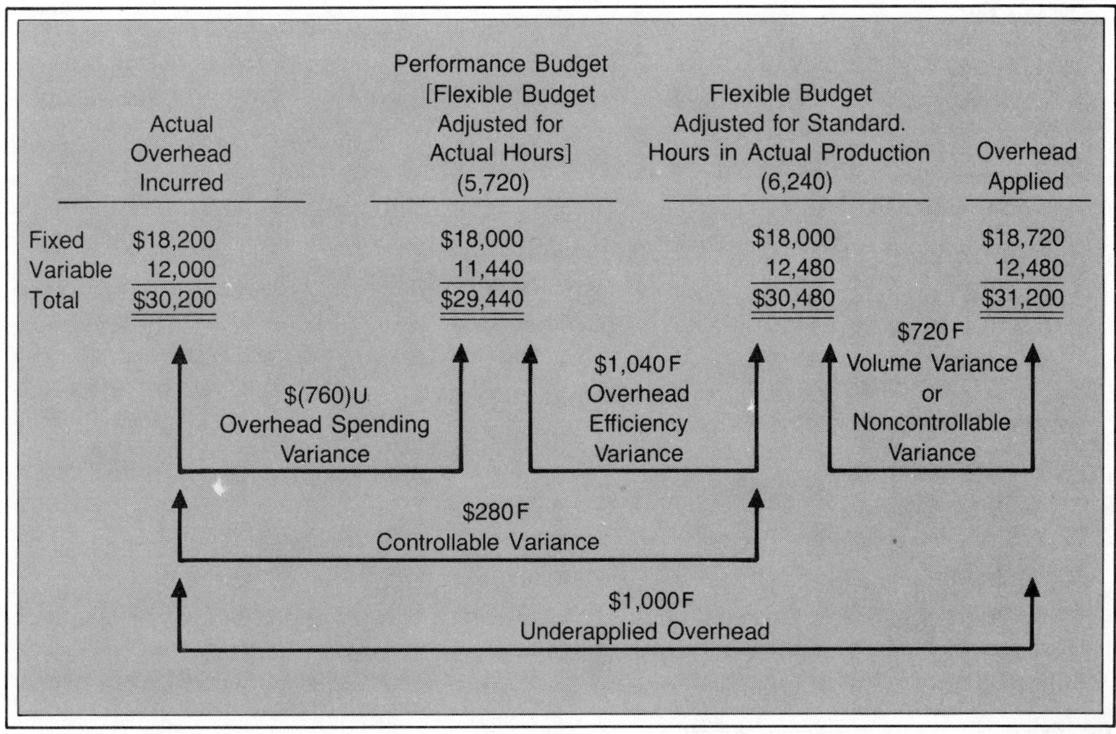

EXHIBIT 7–7
Overhead variance analysis worksheet

SUMMARY

Overhead is an indirect cost to the products. The overhead rate, overhead dollars divided by some measure of production output, is the accountant's method of allocating these costs to the product. The application of overhead to products requires the accountant to select a measure, such as units of output, machine hours, direct labor hours, or direct labor dollars, that best describes a cause-and-effect relationship between the overhead cost and the production output.

There are two types of overhead rates. The first is an historical overhead rate, where actual overhead cost is applied to the Work-in-Process Inventory after the production for the accounting period is completed. There is no under- or overapplied overhead with historical overhead rates since actual overhead is applied using an actual activity measure. The second is a predetermined overhead rate that requires the accountant to estimate both overhead costs and production output before actual production begins. When a predetermined overhead rate is used, the actual overhead costs incurred are recorded in the Overhead Control account. Overhead applied to Work-in-Process Inventory is recorded in the Overhead Applied account. The difference between the two accounts is the under- or overapplied overhead.

The selection of the predetermined overhead volume measure is important because the fixed costs in overhead will vary per unit of output with changes in output. Overhead rates may be based on three different volume measures: first, practical capacity, the maximum volume sustainable in the long run; second, normal volume, the volume necessary to meet sales demand in the long run; and third, expected or budgeted volume, the volume planned for the coming accounting period.

In firms that have a departmental organization, it is often necessary to calculate departmental overhead rates. This process requires the apportionment of indirect costs to the departments and the allocation of service department costs to producing departments. Separate overhead rates are then calculated for each producing department. The departmentalization of overhead costs is useful in determining departmental overhead rates, but it does not identify controllable and noncontrollable costs. For this reason, many firms recast their costs for management reports into a responsibility accounting format that identifies costs with the responsibility centers exercising control over them.

SUPPLEMENTARY READING

Beckett, John A. "A Study of the Principles of Allocating Costs." *The Accounting Review,* July, 1951.

Bergquist, Richard E. "Direct Labor v. Machine Hour Costing." *Management Accounting,* May, 1971.

Brummet, R. Lee. *Overhead Costing.* (Ann Arbor: Michigan Business Studies, Vol. XIII, No. 2, 1957).

Copeland, Ben R. "Analyzing Burden Variance for Profit Planning and Control." *Management Services,* January–February, 1965.

DeCoster, Don T. "Measurement of the Idle-Capacity Variance." *The Accounting Review,* April, 1966.

National Association of Accountants. *Accounting for Costing of Capacity.* New York: National Association of Accountants, 1963.

Sharp, Harold E. "Control and Management of Indirect Expenses." *Management Accounting,* February, 1973.

*Thomas, Arthur L. "On Joint Cost Allocations." *Cost and Management,* September/October, 1974.

QUESTIONS

7-1 What criteria can be used to determine an acceptable base for allocating overhead to the products?

7-2 Compare the advantages and disadvantages of predetermined overhead rates and historical overhead rates. When are the effects of the two overhead rates identical?

7-3 Define the following bases for the determination of overhead rates: *unit of product, machine hours, direct labor hours,* and *direct labor dollars.* Under what circumstances should each be used? Name an industry that might use each type of overhead base.

7-4 What is the difference between departmental overhead rates and a blanket overhead rate? What are the major disadvantages of a blanket overhead rate? Major advantages?

7-5 The establishment of departmental overhead rates requires a four-step sequential process. What are these steps? Give examples.

7-6 Define and explain the differences among *practical capacity, normal volume,* and *expected (budgeted) volume.*

7-7 "The spending variance indicates to management how well costs were controlled in comparison with the firm's plans. The volume variance has little management usefulness." Do you agree or disagree? Why?

7-8 The most important criterion in choosing an allocation base for apportioning expenses to departments is the discovery of any cause-and-effect relationships that exist. Why is this so? How can cause-and-effect relationships be determined?

7-9 What is a *service department?* Name a few in a manufacturing setting. Name a few in a university setting.

7-10 "The basic rule of decision making is to examine only those costs that differ between alternatives." This statement seems to be contradictory with the cost allocation procedures. Is it? Why or why not?

EXERCISES

7-11 *(True or False).* Indicate whether the following statements are *true* or *false.*

1. The machine-hour basis of applying overhead is appropriate where direct labor costs are relatively low and machine costs are relatively high.

2. The historical overhead rate is generally preferred over the predetermined overhead rate because it is precise and the predetermined overhead rate is only an estimate.

3. If activity fluctuates widely during a year because of seasonal variations, the historical overhead rate will provide more constant unit costs from month to month than will a predetermined overhead rate.

4. The overhead spending variance is the difference between actual overhead costs and the flexible budget adjusted for actual hours.

5. The volume variance is the difference between fixed overhead applied and the flexible budget allowance for fixed costs.

6. The volume variance will usually be larger if overhead is applied with an historical overhead rate than if it is applied with a predetermined overhead rate.

7. The distinction between direct and indirect costs is their traceability to cost objectives.

8. Allocation of overhead costs to producing departments is necessary to identify operating inefficiencies in service departments.

9. Fixed overhead rates fluctuate because the fixed costs interact with changes in production volume.

10. Practical capacity is the volume necessary to meet sales needs for the coming year.

7-12 *(Matching).* Match the following terms and descriptions.

1. Direct costs
2. Responsibility accounting
3. Indirect costs
4. Predetermined overhead rates
5. Practical capacity
6. Expected volume
7. Normal volume
8. Spending variance
9. Efficiency variance
10. Volume variance

A. Volume needed to meet sales over a three- to five-year period.
B. Estimated overhead divided by estimated direct labor hours.
C. Output capability of the existing plant in sustained operations over a long period of time.
D. The concept that an individual manager is held accountable for those activities he can directly affect.
E. Costs that can logically be associated with some costing objective.

F. Costs that must be allocated.
G. Absorption costing variance due to producing more or less units than planned.
H. Variance due to actual time worked being more or less than standard.
I. Planned level of operations.
J. Deviation of actual costs from a budget allowance.

7-13 *(Computing Fixed Overhead Variances).* The Purple Butte Company uses a standard absorption costing system to accumulate product costs. Budgeted fixed overhead is $10,000 at the normal monthly activity of 5,000 direct labor hours. The direct labor standard is 2 hours per unit at a standard wage rate of $8.00 per hour.

REQUIRED:
Compute the fixed overhead spending variances and the fixed overhead volume variances under each of the following independent conditions. Indicate whether the variances are favorable or unfavorable.
A. During September, 2,050 units were produced; actual labor hours were 4,300; and actual fixed overhead costs were $9,600.
B. During January, 2,500 units were produced; actual labor hours were 4,900; and actual fixed overhead costs were $9,800.
C. During March, 3,100 units were produced; actual labor hours were 6,200; and actual fixed overhead costs were $10,350.

7-14 *(Computing Labor and Overhead Variances with Absorption Costing).* Mike Herzog operates a small business with wide seasonal fluctuations. Budgeted overhead is $12,000 per month plus $2.00 per direct labor hour at the normal volume of 1,000 units. The standard labor cost per unit of production is 3 hours at $5.00 per hour. During June, 800 units were produced which required 2,500 direct labor hours at a total labor cost of $12,000. Actual overhead amounted to $17,200, of which $5,500 was variable.

REQUIRED:
Compute the following variances:
A. Labor efficiency variance.
B. Variable overhead efficiency variance.
C. Variable overhead spending variance.
D. Fixed overhead spending variance.
E. Fixed overhead volume variance.

7-15 *(Development of Overhead Rates).* The Eastclox Company has decided to develop a predetermined overhead rate for application of overhead to their products. The company uses a standard absorption costing system. The plant engineer gathered the following production data, all of which are within the relevant range.

Plant capacity	36,000 direct labor hours
Normal (average) level of production	24,000 direct labor hours
Expected level of production for 19X8	20,000 direct labor hours
Hours required for one unit of production	10 direct labor hours

The cost accountant, in a study of overhead costs, believed that the two most representative volume-cost years were as follows:

	Volume	*Overhead Costs*
19X4	30,000 direct labor hours	$147,000
19X7	21,000 direct labor hours	$124,500

REQUIRED:

A. Compute the predetermined overhead rate at each of the following levels:
   1. Plant capacity.
   2. Normal (average) level of production.
   3. Expected level of production for 19X8.

B. Assuming that during 19X8 the company produced 2,500 units, worked 26,000 actual hours, and incurred overhead costs of $138,500 compute the volume variance using each of the overhead rates developed in Part A above.

C. Using the data in Part B above, compute the overhead spending variance.

7-16 *(Development of Overhead Rate).* Princely Printers has been in business for one year. Because the owner is concerned with both cost control and product pricing, she calculates an historical overhead rate at the end of each month. She then uses this overhead rate to price the next month's business. She feels that this practice keeps her aware of all changes in costs and at the same time makes possible product pricing that is up-to-date. The following three months are typical of her overhead costs and volume.

	April	*August*	*December*
Direct labor hours	800	320	832
Overhead costs	$2,400	$1,680	$2,448

REQUIRED:

A. Assume that a particular printing order had the following material and labor costs:

Paper stock	$120
Labor (10 hours at $6.00)	60

Compute the price the owner of the print shop would charge a customer in the months of May, September, and January if she added a profit margin of 10% on total cost.

B. If you were a customer of Princely Printers and you could plan your printing needs in advance, when would you have your printing done? Why?

C. Devise a predetermined overhead rate that would provide Princely Printers with a constant price throughout the year. Assume that the direct labor hours total 7,200 for the year.

7-17 *(Bases for Allocation of Service Departments).* The Full Cost Company has ten service departments, as shown in the following list. It is company policy to allocate the costs of all service departments to the four producing departments in order to compute department overhead rates.

a. Building and grounds
b. Factory personnel department
c. General factory administration
d. Inventory storeroom
e. Cafeteria (operating loss)
f. Product engineering
g. Quality control
h. First aid
i. Cost accounting
j. Standby power generation plant

REQUIRED:
For each service department:

A. Indicate an order of allocation and state your reasons for choosing this order.

B. Indicate the basis of allocation (i.e., square feet, number of employees, etc.) and why this allocation basis was selected.

7-18 *(Allocation of Service Department Costs).* Culbertson Clinic, a not-for-profit medical clinic serving the low-income population of Culbertson, needs cost data to justify its grant from the state. During the budgetary allocation process last year they received a grant of $20,000; this was based upon 2,000 forecasted patient visits at an average rate of $10.

At a recent board of directors meeting the granting agency has decided to change the funding formula. No longer will grants be made on an "average" visit. The clinic is now required to determine the historical costs for the past year, by type of service provided, and then use this data in their grant request.

The director of the clinic prepared the following data relative to the clinic:

There are two service departments, occupancy and administration, and two producing departments, medical services and X-ray. Data for these four departments for the last year are:

	Occupancy	*Administration*	*Medical*	*X-ray*
Direct costs	$3,000	$3,800	$12,000	$2,500
Number of patient visits			1,500	600
Square footage		2,000	3,000	1,000
Number of personnel	1	2	6	2

Grantor rules require that occupancy be allocated on the basis of square foot occupied by a department and administration on the basis of number of personnel.

REQUIRED:

A. Show the sequential allocation of the service department costs to the producing departments.

B. Determine the cost per patient visit for the year.

C. Prepare a grant request for the coming year assuming that forecasted patient visits are 1,800 to medical services and 650 to X-ray.

7-19 *(Overhead Rates)*. The Wayne Company uses a job cost system to determine the cost of its products. A predetermined overhead rate is used to apply overhead to individual jobs. The rate is based upon direct labor hours in Department A and machine hours in Department B. The following production and cost estimates were made at the start of the year.

	Department A	*Department B*
Direct materials	$300,000	$100,000
Direct labor	$480,000	$ 80,000
Variable overhead	$240,000	$200,000
Fixed overhead	$240,000	$160,000
Machine hours	60,000	90,000
Direct labor hours	160,000	20,000

REQUIRED:

A. What are the predetermined overhead rates for both Departments A and B under absorption costing?

B. Assume that costs and production data for Job #1932 were as follows:

	Department A	*Department B*
Direct materials	$30	$20
Direct labor	$40	$15
Direct labor hours	14	4
Machine hours	2	5

How much overhead should be charged to Job #1932 under absorption costing?

C. What is the total cost for Job #1932? What is the variable cost for Job #1932?

7-20 *(Overhead Variances for Performance Assessment).* The factory manager of the Hobert Ringer Company was severely criticized by the vice-president of operations for overspending at a time when sales (and production) had dropped unexpectedly. The vice-president had studied the cost reports of every responsibility center for excessive costs. In the factory cost report he found the following data concerning overhead expenses.

OVERHEAD EXPENSES

September 19X6

	Actual	*Budget*	*Variance*
Direct labor hours	24,000	30,000	6,000 Unfavorable
Actual overhead	$80,000	$90,000	$10,000 Favorable
Overhead applied	72,000	90,000	18,000 Unfavorable
Underapplied overhead	$ 8,000	0	$ 8,000 Unfavorable

The factory manager was confused. Labor hours were exactly at standard, and he was certain that he had controlled the overhead costs to the best of his ability. He reviewed the previous cost reports and noticed that the budgeted amounts had been the same since January 1, 19X6. He came to you for assistance.

You found that the predetermined overhead rate would have been $4 if the expected level of production for the year had been 240,000 units.

REQUIRED:

A. Compute the overhead variances for September, 19X6.

B. Prepare a report to the vice-president of operations explaining the cause of the "overspending." Explain fully, using your analysis from Part A above.

7-21 *(Incomplete Data).* Three independent situations involving overhead follow. In each case you are to determine the amount where the question mark appears.

	Case A	*Case B*	*Case C*
1. Flexible budget for fixed costs	$1,000	?	$4,000
2. Flexible budget for variable costs per direct labor hour	$ 4	$ 3	$ 1
3. Planned hours for month	1,000	500	4,000
4. Budgeted overhead for month	?	?	?
5. Fixed overhead rate per direct labor hour	?	$ 4	$ 1
6. Actual direct labor hours worked	1,200	500	?
7. Standard direct labor hours allowed for units produced	1,200	600	2,800
8. Overhead applied to production (absorption costing)	?	$4,200	?
9. Overhead applied to production (variable costing)	?	?	2,800
10. Performance budget for variable overhead based on actual hours	$4,800	$1,500	$3,000
11. Actual fixed overhead	$ 800	$2,100	?
12. Variable overhead efficiency variance	$ 0	?	$ (200) U
13. Fixed overhead spending variance	?	?	$ 500 F
14. Fixed overhead volume variance	$ 200 F	?	?

7-22 *(Conversion from Variable to Absorption Costing)*. An income statement for the Glass Horseshoe Company is presented below.

GLASS HORSESHOE COMPANY
INCOME STATEMENT
For the Year 19X1

Sales (25,000 units @ $20		$500,000
Variable costs:		
Cost of sales	$300,000	
Selling expenses	50,000	350,000
Standard contribution margin		$150,000
Variances from standard		30,000
Adjusted contribution margin		$120,000
Fixed costs:		
Production	$ 60,000	
Selling and administration	40,000	100,000
Net income		$ 20,000

Beginning and ending inventories of finished goods were 5,000 and 10,000 units, respectively. Planned production in 19X1 was 20,000 units, which was identical with the actual production of the previous year; actual production in 19X1 was 30,000 units. Planned cost behavior patterns were the same in both years. During 19X0 there were no variances from standard. The variances from standard in 19X1 were due to permanent price changes.

REQUIRED:
Convert the income statement to absorption costing for external reporting.

7-23 *(Allocation of Service Department Costs).* The Constance Corporation is a manufacturing concern with three separate production departments. The following statistics have been kept concerning these departments.

	Department 1	*Department 2*	*Department 3*
Direct labor hours	40,000	25,000	22,000
Number of employees	450	220	240
Factory floor space (square feet)	12,000	6,000	4,000
Machine hours worked	3,000	8,000	5,000

The firm is trying to determine the most appropriate base with which to allocate the following costs.

Factory maintenance	$24,200
Depreciation of factory building	$33,000
Employee cafeteria	$24,300
Depreciation of machinery	$32,000
Supervisory salaries	$65,520

REQUIRED:

A. What method of allocation would you recommend for each indirect cost? Why?

B. Does the order of allocation matter in this situation (i.e., depreciation of building allocated before factory maintenance, etc.)? Why or why not?

C. Prepare a schedule that shows your allocations and the total costs charged to each of the three producing departments. Round to the nearest whole percentage.

D. Would your allocation for factory maintenance change if you discovered that it was incurred almost entirely to service the factory machinery? How?

7-24 *(Essay on Volume Measures).* The Cox Company, manufacturer of a single product, operated at 80% of normal volume in 19X8. Since Cox bases its overhead rate on normal volume, the company had a substantial amount of underapplied overhead for the period.

Early in 19X9 Cox received an order for a substantial number of units, at 30% off the regular $7.00 sales price. The controller wants to accept the order because $.80 of the total manufacturing cost of $5.00 per unit is fixed overhead and because the additional units can be produced within the company's practical capacity.

The president of Cox Company wants to know if you agree with the controller.

REQUIRED:

A. Differentiate among practical capacity, normal volume, and expected volume.

B. Discuss the financial considerations that the president should review before accepting or rejecting the order.

C. Because of this order, the financial statements of the Cox Company as of December 31, 19X9 are likely to show overapplied overhead.

1. What is overapplied overhead?

2. What are likely to be the major causes of overapplied overhead in 19X9?

3. How, if at all, should overapplied overhead be treated in the financial statements as of December 31, 19X9? *(CPA adapted)*

7-25 *(Departmentalization of Costs: Multiple Choice).* The Parker Manufacturing Company has two production departments (fabrication and assembly) and three service departments (general factory administration, factory maintenance, and factory cafeteria). The following is a summary of costs and other data for each department prior to allocation of service department costs for the year ended June 30, 19X3.

The costs of the general factory administration department, factory maintenance department, and factory cafeteria are allocated on the basis of direct labor hours, square footage occupied, and number of employees, respectively.

	Fabrication	Assembly	General Factory Administration	Factory Maintenance	Factory Cafeteria
Direct labor costs	$1,950,000	$2,050,000	$90,000	$82,100	$87,000
Direct material costs	$3,130,000	$ 950,000	—	$65,000	$91,000
Manufacturing overhead costs	$1,650,000	$1,850,000	$70,000	$56,100	$62,000
Direct labor hours	562,500	437,500	31,000	27,000	42,000
Number of employees	280	200	12	8	20
Square-footage occupied	88,000	72,000	1,750	2,000	4,800

REQUIRED:

Round all final calculations to the nearest dollar.

1. Assuming that Parker elects to distribute service department costs directly to production departments without inter-service department cost allocation, the amount of factory maintenance department costs that would be allocated to the fabrication department would be
   a. $0
   b. $111,760
   c. $106,091
   d. $91,440

2. Assuming the same method of allocation as in Item 1, the amount of general factory administration department costs allocated to the assembly department would be
   a. $0
   b. $63,636
   c. $70,000
   d. $90,000

3. Assume that Parker elects to distribute service department costs to other service departments (starting with the service department with the greatest total costs) as well as the production departments. (Note: Once a service department's costs have been reallocated, no subsequent service department costs are recirculated back to it.) The amount of factory cafeteria department costs allocated to the factory maintenance department would be
   a. $0
   b. $96,000
   c. $3,840
   d. $6,124

4. Assuming the same method of allocation as in Item 3, the amount of factory maintenance department costs allocated to the factory cafeteria would be
   a. $0
   b. $5,787
   c. $5,856
   d. $148,910

(CPA adapted)

PROBLEMS

7-26 *(Comparison of Variable and Absorption Costing)*. Raycon Corporation produces medical equipment to special order. During the month only one job was started and was in process (Job #1252). The data pertaining to the month were:

Direct materials and labor	$40,680
Variable indirect materials and labor	$12,300
Fixed overhead	$13,700
Administration and selling expenses	$ 5,250
Direct labor hours	3,950

Raycon's flexible budget for factory overhead is $12,000 + ($3.00 per direct labor hour).

REQUIRED:

A. *1.* If Raycon uses an absorption costing system and applies overhead to Work-in-Process upon an expected activity level of 4,000 direct labor hours, determine the balance in the account "Work-in-Process—Job #1252" at the end of the month.

2. If Job #1252 was finished during the month and was sold for $74,950, what was the net income for the month? Prepare an income statement that explicitly recognizes Over- or Underapplied Overhead.

B. *1.* If Raycon uses variable costing, what is the balance in the "Work-in-Process—Job #1252" account at the end of the month, assuming that overhead is applied on an expected activity level of 3,000 direct labor hours?

2. What is the net income for the month if Job #1252 was finished during the month and sold for $74,950? Prepare an income statement that explicitly recognizes Over- or Underapplied Overhead.

7-27 *(Departmental Overhead Rates)*. The Raintree Manufacturing Company uses an absorption costing system with a predetermined rate for the application of overhead to production. Overhead is applied on a machine-hour basis in Department A and a direct labor-hour basis in Department B. The firm made the following projections at the beginning of the year.

	Department A	*Department B*
Direct labor cost	$32,000	$48,750
Overhead	$36,000	$37,500
Direct labor hours	1,000	5,000
Machine hours	250	1,250

REQUIRED:

A. Compute the predetermined overhead rate for each department.

B. The cost sheet for Job #125 shows costs and activity levels as follows:

	Department A	*Department B*
Direct materials	$18	$32
Direct labor	$24	$16
Direct labor hours	3	2
Machine hours	1	12

1. How much overhead should be applied to Job #125?
2. What is the total cost of Job #125?

C. At the end of the year the actual overhead data were as follows:

	Department A	*Department B*
Direct labor cost	$36,000	$42,000
Overhead	$42,000	$36,000
Direct labor hours	1,200	4,800
Machine hours	300	1,100

Determine the amount of under- or overapplied overhead by department, and indicate if it was overapplied or underapplied.

D. What would be the historical overhead rate based upon a plant-wide overhead rate using direct labor cost as basis of application? If this historical rate is used, how much overhead would be applied to Job #125?

7-28 *(Comparison of Alternative Costing Methods).* The Soggy Company has sales of $500,000 in both May and June (100,000 units at $5.00 per unit). The following production costs apply to each of the two months.

Fixed costs per month	$300,000
Variable costs per unit	$ 1.10

Production for May was 100,000 units. Production for June was 300,000 units, the output at 100% of practical capacity. The May 1 finished goods inventory was zero.

REQUIRED:

A. Compute the cost of the ending inventory at the end of June, assuming that the company used historical (actual) absorption costing to cost the inventory.

B. Compute the cost of the ending inventory at the end of June, assuming that the company used variable costing.

C. Compute the unit cost of production during the month of May, assuming that the company used absorption costing with a predetermined overhead rate based upon practical capacity.

D. Compute the contribution margin of the Soggy Company.

E. Compute the net income for the month of May, assuming that the company used variable costing.

F. Compute the net income for the month of June, assuming that the company used absorption costing with a "normal" overhead rate based upon a normal activity level of 200,000 units.

7-29 *(Comparison of Costing Methods).* Four-Ways Incorporated had income statements prepared by four different accountants. Accountant 1 advocated historical absorption costing using actual overhead; Accountant 2 advocated historical absorption using predetermined overhead; Accountant 3 advocated standard absorption costing; and Accountant 4 advocated standard variable costing. The four income statements are presented below:

	Income Statement A	*Income Statement B*	*Income Statement C*	*Income Statement D*
Sales	$100,000	$100,000	$100,000	$100,000
Cost of sales	63,000	40,000	67,000	60,000
Margin	$ 37,000	$ 60,000	$ 33,000	$ 40,000
Variances:				
Material	$ 0	$ (3,000)	$ 0	$ (3,000)
Labor	0	0	0	0
Overhead	(8,000)	0	0	(8,000)
Total	(8,000)	(3,000)	(0)	(11,000)
Adjusted margin	$ 29,000	$ 57,000	$ 33,000	$ 29,000
Period costs	15,000	39,000	15,000	15,000
Net income	$ 14,000	$ 18,000	$ 18,000	$ 14,000

There were no price, rate, or spending variances during the month.

REQUIRED:

A. Match each accountant with the appropriate income statement.
B. Was the ending inventory larger, smaller, or equal to the beginning inventory? Explain.
C. Was production above, below, or equal to plan? Explain.
D. Determine the following amounts:
 1. Material usage variance.
 2. Variable overhead efficiency variance.
 3. Amount of fixed overhead.
 4. Amount of selling and administrative expense.
 5. If 10,000 units were sold, what was the standard absorption cost per unit?
 6. If 10,000 units were sold, what was the standard variable cost per unit?

7-30 *(Analysis of Overhead Variances—Different Costing Methods).* Hot Heater Manufacturing Company estimated the following overhead costs for 19X8.

Variable overhead:	
Indirect labor	$ 4,500
Factory supplies	2,700
Fixed overhead:	
Heat and light	800
Factory depreciation	5,200
Factory administration	8,400
	$21,600

The Hot Heater Company planned to produce 600 units using a total of 1,800 direct labor hours. Cost behavior studies have shown that changes in variable overhead costs relate closely to changes in direct labor hours.

REQUIRED:

A. Calculate the predetermined overhead rate based upon direct labor hours for:
1. Historical absorption costing
2. Standard absorption costing
3. Standard variable costing

B. Assume that actual production for 19X3 was 500 units requiring 1,600 hours. Prepare the journal entry to apply overhead costs under:
1. Historical absorption costing
2. Standard absorption costing
3. Standard variable costing

C. Assume that actual production in 19X3 was 500 units requiring 1,600 hours and actual overhead costs were:

Indirect labor	$4,000
Factory supplies	$2,200
Heat and light	$ 850
Factory depreciation	$5,200
Factory administration	$8,500

1. Determine the amount of under- or overapplied overhead under historical absorption costing.
2. Compute the usual overhead variances under standard absorption costing and prepare a report to the factory manager indicating how well she controlled her factory overhead costs during 19X3.
3. Compute the usual variances under standard variable costing and prepare a report to the factory manager indicating how well she controlled her overhead costs during 19X3.

7-31 *(Departmentalization of Costs for Decision Making).* Thrift-Shops, Inc. operates a chain of three food stores in a state that recently enacted legislation permitting municipalities within the state to levy an income tax on corporations operating within their respective municipal limits. The legislation establishes a uniform tax rate, which the municipalities may levy, and regulations which provide that the tax is to be computed on income derived within the taxing municipality after a reasonable and consistent allocation of general overhead expenses. General overhead expenses have not been allocated to individual stores previously and include warehouse, general office, advertising, and delivery expenses.

Each of the municipalities in which Thrift-Shops, Inc. operates a store has levied the corporate income tax as provided by state legislation, and management is considering two plans for allocating general overhead expenses to the stores. The 19X9 operating results before general overhead and taxes for each store were as shown in the accompanying statement.

	Store			
	Ashville	*Burns*	*Clinton*	*Total*
Sales (net)	$416,000	$353,600	$270,400	$1,040,000
Less: Cost of sales	215,700	183,300	140,200	539,200
Gross margin	$200,300	$170,300	$130,200	$ 500,800
Less local operating expenses:				
Fixed	$ 60,800	$ 48,750	$ 50,200	$ 159,750
Variable	54,700	64,220	27,448	146,368
Total	115,500	112,970	77,648	306,118
Income before general overhead and taxes	$ 84,800	$ 57,330	$ 52,552	$ 194,682

General overhead expenses were as follows:		
Warehousing and delivery expenses:		
Warehouse depreciation	$ 20,000	
Warehouse operations	30,000	
Delivery expenses	40,000	$ 90,000
Central office expenses:		
Advertising	$ 18,000	
Central office salaries	37,000	
Other central office expenses	28,000	83,000
Total general overhead		$ 173,000

Additional information includes the following:

1. One-fifth of the warehouse space is used to house the central office, and depreciation on this space is included in other central office expenses. Warehouse operating expenses vary with quantity of merchandise sold.

2. Delivery expenses vary with distance and number of deliveries. The distances from the warehouse to each store and the number of deliveries made in 19X9 are illustrated in the following tabulation.

Store	*Miles*	*Number of Deliveries*
Ashville	120	140
Burns	200	64
Clinton	100	104

3. All advertising is prepared by the central office and is distributed in the areas in which stores are located.
4. As each store was opened, the fixed portion of central office salaries increased $7,000 and other central office expenses increased $2,500. Basic fixed central office salaries amount to $10,000 and basic fixed other central office expenses amount to $12,000. The remainder of central office salaries and the remainder of other central office expenses vary with sales.

REQUIRED:

A. For each of the following plans for allocating general overhead expenses, compute the income of each store that would be subject to the municipal levy on corporation income.

Plan 1. Allocate all general overhead expenses on the basis of sales volume.

Plan 2. First, allocate central office salaries and other central office expenses evenly to warehouse operations and each store. Second, allocate the resulting warehouse operations expenses, warehouse depreciation, and advertising to each store on the basis of sales volume. Third, allocate delivery expenses to each store on the basis of delivery miles times number of deliveries.

B. Management has decided to expand one of the three stores to increase sales by $50,000. The expansion will increase local fixed operating expenses by $7,500 and require ten additional deliveries from the warehouse. Determine which store management should select for expansion to maximize corporate profits. *(CPA adapted)*

7-32 *(Comprehensive Standard Absorption Costing—Journal Entries)*. The Old Paint Glue Factory produces a glue product for home use. The company has developed standards for its manufacturing costs. The standard cost card for one case of glue follows.

Standard Cost Card One Case	
Material:	
Material H (2 liters @ $4.00)	$ 8.00
Containers (10 @ $.10)	1.00
Direct labor (.5 hours @ $8.00)	4.00
Variable overhead (.5 hours @ $2.00)	1.00
Fixed overhead (.5 hours @ $4.00)	2.00
Total standard cost	$16.00

The overhead standards are based on the flexible budget of $y_c =$ \$16,000 + \$2.00 per direct labor hour.

At the beginning of the month, inventories consisted of 1,000 liters of raw material H and 400 completed cases in the finished goods. Containers are purchased as they are used. During the month, 6,000 cases of glue were produced and transferred to finished goods. The beginning and ending Work-in-Process Inventories are zero.

Transactions for the month are listed below.

1. Purchased the following materials on account:

Material H:	20,000 liters @ $3.80	$76,000
Containers:	62,000 @ $.09	5,580
		$81,580

2. Materials issued to production during the month:

Material H:	13,600 liters
Containers:	62,000 containers

3. Direct labor for the month was 2,800 hours @ $8.10 per hour.

4. Actual overhead incurred during June was $6,500 for variable overhead and $18,000 for fixed overhead.

5. Sales for the month were 6,200 cases at $24 per case.

6. Actual selling and administrative costs were $30,000, of which $8,000 were variable.

REQUIRED:

A. Prepare all necessary journal entries for June (assume standard absorption costing).
B. Post the transactions to T-Accounts.
C. Prepare an income statement.
D. How did actual production compare with planned production?

7-33 *(Absorption and Variable Costing).* Flear Company has a maximum productive capacity of 210,000 units per year. Normal volume is 180,000 units per year. Fixed overhead is $360,000 per year, and variable production costs are $11 per unit. Variable selling expenses are $3.00 per unit, and fixed selling expenses are $242,000 per year. The unit sales price is $20.

During 19X1 the company produced 160,000 units and sold 150,000. The beginning inventory consisted of 10,000 units. Cost of the beginning inventory was $130,000 under absorption costing ($11 variable and $2.00 fixed cost per unit) and $110,000 under variable costing ($11 variable cost per unit).

REQUIRED:

A. What is the breakeven point expressed in dollar sales?
B. How many units must be sold to earn a net income of $60,000 per year?
C. How many units must be sold to earn a net income of 10% on sales?
D. Assuming that the predetermined overhead rate of $2.00 per unit was based upon normal volume, compute the cost of production under absorption costing in 19X1. Compute the volume variance under absorption costing.
E. Compute the cost of production under variable costing in 19X1. Why is there no volume variance under variable costing?
F. Assuming that the volume variance under absorption costing is added to Cost of Goods Sold, prepare income statements for 19X1 under:
  1. Absorption costing
  2. Variable costing
G. Briefly account for the difference in net income between the two income statements. *(CPA adapted)*

7-34 *(Comprehensive Problem Comparing Standard Absorption and Standard Variable Costing).* The Spiller Spline Company uses a standard costing system to account for its single product. Events for the month of December follow:

Flexible budget for overhead is $300 per month plus $2.00 per direct labor hour.
Standard material cost: $.80 per foot.
Standard direct labor wage rate: $5.00 per hour.
Planned production: 600 units.
Standard material per finished unit: 2 feet.
Standard direct labor per finished unit: .5 hours.
Materials purchased: 800 feet, $800.
Materials used: 900 feet.
Direct labor costs for December: 260 hours @ $4.50.
Overhead for the month: $900, of which $340 is fixed.
Finished units produced: 500.
Units sold: 800 @ $10.
Selling and administration expenses: $1,000, of which $320 is variable.
Beginning and ending inventories of Work-in-Process are zero.

REQUIRED:

A. Prepare journal entries and an income statement for the month's events using standard absorption costing.

B. Prepare journal entries and an income statement for the month's events using standard variable costing.

7-35 *(Journal Entries Under Standard Absorption Costing).* The Terry Company manufactures a commercial solvent that is used for industrial maintenance. This solvent is sold by the drum and generally has a stable selling price. Due to a decrease in demand for this product, Terry produced and sold 60,000 drums in December 19X6, which is three-fourths of normal volume.

The following information is available regarding Terry's operations for the month of December 19X6:

1. Standard costs per drum of product manufactured were as follows:

Materials:	
10 gallons of raw material	$20
1 empty drum	1
Total materials	$21
Direct labor:	
1 hour	$ 7
Factory overhead (fixed):	
Per direct labor hour	$ 4
Factory overhead (variable):	
Per direct labor hour	$ 6

2. Costs incurred during December 19X6 were as follows:

Raw materials:	
600,000 gallons were purchased at a cost of $1,150,000.	
700,000 gallons were used.	
Empty drums:	
85,000 drums were purchased at a cost of $85,000.	
60,000 drums were used.	
Direct labor:	
65,000 hours were worked at a cost of $470,000.	
Factory overhead:	
Depreciation of building and machinery (fixed)	$230,000
Supervision and indirect labor (semivariable)	360,000
Other factory overhead (variable)	76,500
Total factory overhead	$666,500

3. The flexible budget for supervision and indirect labor is \$90,000 + \$4.50 per direct labor hour.

REQUIRED:

Prepare journal entries for December 19X6 assuming that the firm uses absorption costing. Set forth all variances in your entries. *(CPA adapted)*

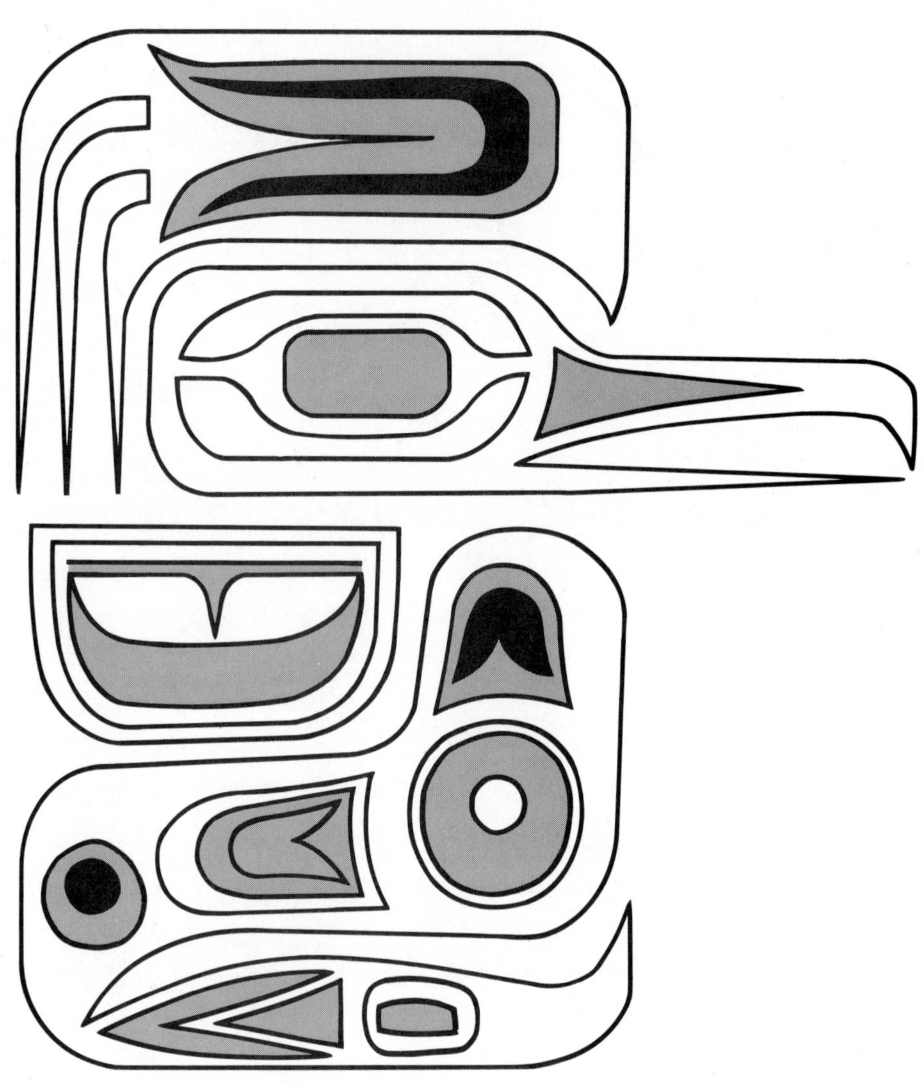

PART 3

PLANNING AND CONTROL SYSTEMS FOR DECISION IMPLEMENTATION

Budgeting: A Systematic Approach to Planning

THE PLANNING PROCESS
- *Goals*
- *Objectives*
- *Budgets*

THE CONTROL PROCESS

MASTER BUDGET
- *Profit Plan*
- *Cash Budget*
- *Capital Expenditures Budget*
- *Projected Statement of Financial Position*

TIME DIMENSIONS OF BUDGETING

DEVELOPMENT OF A MASTER BUDGET
- *Projected Profit Plan*
- *Projected Cash Budget*
- *Projected Statement of Financial Position*

NEW APPROACHES TO BUDGETING

SUMMARY

A decision involves change—an action in addition to or in place of past actions. Each decision can be treated as a unique, independent activity, but this approach can be dangerous. In practice, each decision affects other areas in the operation. A pricing decision will affect the production volume; the production volume in Department A will affect the production volume of Department B; raw material purchases will affect not only the cost of production, but also the cash flow of the firm.

Management has the responsibility of coordinating its plans into an integrated whole. Without coordination the individual managers may actually work at cross-purposes; what seems to be a good decision from one department's point of view can be a bad decision from the standpoint of the total firm. One way to provide coordination is through the budget—a summary of the planned results of individual departmental decisions, expressed in financial terms. This chapter presents an overview of the budgeting process. In the next chapter we will examine how the budgeting program relates to the control process.

THE PLANNING PROCESS

The purpose of business planning is to reduce uncertainty about the future and, through coordination of plans, to increase the chances of making a satisfactory profit. Within a planning system is the basic assumption that management can plan its activities and, through these plans, manipulate or control the relevant variables that determine the destiny of the firm. Among the variables subject to control are employee quality and quantity, capital sources, product lines, production methods, and the cost structure of the firm. Other relevant variables affect the operations of the firm but are external to it. These are not subject to manipulation by management. Management can, however, anticipate the direction and magnitude of these variables to maximize their favorable consequences or minimize their unfavorable consequences. Examples of external variables not subject to control are population changes, national economic growth, competitive activities of other firms, and governmental action.

As stated in Chapter 1, the planning process begins with the establishment of the firm's goals. The action management takes to achieve these goals leads to decisions and, in turn, to the development of the budget. An illustration of the planning process and its interrelationship with the control process is presented in Exhibit 8–1. The budget is not only an expression of management's plans, but also a basis of comparison with actual results in the control process.

Goals

Goals are statements of the desired position of the firm in the future. They are directional and motivational in nature and are seldom quantified. Generally, they are statements about the desired direction the relevant variables should

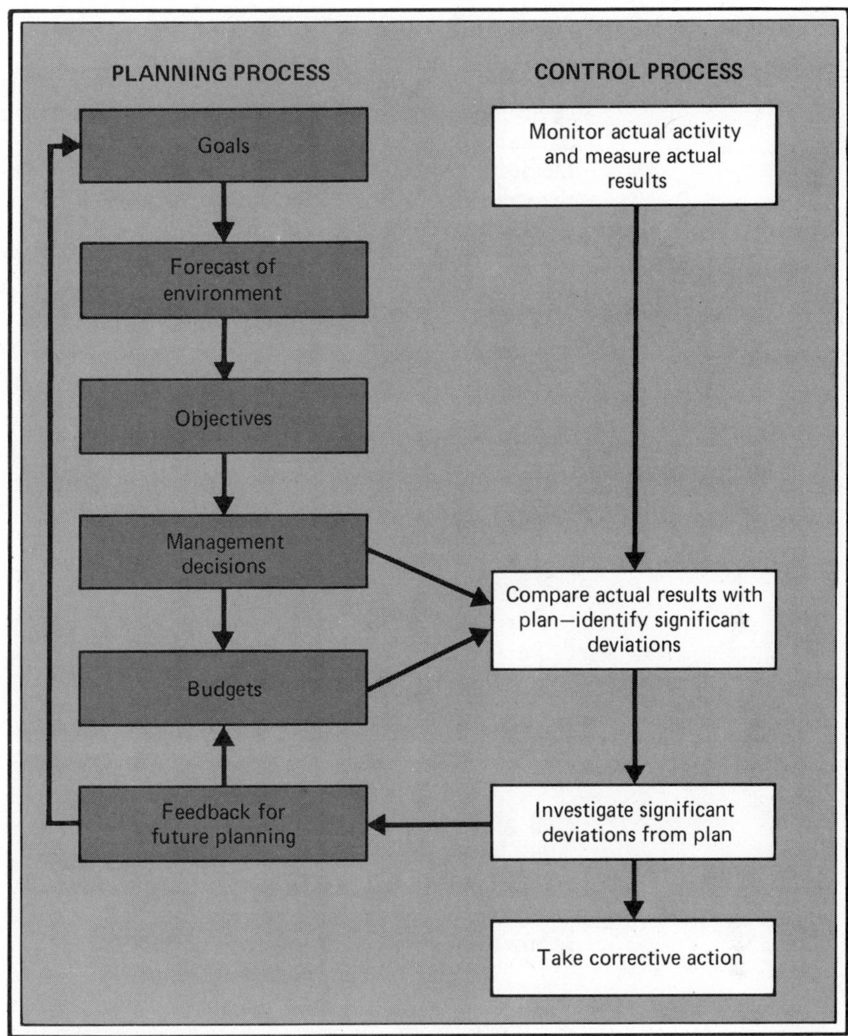

EXHIBIT 8-1
Planning and control process

take in determining the long-range destiny of the firm. A primary goal is survival of the firm. Survival, however, is dependent upon earning satisfactory profits. Thus, a fundamental goal is often stated as "an adequate profit to sustain the investment in the long run." Subgoals of this profit goal may include desired product lines, competitive position, and organizational structure. Other goals may be less profit-oriented, such as goals of community service, technological advancement, or political influence.

Objectives

Objectives provide a quantitative and time framework for the goals within the environmental constraints. They are specific performance targets and calendar dates by which desired accomplishments should be attained. For example, the profit *goal* may be to earn satisfactory profits across time so as to increase the value of the firm to the stockholders. The profit *objective,* however, may specify a 20% rate of return on investment, a 6% profit on sales, or, in some cases, a specific dollar amount of profit. Objectives provide targets that, if attained, will achieve the firm's goals.

Budgets

In a business enterprise a **budget** is the formal statement of management's goals and objectives expressed in financial terms for a specific future period of time. The budget permeates every level of activity, integrating revenue plans, expense plans, asset requirements, and financing needs. The comprehensive master budget includes and unifies each manager's activities. This coordinating role is a major, if not *the* major, function of the budget. In most firms there are many decision makers; failure to bring their plans into congruence with the firm's objectives can result in each manager's marching to a different drummer. The budget may be thought of as the network that ties the decisions of the subsystems into a firm-wide system.

THE CONTROL PROCESS

One of the basic functions of budgeting is to provide a benchmark for controlling actual performance, as shown in Exhibit 8–1. The control process involves a number of steps. First, the accounting system monitors actual performance in financial terms. A complete control system will provide actual results for each area of responsibility.

Second, actual performance is compared with the plan and any significant deviations from the plan are identified. The principle of **management by exception** suggests that as long as operations conform with the plan, the activity is in control and no intervention is required. Only exceptional or significant variances require management action. Where possible, control limits that represent the range of normal deviations from plan should be developed for each variable measured.

Third, there must be a feedback mechanism, through reports to management, to inform operating management of deviations from plans. Ideally, feedback is made as soon as possible after the activity is performed.

Fourth, action may be required. Where there is a deviation from the plan, corrective action should be taken to bring all future activities in line with the plan. Action may involve enforcing existing policies, retraining employees, or changing the manufacturing process. If the deviation is a result of a plan that is unrealistic or incorrect, the plan may have to be revised.

MASTER BUDGET

The **master budget** is expressed in financial terms and sets out management's plans for the operations and resources of the firm for a given period of time. The term *budget* alone usually refers to the master budget, a comprehensive document with many component schedules or sub-budgets. Exhibit 8–2 presents an illustration of interrelationships of the subcomponents of a master budget. The master budget is usually presented in four parts: a *profit plan* for operations, a *cash budget,* a *projected statement of financial position,* and a *capital expenditures budget.* Supporting schedules or budgets are prepared for all the necessary inputs, such as purchases of material and the costs of the various areas of responsibility. The supporting schedules should present data in as much detail and from as many different dimensions as management considers useful and economically feasible.

Profit Plan

The **profit plan** is the operating plan detailing revenue, expenses, and the resulting net income for a specific period of time. The format is usually a projected income statement. The profit plan reflects the results of the short-range decision models. It is the firm's optimal plan in light of management's expectations of the future. It is a **static budget** because only one level of sales activity is expected; all other plans are based on that level. The profit plan should be detailed by areas of responsibility within the firm and by other significant dimensions, such as product lines and sales territories.

Cash Budget

A critical resource in the firm is cash. Advance knowledge of cash needs allows the firm to provide for optimal liquidity and to find the best way of financing the business. The **cash budget** converts all planned actions into cash inflows and cash outflows so management can visualize its plans in terms of their cash impact. With knowledge of future cash status, management can plan expense payments, credit policies, the timing of capital additions, and borrowing needs.

Capital Expenditures Budget

The **capital expenditures budget** is a formal list of all approved plans for the procurement or disposition of productive assets. The budgeting process for capital expenditures differs from that of the profit plan and other parts of the master plan. As shown in Exhibit 8–2 the need for capital expenditure projects is based upon long-term sales and product forecasts. Capital expenditures are approved by *individual project* throughout the year as the need and opportu-

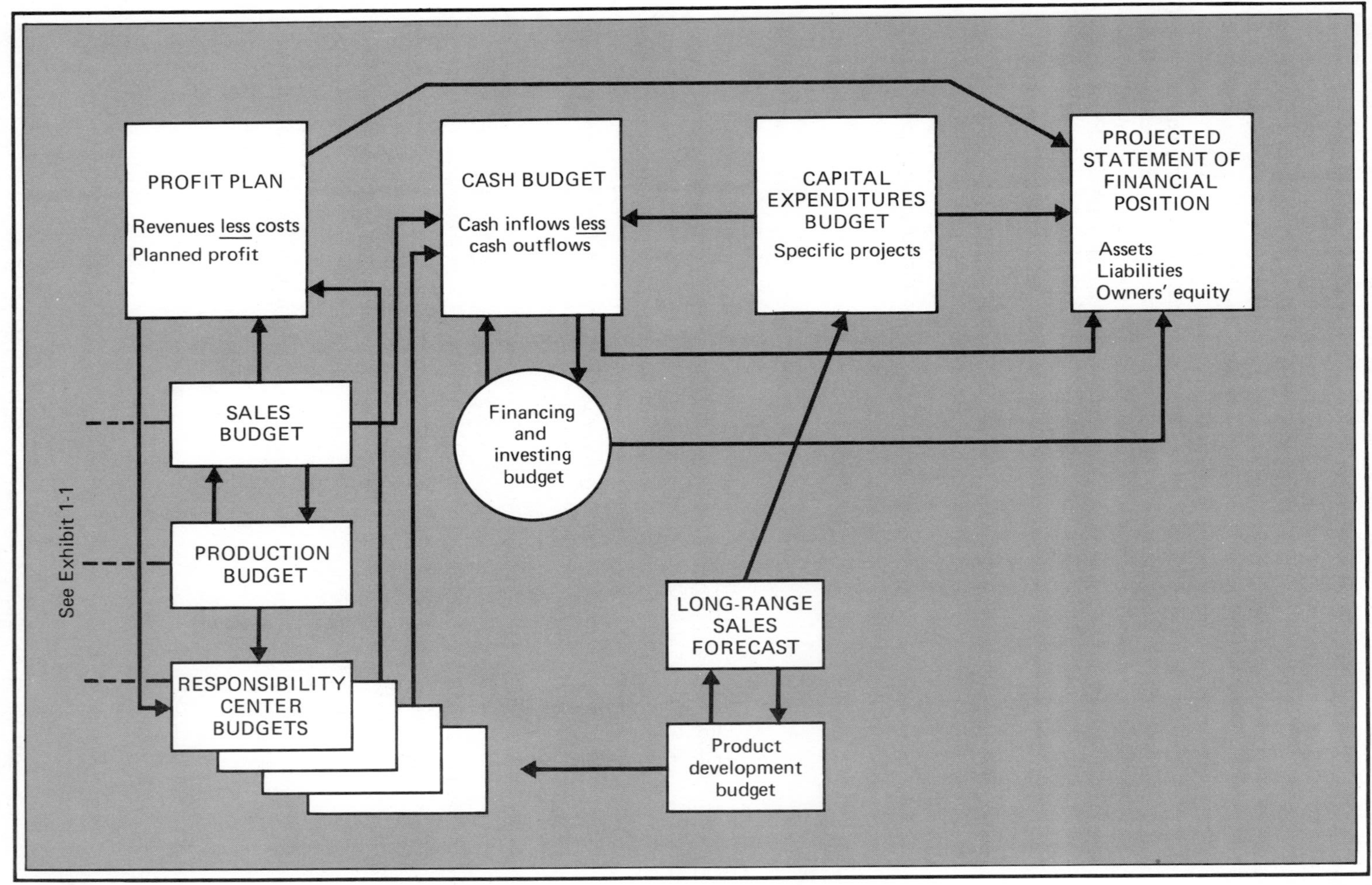

EXHIBIT 8–2
Interrelationships of subcomponents of master budget

nity arise. As proposals are developed in the organization, they are screened; those which meet the long-range decision rules are ranked in order of desirability. Final approval comes from an investment committee, often the board of directors. Many worthwhile projects may not be approved because funds are not available.

Instead of listing all specific projects, the capital expenditures budget may identify only the large projects that require a long lead time, such as a new plant or a large piece of equipment. The remainder of the capital expenditure budget may be presented as a lump sum of funds available for smaller projects. Each manager is then given authorization to approve projects of limited amounts, with an annual maximum. For example, a foreman may approve purchases of tools or small equipment of less than $100, with an annual limit of $1,000, while the plant manager may approve capital expenditures up to $1,000, with an annual limit of $10,000.

Projected Statement of Financial Position

The **Projected Statement of Financial Position** is a formal statement of the resources of the firm and their sources at the *end* of the budget period. The interrelationship of profit planning is presented in Exhibit 8–2. The projected balances of the assets and liabilities for the projected statement of financial position are the results of the many decisions made in the development of the profit plan, cash budget, and capital expenditures budget.

TIME DIMENSIONS OF BUDGETING

Exhibit 8–3 illustrates the time dimensions of budgeting. The *vertical* columns relate to particular periods of time (in this case, years) for which operating plans and resource budgets are prepared. The *horizontal* rows relate to long-range decisions for specific projects. The horizontal row entitled *continuing operations* represents the operating activities of completed long-range decisions for sales, production, and distribution. When selected Projects A, B, and C were undertaken in previous years, each became an unidentifiable part of continuing operations. Let's assume that these projects involved machines on an assembly line used to manufacture several different products. Once Machine A was installed, separate accountability was lost; its costs and revenues were commingled with those of other activities. The same was true of Machines B and C.

Other projects, such as Project D, maintain their identity and accountability for revenues and costs. An example of a project that would maintain its identity is the acquisition of a separate operating division in another geographic location, intended to provide diversity to the company. In the time-dimensional plan, Project D was added in a previous year and is expected to be replaced by Project F in five years. Project E is included in the capital expenditures budget for next year. The vertical columns represent horizons, in years. The master budget, shown in the Year 1 column, includes the profit

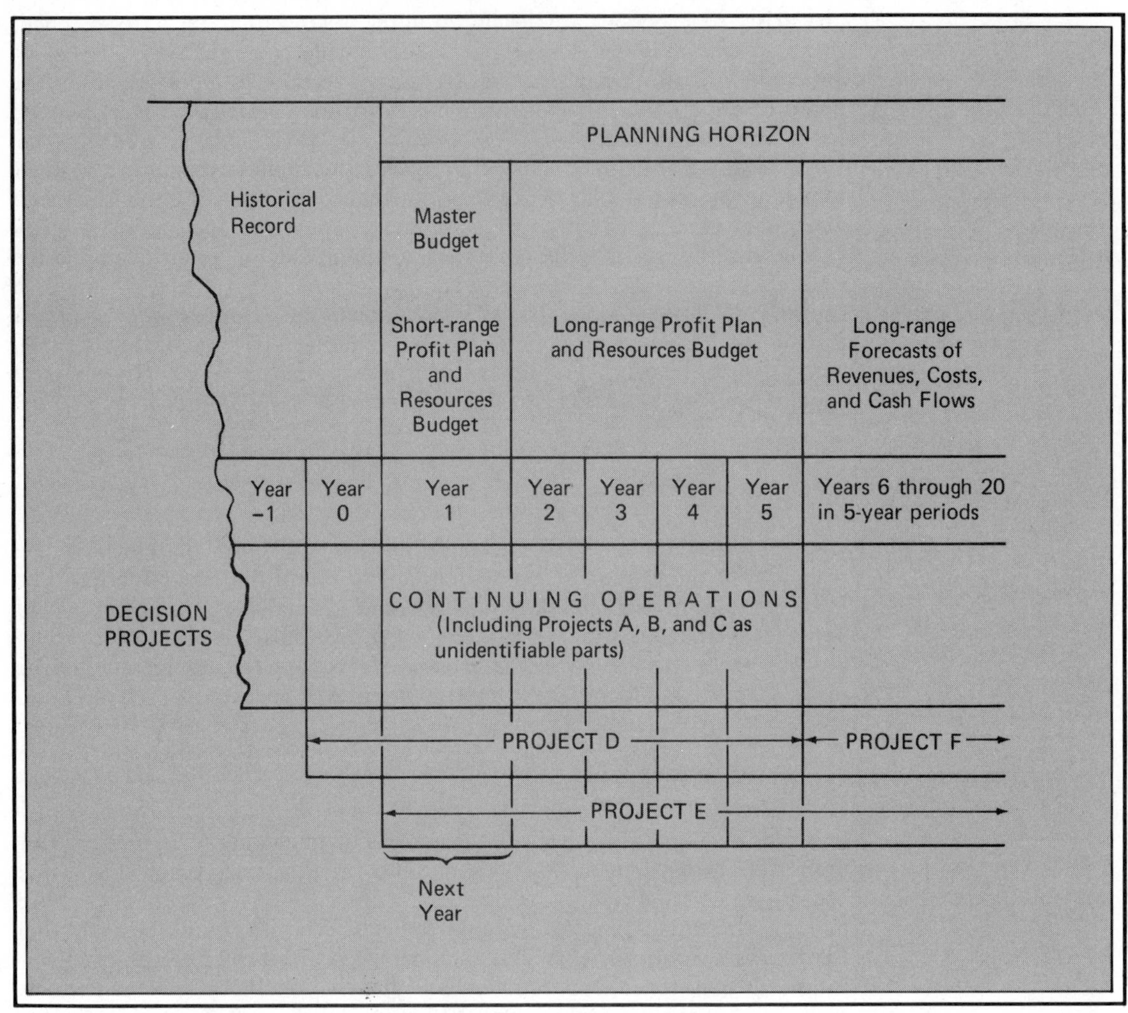

EXHIBIT 8–3
Time dimensions of budgeting

plan and resources budget for the next year. Typically, the master budget is prepared with month-by-month detail. Many firms also prepare a long-range profit plan and resources budget for the next few years (in our example, four years), but in considerably less detail than the master budget. Finally, many firms prepare long-range budgets far into the future. These are shown in the last vertical column. In one way these plans represent a broad statement of the firm's objectives in financial terms. They identify the need for new products, new plants, and other changes that may require long lead times. The long-range planning horizon for many companies, such as those involved in natural resources, is very long—often 50 to 100 years.

DEVELOPMENT OF A MASTER BUDGET

The remainder of this chapter is devoted to a step-by-step development of a master budget for the Donnell Company. Normally, the master budget would be prepared on a monthly basis; however, to keep our illustration as simple as possible, we have presented the data on a quarterly basis. We start with the basic goals of the Donnell Company, develop the various budget schedules, which culminate in the annual profit plan, cash budget, and projected statement of financial position (we have not included a capital expenditures budget).

The Donnell Company produces two sizes of plastic terrariums–a one-gallon size, which they term "small," and a five-gallon size, which they term "large." The terrariums are made from a common plastic raw material; the products differ only because of the size of the molds used in the forming process. The products are then packaged and prepared for shipment in the packing process. The sales patterns for the terrariums are highly seasonal.

Management had previously spent considerable thought on establishing the firm's long-run goals. Their fundamental goal was to earn a minimum profit that would ensure maintenance of the firm's value. To achieve this profit they had decided that they did not want to expand into new markets, that little research and development expense was justified, and that minimal promotion and advertising was needed since their outlets were assured. With their market decisions stabilized they decided to focus their attention on product quality and cost efficiency as the best way of ensuring satisfactory profits. To accomplish this they hired a quality control expert and installed both a standard cost system and a planning budget. To compensate for any negative personnel feelings about the use of standards and budgets they set a goal of minimum employee turnover or layoffs.

Projected Profit Plan

Since one of the basic purposes of the budgetary process is to remove uncertainty by projecting revenues, costs, and resources for future periods, the firm must begin by forecasting its environment. Three forecasts are necessary for a good budget: (1) the sales forecast, (2) cost behavior patterns for the firm, and (3) product costs, which are best stated in standard costs.

Step 1—Development of the Sales Forecast

A budgeting system must start with an estimate of the output demanded from the organization. In the private sector this output is measured by sales of goods and services. The amount of goods and services to be sold by a firm is a combination of what the market will absorb (*demand*) and what the productive capacity and cost structure of the firm will allow (*supply*). The sales forecast, or demand curve (a continuous curve showing a forecast of sales at different prices), provides an estimate of the potential sales market.

Sales for a particular company depend upon many factors. Too often the price factor is overemphasized. Nonprice factors, such as customer service and promotion, may have a greater impact on sales volume than price. In order to plan its sales, a firm must have knowledge of the market in which it operates. Ideally, it knows the impact of each relevant variable on product sales, including the effect of price, customer service, and promotion. It is more likely, however, that a firm has only partial information and must turn to market research to supply the needed market data.

There are two approaches to sales forecasting. One, which we will term a *macro* approach, develops a model to forecast total sales. The other projects sales by product, customer, territory, or salesperson, and then groups these individual estimates into an overall sales forecast. We will call this a *micro* approach.

MACRO APPROACH

Where a firm is fortunate enough to have both a picture of its demand curve and a knowledge of its own cost structure, the optimum sales level may be determined by economic analysis. In Chapter 12 we will examine demand curves and the economic approach to pricing. Unfortunately, the demand curve is difficult, if not impossible, to determine in practice. Seldom will a firm have reliable knowledge of more than a very small segment of the demand curve. Market research is one way to develop information about the market so that a picture of demand may be drawn.

Another method used in estimating total sales is the development of a mathematical model that describes the relationship between relevant variables and company sales. Simple regression analysis, demonstrated in Chapter 2 to measure the relationship between costs and volume, may be used to measure the relationship between sales of the firm (the dependent variable) and some relevant variable upon which sales depend (the independent variable). Ideally, changes in the independent variable will lead (precede) changes in the company sales. For example, for a company selling a product used in home construction, the number of residential building permits issued in the market area may be closely related to potential sales. If there is a good relationship between sales and building permits issued, and permits lead sales by one period, then regression analysis will provide an estimate of the *next* period's sales based upon housing starts in *this* period. Seldom, however, does one find such a clear relationship.

Where sales are influenced by more than one variable, multiple regression provides a mathematical statement of the relationship between sales and several variables. Instead of using only building permits, as in our earlier example, the firm might also use consumer disposable income and the availability of mortgage money in a multiple regression model. We have limited our discussion in this text to simple regression.

Another approach to forecasting total sales is market-share analysis. By applying a company's expected share of the market to economic forecasts of an entire market or industry, a projection of that firm's sales is obtained. For example, assume that one pharmaceutical firm's share of all drug sales in the country is 10%. Further, assume that all legitimate drug sales may be positively related to 1% of personal disposable income. The firm can use government forecasts of personal disposable income, to estimate total drug sales and forecast its share of these sales.

MICRO APPROACH

A company's sales force is a potential source of information about future sales. Salespeople can vary from order-takers with very little knowledge of the market to technical specialists who may have a better knowledge of customer needs than the customers themselves. A salesperson with good customer relationships and a knowledge of the market can often project sales with a high degree of accuracy. Total sales projections for the company can be constructed by compiling the salespeople's projections of sales by product or territory.

One possible weakness of these forecasts is that a salesperson's own goals may influence his projection. Where the projection serves as a performance measurement, the salesperson may attempt to set an easily attainable sales level with low quotas to look successful. On the other hand, if the sales projection is not a performance measurement, a salesperson's optimistic projections may reflect his hopes rather than his objective opinion of the marketplace.

In some industry settings it is also possible to ask the customers about their purchasing plans. This method would be most feasible where the number of customers is small and the customer and the firm have constant interaction. One instance of this interaction is the situation where the customer and supplier share in the design or construction of the product.

If at all possible, the sales forecast should be based upon more than one projection. A projection of total sales, through regression analysis or share of the market, for instance, should be compared with a composite estimate such as an aggregate of the sales staff's forecasts. If the projections differ significantly, further investigation may be needed.

Let's assume that the Donnell Company uses the following methods of projecting sales to produce a composite that may be called "executive opinion."

1. Sales of the company's products appear to be related to consumer disposable income in the market area of the firm. The market research staff prepared a trend analysis, fitting a line to the past data and projecting the line for the next year. The regression equation of past data is $y_s = \$40{,}000 + .0034\ (x)$, where x is the consumer disposable income. An economic forecast by the major bank in the area projected consumer disposal income for 19X2 at \$200 million. Using this estimate, sales for 19X2 were projected as follows:

$$y_s = \$40{,}000 + .0034\ (x)$$
$$y_s = \$40{,}000 + .0034\ (\$200{,}000{,}000)$$
$$y_s = \$720{,}000$$

2. The sales manager also compiled sales forecasts by each salesperson and arrived at the following range of expected sales. This range was based upon the belief that the product was so competitive that the sales price was beyond the control of the firm.

   Small terrarium @ $5.00 each—75,000 to 90,000 units
   Large terrarium @ $8.00 each—37,000 to 44,000 units

   The sales manager decided to assess the salespersons' ranges through the use of statistical decision theory. This approach seemed appropriate because of uncertainity about the future sales and the use of probability analysis is one way to deal with this uncertainty.

   Probability analysis is based upon the assumption that there is a statistical chance (probability) that some specific event will occur. When a range of possile outcomes can be expected the manager must first identify them. Second, the manager must assign probabilities to these possible outcomes. For example, if the manager were to flip a coin he might assign a 50% chance of a tails, or a probability of .5, and a 50% chance of a heads, or a probability of .5. The sum of the probabilities must always equal 1.0 since probability analysis assumes the events are all-inclusive and each event is mutually exclusive (no two events can happen at the same time). Third, the manager multiplies each of the possible outcomes by the probability of its occurance and sums the results. This sum is called the **expected value.**

   Using probability analysis the sales manager prepared the following analysis based upon subjective probabilities:

	Possible Outcomes of Sales in Units	*Probability Outcome will Occur*	*Expected Value*
Small	75,000	.30	22,500
	80,000	.40	32,000
	85,000	.20	17,000
	90,000	.10	9,000
		1.00	80,500
Large	37,000	.15	5,550
	39,000	.40	15,600
	41,000	.30	12,300
	43,000	.15	6,450
		1.00	39,900

   Using probability analysis the expected sales would be 80,500 small units and 39,900 large units.

3. The sales manager also noted that last year's sales were $675,000;

the firm's sales had been growing at approximately 7% per year. At this growth rate, next year's sales would be $722,250.

4. Upon the basis of this knowledge of the market and the established selling price, a management committee made a final sales forecast as follows:

Small terrarium 80,000 units @ $5.00 each	$400,000
Large terrarium 40,000 units @ $8.00 each	320,000
Total sales forecast	$720,000

5. The sales of the company's products are highly seasonal. The following historical pattern of sales is expected to continue into 19X2.

Quarter	Small Terrarium	Large Terrarium
1	10%	20%
2	20%	15%
3	60%	50%
4	10%	15%
	100%	100%

It was decided to use this pattern in the budget estimates.

Step 2—Development of Cost Behavior Patterns by Responsibility Area

Effective planning and control systems are structured around the implicit or explicit areas of responsibility within the organization. Responsibility areas may be departments (drilling department or maintenance department), product lines (pickles or mustard), territories (West or South), or any other type of identifiable unit or combination of units. The specific types of responsibility areas depend upon the nature of the firm and its activities.

Ideally, the budgetary system is tailored to the relevant organization level and the particular individual involved. Budgetary reports should include the specific revenues and costs over which the manager has control. A cost or benefit is controllable by an individual if it is directly affected by his decisions, regardless of how the cost or benefit is actually accounted for within the data system. For example, if a salesperson accepts a rush order that requires exceptional production costs, such as additional setups and overtime, the cost report for his marketing unit should bear the additional production costs. The production department has no control over the delivery date that gave rise to the additional costs. Care must be taken, however; excessive zeal in pinpointing responsibility may lead to interdepartmental conflict that is more detrimental to the company than lack of control over the particular cost. Where control is shared, the assignment of responsibility must be decided by the superior who is responsible for the common activity. One overriding principle is that arbitrary allocations of costs should not enter into a responsibility cost system.

We are using the term **responsibility center** in a broad sense. It could be as small as an individual machine or as large as the Chevrolet division of General Motors. It could be a sales department in a department store, a service department, a specific production line, a warehouse unit, a group of salesmen, or a tax section in the accounting department. Size is not the criterion for development of a responsibility center. The important criteria are (1) that a subdivision relevant to operating performance is separable and identifiable, and (2) that there are relevant measures of performance.

Accountants usually classify responsibility centers into three classes: cost centers, profit or contribution margin centers, and investment centers. Each class has different characteristics in regard to the financial data available for performance assessment.

COST CENTERS

A **cost center** is a responsibility center where costs (expenses) are the principal planning and control data. Performance is assessed by comparing the actual expenses with the performance budget, which shows the expenses the center should have incurred, given their actual activity. Any variances between actual and budgeted expenses are the primary focus of management assessment. In firms where the budgetary process is underdeveloped, the control data may consist of a comparison of current expenses with past expenses.

It is difficult to assess the effectiveness and efficiency of a cost center, even with a budget, because the financial impact of decisions is measured only by costs. There is no corresponding *financial* measure of what the cost center accomplished. If not done carefully, the analysis of a cost center may lead to the assumption that "the best cost center is the one that spends the least." This attitude ignores benefits contributed by the cost center to the overall firm.

Because no financial benefits are traced to cost centers, most firms mix financial and nonfinancial data in performance assessment. The consumption of the department is measured in financial terms—costs, whereas the benefits are measured in nonfinancial terms—number of units produced, number of customers waited on, or number of invoices processed, for example. It is impossible to determine whether the efficiency of the cost center is acceptable without relating the financial and nonfinancial data. Comparison with the budget will tell whether actual performance conformed with planned expenditures, but it will not tell whether this performance was effective.

PROFIT OR CONTRIBUTION MARGIN CENTERS

In a **profit center,** or **contribution margin center,** both cost and revenue data are measurable in financial terms, which provides greater scope in assessing performance. The profit center is more sophisticated, in terms of management planning and control potential, than a cost center, where only costs are measurable. Because outputs as well as inputs may be measured in a profit center, its ability to earn a "satisfactory profit" may be assessed.

Because the manager of a profit center should be held accountable only for the revenues and costs he can control through his decisions, the allocation of indirect costs should be avoided. The inclusion of an allocated portion of service department costs will only confuse the issue. Accordingly, many firms prefer to think in terms of contribution margin centers rather than profit centers. In a contribution margin center the manager's controllable costs are deducted from his controllable revenue. The resulting contribution margin is his contribution to the firm's joint costs and, ultimately, net income.

Implicit to the profit center concept is the assumption that a manager's economic decisions affect the profits of his division. Thus, there can be an effective assignment of responsibility for both costs and revenues. Second, it is assumed that an increase in the profit center's net income will act to increase the net income of the firm. Without this implied relationship, a manager could optimize his division's net income to the detriment of the firm's net income. Third, and very important, is the assumption that the profit center's activities are not significantly dependent upon the actions of the other divisions. It must have some autonomy.

INVESTMENT CENTERS

In an **investment center,** performance is measured not only by net income, but also by relating this net income to the asset investment. The investment center concept makes it possible to assess the efficiency of investment utilization; the rate of return on investment may be used in performance evaluation. Investment centers are treated as individual businesses where the manager is responsible for all activities—costs, revenues, and investments.

The Donnell Company has the following organizational structure:

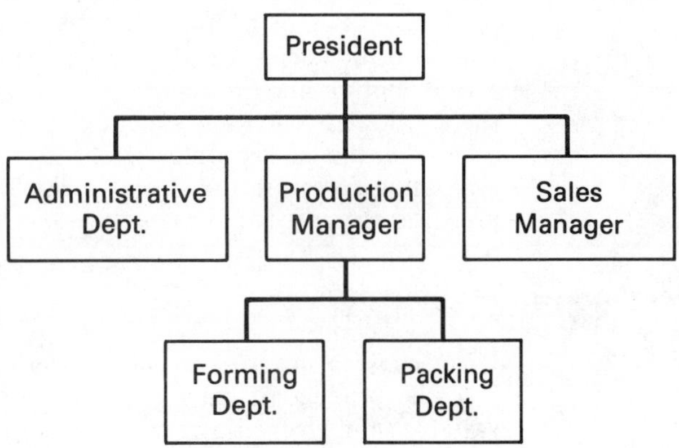

OVERHEAD COSTS:				
	FACTORY RESPONSIBILITY CENTERS			
	Forming	*Packing*	*Factory Management*	*Total*
Variable (per labor hour)	$4.00	$1.00	None	
Fixed (per year)				
Depreciation	$32,000	$ 4,000	$ 4,000	$ 40,000
Supervisory salaries	12,000	8,000	40,000	60,000
Total	$44,000	$12,000	$44,000	$100,000
MARKETING COSTS:				
Variable (per unit sold)	$.50 for small terrarium $.80 for large terrarium			
Fixed (per year):				
Depreciation				$ 24,000
Supervisory salaries				56,000
Total				$ 80,000
ADMINISTRATIVE COSTS:				
Fixed (per year):				
Depreciation				$ 4,000
Salaries				$ 36,000
Total				$ 40,000

EXHIBIT 8–4
Cost behavior patterns

The production areas, including the forming and packing departments and the production manager's administrative areas, are cost centers. The corporate administrative department is also a cost center. The marketing department is a contribution margin center. The firm as a whole is an investment center; there are no division investment centers.

On the basis of this organizational structure, and the methodology of separating costs into fixed and variable shown in Chapter 2, the company prepared the cost behavior patterns shown in Exhibit 8–4.

Step 3—Development of Product Costs

Using engineering studies and the overhead cost behavior patterns in Exhibit 8–4, the production manager together with the supervisors, developed the variable standard cost cards shown in Exhibit 8–5. These standards are considered tight, but achievable during 19X2.

STANDARD COST CARD
Small Terrarium

	Forming Department	Packing Department	Total
Direct Material:			
Plastic—1 pound	$ .40		$ .40
Carton—1 gallon		$.30	.30
			$ .70
Direct Labor:			
.1 hours @ $5.00	.50		$ .50
.1 hours @ $3.00		.30	.30
			.80
Variable Overhead:			
.1 hours @ $4.00	.40		$ .40
.1 hours @ $1.00		.10	.10
			.50
Total Variable Cost	$1.30	$.70	$2.00

STANDARD COST CARD
Large Terrarium

	Forming Department	Packing Department	Total
Direct Material:			
Plastic—3 pounds	$1.20		$1.20
Carton—5 gallon		$ .60	.60
			$1.80
Direct Labor:			
.2 hours @ $5.00	1.00		$1.00
.1 hours @ $3.00		.30	.30
			1.30
Variable Overhead:			
.2 hours @ $4.00	.80		$ .80
.1 hours @ $1.00		.10	.10
			.90
Total Variable Cost	$3.00	$1.00	$4.00

EXHIBIT 8–5
Standard cost cards

Step 4—Development of Company Objectives

On the basis of their long-run goals and their assessment of the environment for the coming year the management of Donnell Company prepared the objectives for 19X2 shown in Exhibit 8–6.

PROFIT OBJECTIVES	1. Achieve a net income after tax of 12% of reported stockholders' equity at the beginning of the year. 2. Achieve a net income after tax of 8% on sales.
MARKET OBJECTIVE	1. Increase total dollar sales of the company by 7%, and for each product at least 5%.
INVENTORY OBJECTIVES	1. Maintain finished goods inventories at a level equal to 50% of the next quarter's production. 2. Maintain raw materials inventory of plastics at a level equal to 10% of the next quarter's usage. Maintain inventory of boxes at the same level as at the beginning of the year.
MANPOWER OBJECTIVE	1. Move toward a stable work force with no more than 10% turnover through layoffs.

EXHIBIT 8–6
Objectives for 19X2

Step 5—Development of Sales Budget

Where productive capacity of the company is limited, the company may not be able to produce at the level of the sales forecast. In this case the combination of products that generates the largest total contribution margin should be produced. We will assume that the Donnell Company has adequate productive capacity to meet the sales forecast; thus, the sales forecast becomes the sales budget. If production capacity were limited, it would act as a constraint, and a model, such as the linear programming model presented later in Chapter 12, would be used to maximize the contribution margin within the constraints.

	Quarter 1	Quarter 2	Quarter 3	Quarter 4	Total for Year
Sales in Units:					
Small	8,000	16,000	48,000	8,000	80,000
Large	8,000	6,000	20,000	6,000	40,000
Sales in Dollars:					
Small	$ 40,000	$ 80,000	$240,000	$40,000	$400,000
Large	64,000	48,000	160,000	48,000	320,000
Total Sales	$104,000	$128,000	$400,000	$88,000	$720,000

EXHIBIT 8–7
Sales budget

Budgeted sales, by product and quarter, are presented in Exhibit 8–7. Quarterly sales were determined by applying the seasonal pattern to total sales forecasts.

Step 6—Development of Production Budget

The production budget expresses management's plan for factory volume for the year. It provides the activity base for planning the variable production cost levels. The desired ending inventory of finished goods is added to budgeted sales, and the beginning inventory of finished goods is deducted to arrive at required production. Donnell management has established desired finished goods inventory levels at 50% of the sales of the following quarter. The production budget is presented in Exhibit 8–8.

Step 7—Development of Purchasing Budget

The material standards from the standard cost card (Exhibit 8–5) are multiplied by the required production levels in the production budget to determine the amount of materials required for production during the year (Exhibits 8–9 and 8–10). Computation of purchase requirements starts with the materials needed for scheduled production (from the production budget), adds desired ending inventory of raw materials, and, finally, deducts the beginning levels of raw materials to arrive at required purchases of materials.

The company has set the desired material inventory levels at 10% of the next quarter's usage for plastic. Company policy regarding boxes was to maintain a constant inventory; thus, the amount purchased equaled the production requirements.

	Quarter				Total for
	1	2	3	4	Year
Product: Small Size					
Sales (in units)	8,000	16,000	48,000	8,000	80,000
Plus: Desired Ending Inventory of Finished Goods[1]	8,000	24,000	4,000	4,000[2]	4,000
Total	16,000	40,000	52,000	12,000	84,000
Less: Beginning Inventory of Finished Goods[3]	6,000	8,000	24,000	4,000	6,000
Required Production	10,000	32,000	28,000	8,000	78,000
Product: Large Size					
Sales (in units)	8,000	6,000	20,000	6,000	40,000
Plus: Desired Ending Inventory of Finished Goods	3,000	10,000	3,000	4,000[2]	4,000
Total	11,000	16,000	23,000	10,000	44,000
Less: Beginning Inventory of Finished Goods[3]	5,000	3,000	10,000	3,000	5,000
Required Production	6,000	13,000	13,000	7,000	39,000

[1]Assumes ending inventory levels are 50% of next quarter's sales.
[2]Assumes ending inventory level of 4th quarter is based upon next year's sales levels being the same as this year.
[3]Taken from beginning statement of financial position (Exhibit 8–20).

EXHIBIT 8–8
Production budget

Step 8—Development of Departmental Budgets by Responsibility Area

Earlier in this chapter we stressed the need for responsibility accounting. With responsibility reporting, each departmental report should include only those revenues and costs over which the manager has control—those which he can influence or change. In the Donnell Company each revenue and cost has been related to the lowest level of management with the authority to influence or change it.

In the factory the managers of the forming and packing departments are responsible only for costs. Exhibits 8–11 and 8–12 present the department budgets for these two departments.

	Quarter				Total
	1	*2*	*3*	*4*	*for Year*
Production of Small:	10,000	32,000	28,000	8,000	78,000
Plastic per unit	1#	1#	1#	1#	1#
Required plastic for small terrariums	10,000	32,000	28,000	8,000	78,000
Production of Large:	6,000	13,000	13,000	7,000	39,000
Plastic per unit	3#	3#	3#	3#	3#
Required plastic for large terrariums	18,000	39,000	39,000	21,000	117,000
Total Plastic Required	28,000	71,000	67,000	29,000	195,000
Plus: Desired ending inventory of raw materials[1]	7,100	6,700	2,900	2,800	2,800
Total	35,100	77,700	69,900	31,800	197,800
Less: Beginning inventory of raw materials[2]	6,000	7,100	6,700	2,900	6,000
Required purchases in pounds	29,100	70,600	63,200	28,900	191,800
Cost per pound of plastic	$.40	$.40	$.40	$.40	$.40
Required purchases in dollars	$11,640	$28,240	$25,280	$11,560	$ 76,720

[1]Assumes desired inventory levels are 10% of next quarter's production requirements.

[2]Taken from beginning statement of financial position (Exhibit 8-20)

EXHIBIT 8-9
Purchases budget for plastic

In the marketing area, on the other hand, the manager is responsible for both revenues and costs (Exhibit 8-13). The budget should show product contribution, that is, the amount the product contributes toward company fixed costs and net income. Product contribution is computed by deducting standard variable production costs, variable marketing costs, and fixed marketing costs incurred for the particular product or marketing territory.

	Quarter				Total
	1	2	3	4	for Year
Production of Small:	10,000	32,000	28,000	8,000	78,000
Boxes per unit	1	1	1	1	1
Required 1-gal. size boxes	10,000	32,000	28,000	8,000	78,000
Cost per box	$.30	$.30	$.30	$.30	$.30
Required purchases of 1-gal. boxes[1]	$ 3,000	$ 9,600	$ 8,400	$2,400	$23,400
Production of Large:	6,000	13,000	13,000	7,000	39,000
Boxes per unit	1	1	1	1	1
Required 5-gal. size boxes	6,000	13,000	13,000	7,000	39,000
Cost per box	$.60	$.60	$.60	$.60	$.60
Required purchases of 5-gal. boxes[1]	$ 3,600	$ 7,800	$ 7,800	$4,200	$23,400

[1]Assumes no change in inventory levels during the year. Beginning Inventory and ending inventories will each be $5,600. However, this is the total of both styles of boxes and from the information given we cannot determine how many of each style.

EXHIBIT 8–10
Purchasing budget for boxes

	Quarter				Total for
	1	2	3	4	Year
Material	$11,200	$28,400	$26,800	$11,600	$ 78,000
Direct Labor	11,000	29,000	27,000	11,000	78,000
Variable Overhead	8,800	23,200	21,600	8,800	62,400
Total Variable Costs	$31,000	$80,600	$75,400	$31,400	$218,400
Departmental Fixed Costs:					
Depreciation	$ 8,000	$ 8,000	$ 8,000	$ 8,000	$ 32,000
Supervisor's salaries	3,000	3,000	3,000	3,000	12,000
Total fixed costs	11,000	11,000	11,000	11,000	44,000
Total Department Cost	$42,000	$91,600	$86,400	$42,400	$262,400
Physical Data:					
Production:					
Small	10,000	32,000	28,000	8,000	78,000
Large	6,000	13,000	13,000	7,000	39,000
Material used (lbs.)	28,000	71,000	67,000	29,000	195,000
Direct labor hours	2,200[a]	5,800	5,400	2,200	15,600

[a]For example, (1,000 small × .1) + (6,000 large × .2)

EXHIBIT 8–11
Cost budget for forming department

	Quarter 1	Quarter 2	Quarter 3	Quarter 4	Total for Year
Material	$ 6,600	$17,400	$16,200	$ 6,600	$ 46,800
Direct Labor	4,800	13,500	12,300	4,500	35,100
Variable Overhead	1,600	4,500	4,100	1,500	11,700
Total Variable Costs	$13,000	$35,400	$32,600	$12,600	$ 93,600
Departmental Fixed Costs:					
Depreciation	$ 1,000	$ 1,000	$ 1,000	$ 1,000	$ 4,000
Supervisor's salaries	2,000	2,000	2,000	2,000	8,000
Total fixed costs	3,000	3,000	3,000	3,000	12,000
Total Department Cost	$16,000	$38,400	$35,600	$15,600	$105,600
Physical Data:					
Production:					
Small	10,000	32,000	28,000	8,000	78,000
Large	6,000	13,000	13,000	7,000	39,000
Material used					
1-gal. size	10,000	32,000	28,000	8,000	78,000
5-gal. size	6,000	13,000	13,000	7,000	39,000
Direct labor hours	1,600	4,500	4,100	1,500	11,700

EXHIBIT 8–12
Cost budget for packing department

Step 9—Compilation of Departmental Budgets into the Profit Plan

After a flow of information downward through the sales budget and production budget of departmental volume levels, the departmental managers prepare budgets that provide an upward flow of information for compilation at the factory and marketing level. Budgets by these functional areas are then compiled into the profit plan. At each level, review and feedback take place. This process of budget compilation is illustrated in Exhibit 8–14. The upward compilation is illustrated by a solid line and the downward flow of information, including the process of review and feedback, by a broken line.

The first level of budget compilation for the Donnell Company is illustrated in the factory cost budget (Exhibit 8–15). The factory cost budget includes a one-line cost summary for each subordinate factory department. For example, the total of the forming department budget from Exhibit 8–11 can be traced into the factory cost budget in Exhibit 8–15.

	Quarter				Total for
	1	2	3	4	Year
Product: Small Terrarium					
Sales	$40,000	$80,000	$240,000	$40,000	$400,000
Variable production costs	16,000	32,000	96,000	16,000	160,000
Contribution margin from production	$24,000	$48,000	$144,000	$24,000	$240,000
Variable selling costs	4,000	8,000	24,000	4,000	40,000
Contribution margin from operations	$20,000	$40,000	$120,000	$20,000	$200,000
Product: Large Terrarium					
Sales	$64,000	$48,000	$160,000	$48,000	$320,000
Variable production costs	32,000	24,000	80,000	24,000	160,000
Contribution margin from production	$32,000	$24,000	$ 80,000	$24,000	$160,000
Variable selling costs	6,400	4,800	16,000	4,800	32,000
Contribution margin from operations	25,600	19,200	64,000	19,200	128,000
Total Contribution Margin	$45,600	$59,200	$184,000	$39,200	$328,000
Less: Fixed Marketing Costs					
Depreciation	$ 6,000	$ 6,000	$ 6,000	$ 6,000	$ 24,000
Supervisor's salaries	14,000	14,000	14,000	14,000	56,000
Total fixed costs	20,000	20,000	20,000	20,000	80,000
Marketing Contribution	$25,600	$39,200	$164,000	$19,200	$248,000

EXHIBIT 8–13
Contribution margin budget for marketing department

Because a responsibility accounting system groups accounting data by responsibility area, other possible aggregations, such as by type of cost, are lost; they must be presented as supplementary information. A summary by type of cost is presented at the bottom of the factory cost budget.

The profit plan by quarter is presented in Exhibit 8–16. It is a consolidation of decisions made to allocate the firm's resources in the short run. All the efforts to project sales, and to determine optimum product mix and departmental costs were necessary to develop the profit plan. The goals of the individual managers have been brought together and may now be related to company goals, and the profit plan can be compared with company objectives.

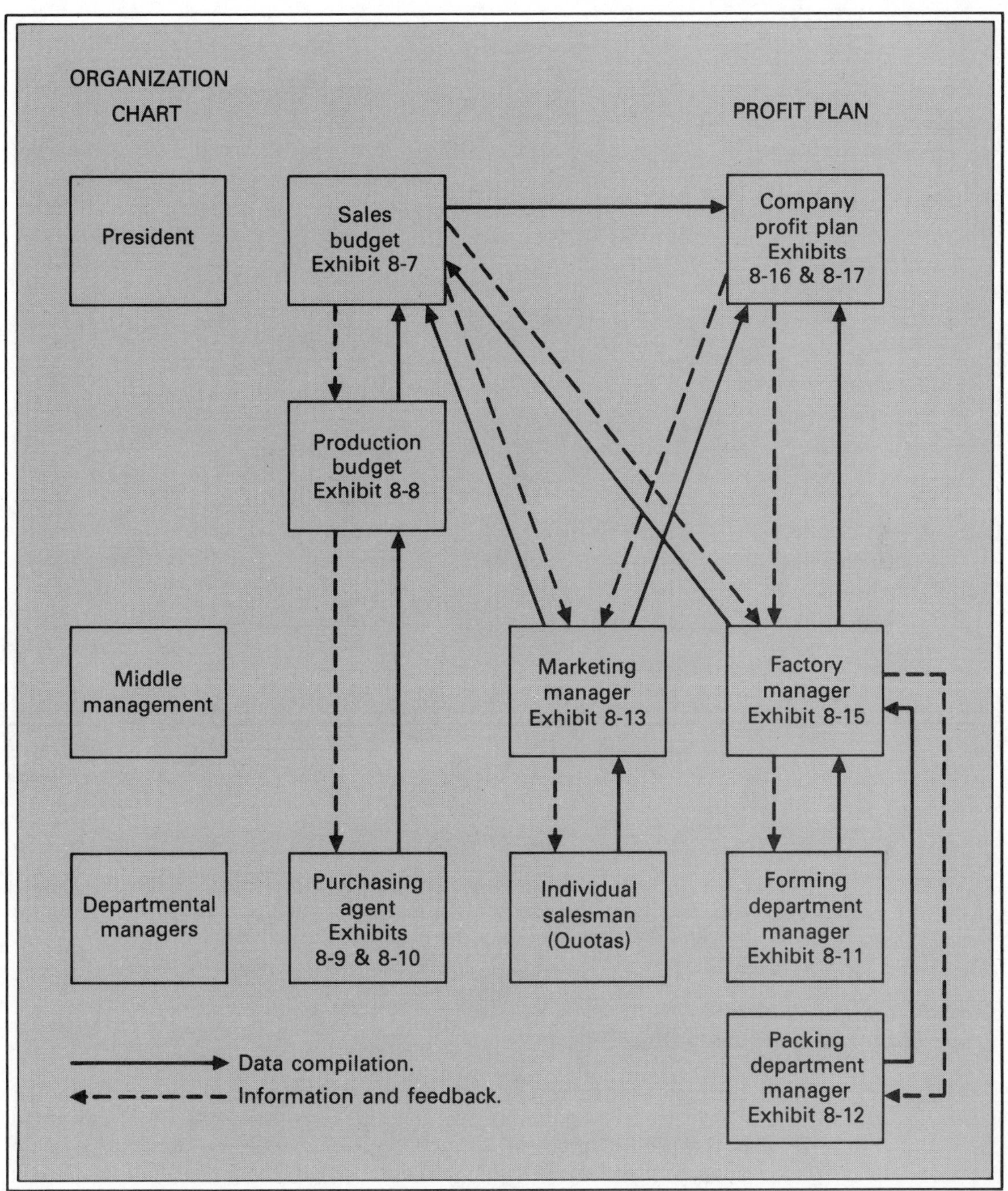

EXHIBIT 8–14
Illustration of compilation of departmental budgets into profit plan

	Quarter 1	Quarter 2	Quarter 3	Quarter 4	Total for Year
Costs Controllable by Subordinate Department:					
Forming department	$42,000	$ 91,600	$ 86,400	$42,400	$262,400
Packing department	16,000	38,400	35,600	15,600	105,600
Total	$58,000	$130,000	$122,000	$58,000	$368,000
Costs Controllable by Factory Manager Directly:					
Depreciation	$ 1,000	$ 1,000	$ 1,000	$ 1,000	$ 4,000
Supervisory salaries	10,000	10,000	10,000	10,000	40,000
Total	11,000	11,000	11,000	11,000	44,000
Total Factory Costs	$69,000	$141,000	$133,000	$69,000	$412,000
Summary of Costs					
Material	$17,800	$ 45,800	$ 43,000	$18,200	$124,800
Direct labor	15,800	42,500	39,300	15,500	113,100
Variable overhead	10,400	27,700	25,700	10,300	74,100
Total variable costs	$44,000	$116,000	$108,000	$44,000	$312,000
Fixed costs	25,000	25,000	25,000	25,000	100,000
Total factory costs	$69,000	$141,000	$133,000	$69,000	$412,000

EXHIBIT 8–15
Cost budget for factory manager

An alternative profit plan by product is presented in Exhibit 8–17. This plan highlights the contribution margin of each product; in this respect, it provides different data than the profit plan in Exhibit 8–16 does.

Step 10—Comparison of Profit Plan with Corporate Objectives

The profit plan is the focal point of the master budget. It shows the profit that management can expect to earn, given the resources and facilities committed. Is the planned profit of $50,000 enough? Earlier we presented a set of company objectives (Exhibit 8–6) developed by the president of the Donnell Company in consultation with functional managers. A comparison of these objectives and the profit plan is presented in Exhibit 8–18. The profit plan met or exceeded all company objectives with two exceptions. Net income as a

	Quarter 1	Quarter 2	Quarter 3	Quarter 4	Total for Year
Sales	$104,000	$128,000	$400,000	$ 88,000	$720,000
Variable Costs:					
Production	$ 48,000	$ 56,000	$176,000	$ 40,000	$320,000
Marketing	10,400	12,800	40,000	8,800	72,000
Total variable costs	58,400	68,800	216,000	48,800	392,000
Contribution Margin	$ 45,600	$ 59,200	$184,000	$ 39,200	$328,000
Fixed Costs:					
Production	$ 25,000	$ 25,000	$ 25,000	$ 25,000	$100,000
Marketing	20,000	20,000	20,000	20,000	80,000
Administration	10,000	10,000	10,000	10,000	40,000
Total fixed costs	55,000	55,000	55,000	55,000	220,000
Operating Income	$ (9,400)	$ 4,200	$129,000	$(15,800)	$108,000
Interest Expense	2,000	2,000	2,000	2,000	8,000
Income before Taxes	$ (11,400)	$ 2,200	$127,000	$(17,800)	$100,000
Income Taxes (50%)					50,000
Net Income after Taxes					$ 50,000

EXHIBIT 8–16
Profit plan, by quarter

	Small Terrarium		Large Terrarium		Total for Year
	Per Unit	For Year	Per Unit	For Year	
Sales	$5.00	$400,000	$8.00	$320,000	$720,000
Variable Costs:					
Production	$2.00	$160,000	$4.00	$160,000	$320,000
Marketing	.50	40,000	.80	32,000	72,000
Total variable costs	2.50	200,000	4.80	192,000	392,000
Contribution Margin	$2.50	$200,000	$3.20	$128,000	$328,000
Fixed Costs:					
Production					$100,000
Marketing					80,000
Administration					40,000
Total fixed costs					220,000
Operating Income					$108,000
Interest Expense					8,000
Income Before Taxes					$100,000
Income Taxes (50%)					50,000
Net Income After Taxes					$ 50,000

EXHIBIT 8–17
Profit plan, by product line

PROFIT OBJECTIVES	19X2 PROFIT PLAN PROJECTIONS
Achieve a net income after tax of:	
1. 12% of reported owners' equity at the beginning of the year.	14.9% on reported owners' equity ($50,000 ÷ $336,000)
2. 8% on net sales	6.9% on net sales ($50,000 ÷ $720,000)
MARKET OBJECTIVE	
1. Increase dollar sales of the company by 7%	6.7% increase in sales 19X2 $720,000 19X1 $675,000 ($45,000 ÷ $675,000)
INVENTORY OBJECTIVES	
1. Maintain finished goods inventory at 50% of next quarter's sales.	Inventory-level objectives were achieved by the end of the first quarter.
2. Maintain material inventories at 10% of next quarter's usage for plastic; no change for boxes.	
MANPOWER OBJECTIVE	
1. Move toward a stable work force with no more than 10% turnover through layoffs.	The manpower objective and inventory level objectives are in conflict. Direct labor hours in the two production departments totaled 3,800, 10,300, 9,500, and 3,700 by quarter. If a stable work force is to be maintained, the company must produce for inventories in Quarters 1 and 4.

EXHIBIT 8–18
Comparison of profit plan with Donnell Company objectives

percent of sales was only 7%, when the objective was 8%. The second involves a conflict in objectives. In a highly seasonal market the company cannot hold inventories at a percentage of the next quarter's sales *and* maintain a stable work force. If a stable work force is to be achieved, the company must build inventories in periods of low sales activity.

Projected Cash Budget

The final cash budget for the Donnell Company for 19X2 is presented in Exhibit 8–19. The particular form of the cash budget is not important so long as cash flows from operations—the continuing source of funds—are separated from other cash flows.

	Quarter				Total for
	1	2	3	4	Year
Cash Flows from Operations					
Sources:					
Collections from customers[1]					
Previous quarter	$ 50,000[A]	$ 52,000	$ 64,000	$200,000	$366,000
Current quarter	52,000	64,000	200,000	44,000	360,000
Total	$102,000	$116,000	$264,000	$244,000	$726,000
Uses:					
Payments to suppliers[2]	$ 20,000[A]	$ 18,240	$ 45,640	$ 41,480	$125,360
Direct labor[3]	15,800	42,500	39,300	15,500	113,100
Variable overhead[4]	10,000[A]	10,400	27,700	25,700	73,800
Variable selling costs[4]	9,000[A]	10,400	12,800	40,000	72,200
Fixed costs[5] (excluding depr.)					
Production	15,000	15,000	15,000	15,000	60,000
Marketing	14,000	14,000	14,000	14,000	56,000
Administrative	9,000	9,000	9,000	9,000	36,000
Income taxes[9]	10,000[A]	12,500	12,500	12,500	47,500
Total uses	102,800	132,040	175,940	173,180	583,960
Net Cash Flow from Operations	$ (800)	$ (16,040)	$ 88,060	$ 70,820	$142,040
Other cash flows:					
Interest expense[6]				8,000	8,000
Payment on debt[6]				20,000	20,000
Dividends[7]			30,000		30,000
Capital additions[8]				70,000	70,000
Net Change in Cash	$ (800)	$ (16,040)	$ 58,060	$ (27,180)	$ 14,040
Beginning Balance	25,000	24,200	8,160	66,220	25,000
Ending Balance	$ 24,200	$ 8,160	$ 66,220	$ 39,040	$ 39,040

[A]From beginning statement of financial position (Exhibit 8-20).
[1]For numbered footnotes, see discussion in text.

EXHIBIT 8-19
Cash budget

Each firm must study its past cash flows to determine the method it will use to decide when cash will be received or spent. First, costs must be separated into those that require cash and those that do not. Depreciation, for example, is a noncash cost. Next, the firm must determine timing of receipts and disbursements for the cash items. These schedules will be the result of the behavior of the company's customers, supplier policy, and the policy of top management. The cash budget in Exhibit 8–19 was built upon the following cash flow assumptions (these assumptions are indicated on the cash budget by a footnote number which corresponds to the numbers below).

1. Cash receipts from sales were based upon the assumption that 50% of sales were collected in the quarter of the sale and the balance in the following quarter (see Exhibit 8–7). One-half of the sales in the fourth quarter will become Accounts Receivable on the ending statement of financial position.
2. Cash payments to suppliers were determined on the assumption that the suppliers are paid in the quarter following the purchase (see Exhibits 8–9 and 8–10). The purchases in the fourth quarter will become Accounts Payable on the ending statement of financial position.
3. Cash payments to workers were based upon the assumption that payrolls are paid in the quarter that the workers work (see Exhibit 8–15).
4. Payments for variable costs were based upon the assumption that these costs are paid in the quarter following the incurrence of the cost (see Exhibit 8–16). The unpaid variable costs in the fourth quarter will appear on the ending statement of financial position as Accrued Liabilities.
5. Cash payments for fixed costs, excluding depreciation, are scheduled to be paid in the quarter which the costs are incurred (see Exhibit 13–4).
6. Cash payments for annual interest and payment on long-term debt are scheduled on the assumption that payment is made in the last month of the year.
7. Cash payments for dividends are scheduled on the assumption that a dividend will be declared by the Board of Directors which will be payable in the third quarter.
8. Cash payments for capital additions will come from the capital additions budget, which was not presented in our example. We have assumed that payment would be made in the fourth quarter.
9. Cash payments of taxes were scheduled on the assumption that taxes are paid quarterly. In the first quarter we will pay the taxes of the last quarter of the previous year. This year's taxes will be paid in the second, third, and fourth quarter of this year with one-fourth of the tax liability shown on the ending statement of financial position. This liability will be paid in the first quarter of next year.

If we look at the cash flow column for the year as a whole, the Donnell Company appears to have no problem with liquidity. However, if we look at the individual quarters, we get a different picture. The difference between the seasonal pattern in sales and the production pattern results in uneven cash flows during the year. At the end of the second quarter, the cash balance is projected to decline to a low of $8,160. Management must decide if this is unusually low.

There are four nonoperating cash flows in Exhibit 8–19. Two are the interest and principal payments on the long-term debt. The third item is the dividends declared by the board of directors. In a real world setting this would probably be decided *after* the cash budget, excluding dividends, was prepared. In this way the board of directors could ensure that cash would be available when needed. The fourth item is a major ($70,000) plant addition from the capital additions budget (Note: this budget is not shown for the Donnell illustration).

Projected Statement of Financial Position

The master budget is completed with the preparation of the projected statement of financial position, which shows the consequences of planned operating actions on the financial resources of the firm. Planning and control of the various financial resources are interwoven through the various planning steps in developing the profit plan, cash budget, and capital expenditures budget. The projected statement of financial position consolidates the results.

The projected statement of financial position for the Donnell Company is presented in Exhibit 8–20. The source of each amount in the projected statement of financial position is explained by reference to the exhibits and schedules.

Cash, $39,040 is the ending cash balance from the cash budget (Exhibit 8–19).

Accounts receivable, $44,000, represents one-half the sales of the last quarter.

Inventory of finished goods, $24,000, is determined from the production budget (Exhibit 8–8). Ending inventory was planned at the level of 50% of the next quarter's sales. The unit costs were taken from the standard cost card (Exhibit 8–5).

Products	*Number of Units*		*Variable Standard Cost*		*Inventory*
Small	4,000	×	$2.00	=	$ 8,000
Large	4,000	×	$4.00	=	16,000
					$24,000

Since this statement of financial position is for management only, there is no need to convert from variable to absorption costing.

DONNELL COMPANY
STATEMENT OF FINANCIAL POSITION

	ACTUAL *December 31, 19X1*	*PROJECTED* *December 31, 19X2*
ASSETS		
Current Assets:		
Cash	$ 25,000	$ 39,040
Accounts receivable	50,000	44,000
Finished goods inventory	32,000	24,000
Materials inventory	8,000	6,720
Total current assets	$115,000	$113,760
Fixed Assets:		
Land	$ 40,000	$ 40,000
Buildings and equipment	440,000	510,000
Accumulated depreciation	(110,000)	(178,000)
Total fixed assets	370,000	372,000
TOTAL ASSETS	$485,000	$485,760
LIABILITIES AND STOCKHOLDERS' EQUITY		
Current Liabilities:		
Accounts payable	$ 20,000	$ 18,160
Accrued liabilities	19,000	19,100
Income taxes payable	10,000	12,500
Current portion of debt	20,000	20,000
Total current liabilities	$ 69,000	$ 69,760
Long-term debt (8%, $20,000 maturing each year)	80,000	60,000
Total liabilities	$149,000	$129,760
Stockholders' Equity:		
Common stock, $10 par, 20,000 shares issued and outstanding	$200,000	$200,000
Retained earnings	136,000	156,000
Total stockholders' equity	336,000	356,000
TOTAL LIABILITIES AND STOCKHOLDERS' EQUITY	$485,000	$485,760

EXHIBIT 8–20
Statement of financial position

Materials inventory, $6,720, was determined from the purchases budget (Exhibits 8–9 and 8–10) where estimated ending inventories of plastic were projected at 25% of the following quarter's usage, and the ending inventory of boxes was the same as the beginning inventory.

Materials	*Number of Units*		*Variable Standard Cost*		*Inventory*
Plastic	2,800	×	$.40	=	$1,120
Packing	—		—		5,600
					$6,720

Land is unchanged from the beginning statement of financial position.

Building and equipment, $510,000, includes the total of the beginning balance from the beginning statement of financial position and the $70,000 of capital expenditures made during the year.

Beginning balance	$440,000
Capital expenditures	70,000
Ending balance	$510,000

Accumulated depreciation, $178,000, includes the beginning balance of $110,000, and the sum of the depreciation from Exhibit 8–4 amounting to $68,000 for the year.

Accounts payable, $18,160, represents the last quarter's purchases from Exhibits 8–9 and 8–10.

Accrued liabilities, $19,100, includes the unpaid balance of variable costs.

Variable Overhead:	
Forming (Exhibit 8–11)	$ 8,800
Packing (Exhibit 8–12)	1,500
Variable Selling (Exhibit 8–13):	
Small	4,000
Large	4,800
Total	$19,100

Income taxes payable, $12,500, represents the final one-fourth of estimated taxes for 19X2.

Current portion of debt, $20,000, represents the payment due in the final quarter of 19X2. The current portion is the amount due during the year after the balance sheet date.

Long-term debt, $60,000, represents the balance of the long-term debt due beyond one year from the balance sheet date. The current portion is transferred to current liabilities.

Common stock, \$200,000, remained unchanged from the beginning amount.

Retained earnings, \$156,000, represents the beginning balance of retained earnings plus the net income from the profit plan (Exhibit 8–16) less the dividends paid in the cash budget (Exhibit 8–19).

Beginning balance	\$136,000
Plus net income	50,000
Less dividends	(30,000)
Ending balance	\$156,000

NEW APPROACHES TO BUDGETING

This overview of the budgetary process uses an **iterative** (sequence of steps) approach to budgeting. Tentative projections made by operating divisions undergo any necessary revision as the budget is coordinated and resource needs are compared with available resources. For example, a change in the sales estimate or product mix will require revision of many budget schedules. A pervasive change is a costly process.

Recent advancements in firm modeling have provided mathematical techniques for budgeting, including linear programming. Introduced in Chapter 12 as a solution to product-mix problems, linear programming may also be used to develop a model of the budgetary process. For example, in setting the budget subsystem for production, the inventory and financing decisions would provide constraints to the linear programming model. The model provides an optimal set of resource levels, given management's objectives. The set of resource levels may then be translated into a master budget. A real advantage of linear programming is that, as a by-product of the model, we can see the impact upon the resources when we vary the constraints. The use of a linear programming model requires mathematical skills and computer capabilities not possessed by many companies and is beyond the scope of this text.

Another modeling advancement that is gaining popularity is the computerized simulation of a firm. **Simulation** is a natural extension of the traditional budgeting process. First, a mathematical statement of the interrelationship of accounts is developed. Then, a simulation model is used to incorporate the relationships among the variables affecting the budget. As an example, a food-processing firm developed a successful profit planning system using a computerized simulation model. The firm's major product was pickles. After testing several different combinations of cucumber sizes on costs and profit to determine the best product mix, the firm was able to contract growers to produce the sizes and varieties that provided the optimal input. After the profit plan was adopted, the impact of any changes in the relevant variables, such as crop shortages due to bad weather, rising costs, or changes in consumer demand, could be tested quickly. It is not economically possible to determine the impact of similar changes in a traditional, manually prepared profit plan.

Further discussion of these mathematical approaches to budgeting is beyond the scope of this book. It should be clear, however, that a computerized model of the budgetary process can improve the planning process. By including more variables and examining more alternatives, the firm should be able not only to reach a better plan, but also to react to external changes.

SUMMARY

The master budget is management's principal vehicle for coordinating the firm's plans. Without the integrating features of the budget there is a danger that the various responsibility centers will act to optimize their own performance to the detriment of the total firm. To achieve its long-run goals and objectives, management must plan and control actual operations. The budget serves as a focus of the planning process, as an integrative tool for the many plans, and as a reference for control. By comparing actual results with plans on a timely basis, management can ensure that actual performance is congruent with the plans.

The master budget is composed of four separate subcomponents. The profit plan is the operating plan detailing revenues, expenses, and net income in the form of a projected income statement. The projected statement of financial position includes the planned asset, liability, and equity levels. The cash budget shows the effects of management's plans on cash inflows and outflows. The capital expenditures budget details planned procurements and disposals of the major production assets.

SUPPLEMENTARY READING

Copulsky, William. *Practical Sales Forecasting*. New York: American Management Association, 1970.

*DeCoster, Don T. "The Budget Director and PERT." *Business Budgeting,* March, 1964.

*Hall, William K. "Forecasting Techniques for Use in the Corporate Planning Process." *Managerial Planning,* November–December, 1972.

Irvine, V. Bruce. "Budgeting: Functional Analysis and Behavioral Implications." *Cost and Management,* March–April, 1970.

*Livingstone, J. Leslie. "Organization Goals and the Budget Process." *Abacus,* June, 1975.

Malcom, R. E. "Improving Forecast Effectiveness." *Managerial Planning,* July–August, 1970.

Pryor, LeRoy J. "Simulation: Budgeting for a 'What if . . . '." *The Journal of Accountancy,* November, 1970.

Sandbulte, Arend J. "Sales and Revenue Forecasting." *Management Accounting,* December, 1969.

Wallace, M. E. "Behavioral Consideration in Budgeting." *Management Accounting,* August, 1966.

Welsch, Glenn A. "Budgeting for Management Planning and Control." *The Journal of Accountancy,* October, 1961.

Welsch, Glenn A. *Budgeting: Profit Planning and Control.* Englewood Cliffs, N.J.: Prentice-Hall, Inc., 1971.

QUESTIONS

8-1 What is the primary purpose of planning?

8-2 What is the interaction between the budget and planning? The budget and control?

8-3 Define *goals, objectives,* and *budgets.* What are the interrelationships among them?

8-4 Define *master budget, profit plan, performance budget,* and *cash budget.* What is the primary purpose of each?

8-5 The control process may be illustrated through a number of steps. List the steps of the control process and indicate the importance of each.

8-6 Explain the concept *management by exception.* Explain the use of management by exception in both quantitative and nonquantitative areas.

8-7 What is the relationship between the profit plan and the cash budget?

8-8 Distinguish between macro and micro approaches to sales forecasting. Give examples of techniques used in each.

8-9 List the steps necessary to develop a profit plan. Is the order of the steps critical? Explain.

8-10 What is the difference between a sales forecast and a sales budget? Are they always the same? Why or why not?

EXERCISES

8-11 *(True or False)*. Indicate whether the following statements are *true* or *false*.

1. Objectives provide broad direction to the firm and typically are not quantified.

2. To be successful, the planning and control system must reflect only the formal organizational structure. Informal patterns of authority and responsibility must be ignored in the system.

3. The capital expenditures budget is based on the projected statement of financial position.

4. A cost is controllable by an individual if his or her decision will directly affect the cost, regardless of where the cost is actually incurred.

5. It is unusual for a firm to prepare the responsibility center budgets before the production budget.

6. The master budget is composed of the profit plan, the cash budget, the budgeted statement of financial position, and the performance budget.

7. The sales budget is the sales forecast modified by any constraints the firm might face.

8. The attitude of top management is crucial to the success or failure of the budgetary system.

9. The sales budget is another name for the sales forecast.

10. Two budgets that serve as inputs to the profit plan are the cash budget and the capital expenditures budget.

8-12 *(Matching)*. Match the following terms and definitions.

1. Goals
2. Master budget
3. Profit plan
4. Capital expenditures budget
5. Objective
6. Performance budget
7. Balance sheet
8. Responsibility accounting
9. Management by exception
10. Sales forecast

A. An operating budget for a specific future period of time.

B. A budget prepared after the fact, showing what costs should have been at the actual level of activity.

C. The practice of focusing attention on those activities where the actual performance differs significantly from planned performance.

D. A set of statements providing broad direction for the firm.

E. An integrated statement of resource levels and their sources.

F. A system that relates costs to organizational structure.

G. An integrated plan of action for the firm as a whole, expressed in financial terms.
H. The most important input for budget preparation. All estimates of activity depend upon this information.
I. A budget reflecting long-range decisions of the company.
J. A quantitative benchmark for measuring company achievement.

8-13 *(Sales Budget and Expected Value).* The Ideal Home Products Company is about to introduce a new product. Most of the company's products have four-year sales lives. Sales peak in Year 3 and decline dramatically in Year 4.

The marketing department has developed the following data for the new product.

Probability of Occurrence		Estimated Sales			
		Year 1	*Year 2*	*Year 3*	*Year 4*
Most optimistic estimate	25%	$300,000	$600,000	$1,200,000	$200,000
Most likely estimate	60%	$100,000	$400,000	$ 800,000	$100,000
Most pessimistic estimate	15%	$ 50,000	$100,000	$ 50,000	$ 10,000

REQUIRED:

Prepare a sales budget by year for this new product, taking into account the probability of the most optimistic, most likely, and most pessimistic sales levels occurring. (Note: An expected value for sales may be determined by multiplying amount of estimated sales times the probability of occurrence.)

8-14 *(Sales Forecast—Demand Curve).* Aquarius Jewelry Company undertook a thorough research of the market for the company's single product. Data concerning demand for the company's product is as follows:

Price	*Quantity Demanded (Units)*
$5.00	100,000
$4.00	300,000
$3.00	600,000
$2.50	1,100,000
$2.00	2,000,000
$1.50	3,400,000
$1.00	5,000,000

Plant capacity is two million units. Fixed costs are $1,500,000; variable costs are $.75 per unit.

REQUIRED:

A. Determine the optimum level of production and sales.

B. Prepare a profit plan for the company at the optimum level using a contribution margin approach.

8-15 *(Sales Forecast).* The management of the Bright Light Company is attempting to develop a forecast of the company's sales for 19X7. The following estimates were derived independently.

Trend-line estimate (projection of past sales trend)	$4,600,000
Composite of salesmen's estimates	$4,500,000
Sales manager's planned sales quota	$5,200,000
Share of the market (Bright Light's share of the market for lights has been 8%. The total market for lights has been estimated at $62,500,000 by the State University business research department.)	?
Simple regression of sales with disposable income: (Regression equation: $y_s = \$1{,}000{,}000 + .01(x)$, where (x) is disposable income in the market area. Standard error: $100,000. Disposable income in the market area was estimated by the Department of Commerce at $380,000,000.)	?

The salesmen expect their estimates to be used as sales quotas and the sales manager expects his estimate to be a maximum for bonus purposes.

REQUIRED:

Prepare a sales forecast from the five projections. Explain how you considered or weighted the various projections.

8-16 *(Purchases Budget; Cash Payments).* Crazy Mary Wholesale Company distributes specialty food products. The company has serious cash flow problems and has come to you for assistance. The sales budget for the first six months of 19X7 follows.

January	$100,000	April	$240,000
February	$150,000	May	$180,000
March	$200,000	June	$150,000

The inventory policy of the firm is to maintain an inventory equal to sales for the next one and one-half months. The beginning inventory was in conformity with this policy. Purchases are subject to terms of 2/10, *n*/60. (A 2% discount is allowed on payments within 10 days of the purchase; the balance is due within 60 days.) Fifty percent of all purchases are made during the last 10 days of each month. It is the policy of the firm to take full advantage of credit terms but never to miss a discount. Purchases during December were $100,000, and sales were $120,000.

The company has a gross margin of 40%. Operating expenses are $20,000 per month plus 10% of sales, including depreciation of $4,000 per month. Sixty percent of expenses are paid in the month of the expense; the balance is paid in the following month.

REQUIRED:

A. Prepare a purchases budget for the first three months of 19X7.
B. Determine the cash payments to suppliers and the cash payments for expenses during the first three months of 19X7.

8-17 *(Cash Budget for College Student).* Fred Lutz, a student at Southwestern University, is planning his program for his junior year. Fred has saved $3,440 from summer work with a construction company. He has arranged for a part-time job at $3.00 per hour. He must carry five three-hour courses each term and cannot work more than 20 hours per week.

Fred will share an apartment near campus with a friend. The rent is $150 per month, and food is expected to cost each roommate $125 per month. Tuition is $90 per credit-hour; books and supplies, $30 per course; and other fees and organization dues, $50 per semester.

His two trips home, between terms and at spring break, will cost approximately $50 each. His parents will cover any costs while at home. They are not financially able to assist him with his educational expenses, however.

Fred expects to spend an average of $20 per week on social activities. He does not own a car and is able to walk or bicycle to work and campus. His roommate has a car and Fred will help with gas when he shares the car. He will have to use his social activities budget to cover this expense.

REQUIRED:

A. Assuming a nine-month academic year and two terms, prepare a cash budget for expenses.
B. How many hours per week must Fred work in order to cover his expenses? If he works 20 hours per week, how much extra money will he have?

8-18 *(Production Budget with Capacity Constraints).* Sunny Sports, Inc. produces a product for summer use. As a result, sales show a strong seasonal pattern.

Quarter	Percentage of Annual Sales
1	10%
2	25%
3	50%
4	15%

Demand for the company's product has grown to the point where 1,200,000 units should be sold in both 19X2 and 19X3. The company has established an inventory policy that requires the ending inventory to be equal to 25% of the next quarter's sales. A total of 25,000 finished units are on hand at the beginning of 19X2. Practical capacity of the company's plant is 1,600,000 units per year (400,000 per quarter). The management of the company has not permitted overtime in the past.

REQUIRED:

A. Prepare a production budget by quarter for 19X2.

B. If Summer Sports, Inc. could not replace skilled employees laid off during slack seasons, how would your production budget and inventory policy change? What information would you need to establish a production budget that optimizes production and storage costs?

8–19 *(Continuation of Exercise 8–18; Purchases Budget).* The product produced by Sunny Sports, Inc. in Exercise 8–18 requires two types of raw material. Each finished unit requires two pounds of Material A and four units of Material B. Raw materials equal to one-fourth of the following quarter's production are to be on hand at the end of each quarter. The January 1, 19X2, inventory meets this requirement. The standard costs of the raw materials are $2.00 per pound for Material A and $1.00 per unit for Material B.

REQUIRED:

A. Prepare a purchases budget for the two raw materials, by the quarter and for the year.

B. What changes in the purchasing budget would you recommend if the per-quarter inventory holding costs were equal to 7% of the units held, and you expected a 25% increase in the price of Material B in quarter 3?

8–20 *(Sales Budget; Production Budget).* The Pacific Manufacturing Company anticipates a sales volume of $500,000 (25,000 units) for 19X1. The beginning inventory level is 1,200 units. Objectives of the company for 19X2 include a growth rate of 15% in sales.

REQUIRED:

A. Assuming the following seasonal sales pattern, prepare a sales budget by quarter for 19X1.

First quarter	10%
Second quarter	30%
Third quarter	50%
Fourth quarter	10%

B. Assume that productive capacity is 9,000 units per quarter (3,000 units per month). Assume also that the product is perishable and cannot be stored for more than one-half quarter. Prepare a production budget by quarter for the next year.

C. Assume that the product is not perishable and that one of the company's goals is a stable work force. Prepare a new production budget by quarter for the next year. Will the revision of the production budget have any impact upon the sales budget? Other than timing of variable production costs, what changes in costs will arise because of your change in the production schedule?

8–21 *(Cash Budget; Statement of Financial Position).* You have just been elected treasurer of the Farmville Racquet Club for the year 19X1. The accounting records are limited to a checkbook and a desk drawer full of invoices and receipts. The board of governors has asked you to prepare a financial plan for the next year. Disturbed by the decline in cash during the past year, the board must consider a dues increase. The present cash balance is $3,000; the board wants a cash balance of $5,000 by year-end.

An examination of the records produced the following information. There are 200 members who have paid dues of $50 per year and $3.00 per hour for use of the tennis courts. The club owns four courts, each of which is used an average of five hours per day for approximately 300 days per year.

In addition to the $3,000 in the bank, club assets consist of receivables from members of $2,000, half of which apply to members who have moved away and should be written off, and land and tennis courts worth $50,000. The club owes $600 for maintenance performed in 19X0.

For managing the club, a tennis pro is paid one-third of the court fees billed. The pro also gives lessons and sells equipment. Cash payments last year, in addition to the payment to the tennis pro, were: maintenance $12,000, utilities $3,000, property taxes $2,000, new playing surface $10,000, and miscellaneous $1,000. During 19X1, taxes and utilities are expected to increase by 50%, new surfaces will cost $6,000, and miscellaneous expenses will be $1,000. Maintenance costs and the contract with the pro are expected to remain unchanged. At the end of the year, 5% of 19X1 court fees are expected to be outstanding; and unpaid maintenance expenses should be $1,000.

The board does not want you to consider depreciation.

REQUIRED:

A. Prepare a statement of financial position at the beginning of 19X2.
B. Prepare a cash budget for 19X1 that will achieve the cash flow objectives of the board. How much will dues have to be increased?
C. Assuming that dues are increased, prepare a projected statement of financial position at December 31, 19X1.

8–22 *(Cash Budget; Profit Plan).* Karen Brotherston graduated three years ago from State University with a major in accounting. Since graduation she has been working for a large CPA firm in Urbanville. She has had excellent training and challenging assignments from the CPA firm, but wants to live in a smaller city. One of the CPA's in her home town wants to retire at the end of June and will sell his practice.

For the past few years he has withdrawn about $20,000 per year. Karen may purchase the practice for $20,000, payable 25% down and one-fourth at the end of each of the next three years without interest. His billings to clients last year, by quarter, were: January through March, $18,000; April through June, $9,000; July through September, $6,000; and October through

December, $9,000. Of a quarter's billings, 5% are uncollectible and 20% of the balance are collected in the next quarter. Because of the change in ownership, Ms. Brotherston can expect her billings to be only half the previous billings for the first quarter she owns the practice (July through September), two-thirds in the next quarter, and from then on equal to the previous owner's billings. She expects his pattern of cash collections to continue.

Office rent, telephone expense, and secretarial expense will be $600 per month. Part-time help will be used after business increases and will cost $500 during October through December, $1,800 during January through March, and $800 during April through June. Automobile expenses will be $40 per month plus 2% of billings to clients. The state recently enacted continuing education requirements. Karen will spend $400 in the first quarter and $800 in the second quarter she owns the business to meet these requirements. Other expenses will be 8% of billings. Two-thirds of automobile and other expenses will be paid in the month of the expense; one-third in the month following the expense. The remaining expenses will be paid in the month the expense is incurred.

The $20,000 purchase price includes $2,000 of equipment, $2,000 of accounts receivable, and $16,000 for the clients' files. The equipment is old and is to be depreciated over two years; the amount allocated to clients' files will be amortized over four years.

Karen has accumulated $6,000 in savings and will invest the entire amount in the practice. She believes she must withdraw at least $600 per month for personal living expenses for the first year.

REQUIRED:

A. Assuming that Karen Brotherston purchases the accounting practice on July 1, prepare a profit plan by quarter for the first year she owns the business.

B. Prepare a cash budget by quarter for the first year.

C. How much revenue is needed each quarter to break even?

8-23 *(Sales Budget and Profit Plan Using Expected Values).* Ivan's Enterprises designs and manufactures toys. Past experience indicates that the product life cycle of a toy is three years. Promotional advertising produces large sales in the early years, but there is a substantial sales decline in the final year of a toy's life.

Consumer demand for new toys placed on the market tends to fall into three classes. About 30% of the new toys sell well above expectations, 60% sell as anticipated, and 10% have poor consumer acceptance.

The management of Ivan's Enterprises has decided to produce a new toy. The following sales projections were made after carefully evaluating consumer demand for the new toy.

Consumer Demand for New Toy	Chance of Occurring	Estimated Sales Year 19X7	Year 19X8	Year 19X9
Above average	30%	$1,200,000	$2,500,000	$600,000
Average	60%	$ 700,000	$1,700,000	$400,000
Below average	10%	$ 200,000	$ 900,000	$150,000

Variable production costs are estimated at 30% of sales. Fixed production expenses, excluding depreciation, related to the new toy are estimated at $50,000 per year. New machinery costing $860,000 will be installed by January 1, 19X7, to produce the new toy. The new machinery will be depreciated by the sum-of-the-years'-digits method. There is no other use anticipated for the equipment. It will be sold at the end of the third year at its salvage value, expected to be $110,000. A vacant portion of the plant that has no other prospect for use will be used to produce the toy. Rent expense apportioned to this space is $20,000 per year.

Advertising and promotional expenses are expected to be $100,000 the first year, $150,000 the second year, and $50,000 the third year. Assume that state and federal taxes will total 60% of income.

REQUIRED:

A. Prepare a sales budget for this new toy in each of the three years, taking into account the probability of above-average, average, and below-average sales occurring.

B. Prepare a profit plan for the new toy for each of the three years of its life.

(CPA adapted)

8-24 *(Profit Plan and Cash Budget).* Two students formed a company, Paint Your House, to earn enough money during the summers to pay for their last year of undergraduate studies and for one year of graduate school. Both men will live with their parents during the summer, and each expects to spend no more than $50 per week for personal expenses. Each student wants to save at least $5,000 during the summer. They have lined up a number of customers and expect to work all 16 weeks during the summer. Ignore income taxes.

The venture will be operated as a partnership with each individual investing $1,000. They have located a used van in good shape for $600; insurance and licenses for the summer are $120. Painting equipment will cost another $600. The van and equipment should last for two summers.

The painters will charge an average of $.15 per square foot painted, including $.03 per square foot for paint. The average house contains approximately 8,000 square feet, which can be painted in approximately one week (50 hours each).

Painting expenses are expected to include the following:

Paint will cost 10% less than the customer is charged.
Painting supplies will cost $.01 per square foot.
Operation of the van is expected to cost $180 for repairs plus $.10 per mile.
Painting an average house should involve 160 miles of travel.
Miscellaneous expense should cost $200 for the summer.

REQUIRED:

A. Prepare a profit plan for the summer.

B. Prepare a cash budget for the summer.

C. How much will they lose for each day of bad weather that cannot be made up? Assume that an average week is five 10-hour days.

8-25 *(Profit Plan and Cash Budget for Health Center).* Mesa County Health Association is a nonprofit health association organized to provide health care for a low-income rural population. Medical service will be provided to all residents of the county regardless of their ability to pay. About 30% of the patients who come to the health center are financially able to pay for medical services. The balance of the costs of the health center will be covered by a federal grant. The executive committee of the health center has asked you to prepare a budget to support the grant request.

Mesa County Health Association serves a rural county with about 18,000 residents, of whom 40% are expected to become patients of the health center. Each patient is expected to average five visits per year. Assume that the visits are spread evenly throughout the year.

Physicians will be employed by the health center. Each physician can see 500 patients per month. One nurse is required for each 300 patient visits per month. The average physician's salary is $4,000 per month and nurses receive $1,000 per month. Physicians may be hired on a half-time basis if necessary. All other employees will be full-time employees.

Operating costs of the health center include the following:

Medical supplies	$3.00 per patient visit
Lab and X-ray technicians	$3,000 per month
Rent	$12,000 per year
Administration	$3,800 per month plus $.50 per visit
Other expenses	$1,000 per month plus $.20 per visit

The physicians and "other expenses" are paid in the month following the month in which the expense is incurred. The remainder of the expenses are paid in the month the expense is incurred. The grant will be received in equal monthly installments. Assume a two-month delay in payment by the patients who are paying their own bills.

All facilities except an X-ray unit costing $4,800 will be leased. The equipment will be depreciated on a straight-line basis over four years.

The health center has a beginning cash balance of $15,000. A local grant was received from the community to provide working capital and purchase the X-ray equipment.

REQUIRED:

A. Determine the projected expenses for the year. What billing rate will be required to cover all costs?

B. Prepare a profit plan for the year.

C. Prepare a cash budget for the year.

PROBLEMS

8-26 *(Profit Plan, Cash Budget, Projected Statement of Financial Position).* Exotic Imports, Inc. was organized to import unusual gift items. The statement of financial position on April 1, 19X0, the date the company was organized, follows.

EXOTIC IMPORTS, INC.
STATEMENT OF FINANCIAL POSITION
April 1, 19X0

Assets		*Equities*	
Cash	$ 30,000	Capital stock	$100,000
Land	20,000		
Buildings and equipment	50,000		
	$100,000		$100,000

Sales for the first six months are expected to be as follows:

April	$ 40,000	July	$200,000
May	$ 60,000	August	$250,000
June	$120,000	September	$100,000

The owners are worried about the cash position of the company for the first three months of operations. They believe that cash flows will be favorable after June. The company plans to borrow any amount needed to carry it through the first quarter as soon as a minimum cash balance of $10,000 is reached. A line of credit has been arranged at the bank requiring interest of 1% per month on the money borrowed. Interest will be paid at the time the loan is repaid.

The gross margin on sales is expected to be 60%. The company plans to carry an inventory equal to expected sales for the next two months. Purchases are paid in the following month.

Variable selling expenses are expected to equal 20% of sales. Fixed selling and administrative expenses are expected to be $30,000 per month, including $1,000 of depreciation. Eighty percent of the expenses will be paid in the month of expense, the balance will be paid in the following month.

Sixty percent of sales are expected to be cash sales. The balance of sales will be credit card sales with 25% collected in the month of sale and 75% in the following month.

REQUIRED:

A. Prepare a profit plan by month for the first three months of operations.
B. Prepare a cash budget by month for the first three months of operations. How much does the company have to borrow to maintain a minimum cash balance of $10,000? How soon?
C. Prepare a projected statement of financial position at June 30, 19X0.
D. Compute the breakeven point in sales dollars, ignoring any interest cost. Does it appear that the problems of liquidity will be solved and that the firm will be profitable after June?

8-27 *(Multiple Choice; Comprehensive Problem).* Tomlinson Retail Company seeks your assistance to develop cash and other budget information for May, June, and July, 19X3. On April 30, 19X3, the company had cash of $5,500, accounts receivable of $437,000, inventories of $309,400, and accounts payable of $133,055.

The budget is to be based on the following assumptions.

1. Sales
  a. Each month's sales are billed on the last day of the month.
  b. Customers are allowed a 3% discount if payment is made within 10 days after the billing date. Receivables are recorded at the full amount.
  c. Sixty percent of the billings are collected within the discount period, 25% are collected by the end of the month, 9% are collected by the end of the second month, and 6% prove uncollectible.

2. Purchases
  a. Fifty-four percent of all purchases of material and selling, general, and administrative expenses are paid in the month purchased and the remainder in the following month.
  b. Each month's units of ending inventory is equal to 130% of the next month's units of sales.
  c. The cost of each unit of inventory is $20.
  d. Selling, general, and administrative expenses, of which $2,000 is depreciation, are equal to 15% of the current month's sales.

Actual and projected sales are as follows:

19X3	*Dollars*	*Units*
March	$354,000	11,800
April	$363,000	12,100
May	$357,000	11,900
June	$342,000	11,400
July	$360,000	12,000
August	$366,000	12,200

REQUIRED:

1. Budgeted cash collections during May are
  a. $333,876
  b. $355,116
  c. $340,410
  d. $355,656

2. The amount of sales discounts taken by customers during June are
  a. $6,426
  b. $6,534
  c. $10,260
  d. $10,710

3. The balance of accounts receivable at the end of May, assuming that no uncollectible accounts are written off during May, is
  a. $357,000
  b. $417,984

c. $453,590
d. $460,124

4. The budgeted number of units of inventory to be purchased during May is
   a. 14,820
   b. 11,250
   c. 11,900
   d. 15,470
5. The budgeted payments to suppliers during May for purchases of merchandise are
   a. $225,000
   b. $230,428
   c. $236,800
   d. $240,020
6. The budgeted selling, general, and administrative expenses during June are
   a. $26,622
   b. $49,300
   c. $50,335
   d. $51,300
7. Budgeted cash payments during May are
   a. $278,550
   b. $281,978
   c. $282,392
   d. $283,978
8. The projected balance of accounts payable at the end of May is
   a. $103,500
   b. $127,213
   c. $127,627
   d. $225,000
9. The projected balance of cash at the end of May is
   a. $5,500
   b. $51,484
   c. $56,984
   d. $108,948
10. The budgeted net income for May is
   a. $51,484
   b. $65,450
   c. $67,030
   d. $78,450

(CPA adapted)

8-28 *(Sales Budget, Production Budget).* The Wicker Works produces a line of three straw products: a hamper, a chest, and a large basket. The company does not have a formal budgetary system. Management has described its planning and control system as "experience and good judgment."

Sales during the current year were $700,000. The sales manager believes that sales will increase by about 10% each year, and projects sales at

$770,000 for the coming year. The production manager is planning to increase production by about 10%. Planned production by product would be:

Hamper	12,000 units
Chest	500 units
Basket	42,000 units

The controller compiled the following information.

	Last Year's Sales		Ending Inventory
	Amount	*Unit Price*	
Hamper	$360,000	$20	1,500 units
Chest	60,000	$25	3,000 units
Basket	280,000	$ 7	3,000 units
	$700,000		

In addition, the controller found that with the exception of the last quarter, when sales were about 40% of the annual total, sales were fairly uniform throughout the year. The controller believes that the inventory policy should require an ending level of one-half of the next quarter's sales.

REQUIRED:

A. Prepare a sales budget and production budget by quarter and in total for the year.

B. Write a brief recommendation to top management detailing your reasons for recommending implementation of the budget process for all departments.

C. If you could have any two specific pieces of additional information to help persuade management to adopt a budgeting system, what would you request? Why?

8-29 *(Profit Plan for Newspaper).* The Metropolitan News, a daily newspaper, services a community of 100,000. The paper has a circulation of 40,000, with 32,000 copies delivered directly to subscribers. The rate schedule for the paper is as follows.

	Daily	*Sunday*
Single issue price	$0.15	$0.30
Weekly subscription (Includes daily and Sunday)	$1.00	

The paper has experienced profitable operations, as can be seen from the Income Statement for the Year Ended September 30, 19X4 (000 omitted).

Revenue:		
Newspaper sales	$2,163	
Advertising sales	1,800	$3,963
Costs and expenses:		
Personnel costs:		
Commissions:		
Carriers and sales	$ 365	
Advertising	48	
Salaries:		
Administration	250	
Advertising	100	
Equipment operators	500	
Newsroom	400	
Employee benefits	188	$1,851
Newsprint		834
Other supplies		417
Repairs		25
Depreciation		180
Property taxes		120
Building rental		80
Automobile leases		10
Other		90
Total costs and expenses		3,607
Income before income taxes		$ 356
Income taxes		142
Net income		$ 214

The Sunday edition usually has twice as many pages as the daily editions. Analysis of direct edition variable costs for 19X3–X4 is shown in the following schedule.

	Cost per Issue	
	Daily	*Sunday*
Paper	$0.050	$0.100
Other supplies	0.025	0.050
Carrier and sales commissions	0.025	0.025
	$0.100	$0.175

Several changes in operations are scheduled for the next year, and there is a need to recognize increasing costs.

1. The building lease expired on September 30, 19X4, and has been renewed with a change in the rental fee provisions from a straight fee to a fixed fee of $60,000 plus 1% of newspaper sales.

2. The advertising department will eliminate the payment of a 4% advertising commission on contracts sold by its employees. An average of two-thirds of the advertising has been sold on a contract basis in the past. The individual salaries of the four who solicited advertising will be raised from $7,500 to $14,000. Other advertising salaries will be increased by 6%.

3. Automobiles will no longer be leased. Employees whose jobs require automobiles will use their own and be reimbursed at $0.15 per mile. The leased cars were driven 80,000 miles in 19X3–X4, and it is estimated that the employees will drive some 84,000 miles next year on company business.

4. Cost increases estimated for next year:
   a. Newsprint: $0.01 per daily issue and $0.02 for the Sunday paper
   b. Salaries:
      (1) Equipment operators 8%
      (2) Other employees 6%
   c. Employee benefits (from 15% of personnel costs, excluding all commissions, to 20%) 5%

5. Circulation increases of 5% in newsstand and home delivery are anticipated.

6. Advertising revenue is estimated at $1,890,000, with $1,260,000 from employee-solicited contracts.

REQUIRED:

A. Prepare a profit plan for the Metropolitan News for the 19X4–X5 fiscal year using a format that shows the total variable costs and total fixed costs for the newspaper. (Round calculations to the nearest thousand dollars.)

B. The management of Metropolitan News is contemplating one additional proposal for the 19X4–X5 fiscal year—raising the rates for its newspaper to the amounts as computed.

	Daily	*Sunday*
Single issue price	$0.20	$0.40
Weekly subscription		
(Includes daily and Sunday)	$1.25	

It is estimated that the newspaper's circulation will decline to 90% of the currently anticipated 19X4–X5 level for both newsstand and home delivery sales if this change is initiated. Advertising revenue will not be affected by the change. Calculate the effect on the projected 19X4–X5 income if this proposed rate change is implemented. *(CMA adapted)*

8-30 *(Comprehensive Master Budget for Pharmacy)*. The Nelson Pharmacy has completed its first year of business in a new shopping center. The owners are very optimistic about the future and plan a number of changes that will expand the business. They plan to develop a budgetary system for planning and control of operations. The following data were accumulated.

1. Sales and merchandise costs for 19X0:

Department	*Sales*	*Gross Profit*	*Inventory Turnover (Ending Inventory)*
Prescription drugs	$ 60,000	60%	4 times
Patent medicine	$100,000	40%	6 times
Cosmetics	$ 50,000	20%	10 times
Sundries	$ 90,000	30%	7 times

2. Operating expenses for 19X0:

Expense	*Amount*	*Traceable to Department*	*Cost Behavior Pattern Fixed and Variable*
Salaries	$40,000	40% prescriptions 20% patent medicine	$40,000 + $0
Advertising	$12,000	50% cosmetics	$12,000 + $0
Rent	$18,000		$0 + 6% of sales
Depreciation of fixtures	$10,000		$10,000 + $0
Miscellaneous	$15,000		$ 6,000 + 3% of sales

3. Statement of Financial Position at the end of 19X0:

Statement of Financial Position

Cash	$ 3,500	Accounts payable	$15,000
Accounts receivable	12,500	Accrued expenses	12,000
Inventory	29,000		
Fixtures and equipment	50,000	Capital stock	40,000
Accumulated depreciation	(10,000)	Retained earnings	18,000
	$ 85,000		$85,000

4. A number of policy changes have been made that will change the character of the store. The following results are expected.

Department	Percentage Increase in Sales	New Gross Margin Percentage	New Inventory Turnover (End of Year)
Prescription drugs	100%	60%	4 times
Patent medicine	50%	40%	6 times
Cosmetics	100%	25%	15 times
Sundries	300%	20%	8 times

5. Other information:

At the end of 19X1, accounts receivable are expected to be $25,000, accounts payable $60,000, and accrued expenses $20,000. Salaries will be increased to $50,000 and miscellaneous expense will become $10,000 + 4% of sales. All other cost-volume relationships will be maintained. The stockholders expect the maximum cash dividend possible that will leave a balance of $10,000 in cash.

REQUIRED:

A. Prepare a profit plan for 19X1 following a contribution margin approach.
B. Prepare a cash budget for 19X1.
C. Prepare a projected statement of financial position at the end of 19X1.
D. Did the changes improve the profitability of the company? Explain.

8-31 *(Cash Budget for University).* Valley University is developing its budget for the coming academic year. You are supplied with the following information.

1. Statistics for the *current* academic year:

Average number of students per class	25
Average number of credit-hours carried per student per year	32
Present enrollment	3,100
Average faculty teaching load in credit-hours per year (6 classes of 4 credit-hours each)	24
Average salary of faculty members	$20,000
Scholarships (tuition-free scholarships)	35
Tuition (per credit-hour)	$ 80

2. Projected enrollment data for 19X1–19X2:

Student enrollment is expected to increase by 10%. Valley University expects to add five new tuition-free scholarships.

3. Budgeted revenue for 19X1–19X2:

Intercollegiate athletics	$200,000
Net income from food services, dormitories, and bookstore	$250,000
Income from endowments	$105,000

The board of regents approved a tuition increase of $2.00 per credit-hour.

4. Budgeted expenditures for 19X1–19X2:

Faculty salaries are to be increased by 5%	
Additional merit increases for faculty members	$ 250,000
Faculty retirement and benefits—20% of faculty salaries	
Eight faculty members will be on leave with full pay	
Administration and general operation	$ 680,000
Academic department direct costs (secretarial, grading, supplies, etc.) $10 per credit-hour	
Athletics	$ 180,000
Library	$ 450,000
Intramural sports	$ 200,000
Building and grounds (maintenance and operation of physical facilities)	$ 800,000
Interest and principal payment on long-term debt (Long-term debt at the beginning of 19X1–19X2 consisted of a 6%, $900,000 debt that requires annual payments of $100,000 plus interest at the end of each year.)	$ 154,000
Building construction	$1,000,000

5. An annual contribution campaign is held each year to "balance the budget."

REQUIRED:

A. Determine the amount of
   1. Expected enrollment
   2. Total credit-hours to be carried
   3. The number of faculty needed

B. Prepare a cash budget for 19X1–19X2. Your budget should include direct cost per student-hour and should separate operating expenses from capital expenditures and reduction of debt.

8–32 *(Profit Plan for Hospital).* The administrator of Appletown Hospital has asked you to prepare an operating budget (profit plan) for the next year ending June 30, 19X2, and presented you with a number of service projections for the year. The following are estimated room requirements for inpatients by type of service.

Type of Patient	Total Patients Expected	Average Number of Days in Hospital	Percentage of Regular Patients Selecting Types of Service		
			Private	Semiprivate	Ward
Medical	2,100	7	10%	60%	30%
Surgical	2,400	10	15%	75%	10%

Daily rentals per patient are $40 for a private room, $35 for a semiprivate room, and $25 for a ward.

Operating-room charges are based on man-minutes (number of minutes the operating room is in use multiplied by number of personnel assisting in the operation). The per-man-minute charges are $.13 for inpatients and $.22 for outpatients. Studies for the current year show that operations are divided by type as follows:

Type of Operation	*Number of Operations*	*Average Number of Minutes Per Operation*	*Average Number of Personnel Required*
A	800	30	4
B	700	45	5
C	300	90	6
D	200	120	8
	2,000		
Outpatient	180	20	3

The following is a budget of direct costs for the year ending June 30, 19X2, by departments.

Service departments:	
Maintenance of plant	$ 50,000
Operation of plant	27,500
Administration	97,500
All others	192,000
Revenue-producing departments:	
Operating room	68,440
All others	700,000
Total direct costs	$1,135,440

All service department costs are to be allocated to the revenue-producing departments. The following information is provided for cost-allocation purposes.

	Square Feet	*Salaries*
General services:		
Maintenance of plant	12,000	$ 40,000
Operation of plant	28,000	25,000
Administration	10,000	55,000
All others	36,250	102,500
Revenue-producing departments:		
Operating room	17,500	15,000
All others	86,250	302,500
	190,000	$540,000

Bases of allocations:
Maintenance of plant—salaries
Operation of plant—square feet
Administration—salaries
All others—8% to operating room
92% to other revenue-producing services

REQUIRED:
Prepare schedules showing the computation of:

A. The number of patient days (number of patients multiplied by average stay in hospital) expected by type of patients (medical or surgical) and type of room service (private, semiprivate, or ward).
B. Expected gross revenue from room service.
C. The total number of man-minutes expected for operating-room services for inpatients and outpatients. For inpatients, show the breakdown of total operating-room man-minutes by type of operation.
D. Expected gross revenue from operating-room services.
E. Cost per man-minute for operating-room services, assuming that the step-down method of cost allocation is used. (Costs of the general services departments are allocated first to the general services departments that they serve and then to the revenue-producing departments.)
F. Operating budget (profit plan) showing the budget for each revenue-producing center and the entire hospital. *(CPA adapted)*

8-33 *(Comprehensive Profit Plan).* Handy Co. produces and sells a single product. The 19X2 sales budget by quarter, in number of units, was:

First quarter	21,000 Units
Second quarter	24,000 Units
Third quarter	30,000 Units
Fourth quarter	36,000 Units

The long-range sales forecast shows expected sales for 19X3 at approximately 3,000 units per month above the 19X2 expected sales level.

The established inventory policy of the company is to maintain a supply of raw materials equal to one-third of the next quarter's needs and a supply of finished goods equal to 50% of the next quarter's budgeted sales. On January 1, 19X3, inventories consisted of 20,000 units of finished goods and 80,000 pounds of raw materials.

Standard costs for material and labor and a flexible budget for other costs are as follows:

Materials	(5 pounds @ $2.00) =	$10.00
Labor	(2 hours @ $4.00) =	$8.00
Factory overhead		$60,000 per month plus $3.00 per direct labor hour
Marketing and administrative costs		$25,000 per month plus 10% of sales

The established selling price is $40 per gadget.

REQUIRED:

A. Prepare the following budgets for the first two quarters of 19X3:
   1. Sales budget
   2. Production budget
   3. Purchasing budget
   4. Factory cost budget
   5. Profit plan

B. The executive committee of top management officers has established a profit objective of at least breakeven operations in each quarter and an overall rate of profit of 12% of sales. What is the breakeven point per quarter? If budgeted net income is $475,000 for the year, does the profit plan meet company objectives?

8-34 *(Comprehensive Profit Plan).* Modern Products Corporation, a manufacturer of molded plastic containers, determined in October 19X8 that it needed cash to continue operations. The corporation began negotiating for a one-month bank loan of $100,000 that would be discounted at 6% per annum on November 1, that is, the interest would be deducted in advance and the corporation would pay $100,000 on December 1. In considering the loan, the bank requested a projected income statement and a cash budget for the month of November.

The following information is available.

1. Sales were budgeted at 120,000 units per month in October 19X8, December 19X8, and January 19X9 and at 90,000 units in November 19X8. The selling price is $2.00 per unit. Sales are billed on the fifteenth and last day of each month on terms of 1/10, net 30. Past experience indicates that sales are even throughout the month, and 50% of the customers pay the billed amount within the discount period. The remainder pay at the end of 30 days, except for bad debts, which average 1% of gross sales.

2. The inventory of finished goods on October 1 was 24,000 units. The finished goods inventory at the end of each month is to be maintained at 20% of the sales anticipated for the following month. No Work-in-Process Inventory remains at the end of any month.

3. The inventory of raw materials on October 1 was 22,800 pounds. At the end of each month the raw materials inventory is to be maintained at not less than 40% of the production requirements for the following month. Materials are purchased as needed in minimum quantities of 25,000 pounds per shipment. Raw material purchases for each month are paid in the succeeding month on terms of net 30 days.

4. All salaries and wages are paid on the fifteenth and last day of each month for the period ending on the date of payment.

5. All manufacturing overhead, selling, and administrative expenses are paid on the tenth of the month following the month in which they were incurred. Selling expenses are 10% of gross sales. Administrative expenses, which include depreciation of $500 per month on office furniture and fixtures, total $33,000 per month.

6. The standard cost of a molded plastic container, based on normal production of 100,000 units per month, is as follows:

Materials (½ pound)	$ .50
Labor	.40
Variable overhead	.20
Fixed overhead	.10
Total	$1.20

Fixed factory overhead includes depreciation on factory equipment of $4,000 per month.

REQUIRED:

A. Prepare a sales budget for October, November, and December.
B. Prepare a production budget for October, November, and December.
C. Prepare a purchases budget for October and November.
D. Prepare a projected income statement (profit plan) for November.
E. Prepare a cash budget for November and December. The cash balance on November 1, before the loan is granted, is expected to be $10,000.

(CPA adapted)

8–35 *(Comprehensive Master Budget).* Famous People Miniatures Inc. was formed six months ago to produce a line of small plastic miniatures of famous people. The product was an immediate success. Because of the unexpected demand for the product and higher level of production, the initial cash was exhausted and payables were delayed. Because of these delays in payment, creditors are demanding payment on delivery of any additional materials. The bookkeeper is far behind and has never prepared financial statements. The bank will not grant a loan until a planning and control system is implemented and a master budget is prepared.

The following data were drawn from documents, accounting records, and contacts with creditors.

1. The owners invested $50,000 when the company was formed. Equipment was purchased with a note and the building was rented. Assets at the present time consist of: cash, $800; accounts receivable, $30,000; inventory of plastic compound (6,000 pounds), $1,200; and equipment, $48,000. Liabilities consist of accounts payable, $10,000 (now past due), notes payable on equipment, $30,000, and accrued interest on note, $1,800.

2. The cost records are in very poor shape. The following data, however, are accurate. Each miniature requires two pounds of a plastic compound, costing $.20 per pound. Six miniatures may be produced per hour of labor. Direct labor employees are paid $6.00 per hour. The equipment was expected to have a useful life of four years at the time of purchase. Overhead and selling and administrative expenses for two months were as follows:

	October	December
Overhead costs (excluding depreciation)	$ 9,600	$10,860
Selling and administrative expenses	$10,900	$12,160
Hours worked	500	1,200
Units sold	3,000	7,200

3. With the present equipment, production capacity is 1,600 hours of direct labor per month.

4. The established selling price is $5.00 per unit. For the first half of 19X1, demand is expected to be 7,200 units per month, increasing to capacity for the last six months.

5. By the end of 19X1 the company expects to have an inventory of raw materials equal to two months use of plastic compound and 3,000 finished units on hand. Uncollected receivables will be equal to 1½ months of sales. Accounts payable should be $6,000, and accrued expenses (excluding interest) should be $10,000.

6. The note payable for equipment is due in three annual installments of $10,000 each, beginning on Jan. 1, 19X1. Interest is 12% on the unpaid balance payable with each installment.

7. If the cash budget shows that the loan can be repaid, the bank has agreed to lend the company $50,000 on January 1, 19X1, to be repaid with interest at 12% on December 31, 19X1.

REQUIRED:

A. How many units must be produced and sold per month during 19X1 to break even? How much income will be generated in the month the company operates at capacity?

B. Prepare a statement of financial position as of December 31, 19X0. The owner wants to know the amount of the loss for the first six months of operation.

C. Prepare a sales budget for 19X1.

D. Prepare a production budget for 19X1.

E. Prepare a purchases budget for 19X1.

F. Prepare a departmental budget for the factory for 19X1.

G. Prepare a profit plan for 19X1.

H. Prepare a cash budget for 19X1.

I. Prepare a projected statement of financial position at the end of 19X1.

8-36 *(Evaluation of Budget Process).* Clarkson Company is a large multidivision firm with several plants in each division. A comprehensive budgeting system is used for planning operations and measuring performance. The annual budgeting process commences in August, five months prior to the beginning of the fiscal year. At this time the division managers submit proposed budgets for sales, production and inventory levels, and expenses. Capital expenditure requests also are formalized at this time. The expense budgets include direct labor and all overhead items, which are separated into fixed and variable components. Direct materials are budgeted separately in developing the production and inventory schedules.

The expense budgets for each division are developed from its plants' results, as measured by the percent variation from an adjusted budget in the first six months of the current year and a target expense reduction percentage established by the corporation.

To determine plant percentages, the plant budget for the just completed half-year period is revised to recognize changes in operating procedures and costs outside the control of plant management (e.g., labor wage-rate changes, product style changes, etc.). The difference between this revised budget and the actual expenses is the controllable variance, and is expressed as a percentage of the actual expenses. This percentage is added (if unfavorable) to the corporate target expense reduction percentage. A favorable plant variance percentage is subtracted from the corporate target. If a plant had a 2% unfavorable controllable variance and the corporate target reduction was 4%, the plant's budget for next year should reflect costs approximately 6% below this year's actual costs.

Next year's final budgets for the corporation, the divisions, and the plants are adopted after corporate analysis of the proposed budgets and a careful review with each division manager of the changes made by corporate management. Division profit budgets include allocated corporate costs; plant profit budgets include allocated division and corporate costs.

Return on assets is used to measure the performance of divisions and plants. The asset base for a division consists of all assets assigned to the division, including its working capital, and an allocated share of corporate assets. Recommendations for promotions and salary increases for the executives of the divisions and plants are influenced by how well the actual return on assets compares with the budgeted return on assets.

The plant managers exercise control only over the cost portion of the plant profit budget because the divisions are responsible for sales. Only limited control over the plant assets is exercised at the plant level.

The manager of the Dexter Plant, a major plant in the Huron division, carefully controls his costs during the first six months so that any improvement appears after the target reduction of expenses is established. He accomplishes this by careful planning and timing of his discretionary expenditures.

During 1973 the property adjacent to the Dexter Plant was purchased by Clarkson Company. This expenditure was not included in the 1973 capital expenditure budget. Corporate management decided to divert funds from a project at another plant since the property appeared to be a better long-term investment.

Also during 1973, Clarkson Company experienced depressed sales. In an attempt to achieve budgeted profit, corporate management announced in August that all plants were to cut their annual expenses by 6%. In order to accomplish this expense reduction, the Dexter Plant manager reduced preventive maintenance and postponed needed major repairs. Employees who quit were not replaced unless it was absolutely necessary to do so. Employee training was postponed whenever possible. The raw materials, supplies, and finished goods inventories were reduced below normal levels.

REQUIRED:
Evaluate the budget procedure of Clarkson Company with respect to its effectiveness for planning and controlling operations. *(CMA adapted)*

Budgetary Control, Responsibility Accounting, and Their Behavioral Implications

The control process begins after the planning process is completed and as the decisions are being implemented. The accounting system performs a monitoring role by accumulating actual performance data, comparing the actual results with the plans, and communicating the results to management. To the extent that relevant data are accumulated accurately and reporting is timely, accounting reports will be useful for control.

In Chapter 8, a master budget including a profit plan, cash budget, and projected statement of financial position was prepared. We will now concentrate on the control process, that is, where actual results of operations are compared with those plans, and reports are prepared for each level of management. This chapter begins with an examination of the requirements of a good reporting system, then presents an analysis of the differences between planned profit and actual profit, and finally, presents a set of reports for the Donnell Company, the illustration in Chapter 8.

BASIC REQUIREMENTS FOR A GOOD REPORTING SYSTEM

Any deviations from the course of action planned in the budget must be identified so that corrective action can be taken. Qualitative standards for good reporting include relevancy, timeliness, and accuracy.

Relevancy

Accounting's role is to provide information relevant to user needs. To be relevant to the needs of management, a reporting system must reflect the factors over which each manager has control and must identify the areas that need management attention. Responsibility accounting and management by exception are ways of stressing relevant data.

RESPONSIBILITY ACCOUNTING

The reporting function of accounting requires the **feedback** of information to management so that performance can be evaluated and, if necessary, actions altered. The reporting function also provides a base of information about the activities over which an individual manager has responsibility. In preparing the budgets in Chapter 8, we included only the costs over which the particular manager had control.

Some accountants have suggested that reports should include information beyond a manager's present scope of responsibility in order to prepare the manager for broader managerial responsibilities in the future. However, performance evaluation is too important to the individual manager to use the report for professional development. There are other ways to develop the interests of a departmental manager in firm-wide activities. These could include training programs, committee memberships, staff meetings, and participative management.

Exhibit 9–1 summarizes the types of continuing information needs at the various levels of a firm. At the lower levels in the organization, emphasis is almost exclusively on nonfinancial information. Group leaders and individual workers are measured in nonfinancial terms: How many hours must they work? How many units must they produce? How much scrap is allowed? The individual worker is not involved with accounting reports. Here information needs are met by nonfinancial data accumulated in the factory, and performance is evaluated in nonfinancial terms when actual results are compared with the standards. The time frame of information at this level is very short. Most information is concerned with hour-by-hour or day-by-day activities.

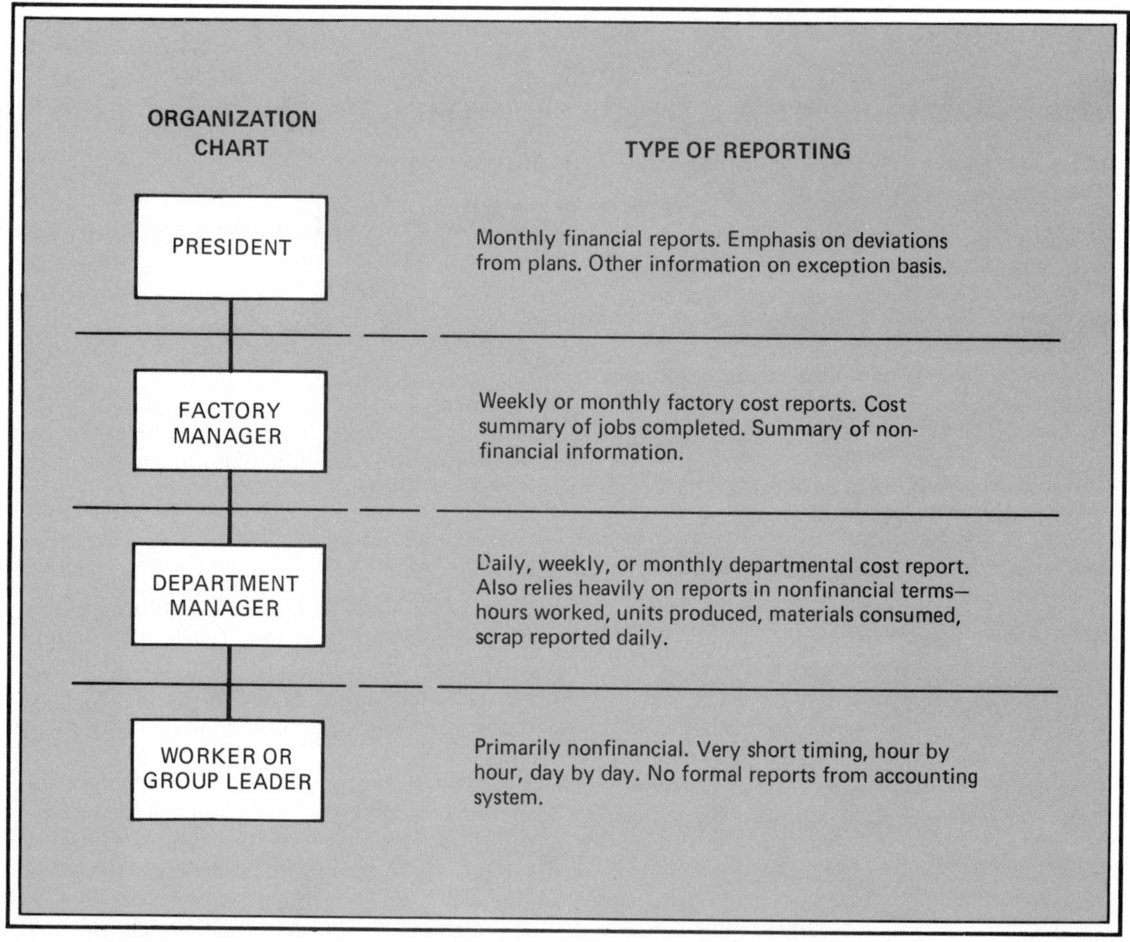

EXHIBIT 9–1
Reporting to different levels of management

At the department manager level there is concern over costs. The department is identified as a cost center, and costs for which the manager is responsible are accumulated for the department. However, the department manager also deals in physical quantities on a day-to-day basis. Many of the objectives of the department are expressed in physical terms, and the technical standards, in physical terms, provide guides for performance measurements. From the summaries of labor tickets the manager should know roughly what the labor efficiency variance will be before it is computed and reported by the accounting department. Having approved any excess materials requisitions for material usage beyond standard, the manager would know if the material usage variance were unfavorable and would know its approximate amount. The accounting system should later verify what the department manager already knows. The time horizon of the department manager is limited to a relatively short period, probably the time covered by a production schedule.

At the level of vice-president for manufacturing (factory manager in our illustration), the concern of the manager has moved from physical (nonfinancial) measures to financial measures. The manager is not responsible for profit, but is involved in a wide range of decisions that are measurable in financial terms. Although the factory manager does receive information in physical terms, most of the data are also converted to financial terms to allow summarization.

At the level of top management, the president is concerned with the attainment of objectives and plans for the future. The amount of information needed depends upon management style. If decisions are decentralized, top management establishes company goals and objectives and expects subordinates to administer the continuing activities of the company. As long as subordinates are meeting their objectives, the president deals only in summary information. If decisions are centralized, the president needs more information, in greater depth, about the operations of the company.

Similar levels of reporting exist in the marketing area. At the lowest level, the salespeople are interested in quantity sold, number of calls, number of customers, and other data related to the selling effort. The product or territory manager's interests are restricted to products, territories, and customers. The sales manager is interested in demand for the company's product, the actions of competitors, and income or contribution margin. However, there is a basic difference between the information concerns of the marketing and manufacturing areas. The marketing area is a profit center where the manager has responsibility for both revenues and costs. In the manufacturing area, the manager has responsibility only for costs.

MANAGEMENT BY EXCEPTION

Another aspect of relevancy is the concept of management by exception. Reports should emphasize exceptional deviations from plans. If plans are well prepared, management may expect activities to proceed according to plan. The reporting system should provide some basis for the manager to separate significant favorable or unfavorable deviations, which should be investigated further, from those that are insignificant. Ideally, the reporting system would report deviations from plans based upon the probability of their occurrence. Then, based on past experiences and the nature of the cost, if a deviation from the plan is beyond an acceptable level it would be treated as exceptional.

In Chapter 2, when past costs were plotted on a scattergraph, two observations were made about the data. First, the graph showed the behavior pattern of the cost in relation to activity increases; second, not all the observations fell on the line. Some variations are likely. From estimates and measures of the variations, control limits may be developed which will provide a basis that indicates when a variation is normal and does not need investigation and when a variation is significant and should be investigated. For example, scattergraphs for two costs follows:

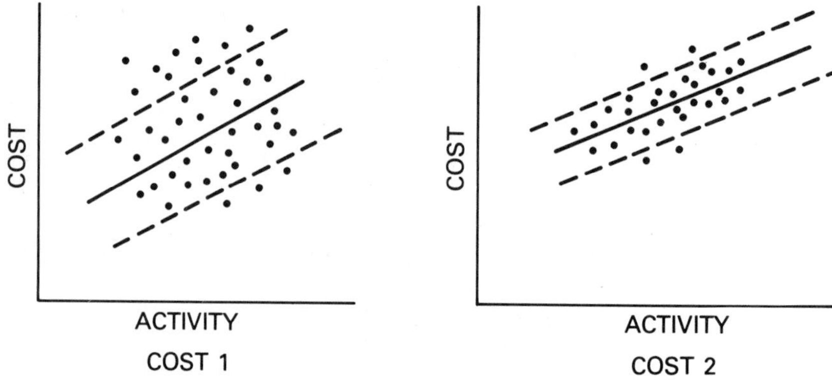

Historically, Cost 1 has varied widely in relation to activity levels; on the other hand, Cost 2 has shown little variation. If control limits of the same width were used for both costs, management could waste time investigating normal variances in Cost 1 and pass up abnormal variances in Cost 2. It is beyond the scope of this book to present the probability concepts necessary to build statistical control charts. However, it is important to recognize that different cost variation patterns call for different types of control applications and that cost control charts can be based upon statistical techniques.

Timeliness

One dimension of timeliness is the date a report is received. A major criticism of accounting reports is that they are often delayed until the information content is no longer useful. To be useful for a decision, a report must be received before the decision is made. If information is to be useful for control, it must be received as soon as possible after the measured action takes place. A cost report for the month of May that arrives in the middle or latter part of June is not useful to management for operational control. A delay of several days to improve the precision of a report may make the report worthless. Out-of-date information is not useful, regardless of how precise it may be.

Another dimension is the period of time covered by the reports. Out of tradition, reports are issued weekly, monthly, or for some other set period of time. A fixed reporting schedule is adequate only if the planning and control process fits naturally into the time periods used. Where there are special problems, such as an unusual production quantity decision or a capital expenditures decision, regular reports are inadequate. For these nonroutine decisions special reports must be prepared.

Accuracy

Accounting reports have an aura of precision that is not warranted. It is taken for granted by most managers that the accounting system will produce information in an objective manner. The accuracy of the data, however, is dependent upon many factors, including the nature of the accounting classification system, the reliability of the source documents, and the interpretations given to events and transactions.

One possibility for error stems from errors in the data input that originate elsewhere in the firm. Labor records are a good example. If excessive pressure is exerted on foremen to have their subordinates meet time standards, the employees may falsify their records by averaging the time spent on several activities in order to hide large deviations from standard. This action may even be condoned or encouraged by the foremen.

As an example, consider the following two activities:

	Process A	*Process B*
Standard labor	1,000 hours	1,000 hours
Actual labor	940 hours	1,150 hours

If we assume that any deviation over 5% will result in an investigation and pressure for improved future performance, employee time tickets may be falsified to show approximately 1,045 hours on each process, both safely within the 5% limit. The accountant using the data may be completely unaware of the smoothing of labor deviations. Unfortunately, this kind of error can have a significant impact upon subsequent decisions because the decision maker is misled about the facts.

Empirical research on the accuracy of labor data has revealed errors of 20% to 25% in the recording of labor hours on particular jobs.[1] The management accountant must take pains to ensure that his data sources provide accurate information.

---

[1]Sam E. Scharff, "The Industrial Engineer and the Cost Accountant," *N.A.A. Bulletin* (March, 1961), pp. 17–18.

LEVEL OF DETAIL IN REPORTING

As shown in Exhibit 8–1, the control process begins with the accumulation of actual results of operations through the accounting system and supplementary schedules. The next step in the control process is the comparison of the actual results with the plan and an identification of significant deviations. This comparison is the critical step in determining what corrective action must be taken by management.

The importance of a deviation depends on its impact upon net income and its potential contribution to increased management control. The depth of detail in reporting should vary depending on the circumstances and the needs of the particular manager. When the need for greater detail is important to pinpoint areas needing management action, the analysis should be carried further. Expansion of the analysis should continue until the cost of additional detail is not justified by the benefits obtained from further information. In a responsibility reporting system tailored to individual managers, different managers at the same organizational level may require different degrees of analysis in order to exercise the appropriate level of control.

For our illustrations in this chapter we will use the master budget information developed for the Donnell Company in Chapter 8. We will also assume that the Donnell Company is in the fourth quarter of the year 19X2 and that the actual results have been accumulated. A summary of the actual results is shown in the income statement in Exhibit 9–2. Our illustration of performance analysis will refer only to the fourth quarter. However, some reports shown later in the chapter will include the results for the entire year. In the illustration of performance analysis, income will refer to income before taxes. We will begin with the broadest level of analysis and then systematically develop greater detail through a series of levels.[2] (Exhibit 9–10 shows a summary of the following discussion.)

Level 1: *Aggregate Analysis*

One mode of aggregate analysis is to compare the results from this accounting period with those from the previous accounting period. While such a comparison may be functional in an actual situation, it is a relatively weak analysis in theory since it assumes that all conditions of operations were similar in the two accounting periods. Changes in volume or sales mix, cost structures, economic conditions, operating procedures, and price levels all act to weaken the value of historical comparisons.

The control comparison is relatively stronger, at least in theory, where there is a planning budget. With a planning budget the comparison can be made between the profit plan and the actual results. Since the planning

---

[2]The concept of reporting levels is adapted from: John Shank and Neil C. Churchill, "Variance Analysis: A Management-Oriented Approach," *The Accounting Review*, October, 1977.

DONNELL COMPANY
ACTUAL INCOME STATEMENT
Fourth Quarter, 19X2

Sales:		
Small: (6,000 × $5)	$ 30,000	
Large: (12,000 × $10)	120,000	
Total		$150,000
Variable production costs:[A]		
Materials used:[B]		
Plastic	$ 17,300	
Small boxes	2,100	
Large boxes	7,500	$ 26,900
Labor:		
Forming Dept. (2,800 hours × $5.15)	$ 14,420	
Packing Dept. (1,900 hours × $3.20)	6,080	20,500
Overhead:		
Forming Dept.	$ 11,000	
Packing Dept.	1,800	12,800
Total variable costs of production		60,200
Contribution margin from production		$ 89,800
Variable costs of marketing		14,600
Contribution margin from operations		$ 75,200
Fixed costs:[C]		
Forming Dept. ($8,000 + $3,300)	$ 11,300	
Packing Dept. ($1,000 + $1,800)	2,800	
Factory Administration ($1,000 + $9,000)	10,000	
Marketing ($6,000 + $16,000)	22,000	
Administrative Costs ($1,000 + $8,000)	9,000	
Total fixed costs		55,100
Operating income		$ 20,100
Interest expense		2,000
Income before taxes		$ 18,100

[A]Actual production was 6,000 small; 12,000 large.

[B]

	Actual Purchases	Inventory Increase at Standard Cost	Material Used
Plastic	45,000 × $.42	4,000 × $.40	$17,300
Small boxes	6,000 × $.35	none	2,100
Large boxes	15,000 × $.58	2,000 × $.60	7,500

[C]Depreciation expense listed first; salaries next.

EXHIBIT 9–2
Historical income statement for Donnell Company

budget was based upon volumes, mixes, cost structures, and operating conditions predicted for the accounting period, the comparison is relatively strong.

The first level of analysis with a planning budget simply identifies the fact that income for the quarter is different from planned income.

Planned income (loss) for Quarter 4 (from Exhibit 8–16)	$(17,800)
Actual income for Quarter 4 (from Exhibit 9–2)	18,100
Variance in income	$ 35,900 F

For the Donnell Company actual income exceeded planned income by $35,900.

Level 2: Planning Budget Analysis

The second level of analysis compares actual and planning budget data for each item on the income statement. Using only major items, the analysis would be:

	Profit Plan	*Actual*	*Variance*
Sales	$ 88,000	$150,000	$62,000 F
Expenses	105,800	131,900	(26,100) U
Profit (loss)	$(17,800)	$ 18,100	$35,900 F

The analysis at this level is concerned with comparing actual results with the profit plan. The same mode of analysis for the major expense categories in the income statement follows.

	Profit Plan	*Actual*	*Variance*
Variable production costs	$ 40,000	$ 60,200	$(20,200) U
Variable selling costs	8,800	14,600	(5,800) U
Fixed production costs	25,000	24,100	900 F
Fixed marketing costs	20,000	22,000	(2,000) U
Fixed administration costs	10,000	9,000	1,000 F
Interest on debt	2,000	2,000	0
Total	$105,800	$131,900	$(26,100) U

This analysis may be called a "static" or "fixed" analysis because the plan is not adjusted to the actual level of activities with the flexible budget.

Level 3: Performance Budget Analysis

The planned level of activity is seldom achieved exactly. When the actual level of performance differs from planned performance, a **performance budget** can be prepared *after the fact* to show what revenues and costs should have been at the *actual* level of activity. For performance assessment, it would be a weak analysis to use a profit plan based upon a level of activity that differs from the actual level of activity. The performance budget is the flexible budget, discussed in Chapter 2, adjusted to the actual level attained. For example, the Donnell Company expected to sell 6,000 large terrariums during the fourth quarter but, because of unexpected demand for the product, actually sold 12,000 large terrariums. The profit plan with revenues and costs based upon 6,000 terrariums would be a relatively weak measurement base. A performance budget showing revenues and costs that should have been incurred at 12,000 units is better for evaluating actual performance.

Using the performance budget and the actual results it is possible to derive activity variances and price, spending, and efficiency variances.

ACTIVITY VARIANCE

The impact of differences between planned and actual activity levels is determined by comparing the profit plan with the performance budget. Because both plans are prepared using standard (budgeted) prices and costs, the only difference between them is due to changes in the volume level. The profit plan is the result of the *planned* level of activity times the planned unit revenues and costs (see Exhibit 8–16 where the profit plan was developed). The performance budget is the result of the *actual* level of activity times the planned unit revenues and costs. The following analysis shows a comparison of the profit plan with the performance budget.

The performance budget sales for small terrariums is 6,000 units times the budgeted sales price of $5.00 per unit, or $30,000; for large terrariums, it is 12,000 units times $8.00, or $96,000. The variable production costs total $60,000, representing the 6,000 actual small terrariums sold times their standard cost of $2.00 ($12,000), plus the 12,000 actual large terrariums sold times their standard cost of $4.00 ($48,000). The $57,000 of fixed costs are budgeted operating fixed costs of $55,000 plus the $2,000 of interest expense. Fixed costs in the performance budget are the same as in the profit plan, since fixed costs do not change with volume changes.

If the planned selling prices and costs were used, the actual volume would have resulted in a net loss of $3,600. However, with the same selling prices and costs at the planned volume, the loss would have been $17,800. Because a higher volume of large terrariums was sold, the revenues increased $38,000. There would be an expected increase in variable costs of $23,800. In

	Profit Plan	*Performance Budget*	*Activity Variance*
Units sold:			
Small	8,000	6,000	(2,000) U
Large	6,000	12,000	6,000 F
Sales revenue:			
Small	$ 40,000	$ 30,000	$(10,000) U
Large	48,000	96,000	48,000 F
Total	$ 88,000	$126,000	$ 38,000 F
Expenses:			
Variable production	$ 40,000	$ 60,000	$(20,000) U
Variable marketing	8,800	12,600	(3,800) U
Fixed costs	57,000	57,000	0
Total	105,800	129,600	(23,800) U
Net Income (Loss)	$ (17,800)	$ (3,600)	$ 14,200 F

summary, there is a $14,200 profit increase over the planned profit because of increased activity.

There is another way to determine the $14,200 activity variance. Since the variable costs increase directly with volume, as does the total sales revenue, the variance could be measured by the planned contribution margin.

	Planned Sales in Units	*Actual Sales in Units*	*Activity Variance in Units*	*Planned Contribution Margin*	*Activity Variance in Dollars*
Small	8,000	6,000	(2,000)	$2.50	$ (5,000) U
Large	6,000	12,000	6,000	$3.20	19,200 F
					$14,200 F

PRICE, EFFICIENCY, AND SPENDING VARIANCES

In addition to the variance in activity, it is highly probable that the firm's actual profit differed from the profit in the profit plan because the prices, efficiencies, or spending rates were different from those planned. By comparing the actual results (which are actual quantities times the actual prices and costs) with the performance budget (which are actual quantities times the planned prices and costs), the price, efficiency, and spending variances can be isolated.

	Performance Budget	*Actual*	*Price, Efficiency, Spending Variances*
Sales revenue:			
Small	$ 30,000	$ 30,000	$ 0
Large	96,000	120,000	24,000 F
Total	$126,000	$150,000	$24,000 F
Expenses:			
Variable production	$ 60,000	$ 60,200	$ (200) U
Variable marketing	12,600	14,600	(2,000) U
Fixed costs	57,000	57,100	(100) U
Total	129,600	131,900	(2,300) U
Net income (loss)	$ (3,600)	$ 18,100	$21,700 F

Sales price increases on the large terrariums acted to increase profits by $24,000. At the same time, actual costs were $2,300 above the performance budget. Thus, because of price, efficiency, or spending variances, profits were $21,700 larger than planned.

Because of increased activity, the profit was $14,200 larger than planned, and because of price and spending differences, profits were $21,700 larger than planned. The total variance is $35,900 ($14,200 + $21,700). This is the difference between the profit in the profit plan and the actual results. The total of the price, efficiency, and spending variances was $21,700. This variance can be decomposed (broken down) into sales price variances and cost variances.

SALES PRICE VARIANCES

The sales price variance is $24,000, favorable. It is the difference between (a) actual sales in units times standard sales prices in the performance budget ($126,000), and (b) actual sales in units times the actual sales price in the actual income statement ($150,000). During the fourth quarter, the price of the large terrariums was increased $2.00. Since 12,000 large terrariums were sold in the quarter, the total sales price variance of $24,000 resulted from this price increase.

COST VARIANCES

The total of the cost variances was $2,300. This total can be decomposed by the nature of costs incurred: direct materials, direct labor, variable overhead, variable marketing costs, and fixed costs.

As a starting point we will use the standard costs for the products shown in Exhibit 8–5. The first column below shows these standard costs times the actual units produced; the second column shows the actual costs

Variance	Calculational Formula	Cost Variances	
Material price variance	(Standard price per unit of materials − Actual price per unit of materials) × Actual quantity of materials purchased	Plastic ($.40 − $.42) 45,000	$ 900 U
		Small Box ($.30 − $.35) 6,000	300 U
		Large Box ($.60 − $.58) 15,000	300 F
		TOTAL	900 U
Material quantity variance	[(Actual units produced × Standard quantity per unit) − Actual quantity of materials used] × Standard price per unit of materials	Plastic [(6,000 × 1) + (12,000 × 3) − 41,000] $.40	$ 400 F
		Small Box [(6,000 × 1) − 6,000] $.30	0
		Large Box [(12,000 × 1) − 13,000] $.60	600 U
		TOTAL	$ 200 U
Labor price (rate) variance	(Standard wage rate per hour − Actual wage rate per hour) × Actual hours worked	Forming ($5.00 − $5.15) 2,800	$ 420 U
		Packing ($3.00 − $3.20) 1,900	380 U
		TOTAL	800 U
Labor efficiency variance	[(Actual units produced × Standard labor hours per unit) − Actual labor hours worked] × Standard wage rate per hour	Forming [(6,000 × .1) + (12,000 × .2) − 2,800] $5	1,000 F
		Packing [(18,000 × .1) − 1,900] $3	300 U
		TOTAL	700 F
Variable overhead efficiency variance	[(Actual units produced × Standard labor hours per unit) − Actual labor hours worked] × Standard variable overhead rate per hour	Forming [(6,000 × .1) + (12,000 × .2) − 2,800] $4	800 F
		Packing [(6,000 × .1) + (12,000 × .1) − 1,900] $1	100 U
		TOTAL	700 F
Variable overhead spending variance	(Standard variable overhead rate per hour × Actual hours worked) − Actual variable overhead costs	Forming ($4 × 2,800) − $11,000	200 F
		Packing ($1 × 1,900) − $1,800	100 F
		TOTAL	300 F

EXHIBIT 9–3
Standard cost variances

incurred during the quarter. The production budget in the profit plan (Exhibit 8–8) had called for an increase in inventory of large terrariums but the unexpected sales increase made this impossible, and actual units produced equaled the units sold.

	Standard Costs for 6,000 Small and 12,000 Large	*Actual Costs for 6,000 Small and 12,000 Large*	*Total Variance*
Direct materials	$25,800	$26,900[a]	$(1,100) U
Direct labor	20,400	20,500	(100) U
Variable overhead	13,800	12,800	1,000 F
Total	$60,000	$60,200	$ (200) U

[a]Actual material purchases were $29,700; however, the raw materials inventory increased $2,800.

Following the methods explained in Chapter 6, the variable production costs can be further analyzed into their price, efficiency, and spending variances as shown in Exhibit 9–3.

Variable marketing costs can be analyzed also in terms of actual units sold.

	Standard Costs for 6,000 Small and 12,000 Large	*Actual Costs for 6,000 Small and 12,000 Large*	*Total Variance*
Variable marketing costs	$12,600	$14,600	$(2,000) U

The fixed costs should not be influenced by activity. Therefore the spending analysis will not change from Level 2 where the fixed costs were detailed. The difference between the planned and actual total fixed costs amounted to $100 unfavorable.

The cost variances may be summarized as follows:

Material price variance		$ (900) U
Material quantity variance		(200) U
Labor price (rate) variance		(800) U
Labor efficiency variance		700 F
Variable overhead efficiency variance		700 F
Variable overhead spending variance		300 F
Variable marketing costs		(2,000) U
Fixed production costs:		
Forming	$ (300) U	
Packing	200 F	
Administration	1,000 F	900 F
Fixed marketing costs		(2,000) U
Fixed administrative costs		1,000 F
Interest on debt		0
Total		$(2,300) U

Level 4: Departmental Performance Analysis

At the heart of the responsibility reporting system are the departmental reports. In this section reports for a manufacturing department manager, the vice-president of manufacturing, the vice-president of marketing, and some of the reports for top management are presented.

DEPARTMENTAL COST REPORT—FORMING DEPARTMENT

The departmental budget for the Donnell Company's forming department was developed in Exhibit 8–15 as a part of the profit plan. Our reporting example continues with the same department. The departmental budget in the profit plan was a *static budget*; only one level of activity was planned. However, in management reports, the performance budget should be adjusted to show what the costs should be at the *actual level* of activity.

A departmental cost report for the forming department is illustrated for the fourth quarter and year-to-date in Exhibit 9–4. Each part of the report contains three cost columns: a performance budget, actual costs for the period, and the variances of actual costs from the performance budget.

The fourth quarter performance budget is based upon the actual production of 6,000 small terrariums and 12,000 large terrariums. For example, the performance budget for material is the 6,000 small units produced times their standard cost of $.40 per unit plus the 12,000 large units produced times their standard cost of $1.20 per unit (see the standard cost card in Exhibit 8–5). For labor, it is the 6,000 small units times $.50 plus the

	QUARTER 4			*YEAR-TO-DATE*		
	Performance Budget	*Actual*	*Variance*	*Performance Budget*	*Actual*	*Variance*
MATERIAL—Plastic	$16,800	$16,400		$104,400	$100,000	
Material quantity variance			$ 400 F			$ 4,400 F
DIRECT LABOR	15,000	14,420		99,000	106,500	
Labor efficiency variance			1,000 F			6,000 U
Labor rate variance			420 U			1,500 U
VARIABLE OVERHEAD	12,000	11,000		79,200	90,000	
Variable overhead spending variance			200 F			6,000 U
Variable overhead efficiency			800 F			4,800 U
TOTAL VARIABLE COSTS	$43,800	$41,820	$1,980 F	$282,600	$296,500	$13,900 U
FIXED COSTS:						
Depreciation	$ 8,000	$ 8,000	$ 0	$ 32,000	$ 32,000	$ 0
Supervisory salaries	3,000	3,300	300 U	12,000	12,800	800 U
Total	11,000	11,300	300 U	44,000	44,800	800 U
TOTAL DEPARTMENTAL COSTS	$54,800	$53,120	$1,680 F	$326,600	$341,300	$14,700 U
PHYSICAL DATA:						
Units produced:						
Small		6,000			72,000	
Large		12,000			63,000	
Plastic used (pounds)		41,000			272,000	
Direct labor hours		2,800			21,000	

EXHIBIT 9–4
Forming department cost report for Donnell Company

12,000 large units produced times $1.00. The actual costs are shown in Exhibit 9–2. The variances for variable costs were calculated above.

FACTORY COST REPORT

The factory cost report focuses on the control of all manufacturing costs. Therefore, the costs of each subordinate department are shown as a single-line summary. If more information is desired by the factory manager, the individual cost report for any subordinate department may be examined.

	QUARTER 4			YEAR-TO-DATE		
	Performance Budget	*Actual*	*Variance*	*Performance Budget*	*Actual*	*Variance*
COSTS CONTROLLABLE BY SUBORDINATE DEPARTMENTS						
Forming department	$54,800	$53,120	1,680 F	$326,600	$341,300	$14,700 U
Packing department	19,200	20,280	1,080 U	125,400	132,350	6,950 U
PURCHASING—Material price variance	0	900 U	900 U	0	7,050	7,050 U
Total	$74,000	$74,300	$ 300 U	$452,000	$480,700	$28,700 U
FIXED COSTS COMMON TO FACTORY						
Depreciation	$ 1,000	$ 1,000	$ 0	$ 4,000	$ 4,000	$ 0
Supervisory salaries	10,000	9,000	1,000 F	40,000	38,000	2,000 F
Total	11,000	10,000	1,000 F	44,000	42,000	2,000 F
TOTAL FACTORY COSTS	$85,000	$84,300	$ 700 F	$496,000	$522,700	$26,700 U
SUMMARY OF FACTORY COST VARIANCES:						
Material price variance			$ 900 U			$ 7,050 U
Material quantity variance			200 U			1,550 F
Labor efficiency variance			700 F			7,500 U
Labor rate variance			800 U			2,600 U
Variable overhead spending variance			300 F			6,400 U
Variable overhead efficiency variance			700 F			5,300 U
Fixed overhead spending variance			900 F			600 F
Total			$ 700 F			$26,700 U

EXHIBIT 9–5
Factory cost report for Donnell Company

The factory cost report is presented in Exhibit 9–5 where actual costs are compared with the performance budget. In this report, as in other cost center reports, inclusion of the profit plan is not necessary. The performance budget for the factory is prepared by applying the flexible budget to the actual level of production in the plant as a whole. However, the budget figures for the subordinate departments come from the summary of their departmental reports. Only the costs under direct control of the plant manager are detailed in this report.

A summary of the variances from budget is presented as a part of the report in our example. Since control is exercised over most of the variances in subordinate departments, the summary gives the factory manager an overview of cost control. There may be overall patterns that cannot be determined from individual reports.

DEPARTMENTAL REPORT—MARKETING

The marketing departments are profit centers. Selling more or fewer units than planned will affect the income of the period. The activity variance is the increased contribution margin from the sale of more units than predicted in the profit plan or the reduced contribution margin from selling fewer than planned.

Because of the possible activity variance, reports for marketing areas should show the profit plan as well as the performance budget and actual results. Exhibit 9–6 illustrates a report prepared for the marketing manager for Quarter 4 and the year-to-date. The first column in the report, headed *Profit Plan,* is the budget developed for this area in Chapter 8 as part of the total profit plan (Exhibit 8–16). At that time the sales manager expected to sell 8,000 small and 6,000 large terrariums and prepared a marketing budget for that sales volume. During the quarter 6,000 small and 12,000 large terrariums were actually sold, and the performance budget was prepared for this level. The activity variance which is the difference between the two budgets, shows that contribution margin was increased by $14,200 as a result of the change in sales volume. This variance was examined in detail earlier in the chapter.

REPORTS TO TOP MANAGEMENT

Reports to top management should do three things: first, for control they should explain the difference between the profit in the profit plan and actual profit, drawing management's attention to significant problem areas; second, they should show the aggregate data used in financial reports; third, they should provide feedback about the achievement of goals and objectives.

One way to show why planned and actual profit differed is a summary report called the report on profit plan. The report shows only variances from the plan. To be effective, the differences should be grouped by responsibility centers (manufacturing, marketing, and administration). The report on profit

	QUARTER 4				
				Variances	
	(a) Profit Plan	(b) Performance Budget	(c) Actual	(a − b) Activity	(b − c) Price, Efficiency, Spending
PRODUCT—SMALL:					
Sales	$40,000	$30,000	$ 30,000	$(10,000) U	$ 0
Variable production costs	16,000	12,000	12,000	4,000 F	0
Contribution margin from production	$24,000	$18,000	$ 18,000	$ (6,000) U	0
Variable selling costs	4,000	3,000	2,600	1,000 F	400 F
Contribution margin from operations	$20,000	$15,000	$ 15,400	$ (5,000) U	$ 400 F
PRODUCT—LARGE:					
Sales	$48,000	$96,000	$120,000	$ 48,000 F	$ 24,000 F
Variable production costs	24,000	48,000	48,000	(24,000) U	0
Contribution margin from production	$24,000	$48,000	$ 72,000	$ 24,000 F	0
Variable selling costs	4,800	9,600	12,000	(4,800) U	(2,400) U
Contribution margin from operations	$19,200	$38,400	$ 60,000	$ 19,200 F	$ 21,600 F
CONTRIBUTION MARGIN FROM ALL PRODUCTS:	$39,200	$53,400	$ 75,400	$ 14,200 F	$ 22,000 F
Less fixed marketing costs:					
Depreciation	$ 6,000	$ 6,000	$ 6,000	$ 0	$ 0
Supervisory salaries	14,000	14,000	16,000	0	(2,000) U
Total	$20,000	$20,000	$ 22,000	0	$ (2,000) U
Marketing contribution	$19,200	$33,400	$ 53,400	$ 14,200 F	$ 20,000 F

EXHIBIT 9–6
Marketing department report for Donnell Company

plan represents the final step in the responsibility accounting system. The report for the Donnell Company for the fourth quarter and the year-to-date is shown in Exhibit 9–7. For the year-to-date the marketing area accounted for

DONNELL COMPANY
REPORT ON PROFIT PLAN
19X2

	Fourth Quarter		*Year-to-date*	
Planned net income from profit plan		$(17,800)		$50,000
Variances due to marketing:				
Activity variance	$14,200		$49,000	
Selling price variance	24,000		24,000	
Marketing costs	(4,000)	34,200	(5,000)	68,000
Variances due to production:				
Material price variance	$ (900)		$ (7,050)	
Material quantity variance	(200)		1,550	
Labor efficiency variance	700		(7,500)	
Labor rate variance	(800)		(2,600)	
Variable overhead efficiency variance	700		(6,400)	
Variable overhead spending variance	300		(5,300)	
Fixed overhead spending variance	900	700	600	(26,700)
Variances due to administration:				
Administrative costs	$ 1,000		$ 2,000	
Income taxes	N/A	1,000	(21,650)	(19,650)
Actual net income		$ 18,100		$71,650

EXHIBIT 9–7
Report on profit plan for Donnell Company

$68,000 of additional operating income through additional sales ($49,000 activity variance), increased selling prices (shown by the selling price variance of $24,000) less increased marketing costs of $5,000. With the exception of the material quantity variances, and the fixed cost spending variance, all factory cost variances are unfavorable and accounted for $26,700 of the variation from plan.

In addition to the report on profit plan, top management would also receive the traditional financial statements: income statement, a statement of financial position (balance sheet), and a cash flow statement or a statement of changes in financial position. Exhibit 9–2 presented an income statement based upon historical costs shown only as a data base to illustrate different levels of analysis. When a firm uses standard variable costing, as does the Donnell Company, this historical cost statement would not be prepared and

DONNELL COMPANY
INCOME STATEMENT
Fourth Quarter, 19X2

	(a) Profit Plan	(b) Performance Budget	(c) Actual	Variances: (a − b) Activity	Variances: (b − c) Price, Efficiency, Spending
Sales	$ 88,000	$126,000	$150,000	$ 38,000 F	$24,000 F
Variable costs:					
Production	$ 40,000	$ 60,000	$ 60,200	$(20,000) U	$ (200) U
Marketing	8,800	12,600	14,600	(3,800) U	(2,000) U
Total	48,800	72,600	74,800	(23,800) U	(2,200) U
Contribution margin	$ 39,200	$ 53,400	$ 75,200	$ 14,200 F	$21,800 F
Fixed costs:					
Production	$ 25,000	$ 25,000	$ 24,100	—	$ 900 F
Marketing	20,000	20,000	22,000	—	(2,000) U
Administration	10,000	10,000	9,000	—	1,000 F
Total	55,000	55,000	55,100	—	(100) U
Net operating income	$(15,800)	$ (1,600)	$ 20,100	$ 14,200 F	$21,700 F
Interest expense	2,000	2,000	2,000	—	—
Net income before taxes	$(17,800)	$ (3,600)	$ 18,100	$ 14,200 F	$21,700 F

EXHIBIT 9–8
Quarterly income statement for management of Donnell Company

the data for performance assessment would come directly from the accounting system. The income statement given to top management would be based upon standard variable costing. Income statements for the fourth quarter and the year-to-date are shown in Exhibits 9–8 and 9–9. Other financial statements are not illustrated. For the year, actual income exceeded the profit plan by $21,650 ($71,650 − $50,000). Actual earnings per share were $3.58 versus a planned earnings per share of $2.50.

As a final step, top management needs a comparison of the actual results with the original objectives. Exhibit 8–18 shows the objectives of the firm for 19X2. Exhibit 9–10 shows a comparison of the actual results for 19X2 with the original objectives. Overall, the firm exceeded its objectives. The only problems were in the area of inventory management which were anticipated. Because of the wide variations in sales, the firm found it difficult to maintain a stable work force; it was also difficult to maintain the plastic inventory at the desired level because of the large favorable increase in sales.

DONNELL COMPANY
INCOME STATEMENT
For the year 19X2

	(a) Profit Plan	(b) Performance Budget	(c) Actual	Variances: (a − b) Activity	Variances: (b − c) Price, Efficiency, Spending
Sales	$720,000	$850,000	$874,000	$130,000 F	$24,000 F
Variable Costs:					
Production	$320,000	$388,000	$388,000	$ (68,000) U	—
Marketing	72,000	85,000	87,000	(13,000) U	$ (2,000) U
Total	392,000	473,000	475,000	(81,000) U	(2,000) U
Contribution margin	$328,000	$377,000	$399,000	$ 49,000 F	$22,000 F
Variances from standard			(27,300)		(27,300) U
Contribution margin adjusted	$328,000	$377,000	$371,700	$ 49,000 F	$ (5,300) U
Fixed Costs:					
Production	$100,000	$100,000	$ 99,400	—	$ 600 F
Marketing	80,000	80,000	83,000	—	(3,000) U
Administration	40,000	40,000	38,000	—	2,000 F
Total	220,000	220,000	220,400	—	(400) U
Net operating income	$108,000	$157,000	$151,300	$ 49,000 F	$ (5,700) U
Interest expense	8,000	8,000	8,000	—	—
Net income before taxes	$100,000	$149,000	$143,300	$ 49,000 F	$ (5,700) U
Income taxes (50%)	50,000	74,500	71,650	(24,500) U	2,850 F
Net income after taxes	$ 50,000	$ 74,500	$ 71,650	$ 24,500 F	$ (2,850) U
Earnings per share	$2.50	$3.73	$3.58		

EXHIBIT 9–9
Annual income statement for management of Donnell Company

Summary and Extensions of Performance Analysis

A table showing the analysis of levels is presented in Exhibit 9–11. This table gives an overview of the previous discussion of how we decomposed the difference between planned profits and actual profits. Ideally, each step in the decomposition will provide additional insights to management.

These are not the only performance measures that could be derived. With additional information many of the variances could be decomposed further. For example:

19X2 PLAN	*19X2 ACTUAL RESULTS*
PROFIT OBJECTIVES: Achieve a net income after tax of: 1. 12% of reported owners' equity at beginning of year. 2. 8% of net sales.	PROFIT RESULTS: 21.3% on reported owners' equity. ($71,650 ÷ $336,000) 8.2% on sales. ($71,650 ÷ $874,000)
MARKET OBJECTIVE: 1. Increase dollar sales of the company by 7%.	MARKET INCREASE: 29.5% increase 19x2 $874,000 19x1 $675,000 ($199,000 ÷ $675,000)
INVENTORY OBJECTIVES: 1. Maintain finished goods inventory of 50% of next quarter's sales. 2. Maintain material inventory at 10% of next quarter's usage for plastic; no change for boxes.	INVENTORY LEVELS: Because of unexpected increase in sales, finished goods inventories and plastic inventories were increased to the following percentage of next quarter's usage: Small terrariums 50% Large terrariums 66⅔% Plastic 26⅔% Inventory of boxes remained unchanged.
PERSONNEL OBJECTIVE: Move toward a stable work force with no more than 10% turnover through layoffs.	PERSONNEL: This objective is not possible to achieve unless inventory is built significantly during periods of low sales.

EXHIBIT 9–10
Comparison of actual results with Donnell Company objectives

The activity variance could be decomposed to show the deviation in profit caused by selling a different product mix than planned.

The material price variance could be decomposed to show the effect of purchasing substitute materials. This could also affect the material quantity variance.

The labor rate variance could be decomposed to show the labor mix variance that would result because work was performed by a worker in a different pay grade than planned.

Cost variances could be decomposed by product line or territories.

The activity variance could be analyzed by product line or sales territories.

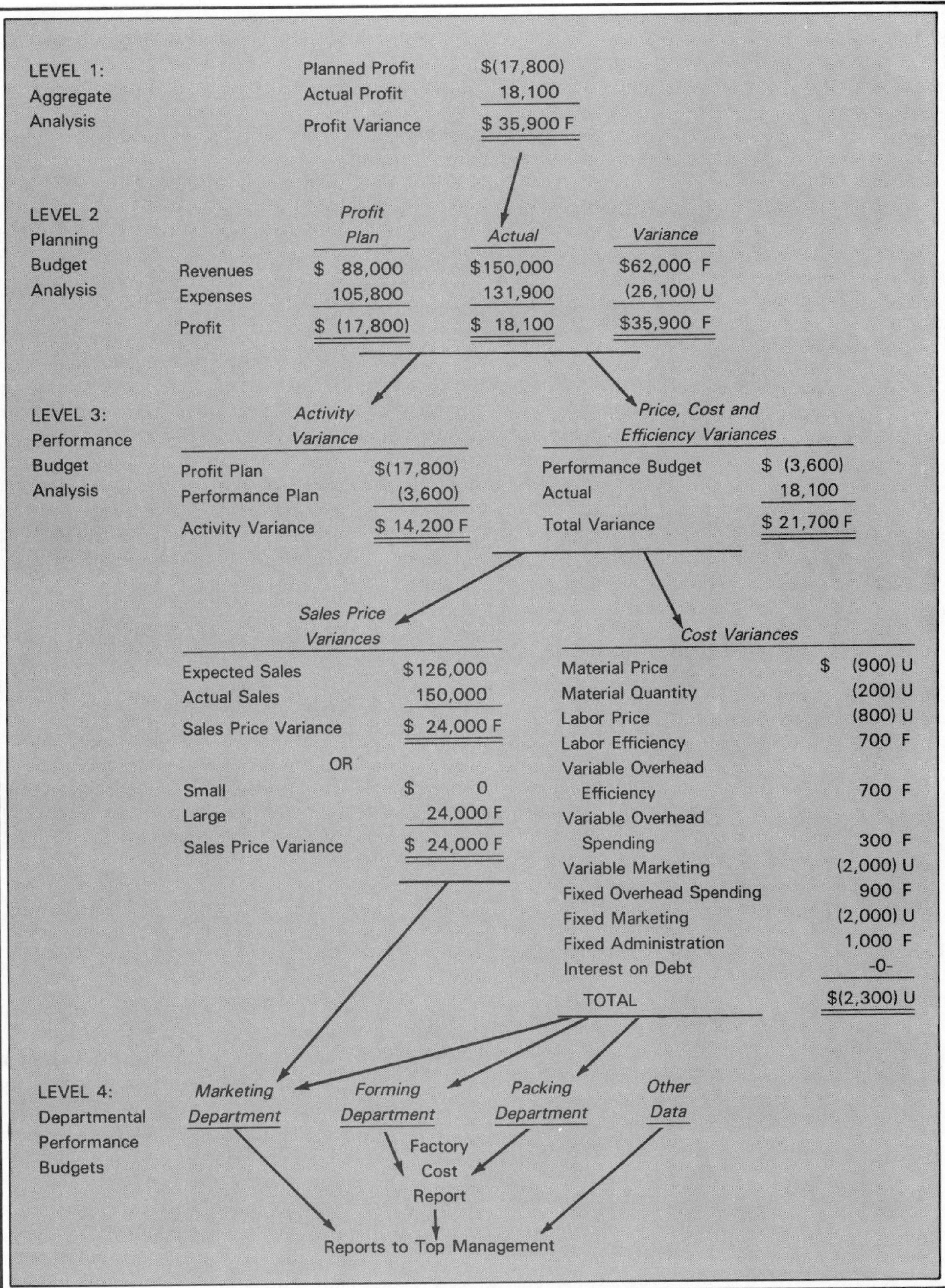

EXHIBIT 9–11
Summary of performance assessment levels

From these examples it should be evident that the possibilities of performance analysis exceed those presented in this book.

Let's carry our discussion of control systems one more step. We have emphasized that the potency of a control system is always relative to other possible control systems. Comparison of a performance budget with actual performance is relatively stronger, at least in theory, than comparison of the planning budget with actual, because the performance budget equalizes the activity level between budget and actual. However, the performance budget may not be the optimum measure. The performance budget is based upon the flexible budget, which was structured upon presupposed operational techniques, pricing structures, cost structures, and market conditions. In this sense the performance budget represents an *ex ante* measure; it is a control tool in that its basic structure was determined in advance.

Even more potent would be *ex post* measures, that is, performance measures that *should* have resulted, considering all actual events, both inside and outside the firm. For example, the activity variance could be analyzed by looking at economy-wide or industry-wide events that could be known only after-the-fact. In a general sense, *ex post* measures are the result of more complete information than *ex ante* measures; therefore, they are relatively stronger.

From this discussion it should be clear that there are no perfect control systems. Each mode of performance analysis can be judged only in terms of its contribution to management. Certainly one principle is that the control system should be no stronger than necessary, given the objectives of management. Control systems should be developed only to the extent that the benefits from the data outweigh the costs of obtaining them.

Finally, it should be emphasized that budgetary and accounting systems are only one component of the complete control system. Generally, accounting systems address themselves to evaluating efficient behavior; they do not focus upon organizational effectiveness.

THE COST OF VARIANCE INVESTIGATION

In recent years information economics has paid increasing attention to when a variance should or should not be investigated further. The basic principle is that variance investigation should be undertaken whenever the expected savings from the investigation outweigh the costs of the investigation.

For example, assume that the Milling Department has an unfavorable labor efficiency variance of $500 this month which the manager considers significant. The departmental manager believes that this variance will continue for the next 3 months unless he calls in a team of experts to discover the cause. There is a 20% chance that the cause is random and that the variance will cease regardless of the action he takes. If the manager calls the efficiency experts the department will have to absorb their expenses of $1,000. Even if the team is called past experience has shown there is a 10% chance they will fail to discover the cause of the variance. Based upon this data the manager prepared the following decision table.

Possible outcome	*Cost of possible outcome*	*Probability of possible outcome*	*Expected value*
Do Not Investigate:			
Variance is random and will cease	$ 0	.20	$ 0
Variance will continue	$1,500	.80	1,200
		1.00	$1,200
Investigate Further:			
Variance is random and will cease	$1,000	.20	$ 200
Variance cannot be corrected[1] (.80 × .10)	$2,500	.08	200
Variance can be corrected[2] (.80 × .90)	$1,000	.72	720
		1.00	$1,120

[1]The 10% probability that the variance cannot be corrected applies to only 80% of the possibilities.
[2]The 90% probability that the variance will be corrected applies to 80% of the possibilities.

In this example the expected costs of not investigating are $1,200; the expected costs of an investigation are $1,120. Therefore it would be cost advantageous to investigate the variance further.

HUMAN ASPECTS OF BUDGETARY CONTROL

There is a tendency to overemphasize the mechanical aspects of the budgetary system and to expect it to work without regard to the interpersonal relationships implied therein. However, goals and objectives are achieved through people. It is important that we examine the effects of budgets on people and the effects of people on the budget. The human element is an extremely complex issue; oversimplification is easy in our brief discussion. A review of behavioral research literature reveals that the studies have raised more questions regarding human behavior than they have answered.

Early budgetary literature adopted a mechanical and materialistic view of human behavior. This view of the behavior of workers and managers was based upon a number of assumptions:

1. Employees are primarily motivated by monetary rewards.
2. Work is an unpleasant task and people avoid work whenever possible.

3. Human beings are ordinarily inefficient and wasteful.
4. There is one best way of behaving and this can be discovered through research and taught to individuals.[3]

These assumptions led to the belief that responsibility had to be established and external pressure applied to achieve the desired results. In practice, a high level of performance through budgets has often been accompanied by several unfavorable consequences, including excessive pressure on employees, hostility toward the budget, and conflict among departments.[4]

Excessive Pressure

Behavioral research has provided some information on the effects of pressure in the management process. It appears that individuals and groups work best with some kind of pressure. One researcher[5] found that when benchmarks are too loose, motivation diminishes; as they are tightened, motivation increases. However, when a benchmark becomes too tight, motivation is poor. Another researcher[6] found the results of empirical findings to indicate that established performance requirements should be achievable not more than 40% of the time, but not less than 25% of the time. It would be inappropriate to treat these percentages as irrefutable facts, but it is clear that the degree of difficulty encountered by workers to attain the planned activity level will have a motivational impact.

Responsibility accounting identifies individual responsibility for budgeted costs and deviations from plan. Management by exception implies that significant deviations from the plan will cause the superior to exert pressure for correction. Excessive pressure can result in growing antagonism toward the budget. It is possible for a firm to create a situation where budgetary success means failure for worker and managers. In such a situation, the planning and coordinating function of the budget can be completely negated as the budget becomes something to be feared.

Interdepartmental Conflict

Responsibility accounting focuses attention upon limited areas of responsibility and tends to cause managers to overemphasize departmental goals. The lower-line managers may attempt to direct budgetary pressure away from

---

[3]E. H. Caplan, *Management Accounting and Behavioral Science* (Reading, Mass.: Addison-Wesley, 1971).

[4]Chris Argyris, "Human Problems with Budgets," *Harvard Business Review* (January–February, 1953).

[5]G. H. Hofstede, *The Game of Budget Control* (New York: Van Nostrand, 1967).

[6]R. L. M. Dunbar, "Budgeting for Control," *Administrative Science Quarterly* (March, 1971), pp. 88–96.

themselves by shifting the blame to other departments. This departmental overemphasis can operate against the organization's goals and objectives.

Participation and Motivation

Participation by the managers in preparing the budget has been advocated as a way to increase employee motivation and reduce organizational conflict. The call for such participation is widespread in accounting literature. Most current management theorists and management accountants believe that employee initiative, performance, and morale are increased with employee participation. The value of participation rapidly becomes interwoven with the theory of organizational structures.

Caplan[7] classified organizational structures and their effects upon accounting into two extremes. The "classical" organization emphasizes profit maximization, formal and hierarchical structure, economic rewards, and the inherent laziness and inefficiency of employees. The "modern" organization is characterized by coalitions of individuals who are adaptive problem-solvers, motivated by a variety of psychological, social, and economic drives and needs. The modern organization certainly appears to be more conducive to true employee participation.

One indication that an organization encourages active employee participation is the existence of good superior-subordinate relationships fostered by (1) frequent person-to-person contacts; (2) the use of results in performance appraisal; (3) the use of departmental meetings to review actual results; and (4) the creation of a "game" spirit (margin for error, tolerance, and slack).[8]

A closer look at this list provides further insights into the planning and control process. First, participation is achieved on a personal basis. A formal, indirect mode of communication creates the danger of pseudoparticipation. Pseudoparticipation, which pretends to be participation but is not, is a form of deceit; the result can be a decrease in motivation. Second, the achievement of the goal or budget should bear directly upon the reward received by the employee. Further, direct, clear feedback allows the employee to adjust aspiration levels and strive to achieve desired rewards. Finally, a certain amount of leeway, termed *slack*, gives the employee some freedom of movement and action. It keeps employee pressure at an accepted level.

Slack

An individual in an organization is motivated to achieve two sets of goals: personal and organizational. A manager's personal goals within the organization may relate to income, status, size of staff, or discretionary control over the

[7]Caplan, *Management Accounting and Behavioral Science.*

[8]Hofstede, *Game of Budget Control.*

allocation of resources. Where a budget serves to measure performance, a manager will strive to set the budget so that it can be achieved and still meet top management's objectives. To avoid the stigma attached to failure, a manager will attempt to introduce a cushion, or slack.

Slack can be thought of as a budgetary lubricant. Some slack is necessary to reduce friction between individual and organizational goals and to give managers room to perform. It has been shown that success causes people to raise their levels of aspiration and that failure causes them to lower their aspirations. The provision of slack is one way employees attempt to avoid failure.

Every firm operates with slack; perfection of the traditional economic model is not possible. Resources cannot be perfectly allocated. The treasurer introduces slack by maintaining excessive cash balances; division management understates sales projections; line management requests employee positions that will be filled only as budgetary expectations are met; and manufacturing costs are based on estimates that do not reflect improvements. Slack tends to grow in good years, when satisfactory profits are easily attainable; in bad years slack is voluntarily decreased throughout the firm. Cost-cutting campaigns are attempts to reduce excessive slack that will jeopardize long-run profit objectives of the firm through inefficiency. Too much pressure to reduce slack will create conflict in the system and may result in system failure. The solution is to find a level of slack that maintains efficiency and avoids the conflict caused by excessive pressure.

SUMMARY

To be effective, reports must be relevant to management needs. Two dimensions of relevancy exist: First, the concept of responsibility accounting requires that costs and revenues be identified with the manager responsible for their incurrence. Second, the concept of management by exception requires that significant deviations from plan be identified so that the cause may be determined and action taken, if necessary, to prevent future variances. To ensure their effectiveness, reports to management must also be timely and accurate.

At the bottom of the chart of organization, the information needs are primarily nonfinancial and involve a limited time horizon. Moving upward through the chart, there is increasing emphasis upon financial planning. At the top, the reporting process serves to explain deviations from plan.

The differences between actual profit and planned profit can be decomposed into a number of levels. Static analysis consists of comparing the actual results with the planning budget. More appropriate for managerial control is the comparison of the actual results with the performance budget. The performance budget is the flexible budget and standard costs adjusted to the actual volume.

The proper administration of the budget for planning and control depends not only upon the technology, but also upon the impact it has on the persons affected. Paramount here are the problems of pressure, motivation, and slack.

SUPPLEMENTARY READING

Calas, Robert. "Variance Analysis in Profit Planning." *Management Accounting,* July, 1971.

Higgins, John A. "Responsibility Accounting." *The Arthur Anderson Chronicle,* April, 1952.

Holmes, Robert W. "An Executive Views Responsibility Reporting." *Financial Executive,* August, 1968.

Kellogg, Martin N. "Fundamentals of Responsibility Accounting." *N.A.A. Bulletin,* April, 1962.

Kiessling, J. R. "Profit Planning and Responsibility Accounting." *Financial Executive,* July, 1963.

Koehler, Robert W. "Statistical Variance Control: Through Performance Reports and On-the-Spot Observation." *Management Accounting,* December, 1969.

*Morris, R. D. F. "Budgetary Control is Obsolete." *The Accountant,* May 18, 1968.

Netten, E. W. "Responsibility Accounting for Better Management." *The Canadian Chartered Accountant,* September, 1963.

*Pick, John. "Is Responsibility Accounting Irresponsible?" *The New York Certified Public Accountant,* July, 1971.

*Schiff, Michael, and Arie Y. Lewin. "Where Traditional Budgeting Fails." *Financial Executive,* May, 1968.

Walker, Charles W. "Profitability and Responsibility Accounting." *Management Accounting,* December, 1971.

QUESTIONS

9-1 What ideas underlie the concept of management by exception?

9-2 At what levels in the organization are accounting data most useful? Why? What types of information are used at other levels?

9-3 What are some causes of inaccuracy in accounting reports? Discuss the trade-off between accuracy and timeliness in reporting to management.

9-4 Why does the profit plan for a department usually differ from the performance budget? When will they become the same?

9-5 From what sources is the performance budget developed?

9-6 How is the absorption costing fixed overhead rate used in performance evaluation?

9-7 What is a control limit? How is it used by management?

9-8 How do reports for cost centers differ from reports for profit centers? Give an example of each type of center.

9-9 How does the activity variance affect net income? What types of departments have activity variances?

9-10 What changes must be made in the report to top management for external reporting? Why?

EXERCISES

9-11 *(True or False)*. Indicate whether the following statements are true or false.

1. In applying the concept of responsibility accounting, only costs that are applicable to the decisions within in the responsibility center should be reported to the manager.

2. The most important concept of responsibility accounting is that the responsibility center should bear its fair share of all costs.

3. The level of performance analysis that compares actual and planned performance may be referred to as "static" analysis.

4. The performance budget is equal to the profit plan plus or minus the activity variance.

5. Under the concept of management by exception, management should not intervene in a subordinate's activities as long as the plan is being achieved.

6. The report on profit plan is just another name for the actual income statement.

7. The profit plan is prepared to plan, as well as to control, the financial resource structure and composition of the firm.

8. Internal reporting to management may use either variable costing or absorption costing.

9. An activity variance shows the efficiency of the marketing effort, whereas the volume variance shows the efficiency of the manufacturing effort.

10. Slack is introduced into the planning budget to increase pressure on the workers.

9-12 *(Matching)*. Individuals at several levels in the organizational structure of a firm are listed below. Match the reporting concept on the right with the appropriate individual. A particular concept may apply to more than one individual.

1. Stockholder
2. Member of board of directors
3. President
4. Vice-president (marketing or manufacturing)
5. Factory manager or marketing product manager
6. Factory department foreman
7. Group leader
8. Worker or salesperson

A. Primary information for planning and control is financial.
B. Primary information for planning and control is nonfinancial.
C. Information must meet externally imposed requirements.
D. If a good control system is present, user is more concerned with planning information.
E. Practices management by exception in use of information.
F. Time frame is very short, perhaps daily or hourly.
G. Receives no formal reports from accounting system.
H. Receives monthly reports and additional reports for shorter periods on an exception basis.
I. Receives only historical information and the most general of projections.
J. All planning and control information may be received orally.

9-13 *(Matching).* Match the following terms and definitions.

1. Control
2. Planning
3. Responsibility accounting
4. Management by exception
5. Feedback
6. Activity variance
7. Material usage variance
8. Report on profit plan
9. Generally accepted accounting principles
10. Relevancy

A. A step in the control process that informs of progress.
B. Meaningful and usable.
C. Variance arising from volume of material used.
D. Variance arising from volume of goods sold.
E. A system of reporting that conveys information about the activities over which an individual manager has control.
F. External constraints imposed upon financial reporting outside the firm.
G. Leaving well enough alone.
H. Process of measuring and correcting actual performance to ensure that a firm's objectives and plans are accomplished.

I. Explanation of differences between planned net income and actual net income.
J. Process of selecting goals, objectives, and the actions required to attain them.

9-14 *(Control Report for Overhead Costs).* The Conners Bag Company recently completed an analysis of overhead cost behavior patterns. The linear equation for each overhead item follows.

	Best Fit Line $y_c = a + b(x)$*		*Standard Error of Estimate*
	a	*b*	
Overtime premium	$ 0	$1.00	$ 25
Supplies	$ 0	$ .20	$ 75
Fringe benefits	$1,000	$ 0	$ 10
Power	$1,000	$7.40	$400
Utilities	$ 500	$ .50	$ 25
Contracted janitorial service	$ 600	$ 0	$ 0
Supervisory salaries	$1,200	$ 0	$ 20
Repairs	$ 250	$ .50	$ 25
Miscellaneous	$ 100	$2.80	$200

*(x) is direct labor hours.

The profit plan for September called for 500 direct labor hours. The actual direct labor hours were 700, however, and the following actual costs were incurred.

Overtime premium	$ 500
Supplies	$ 325
Fringe benefits	$1,000
Power	$5,800
Utilities	$ 765
Janitorial service	$ 600
Supervisory salaries	$1,200
Repairs	$1,300
Miscellaneous	$1,800

REQUIRED:

A. Which overhead costs are fixed? Which are variable? Which are mixed?
B. Prepare a report to the departmental manager on overhead costs for September. Which variances bear further investigation?

9–15 *(Historical Cost Comparisons).* In an analysis of company expenses, the management of the S. Simon Company compared this year's expenses against last year's.

	This Year	*Last Year*	*Difference (Increase) Decrease*
Direct labor	$ 50,000	$ 65,000	$15,000
Supervisory salaries	31,000	30,000	(1,000)
Indirect labor	35,000	40,000	5,000
Maintenance	7,000	5,000	(2,000)
Power	18,000	13,000	(5,000)
Depreciation	8,000	6,500	(1,500)
Insurance	2,400	1,700	(700)
Total	$151,400	$161,200	$ 9,800

REQUIRED:

A. Comment upon the expense comparison as a tool for analyzing company performance. What are the advantages and disadvantages of the comparison above?

B. What other information would you consider necessary? Explain.

9–16 *(Labor Variances).* The Lark Company has a labor union contract that guarantees a minimum wage of $500 per month to each direct labor employee with at least 12 years of service. A total of 100 employees currently qualify for coverage. All direct labor employees are paid $5.00 per hour.

The direct labor budget for 19X7 was based on the annual usage of 400,000 hours of direct labor × $5.00, or a total of $2,000,000. Of this amount, $50,000 (100 employees × $500) per month (or $600,000 for the year) was regarded as fixed. Thus, the budget for any given month was determined by the formula, $50,000 + ($3.50 × Direct labor hours worked).

Data on performance for the first three months of 19X7 follow. (*U* means unfavorable; *F* means favorable.)

	January	*February*	*March*
Direct labor hours worked	22,000	32,000	42,000
Direct labor costs budgeted	$127,000	$162,000	$197,000
Direct labor costs incurred	110,000	160,000	210,000
Variance	$ 17,000 F	$ 2,000 F	$ 13,000 U

The factory manager was perplexed by the results showing favorable variances when production was low and unfavorable variances when production was high; the employees' output per hour of work was constant throughout the three months. He expected little or no labor variance during these three months.

REQUIRED:

A. Why did the variances arise? Explain.

B. Prepare a graph with labor costs on the vertical axis and labor hours on the horizontal axis. Plot one line for budgeted labor costs and another for actual labor costs. Determine the flexible budget equation for each line.

C. Does this direct labor budget provide a basis for controlling direct labor cost? Explain, indicating any changes you think should be implemented to facilitate performance evaluation of direct labor employees.

D. For inventory valuation purposes, how should per-unit standard costs for direct labor be determined in a situation such as this? Explain, assuming that in some months fewer than 10,000 hours are expected to be utilized.

(CPA adapted)

9-17 *(Accuracy of Accounting Information).* Arnie Jenson, president of Green River Woodworking, has just received a request for an additional 700 special-order kitchen cabinets from Ramsey Construction. After reviewing Job 52, a recently completed job for the same type of cabinet, he accepted the order. Data from Job 52 follow.

	Job 52		
	Standard	*Actual*	*Efficiency Variance*
Sales	$15,000	$15,000	
Variable costs:			
Material	$ 2,000	$ 1,950	$ 50
Labor	8,000	8,400	(400)
Variable overhead*	2,000	2,100	(100)
Total variable costs	12,000	12,450	$(450)
Contribution margin	$ 3,000	$ 2,550	
Identifiable fixed costs	2,000	1,050	
Product margin	$ 1,000	$ 1,500	

*Applied on the basis of labor hours. Standard wage rate is $8.00 per hour.

Arnie was not concerned about the $400 variance in labor because Job 52 was a new job. He reasoned that performance should improve on the second job.

While walking through the factory on the way to his office, he overheard Ollie Ajax, the group leader for special cabinet construction, talking to another group leader. "... those work tickets on Job 52," Ajax was saying. The other man answered, "You mean you plugged the labor hours too?" "Of course," replied Ajax, "Johnson [the foreman] hits the roof if the variances are over 50 hours on any job. We just keep them under 50 hours and everyone is happy. Saves having to explain to the boss and get chewed out. Why, I bet we were at least 30% over standard on that Ramsey job. There is no way we can make standard on that type of job. We loaded the hours on other jobs."

REQUIRED:

A. Assuming the 30% estimate of labor variance on Job 52, correct the report that was presented to Mr. Jenson.
B. Were any costs other than labor affected?
C. How would the additional information have affected his decision?
D. What suggestions do you have concerning the control system and reporting to management?

9-18 *(Cost of Variance Analysis)*. Joe Ada, the manager of the personnel department received his management report for the month of July which showed an unfavorable spending variance for computer services of $400. Joe believed that the unfavorable variance was the result of excessive time usage on the computer caused by an inefficient software program that used too many calculational steps. He had to make a choice between continuing to use the program for the next six months until a new computer software package was implemented or calling in a programmer now to correct the fault. He believed that there was a 20% chance he was wrong about the program and that the cost variance would not occur again and an 80% chance he was correct and that the cost overrun would occur again. He estimated that the computer programmer would cost the department $900 and that even if the programmer was called there was only a 60% chance that the new program would correct the fault.

REQUIRED:

Prepare a decision table indicating what action you believe that Joe should take.

9-19 *(Explanation of Fluctuations in Profit)*. The Burnaby Company manufactures a single product with the following standard costs and selling price per unit.

Raw material	$0.20
Direct labor	.60
Variable overhead	.20
Fixed overhead*	.50
Total cost	$1.50
Selling price	2.00
Profit	$0.50

*Based on standard volume of 10,000 units per month.

During the first three months of the year, production, sales, and profits were:

	Month		
	1	*2*	*3*
Production in units	10,000	15,000	5,000
Sales in units	10,000	5,000	15,000
Profit in dollars	$ 5,000	$ 5,000	$ 5,000

Inventories and cost of goods sold are accounted for at standard cost. There have been no variances except for those due to volume of goods produced, and those variances have been charged in total to cost of goods sold each month.

Management is unable to understand why profits have been the same each month despite substantial changes in sales volume. Pointing to the indicated profit of $.50 per unit, the president questions the correctness of the third-period profit of $5,000, when 15,000 units were sold.

REQUIRED:
Prepare a presentation for management to explain what has happened. Comment on your presentation. *(Canada SIA adapted)*

9–20 *(Report on Profit Plan).* The following income statement was prepared for the president of Charlie Horse Saddle Company.

				Variances	
	Profit Plan	*Performance Budget*	*Actual*	*Activity*	*Price Efficiency Spending*
Sales	$36,000	$27,000	$31,500	$(9,000)	$ 4,500
Variable production costs	24,000	18,000	18,000	6,000	—
Contribution margin	$12,000	$ 9,000	$13,500	$(3,000)	$ 4,500
Production variances:					
Material price			(2,500)		(2,500)
Material usage			500		500
Labor rate			(200)		(200)
Labor efficiency			800		800
Variable overhead spending			(1,000)		(1,000)
Variable overhead efficiency			200		200
Contribution margin adjusted	$12,000	$ 9,000	$11,300	$(3,000)	$ 2,300
Fixed costs:					
Manufacturing	3,000	3,000	3,200		(200)
Administration	2,000	2,000	2,100		(100)
Net income	$ 7,000	$ 4,000	$ 6,000	$(3,000)	$ 2,000
Saddles sold	120	90	90		

The Charlie Horse Saddle Company has been in business for many years. Production is to order, primarily from repeat customers, so there are no significant marketing costs. A standard variable costing system was implemented, and the owner is confused by the first report. He wants a simple explanation of why net income is $1,000 lower than planned.

REQUIRED:
Prepare a simple report for the owner that explains, by area of responsibility, why actual net income exceeded planned net income.

9-21 *(Factory Cost Report).* As part of your on-the-job training for Bigfoot Skis, you have been assigned the task of assisting in preparation of monthly performance reports. You are given the following data for the finishing department for May.

Standard Cost per Unit		*Actual Total Costs*	
Labor: Sanding (2 hours @ $3)	$ 6.00	Labor: Sanding	$12,000
Coating (1 hour @ $5)	5.00	Coating	8,500
Material (½ pound @ $24 per pound)	12.00	Material	30,000
Variable overhead (3 hours @ $4)	12.00	Variable overhead	27,000
		Rejects	3,000
Total	$35.00		$80,500

Any variance due to fluctuations in material price is isolated and reported as purchased. Variances in labor rates are isolated by the payroll department. Actual fixed costs were $10,000 and did not vary from budget.

Bigfoot Skis had planned to produce 2,000 pairs of skis this month. However, only 1,800 were produced and an additional 100 had to be scrapped because one batch of material was allowed to harden before it was applied to the skis. Several of the 1,800 pairs of skis had to be reworked, using overtime and dropping actual performance below budget. The cost of rejects includes the standard costs of prior departments.

REQUIRED:

A. Prepare a report on this month's operations for the finishing department manager. It should be accompanied by a narrative explaining the variances.

B. How much of this information should be presented in the factory cost report to the manager?

9-22 *(Variance Analysis for a Newspaper).* A partial report for the classified ad department of the *Daily Planet* is presented below.

	Profit Plan	Performance Budget	Actual	Activity	VARIANCE Price, Efficiency, Spending Amount	Percentage
Lines sold	25,000	20,000	20,000			
Sales	$50,000	$40,000	$41,000			
Variable costs:						
Original sales	$25,000	$20,000	$23,000			
Corrections	5,000	4,000	4,000			
Write-off due to printing error	2,500	2,000	3,000			
Total	32,500	26,000	30,000			
Contribution margin	$17,500	$14,000	$11,000			
Fixed costs:						
Salaries	$10,000	$10,000	$10,000			
Fringe benefits	500	500	500			
Advertising	1,000	1,000	1,100			
Other	1,000	1,000	1,200			
Total	12,500	12,500	12,800			
Departmental contribution	$ 5,000	$ 1,500	$ (1,800)			

REQUIRED:

A. Compute the variances for April.

B. Management has a policy of investigating only those variances that exceed budget by 10% or more. Which variances should be looked into? What might be the causes of some of the variances?

C. Is 10% an appropriate level for all expenses? Explain.

9-23 *(Departmental Overhead Cost Report).* The Black Lite Company has just introduced the concept of control by responsibility and has decided to use the winding department for the test application. The variable overhead absorption rate for the winding department which is $1.00 per hour, was based on a forecast level of activity of 30,000 hours as follows:

	Fixed	*Variable per Hour*
Forecasted overhead costs:		
Supervision	$16,000	$ —
Materials handling	5,000	.15
Quality inspection	10,000	.10
Overtime premium	—	.08
Clerical	6,000	—
Fringe benefits	3,000	.12
Supplies	7,000	.40
Repairs and maintenance	3,000	.10
Rework	—	.05
Depreciation of machinery	2,500	—
Allocated general plant	7,500	—
Total	$60,000	$1.00

During April the winding department actually worked 28,000 hours and incurred the following actual overhead costs.

Supervision	$15,000
Materials handling	10,700
Quality inspection	13,400
Overtime premium	1,600
Clerical	6,200
Fringe benefits	6,100
Idle time	800
Supplies	16,400
Repairs and maintenance	7,400
Depreciation of machinery	2,600
Allocated general plant	6,900
Total	$87,100

REQUIRED:

A. Prepare a detailed overhead control report for the manager of the winding department recording the favorable or unfavorable variances.

B. Comment briefly regarding the performance of the manager of the winding department in controlling overhead. *(Canada SIA adapted)*

9-24 *(Responsibility Accounting).* In recent years distribution expenses of the Hooper Company have increased more than other expenditures. For more effective control, the company plans to provide each local manager with an income statement for his territory showing monthly and year-to-date amounts for the current and the previous year. Each sales office is supervised by a local manager; sales orders are forwarded to the main office and filled from a central warehouse; billing and collections are also centrally processed. Expenses are first classified by function and then allocated to each territory in the following ways.

Function	*Basis*
Sales salaries	Actual
Other selling expenses	Sales dollars
Warehousing	Sales dollars
Packing and shipping	Weight of package
Billing and collections	Number of billings
General administration	Equally

REQUIRED:

A. Explain responsibility accounting and the classification of revenues and expenses under this concept.

B. What are the objectives of profit analysis by sales territories in income statements?

C. Discuss the effectiveness of Hooper Company's comparative income statements by sales territories as a tool for planning and control. Include in your answer additional factors that should be considered and changes that might be desirable for effective planning by management and evaluation of the local sales managers.

D. Compare the degree of control that can be achieved over production costs and distribution costs and explain why the degree of control differs.

E. Criticize Hooper Company's allocation and/or inclusion of (1) other selling expenses, (2) warehousing expense, and (3) general administration expense. *(CPA adapted)*

9-25 *(Responsibility Accounting).* Monthly departmental performance reports are prepared by the Mulligan Manufacturing Corporation. A Manager of the Month award is given to the manager who has performed best in relation to his budget. A bonus is paid to any department manager whose performance is better than budget. Two departmental reports for the month of May follow.

MARKETING–PRODUCT B
PERFORMANCE REPORT FOR MAY

	Master Budget	*Performance Budget*	*Actual*
Sales revenue	$180,000	$200,000	$210,000
Variable costs:			
Production	90,000	100,000	100,000
Selling	18,000	20,000	26,000
Contribution margin	$ 72,000	$ 80,000	$ 84,000
Departmental fixed costs	20,000	20,000	22,000
Departmental margin	$ 52,000	$ 60,000	$ 62,000

PRODUCTION–ASSEMBLY
PERFORMANCE REPORT FOR MAY

	Master Budget	*Performance Budget*	*Actual*
Subassemblies (material)	$160,000	$200,000	$190,000
Labor ($5.00 per hour)	80,000	100,000	118,000
Variable overhead	48,000	60,000	67,000
Total variable	$288,000	$360,000	$375,000
Departmental fixed costs	80,000	80,000	75,000
Total departmental costs	$368,000	$440,000	$450,000

One of the goals of the company is customer satisfaction. The marketing manager for Product B received the Manager of the Month award for exceptional customer service. He had received several new orders and was commended by many customers for filling rush orders when competitors refused to do so.

The manager of the production-assembly department is extremely unhappy with the company's accounting system. Her department operated near capacity and completed all orders within the promised delivery schedule but had excessive labor and variable overhead costs. She can show that the labor efficiency variance which was unfavorable by 3,000 hours would have been favorable by 1,000 hours if she had been able to produce at the scheduled level without the rush orders.

REQUIRED:

A. Did the manager of the production-assembly department receive a bonus in May? Explain.

B. Why should the manager of the production-assembly department be so unhappy with the accounting system?

C. Recast the performance reports to reflect responsibility accounting.

D. On the basis of your reports from Part B, who should receive a bonus? Explain.

PROBLEMS

9-26 *(Breakeven Analysis; Analysis of Performance).* At the end of 19X3, the following income statement was prepared for The Window Dresser, a custom drapery shop.

THE WINDOW DRESSER
INCOME STATEMENT
For the Year 19X3

Sales (6,500 yards)		$104,000
Cost of goods sold		63,700
Gross margin		$ 40,300
Operating expenses:		
Salaries and commissions	$25,000	
Depreciation	6,000	
Supplies	5,600	
Utilities	700	
Advertising	4,200	41,500
Net loss		$ (1,200)

Ms. Drugge, the owner of the shop, does not believe that her shop should have shown a loss for the year. Although a downturn in the economy of the area resulted in fewer sales than planned, she believes that The Window Dresser should still be above breakeven. She believed that she had increased her selling prices to more than enough to offset the increases in the cost of fabric.

At the beginning of 19X3, Ms. Drugge developed the following planning data.

Sales	10,000 yards @ $15	
Cost of fabric	$9.00 per yard (60% of sales)	
Operating expenses:		
	Fixed	*Variable (% of sales)*
Salaries	$10,000	12%
Depreciation	$ 6,000	—
Supplies	—	5%
Utilities	$ 800	—
Advertising	$ 1,200	3%

REQUIRED:

A. On the basis of the planning data, what was Ms. Drugge's breakeven point in dollars of sales?

B. Considering only the changes in the cost of fabric and her selling price, what is the new breakeven point?

C. Prepare a report to Ms. Drugge explaining the performance for the period.

9-27 *(Factory Cost Report)*. The Adrian Company produces farm equipment at several plants. The business is seasonal and cyclical in nature. The company has attempted to use a planning budget for planning and controlling activities, but the variable nature of the business has caused some company officials to be skeptical about the usefulness of budgeting. The accountant for the Melcher plant has been using a system he calls *flexible budgeting* to help his plant management control operations.

The company president asks him to explain how he applies the system at the Melcher plant, using the following data from the Adrian Company's records.

Budget data for 19X3			Actual data for January, 19X3	
Normal monthly capacity of the plant in direct labor hours		10,000 hours	Hours worked	8,400
Material costs	(6 pounds @ $1.50)	$9.00 per unit	Units produced	3,800
Direct labor costs	(2 hours @ $3.00)	$6.00 per unit	Costs incurred:	
Overhead estimate at normal monthly capacity:			Material (24,000 pounds)	$36,000
Variable (controllable):			Direct labor	25,200
Indirect labor		$ 6,650	Indirect labor	6,000
Indirect materials		600	Indirect materials	600
Repairs		750	Repairs	1,800
Total variable		$ 8,000	Depreciation	3,250
Fixed (noncontrollable):			Supervision	3,000
Depreciation		$ 3,250	Total	$75,850
Supervision		3,000		
Total fixed		6,250		
Total fixed and variable		$14,250		
Planned units for January, 19X3		4,000		
Planned units for February, 19X3		6,000		

REQUIRED:

A. Prepare a factory cost budget for January. Can you use this budget to evaluate performance for January? Explain.

B. Prepare a report to the factory manager of the Melcher plant for January. Your report should utilize a performance budget to compare actual and budgeted costs for the actual activity of the month.

C. Can flexible budgeting be applied to the nonmanufacturing activities of the company? Explain your answer. *(CMA adapted)*

9–28 *(Analysis of Sales Activity and Product Mix).* The Arsco Co. makes three grades of indoor-outdoor carpets. The sales volume for the annual budget is determined by estimating the total market volume for indoor-outdoor carpet and then applying the company's prior-year market share, adjusted for planned changes due to company programs for the coming year. The volume is apportioned between the three grades based upon the prior year's product mix, again adjusted for planned changes due to company programs for the coming year.

The company budget for 19X3 and the results of operations for 19X3 follow.

	Budget (000 omitted from dollar amounts)			
	Grade 1	*Grade 2*	*Grade 3*	*Total*
Sales (units)	1,000 rolls	1,000 rolls	2,000 rolls	4,000 rolls
Sales	$1,000	$2,000	$3,000	$6,000
Variable expense	700	1,600	2,300	4,600
Variable margin	$ 300	$ 400	$ 700	$1,400
Traceable fixed expense	200	200	300	700
Traceable margin	$ 100	$ 200	$ 400	$ 700
Selling and administrative expense				250
Net income				$ 450

	Actual (000 omitted from dollar amounts)			
	Grade 1	*Grade 2*	*Grade 3*	*Total*
Sales (units)	800 rolls	1,000 rolls	2,100 rolls	3,900 rolls
Sales	$810	$2,000	$3,000	$5,810
Variable expenses	560	1,610	2,320	4,490
Variable margin	$250	$ 390	$ 680	$1,320
Traceable fixed expense	210	220	315	745
Traceable margin	$ 40	$ 170	$ 365	$ 575
Selling and administrative expense				275
Net income				$ 300

Industry volume was estimated at 40,000 rolls for budgeting purposes. Actual industry volume for 19X3 was 38,000 rolls.

REQUIRED:

A. Calculate the profit impact of the unit sales activity variance for 19X3 using budgeted variable margins.

B. What portion of the variance, if any, can be attributed to the state of the carpet market?

C. What is the dollar impact on profits (using budgeted variable margins) of the shift in product mix from the budgeted mix? *(CMA adapted)*

9-29 *(Hospital Department Performance Report).* The Argon County Hospital is located in the county seat. Argon County is a well-known summer resort area. Its population doubles during the vacation months (May–August), and hospital activity more than doubles during these months. The hospital is organized into several departments. Although it is relatively small, its pleasant surroundings have attracted a well-trained and competent medical staff.

An administrator was hired a year ago to improve the business activities of the hospital. Among the new ideas he has introduced are responsibility accounting and quarterly cost reports supplied to department heads. Previously, cost data had been presented to department heads only infrequently. Excerpts from the announcement and the report received by the laundry supervisor follow.

> The hospital has adopted a responsibility accounting system. From now on you will receive quarterly reports comparing the costs of operating your department with budgeted costs. The reports will highlight the differences (variations) so you can zero in on the departure from budgeted costs (this is called *management by exception*). Responsibility accounting means you are accountable for keeping the costs in your department within the budget. The variations from the budget will help you identify what costs are out of line, and the size of the variation will indicate which ones are the most important. Your first such report accompanies this announcement.

ARGON COUNTY HOSPITAL
PERFORMANCE REPORT–LAUNDRY DEPARTMENT
July–September 19X3

	Budget	*Actual*	*(Over) Under Budget*	*Percentage (Over) Under Budget*
Patient days	9,500	11,900	(2,400)	(25)
Pounds of laundry processed	125,000	156,000	(31,000)	(25)
Costs:				
Laundry labor	$ 9,000	$12,500	$(3,500)	(39)
Supplies	1,100	1,875	(775)	(70)
Water and water heating and softening	1,700	2,500	(800)	(47)
Maintenance	1,400	2,200	(800)	(57)
Supervisor's salary	3,150	3,750	(600)	(19)
Allocated administration costs	4,000	5,000	(1,000)	(25)
Equipment depreciation	1,200	1,250	(50)	(4)
	$21,550	$29,075	$(7,525)	(35)

Administrator's comments: Costs are significantly above budget for the quarter. Particular attention needs to be paid to labor, supplies, and maintenance.

The annual budget for 19X3 was constructed by the new administrator. Quarterly budgets were computed as one-fourth of the annual budget. The administrator compiled the budget from analysis of the prior three years' costs. The analysis showed that all costs increased each year, with more rapid increases between the second and third year. He considered establishing the budget at an average of the prior three years' costs, hoping that the installation of the system would reduce costs to this level. However, in view of the rapidly increasing prices, he finally chose 19X2 costs less 3% for the 19X3 budget. The activity level measured by patient days and pounds of laundry processed was set at 19X2 volume, which was approximately equal to the volume of each of the past three years.

REQUIRED:

A. Comment on the method used to construct the budget.

B. What information should be communicated by variations from budgets?

C. Recast the budget to reflect responsibility accounting, assuming the following:

1. Laundry labor, supplies, water and water heating and softening, and maintenance are variable costs. The remaining costs are fixed.

2. Actual prices are expected to be approximately 20% above the levels in the budget prepared by the hospital administrator. *(CMA adapted)*

9–30 *(Cost Reports for Several Levels).* Sisul Metal Products Company has three different plants in its manufacturing operations. Each plant performs a different step on the product.

The foundry plant has two producing and two service departments. Costs of the maintenance and administration cost centers are reallocated to the producing departments. Data for May for the foundry plant, by department, are in the accompanying report.

The foundry plant incurred no variances in labor rates during the month; the only variance in material price was an unfavorable price variance of $1,000 in the casting department. All budgets were prepared from flexible budget data for the company at the actual level of operation.

The two other plants are the grinding plant and the finishing plant. Summary data from the cost reports of these two plants are:

	Budget	*Actual*
Grinding plant	$40,000	$38,000
Finishing plant	$50,000	$55,000

Costs incurred by the vice-president of manufacturing for the month were:

	Budget	*Actual*
Salaries	$6,000	$5,800
Supplies	300	280
Depreciation	1,000	1,000
	$7,300	$7,080

FOUNDRY PLANT
COST REPORT

	PRODUCING DEPARTMENTS			
	Casting		Burring	
	Budget	*Actual*	*Budget*	*Actual*
Materials used	$ 8,000	$ 8,800	$ 3,000	$ 3,100
Direct labor	6,000	4,800	15,000	15,800
Indirect labor	4,000	4,400	2,000	2,200
Supplies	1,000	800	2,000	2,400
Depreciation	7,000	7,000	5,000	5,000
Allocation of maintenance	4,500	5,500	4,500	5,000
Allocation of administration	1,800	1,500	4,500	5,100
	$32,300	$32,800	$36,000	$38,600

	SERVICE DEPARTMENTS			
	Maintenance		Administration	
	Budget	*Actual*	*Budget*	*Actual*
Indirect labor	$ 4,000	$ 5,000	$ 5,000	$ 5,400
Supplies	3,000	3,500	300	200
Depreciation	2,000	2,000	1,000	1,000
Allocation to producing departments	(9,000)	(10,500)		
Allocation to producing departments			(6,300)	(6,600)
	$ 0	$ 0	$ 0	$ 0

REQUIRED:

A. Prepare departmental cost reports for the supervisors of the casting and maintenance departments. Your reports should isolate variations from plans that are clearly under their responsibility.

B. Prepare a factory cost report for the manager of the foundry plant.

C. Prepare a cost report for the vice-president of manufacturing.

9-31 *(Reporting Under Absorption and Variable Costs).* The Little Plunker Piano Company manufactures an average of 50 pianos per month. Data on the manufacturing process includes:

Standard prime costs		
Standard labor	30 hours	@ $ 6.00
Standard material:		
Music assembly	1	@ $50
Case	40 ft.	@ $ .50
Variable overhead		
Supplies	$600 per month	
Power	$450 per month	
Other	$150 per month	
Fixed overhead		
Supervision	$1,500 per month	
Rent	$1,800 per month	

The February plan called for production of 50 pianos. However, only 40 were produced. Actual costs for the month were:

Labor (1,100 hours)	$7,040
Material	
42 music assemblies	$2,184
1,500 ft. of case material	$ 900
Supplies	$ 430
Power	$ 500
Other	$ 300
Supervision	$1,050
Rent	$1,800

REQUIRED:

A. Assuming standard variable costing:
  1. Compute the standard unit cost.
  2. Determine the factory cost variances.
  3. Prepare a performance report for the factory.

B. Assuming standard absorption costing:
  1. Compute the standard unit cost.
  2. Determine the factory cost variances that are different under absorption costing.
  3. Prepare a performance report for the factory. How is it different from the performance report under standard variable costing?

9–32 *(Comprehensive Master Budget and Reports to Management).*

Part A–(Master Budget).
Two women who had been working in pottery as a hobby received so many requests for stoneware dishes that they decided to produce the sets commercially. They formed a company, withdrew their savings, refinanced their homes, purchased equipment, rented an old barn, and started busines as The

Crockery Barn. They need additional financing from the bank and come to you for assistance in financial planning. Upon formation, the company has the following assets:

Cash	$ 2,000
Equipment	$20,000

The women expect to sell 500 sets of dishes at $100 per set during the first six months. They believe an inventory of 20 finished sets is needed to fill rush orders. Because of drying time required, there will always be 20 half-finished sets in production. Costs (except depreciation and interest) for the first six months should be:

Production	$10,000 plus $50 per set produced
Selling and administration	$5,000 plus $10 per set sold

Purchases and sales will be on account, with average balances of $20,000 for accounts receivable and $4,000 for accounts payable. Other payments will be made in the month the costs are incurred. A minimum cash balance of $2,000 is necessary.

The bank is willing to grant a two-year loan of up to $25,000 with 10% interest payable at maturity. Equipment is to be depreciated by the straight-line method over an estimated useful life of five years.

REQUIRED:

1. Prepare a master budget for the first six months of operations. Your master budget should include a profit plan, a cash budget, and a projected statement of financial position. The contribution margin approach is to be used.
2. Compute the breakeven point and margin of safety. Do not consider interest expense in your calculations.

Part B–(Reports to Management).
At the end of the first six months of operations The Crockery Barn asked you to continue your financial consultation.

Orders for the first six months exceeded expectations and the women actually sold 600 sets of dishes at an average price of $110. Inventory levels were maintained at 20 finished sets and 20 half-finished sets.

Actual costs were as follows:

Production:	
Variable	$ 60 per set
Fixed	$11,000
Selling and administration:	
Variable	$ 8 per set
Fixed	$ 5,500
Interest expense	$ 700
Depreciation of equipment	$ 2,000

REQUIRED:

A. Prepare an income statement showing profit plan, performance budget, actual results, and variances.

B. Prepare a report on profit plan that explains the difference between planned net income and actual net income.

C. Comment upon the performance of The Crockery Barn.

9-33 *(Comprehensive Planning and Control).*

Part A–(Master Budget).
Parkland Doctors' Clinic serves a suburban community of about 24,000 population, of which 25% are expected to become patients of the clinic. Each patient is expected to average five visits per year. You may assume that patient visits occur evenly throughout the year. Normally, about 5% of the billings of $17 per patient visit are not collected. Accounts receivable at the end of the year is expected to be equal to an average month's net billings.

Each doctor can serve about 600 patient visits per month. A half-time consulting physician is available if the patient load requires less than a full-time doctor. (For example, if 3,750 patient visits require 6¼ doctors, one half-time and six full-time doctors would be hired.) One nurse is required for each 500 patient visits per month. The average individual doctor's salary is $4,000 per month; a nurse's average salary is $1,000 per month. Doctors are paid in the following month; all other personnel are paid in the month service is performed.

Operating costs for the clinic include:

Administrative salaries	$5,000 per month
Lab and X-ray technicians	$4,000 per month
Medical supplies	$1.50 per patient visit
Rent	$24,000 per year
Medical and financial records	$1,000 per month plus $.25 per patient visit
Other operating costs	$500 per month plus $.15 per patient visit

Medical supplies are purchased monthly on 30-day terms. The medical and financial records are maintained by a computer service bureau. Payment is made in the month following service. All other operating costs are paid in the month of service.

The statement of financial position at the end of 19X1 follows.

PARKLAND DOCTORS' CLINIC
STATEMENT OF FINANCIAL POSITION
December 31, 19X1

Assets		*Equities*	
Cash	$10,000	Accounts payable	$12,500
Accounts receivable (net)	25,000	Salaries payable	4,000
Supplies	2,000	Owners' equity	20,500
	$37,000		$37,000

REQUIRED:

1. Prepare a profit plan for 19X2.
2. Prepare a cash budget for 19X2. Assume a desired minimum cash balance of $5,000. A line of credit is available if needed. (Ignore interest expense.)
3. Prepare a projected statement of financial position at the end of 19X2.

Part B–(Reporting to Management).

During 19X8 the following actual events were recorded for the Parkland Doctors' Clinic.

1. Patient visits amounted to 28,000 in 19X8. The billing rate through the year was $17 per patient visit. The collection rate was better than anticipated. Only 3% of 19X8 billings were considered uncollectible.
2. Costs for 19X8:

Doctors' salaries (December salaries $14,000)	$200,000
Nurses' salaries	$ 62,000
Administrative salaries	$ 60,000
Lab and X-ray technicians' salaries	$ 45,000
Medical supplies	$ 39,200
Rent	$ 24,000
Medical and financial records	$ 19,000
Other costs	$ 11,000

3. Other information:
During the last month of 19X8 there were 2,000 patient visits. Supplies of $2,800 were purchased, and the bill for medical and financial records was $1,500. The inventory of supplies at the end of 19X8 was $2,000.

REQUIRED:

1. Prepare an income statement for 19X8 for the Parkland Doctors' Clinic. Your income statement should compare actual results with plans and identify variances.
2. Prepare a cash flow statement for the year.
3. Prepare a statement of financial position at the end of 19X8.

9-34 *(Comprehensive Planning and Control Problem).* The Theobold Toy Company was formed to produce a plastic doll that has been shown by market tests to have immediate consumer acceptance. The following balance sheet was prepared on January 2, 19X1, when the company was formed.

THEOBOLD TOY COMPANY
BALANCE SHEET
January 2, 19X1

Assets		*Equities*	
Cash	$ 50,000	Capital Stock	$150,000
Equipment	100,000		
	$150,000		

On the basis of future earnings potential, the bank approved a loan of $100,000, to be repaid $50,000 at the end of 19X1 and $50,000 at the end of 19X2. Interest at 12% per year is to be paid at the end of each year. However, before the company can receive any cash from the loan, it must submit a profit plan, a cash budget, and a projected statement of financial position.

The sales forecast for the first year estimated sales of 250,000 dolls at $5.00 each. The company wants an inventory of 50,000 dolls by year-end. An inventory of raw materials (plastic) for 20,000 dolls must be maintained.

The following costs are expected for the first year.

Plastic for production of dolls	$1.00 per doll
Direct labor	$ .50 per doll
Factory overhead	$20,000 per month plus $.50 per doll produced
General and selling	$10,000 per month plus $.50 per doll sold

Depreciation of equipment (not included in factory overhead above) will be computed on a straight-line basis with a five-year life.

All doll sales and material purchases will be on credit. At the end of the year, sales of 50,000 dolls and purchases of $60,000 of plastic will not be paid. Other cash payments will be made as the cost is incurred.

Actual sales did not reach management's expectations; 220,000 dolls were produced and 200,000 sold. The selling price was reduced to $4.80. Actual costs follow.

Plastic used in production	$198,000
Direct labor	$110,000
Factory overhead ($244,000 fixed)	$355,000
General and selling ($90,000 fixed)	$200,000
Depreciation of equipment	$ 20,000
Interest expense	$ 12,000

When management saw that projected sales would not be achieved, they reduced purchases of materials, buying only what was to be used, and paid cash. At the end of the year, only 20,000 units of sales were uncollected.

REQUIRED:

A. Prepare the following for the bank:
   1. Profit plan for the year, using variable costing.
   2. Cash budget for the year.
   3. Projected statement of financial position.
   4. Compute the breakeven point in units and the margin of safety.

B. What is the role of each of the requirements in Part A in the master budget?

C. Prepare an analysis of operations for the first year of business including the following:
   1. Income statement for the year showing profit plan, performance budget, actual results, and variances. (Note: the company does not use a standard cost system.)
   2. Prepare a report on profit plan that explains the difference between planned net income and actual net income.
   3. At the end of the year, actual cash is greater than planned and net income is less than planned. Explain why this is true. Prepare a report that compares actual cash receipts and disbursements with planned receipts and disbursements.
   4. Prepare a statement of financial position at the end of 19X1.

9-35 *(Comprehensive Reporting to Different Levels of Management).* The Alberta Manufacturing Company Ltd. produces a single product and uses a standard cost system. The standards for cost and price for each unit are shown in the following tabulation.

Material: 4 yards of Cloth X @ $2.88	$11.52	
3 yards of Cloth Q @ $2.16	6.48	$18.00
Direct labor: 5 hours @ $2.00		10.00
Factory overhead: Based on direct labor hours (⅓ fixed)		7.50
Cost to manufacture		$35.50
Selling expense (⅔ fixed)		7.20
Total cost		$42.70
Net profit		5.30
Selling price		$48.00

Materials are recorded in the Raw Materials Inventory account at standard cost,and any variances therefrom, as well as all other variances, are assigned to the operations of the current year as period costs.

For the year ended March 31, 19X2, budgeted production and sales were 12,000 units; actual sales totaled 15,000 out of 18,000 units produced. There were no beginning inventories.

An examination of the accounts discloses the following:

1. During the year, 250,000 feet of Cloth X were purchased at $1.00 per foot and 180,000 feet of Cloth Q were purchased at $.70 per foot. Materials issued were 230,000 feet of X and 175,000 feet of Q.
2. Direct labor cost was $180,500. Hourly wage rates averaged 5% less than standard.
3. Actual factory overhead was $120,000, of which $35,000 was fixed.
4. Actual selling expenses totaled $107,600, of which $60,000 was fixed.
5. A special sale of 2,000 units was made at a price of $44 each; the other 13,000 units were sold at the planned price.

REQUIRED:

The president of Alberta Manufacturing Co. Ltd. has hired you as a consultant to analyze the operations of the company and explain fully the deviations from plan.

A. Assuming standard variable costing, prepare a report to the purchasing manager, a report to the sales manager, a report to the factory manager, and a report to the president. Each report should deal with the area for which the particular manager has responsibility. In addition, a brief written analysis should accompany each report. Seldom have variances exceeded 5% of standard in the past.

B. Prepare an income statement in accordance with generally accepted accounting principles for inclusion in the annual report. You may assume that the standards are accurate. *(Canada SIA adapted)*

10 Measurement of Divisional Performance

Throughout this text we stress management's role in making decisions that allocate the firm's resources. In evaluating the results of those decisions, we have stressed the importance of establishing responsibility centers and the use of responsibility accounting. Under responsibility accounting, costs, revenues, and, in some cases, investment in resources are assigned to the manager who exercised control over them. Our illustrations in the previous chapters have concerned only cost centers and profit centers; that is, those units of the firm in which responsibility extended only over costs or, in some units, costs and revenue. An entirely different dimension is added when management's responsibility is extended to cover resource investment, as is the case in an investment center.

DIVISIONALIZATION

A **division** (investment center) is a responsibility center where the manager is held accountable for both production and marketing operating decisions, as well as decisions involving investments in the resources necessary to carry them out. Division management is concerned not only with *how* operations are carried on, but also *what* operations are to be carried on. All the conditions for overall evaluation of a company are present in a division. Corporate goals and objectives provide constraints on the divisions. However, within those broad constraints, a division may operate as a separate company. It may be identified along geographic lines, as Eastern and Western divisions, along product lines, as Chevrolet and Cadillac divisions, or along separate industry lines, as in food products and leisure-time products divisions.

Business firms establish separate divisions for several reasons. The most important is to provide a natural separation of activities that allows decentralization. Decentralization provides a climate of individual management responsibility in decision making, as well as in the administration of the decisions. Complementing decentralization is the ability to measure a division's performance in terms of corporate objectives, principally through the measurement of return on investment. Because the performance measure is compatible with overall corporate objectives, division management may be given a high degree of freedom in the management of resources. The ultimate test of the effectiveness of management decisions is whether they provide the firm with a satisfactory overall rate of return on the assets committed. It is the ability to measure return on investment that makes decentralized administration attractive.

Several conditions must be present, however, for divisionalization to operate successfully.[1] First, each division must be independent of other divisions. Unless separation is possible, performance measurement as an individual division is illusory. The more difficult it is to separate profit and investment measures, the less probable it is that a division makes independent

[1]David Solomons, *Divisional Performance, Measurement and Control* (Homewood, Ill.: Richard D. Irwin, Inc., 1965).

decisions. Interdivisional transactions may cause measurement problems but they do not preclude separate divisional status. Second, the decisions of one division to increase its own income must not be allowed to reduce corporate income. It would be dysfunctional to allow a division to compete with other divisions or deal with other divisions in such a way as to cause overall corporate income to decline. This situation may arise if division boundaries are poorly drawn or corporate goals and objectives are not clearly stated. Finally, it is important to decentralization that corporate management refrain from making decisions for the divisions; divisions must be free to make decisions themselves. Corporate management should step in only as an emergency measure.

RETURN ON INVESTMENT

Simply stated, **return on investment** (ROI) is found by dividing net income by some measure of investment. The major purpose of return on investment analysis is the measurement, both absolutely and relatively, of the success of the company or its subdivisions. Return on investment analysis relates the net income, as determined on the income statement, to the resources, as measured on the statement of financial position. There are two components to the return on investment calculation: profit margin and investment turnover. **Profit margin,** sometimes called *profit as a percentage of sales,* is found by dividing net income by sales. **Investment turnover** is sales divided by investment in assets. Return on investment is the product of two components:

$$\text{Return on investment} = \text{Profit margin} \times \text{Investment turnover}$$

Stated in formula form, return on invstment is as follows:

$$\text{Return on investment} = \frac{\text{Net income}}{\text{Investment}} = \frac{\text{Net income}}{\text{Sales}} \times \frac{\text{Sales}}{\text{Investment in assets}}$$

The return on investment may be increased by increasing the profit margin, by increasing the investment turnover, or by some combination of the two. Planning and evaluation of operations is enhanced by the ability to examine each component separately. To illustrate the components of return on investment, let's assume that a firm has budgeted sales of \$500,000, costs of \$400,000, net income of \$100,000, and investment in assets of \$250,000. The return on investment is computed as:

$$\begin{aligned}\text{Return on investment} &= \frac{\text{Net income}}{\text{Investment}} = \frac{\text{Net income}}{\text{Sales}} \times \frac{\text{Sales}}{\text{Investment}} \\ &= \frac{\$100{,}000}{\$250{,}000} = \frac{\$100{,}000}{\$500{,}000} \times \frac{\$500{,}000}{\$250{,}000} \\ &= 40\% = 20\% \times 2 \text{ times}\end{aligned}$$

If, through cost reduction, the firm is able to increase the net income as a percentage of sales by 3%, the return on investment will increase by 6%. The investment turnover acts as a multiplier.

$$\text{Return on investment} = 46\% = 23\% \times 2 \text{ times}$$

Suppose instead that the firm is able to speed up collection of receivables and reduce inventories through better planning. The turnover component of the return on investment calculation would be increased. If working capital could be decreased by $25,000, the total investment in assets would decrease and the investment turnover would increase to 2.2 times. The return on investment would increase to 44%.

$$\begin{aligned} \text{Return on investment} &= \frac{\text{Net income}}{\text{Sales}} \times \frac{\text{Sales}}{\text{Investment in assets}} \\ &= \frac{\$100{,}000}{\$500{,}000} \times \frac{\$500{,}000}{\$225{,}000} \\ &= 20\% \times 2.2 \text{ times} \\ &= 44\% \end{aligned}$$

Measurement of Return on Investment Components

To use return on investment analysis in management assessment, it is important that measures of net income and investment be clearly understood by all concerned. There are some variations in practice in both the measurement of net income and the measurement of investment.

The net income figure used in calculating return on investment is usually taken directly from the financial statements. Generally accepted accounting principles guide the determination of income for external reporting. To the extent that these principles are followed for internal income measurements, internally reported income will be consistent with income for external reporting. In this case, inventories will be costed under full-absorption costing, and all assets and liabilities will be recorded at historical cost.

Net income for internal reports used in measuring divisional performance can differ from generally accepted accounting principles in two important respects. First, when products or other assets are transferred between divisions of the company, proper evaluation of the divisions may require that transfer prices be based upon market prices or other values. The use of a transfer price based upon some measure other than historical cost will result in intercompany profit in divisional inventories or other assets acquired from other divisions. Transfer pricing will be discussed later in this chapter.

Second, because of its usefulness in short-range decisions, variable costing may be used for internal profit measurement. This should not be troublesome to management. The income principles used in calculating divisional rates of return may or may not conform to generally accepted accounting principles. It is more important that the net income measure be understood and used consistently throughout the firm.

The measurement of investment is even less standardized than the net income measure. The most readily available measure of investment is the book value of assets shown on the statement of financial position.[2] However, this measure has an inherent weakness. Over time, the carrying value of the assets decreases through depreciation charges. As long as the net income remains relatively constant, the return on investment will increase because of the declining investment base. If a manager holds net income reasonably constant and makes no new investments, his rate of return will show improving performance. The ultimate result is a decline in the firm's productive capacity as the plant wears out.

There are several ways to overcome this defect in return on investment analysis. One approach is to use the original cost of the asset before any deduction for depreciation, providing a constant return on investment if earnings are constant. Another approach is to use a method of depreciation with increasing charges over the life of the asset. The result is a constant rate of return on investment; each year a lower income is related to a smaller asset base.

As another way of overcoming the ROI defect some firms use only **productive assets** in their investment base. Under this method, assets not currently committed to productive use are excluded from the investment base. Assets such as idle plants, land held for possible plant expansion or for speculative purposes, and obsolete inventories are examples of nonproductive assets. If any assets are removed from the base, earnings related to them should be excluded from the net income. This definition of the investment base is not particularly useful. If the firm has nonproductive resources, it has capital invested that is not earning a satisfactory return. The mere existence of idle resources implies that management may not be using its resources wisely; exclusion of these assets from the investment base may serve as a disguise.

Any return on investment calculation that uses historical cost to measure the investment base may be overstating the return in a period of inflation. As the asset base increases in value because of a change in the price level, the company may be misled about the rate of return being achieved. As an example, assume that Stagnation, Inc. has reported assets of $100,000 and income of $20,000 in its most recent financial statements. The return on investment, based upon depreciated cost, is 20% ($20,000 ÷ $100,000). Let's assume that since the assets were acquired, their replacement cost has doubled, primarily because of an increase in construction costs. In many cases meaningful rates of return can be found by restating the value of the assets on the statement of financial position and the depreciation expense on the income statement to reflect their current replacement costs. The following comparison shows return on investment for assets at original cost and at replacement cost.

[2]**Book value** is original cost less the accumulated depreciation to date.

	Original Cost		*Replacement Cost*	
Assets	$100,000		$200,000	
Operating income	$ 30,000		$ 30,000	
Depreciation	10,000		20,000	
Net income	$ 20,000		$ 10,000	
Return on investment	$\left(\frac{\$20{,}000}{\$100{,}000}\right)$	= 20%	$\left(\frac{\$10{,}000}{\$200{,}000}\right)$	= 5%

To the management of Stagnation, Inc. it appears that a rate of return on investment of 20% is being earned. In reality, the return is only 5% when replacement costs are considered. If the replacement costs had been higher than $200,000, and if accelerated depreciation had been used, the company could show a loss when replacement costs are used.

The rates of return among divisions within the same company may not be comparable if their asset bases were acquired at different times. The carrying costs of recently acquired assets are usually relatively close to replacement costs, whereas the carrying costs of old assets may be substantially different. For a proper comparison of two different divisions, it may be necessary to restate each unit's assets and depreciation expenses at current replacement costs.

In many companies with decentralized divisions, the home office centralizes some corporate activities, such as cash management or billing and collection of receivables. In cases where corporate assets are pooled or where assets are shared among divisions, the common, or jointly shared, assets must be allocated to the benefiting divisions for the proper measurement of their individual investments. Difficulty in identification of assets with separate divisions may indicate that the responsibility center should be identified as a cost or profit center rather than an investment center.

The most commonly apportioned assets include cash, receivables, and inventories.

Cash. To provide better control and use of this resource, cash is often managed by the central office. Only the cash balance necessary to cover local transactions should be allocated to a particular division. As a result, many divisions include a smaller amount of cash in their asset base than would be necessary if they were truly separate businesses.

Receivables. Where the division maintains its own receivables, there is no need for allocation. The investment base would simply include the ending balances of accounts receivable held by that division. Where receivables are maintained by the central office, the allocation is often based upon receivables turnover. The investment base would include the amount of receivables generated by the firm's credit and collection policies applied to the division's sales.

Inventories. Inventories are usually maintained and controlled by the individual division. Where there is the case, there is no need for apportionment. If the inventories and their levels are centrally controlled, they can be apportioned by applying an inventory turnover to actual sales volume or material consumption.

Performance Assessment Through Return on Investment Analysis

Return on investment analysis can be used to provide information about specific aspects of a manager's decisions. Separation of the overall rate of return into profit margin and investment turnover enables a manager to see the overall effects of his decisions. To illustrate this point, let's assume that a corporation has three independent divisions and that top management's overall goal is a total return on investment of 24%. This goal is illustrated in graphic form in Exhibit 10–1. The vertical scale measures investment turnover (Sales ÷ Investment). Profit margin (Net income ÷ Sales) is shown on the horizontal scale. The desired rate of 24% may be attained by any combination of investment turnover and profit margin shown on the curve. For example, a 24% return could be achieved with an investment turnover of twelve and a profit margin of 2%; it could also be obtained with an investment turnover of six and a profit margin of 4%.

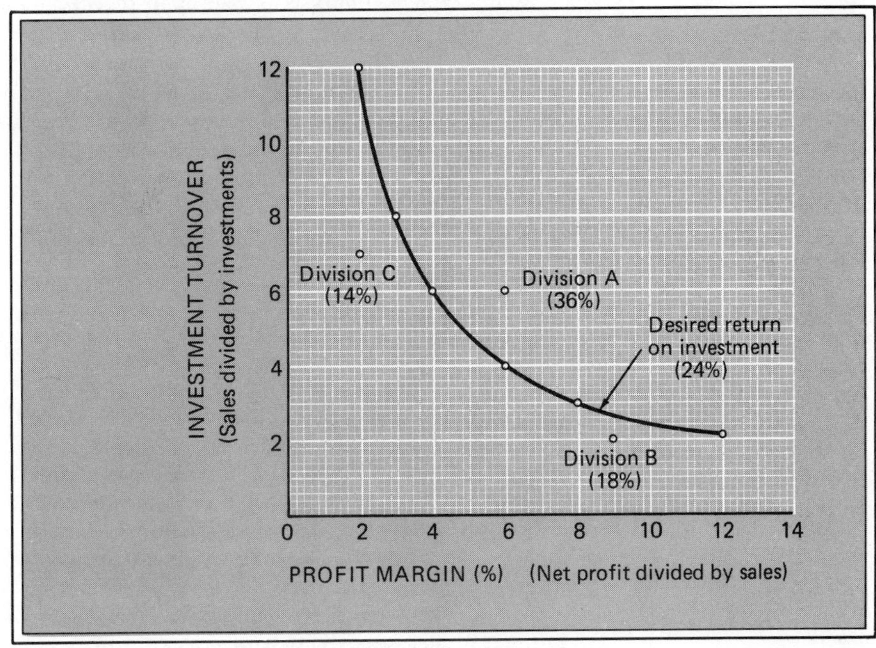

EXHIBIT 10–1
Divisional performance assessment through return on investment analysis

Actual rates of return on investment for the three divisions are shown on Exhibit 10–1. Division A shows a rate of return of 36%. The investment turnover is six times per year and the profit margin is 6%. Division A achieved results above the desired rate.

The manager of Division B did not achieve the desired rate of return. He obtained an 18% return with an investment turnover of two and a profit margin of 9%. On the surface, the 9% margin seems satisfactory, but the turnover seems low. If the investment turnover had been increased to three, the division would have earned a satisfactory rate of return of 27%. The low turnover indicates that the manager did not utilize his assets properly in relation to sales. He should begin his assessment by studying his asset structure to see if nonproductive assets are excessive. Perhaps he has excess inventory, idle cash, or unused plant capacity. It is also possible that he has misinterpreted the demand for the product or has not actively pursued additional sales.

Division C's 14% rate of return also did not achieve the desired rate. The investment turnover of seven seems to be adequate, indicating good utilization of the assets. The profit margin of 2% seems low, however. It could perhaps be improved by a study of the cost structure; a low profit margin may be indicative of poor cost control. The manager should assess the production facilities in an attempt to lower manufacturing costs, and he should test other costs, particularly those such as advertising, to ensure that they are being incurred wisely.

This type of analysis is useful in directing the manager's attention toward broad areas for improvement, but it does not determine what should be done. The ability to interpret the profit margin and investment turnover depends upon the specific business or industry involved. For example, a retail grocery store typically has a low profit margin and a high investment turnover. A steel mill, on the other hand, would have a relatively high profit margin and, with a heavy investment in plant and equipment, a relatively low investment turnover. The manager must relate rate of return analysis to the specific situation.

Overemphasis upon Return on Investment Analysis

There is no question that the rate of return on investment is a valuble measure of *overall firm or divisional performance.* It relates the resources to their utilization better than any other single measure. It also allows the comparison of one firm with another, or one division with another. If a given firm consistently earns a rate of return of 5% while another firm earns 25%, we would expect investors to prefer the firm with a 25% return. In the long run, capital investment will flow away from firms with low rates of return toward those with higher return rates.

There are many advantages in using investment centers and return on investment to measure performance. First, return on investment is a generally accepted measure of overall performance. As a measure of divisional performance, it is compatible with a firm-wide rate of return analysis. In addition, it corresponds to the inituitive view that investments are made with the goal of achieving a desired rate of return.

Second, return on investment analysis, since it is a ratio, provides a common denominator allowing comparisons of different activities. Retailing activities can be compared with wholesaling activities, steel companies can be compared with fabrication companies, and one company can be compared with other companies in the same industry.

Third, rate of return can be easily understood and interpreted.

Finally, return on investment analysis can provide a solid incentive for optimal utilization of the firm's assets. It encourages managers to obtain assets that will provide a satisfactory return on investment and to dispose of assets that are not providing an acceptable return. In this sense, the return on investment analysis of divisions corresponds and integrates well with the way long-range capital investment decisions are made.

It would be simplistic, however, to assume that return on investment is always the best method of measuring performance. Its limitations must be considered. First, many subjective judgments contribute to a measurement of the investment base. In most firms there must be some allocation of the centrally controlled assets; any apportionment is subject to arbitrary interpretation.

Second, the rate of return represents a single control point that can be manipulated by the manager. Earlier we pointed out that one way to increase the rate of return is to make no new capital investments. Because book values decline due to depreciation, the investment base will continually decrease in value, causing the rate of return to increase. This effect could lead to a situation where the manager's favorable performance assessment is jeopardizing the long-range profit potential of the firm.

A third shortcoming of overemphasis upon divisional rate of return in evaluating performance is that it can distort the overall allocation of firm resources. To illustrate, let's assume that a firm is currently earning an overall rate of return of 15%, but that Division A is earning a net income of $20,000 on capital investments of $100,000. Division A's 20% return ($20,000 ÷ $100,000) exceeds the 15% corporate rate of return. Assume that the manager of Division A has the opportunity to purchase a new asset that would earn $1,800 on an investment of $10,000. The firm has the needed $10,000 to purchase the asset. Investment in the new asset would yield an 18% return on investment ($1,800 ÷ $10,000), which is greater than the overall company return of 15%. However, if the new project is undertaken by Division A, its rate of return will fall to 19.8% ($21,800 ÷ $110,000). Further assume that the next best alternative use of the $10,000 is a project desired by Division C, whose operations are currently earning only 10%. If Division C can earn 14% on the new investment, it will increase its rate of return but reduce the overall corporate rate of return. Thus, what is good for Division C will be bad for the company as a whole, and what is bad for Division A will be good for the company as a whole. For reasons shown in this example, many firms use a firm-wide capital investment committee to oversee major investments.

RESIDUAL INCOME

As an alternative to the rate of return, General Electric Company developed the concept of residual income to measure divisional performance. **Residual income** is the incremental income of a division after deducting an interest charge based upon the value of the division's investment in assets. The company's average cost of capital is usually used as a measure of the interest charges. For example, assume that Division S has a budgeted net income of $100,000 this year, with a budgeted investment of $500,000. The cost of capital for the corporation is 15%. The income objective for the division, in terms of residual income is:

Divisional income	$100,000
Cost of capital used by division (15% × $500,000)	75,000
Residual income of Division S	$ 25,000

A principal advantage of residual income is that it encourages capital investment any time the manager can exceed the firm's cost of capital. Any new investment will increase the division's residual income if it yields an income higher than the cutoff (required) percentage. A second advantage is that it allows different rates of return for different assets. For example, a manager can use a different cost of capital for risky projects than he does for stable, relatively certain projects. In this way the performance measure can be made consistent with the decision rules employed in capital investment decisions.

Residual income as a performance measure overcomes some of the shortcomings of return on investment analysis, but it is not a perfect measure. Most of the problems in measuring divisional income and divisional investment discussed earlier in this chapter are present in the measurement of residual income. There is an additional problem of deriving a fair and equitable measure of cost of capital. (Calculation of the cost of capital will be discussed in Chapter 14.)

Setting a residual income target is a unique challenge. The target must be set in dollars. The division manager is then evaluated by his success in meeting or bettering the target. Exhibit 10–2 shows why residual income may be a better measure of divisional performance than return on investment. As the capital investment increases, the divisional income curve first increases at a rate reflecting an increasing return on investment, then slows to a constant rate of return, and, finally, flattens out to reflect a declining rate of return. The cost of capital, line K, and three different rates of return, lines R_1, R_2, and R_3, are shown as straight lines. Residual income is the dark area between divisional income and cost of capital. Residual income peaks at point E_2 and remains fairly constant between points E_2 and E_3.

A division manager could earn an equal or larger rate of return at any investment level between I_1 and I_2 than at any other level of investment, although this higher rate of return would not result in higher income for his

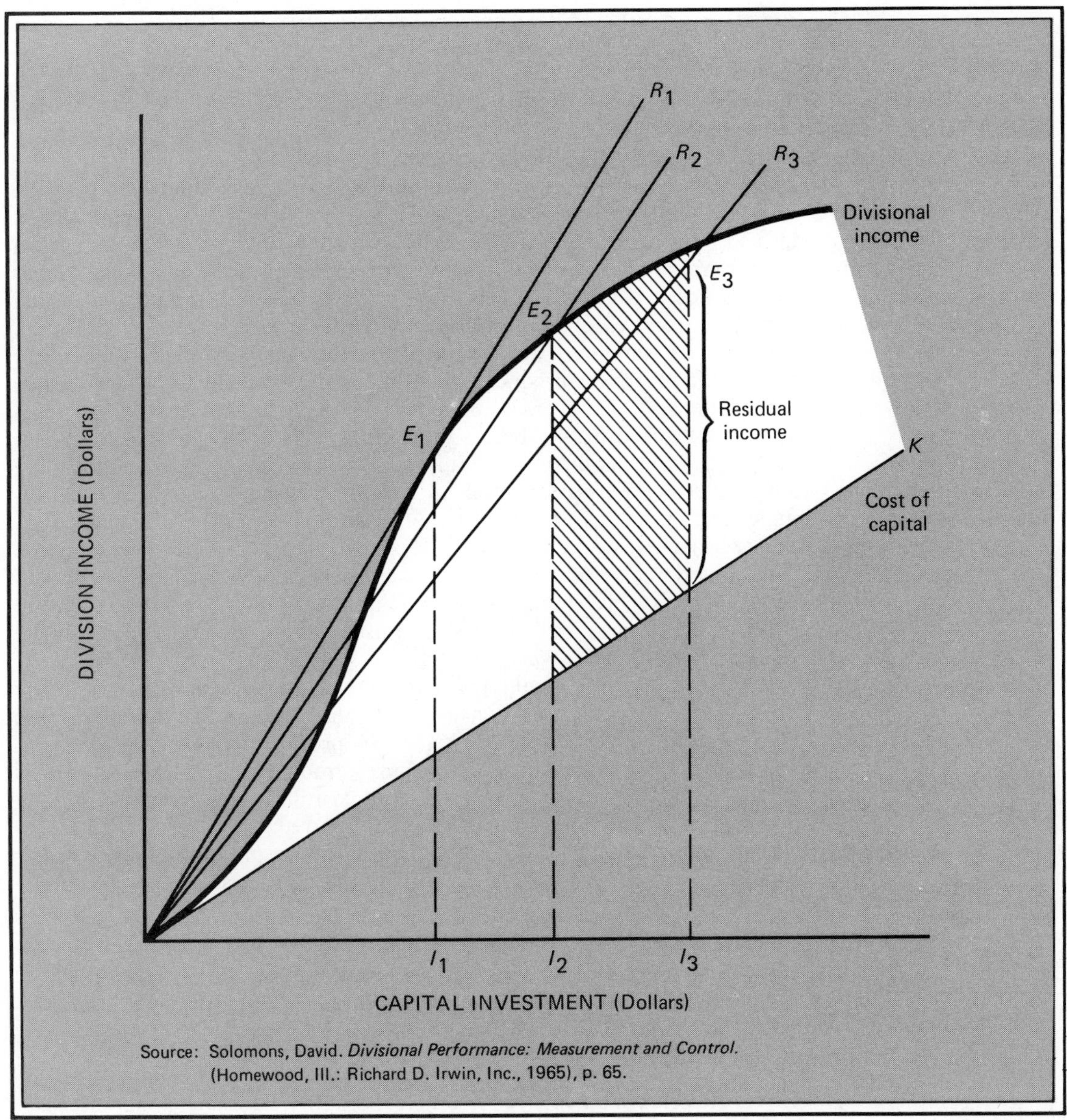

Source: Solomons, David. *Divisional Performance: Measurement and Control.* (Homewood, Ill.: Richard D. Irwin, Inc., 1965), p. 65.

EXHIBIT 10–2
Residual income and return on investment

division. In this illustration the highest rate of return (R_1) can be achieved at only investment level I_1. Yet, a higher level of divisional income and residual income can be achieved with the larger investment level at I_2. In this case the target residual income should be set between points E_2 and E_3, even though the rate of return is lower. It is only within this range that the residual income available to cover home office expenses and profits is highest.

INTRAFIRM TRANSFER PRICING

Divisional income as a control measure is based upon the view that the divisions operate much like independent companies. It is assumed that a division buys its resources in one market and sells its products or services in another. Yet products and services are often exchanged between divisions. For this practice it is necessary to establish a **transfer price,** the price at which goods and services are transferred among divisions. *Any price* can be a transfer price, whether based upon a price that would exist in an independent market, the cost to the producing division, or an arbitrarily established price.

There is no simple measure of transfer price that can meet all the needs of a decentralized firm. Obviously the transfer price of goods and services between divisions has an important impact upon the income of both the selling and purchasing divisions, as well as on the differential costs used in short-range decisions. Any transfer price that is not the price a division would pay in the open marketplace results in an arbitrary allocation of income among the divisions and weakens the measurement of divisional performance. The task of management is to develop a transfer pricing system that (1) allows a measure of performance to reflect the division's use of resources and (2) allows the optimal allocation of the firm's resources.

Where there is an intermediate market that is competitive and the divisions are independent (a division may either buy or sell externally if it is more profitable), these open-market prices provide the best transfer price. However, when corporate policy requires trading among the company's divisions, a portion of the control over resource utilization is removed from the divisions and their profit responsibility is blurred. For decentralization to work in these cases, there must be an arbitration procedure to settle any disputes regarding transfer prices and the subsequent assessment of management performance.

Transfer Pricing for Measuring Management Performance

The best transfer price for measuring management performance is one that reflects the price in an open, competitive market. Where such a market exists for the products being transferred, it provides a value for the inputs used and a value for the outputs produced. These market prices are the best measure of revenue for the selling division and of cost inputs for the buying division. A major drawback in the use of market prices is that few markets are perfectly competitive. In many instances no intermediate market exists for the products or services being transferred. One way to establish market prices is through bids from outside firms. However, unless the divisions actually purchase from these external suppliers occasionally, the bids may not be representative. If the supplier is aware that the bid is simply to establish an internal transfer price and will probably not result in an order, the quoted price may be unrealistic.

For market prices to have maximum effectiveness in management performance measurement, both the buying and selling divisions must be able to act independently. The divisions must be free to buy or sell their products in any market. If there is no intermediate market for the products or services, or if corporate policy requires interdivisional trading, negotiated market prices may be necessary. Here, a price is negotiated between the buying and selling units, often with the aid of a corporate arbitrator. Without some external market for comparison, these negotiated market prices can be artificial, just as the cost-plus-fixed-markup transfer price is artificial. Too great a reliance upon arbitration tends to centralize decisions and weaken the ability to measure divisional performance.

In circumstances where there are no competitive market prices and a negotiated transfer price cannot be established, the company cannot establish profit or investment centers. It can only use cost centers for management performance evaluation. By using standard costs as the transfer prices for cost centers, the selling divisions are encouraged to have good cost control. The manager of a selling division would be evaluated as the manager of any other cost center. His performance would be measured by the question, "How well did he control costs subsequent to the transfer?"

In responsibility accounting, a division's performance should reflect only revenues and costs subject to the control of the division. Artificial prices, such as a constant markup on cost allow divisional income to be measured and therefore give an appearance of a profit center. An artificial transfer price with an arbitrary markup does not fit the requisite of controllability. Control over revenue is not present and the divisions are not true profit centers. Therefore, artificial prices are not useful in assessing managerial performance. The measure of a specific division's performance should also be independent of performance measurements used to assess other divisions in the company.

Transfer Prices for Decisions

The ideal transfer price for management decision making is the price that would be used by the corporation if it were not organized into divisions. Such a price would emphasize the well-being of the company as a whole, rather than of the individual divisions. For decision-making purposes, the transfer price should reflect the opportunity cost of the goods or services transferred between the divisions. An optimal allocation of resources takes place only if the goods or services are priced on transfer at the opportunity cost that would be incurred to obtain the goods or services elsewhere when they are needed. Where an intermediate market exists, the goods and services are available from external sources and the open-market price is the best measure of opportunity cost.

Where no intermediate market exists, only top management may be in a position to know the opportunity costs of a particular exchange. It may be necessary for top management to prescribe a transfer price or arbitrate in the negotiations so that decisions reflect corporate objectives and coordinate the activites of all divisions. One widely used approach uses the variable costs incurred by the selling division as the transfer price charged to the buying division.[3] The use of variable costs allows each divisional manager to assess the differential costs more accurately. When used as a transfer price, standard variable costs, representing what costs should be, are preferred over actual variable costs. The selling division is thus prevented from passing inefficiencies on to the buying division.

The manager of the selling division cannot be expected to accept readily a price as a performance measure that will produce a large loss for his division even if it is best for the firm as a whole. In fact, if variable costs are used as the transfer price, and there is no intermediate market, the manager of the selling division should be indifferent between selling to another division of the company as he would about closing down. In either case the selling division's loss would be equal to the fixed costs of the division.

Top management support is essential in negotiations between divisions to show each division the effect of the transfer pricing policy on firm-wide profits. The transfer prices used must recognize the economic reality of the division's environment for decision making and at the same time be fair to division managers for performance evaluation.

Tranfer Prices for External Reporting

Under generally accepted accounting principles, assets must be stated at cost, and revenue is not recognized until a sale is completed with an outside party. The only transfer price appropriate for external reporting is an actual cost based upon full-absorption costing. In this way the inventory is stated at the full cost required to bring the goods to the condition for resale.

When divisional financial statements are consolidated into financial statements for the firm as a whole, all interdivisional profits resulting from tranfer prices must be eliminated from assets on hand. All interdivisional payables, receivables, purchases, and sales must also be eliminated.

Transfer Pricing Case

To illustrate some of the problems of transfer prices, let's assume that the Rex Company produces industrial chemicals. Three divisions are evaluated on the basis of their divisional income and return on investment. Division R extracts material from animal by-products. The resulting product, Product R, is sold

[3]For a microeconomic analysis of transfer prices in differing marketplaces, see J. Hirshleifer, "Economics of the Divisionalized Firm," *Journal of Business* (April, 1957), pp. 96–108.

to Division E, as well as to outside customers, for $100 per barrel. Division R, which has idle capacity, has a contribution margin ratio of 40%. Division E processes Product R into a number of other products. One of these products, Product E, is sold primarily to Division X. Product E requires $110 of variable costs, in addition to the cost of one barrel of Product R. Division E has a contribution margin ratio of 30%. Division X combines one unit of Product E with other ingredients in a process that incurs an additional $100 in variable costs. The result is an industrial cleaner, Product X, which is sold to outsiders for $500 per unit. A diagram of the product flow follows.

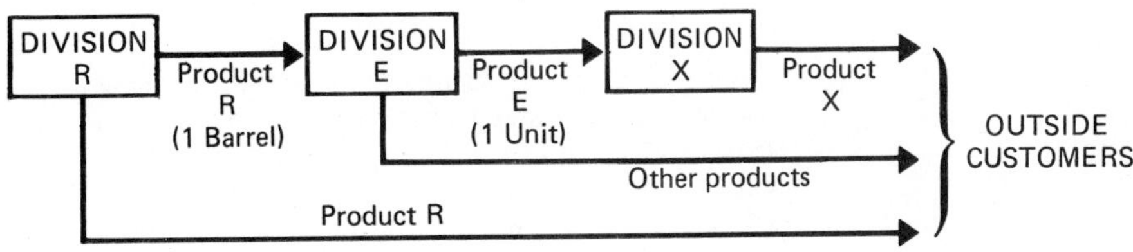

Each division buys and sells externally as well as to other divisions. Top management wishes each division to operate independently.

Division X's purchasing agent requested bids from Division E and one outside company that also makes Product E. The bids were $300 per unit from Division E and $250 per unit from Mohawk Chemical Company. The manager of Division E does not want to match the low price of Mohawk and has requested that corporate top management require Division X to purchase Product E from him at the bid price of $300. The Division E manager bases the request upon two arguments. First, it is widely known that Mohawk Chemical Company has idle capacity in the plant that manufactures Product E; this implies that Mohawk is "underpricing" their product and that they will not attain their normal profit margin. Second, the manager feels that if his division is to maintain its average contribution margin ratio of 30%, the selling price must be $300. This figure was determined as follows:

Variable Costs:			
Transfer price from Division R	$100		
Variable costs of Division E	110	$210	70%
Contribution margin		90	30%
Selling Price		$300	100%

The controller prepared the following tabulation which shows the contribution margins from a company-wide standpoint under the two alternatives.

	Buy Internally	*Buy from Mohawk*
Selling price of Product X	$500	$500
Variable costs:		
Division R	$ 60	$ 0
Division E	110	0
Division X	100	100
External purchase price	0	250
Total variable costs	270	350
Contribution margin	$230	$150

Clearly, this analysis shows that Division X, from the company-wide standpoint, should purchase from Division E. The company would earn an extra $80 per unit ($230 − $150) contribution margin. In this case what is good for the company as a whole would not satisfy the divisional managers. Division X would want to purchase externally; top management would want the transfer to take place internally. If top management allows individual action, Division E would have no tranfer selling price, since they would not make a sale; Division X would be held accountable for the actual purchase price of $250, the price they would pay Mohawk. The Division E manager's willingness to forego this sale will depend upon the marketplace for Product E and the alternative uses of Division E capacity. If the actual market price for Product E is $250, as bid by Mohawk, and if Division E cannot use the productive capacity for any other purposes, then Division E is in a weakened bargaining position. The manager should be willing to sell Product E at any price greater than the variable costs of $210 ($100 + $110). He should be willing to meet or better the Mohawk price of $250, since it will provide a positive contribution margin.

If the manager of Division E has alternative uses other than the manufacture of Product E, the problem changes. Anytime the manager of Division E can obtain a contribution margin from outsiders of more than $80 ($230 − $150) from the productive capacity, the firm would want him to sell to outsiders and Division X to buy from Mohawk. Division E would receive the benefits of the actual selling price to the outsider; Division X would be held accountable for the actual purchase price from Mohawk of $250. Anytime the contribution margin of Division E falls below $80 per unit of capacity, the firm would want Division X to purchase its materials from Division E and the problem of independence would arise again. Here, the minimum Division E selling price would be the variable costs plus the actual contribution margin obtainable from the outsiders; Division X's purchasing price would be $250, the lowest offer. In this case the firm may have to use different prices in the different divisions. Each division could be allowed to use the transfer price determined by the best market price available.

This case illustrates that the question of suitable transfer prices for the two functions of management performance assessment and decision optimization does not have an easy answer. The firm must give serious consideration to its goals and objectives in using transfer prices before adopting a particular measure.

MULTIPLE PERFORMANCE MEASURES

Throughout the previous chapters we have stressed financially quantifiable data for judging the effectiveness of management decision making. Financial measures such as the rate of return on investment are valid and useful, but they are not the only suitable measures. Many nonfinancial measures are also valuable.

When a method of assessment emphasizes a small number of financial measures to the exclusion of others, the system can be more easily manipulated. This is true even though the measure is inherently valid. There is no question that rate of return on investment and net income for the period, as examples, are valid measures of performance. However, reliance upon a single control tool can distort the decision-making process. The manager who maximized his rate of return by delaying potentially profitable capital investment is an example.

Many firms prefer multiple goals and multiple performance measures, both financial and nonfinancial. General Electric Company is an example of a firm that has developed a series of multiple goals for assessing management performance. Goals are stated for each of the following areas.

1. Profitability
2. Market position
3. Productivity
4. Product leadership
5. Personnel development
6. Employee attitudes
7. Public responsibility
8. Balance between long-range and short-range goals

Three observations may be made from a close examination of these eight goals. First, the measures to assess performance are both financial and nonfinancial. Profitability and productivity may be financial measures. Employee morale and personnel development measures are certainly nonfinancial and highly subjective. The mixture of subjective and objective assessment measures taxes the measurement skill of the accountant and the evaluation skills of management.

Second, the goals are somewhat contradictory. For example, increasing profitability through increasing employee productivity may lower employee morale. Also, maintaining product leadership may call for research and development costs that lower short-range profitability. The manager should not emphasize one goal by jeopardizing another; he must seek an optimal balance.

Third, multiple goals will increase pressure upon the managers. An attempt to meet many criteria simultaneously can be frustrating and confusing. The proper balance of goals and performance measures is difficult to set. While many of the concepts presented in this text appear highly quantitative and objective, we can never overlook the fact that the setting of goals, the evaluation of actual performance, and the development of a system to measure management decisions are highly subjective. Management accounting relies upon scientific methods, but it always has been and always will be an art.

SUMMARY

A widely used test of the effectiveness of management's decisions is the rate of return on investment. The return on investment is:

$$\text{Return on investment} = \frac{\text{Net income}}{\text{Investment}}$$

$$= \frac{\text{Sales}}{\text{Investment}} \times \frac{\text{Net income}}{\text{Sales}}$$

where (Sales ÷ Investment = Investment turnover) and (Net income ÷ Sales = Profit margin).

While conceptually sound and easy to determine, the rate of return on investment has limitations. It focuses management's attention upon a single measure and can result in optimizing the measure rather than optimizing the decisions. For example, failure to make new capital investments will increase the rate of return and simultaneously reduce the company's long-range profit potential. The use of residual profit as a measure of divisional performance is one way of overcoming some of the shortcomings of return on investment analysis.

Where there are responsibility centers that rely upon each other for their production inputs, the problems of interdivisional transfer pricing exist. With profit centers or investment centers, a firm must develop transfer prices when the divisions exchange goods or services. There are many possible transfer prices. To obtain optimum utilization of company resources, transfer prices based upon variable costs seem best. For management performance assessment, transfer prices based upon current market prices or standard costs seem best. For external reporting purposes, transfer prices based upon full cost with no added profit margin conform to generally accepted accounting principles.

There is no single performance measure that can fulfill all management's needs. Overemphasis upon one measure, although that measure seems appropriate, can be detrimental. The best control system includes many performance measures, such as budgets, cost standards, product leadership, and technical standards; and many nonquantifiable measures, such as personnel attitudes and public responsibility. If a firm is to achieve a goal of long-run profitability and stability, it must consider *all* the relevant factors.

SUPPLEMENTARY READING

Bierman, Harold, Jr. "Pricing Intracompany Transfer." *The Accounting Review,* July, 1959.

*Bierman, Harold, Jr. "ROI as a Measure of Managerial Performance." *Financial Executive,* March, 1973.

Clayden, Roger. "A New Way to Measure and Control Divisional Performance." *Management Services,* September–October, 1970.

Dearden, J. "Interdivisional Pricing." *Harvard Business Review,* January–February, 1960.

Dearden, J. "Limits on Decentralized Profit Responsibility." *Harvard Business Review,* July–August, 1962.

Dearden, J. "The Case Against ROI Control." *Harvard Business Review,* May–June, 1969.

Fremgen, James M. "Transfer Pricing and Management Goals." *Management Accounting,* December, 1970.

Mauriel, John J., and Robert N. Anthony. "Misevaluation of Investment Center Performance." *Harvard Business Review,* March–April, 1966.

National Association of Accountants. *Accounting for Intra-Company Transfers.* New York: National Association of Accountants, 1956.

*Sharav, Itzhak. "Transfer Pricing—Diversity of Goals and Practices." *The Journal of Accountancy,* April, 1974.

Shillinglaw, Gordon. "Problems in Divisional Profit Measurement." *N.A.A. Bulletin,* March, 1961.

Solomons, David. *Divisional Performance: Measurement and Control.* Homewood, Ill.: Richard D. Irwin, Inc. 1965.

QUESTIONS

10-1 What does *decentralization* mean? What are its advantages and disadvantages?

10-2 What are some of the disadvantages of using division profit as the measure of performance?

10-3 "The rate of return on investment is the best measure of overall firm performance." Do you agree? Explain.

10–4 Explain the concepts:

Current replacement cost of assets as a measure of investment
Productive assets as an investment base
Gross book value as an investment base

10–5 What are the two components of return on investment? Explain how they interact.

10–6 The development of a profit center requires four conditions, or assumptions, on the part of the firm. List and explain why each is necessary to a profit center.

10–7 "The investment center provides greater control than a profit center." Explain.

10–8 Define *residual income.* What are the advantages of using residual income for performance evaluation? The disadvantages?

10–9 What is a *transfer price?* Under what conditions are transfer prices necessary?

10–10 If a market-based transfer price can be determined, why is it usually considered the best transfer price to use?

EXERCISES

10–11 *(True or False).* Indicate whether the following statements are true or false.

1. An investment center is a responsibility center where the manager has responsibility for revenue, costs, and investment.
2. The extent of decentralization is indicated by the geographic location of the responsibility center in relation to the corporate office.
3. Return on investment is determined by dividing residual income by assets employed.
4. Contribution margin is a better measure of performance than net expenses for a cost center.
5. The use of residual income to evaluate division performance should result in expansion through new investments as long as the income from a new investment exceeds the cost of capital.
6. The use of return on investment to evaluate division performance may result in the rejection of an otherwise profitable expansion.
7. Any price used to measure the transfer of goods or services between parts of a company is called a transfer price.

8. The best transfer price for management decision making is one based on full cost.

9. The best transfer price for measuring management performance is one based on an independent market price.

10. The most important factor in the choice of a transfer price is to motivate managers.

10–12 Match the following terms and definitions.

1. Division
2. Return on investment
3. Profit margin
4. Investment turnover
5. Profit center
6. Residual income
7. Replacement cost
8. Transfer price
9. Investment center
10. Historical cost

A. A responsibility center accountable only for revenues and costs.
B. Division contribution less charge for cost of capital.
C. Consideration actually given for an asset.
D. Net income divided by investment.
E. Sales divided by investment.
F. Net income divided by sales.
G. Interdivisional sales price.
H. Another name for decentralized investment center.
I. Consideration that would be given to purchase an asset now.
J. Responsibility center with control over resources as well as revenues and costs.

10–13 *(Incomplete Data and Return on Investment).* In the following four cases, determine the amount where the question mark appears.

	A	*B*	*C*	*D*
Net income	$100	$?	$?	$ 600
Cost of capital	$ 40	$?	$ 540	$ 300
Sales	$400	$1,000	$ 900	$?
Investment base	$200	$?	$2,700	$1,500
Profit margin	?%	20%	33 ⅓ %	?%
Investment turnover	? time(s)	1 time	? time(s)	4 times
Return on investment	?%	?%	11%	?%
Residual income	$?	$ 0	$?	$ 300

10–14 *(Return on Investment).* A common measure of a manager's performance is return on net worth. This is a particularly important measure from the stockholder's point of view. This ratio can be expressed as the product of three other ratios as shown below:

$$\frac{\text{Return on}}{\text{net worth}} = \frac{\text{Net income}}{\text{Net worth}} = \overset{\underline{1}}{\frac{\text{Net income}}{\text{Sales}}} \times \overset{\underline{2}}{\frac{\text{Sales}}{\text{Assets}}} \times \overset{\underline{3}}{\frac{\text{Assets}}{\text{Net worth}}}$$

REQUIRED:

A. Discuss the return on net worth as a management goal and as a measurement of management performance.

B. What management activities are measured by each of the ratios 1, 2, and 3?

C. Would separation of the return on net worth into the three ratios and use of these ratios for planning targets and performance measures result in goal congruence (or improvement toward goal congruence) among the responsible managers? Explain your answer. *(CMA adapted)*

10–15 *(Graphic Presentation of Return on Investment).* The Gold Bracelet Custom Manufacturing Company desired a return on investment of 36%. The following were actual results by sales outlet.

	Investment Turnover	*Profit Margin*
Outlet A	4 times	6%
Outlet B	9 times	5%
Outlet C	6 times	6%

REQUIRED:

A. Compute the return on investment for each outlet.

B. Illustrate graphically each outlet's return on investment and the company's desired return on investment.

C. List some possible reasons for the performance of Outlets A and B.

10–16 *(Investment by Division).* The Corn Products Division of Cobb Company has prepared the following profit plan for 19X7.

Sales	$5,000,000
Variable costs	$2,500,000
Fixed costs	1,500,000
Total costs	4,000,000
Income	$1,000,000
Assets employed by the division	$4,000,000

The entire company has projected a rate of return of 15%. The cost of capital for the company is 12%.

The division is considering the following investment in new equipment for a new product.

Cost of equipment	$200,000
Expected annual sales	$300,000
Variable costs	40% of sales
Annual fixed costs (including depreciation of equipment)	$140,000

Other divisions have submitted proposals for new projects that will provide a return on investment of approximately 15%.

REQUIRED:

A. As manager of the Corn Products Division, would you accept or reject the proposal? Explain.

B. As president of Cobb Company, would you want the division to accept or reject the proposal? Explain.

C. What would you recommend to avoid problems of this nature in the future?

10-17 *(Transfer Price for Decisions).* The Billings Bag Company has several divisions that produce a number of packaging products. The Bag Division purchases fibers from the Finished Fibers Division, as well as from several outside companies, for the production of bags. In May the Bag Division received an order for one million bags at $12 per thousand and requested bids for finished fibers from a number of companies, as well as from the Finished Fibers Division. Three bids were considered:

1. The Finished Fibers Division bid will result in a materials cost of $6.00 per thousand bags based upon full cost. Finished Fibers Division is operating at 65% of capacity and earning a contribution margin of 40%.
2. A bid resulting in a materials cost of $5.00 per thousand bags was received from the Himalayas Company. This company will buy its raw material from the Import Division of the Billings Bag Company. Raw materials account for $1.50 of the $5.00. The Import Division earns a contribution margin ratio of 50%.
3. The lowest bid, resulting in a materials cost of $4.50 per thousand, was received from the Andes Company, a completely independent company.

REQUIRED:

A. From whom should the Bag Division manager buy if he acts in conformity with his division's goals?

B. From whom should the Bag Division manager buy if he acts in conformity with corporate goals?

C. If you were the president of Billings Bag Company, what would you do to maximize the corporation's net income and yet maintain decentralization?

10-18 *(Determining Transfer Prices)*. Cubbage Enterprises, Inc. has several divisions that have interdivisional sales of components. The company is fully decentralized. Individual divisions may purchase or sell in any market consistent with the division's goals. The Electronics Division purchases most of its wire from the Metal Products Division. The two divisions are in the process of negotiating the price for the wire the Electronics Division will purchase next quarter. The following information was accumulated for the decision.

1. Costs of Metal Products Division (per spool for 12,000 spools, 60% of capacity):

Material	$30
Direct labor	15
Variable overhead	10
Fixed overhead	20
Fixed selling and administration costs	10
Fixed central corporate costs	6
	$91

2. The Metal Products Division has a net income objective of 9% of sales. Pricing has been consistent with this rule.

3. The current market price for the wire has dropped to $75 per spool.

REQUIRED:

A. Determine the selling price that would allow the Metal Products Division to achieve its income objective.

B. What price should the Electronics Division offer to pay for wire to maximize its income?

C. What is the minimum price the Metal Products Division could charge and be no worse off than if the Electronics Division purchased from the outside?

D. What price should top corporate management use in evaluating whether to have the wire made by the Metal Products Division or purchase it from the outside?

10-19 *(Return on Investment and Residual Income).*

Part A.

The Circle B Manufacturing Company, a decentralized producer of building materials, has a firm-wide goal of 18% return on investment and a cost of capital of 15%. The following data relate to the operating divisions.

	Income	*Investment*
Division D	$30,000	$200,000
Division E	$50,000	$250,000
Division F	$20,000	$ 80,000

REQUIRED:

1. Compute the return on investment for each division.
2. Compute the residual income for each division.
3. Rank the divisions according to performance.

Part B.
The Circle B Manufacturing Company is considering the purchase of a new venture that would be placed in one of the existing operating divisions. The project will have assets of $30,000 and earn $5,400 per year.

1. What will the new project do to each of the performance measures in Part A above.
2. If the asset is acquired, in which division should it be placed?

10–20 *(Performance Measures).* You have been asked by corporate management to evaluate three divisions of the Many Products Company. The cost of capital is 10%.

	Divisions		
	Wood Products	*Metal Products*	*Chemical Products*
Sales	$240,000	$300,000	$450,000
Net income	$ 24,000	$ 24,000	$ 63,000
Productive assets—original cost	$ 80,000	$ 75,000	$300,000
Productive assets—replacement cost	$160,000	$225,000	$300,000
Asset life	30 years	30 years	30 years

REQUIRED:

A. Compute and rank all performance measures available using the above data, first using original cost of the assets, then using replacement cost.
B. Which division has the best overall performance? Explain.

10–21 *(Determining Transfer Prices).* The Chemical Division of Southeast Industries produces a chemical product called Gluck used in paints and many industrial products. The Industrial Products Division, another Southeast Industries Division, uses Gluck in several of its products but has always purchased Gluck from outside suppliers.

The internal auditor for Southeast Industries has examined a number of profit improvement ideas and recommends that the Industrial Products Division purchase Gluck from the Chemical Division. At the present time the Chemical Division is operating at 50% of capacity. The annual requirements of the Industrial Products Division have been 3,000 barrels at $180 per barrel. The audit team found that variable selling costs would be reduced to $10 per unit on intercompany sales.

The internal audit team developed the following data concerning the production of Gluck during the past year.

Chemical Division

Capacity	10,000 barrels per year
Unit selling price	$ 200
Variable production costs	$ 116
Variable selling costs	$ 20
Fixed production costs	$200,000
Allocated fixed corporation costs	$ 88,000

REQUIRED:

A. What is the breakeven point for the Chemical Division? How much income did the division earn last year?

B. What is the highest transfer price that can be justified on intercompany sales of Gluck? Explain.

C. What is the lowest transfer price that can be justified on intercompany sales of Gluck? Explain.

D. The Industrial Products Division can purchase Gluck from Bayou Chemicals at $170 per barrel. Should the Chemical Division be required to meet this price? Explain.

E. What is your answer to B and C if the Chemical Division is operating at capacity? Explain.

10–22 *(Measures of Profitability).* A year ago the Dennison Company instituted a bonus system for division managers. A bonus will be paid to the division manager who produces the highest income in relation to the investment in productive assets. Each division manager claimed the bonus for 19X4 and produced calculations to prove the point. The following data were used by the division managers.

Division	*Original Cost of Productive Assets*	*Age of Assets*	*Net Income (computed in accordance with GAAP)*
Purple Sage	$500,000	10 years	$67,500
Blue Mountain	$400,000	8 years	$56,000
Sandy Beach	$300,000	5 years	$43,500

All assets have a 10-year remaining life. Dennison Company's cost of capital is 12%.

REQUIRED:

Determine the method each plant manager used to determine profitability.

10–23 *(Evaluation of Old and New Plants).* The Caustic Chemical Company produces the same chemical in two different plants. New Plant was put into production two years ago and has operated near capacity since opening. The corporate management is very pleased with the operating results for New Plant. Old Plant has been in operation for many years. Because the market cannot absorb the total production of the two plants, production has fluctuated widely at Old Plant and remained at capacity in New Plant. Because of these fluctuations in volume, Old Plant has had unfavorable labor and variable overhead efficiency variances.

Corporate management evaluates the plants on the basis of net income and return on investment. Data for the two plants are presented below. Assume a 20% cost of capital.

	Old Plant		*New Plant*	
Capacity in barrels	1,000,000		2,000,000	
Investment in assets	$2,000,000		$10,000,000	
Selling price of product per unit	$16		$16	
Operating costs:				
	Standard	*Actual*	*Standard*	*Actual*
Material per unit	$5	$5	$5	$5
Labor per unit	$6	$6.40	$2	$2
Variable overhead per unit	$1	$1.10	$2	$2
Fixed overhead per year	$1,000,000		$10,000,000	
Actual level of operations (Percent of capacity)	50%		100%	

REQUIRED:

A. Prepare an income statement for each plant. Compute the return on investment and residual income for each. Comment upon the performance of each.

B. How should production be distributed between the plants if the market remains 2,500,000 barrels per year?

C. Devise a way to evaluate the performance of the plants that will be fair to Old Plant.

10-24 *(Divisional Bonuses and Transfer Prices).* The owner of the Nibler Equipment Company is nearing retirement age and wants to provide incentives for key employees who hold management positions with the firm. He formally organized the business into three divisions: New Equipment Sales, Used Equipment Sales, and Equipment Repairs and agreed to pay each manager 50% of the net income of the division as a bonus. To measure income by division, Mr. Nibler will charge each division rent based on the value of the space used and a management fee based on divisional sales to cover Mr. Nibler's salary and other administrative costs. Each division is to operate as an independent business with responsibility for purchasing, marketing, and sales. Corporate goals relating to quality of service and fairness to the customer are to be maintained.

Income statements for the first quarter of operations as separate divisions follow.

NEW EQUIPMENT SALES DIVISION
INCOME STATEMENT
Quarter 1, 19X3

Sales of new equipment		$325,000
Trade-in allowance in excess of appraised value of used equipment		25,000
Net sales		$300,000
Operating expenses:		
Cost of equipment sold	$210,000	
Direct operating expenses of division	30,000	
Rent	20,000	
Management fee	18,000	278,000
Net income		$ 22,000

USED EQUIPMENT SALES DIVISION
INCOME STATEMENT
Quarter 1, 19X3

Sales of used equipment		$175,000
Trade-in allowance in excess of appraised value of used equipment		15,000
Net sales		$160,000
Operating expenses:		
Cost of used equipment sold	$105,000	
Direct operating expenses of division	20,000	
Rent	8,000	
Management fee	9,600	142,600
Net income		$ 17,400

The New Equipment Sales Division and Used Equipment Sales Division take trade-ins from customers. The Used Equipment Sales Division must establish the appraised price and must purchase the used equipment from the New Equipment Division at the appraised price. If the New Equipment Division manager believes that the appraised price is too low, he may sell the used equipment on the wholesale market. If service is needed on used equipment, the repair manager will estimate the cost and bill the selling divisions at the estimate. If the actual cost exceeds the estimate the Repair Division must bear the added costs. For years the Service Division (earlier the service department) has provided service work for the selling divisions at cost.

The New Equipment Sales Division recently sold a new piece of equipment and accepted a used piece of equipment in trade. The following

EQUIPMENT REPAIR DIVISION
INCOME STATEMENT
Quarter 1, 19X3

	Repair work for outside customers	*Repair work for other divisions*	*Total*
Charges to customers	$75,000	$20,000	$95,000
Variable cost of work performed	52,500	21,000	73,500
Gross margin	$22,500	$ (1,000)	$21,500
Operating costs:			
Direct operating expenses of division			$ 6,000
Rent			6,000
Management fees			5,700
Total			17,700
Net income			$ 3,800

information relates to the sale.

List price of machine (sales are normally made at list price)	$12,000
Cost of equipment sold	$ 8,400
Trade-in allowed on old equipment	$ 2,000
Appraisal value in present condition (determined by Used Equipment Sales Division)	$ 1,300
Cost of estimated repairs required (determined by Equipment Service Division)	$ 600

When the repairs were actually performed, additional internal damage not apparent in the estimate raised the repair cost to $1,000. The best price the Used Equipment Sales Division could finally get for the used equipment was $1,800.

REQUIRED:

A. How much did each manager earn or lose on the transaction?

B. When the service manager saw the income statement, he became very angry and said that he had been taken by the other managers for the last time. He will now charge full price for all service. What should the service manager have charged for the service on the trade-in equipment? Using this new charge, recompute the amount each division gained or lost on the transaction.

C. If the internal repair work was performed equally for each sales division, determine the amount of bonus each manager would have earned if the service manager had charged the "full price" for service.

D. The management fee consists of the president's salary, accounting, credits and collections, and other administrative costs of the company. Comment upon the manner in which the management fee is charged to each division. How would you establish a transfer price for this "service"?

10-25 *(Transfer Prices).* Fictum Farms, Inc. produces wheat and soybeans. When the crops are harvested, they are transferred from the Harley producing division to the Kenneth selling division, where they are dried and stored for sale at the best price.

During 19X2, 90,000 bushels of wheat and 60,000 bushels of soybeans were produced. At the time of harvest, wheat was selling at $3.00 per bushel and soybeans at $4.00 per bushel. The entire crop was sold before the end of the fiscal year, at $4.00 per bushel of wheat and $7.00 per bushel of soybeans. At the end of fiscal year 19X2, the prices were $4.50 for wheat and $7.50 for soybeans.

The income statement for the fiscal year follows.

Sales		$780,000
Operating expenses:		
Variable production costs	$300,000	
Variable selling costs	30,000	
Fixed production costs	100,000	
Fixed selling costs	10,000	440,000
Net income		$340,000

REQUIRED:

A. The president of the corporation, Mr. Vern, wants to see how each division performed. Prepare separate income statements for each division. Explain the transfer price you used.

B. Explain how your income statements will assist in the following roles.

1. Evaluation of performance
2. Awarding of bonuses
3. Decision of when to sell the grain (sell or store longer)

PROBLEMS

10-26 *(Performance Measurement Through Return on Investment).* Two identical small companies, A and B, manufacture cleaning compounds under identical franchises from a larger company. Their franchises give each an exclusive right to sell anywhere within 300 miles of its factory and require each to show substantial increases in sales until a volume is reached that indicates satisfactory cultivation of its entire franchised territory. Each has 10 salesmen, and each president estimates that 100 salesmen would provide optimal coverage (measured by return on investment) of his allotted territory.

At the beginning of Year 2 each company had $10,000 cash available for investment. The companies considered various methods of utilizing the

$10,000 available cash to improve their operations. Each company adopted a different plan.

Company A

The president of Company A investigated his costs of raw materials and discovered that his company bought liquid raw materials in carload lots. He estimated a prospective saving of $8,000 per year on raw materials costs if such liquids were purchased in tank cars instead of boxcars, and that an investment of $10,000 would be needed in underground storage tanks to make use of tank cars feasible.

Company A acquired the storage tanks. Liquid raw materials were purchased in tank cars and the predicted $8,000 annual saving on purchased raw materials was realized in all subsequent years.

Company B

Company B, on the other hand, decided to expand its sales force. The $10,000 cash available at the beginning of Year 2 would be used during the year to recruit and train five additional salesmen. Since the entire $10,000 would be written off as an expense in Year 2, the after-tax profits would be reduced by $5,000. However, in Year 3 and subsequent years, this 50% increase in salesmen would increase sales by 50%, and annual sales could be expected to go to $300,000. Furthermore, since breakeven volume was $100,000 and the company made a $10,000 profit on $200,000 sales, it could be expected to make a $20,000 profit on $300,000 sales. This would defend its territorial rights under its franchise.

The results for both companies are condensed in the following schedule.

	Year 1		Year 2		Year 3	
	A	*B*	*A*	*B*	*A*	*B*
Sales	$200,000	$200,000	$200,000	$200,000	$200,000	$300,000
Net income:						
Before taxes	$ 20,000	$ 20,000	$ 27,000*	$ 10,000†	$ 27,000	$ 40,000
After taxes	$ 10,000	$ 10,000	$ 13,500	$ 5,000	$ 13,500	$ 20,000
Total assets	$ 50,000	$ 50,000	$ 59,000	$ 50,000	$ 58,000	$ 50,000
Return on investment	20.0%	20.0%	22.9%	10.0%	23.2%	40.0%
Cash flow (to be paid in dividends)			$ 14,500	$ 15,000	$ 14,500	$ 20,000

Calculation of figures:

*Net income of A in Year 1	$20,000
Add: Reduction in raw materials costs	8,000
	$28,000
Deduct: Depreciation, 10% of $10,000	1,000
Net income of A in Year 2	$27,000
†Net income of B in Year 1	$20,000
Deduct: Expense of training salesmen	10,000
Net income of B in Year 2	$10,000

(Training expenses entirely written off in Year 2)

REQUIRED:
Is the return on investment a good measure of the relative performance of Companies A and B in Year 2 and 3? Discuss fully. *(Canada SIA adapted)*

10-27 *(Setting Transfer Prices).* Two divisions of the Conglomerate Company, Inc. are attempting to establish a transfer price for intercompany transfers. Selling Division provided the following data.

Income Statement		*Units*	
Sales	$200,000	Capacity in units	30,000
Variable costs	60,000	Units produced	20,000
Fixed costs	120,000	Units sold to buying division	12,000
Net income	$ 20,000	Units sold to others	8,000
			20,000

Buying Division is expanding production to a level that will require 24,000 units. An outside company has offered to provide the units at $9.00 each. Buying Division asked Selling Division for a price quote.

REQUIRED:

A. What price should Selling Division charge to achieve the same amount of net income?

B. What price should Selling Division charge to maintain a 10% rate of profit?

C. What transfer price should be used in evaluating the performance of Buying Division? Selling Division?

D. What transfer price should the top management of Conglomerate Company use in deciding whether to have Selling Division make the product or buy it outside?

10-28 *(Transfer Prices and Profit Centers).* A. R. Oma, Inc. manufactures a line of men's perfumes and after-shaving lotions. The manufacturing process is basically a series of mixing operations with the addition of certain aromatic and coloring ingredients; the finished product is packaged in a company-produced glass bottle and packed in cases containing six bottles.

A. R. Oma feels that the sale of its product is heavily influenced by the appearance and appeal of the bottle and has, therefore, devoted considerable managerial effort to the bottle production process. This has resulted in the development of certain unique bottle production processes in which management takes considerable pride.

The two areas (perfume production and bottle manufacture) have evolved over the years in an almost independent manner; in fact, a rivalry has developed between management personnel as to which division is the more important to A. R. Oma. This attitude is probably intensified because the bottle manufacturing plant was purchased intact 10 years ago, and no real interchange of management personnel or ideas (except at the top corporate level) has taken place.

Since the acquisition, all bottle production has been asborbed by the perfume manufacturing plant. Each area is considered a separate profit center and evaluated as such. As the new corporate controller, you are responsible for the definition of a proper transfer value to use in crediting the bottle production profit center and in debiting the packaging profit center.

At your request, the Bottle Division general manager has asked certain other bottle manufacturers to quote a price for the quantity and sizes demanded by the Perfume Division. These competitive prices are:

Volume	*Total Price*	*Price per Case*
2,000,000 eq. cases*	$ 4,000,000	$2.00
4,000,000	$ 7,000,000	$1.75
6,000,000	$10,000,000	$1.67

*An *equivalent case* represents 6 bottles each.

A cost analysis of the internal bottle plant indicates that it can produce bottles at the following costs.

Volume	*Total Price*	*Cost per Case*
2,000,000 eq. cases	$3,200,000	$1.60
4,000,000	$5,200,000	$1.30
6,000,000	$7,200,000	$1.20

(Your cost analysts point out that these costs represent fixed costs of $1,200,000 and variable costs of $1.00 per equivalent case.)

These figures have given rise to considerable corporate discussion as to the proper value to use in the transfer of bottles to the Perfume Division. This interest is heightened because a significant portion of a division manager's income is an incentive bonus based on profit center results.

The Perfume Production Division has the following costs in addition to the bottle costs.

Volume	*Total Cost*	*Cost per Case*
2,000,000 cases	$16,400,000	$8.20
4,000,000	$32,400,000	$8.10
6,000,000	$48,400,000	$8.07

After considerable analysis, the marketing research department has furnished you with the following price-demand relationship for the finished product.

Sales Volume	Total Sales Revenue	Sales Price per Case
2,000,000 cases	$25,000,000	$12.50
4,000,000	$45,600,000	$11.40
6,000,000	$63,900,000	$10.65

REQUIRED:

A. The A. R. Oma Company has used market-price transfer prices in the past. Using the current market prices and costs, and assuming a volume of 6,000,000 cases, calculate the income for the Bottle Division, the Perfume Division, and the corporation.

B. Is this production and sales level the most profitable volume for the Bottle Division? The Perfume Division? The corporation? Explain your answer.

C. The A. R. Oma Company uses the profit center concept for divisional operation.

1. Define *profit center.*

2. What conditions should exist for a profit center to be established?

3. Should the two divisions of the A. R. Oma Company be organized as profit centers? *(CMA adapted)*

10–29 *(Measuring Division Performance).* George Johnson was hired on July 1, 1969, as assistant general manager of the Botel Division of Staple, Inc. It was understood that he would be elevated to general manager of the division on January 1, 1971, when the current general manager retired, and he was. In addition to becoming acquainted with the division and the general manager's duties, Mr. Johnson was specifically charged with the responsibility for development of the 1970 and 1971 budgets. As general manager in 1971, he was, obviously, responsible for the 1972 budget.

The Staple Company is a multiproduct company that is highly decentralized. Each division is quite autonomous. The corporation staff approves division-prepared operating budgets but seldom makes major changes in them. The corporate staff actively participates in decisions requiring capital investment (for expansion or replacement) and makes the final decisions. The division management is responsible for implementing the capital program. The major method used by the Staple Corporation to measure division performance is contribution return on division net investment. The budgets that follow were approved by the corporation. Revision of the 1972 budget is not considered necessary, even though 1971 actual departed from the approved 1971 budget.

BOTEL DIVISION (000 Omitted)

Accounts	Actual			Budget	
	1969	*1970*	*1971*	*1971*	*1972*
Sales	$1,000	$1,500	$1,800	$2,000	$2,400
Less division variable costs:					
Material and labor	$ 250	$ 375	$ 450	$ 500	$ 600
Repairs	50	75	50	100	120
Supplies	20	30	36	40	48
Less division managed costs:					
Employee training	30	35	25	40	45
Maintenance	50	55	40	60	70
Less division committed costs:					
Depreciation	120	160	160	200	200
Rent	80	100	110	140	140
Total	600	830	871	1,080	1,223
Division net contribution	$ 400	$ 670	$ 929	$ 920	$1,177
Division investment:					
Accounts receivable	$ 100	$ 150	$ 180	$ 200	$ 240
Inventory	200	300	270	400	480
Fixed assets	1,590	2,565	2,800	3,380	4,000
Less accounts and wages payable	(150)	(225)	(350)	(300)	(360)
Net investment	$1,740	$2,790	$2,900	$3,680	$4,360
Contribution return on net investment	23%	24%	32%	25%	27%

REQUIRED:

A. Identify Mr. Johnson's responsibilities under the management and measurement program previously described.

B. Appraise the performance of Mr. Johnson in 1971.

C. On the basis of your analysis, recommend to the president any changes in the responsibilities assigned to managers or in the measurement methods used to evaluate division management. *(CMA adapted)*

10–30 *(Transfer Pricing System).*

Birch Paper Company*

"If I were to price these boxes any lower than $480 a thousand," said James Brunner, manager of Birch Paper Company's Thompson division, "I'd be countermanding my order of last month for our salesmen to stop shaving their bids and to bid full-cost quotations. I've been trying for weeks to improve the quality of our business, and if I turn around now and accept this job at $430 or $450 or something less than $480, I'll be tearing down this program I've been working so hard to build up. The division can't very well show a profit by putting in bids that don't even cover a fair share of overhead costs, let alone give us a profit."

Birch Paper Company was a medium-size, partly integrated paper company, producing white and kraft papers and paperboard. A portion of its paperboard output was converted into corrugated boxes by the Thompson division, which also printed and colored the outside surface of the boxes. Including Thompson, the company had four producing divisions and a timberland division, which supplied part of the company's pulp requirements.

For several years, each division had been judged independently on the basis of its profit and return on investment. Top management had been working to gain effective results from a policy of decentralizing responsibility and authority for all decisions except those relating to overall company policy. The company's top officials believed that in the past few years the concept of decentralization had been successfully applied and that the company's profits and competitive position had definitely improved.

Early in 1957, the Northern division designed a special display box for one of its papers in conjunction with the Thompson division, which was equipped to make the box. Thompson's staff for package design and development spent several months perfecting the design, production methods, and materials to be used. Because of the unusual color and shape, these were far from standard. According to an agreement between the two divisions, the Thompson division was reimbursed by the Northern division for the cost of its design and development work.

When all the specifications were prepared, the Northern division asked for bids on the box from the Thompson division and from two outside companies. Each division manager was normally free to buy from whatever supplier he wished; and even on sales within the company, divisions were expected to meet the going market price if they wanted the business.

In 1957, the profit margins of converters such as the Thompson division were being squeezed. Thompson, as did many other similar converters, bought its paperboard, and its function was to print, cut, and shape it into boxes. Though it bought most of its materials from other Birch divisions, most of Thompson's sales were made to outside customers. If Thompson got the order from Northern, it probably would buy its linerboard and corrugating medium from the Southern division of Birch. The walls of a corrugated box consist of outside and inside sheets of linerboard sandwiching the fluted corrugating medium. About 70 percent of Thompson's out-of-pocket cost of $400 for the order represented the cost of linerboard and corrugating medium. Though Southern had been running below capacity and had excess inventory, it quoted the market price, which had not noticeably weakened as a result of the oversupply. Its out-of-pocket costs on both liner and corrugating medium were about 60 percent of the selling price.

The Northern division received bids on the boxes of $480 a thousand from the Thompson division, $430 a thousand from West Paper Company, and $432 a thousand from Eire Papers, Ltd. Eire Papers offered to buy from Birch the outside linerboard with the special printing already on it, but would supply its own inside liner and corrugating medium. The outside liner would be supplied by the Southern division at a price equivalent of $90 a thousand boxes, and it would be printed for $30 a thousand by the Thompson division. Of the $30, about $25 would be out-of-pocket costs.

Since this situation appeared to be a little unusual, William Kenton, manager of the Northern division, discussed the wide discrepancy of bids with Birch's commercial vice-president. He told the vice-president: "We sell in a very competitive market, where higher costs cannot be passed on. How can we be expected to show a decent profit and return on investment if we have to buy our supplies at more than 10 percent over the going market?"

Knowing that Mr. Brunner had on occasion in the past few months been unable to operate the Thompson division at capacity, it seemed odd to the vice-president that Mr. Brunner would add the full 20 percent overhead and profit charge to his out-of-pocket costs. When asked about this, Mr. Brunner's answer was the statement that appears at the beginning of the case. He went on to say that having done the developmental work on the box, and having received no profit on that, he felt entitled to a good markup on the production of the box itself.

The vice-president explored further the cost structures of the various divisions. He remembered a comment that the controller had made at a meeting the week before to the effect that costs which were variable for one division could be largely fixed for the company as a whole. He knew that in the absence of specific orders from top management Mr. Kenton would accept the lowest bid, which was that of the West Paper Company for $430. However, it would be possible for top management to order the acceptance of another bid if the situation warranted such action. And though the volume represented by the transactions in question was less than 5 percent of the volume of any of the divisions involved, other transactions could conceivably raise similar problems later.

Questions

1. In the controversy described, how, if at all, is the transfer price system dysfunctional?

2. Describe other types of decisions in the Birch Paper Company in which the transfer price system would be dysfunctional.

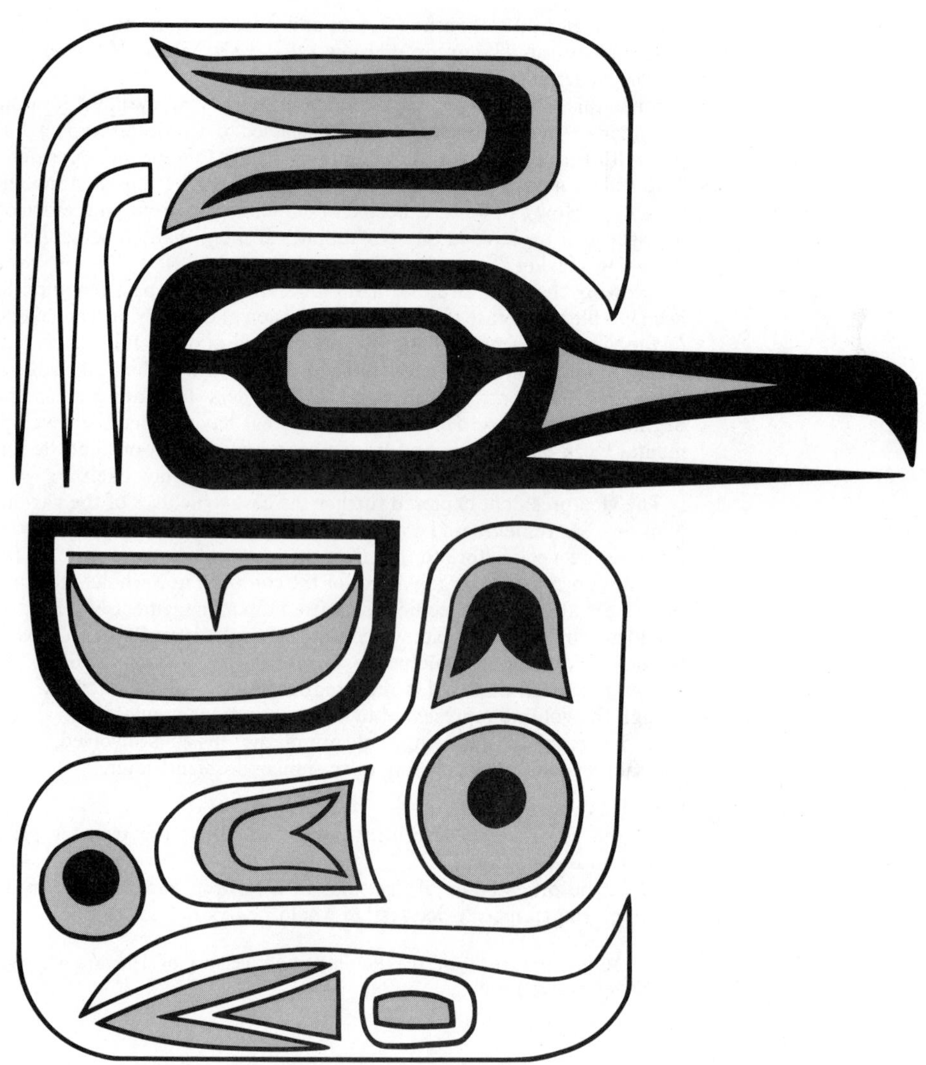

PART 4

THE USE OF DATA IN MAKING OPERATING DECISIONS

11 Revenue and Pricing Decisions

One of the most important operating decisions management must make is establishing the selling prices for its products and services. A company's long-range survival depends upon its pricing decisions. In the long run the firm's prices must be sufficient to cover all costs and leave a profit margin adequate to reward the financial investors for the use of their funds. If the firm's revenue consistently fails to cover costs and provide a satisfactory profit, the investors will seek new opportunities and the firm will fail.

In this chapter we will look at how accounting and economic data can be used by management to make pricing decisions. We will study pricing from three different perspectives. First, we will examine pricing where there is an established marketplace. The economic theory of pricing, as shown by the supply and demand curves, is relevant here. Second, we will examine pricing decisions where prices are determined by costs plus a profit percentage. Third, we will look at the role of the contribution margin approach in pricing decisions.

OPEN MARKET PRICING

A large segment of microeconomic theory is devoted to pricing and the resultant volume decision. Economic theory assumes that there is a known, open, and free marketplace for the goods and services being offered for sale. There are two key elements in assessing the market structure. The first concerns the number of buyers and sellers in the marketplace. Typically, the larger the number of buyers and sellers, the more competitive the market.

Second, the market structure is influenced by the extent to which the product is standardized. If other products are reasonable substitutes for the ones offered for sale, there will be increased competition. For example, in the transportation industry a plane, a bus, and a railroad may be in competition to provide service between two points. The more easily one mode of transportation can be substituted for another, the greater the competition. Also, the nature of the product can determine the market structure. For example, with a highly perishable product, such as fresh strawberries, it is impossible to compete in many geographic markets without incurring excessive transportation and distribution costs.

The Economic Theory of Price

The basic factors in economic theory are the supply of the product and the demand for it. It seems obvious that the quantity of the product that customers will buy over a period of time depends upon the price. The higher the price, the fewer the units of product customers will be willing to buy; the lower the price, the more units of product they will buy. A typical demand curve (*dd*) is shown in Exhibit 11–1. The **demand curve** relates the market prices and the quantity of the product the *customers* want to buy. The demand curve slopes downward and to the right, showing that when the price is

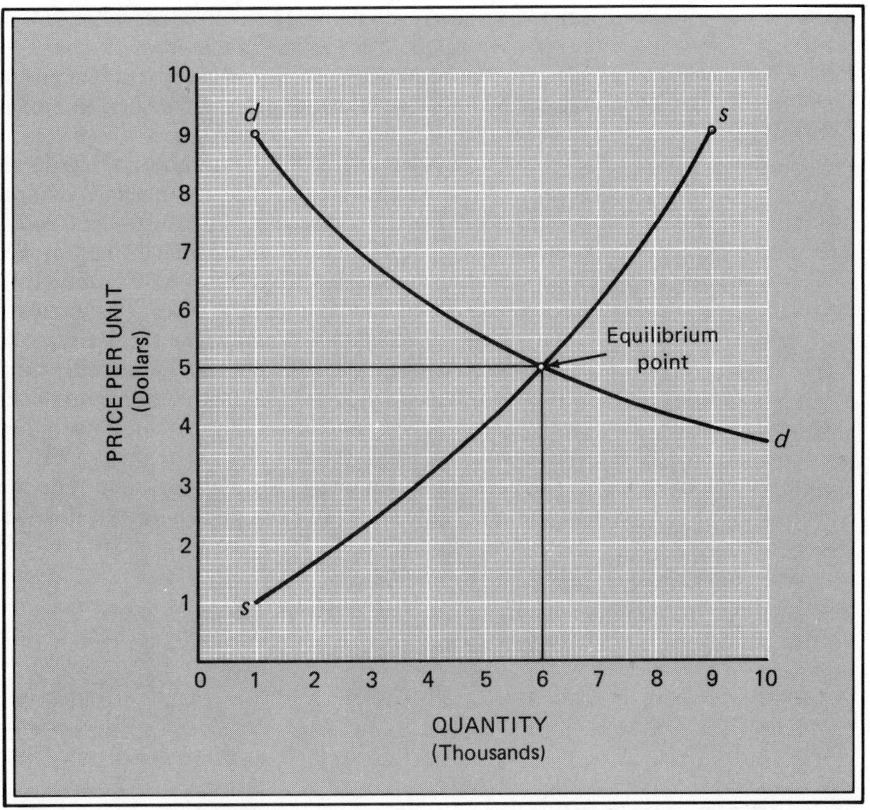

EXHIBIT 11–1
Supply and demand curves

increased, customers will be willing to buy a smaller quantity, and when prices are lowered, customers will buy a larger quantity.

The **supply curve** relates the market prices and the quantity of product that the *suppliers* or *producers* are willing to supply. As shown in Exhibit 11–1 the supply curve (*ss*) rises upward to the right. At a higher price the supplier will increase output. However, as production increases, the supplier ultimately faces diminishing returns on the productive facilities. **Diminishing returns** recognizes that as the use of production facilities increases, it takes more productive energy per unit to produce one additional unit. Workers become tired and inefficient, machines break down more often, factories become crowded, and premium prices must be paid to get material and labor.

How do supply and demand interact to determine the market price? The demand schedule shows us the quantities demanded by the customers combined with the prices they are willing to pay. We can then say, "If customers demand so much, the price will be thus and so." The supply schedule shows us how much the producers are willing to produce at various prices. We can then say, "If so much product is available, the price is thus and so, and the producers will provide so much product." However, neither schedule alone tells what the price will be or how much will be produced by the suppliers or purchased by the customers.

The market price will be determined at the intersection point of the supply and demand curves. At this **equilibrium point** the amount the producers will provide equals the amount the customers demand, and the market is cleared. This point is shown on Exhibit 11–1 where the equilibrium price is $5.00 and the equilibrium quantity is 6,000 units. If the market price were to increase, to $9.00 for example, the quantity supplied would increase to 9,000 units. The increased price would cause the quantity demanded to decrease to 1,000 units. At $9.00 the quantity supplied would exceed the quantity demanded. At a point lower than the equilibrium price, say, $4.00 per unit, the quantity demanded would exceed the quantity supplied, and the buyers would "bid" the price up.

The previous discussion has assumed that the changes taking place were in the quantity supplied or the quantity demanded. The difference in the quantity demanded is shown in the graph on the left. The movement is along a single demand curve.

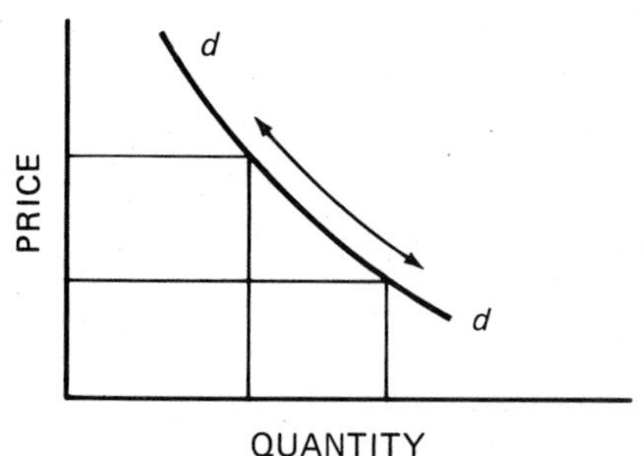

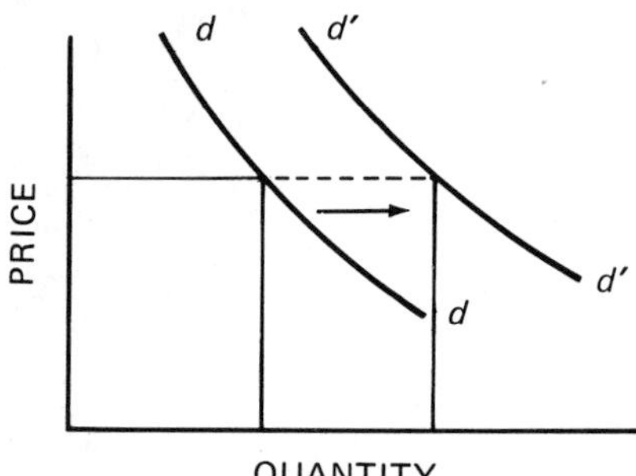

It is also possible that the supply or demand curve might shift. For example, the graph on the right shows a difference in the customer demand that is independent of price differences. The demand curve could shift because of changes in consumer tastes, consumer income, or the prices of related products that could be substituted. In the same way, the supply curve could shift because of changes in the factors of production or the cost of the inputs.

What happens if the producers decrease the supply of the product available? Exhibit 11–2 shows how the original supply curve *ss* has shifted to the left and become supply curve *s′s′*. The demand has not changed, but the equilibrium price has moved from $5.00 at point *E* to $6.00 at point *E′*. This new price would bring the supply and demand into equilibrium again at 4,000 units. What would happen if the demand for the product increases and the supply curve stays the same? Exhibit 11–3 shows the demand curve shifting to the right from *dd* to *d′d′*. The increased demand and the constant supply curve

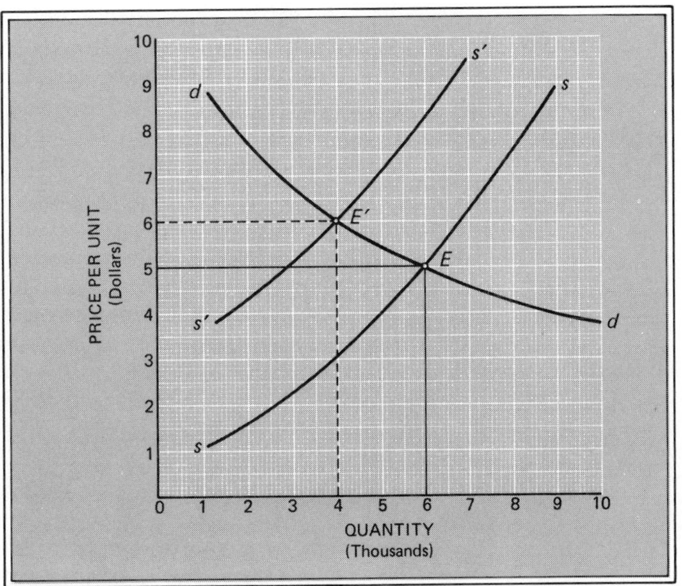

EXHIBIT 11–2
Effects of shift in supply curve

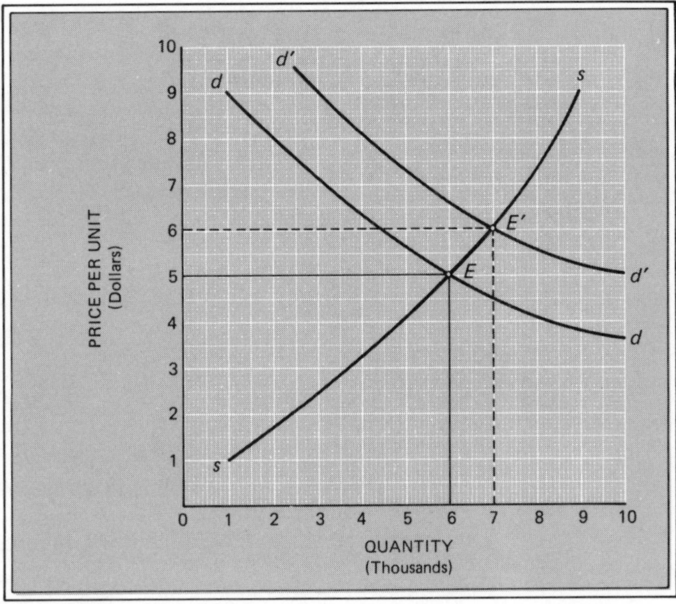

EXHIBIT 11–3
Effects of shift in demand curve

have forced an increase in the price needed for equilibrium from the original \$5.00 price at point E to \$6.00 at point E'.

The way in which a change in price affects the demand is called **price elasticity.** If a small decrease in price creates a large increase in quantity sold, the demand is called *elastic.* If a substantial decrease in price is required to increase quantity sold, demand is called *inelastic.* The raising or lowering of the price of an inelastic product would have little or no effect on the amount of product sold. Whether a product has elastic or inelastic demand characteristics can be vital to decisions regarding price changes. While a manager may be able to see broad stages of price elasticity, it is often difficult to perceive it specifically enough for a given decision.

The scope of the demand curve for a particular firm depends upon its market structure; that is, the degree of competition in the market for the product. There are four broad classes of market structures: pure competition, pure monopoly, monopolistic competition, and oligopoly.

PURE COMPETITION

In a purely competitive market there are a large number of buyers and sellers; each firm's transactions are so small in relation to the total market that they do not affect the price of its product or service.[1] The price is determined in the marketplace. The firm can sell as much as it wishes if it sells at the market price. More importantly, it cannot sell *any* product at a higher price. The firm's demand curve is horizontal. The price is constant and the average revenue and the marginal revenue are equal. However, the industry demand curve will be shaped like the curve in Exhibit 11–1. A purely competitive firm (1) can sell nothing above the equilibrium price, (2) can sell all it produces at exactly that price, and (3) would have no reason to lower its price below the existing market price. Management's decision in a purely competitive market is to select the output (volume) level that maximizes the firm's profits; it must accept the going price.

PURE MONOPOLY

In a pure monopoly there is only one producer. The industry consists of one firm. In a monopoly the industry demand curve is the same as the demand curve for the firm. Since the industry demand curves are downward-sloping, the demand curve of the monopolist will slope downward to the right. For profit maximization the firm should operate at the output level where its marginal cost equals the marginal revenue. This point will simultaneously determine the optimum price and output level. The monopolistic firm can determine either the price or the quantity, but not both. Given one, the other is determined automatically by the market.

---

[1]Other assumptions of pure competition include: perfect homogeneity of the products; free entry and exits to the market; and perfect information about price, cost, and quality by the buyers and sellers in the market.

MONOPOLISTIC COMPETITION

It is very rare to find pure competition or pure monopoly. Most firms have some competition, although not pure competition. In the monopolistic competitive market structure the customers believe that there are differences between the products of different firms. These firms have a number of competitors producing substitutable products. Nevertheless, they have some control over their pricing policies. These firms face downward-sloping demand curves, in contrast to the horizontal demand curve in a purely competitive market.

If a firm is successful in differentiating its product from the products of other firms, it will have greater flexibility in pricing and output decisions. A firm with strong product differentiation and loyal customers has greater control over its prices. Exhibit 11–4 shows the demand curves for two firms. The demand curve d_1 shows a firm whose customers differentiate its product only slightly from those of competitors. The demand curve is almost horizontal, indicating active competition. Demand curve d_2 shows a firm that has been successful in differentiating its products from other products available, with a resulting decrease in the competition from other firms.

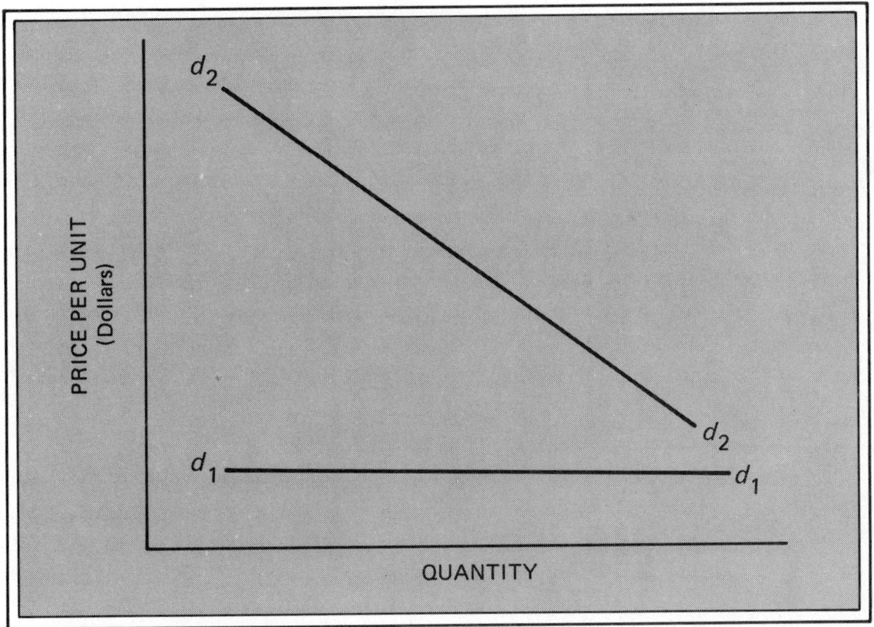

EXHIBIT 11–4
Demand curves for two firms in monopolistic competition

OLIGOPOLY

In an oligopoly there are a few large sellers, each with a large share of the market. These firms interact. The revenue of a given seller depends upon the reactions of his competitors to changes in his selling prices. An action taken by one firm will cause a reaction by others. If an oligopolistic seller raises his prices and his competitors raise theirs, or if he lowers his and they lower theirs, his demand curve will have the same general shape as the demand curve for the whole market. In the oligopoly marketplace, the optimal price and output decision depends upon how competing firms react.

Firms joined together in a cartel could set a price to maximize the industry's profits. If the cartel is successful, it can create a monopolistic market. Because of this possibility, formal or informal agreements that restrict prices and outputs have been made illegal in the United States. Also, cartels are difficult to establish for there is often disagreement among the members about how to share the profits; one firm can subvert the cartel to maximize its own profit at the expense of the other firms. An accepable means of reducing uncertainty in an oligopoly is for one firm to establish itself as the leader and price setter. Because of the leader's strength, all other firms must then accept its pricing policy. A firm may become dominant because of its size in relation to others, its cost efficiency, the products it offers, or because of revenue and cost forecasting accuracy.

Pricing: An Art or a Science?

Economic theory provides a relatively clear and straightforward approach to establishing price and volume for pure monopoly, pure competition, and monopolistic competition. Under an oligopolistic market, the approach is more complex and often impossible to specify, since a firm can interact in many ways. Because of this complexity, price leadership by the dominant firm, or firms, is common, and stable prices develop. Also, oligopolistic firms actively engage in nonprice competition such as service improvement, style differences, and advertising.

While the theoretical pricing model developed by the economists is sound, it is difficult to apply directly in practice. First, it assumes that the firm's demand curve is known. Generally management does not have available data that are accurate and reliable enough to give more than a rough picture of the demand curve. Therefore, while firms may consider the shape of the demand curve, they may not be able to do so in an exacting way.

Second, economics assumes that firms are profit maximizers. Many legal and societal goals and constraints influence management's desire for profits. Certainly stability, growth, and security are important to managers, and these can be obtained short of total profit maximization.

Third, many factors besides price affect a firm's demand function. For example, there is a necessary interaction between marketing and distribution policies, promotional and advertising policies, sales staff deployment, customer services offered, and the types of products sold. All these factors have a heavy influence upon the amount of product that can be sold at a specific price.

In a very real sense pricing is an art rather than a science. Economics provides a sound theoretical background that may be difficult to apply in practice. These difficulties in determining the demand functions have led many managements to adopt a trial and error (**heuristic**) approach to pricing.

FULL COST-BASED PRICING

One method of establishing price, particularly where the firm lacks knowledge of the demand curve, is to calculate the cost of the product and then add a percentage markup for net income. This method has been called **cost-based pricing, cost-plus pricing,** or **average cost pricing.** Each term implies that an addition for net income is made to some suitable cost base. This approach is based upon the fact that in the long run the firm must recover *all* of its costs plus a normal profit margin if it is to remain in business. Full cost-based pricing is applicable both to standard or new products offered in the open market and to specially designed, nonstandard products.

Pricing Standard Products

To illustrate how a firm might price standard or new products, let's assume that a firm has budgeted production of 150,000 units requiring the following costs. Management would also like to earn a 15% rate of return on the stockholders' equity of $1,000,000. The **target price,** that is, the price management will seek in the marketplace, will be determined as follows:

	Total	*Per Unit*
Direct materials	$ 150,000	$1.00
Direct labor	250,000	1.67
Variable overhead	125,000	.83
Fixed overhead	75,000	.50
Fixed selling and administrative	300,000	2.00
Total cost	$ 900,000	$6.00
Desired net income (15% × $1,000,000)	150,000	1.00
Target revenue (price)	$1,050,000	$7.00

If the marketplace accepts the price of $7.00, the firm will recover all of its costs and earn the desired rate of return on stockholders' equity at a volume of 150,000 units. If the price is too high, relative to the competition, then we would expect the sales volume to be less than budgeted and the firm to fail in achieving its goals. If the price is too low, relative to the competition, actual volume should exceed the planned volume and the firm will become a price leader. Of course, in a competitive marketplace the firm would be foregoing available profits. In this way, the target price represents the first step in a heuristic approach to setting the selling price.

In the illustration above, the target price was based upon the *total* cost of the firm. As we illustrated in Chapters 4, 5, and 6 on product costing, firms typically do not use cost accounting systems that measure *total* cost per unit of product. Rather, firms measure product costs on either an absorption or variable costing basis. Both of these systems record only designated production costs as product costs; neither system treats the selling and administrative costs as product costs. Thus, in order to develop target prices using these product costs, management must apply a markup percentage to the production costs that includes an allowance for the period costs and the desired rate of return. For example, let's assume that through past experience management has determined that a markup of 75% of the product cost measured through absorption costing will provide a reasonable target price. The determination of the target price of $7.00 would be:

	Total	*Per Unit*
Direct material	$ 150,000	$1.00
Direct labor	250,000	1.67
Variable overhead	125,000	.83
Fixed overhead	75,000	.50
Total cost	$ 600,000	$4.00
Markup (75% of cost)	450,000	3.00
Target revenue (price)	$1,050,000	$7.00

Given the same market constraints, the firm would have to use a markup of 100% of cost if the product costs were determined by variable costing. In this case the target price would be determined as follows:

	Total	*Per Unit*
Direct material	$ 150,000	$1.00
Direct labor	250,000	1.67
Variable overhead	125,000	.83
Total cost	$ 525,000	$3.50
Markup (100% of cost)	525,000	3.50
Target revenue (price)	$1,050,000	$7.00

From this discussion it should be clear that the selection of an absorption or variable costing system is not the pivotal issue in establishing the target price. The important issues are the determination of the markup percentage *relative* to the measured product cost, and the acceptance by the marketplace of the target price. The optimum resolution of the pricing dilemma depends on management's insight into what the market will accept and the relationship of this price to the product cost. If management believes that the firm is in a strong position, they may adjust the markup percentage upward; if they sense a weakening of their market position, they may adjust the markup percentage downward.

Cost-based pricing cannot be considered as a rigid, deterministic formula. It is simply one way of determining the target price on the first trial in a trial-and-error approach. If, as we stated before, the target price is unacceptable to the buyers in the market, the firm will have no choice but to adjust the selling price or to change their product line.

It is also incorrect to assume that a firm will use the same markup percentage for all products in its product line. The markup will vary according to competition, industry custom, and customer acceptance. The percentage markup will also vary according to the company goals of creating an interaction between profit margin and inventory turnover. Many firms have found that a slightly lower profit margin is more than offset by increased volume. Since the basic goal is a satisfactory profit, and profit is a function of both profit margin and turnover, the firm may adopt a range of markup strategies.

In this section the illustration included only one product. In a multiproduct firm, using cost-based pricing is more complex, since the total cost per unit of a specific product is the total of the variable costs of the product plus some apportioned or allocated share of fixed costs. This complexity leads to problems of cost allocations which we will discuss next.

PROBLEMS IN APPORTIONING FIXED COSTS

The proper treatment of the fixed costs presents a problem. As discussed in Chapter 7, the determination of a total cost per unit requires that the fixed costs be apportioned over a specific number of units. The fixed overhead costs in the previous example were $75,000, and the fixed selling and administrative expenses were $300,000. At a production and sales output of 150,000 units, the fixed costs per unit are $2.50 ($375,000 ÷ 150,000 units). If the company's volume increased to 300,000 units, the per-unit fixed cost would drop to $1.25 ($375,000 ÷ 300,000). The per-unit fixed cost would increase to $5.00 ($375,000 ÷ 75,000) if the volume dropped to 75,000 units. Unlike the fixed costs, the variable costs will remain at $3.50 per unit at all levels [($150,000 + $250,000 + $125,000) ÷ 150,000 units].

Assuming that the firm has a policy of adding to its full cost a 10% profit margin, it could have the following prices, depending upon its volume decision.

Number of units	*75,000*	*100,000*	*150,000*	*300,000*
Variable costs per unit	$3.50	$3.50	$3.50	$3.50
Fixed costs per unit	5.00	3.75	2.50	1.25
Total costs per unit	$8.50	$7.25	$6.00	$4.75
10% markup on cost	.85	.73	.60	.48
Selling price	$9.35	$7.98	$6.60	$5.23

When the decision maker selects 150,000 units as the most likely sales volume, he anticipates that the net income per unit will be $.60. Let's assume that on the basis of this budget a selling price of $6.60 is established and, because of an unexpected market penetration, actual sales were 200,000 units. The actual net income and the budgeted net income are shown in Exhibit 11–5.

	Budgeted		Actual	
Sales	(150,000 x $6.60)	$990,000	(200,000 x $6.60)	$1,320,000
Variable costs	(150,000 x $3.50)	525,000	(200,000 x $3.50)	700,000
Contribution margin	(150,000 x $3.10)	$465,000	(200,000 x $3.10)	$ 620,000
Fixed costs		375,000		375,000
Net income before taxes		$ 90,000		$ 245,000

EXHIBIT 11–5
Effects of volume changes upon net income

There is a difference between the budgeted net income per unit of $.60 and the actual net income per unit of $1.225 ($245,000 ÷ 200,000 units) because the actual fixed cost per unit at 200,000 units is $1.875 ($375,000 ÷ 200,000 units); it was originally budgeted at $2.50. The difference between the $2.50 budgeted fixed costs per unit and the $1.875 actual fixed costs per unit is $.625, which is also the difference between the actual net income per unit of $1.225 and the budgeted net income of $.60.

PROBLEMS IN APPORTIONING JOINT COSTS

There is a major problem with firms that have multiple products. The price based upon full cost assumes that there is a satisfactory way to allocate all manufacturing costs and, in some cases, selling and administrative costs among the several products. There are no absolute criteria for the allocation of these **joint** costs. Joint costs are not inherently traceable to individual products or product lines, and some method must be found to apportion them. To examine this problem of joint costs, let's assume that a firm manufactures two products with the following cost and production data.

	Product A		Product B
Selling price per unit	$ 6		$ 15
Variable costs per unit	$ 4		$ 9
Labor hours per unit	1		3
Units produced per year	15,000		10,000
Joint costs of production		$120,000	

The joint costs represent costs incurred that are applicable to both products. To arrive at a full cost for each product, the joint costs must be allocated. The variable costs per unit of product, the labor hours used per unit of product, the quantity of each product manufactured, and the relative sales value of each product manufactured are all possible bases of allocating the joint costs. The method chosen should be simple, easy to measure, and relate the "cause" (activity base used to apportion) with the "effect" (cost).

The joint costs could be apportioned on the basis of variable costs.

	Variable Costs	Ratio	Joint Costs
Product A (15,000 × $4)	$ 60,000	60/150	$ 48,000
Product B (10,000 × $9)	90,000	90/150	72,000
Total	$150,000	150/150	$120,000

The joint costs could also be allocated on the basis of total labor hours as shown below.

	Total Labor Hours	Ratio	Joint Costs
Product A (15,000 × 1)	15,000	15/45	$ 40,000
Product B (10,000 × 3)	30,000	30/45	80,000
Total	45,000	45/45	$120,000

An allocation based upon the number of units produced would assign the following joint costs.

	Total Units Produced	Ratio	Joint Costs
Product A	15,000	15/25	$ 72,000
Product B	10,000	10/25	48,000
Total	25,000	25/25	$120,000

Where the selling prices of the products are similar, the joint costs can be allocated on the basis of the quantity of products produced. Where the selling prices of the products differ widely, the most common basis of allocating joint costs is the **relative sales-value basis.** Using the relative sales-value basis, the allocation would be:

	Total Units Produced	*Selling Price Per Unit*	*Sales Value*	*Ratio*	*Joint Costs*
Product A	15,000	$ 6	$ 90,000	90/240	$ 45,000
Product B	10,000	$15	150,000	150/240	75,000
Total	25,000		$240,000	240/240	$120,000

Notice that the effect of this allocation is to provide a constant gross margin percentage for each product at the point of split-off. This fact makes the relative sales-value method unsuitable for management decisions, although it is useful in inventory costing. The gross profit margins, after the allocation of the joint cost, is:

	Product A		*Product B*	
Sales Value	$90,000	100%	$150,000	100%
Less apportioned joint cost	45,000	50%	75,000	50%
Gross Margin	$45,000	50%	$ 75,000	50%

If the joint costs were apportioned on the basis of variable costs, Product A would receive two-fifths of the $120,000 joint costs or $48,000. Since 15,000 units of Product A were produced, the full cost would be [$4.00 + ($48,000 ÷ 15,000 units)], or $7.20. If the joint costs had been apportioned on the basis of total labor hours, Product A would receive one-third of the $120,000 joint costs, and the full cost would be [$4.00 + ($40,000 ÷ 15,000 units)], or $6.67. If the joint costs had been apportioned on the basis of number of units produced, Product A would receive 60% of the $120,000 joint costs, and the full cost would be [$4.00 + ($72,000 ÷ 15,000 units)], or $8.80. If the relative sales-value basis were used, Product A would receive 37.5% of the joint costs, and the full cost would be [$4.00 + ($45,000 ÷ 15,000 units)], or $7.00. The full cost and therefore the price will be affected by the joint fixed-cost allocation base chosen. This analysis may be inappropriate when the market conditions are considered.

A second word of caution is necessary. The joint costs often include a large proportion of fixed cost. There is a danger that the unit cost *after* the allocation of joint costs will be viewed by the decision maker as a variable cost. One must be careful not to treat allocated fixed costs as variable costs.

STRENGTHS AND WEAKNESSES OF FULL COST-BASED PRICES

Although the cost-based pricing formula is simple, it does not agree with economic theory, because it ignores the relationships between demand and price and between price and volume. The price determined by full cost plus a markup may be so high that there are no customers. If so, some of the volume potential of the firm will be idle. There is a circularity problem. Volume is used to determine price in the cost-based pricing formula, yet the number of units the company sells, and therefore the firm's volume, may depend upon price.

Nevertheless, pricing policies based on full cost are widely used. Why? Certainly, a principal reason is the inability of the decision maker to quantify the demand curve. This inability to apply economic theory leads the business-man to apply intuitive judgment coupled with trial-and-error methods. Many decision makers begin with a full-cost approach and then, on the basis of buyers' reaction, adjust the price. In this way the full cost-based price represents a first approximation—a target price whose markup must be adjusted to meet the actual marketplace.

Another reason for the adoption of full cost-based prices is the belief that they represent a "floor" or "safe" price that will prevent losses. This safety factor is more illusory than real. Although the per-unit sales price will cover the per-unit full cost, losses may still be incurred if the sales volume is miscalculated. The higher the proportion of fixed costs, the more the profit is influenced by sales volume. If the full cost-based price is so high that it drives customers away, the sales volume can be reduced to the extent that actual average cost is greater than the price.

Perhaps the most convincing reason for the use of full cost-based prices is that the costs of a particular firm are comparable with costs of other firms in the industry. One firm's costs are reasonable estimates of its competitors' costs, and hence its prices are likely to be comparable to those of its competitors. If most companies use similar facilities to perform similar activities, they will have similar full costs and, thus, similar prices if they produce at about the same volume level.

Pricing Nonstandard Products

Where there is demand for a product that does not currently exist, such as the space program's lunar vehicle, competition in price only cannot take place. Here, competition is based upon scientific and technical competence, management skills, and past experience, not upon price alone. In these situations price is determined by negotiation and contract commitments.

Although a large number of different contract types are available, two broad classes are typical:

1. In a **fixed price contract** both parties agree to a price that remains unchanged for the life of the contract. A fixed price contract requires past experience with the product or relatively low risk for both the buyer and seller.

2. In a **cost reimbursable contract** the seller is reimbursed all reasonable (allowable) costs incurred in fulfilling the contract plus an agreed upon fee. The buyer assumes a large portion of the risk, since he must reimburse the seller for all allowable costs. The seller should not suffer a loss, although he could fail to make an acceptable rate of return on his productive assets.

Three broad types of cost reimbursable contracts have been widely used. In the **cost-plus-percentage contract** (CPP), the fee is a percentage of the actual costs incurred. If the contract is cost-plus-10%, and the supplier incurred costs of $100,000, the supplier would earn profits of $10,000 on the contract and $110,000 would be the price to the buyer. If the costs were $200,000, the fee would be $20,000 and the total price, $220,000. This contract is potentially dangerous for the buyer because the supplier can indiscriminately incur costs to increase his fee. It has been widely used for government contracting during wartime but it is not widely used today.

In the **cost-plus-fixed-fee contract** (CPFF) the buyer and the seller negotiate a fee based upon budgeted costs. Suppose, for example, that both the supplier and the buyer believe that costs of $500,000 are reasonable to design and manufacture a new lunar lander, and that a fee of 15% of this cost, or $75,000, is fair and adequate. The contract would be for $575,000. If, because of cost overruns, the actual costs were $600,000, the buyer would reimburse the supplier $675,000—the original fee of $75,000 plus all costs allowed in the contract. The actual profit return, based on cost, is 12.5% ($75,000 ÷ $600,000) rather than the planned 15%. Since the extra costs probably consumed company capacity, the lower return on costs may mean that the overall rate of return for the seller will fall below an acceptable rate to maintain the investment.

An **incentive contract** can be used to encourage a supplier to conserve costs. For example, an incentive contract may call for cost-plus-fixed-fee if the company meets or exceeds the original budgeted costs and include a predetermined way for the buyer and seller to share in cost savings when costs are below budget. Assume that a firm has an incentive contract that calls for sharing with the buyer all cost savings in a 50:50 ratio. The original contract was for $500,000 costs and a $75,000 fee. If the firm incurs allowable costs of $460,000 to complete the job, it will be reimbursed $555,000 ($460,000 costs + $75,000 fee + ½ of $40,000 savings). The firm's profit percentage would be raised to 20.7% ($95,000 ÷ $460,000), considerably higher than the 15% originally planned. If the seller is unsuccessful in reducing costs and his actual costs are $600,000, he would receive $675,000 ($600,000 costs + $75,000 fee), and his return would fall to 12.5% ($75,000 ÷ $600,000).

In those situations where the price is determined by a contractual cost-based formula, cost accounting plays a vital role. Because the contract calls for the reimbursement of all allowable costs, both the buyer and the seller have a stake in how costs are defined, measured, and accumulated. For suppliers to the Department of Defense, *Armed Services Procurement Regulations* (ASPR) has been the authoritative guidebook. It specifies which costs are allowable for reimbursement and how costs should be accumulated and apportioned to products.

Difficulties that arose in interpreting and applying ASPR caused Congress to establish the Cost Accounting Standards Board (CASB) in 1970. The CASB is charged with assisting governmental agencies as buyers of goods and services in understanding and negotiating cost-based prices. To accomplish this task, the board has issued standards of cost accounting to which government suppliers must conform. These cost standards are to ensure that the government pays a fair price for the goods it buys on a cost-based contract. It must be recognized that the intent of the CASB is *not* to develop cost data for managerial decision making, but to simplify the pricing and auditing problems of the U.S. government.

CONTRIBUTION MARGIN-BASED PRICING

In addition to serving as a potential cost base for establishing the price of new or standard products, the contribution margin approach is an excellent analytical tool in a number of other pricing decisions. The contribution margin is particularly useful, since it does not require the allocation of joint costs or the determination of an expected volume to allocate the fixed costs. The contribution margin approach uses the incremental view that the only costs relevant to pricing decisions are those costs that would be avoided if the sales order were not accepted. Among those situations where contribution margin approaches are useful are:[2]

1. Pricing policies recognizing price-volume interactions:
   - *A.* Evaluating proposals to increase profits by increasing volume.
   - *B.* Deciding how far to go in meeting competitive prices.

2. Product-line contribution:
   - *A.* Identifying the most profitable product.
   - *B.* Identifying products needing attention for profit improvement.
   - *C.* Improving sales mix.

3. Pricing special orders:
   - *A.* One-time-only orders.
   - *B.* Distress pricing.

Pricing and Volume Interactions

As shown in Chapter 3, the contribution margin approach leads directly into the study of cost, volume, profit, and revenue interactions. Selling prices rarely have a constant relationship to product cost, since competition and

---

[2]Adapted from *N.A.A. Research Report #37,* "Current Applications of Direct Costing" (New York: National Association of Accountants, January, 1961), p. 45.

customer demand also enter into the pricing decision. Net income depends upon a combination of price, volume, sales mix, and cost structures.

To illustrate how the contribution margin can be used in price and volume decisions, assume that a firm has the following cost structure:

Variable production costs	\$6 per unit
Variable selling costs	\$3 per unit
Fixed production costs	\$24,000 per year
Fixed selling costs	\$12,000 per year

Management is considering a target price of \$15 with the goal of a profit of \$9,000 for the year. What volume must the firm achieve? Using the analysis shown in Chapter 3, we can see that the necessary volume to achieve this profit is 7,500 units:

$$\text{Volume necessary to achieve a profit of \$9,000 with a \$15 selling price} = \frac{\$36{,}000 + \$9{,}000}{\$15 - (\$6 + \$3)} = 7{,}500 \text{ units}$$

If the target price was unacceptable in the marketplace and the firm had to lower the price to \$12, the necessary volume would double to 15,000 units:

$$\text{Volume necessary to achieve a profit of \$9,000 with a \$12 selling price} = \frac{\$36{,}000 + \$9{,}000}{\$12 - (\$6 + \$3)} = 15{,}000 \text{ units}$$

From this illustration we can see that the contribution margin leads directly into the cost-volume-profit analysis. It allows management a rapid way of assessing the sensitivity of volume and price interactions.

Now, let's assume that the firm's target price becomes \$12 as a result of management's assessment of the price the market will accept. Accordingly, management plans a production level of 15,000 units which they believe is achievable. On a per-unit basis they can now establish ceiling and floor prices:

Target price		\$12.00 Ceiling Price
Profit (\$9,000 ÷ 15,000)	\$ .60	
Fixed costs (\$36,000 ÷ 15,000)	2.40	3.00
Variable costs		\$ 9.00 Floor Price

The firm has a market-based ceiling price, which is the maximum price within the marketplace that the firm can achieve. This ceiling price represents the goal of the firm in pricing policy. In distressful situations the firm should reduce its price no lower than the floor of \$9.00. Below \$9.00 the firm would be paying the customer to take the goods; at any price above \$9.00 the firm would recover some of the fixed costs. Stated another way, the minimum price they would charge is the price that would result in a contribution margin of zero.

Product Line Contributions

The contribution margin approach allows an examination of the way in which each class of products contributes toward the recovery of fixed costs and profit contribution. Exhibit 11–6 shows a contribution margin income statement by product line. A study of this exhibit helps extend our views of the contribution margin.

	PRODUCT A (10 Units)	PRODUCT B (20 Units)	PRODUCT C (50 Units)	TOTAL
Sales	$3,000	$4,000	$5,000	$12,000
Variable production costs	2,500	2,400	2,500	7,400
Contribution margin from production	$ 500	$1,600	$2,500	$ 4,600
Variable nonproduction costs	500	600	1,000	2,100
Contribution margin	$ 0	$1,000	$1,500	$ 2,500
Separable (direct) fixed costs	300	400	300	1,000
Product margin	$ (300)	$ 600	$1,200	$ 1,500
Apportioned fixed costs	200	400	400	1,000
Net income (loss)	$ (500)	$ 200	$ 800	$ 500

EXHIBIT 11–6
Contribution margin income statements by product line

Since the fixed costs do not change with changes in volume, the important data are those which show the product that contributes most to the company's profits. Product A has a zero contribution margin; Product B has a contribution margin of $50 per unit and a contribution margin ratio of 25% ($1,000 ÷ $4,000); Product C has a contribution margin of $30 per unit and a contribution margin ratio of 30% ($1,500 ÷ $5,000). Product A is not contributing to company profits, and the company appears no better off for having produced it. Both Products B and C are profitable, although Product B returns the highest contribution margin per unit.

This exhibit also shows another important point. Certain fixed costs, shown on the statement as **identifiable or separable fixed costs,** have been specifically identified with the product line. Other fixed costs, shown on the statement as **apportioned fixed costs,** have been allocated. The separable fixed costs are fixed costs that would be avoided if the product line were dropped. Sometimes they are called **avoidable costs.** Where there are separable fixed costs, a better measure of the product line's contribution is the **product margin,** determined after deducting separable fixed costs from the product's contribution margin.

Where the company is already committed to the separable fixed costs or to retention of the product line, the fixed costs directly associated with the product line are not relevant, and the decision maker should look to the contribution margin of the product. In those instances where the company is not yet committed to the product line or the separable fixed costs, the product margin after separable costs is more appropriate for the decision maker. The apportioned fixed costs would not be relevant in either case.

If there is unused capacity, the firm can realize additional profits by increasing the sales of products with a positive contribution margin (Products B and C) and by decreasing the sales of any products with a negative or zero contribution margin (Product A). Which product in Exhibit 11–6 should the company emphasize? While Product C has the highest contribution margin ratio (30%), Product B has the highest unit contribution margin ($50). The firm should produce and sell in such a way as to maximize the *total contribution margin in dollars*—not the contribution margin ratio. With this type of analysis the firm can achieve a better sales mix.

Pricing Special Orders

To illustrate how special-order pricing decisions can be made with a contribution margin approach, let's assume that the C. M. Manufacturing Company has excess productive capacity. Normal plant capacity is 150,000 units per year; current operations are 100,000 units per year. At this level it is operating at two-thirds of capacity. The current production of 100,000 units is sold in the regular markets for $2.00 each. Variable costs are $1.20 per unit and annual fixed costs are $60,000. The following income statement is based upon current production and sales.

C. M. MANUFACTURING COMPANY
CONTRIBUTION MARGIN INCOME STATEMENT
For the Year Ended December 31, 19X6

Sales (100,000 × $2.00)	$200,000
Variable costs (100,000 × $1.20)	120,000
Contribution margin (100,000 × $.80)	$ 80,000
Fixed costs	60,000
Net income	$ 20,000

The firm's full cost is [$1.20 + ($60,000 ÷ 100,000 units)], or $1.80 per unit. Now assume that it receives an offer from a foreign buyer to manufacture and sell an additional 20,000 units at \$1.50. Should it accept the order? The price of \$1.50 is below the full cost of \$1.80 but above the \$1.20 variable cost. If the additional order does not affect the regular market price of \$2.00, only the variable costs are relevant to the decision. The additional order would affect the net income favorably. The following income statement assumes that the special order was accepted.

C. M. MANUFACTURING COMPANY
CONTRIBUTION MARGIN INCOME STATEMENT
For the Year Ended December 31, 19X6

	Regular	*Special*	*Total*
Sales: Regular (100,000 × \$2.00)	\$200,000		
Special (20,000 × \$1.50)		\$30,000	\$230,000
Variable costs:			
Regular (100,000 × \$1.20)	120,000		
Special (20,000 × \$1.20)		24,000	144,000
Contribution margin	\$ 80,000	\$ 6,000	\$ 86,000
Fixed costs			60,000
Net income			\$ 26,000

The special order increased the net income by \$6,000. A contribution margin approach shows this effect. The unit contribution margin on the special order is \$.30 (\$1.50 − \$1.20) and the total contribution margin on the additional order is \$6,000 (\$.30 × 20,000 units).

What would happen to the firm if the special order affected its current market? Assuming that the demand curve was such that *all* products had to be offered at the special-order price, the income statement would then show a loss.

C. M. MANUFACTURING COMPANY
CONTRIBUTION MARGIN INCOME STATEMENT
For the Year Ended December 31, 19X6

Sales (120,000 × \$1.50)	\$180,000
Variable costs (120,000 × \$1.20)	144,000
Contribution margin (120,000 × \$.30)	\$ 36,000
Fixed costs	60,000
Net loss for the year	\$ (24,000)

If the special order infiltrates the regular market, it could jeopardize the firm's profit structure. If special-order pricing dominates, the lower price will increase demand but could, at the same time, reduce net income. This possible effect has caused many people to reject variable cost-based pricing for both long-run and short-run decisions in favor of full cost-based prices. Obviously, before any decision is made to sell a regular product at a special price, serious consideration must be given to the potential effect of this decision on regular sales.

The contribution margin approach holds that the short-run objective of a pricing decision is to maximize the firm's total contribution margin. The contribution margin—the excess of revenues over variable costs—is to cover fixed costs and then to provide a net income. If the contribution margin is maximized, net income will be maximized. It accepts the view that any unit providing a positive contribution margin will enhance the firm's profit picture. To illustrate this view further, let's assume that a firm has the following cost and revenue structure.

Normal selling price at 100% of normal capacity of 100,000 units	$5.00 per unit
Variable production costs	$3.00 per unit
Variable selling costs	$1.00 per unit
Fixed production costs	$30,000 per year
Fixed selling costs	$20,000 per year

It has received an offer to sell 10,000 units per year for the next five years to a special buyer at a special price of $3.50. Once the contract is consummated, the buyer will take delivery of the goods at the factory; no variable selling costs will be required on these 10,000 units. Should the firm accept the offer? Comparative income statements are shown in Exhibit 11–7. According to these income statements, the answer is no. To accept the order would reduce profits by $5,000. What is the minimum price acceptable for this order to maintain current profits? For this decision the fixed costs are not relevant; they do not change as a result of the decision. To maintain the current profit rate there must be an average contribution margin of $1.00 per unit, the current contribution margin. In order for the remaining 90,000 units to achieve this contribution margin, the 10,000-unit special order must also achieve a contribution margin of $1.00. The variable production costs of $3.00 will be the only relevant costs for the special order. The minimum price would be $4.00 ($3.00 variable cost + $1.00 contribution margin). At a price of $4.00 or above, the special order would be acceptable; below $4.00 it would be unacceptable.

To carry the contribution margin approach one step further, let's assume that the company has an excess inventory of 500 units that it cannot sell in its normal market because of a style change. What is the minimum price it can accept for these units and be better off than it would be if it scrapped them? A full cost-based approach might respond $4.50 [($300,000 + $100,000 + $30,000 + $20,000) ÷ 100,000 units]. A deeper analysis shows that the fixed costs remain unchanged. Further, the variable costs to produce the products are not relevant because the units have already been produced. The only relevant cost is the variable selling cost. If the firm could sell the 500 units for $1.10 they would be $50 [($1.10 − $1.00) × 500 units] better off than if it did not sell them. If it sold the units for $.80 each, it would lose an additional $.20 per unit ($1.00 − $.80).

	Without Special Order			*With Special Order*		
Sales	(100,000 × $5.00)		$500,000	(90,000 × $5.00)		$450,000
				(10,000 × $3.50)		35,000
			$500,000			$485,000
Variable costs:						
Production	(100,000 × $3.00)		$300,000	(100,000 × $3.00)		$300,000
Selling	(100,000 × $1.00)		100,000	(90,000 × $1.00)		90,000
			400,000			390,000
Contribution margin	(100,000 × $1.00)		$100,000			$ 95,000
Fixed costs:						
Production		$30,000			$30,000	
Selling		20,000			20,000	
Total			50,000			50,000
Net income			$ 50,000			$ 45,000

EXHIBIT 11–7
Effects of special order upon net income

To carry this illustration one more step, let's assume that the 500 excess units are a seasonal product which is still in style. The firm has the choice of carrying the items in the inventory for six months at a carrying cost of $300 or selling them now for $2.50 each and replacing them later. It is estimated that in six months the variable production costs will have risen to $3.50 because of a new labor contract. The relevant benefits and costs are the revenue potential, the carrying costs they would forego if they sold the units now, and the replacement costs.

	Sell Now; Replace Later	*Hold in Inventory*
Revenue	$ 1,250	
Replacement Costs	(1,750)	
Carrying Costs		$(300)
Net Cost	$ (500)	$(300)

The firm would incur $200 more in costs if they were to sell now and replace the units later. Here, as in the previous illustrations, the only relevant costs are the future differential costs.

A word of warning about the role of the contribution margin approach in pricing special orders seems appropriate at this point. A firm would have no need to accept a lower price for its product if it could sell all it wished at the normal price. For a firm to accept less than the normal price, it must be facing some adverse condition such as idle capacity, a marketplace where there is strong price competition, or a distressful situation, such as a rapid style change. Where the firm is facing pressure from one or more of these conditions, it may be able to increase its profit even though some products are priced below full cost plus markup. Of course, this is not the most desirable situation. Ideally, they would sell their products at the normal price, but in stressful situations some profit (or cost recovery) is better than no profit (or no cost recovery).

If a firm were to constantly reduce its selling prices to just above the variable costs, the volume would have to increase to cover the fixed costs and contribute to profit. There is always the danger that the use of the contribution margin could lead to short-run underpricing and that, as a result, the long-run financial health of the firm would be jeopardized. However, if the information available in the contribution margin approach is used in cost-volume-profit analysis, there is no reason for the short-run attitude to dominate. Certainly, a valuable skill for rational decision makers is the ability to balance long-run and short-run considerations.

PRICE DISCRIMINATION

Because of their size, cost structure, large customer base, or favorable market position, some firms can price their products low enough to drive competitors out of business. However, Congress has passed a number of antitrust laws in order to protect and encourage wholesome competition. In 1914 passage of the Clayton Act created the Federal Trade Commission, an administrative and semijudicial agency empowered to restrict unfair methods of competition and deceptive practices by competitors.

In 1936 the Clayton Act was amended by the Robinson-Patman Act Among the principal subsections of this law are those relating to unfair price discrimination. When a seller is charged by a buyer with discriminating in price between customers, the seller must show that the different prices were the result of cost differentials. However, a seller can justify his lower price by showing that it was made to meet an equally low offer by a competitor. If a firm is considered to have discriminated in price, the Federal Trade Commission can issue an order for it to stop selling at that price.

Since the Robinson-Patman Act deals with price differences to buyers of the same product, it is relevant only to standard products. In a case where the nature of a contract between a buyer and seller allows the seller to effect a cost savings that he shares with the buyer, price discrimination would not exist. Discrimination can exist only where the *same* products and services are provided to different buyers at different prices.

Although prices differ between buyers, price discrimination may not exist. In defense of charges brought under the Robinson-Patman Act, the comparison of cost differences is potentially important. Although it is not the only defense,[3] it is a crucial one; the seller may justify actual differences in price by showing that costs were different. Cost differences are readily justified when the price depends upon the quantity of an individual order or shipment. In these instances the differences in cost must be shown to result from the quantity sold or the method of selling. For example, simply showing that there are differences in the costs of shipping carload lots, as opposed to partial carload lots, may be all that is necessary to justify differences in costs and, hence, prices between orders of two different sizes.

Generally, the cost differences are more readily traced to selling and distribution costs than to production costs. Where the goods are produced for warehouse stock, the costs of manufacturing goods for specific customers are indistinguishable. In these cases, production costs are not relevant because they are not differential costs. However, whether a particular product was identified with a particular customer before it was manufactured or afterward, differences in costs of distribution may be attributed to differences in quantities sold, shipping methods, or modes of selling. Here the Robinson-Patman Act has a positive impact upon management accounting since it has made it necessary that accountants strive to understand and evaluate the firm's distribution costs.

It would be misleading to imply that all firms must constantly be on the defense against price discrimination charges. Most pricing and cost decisions lie outside the scope of the Robinson-Patman Act. A charge of unfair price discrimination must be brought by an injured party stating that the seller discriminated in price between different purchases of goods of like grade and quality in an attempt to lessen competition. Although cost defenses under the Robinson-Patman Act do happen, they are not an everyday event for most firms.

[3]Other defenses could include proving that the price differences were not discriminatory; that in consideration of discounts, allowances, and rebates, the prices were similar; that all business was intrastate; that the goods were not of similar grade or quality; or that the customers had different functional status, such as retailer and wholesaler.

SUMMARY

In economic theory the price and output quantity where the market is in equilibrium is at the intersection of the demand curve and the supply curve. This is true whether the market structure is pure competition, pure monopoly, monopolistic competition, or oligopoly. Market structures affect the shape and slope of the demand curve but do not change the underlying principle that the intersection of the supply and demand curves determines the equilibrium price and output.

While theoretically sound, economic pricing theory is difficult to apply in practice. Because the exact shape of the demand curve is very difficult to measure, many firms rely upon full cost-based prices, although they are less sound theoretically. This approach can best be thought of as a first estimate of price. The actual obtainable price is found by trial and error.

The contribution margin approach offers some insights into the pricing dilemma. In special-order and distress pricing situations, the contribution margin offers a decision attitude that is more relevant than full cost-based prices. Nevertheless, in the long run all revenue must cover all costs and provide an adequate net income to give the investors a reasonable return on their investment. It is not enough to use only full cost or only the contribution margin in pricing decisions. The decision maker should choose the best approach for specific circumstances.

In today's complicated business world there are many influences besides demand that determine price. Governmental and political factors operate to stop unfair price discrimination, in part because the U.S. economic system is based upon the assumption that price competition is desirable. Another cause of the political and legal constraints is the need to protect the consumer from unfair pricing practices. As a result, most pricing decisions of influential monopolies and some oligopolies, such as the railroads, airlines, electric utilities, and telephone companies, are regulated. Their prices are determined by governmental agencies and controlled to provide only a reasonable, normal return on investment.

SUPPLEMENTARY READING

*Brenner, Vincent C. "An Evaluation of Product Pricing Models." *Managerial Planning,* July–August, 1971.

*Corr, Arthur V. "The Role of Cost in Pricing." *Management Accounting,* November, 1974.

*Fuller, K. John. "Impact of CASB Standards." *The C.P.A. Journal,* January, 1976.

Herson, Richard J. L., and Ronald S. Hertz. "Direct Costing in Pricing: A Critical Reappraisal." *Management Services,* March–April, 1968.

Oxenfeldt, Alfred R., and William T. Baxter. "Approaches to Pricing: Economist versus Accountant." *Business Horizons,* Winter, 1961.

National Association of Accountants. *Product Costs for Pricing Purposes.* New York: National Association of Accountants, 1953.

National Association of Accountants. *Cost Control for Marketing Operations.* New York: National Association of Accountants, 1954.

Taylor, Otto F. "Cost Accounting Under the Robinson-Patman Act." *The New York Certified Public Accountant,* June, 1957.

Wright, Howard W. "Uniform Cost Accounting Standards: Past, Present, and Future." *Financial Executive*, May, 1971.

QUESTIONS

11-1 "Short-run pricing decisions determine the long-run survival of the firm." Discuss the validity of this statement.

11-2 Although cost-based pricing formulas are simple to use, they may not be valid in theory. Why or why not? What are some of the reasons this pricing method is so widely used?

11-3 Joint costs are not relevant to production and distribution decisions subsequent to the allocation. Discuss why this is so.

11-4 "The adoption of full cost-based prices prevents losses and ensures the recovery of all costs." Do you agree or disagree? Discuss.

11-5 Explain the difference between *cost-plus-percentage contracts, cost-plus-fixed-fee contracts,* and *incentive contracts.* Which is most advantageous to the seller? To the buyer?

11-6 Discuss the concepts: *cost-based pricing, heuristic (trial-and-error) pricing, common costs in pricing decisions, fixed-price contracts,* and *cost reimburseable contracts.*

11-7 What are the areas of management accounting where the Robinson-Patman Act has had the most impact?

11-8 Define and differentiate among *pure competition, pure monopoly, monopolistic competition,* and *oligopoly.* Give examples of industries that might belong in each classification.

11-9 Although a special order contributed $50,000 to profits, and excess capacity was available, management rejected the order. Give several possible reasons for management's action.

11-10 In today's marketplace many influences determine the price of a product. Name some of these influences and give examples.

EXERCISES

11-11 *(Matching).* Match the following terms and descriptions.

1. Demand curve
2. Relative sales value
3. Equilibrium point
4. Full-cost pricing
5. Product margin
6. Joint cost
7. Pure competition
8. Contribution margin pricing
9. Oligopoly
10. Fixed price contract

A. A cost that is applicable to more than one product.
B. A contract that is used for standard products.
C. A basis for allocating costs that are applicable to more than one product.
D. A way of setting the price particularly applicable to new technology and government contracts.
E. A market in which the sellers interact with each other.
F. A market that will take all that individual sellers offer at a given price.
G. The amounts customers are willing to buy at various prices.
H. The quantity at which supply and demand are equal.
I. Contribution margin less identifiable fixed costs.
J. A way of setting the price particularly applicable to special orders.

11-12 *(True or False).* Indicate whether the following statements are *true* or *false*.

1. Close substitutes for a product cause increased competition.

2. With a typical downward-sloping demand curve, as prices increase, less quantity will be demanded.

3. The upward slope of the supply curve is caused by diminishing returns.

4. In a purely competitive market, if the seller raises his price he will not sell as much of his product, but his profit will increase because of higher profit margins.

5. One danger in using the contribution margin approach to pricing is that the company might not foresee the need for the sales volume necessary to cover fixed costs.

6. The greater the degree of product differentiation, the greater the slope of the demand curve.

7. It is best to use full cost-based prices in establishing distress and special-order pricing policies.

8. Full cost-based prices are theoretically more sound than prices based upon supply and demand curve analysis.

9. With a downward-sloping demand curve, if there is an increase in supply with no change in the demand, price will decrease.

10. The Robinson-Patman Act is based upon the assumption that competition is healthy for the U.S. economy.

11-13 *(Multiple Choice).*

1. In an oligopolistic market there are
a. Many buyers
b. Few buyers
c. Many sellers
d. Few sellers

2. The automobile industry could be described as
a. A pure monopoly
b. Pure competition
c. Monopolistic competition
d. Oligopoly

3. If Products A and B are close substitutes, a substantial reduction in the price of A will
a. Reduce the demand for B
b. Increase the price of B
c. Reduce the supply of A
d. Increase the demand for B

4. In monopolistic competition there are
a. A very few firms producing identical products
b. A large number of firms producing identical products
c. Many firms producing differentiated products
d. A few firms producing identical products and competing through advertising

5. In which of the following market situations are prices likely to be under the control of an individual firm?
a. Pure competition
b. Pure monopoly
c. Monopolistic competition
d. Oligopoly

6. In a competitive industry the demand curve of the individual firm
a. Slopes downward to the right
b. Slopes upward to the right
c. Is the same as the demand curve for the industry
d. Is horizontal
e. Is vertical

7. Which of the following firms is correctly described as a monopolist?
   a. General Motors Corporation, with more than a 50% market share in the automobile industry
   b. British Airways, the only British airline serving the Atlantic air route
   c. A penicillin producer who possesses an expired patent right to produce the product
   d. A jeweler who holds an exclusive right to sell jewelry in the only regional shopping mall for a particular market area
   e. An independent gasoline dealer during a period of gasoline shortage

8. The pricing behavior in an oligopolistic industry is best described by which of the following statements?
   a. An individual firm is not likely to adjust its price to changes in cost immediately because the firm is not certain about the reaction of competitors to its price change. The industry's price, therefore, is likely to be rigid.
   b. Price is likely to rise or fall continuously because each firm possesses substantial market power to manipulate market price.
   c. Cutthroat price competition is the normal feature because competitors try to squeeze each other out until one finally survives and becomes the monopoly.
   d. There is a tendency for the competitors to fix price by explicit price-fixing agreement.
   e. The smallest firm in the industry always leads the price change for the industry.

9. An increase in demand for a particular item will generally cause its demand curve to shift
   a. Downward and leftward
   b. Upward and rightward
   c. Only if supply shifts
   d. Only if the price changes
   e. None of the above

10. Which of the following is the clearest statement of the law of demand?
   a. As income rises, people buy more of all goods and services.
   b. As price increases, the quantity of a good demanded will fall, assuming all other things are equal.
   c. As price decreases, the quantity of a good demanded will fall.
   d. Demand can never exceed supply.
   e. The higher a person's income, the greater the percentage of income saved.

(Some questions CMA adapted)

11-14 *(Market-based Price).* The Quick Clip Company has fixed costs of $200,000 and variable costs of $3.00 per unit. The company is attempting to choose the best of three possible prices. The expected volume of sales at each price is as follows:

Prices	\$3.50	\$4.00	\$4.50
Expected sales (in units)	500,000	300,000	180,000

REQUIRED:
What price shoud be charged? Show your work.

11-15 *(Market-based Price)*. The Leisure and Sporting Goods Division of AMG Corporation made a thorough market study for a new product for leisure activity. Data concerning units demanded at various prices for the new product follows:

Price	*Quantity demanded (units)*
\$12.00	200,000
\$11.00	400,000
\$10.00	1,000,000
\$ 9.00	2,000,000
\$ 8.50	3,000,000
\$ 8.00	5,000,000
\$ 7.50	7,000,000

Plant capacity available for this product is limited to 3,000,000 units. Because the life of the product is expected to be short, the company will not increase capacity. Fixed costs for the product are projected at \$2,000,000 and variable costs at \$7.00 per unit.

REQUIRED:

A. Determine the optimum price that will maximize income.

B. The company is considering a national promotional campaign that will cost \$2,000,000. The campaign should result in the following revised demand schedule.

Price	*Quantity demanded (units)*
\$12.00	300,000
\$11.00	600,000
\$10.00	1,400,000
\$ 9.00	3,000,000
\$ 8.50	5,000,000
\$ 8.00	8,000,000

Determine the optimum price that will maximize income after spending \$2,000,000 on promotion. Should the advertising campaign be undertaken?

11-16 *(Volume and Its Impact on Profits).* The Down Vest Manufacturing Company manufactures a goose down vest that sells for $20. The contribution margin ratio is 40% and total fixed costs are $240,000 per year. The estimate of sales volume for 19X3 was 40,000 units. On the basis of these estimates, the following budgeted income statement was prepared.

Sales	$800,000
Variable costs	480,000
Contribution margin	$320,000
Fixed costs	240,000
Budgeted net income	$ 80,000

Actual sales were 36,000 units and the profit was only $48,000. The president cannot understand why the profit was so low. The budget showed a net profit of $2.00 per unit ($80,000 ÷ 40,000 units), but the actual profit was only $1.33 per unit ($48,000 ÷ 36,000 units).

REQUIRED:

A. Prepare an explanation to the president showing why the actual profit was $1.33 per unit instead of the planned profit of $2.00 per unit.
B. What selling price would have generated the desired $2.00 profit per unit?
C. What selling price would have generated $80,000 of profit?

11-17 *(Cost-based Pricing).* The Seashore Products Corporation has the following cost structure.

Direct materials	$10
Direct labor	15
Variable overhead	6
Fixed overhead	9
Total unit cost	$40

Fixed selling and administrative costs are $120,000; the budgeted production of the firm for the coming year is 60,000 units. In addition, stockholders' equity is $4,000,000, and management feels that a minimum return of 15% on stockholders' equity is necessary to satisfy investors.

REQUIRED:

A. What is the price that must be charged for the product to meet this required return on investment, assuming that all production is sold?
B. Assume that instead of a 15% return on investment, management wanted to earn a profit of $150,000. What price should it charge for the product?
C. Would your answer to Part A change if the budgeted production volume was 90,000 units instead of 60,000 units? Why or why not?

11-18 *(Distress Pricing).* Pierre's Incorporated, a manufacturer of high-fashion coats, still has 10,000 units of one line of coats in stock at the end of the year.

Unfortunately, styles have changed and these units are no longer desired as fashion items. The following costs are associated with these coats.

Variable costs to produce, per unit	$50
Variable costs to sell, per unit	$ 5
Fixed production costs, per unit	$10
Fixed selling costs, per unit	$15

The coats are stored in a public warehouse and have accumulated storage charges of $5,000.

A discount store has offered $25,000 for the lot. They will pick up the coats immediately and no selling costs will be associated with this order.

REQUIRED:

A. Should Pierre's accept the offer? Explain.

B. What costs are relevant to the decision? If Pierre's are sold only through selected specialty shops, are there nonfinancial costs involved in accepting this order? Explain.

C. What is the minimum amount that Pierre's could charge for the coats and be as well off as if the coats were given away to be shredded and used in the production of paper for greeting cards?

11-19 *(Government Contract).* The Zippy Fastener Company has been asked to bid on a government contract to supply 1,000 of a specialty product for use in the space program. An estimate of the costs per unit are:

Direct materials	$25.00
Direct labor (1 hour)	$12.50
Variable overhead	120% of direct labor cost
Fixed overhead	$22.50 per direct labor hour

In addition to the costs above, special equipment costing $5,000 would be required to produce the special order. This equipment would have no resale value.

REQUIRED:

A. Determine the amount of revenue required to make the company no worse off than if it did not receive the bid. The company has adequate production facilities available.

B. What is the minimum price the firm should bid per unit? Explain.

C. What would be the differential cost if the government increased its order from 1,000 units to 1,500 units?

D. What would be the price under a cost-plus-fixed-fee contract if the fee is set at 6%? (Use the original data.)

11-20 *(Government Contract—Incentive).* Flash Jordan Products, Inc. is developing a backpack for the government that would enable individuals to cross rivers and small lakes without boats or bridges. The company is working under a cost-plus-fixed-fee contract that includes a cost incentive provision with a

50:50 ratio. The contract also contains a clause for noncompletion that assesses a penalty of 5% of total cost per month if the delivery date is not met.

Up to this point, actual costs are 20% below the estimated costs of $300,000. However, there have been developmental problems that could postpone the completion date several months. An accelerated work program would finish the job on time, thus avoiding the penalty for late delivery, but it would result in a 20% overrun on costs. If the completion date is not accelerated, but the job is finished one month late (which is best current estimate), costs will exceed the original budget by 10%. The original profit was a fixed fee based on 15% of estimated costs.

REQUIRED:

A. What are your recommendations to management? You should be concerned with the recommendations that will reduce costs and maximize the return to the company.

B. Would your answer differ if you were the government negotiator charged with administering this contract?

11-21 *(Government Contract—Incentive versus Fixed Fee).* The Sno-Horse Company has been in a bidding competition to supply to the government a special sled with the ability to traverse all terrains and to perform many specialized jobs in the snow. It was agreed upon by management and the government negotiators that the cost of designing and manufacturing five prototypes for experimental purposes should be $750,000. They agreed upon a fee of 12% of cost to be included in the contract price.

REQUIRED:

A. Determine the net income and the income as a percentage of costs, assuming a cost overrun of $150,000 on a cost-plus-fixed-fee contract.

B. Determine the net income and the income as a percentage of costs, assuming a cost incentive contract with a 50:50 ratio and actual costs that were 15% below budgeted costs.

C. Which contract in Part A or B would you prefer if you were the management of the Sno-Horse Company? If you were a government negotiator? Why?

11-22 *(Cost-based Pricing).* Walter's Woodworking Company came to you for assistance when the bookkeeper presented the income statement showing a large loss for the second year of operations. The loss of $70,000 was expected for the first year when the company operated at a low level. However, the management of Walter's Woodworking was shocked to discover a loss of $160,000 for the second year.

The president of the company could not understand how they could be operating at near-capacity and losing money. The company was consistently short of cash, a common problem when operations are expanding.

From your preliminary examination you found very poor accounting records. You are satisfied that the data in the financial statements are correct and that there is no significant fraud. The company manufactures a line of kitchen cabinets. Because of the lack of detailed records, it is impossible to develop data about the cost of the product. The selling price was set by the president to undersell competition. Condensed income statements are presented below:

WALTER'S WOODWORKING
INCOME STATEMENT
19X0 and 19X1

	19X0	*19X1*
Sales ($40 each)	$ 100,000	$ 400,000
Operating expenses:		
Beginning inventory of materials	$ 0	$ 20,000
Operating expense	190,000	570,000
Total	$ 190,000	$ 590,000
Ending inventory of materials	20,000	30,000
Expenses for year	170,000	560,000
Net loss	$ (70,000)	$(160,000)
Other data:		
Units produced	2,500 units	10,000 units
Units sold	2,500 units	10,000 units
Assets invested in business	$ 100,000	$ 100,000
Capacity in units	12,000	12,000

REQUIRED:

A. Why did the company lose $160,000 in the second year? How much would the company lose if they operated at capacity?
B. What price must be set to earn a profit of 8% of sales?
C. What price must be set to earn a contribution margin ratio of 30%?
D. What price must be set to earn 15% on the assets invested in the business?

11-23 *(Cost-based Pricing—Different Volume Levels).* The Coverall Company produces a single product called Glocote, some of which is exported. The sales budget indicates that 12,000 liters will be produced and sold in 19X0. The flexible budget for each cost is:

Prime costs	$0 per month plus $2 per liter
Manufacturing overhead	$2,000 per month plus $.50 per liter
Selling and administrative costs	$1,000 per month plus 10% of sales

The board of directors expects a return on investment of 10%. The company has $100,000 invested in productive assets.

REQUIRED:

A. What price per liter must management get for Glocote to obtain its return on investment objective?

B. What would the price per liter be if the company produced and sold 18,000 liters? 6,000 liters?

C. Prepare a profit plan for 19X0 in dollar and percentage form for each level of sales.

11–24 *(Overhead Costs and Pricing Decisions).* The Fanning Company produces two products for which the following cost and production data are estimated.

	Product A	*Product B*
Units produced and sold	20,000	40,000
Direct materials cost, per unit	$4	$ 9
Direct labor costs, per unit	$6	$15
Direct labor hours, per unit	2 hours	5 hours
Variable overhead, per unit	$2	$ 6
Fixed overhead, per month	$360,000	

The Fanning Company prices are set by adding a 30% markup to the full production cost.

REQUIRED:

A. Compute the selling prices of the two products, assuming that the fixed costs are allocated to the products on the basis of total labor hours.

B. Assume that the Fanning Company uses absorption costing with an expected overhead rate based upon direct labor hours to account for its products. The maximum capacity of the plant is 250,000 direct labor hours per month. The government would like to buy 1,000 units of Product B with slight modifications. The government would reimburse all normal costs of production plus a fixed fee of $2,500. The 1,000 units could be produced using the excess capacity, although the required modifications would cost the firm $1,000 for additional set-up time on the machines. Prepare a schedule showing the profit the Fanning Company would earn on this special order.

11–25 *(Special-Order Pricing).* The Riff-Raff Shoe Company produces high-fashion shoes. For one particular shoe, variable production costs were $6.50 and variable selling costs were $1.75. There are identifiable fixed production costs of $34,000 and fixed selling costs of $25,000. At the selling price of $13 per pair, the firm has been able to sell the entire 20,000 pairs it can produce with available capacity. Riff-Raff has been requested to supply a one-time only order of 10,000 pairs of shoes to the Nickel Department Store Chain at a price of $10 per pair. Management estimates that the variable costs of selling these 10,000 pairs will be cut to $.75 per pair and that the fixed identifiable selling costs will be $20,000 instead of $25,000.

REQUIRED:

A. Should management accept this order? Why or why not? Support your conclusions.

B. Assume that fashions have changed to the point where one style of shoe, currently produced and in the inventory, is no longer marketable. Given the costs above, what is the least amount management should ask for these 3,000 pairs of shoes. Why? Will the firm make a profit or sustain a loss? What will be the amount of the profit or loss?

C. Given the original cost data, what is the quantity of shoes that must be sold to break even?

PROBLEMS

11-26 *(Cost-based Pricing—Different Volume Levels).* The Gulf Iron and Fabric Company produces a line of cast iron urns. The variable production costs of one model of urn are $6.75, and fixed production costs are $36,000 per year. Management has followed the policy of determining the selling price by applying a 30% markup to full production cost. Depending upon the market conditions, the company could sell between 9,000 and 18,000 units during the coming year. While management anticipates sales of 12,000 units, it feels that there is a large degree of uncertainty in these predictions and wants information on the other possible sales levels.

REQUIRED:

A. Assuming that production volume and sales volume are equal, determine the fixed cost per unit, the dollar markup per unit, and the selling price per unit at each level of 9,000, 12,000, 15,000, and 18,000 urns.

B. What is the net income at each level of production in Part A? What is the return on sales at each level?

C. Assuming that management priced its product on an anticipated sales volume of 15,000, what would be the differences between budgeted and actual income if actual sales reached 20,000 units? 9,000 units?

11-27 *(Cost Allocations and Pricing Decisions).* In its production process the Rashad Company incurs joint costs of $48,000. The following data concerning possible allocation bases were compiled.

	Variable Production Costs	Labor Hours	Machine Hours	Units Produced	Selling Price
Product A	$45	3	1	1,200	$ 55
Product B	$90	5	4	1,500	$110

REQUIRED:

A. What is the full cost for each product under each of the following allocation bases?

1. Variable costs

2. Labor hours

3. Machine hours

4. Units produced
5. Relative sales-value method

B. Which allocation base do you prefer? Why?
C. Should this full cost be used for pricing decisions? Why or why not?

11-28 *(Establishing Selling Prices to Maintain Gross Profit).* In July 19X7, the Comfortair Heating and Cooling Company sold 100 air-conditioning units for $250 each. Production costs included:

Materials	$75
Direct labor	$40
Overhead	
(90% of direct labor)	$36

Bank loans were used to finance production. Interest expense on an 8% bank loan was equivalent to $2.00 per unit. Federal income taxes at a 40% rate were equivalent to $16 per unit.

On July 1, 19X7, suppliers announced a materials price increase of 20%, and direct labor costs increased $10. On the same day the interest rate increased from 8% to 10%.

REQUIRED:

A. Assuming no change in the rate of overhead in relation to direct labor costs, compute the sales price per unit that will produce the same ratio of gross profit.
B. Assuming that 50% of the overhead consists of fixed costs, compute the sales price per unit that will produce the same ratio of gross profit.

(CPA adapted)

11-29 *(Computation of Incremental Income).* The Eastinghouse Company wants to determine the best sales price for a new appliance with a variable cost of $4.10 per unit. The sales manager has estimated probabilities of achieving annual sales levels for various selling prices, as shown in the following chart.

Sales Level	*Selling Price*			
(Units)	*$4*	*$5*	*$6*	*$7*
20,000	—	—	20%	80%
30,000	—	10%	40%	20%
40,000	50%	50%	20%	—
50,000	50%	40%	20%	—

The division's current profit rate is 5% on annual sales of $1,200,000; an investment of $400,000 is needed to finance these sales.

REQUIRED:

A. Prepare a schedule computing the expected incremental income for each of the sales prices proposed for the new product. The schedule should include the expected sales levels in units (weighted according to the sales manager's estimated probabilities), the expected total monetary sales, expected variable costs, and the expected incremental income.

B. What price should be charged to maximize income? Explain.

C. Assuming that fixed costs of $8,600 are allocated to the new product, and interest rate on the money borrowed to finance the product is 10%, prepare an income statement for the new product. *(CPA adapted)*

11-30 *(Cost-based Pricing—Joint Cost).* The Feed Shed produces three types of chicken feed that are marketed regionally. The same grains and other supplements are used for each mixture, but in different combinations. The following materials costs apply to each type of feed.

Type of Feed	*Variable Costs for Materials per Hundred Weight*	*Estimated Sales*
Lay-a-lot	$5.70	240 tons*
Quickgro	$5.10	900 tons
Shurgro	$4.25	1,200 tons

*Assume 2,000 pounds per ton.

The joint production costs, which consist primarily of mixing tanks and indirect labor, are $105,300. In the past management has based its pricing policies on full cost, but the sales department has recently complained that Feed Shed is being underpriced by competitors and that the firm's share of the market is declining. Management has been using a 20% markup on the full cost determined by apportioning the joint costs on the basis of the quantity produced.

REQUIRED:

A. Determine the selling price per 100-pound bag for each type of feed, assuming full-cost pricing.

B. With additional variable costs of $1.00 per 100-pound bag, Shurgro sales can be increased to 2,400 tons without affecting the sales of Lay-a-lot and Quickgro. However, management believes that the price of Shurgro cannot be raised more than $1.10 per bag over its current cost-based price. If this additional output is produced, the total joint costs will increase from $105,300 to $117,000. Assuming that capacity is sufficient to allow the additional sales, what would you recommend? Explain fully.

11-31 *(Pricing and Cost-Volume-Profit Relationships).* Austin G. Beardslee, Ltd., has recently leased manufacturing facilities for production of a new product. On the basis of studies made by the controller, the following data have been made available to you.

Estimated annual sales	30,000 units	
	Amount	*Per Unit*
Estimated costs:		
Material (variable)	$120,000	$4.00
Labor (½ fixed)	60,000	2.00
Overhead (⅔ fixed)	36,000	1.20
Administrative expense (fixed)	30,000	1.00
Total	$246,000	$8.20

In addition, variable selling expenses are expected to be 15% of sales, and net income is to amount to $2.00 per unit.

REQUIRED:

A. Compute the selling price per unit.
B. Compute a breakeven point expressed in dollars and in units.
C. Prepare a profit plan for the year.
D. Prepare an actual income statement for the year, assuming that the actual annual sales were 40,000 units and all costs were incurred as planned.

11-32 *(Comprehensive Pricing).* Beloxie Enterprises was formed in 19X0 by Mr. Dodson to produce and market a new kind of glue called Silly Glue. Facilities with a capacity of 1,000,000 units per year were leased at the beginning of 19X0 and the following projection of costs was developed.

Production:	$.15 per unit produced plus $100,000 per year
Selling and administration:	$.05 per unit sold plus $50,000 per year

The marketing consultant reported that at a price of $.40 per unit the company would sell all it could produce. However, Mr. Dodson, the inventor of Silly Glue, believed that the product was worth more than $.40 and set a price of $.50.

Exhibit 1

BELOXIE ENTERPRISES
INCOME STATEMENT
19X0

Sales (500,000 units @ $.50)		$250,000
Cost of goods sold:		
Production costs (1,000,000 units)	$250,000	
Less: Inventory (500,000 units @ $.25)	125,000	125,000
Gross margin		$125,000
Selling and administrative expenses		75,000
Net income		$ 50,000

During 19X0 the company produced at capacity, incurring costs exactly as projected, but sold only 500,000 units. Mr. Dodson was delighted when his accountant presented him with the income statement in Exhibit 1 showing a net income of $50,000 for 19X0.

Mr. Dodson examined his costs at 500,000 units and concluded that he would have to raise his price to $.60 in order to cover costs and generate his target profit of $50,000 per year. So far, he had achieved his profit objective in spite of what the consultant had said. He was, however, facing serious cash flow problems and had accumulated a large inventory.

During 19X1, Mr. Dodson sold only 300,000 units at the $.60 selling price. He had reduced production to 300,000 and therefore did not build inventory further. Mr. Dodson was pleased to see a net income of $40,000 for the year (Exhibit 2). Because of the decline in sales, he had expected a lower profit. Again, costs were exactly as projected.

Exhibit 2

BELOXIE ENTERPRISES
INCOME STATEMENT
19X1

Sales (300,000 units @ $.60)		$180,000
Cost of goods sold:		
Beginning inventory (500,000 units @ $.25)	$125,000	
Current production costs (300,000 units @ $.4833)	145,000	
Total available	$270,000	
Ending inventory @ FIFO (200,000 @ $.25, 300,000 units @ $.4833)	195,000[1]	75,000
Gross margin		$105,000
Selling and administrative expenses		65,000
Net income		$ 40,000

[1]Rounding error in unit cost.

At the beginning of 19X2, Mr. Dodson again examined his costs. At the 300,000-unit level of production his unit cost to produce was slightly over $.48, and selling and administrative costs were approximately $.22. At a selling price of $.60 he was losing approximately $.10 on each unit.

Mr. Dodson began planning a new alternative for 19X2. If the price is raised to $.75 per unit, the consultant's report indicated he would sell approximately 200,000 units, which would also be the production budget. By producing and selling less than 300,000 units in 19X2 he will be able to reduce fixed overhead by $20,000 and fixed selling and administrative costs by $15,000. At the same time, a chain of department stores wants to buy 300,000 units of Silly Glue per year at $.30 per unit. There will be no variable selling expenses for these units.

REQUIRED:

A. Assuming that Beloxie Enterprises adopts only the first alternative and raises the price to $.75 units in 19X2, prepare a profit plan for 19X2 that is consistent with the accounting methods employed in the income statements for 19X0 and 19X1. Comment on the amount of the resulting profit or loss.

B. What would be the impact if the special order is accepted? Mr. Dodson questions the wisdom of accepting an order at $.30 per unit when his lowest possible total unit cost would be $.35 at full capacity. What other factors would affect his decision?

C. Assuming the cost structure in years 19X0 and 19X1, what is the breakeven point in units if the selling price is $.50? If it is $.60? How does this compare with the income statements for 19X0 and 19X1?

D. Recast the income statements using variable costing and the contribution margin approach. Comment upon the results when compared with the income statements for 19X1 and 19X2 prepared by the accountant.

E. Develop a demand curve (just determine the amounts at different prices, do not plot a curve) showing units demanded at $.40, $.50, $.60, and $.75. Using this information and the cost structure of the company, develop a pricing strategy for Beloxie Enterprises for the year 19X2. You should consider the special order in your strategy by assuming it will not affect regular sales.

F. On the basis of your pricing strategy in Part E, prepare a profit plan using variable costing and the contribution margin approach for 19X2.

11–33 *(Product Pricing in Sales Regions).* The Justa Corporation produces and sells three products. The three products, A, B, and C, are sold in both a local market and in a regional market. At the end of the first quarter of the current year, the following income statement, showing income by market, was prepared.

	Total	*Local*	*Regional*
Sales	$1,300,000	$1,000,000	$300,000
Cost of goods sold	1,010,000	775,000	235,000
Gross margin	$ 290,000	$ 225,000	$ 65,000
Selling expenses	$ 105,000	$ 60,000	$ 45,000
Administrative expenses	52,000	40,000	12,000
Total expenses	157,000	100,000	57,000
Net income	$ 133,000	$ 125,000	$ 8,000

Management has expressed special concern with the regional market because of the extremely poor return on sales. This market was entered a year ago because of excess capacity. It was originally believed that the return on sales would improve with time, but after a year no noticeable improvement can be seen from the results as reported in the quarterly income statement.

In attempting to decide whether to eliminate the regional market, the following information was gathered.

SALES BY PRODUCTS

	Products		
	A	*B*	*C*
Sales	$500,000	$400,000	$400,000
Variable manufacturing expenses as a percentage of sales	60%	70%	60%
Variable selling expenses as a percentage of sales	3%	2%	2%

SALES BY MARKET FOR EACH PRODUCT

Product	*Local*	*Regional*
A	$400,000	$100,000
B	$300,000	$100,000
C	$300,000	$100,000

The selling expenses in the income statement are for local and regional sales offices and include both variable and fixed costs. If a market is dropped, the sales office will be closed. All administrative expenses are fixed for the period.

Cost of goods sold in the income statement includes both variable costs and fixed costs. Administrative costs and fixed manufacturing costs were allocated to the two markets to develop a full-cost income statement.

REQUIRED:

A. Prepare a quarterly income statement showing contribution margins by region.

B. Assuming that there are no alternative uses for the Justa Corporation's present capacity, would you recommend dropping the regional market? Why or why not?

C. Prepare a quarterly income statement showing contribution margins by products.

D. It is believed that a new product can be ready for sale next year if the Justa Corporation decides to go ahead with continued research. The new product can be produced by simply converting equipment used at present in producing Product C. This conversion will increase fixed costs by $10,000 per quarter. What must be the minimum contribution margin per quarter for the new product to make the changeover financially feasible?

(CMA adapted)

11-34 *(Pricing a Special Order).* E. Berg and Sons build custom-made pleasure boats ranging in price from $10,000 to $250,000. For the past 30 years, the senior Mr. Berg has determined the selling price of each boat by estimating the costs of material and labor, prorating a portion of estimated total overhead, and adding 20% to these estimated costs.

For example, a recent price quotation was determined as follows:

Direct materials	$ 5,000
Direct labor	8,000
Overhead (25% of labor)	2,000
Total estimated costs	$15,000
Plus 20%	3,000
Selling price	$18,000

If the customer rejected the price and business was slack, Mr. Berg would often reduce his markup to as little as 5% over estimated costs. Thus, average markup for the year is estimated at 15%.

Ed Berg, Jr. has just completed a course on pricing and believes the firm could use some of the techniques discussed in the course. The course emphasized the contribution margin approach to pricing and Ed feels such an approach would be helpful in determining the selling prices of their custom-made boats.

At the beginning of each year the overhead rate is established by dividing total estimated overhead by estimated direct labor cost. This year's total overhead, which includes selling and administrative expenses, was estimated at $150,000, of which $90,000 is fixed and the remainder is variable. Direct labor was estimated at $600,000 for the year.

REQUIRED:

A. Assume the customer in the example rejected the $18,000 quotation and also rejected a $15,750 quotation (5% markup) during a slack period. The customer countered with a $15,000 offer.
   1. What is the difference in net income for the year between accepting or rejecting the customer's offer?
   2. What is the minimum selling price Ed Berg, Jr. could have quoted without reducing or increasing net income?

B. What advantages does the contribution margin approach to pricing have over the approach used by the senior Mr. Berg?

C. What pitfalls are there, if any, to contribution margin pricing?

(CMA adapted)

11-35 *(Pricing a Special Order).* The Largo Manufacturing Company makes and sells a single product, VOSTEX, through normal marketing channels. You have been asked by its president to assist in determining the proper bid to submit for a special manufacturing job for the Aztec Sales Company. You have collected the following information.

1. The special job is for MOFAC, a product unlike VOSTEX, even though the manufacturing processes are similar.

2. Additional sales of MOFAC to the Aztec Sales Company are not expected.
3. The bid is for 20,000 pounds of MOFAC. Each 1,000 pounds of MOFAC requires 500 pounds of Material A, 250 pounds of Material B, and 250 pounds of Material C.
4. Largo's materials inventory data follow.

Material	Pounds in Inventory	Acquisition Cost per Pound	Current Replacement Cost per Pound
A	24,000	$.40	$.48
B	4,000	$.25	$.27
C	17,500	$.90	$.97
X	7,000	$.80	$.85

Material X may be substituted for Material A in MOFAC. Material X, made especially for Largo under a patent owned by Largo, is left over from the manufacture of a discontinued product, is not usable in VOSTEX, and has a current salvage value of $180.

5. Each 1,000 pounds of MOFAC requires 180 direct labor hours at $3 per hour (overtime is charged at time and a half). However, Largo is working near its two-shift capacity and has only 1,600 hours of regular time available. The production manager indicates that he can keep the special job on regular time by shifting the production of VOSTEX to overtime if necessary.
6. Largo's cost clerk informs you that the overhead rate at normal production is as follows:

Fixed element	$ .20 per direct labor hour
Variable element	.80 per direct labor hour
Total factory overhead rate	$1.00 per direct labor hour

7. The bid invitation states that a performance bond must be submitted with the bid. A local agent will bond Largo's performance for 1% of the total bid.

REQUIRED:

A. The Largo Manufacturing Company has a net income objective of a 10% return on sales. Compute the bid that will allow Largo to meet this objective if regular sales currently satisfy this objective.

B. Compute the minimum bid (i.e., the bid that would neither increase nor decrease total net income) that Largo Manufacturing Company may submit.

C. Largo's president also wants to know what his new competitor, Melton Manufacturing Company, probably will bid. You assume that Melton's materials inventory has been acquired very recently and that Melton's cost behavior is similar to Largo's. You know that Melton has ample productive capacity to handle the special job on regular time. Compute the minimum bid (i.e., the bid that would neither increase nor decrease total net income) that Melton Manufacturing Company might submit.

(CPA adapted)

12 Production Decisions

In this chapter we explore how the decision maker uses accounting data to make production volume decisions. It is assumed that previous long-range decisions have provided a productive capacity; short-range decisions must be made concerning its use. The topics in this chapter focus upon how best to use existing productive capacity. Questions asked include: "How many units should the firm produce?" "Should it produce more of Product X than Product Y, or more of Product Y than Product X?" "Should a product be dropped?"

CRITERIA FOR DECISION DATA

Each decision made by management is unique. Different decisions call for different data. To be relevant, data must exhibit the characteristics of **differentiality** and **futurity.** Past benefits and costs are the results of a prior decision that cannot be changed. Past costs are generally irrelevant since no future decision can change what has already happened. The role of the past in decision making lies in what can be learned from it. Further, a benefit or cost that is identical in all the available alternatives does not affect the choice and, therefore, is not relevant to the decision.

Crucial to any measure of differential data is the **opportunity cost,** the foregone income that would have been earned had another alternative been chosen. For example, the opportunity cost of burying money in a glass jar in the backyard is the interest that could be earned if the money were put in a savings account at the bank. This is not the only possibility and, therefore, not the only opportunity cost. The money could be invested in high-grade government bonds, $.10 mining stocks, or blue chip stocks. Each would provide a different opportunity cost. When we examine the possible income that a firm could earn or costs that a firm could save in the selection of one alternative over another, we are viewing these as opportunity costs. We don't often use the term *opportunity cost,* but it is implied. When we use the contribution margin to measure the impact of production output decisions, we are treating the contribution margin as an opportunity cost.

THE CONTRIBUTION MARGIN AND PRODUCTION DECISIONS

In Chapters 2 and 3 we stressed the role of fixed and variable costs in determining the contribution margin and in assessing cost-volume-profit interactions. In Chapter 11 we showed how the contribution margin facilitates pricing decisions. Now let's turn our attention to how the contribution margin can be used in making production output decisions. As output is changed, within the relevant range, both variable costs and revenue change. The contribution margin measures the combined effect of changes in revenue and variable costs, allowing a direct measure of the impact of output variations. Fixed costs, on the other hand, do not change and, therefore, are not relevant to production decisions as long as the firm stays within the relevant range or does not change productive capacity.

Adding a New Product

Assume that Product A of the Sultan Company has not achieved the customer acceptance expected and that the company has excess productive capacity. In its search for new products to produce with existing facilities, the Sultan Company narrowed its study to two: Product B and Product C. The following tabulation shows estimated selling prices and costs directly associated with these new products.

	Product B	*Product C*
Selling price per unit	$20 per unit	$2.50 per unit
Costs:		
Direct materials	$10 per unit	$ .80 per unit
Direct labor	$ 3 per unit	$ .45 per unit
Variable overhead	$ 1 per unit	$ .15 per unit
Variable selling costs	$ 2 per unit	$ .50 per unit
Fixed selling costs	$6,000 per year	$10,000 per year

The current fixed overhead of $15,000 per year and fixed selling costs of $5,000 per year would not be affected and are not relevant. The Sultan Company has sufficient excess capacity to produce 4,000 units of Product B or 30,000 units of Product C. Market studies indicate that these units may be sold at the planned market prices.

Which product should be added? Projected income statements show the contribution margin and product margin for the two new products.

	PRODUCT B		**PRODUCT C**	
Number of units	**4,000**		**30,000**	
	Per Unit	*Amount*	*Per Unit*	*Amount*
Sales	$20.00	$80,000	$2.50	$75,000
Direct materials	$10.00	$40,000	$ .80	$24,000
Direct labor	3.00	12,000	.45	13,500
Variable overhead	1.00	4,000	.15	4,500
Variable selling costs	2.00	8,000	.50	15,000
Total variable costs	16.00	64,000	1.90	57,000
Contribution margin	$ 4.00	$16,000	$ .60	$18,000
Identifiable fixed selling costs		6,000		10,000
Product margin		$10,000		$ 8,000

Product C has the highest contribution margin; if there were no additional fixed costs, Product C would be produced. However, these products involve new markets, so additional fixed selling costs are necessary. After subtracting the directly identifiable fixed selling costs from the contribution margin, the result is the **product margin,** the amount that net income will be increased by producing and selling the product. Product B, with a product margin of $10,000, should be produced and sold. Product C will provide only an $8,000 product margin and should be rejected in favor of Product B.

Sell or Process Further: A Single Product

The Sultan Company currently manufactures only Product A, which is sold to other firms who process it further. During normal operations 10,000 units of Product A are produced per year; they sell for $10 each. The following costs are incurred to produce and sell these 10,000 units.

	Product A	
	Per Unit	*Total*
Direct materials	$2.00	$20,000
Direct labor	3.00	30,000
Variable overhead costs	1.00	10,000
Variable selling costs	.25	2,500
Fixed overhead costs	1.50	15,000
Fixed selling costs	.50	5,000
Total unit cost	$8.25	$82,500

As an alternative to producing Product B, the managers of the Sultan Company are considering using their excess capacity to process Product A further. After additional processing, Product A could be sold for $14 per unit. The following are estimates of the *additional* costs of processing 10,000 units of Product A further.

Direct labor	$1.25 per unit
Variable overhead costs	$ .75 per unit
Variable selling costs	$ .50 per unit
Fixed overhead costs	$8,000 per year
Fixed selling costs	$5,000 per year

The following tabulation shows the contribution margin and the product margin of Product A, both with and without the additional processing.

	PRODUCT A					
	Without Further Processing		With Further Processing		Difference from Processing Further	
	Per Unit	*Total*	*Per Unit*	*Total*	*Per Unit*	*Total*
Sales	$10.00	$100,000	$14.00	$140,000	$4.00	$40,000
Variable costs:						
Direct material	$ 2.00	$ 20,000	$ 2.00	$ 20,000	—	—
Direct labor	3.00	30,000	4.25	42,500	$1.25	$12,500
Variable overhead	1.00	10,000	1.75	17,500	.75	7,500
Variable selling costs	.25	2,500	.75	7,500	.50	5,000
Total variable costs	6.25	62,500	8.75	87,500	2.50	25,000
Contribution margin	$ 3.75	$ 37,500	$ 5.25	$ 52,500	$1.50	$15,000
Identifiable fixed costs		—		13,000		13,000
Product margin		$ 37,500		$ 39,500		$ 2,000

The contribution margin would increase if the Sultan Company decided to process the product further. Would the net income increase? The added contribution margin per unit would be $1.50 ($5.25 − $3.75), and the total contribution margin would be increased by $15,000 ($1.50 × 10,000 units). Since the increase in fixed costs is $13,000 ($8,000 + $5,000) and the incremental contribution margin is $15,000, $2,000 would be added to the net income. In this case the product should be processed further.

Let's examine the firm's fixed cost structure. The original per-unit cost included fixed overhead costs of $1.50 and fixed selling expenses of $.50. These were calculated by dividing the total fixed costs of overhead and selling expenses by the number of units normally produced and sold. Therefore, the fixed overhead is $15,000 ($1.50 × 10,000 units) and the fixed selling expenses are $5,000 ($.50 × 10,000 units). The decision to process further does not change this fixed cost structure; these fixed costs are nonrelevant. The practice of stating fixed costs on a per-unit basis is potentially misleading and should be avoided in making differential decisions.

The Sultan Company has considered two different uses for its excess capacity. One alternative was to add a new product. Of those products considered, Product B would make the greatest contribution to income. Another desirable choice was to process Product A further. Which of the two alternatives should be chosen?

	PRODUCE PRODUCT B		PROCESS PRODUCT A FURTHER	
Number of units	4,000		10,000	
	Per Unit	*Amount*	*Per Unit*	*Amount*
Sales	$20.00	$80,000	$4.00	$40,000
Variable costs:				
Direct materials	$10.00	$40,000	—	—
Direct labor	3.00	12,000	$1.25	$12,500
Variable overhead	1.00	4,000	.75	7,500
Variable selling costs	2.00	8,000	.50	5,000
Total variable costs	16.00	64,000	2.50	25,000
Contribution margin	$ 4.00	$16,000	$1.50	$15,000
Identifiable fixed costs		6,000		13,000
Product margin		$10,000		$ 2,000

An income statement comparing the two alternatives shows that the new product will contribute $10,000 toward net income, whereas processing Product A further will contribute only $2,000 toward net income. The excess capacity should be used to produce Product B.

Sell or Process Further: Multiple Products

In many industries the production process consists of taking a single material input and producing more than one final product. In the petroleum industry a barrel of crude oil is refined into fuel oil, premium gasoline, regular gasoline, and many other types of petroleum products. The meat-packing industry produces hamburger, roasts, steaks, and many other products from a single steer. In the lumber industry a single log produces 2 × 4s, 4 × 4s, and 1 × 4s. These production processes are called **joint processes.**

The costs of the barrel of crude oil, the steer, or the log are **joint costs**—costs that are incurred to process a single raw material into more than one manufactured product. At the time joint costs are introduced into the production process, it is impossible to identify one finished product from another. Joint costs represent the costs of a single material, a single production process, or a series of production processes that simultaneously produce two or more finished products.

Assume that the Sprock Manufacturing Company produces three products: D, E, and F. Raw Material X enters the process in Department 1 of the factory. Department 1 separates Material X into Products D, E, and F. During the past year $260,000 of Material X was issued to Department 1. Other costs of operating Department 1 were $140,000. Department 1 output was 100,000 pounds of Product D, 50,000 pounds of Product E, and 200,000 pounds of Product F. The end of the production process in Department 1 is called the **split-off point,** where a single raw material yields two or more different products. Each product has a ready market at this point of split-off. At the point of split-off, Product D sells for $2.00 per pound, Product E for $4.00 per pound, and Product F for $.50 per pound.

After the split-off, Product D could be processed further in Department 2, with the additional cost of $200,000. After the additional processing Product D would sell for $4.50 per pound. After the split-off, Product E could be processed further in Department 3 for $60,000 additional costs. After this additional processing, Product E would sell for $5.00 per pound. Product F is not suitable for further processing and must be sold at the point of split-off. These production possibilities can be shown diagrammatically:

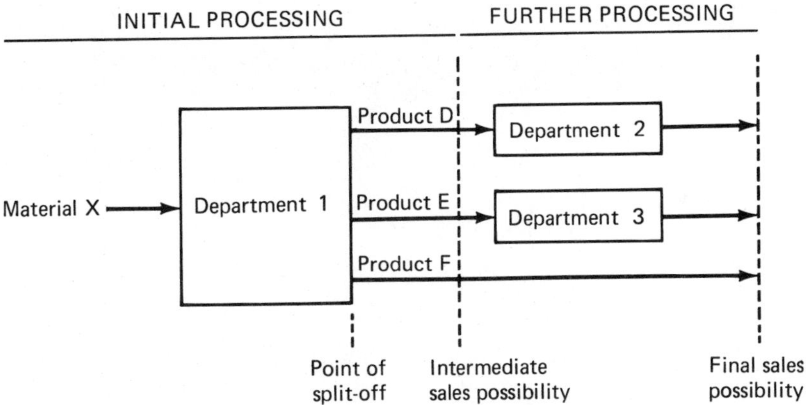

What actions should management take? A comparison of the contribution margins for the products under the possible alternatives is shown in Exhibit 12–1. For Product D the maximum contribution margin is attained when the product is processed further. For Product E the maximum contribution margin is $200,000 when it is sold without further processing. The optimum choice is to process Product D and sell Products E and F at the point of split-off. The following net income figure is based on these choices.

Sales ($450,000 + $200,000 + $100,000)	$750,000
Separable costs of additional processing	200,000
Separable margin	$550,000
Joint costs ($260,000 + $140,000)	400,000
Net income	$150,000

The incremental income from a decision to process a product further is equal to the *additional* revenue gained from selling the product at an

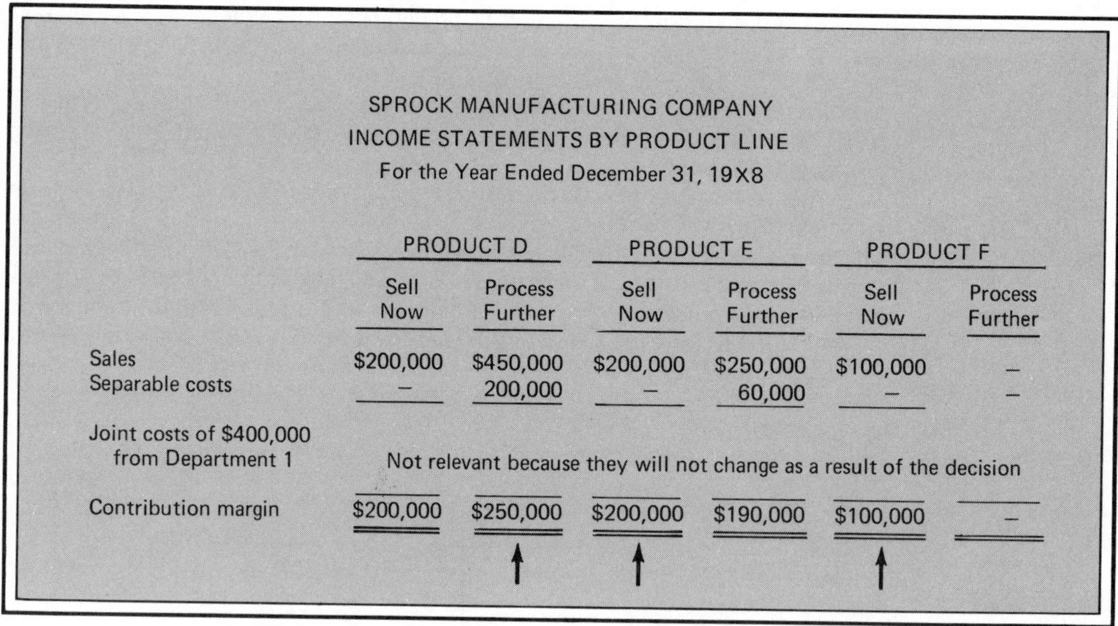

SPROCK MANUFACTURING COMPANY
INCOME STATEMENTS BY PRODUCT LINE
For the Year Ended December 31, 19X8

	PRODUCT D		PRODUCT E		PRODUCT F	
	Sell Now	Process Further	Sell Now	Process Further	Sell Now	Process Further
Sales	$200,000	$450,000	$200,000	$250,000	$100,000	–
Separable costs	–	200,000	–	60,000	–	–
Joint costs of $400,000 from Department 1	Not relevant because they will not change as a result of the decision					
Contribution margin	$200,000	$250,000	$200,000	$190,000	$100,000	–
		↑	↑		↑	

EXHIBIT 12–1
Sell-or-process-further analysis

advanced state of manufacture minus the *additional* processing costs traceable to the product. If this difference is positive, the decision to process further would be profitable in the short run. For example, the incremental revenue of Product D is $250,000; the incremental costs are $200,000; and the incremental income is $50,000. The joint costs ($400,000) are not relevant to the decision; they will not change because of subsequent decisions. In any incremental analysis, joint costs such as these are not relevant. Costs incurred before the point of split-off are common to all products and cannot be treated as incremental costs of the individual products, even if allocated.

A second observation should be made. The decision was made without consideration of alternative uses for Departments 2 and 3. It was assumed that the only choice was to process the products further and that no other opportunity costs were applicable.

You may have noticed an accounting conflict. Joint costs are irrelevant for incremental production decisions because the joint costs do not change as a result of the decision to sell or process further. Yet for inventory costing and income-determination purposes, the financial accountant must allocate joint costs to the products. As shown in Chapter 11, one way to allocate the joint cost is to use the relative sales-value basis either at the point of split-off or after further processing. The following allocation assumes that the Sprock Company uses the relative sales-value basis at the point of split-off.

Product	Units Produced	Selling Price at Split-off	Total Market Value at Split-off		Allocation of Joint Costs
D	100,000	$2.00	$200,000	2/5	$160,000
E	50,000	$4.00	200,000	2/5	160,000
F	200,000	$ .50	100,000	1/5	80,000
Total	350,000		$500,000	5/5	$400,000

After the allocation of the joint costs, the per-unit cost for inclusion in the inventory would be $3.60 for Product D [($160,000 + $200,000) ÷ 100,000 units], assuming that the product was processed further. For Product E, assuming that it was to be sold at the point of split-off, the inventory value would be $3.20 ($160,000 ÷ 50,000 units). For Product F the inventoriable cost would be $.40 ($80,000 ÷ 200,000 units). These unit costs are applicable to inventory costing.

Although the joint cost allocation may be necessary for inventory valuation, it is not useful in management decision making. Regardless of what products are produced or their ultimate disposition, the joint cost has already been incurred; it is not relevant to any decision subsequent to its incurrence.

It may seem inadequate to talk about incremental income for the products rather than net income. To speak of "net" income by product line requires the allocation of joint costs to the various products. Incremental income, on the other hand, is the contribution of the individual products to the firm's joint costs and income. The allocation of joint costs, regardless of how they are allocated, will not change the net income of the firm over time and can mislead the decision maker into believing that the allocated joint costs are relevant in measuring incremental income.

Make or Buy Component Parts

Another important production decision is whether to make or buy component parts. This decision can involve both quantitative and qualitative factors. Many firms, to ensure their flow of finished products, control the total production flow from extraction or manufacture of the raw materials to the completion of the final product. This control creates an operation much less dependent upon suppliers and allows the firm to earn profits from manufacturing its subcomponents. However, the manufacture of subcomponents requires that skilled labor and productive facilities be available. A firm that follows the policy of manufacturing its parts when activity on the final product is slack, and purchasing them when its production facilities are busy on the final product, may find its suppliers less than willing to fill orders on a sporadic basis.

The economic effects of the make-or-buy decision are best seen through the contribution margin approach of measuring incremental income.

The purchase price of the parts plus other incremental costs of procurement, such as ordering and receiving, can be compared with the additional costs of producing the part. As long as the incremental costs of making the part are less than the purchase costs of buying it, the firm should manufacture the part. When the incremental manufacturing costs exceed the purchase costs, the part should be purchased from the supplier.

To illustrate, assume that a firm has prepared the following cost estimate for the manufacture of a subcomponent—a motor casting—based upon an annual production of 5,000 parts.

	Per Unit	*Total*
Direct materials	$ 5	$ 25,000
Direct labor	8	40,000
Variable overhead	4	20,000
Fixed overhead		
(37.5% of direct labor cost)	3	15,000
Total cost per motor casting	$20	$100,000

A supplier has offered to provide the motor casting at a price of $16.50; the firm estimates that costs of ordering, receiving, and inspecting each part will be $1.50. The key to the decision lies in the examination of those costs that will change between the alternatives. Assuming that the productive capacity will be idle if not used to manufacture the part, the incremental analysis is as follows.

	Per Unit		**Total of 5,000 Units**	
	Make	*Buy*	*Make*	*Buy*
Direct material	$ 5	—	$25,000	—
Direct labor	8	—	40,000	—
Variable overhead	4	—	20,000	—
Purchase price plus ordering, receiving, and inspection costs	—	$18	—	$90,000
Total relevant costs	$17	$18	$85,000	$90,000

In this case the company should make the product rather than purchase it from the supplier. The variable costs to produce the part are $17; the purchase costs are $18. The fixed overhead is not relevant to the decision.

Let's carry the illustration one step further. Assume that management can choose to make the motor casting or buy it from the supplier, using the excess capacity to make 5,000 pump housings. Cost and revenue estimates for the pump housing follow.

Pump Housing		
Selling price		$ 25.00
Direct material	$ 8.00	
Direct labor	10.00	
Variable overhead	4.00	
Fixed overhead		
(37.5% of direct labor cost)	3.75	
Total costs		25.75
Net loss per unit		$(.75)

At first glance it would seem unprofitable to produce the pump housing; total costs exceed total revenue by $.75 per unit. Closer examination shows that the variable costs per unit of producing the pump housing are $22 ($8 + $10 + $4), and the contribution margin per unit is $3.00 ($25 − $22). If the motor castings are sold for $26, the total contribution margin for producing and selling motor castings will be $45,000 [($26 − $17) × 5,000 units]. However, if motor castings are purchased and the pump housing produced, the total contribution margin will increase to $55,000.

	Motor Castings		*Pump Housings*		*Total*
Sales	$26	$130,000	$25	$125,000	$255,000
Variable costs	18	90,000	22	110,000	200,000
Contribution margin	$ 8	$ 40,000	$ 3	$ 15,000	$ 55,000

Management's optimum decision would be to produce the pump housing and buy the motor casting. The fixed costs of the factory are not relevant to the make-or-buy decision, although they must be covered before the firm makes a profit.

The previous discussion assumed that the firm did not need additional plant facilities to produce the unit. If the plant had to be enlarged or new equipment purchased, the firm would need to make a long-range capacity decision. The savings from producing the part would have to be compared to the additional investment to ensure an adequate rate of return on the investment. In this situation the make-or-buy alternatives would be an integral input to the capital investment decision shown in Chapters 14 and 15.

As a final example of a make-or-buy decision, suppose that a firm uses a specifically machined gear in its final product. The manager can manufacture the gear or buy it from an outside supplier for $10 each. To manufacture the gear he would incur variable costs of $5.00 per unit, but he would have additional relevant fixed costs specifically identified with the manufacture of the gears of $20,000 per year. Exhibit 12–2 shows that the firm should buy the part if volume is under 4,000 gears per year, but should make the gear if volume is over 4,000 gears per year.

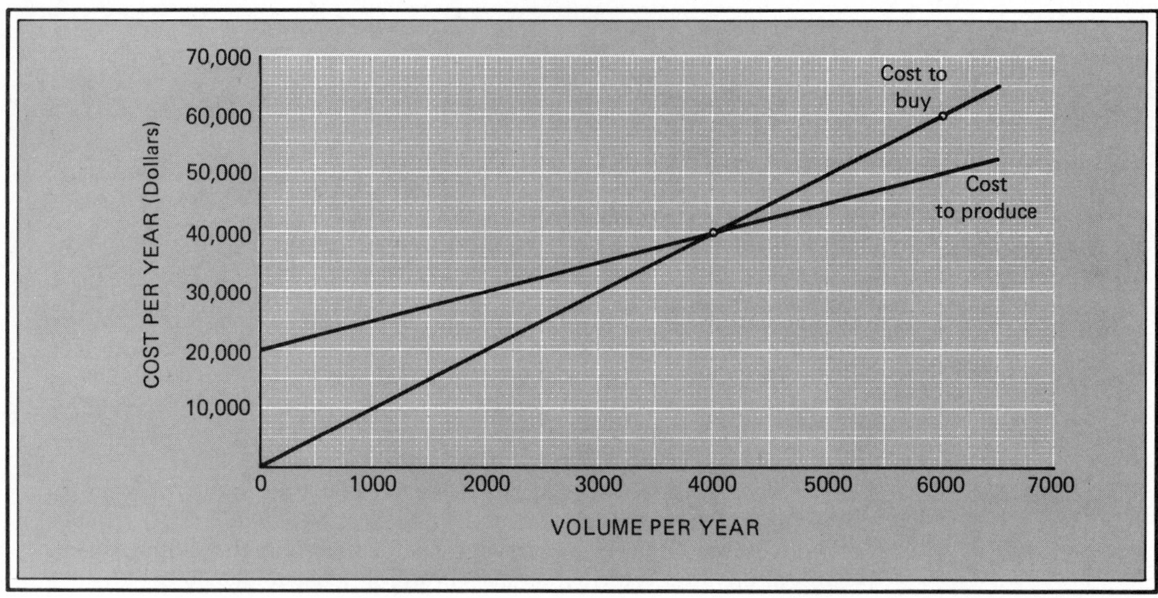

EXHIBIT 12–2
Make-or-buy decisions

Dropping a Product Line

Assume that the Wagner Company manufactures and sells three products: G, H, and I. Income statements for the three products and for the total firm are shown in Exhibit 12–3. Management is considering dropping Product G because it is apparently not contributing to the income of the firm. Recasting the product income statements into a contribution margin format allows us to examine the products according to their respective incremental contribution margins. As shown in the recasted income statements in Exhibit 12–4, the joint costs are common to all products and hence are irrelevant to the decision.

From Exhibit 12–4 the role of the three products in contributing to net income is clearer. Product G has a positive contribution margin to help cover the joint costs, although it is not as large as the contribution margins of the other two products. If Product G were discontinued, the net income would decline.

A customer offered to purchase 2,000 units of Product J at $30 per unit if the Wagner Company would produce them. To produce Product J, the variable costs are estimated at $24,000; the fixed costs specifically identifiable with Product J are $20,000. Because the plant has no idle capacity, one of the existing products would have to be dropped. Would this be profitable? Let's look at the product margin of Product J.

THE WAGNER COMPANY
INCOME STATEMENT
For the Year Ended December 31, 19X7

	Product G	Product H	Product I	Total
Sales	$100,000	$300,000	$200,000	$600,000
Variable costs	60,000	210,000	150,000	420,000
Contribution margin	$ 40,000	$ 90,000	$ 50,000	$180,000
Fixed costs:				
Identifiable to products	$ 30,000	$ 30,000	$ 20,000	$ 80,000
Joint costs allocated on sales basis	10,000	30,000	20,000	60,000
Total fixed costs	40,000	60,000	40,000	140,000
Net income	$ 0	$ 30,000	$ 10,000	$ 40,000

EXHIBIT 12–3
Income statements by product line with apportioned joint costs

THE WAGNER COMPANY
INCOME STATEMENT
For the Year Ended December 31, 19X7

	Product G	Product H	Product I	Total
Sales	$100,000	$300,000	$200,000	$600,000
Variable costs	60,000	210,000	150,000	420,000
Contribution margin	$ 40,000	$ 90,000	$ 50,000	$180,000
Fixed costs identifiable to products	30,000	30,000	20,000	80,000
Product margin	$ 10,000	$ 60,000	$ 30,000	$100,000
Joint costs				60,000
Net Income				$ 40,000

EXHIBIT 12–4
Income statements by product line

Sales (2,000 × $30)	$60,000
Variable costs (2,000 × $12)	24,000
Contribution margin (2,000 × $18)	$36,000
Identifiable fixed costs	20,000
Product margin before joint costs	$16,000

If Product J can be produced in the void left by dropping Product G, it would be economically sound to do so. If, on the other hand, the production of Product J would require the productive time, space, and energy devoted to either Product H or Product I, it would be an unwise choice.

Suppose that management was considering producing one-third more of Product H instead of accepting the offer to produce Product J. The productive facilities used for Product G could be used for this increase. The identifiable fixed costs currently associated with Product G would be associated with the additional units of Product H. The product margin of the incremental quantity of Product H follows.

Sales	$100,000
Variable costs	70,000
Contribution margin	$ 30,000
Identifiable joint costs	30,000
Product margin before joint costs	$ 0

Given these three alternatives, the decision hierarchy should be to produce Product J and, if this is not possible, to produce Product G. Producing an additional one-third of Product H would not be profitable.

Manufacturing the Optimum Product Combination

In assessing production decisions, management must decide how best to allocate the firm's limited production resources. If facilities are not limited, management can produce all it wants of any product. In previous examples we have assumed that the firm was not fully utilizing its productive facilities. With this assumption of idle capacity we were not faced with resource limitations. However, all resources are limited in some way. The maximum amount of resources that can be committed to production is a restriction or **constraint.**

TWO OR MORE PRODUCTS WITH ONLY ONE CONSTRAINT

Assume that a company produces two products, K and L, with the following contribution margins per unit.

	Product K		Product L	
Sales	$6.00	100%	$20.00	100%
Variable costs	4.00	67%	16.00	80%
Contribution margin	$2.00	33%	$ 4.00	20%

The annual fixed costs of production are $36,000, which remain unchanged regardless of the combination of products produced. If there are no production constraints, the product with the highest contribution margin per unit should be produced until demand is satisfied. In our illustration the firm should emphasize Product L, which has a contribution margin per unit of $4.00. When there are no market or production limitations, the decision rule can be stated simply: "Choose the product with the highest contribution margin per unit until the demand is satisfied; then choose the product with the next highest contribution margin per unit." This decision will maximize net income.

Where demand for the product is greater than the production capabilities of the firm, and the production is subject to a single constraint, the firm should maximize the total contribution margin per unit subject to the single production constraint. To illustrate, let's assume that the firm has a production constraint of 100,000 machine hours; the machine capacity is the scarce resource. Further, assume that Product K requires two machine hours to produce and Product L requires five machine hours. One way to express this constraint is to determine the contribution margin per machine hour.

	Product K	Product L
Selling price	$6.00	$20.00
Variable costs	4.00	16.00
Contribution margin	$2.00	$ 4.00
Divided by machine hours required per unit	2	5
Contribution margin per machine hour	$1.00	$ .80

Since Product K returns the highest contribution margin per machine hour, it is the preferred product. The firm should limit its production to Product K as long as the market demand and cost structure are unchanged. There is no advantage in selling Product L instead of Product K.

Another way to view the same data is to prepare comparative income statements assuming that only one product is produced, as shown in Exhibit 12–5. This solution is simple because there is only one constraint that affects both products. In the next section we will examine more complex situations.

	Product K	*Product L*
Sales:		
Product K (50,000 × $6)	$300,000	
Product L (20,000 × $20)		$400,000
Variable costs:		
Product K (50,000 × $4)	200,000	
Product L (20,000 × $16)		320,000
Contribution margin:		
Product K (50,000 × $2)	$100,000	
Product L (20,000 × $4)		$ 80,000
Fixed costs	36,000	36,000
Net income	$ 64,000	$ 44,000

EXHIBIT 12–5
Comparative product income statements

TWO OR MORE PRODUCTS AND TWO OR MORE CONSTRAINTS

A mathematical technique called **linear programming** provides a solution to the problem where there are limited resources and two or more products and/or constraints. Let's assume that the George Sank Company manufactures two styles of lamps: a table lamp and a floor lamp. There are two departments, each with production limitations. Management is considering the use of linear programming to determine the optimum quantity of each product to produce.

A number of requirements must be met if the George Sank Company is to use linear programming appropriately. First, there must be limited resources. For example, the number of machine hours or employee workbenches might be limited. The greater the number of hours spent to manufacture floor lamps, the smaller the number of hours that will be available to make table lamps. Second, alternative courses of action must be available. The production facilities and the market demand must be flexible enough to allow different outputs of floor and table lamps. Third, there must be an objective that the firm is striving to achieve. The most commonly stated objective is to maximize dollar profits. For linear programming the dollar profit is stated as the contribution margin per unit because the total contribution margin is linear to sales volume. Fourth, the variables in the model must be interrelated. Total profit, for example, must reflect profit from the table lamps plus profit from the floor lamps. Finally, the firm's objectives and limitations or constraints must be expressible as linear mathematical equations or inequalities. For example, the firm's dollar contribution margin, stated in linear equation form, would be:

$$\text{Firm's contribution margin} = \begin{bmatrix}\text{Contribution margin per floor lamp} \times \text{Number of floor lamps}\end{bmatrix} + \begin{bmatrix}\text{Contribution margin per table lamp} \times \text{Number of table lamps}\end{bmatrix}$$

To develop the theory of linear programming, let's assume the following cost and production estimates.

Department	Hours Required to Make 1 Unit		Total Production Hours Available
	Floor Lamp	*Table Lamp*	
A	3	4	72
B	6	2	66
Contribution margin per unit	$12	$8	

From this data we can see that to manufacture a floor lamp takes 3 hours in Department A and 6 hours in Department B, for a total of 9 hours. The table lamp requires 4 hours in Department A and 2 hours in Department B, for a total of 6 hours. Department A has a maximum production capability (constraint) of 72 hours; Department B has a constraint of 66 hours. The decision maker must determine the best possible combination of floor and table lamps to realize the maximum total contribution margin, assuming that the contribution margin is $12 for the floor lamp and $8 for the table lamp.

GRAPHIC SOLUTION

In this section we will show a graphic solution.

Step 1. Restate the data in mathematical form. We will use the symbol Q_1 to represent the optimum number of floor lamps and Q_2 to represent the optimum number of table lamps. If P is the maximized contribution margin, the **objective function** that relates output to profit is:

$$P = \$12(Q_1) + \$8(Q_2)$$

The incremental profit of one floor lamp is $12, measured by the contribution margin; the total profit from floor lamps will be $12 times the number produced and sold (Q_1).

The time available to produce the lamps is a production constraint. Certainly, the time used to make the two products cannot exceed the total time available in each of the two departments. The hours available to make one floor lamp times the number of floor lamps produced, plus the hours to make one table lamp times the number of table lamps produced, must be equal to or less than the time available in each department. Expressed mathematically:

$3(Q_1) + 4(Q_2) \leq 72$ for Department A
$6(Q_1) + 2(Q_2) \leq 66$ for Department B

The sign $\leq$ in this inequality statement means *is less than or equal to.* The first statement shows that the hours required in Department A to produce one floor lamp (3) times the number of floor lamps made (Q_1), plus the number of hours needed to make one table lamp (4) times the number of table lamps made (Q_2), must be equal to or less than the total of 72 hours available. These inequalities are capacity constraints on output and, hence, on profits.

If the answers are to be meaningful, they must be positive. It is not conceptually possible to "unmake" a lamp. Thus, all variables in the linear programming model must be equal to or greater than zero. This can be expressed mathematically:

$Q_1 \geq 0$ and $Q_2 \geq 0$

The symbol $\geq$ means *greater than or equal to.* Thus, the solution must be where the values of Q_1 and Q_2 are positive.

The mathematical expressions can now be summarized.

Maximize $P = \$12(Q_1) + \$8(Q_2)$
subject to the constraints of:

$$3(Q_1) + 4(Q_2) \leq 72$$
$$6(Q_1) + 2(Q_2) \leq 66$$
$$Q_1 \geq 0$$
$$Q_2 \geq 0$$

Step 2. Plot the constraints on a graph such as the one shown in Exhibit 12–6. The number of units of Product Q_1 is shown on the x axis and the number of units of Product Q_2 is shown on the y axis. The inequality $3(Q_1) + 4(Q_2) \leq 72$ was plotted by locating the two terminal points, setting Q_1 and then Q_2 equal to zero, and then joining them by a straight line. These terminal points were determined by the following equations.

If all the capacity available were used to make only Product Q_1:

$$3(Q_1) + 4(0) \leq 72$$
$$Q_1 \leq 24$$ (Maximum number of floor lamps the department could produce)

If all the capacity available were used to make only Product Q_2:

$$3(0) + 4(Q_2) \leq 72$$
$$Q_2 \leq 18$$ (Maximum number of table lamps the department could produce)

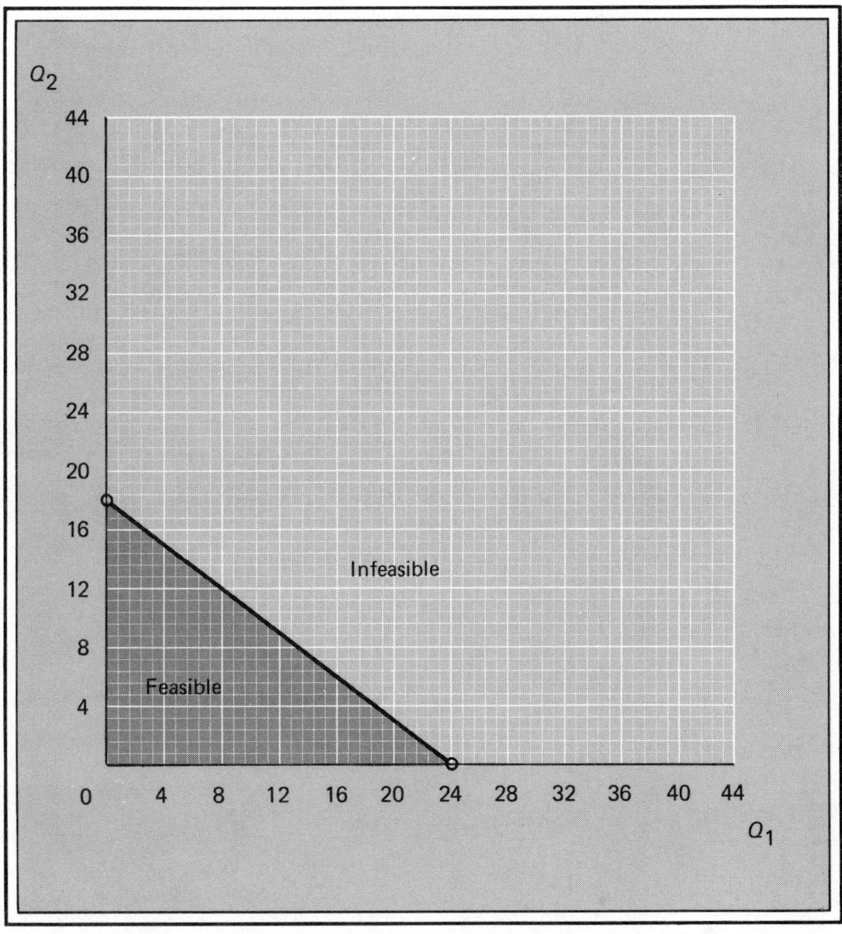

EXHIBIT 12–6
Graphic plot of Department A constraints

On Exhibit 12–6 the first point is where Q_1 is 24 and Q_2 is zero. The second point is where Q_1 is zero and Q_2 is 18. These points were then joined by a straight line. The dark area under the line represents feasible combinations of different production outputs. For example, it is feasible to produce the following combinations from the many possibilities.

$$12(Q_1) + 9(Q_2) = 72 \text{ hours}$$
$$3(Q_1) + 12(Q_2) = 57 \text{ hours}$$
$$17(Q_1) + 4(Q_2) = 67 \text{ hours}$$

Step 3. Plot the constraints for the second department with the same procedures used in Step 2. The plot is shown in Exhibit 12–7. The terminal points are:

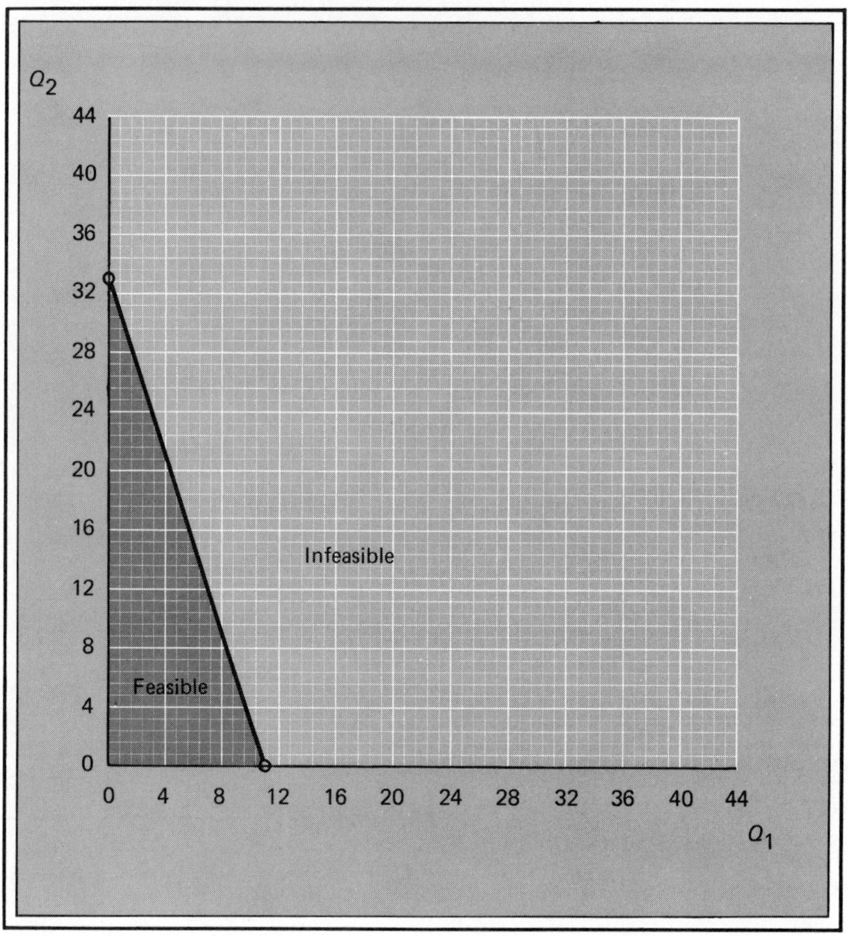

EXHIBIT 12–7
Graphic plot of Department B constraints

$$6(Q_1) + 2(0) = 66 \text{ hours}$$
$$Q_1 = 11 \text{ floor lamps}$$
$$6(0) + 2(Q_2) = 66 \text{ hours}$$
$$Q_2 = 33 \text{ table lamps}$$

Step 4. Combine the two graphs determined in Steps 2 and 3 to show the feasible alternatives for the whole plant. The two inequalities are plotted in Exhibit 12–8. The dark area, included within the points *A-B-C-D*, contains

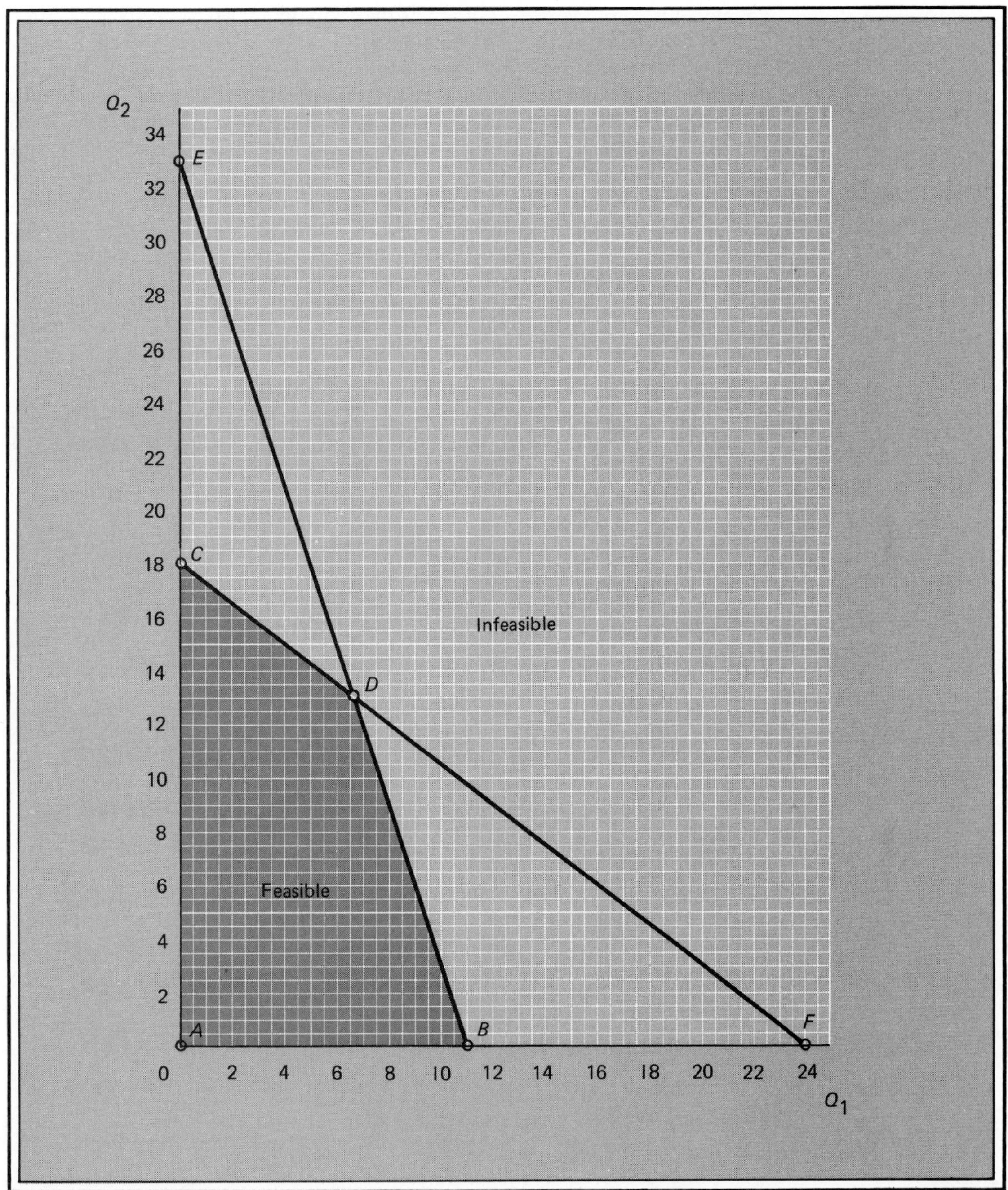

EXHIBIT 12–8
Graphic plot of Departments A and B constraints

all possible combinations of products that satisfy the two original inequalities.

Reading the graph in Exhibit 12–8 for point D we can see that the quantity at point D is 6 floor lamps (Q_1) and 13 table lamps (Q_2). Actually, point D falls somewhat beyond 6 floor lamps and short of 7. We are assuming that the firm wants to produce only completed lamps; it should produce 6. At point D the combination of floor and table lamps does not use all the time available in each department.

Steps 1 through 4 have defined the technical constraints of the plant.

Step 5. Determine the particular combination of products that will maximize total profits. The profit function, previously defined, was:

$$P = \$12(Q_1) + \$8(Q_2)$$

It is a theorem in linear programming that the objective function will be maximized at at least one corner of the feasible region. Therefore, it is necessary to search only the corners for the optimal solution. With the objective function the total contribution margin (P) at points A, B, C, and D would be:

$$
\begin{aligned}
P_A \quad (0,0) &= \$12(0) + \$8(0) = \$0 \\
P_B \quad (11,0) &= \$12(11) + \$8(0) = \$132 \\
P_C \quad (0,18) &= \$12(0) + \$8(18) = \$144 \\
P_D \quad (6,13) &= \$12(6) + \$8(13) = \$176
\end{aligned}
$$

The greatest contribution margin is found at point D.

To further explore the impact of the objective function, let's assume that the objective function, because of changes in demand, becomes:

$$P = \$12(Q_1) + \$3(Q_2)$$

The total contribution margin at each point becomes:

$$
\begin{aligned}
P_A \quad (0,0) &= \$12(0) + \$3(0) = \$0 \\
P_B \quad (11,0) &= \$12(11) + \$3(0) = \$132 \\
P_C \quad (0,18) &= \$12(0) + \$3(18) = \$54 \\
P_D \quad (6,13) &= \$12(6) + \$3(13) = \$111
\end{aligned}
$$

In this case the greatest contribution margin is found at point B. The maximum profit line can be found by calculating the profit for each particular combination of products. Then, the feasible point that yields the highest profit is the optimum choice.

MORE COMPLEX SOLUTIONS

In most firms there are more than two products, several departments, and many constraints. Visualize a company with 15 products manufactured in various combinations through 20 departments. The graphic method would be completely inadequate. A procedure widely used in these complex cases is the **simplex method.** Using matrix algebra, the simplex method works toward the optimal solution by repeating the computational routine over and over until the best solution is reached. A study of the simplex method is far beyond the scope of this book, although the informed decision maker should know that a solution method is available for multiproduct and multiconstraint situations.

SUMMARY

The accountant has a role to play in management's production decisions by providing data on relevant costs. Relevant costs are future costs—estimates of what the decision maker believes *will* happen. They are also differential costs. To be relevant, a future cost must differ among alternatives. For this reason, many fixed costs are not relevant to production decisions. All historical costs are nonrelevant. Joint costs are also nonrelevant for all decisions subsequent to their incurrence.

The contribution margin plays a vital role in short-range production decisions as an estimate of incremental future revenue. To obtain the maximum profit from an existing plant, the decision should be to maximize the total contribution margin of the firm. All decisions on whether to make or buy a component part, to add or drop a product, or to sell a product or process it further hinge upon an analysis of differential contribution margins.

Where there are multiproduct and plant production constraints, linear programming facilitates choosing an optimum product mix. It recognizes the constraints of the departments to determine which outputs are feasible. The objective function, to maximize the product contribution margins, enables management to select the product mix that will maximize total contribution margin.

SUPPLEMENTARY READING

Doney, Lloyd D. "Coping with Uncertainty in the Make or Buy Decision." *Management Accounting,* October, 1968.

Harris, William T., Jr., and Wayne R. Chapin. "Joint Product Costing." *Management Accounting,* April, 1973.

Jaedicke, Robert K. "Some Notes on Product Combination Decisions." *The Accounting Review,* October, 1958.

National Association of Accountants. *Costing Joint Products.* New York: National Association of Accountants, 1957.

National Association of Accountants. *Analysis of Manufacturing Cost Variances.* New York: National Association of Accountants, 1952.

Palmer, B. Thomas. "Management Reports for Multiproduct Plants." *Management Accounting,* August, 1970.

Rinehard, Jack R. "Economic Purchase Quantity Calculations." *Management Accounting,* September, 1970.

Schuba, Kenneth E. "Make-or-Buy Decisions—Cost and Non-Cost Considerations." *N.A.A. Bulletin,* March, 1960.

QUESTIONS

12-1 Discuss the concept of *differentiality* in determining the relevance of benefits and costs for decision making.

12-2 "It is potentially misleading to examine fixed costs on a per-unit basis." Do you agree or disagree? Defend your position.

12-3 "Unit costs determined through the allocation of joint costs are applicable to inventory costing but are not useful for decision making." Do you agree or disagree? Explain.

12-4 "The method chosen to allocate joint costs to individual products can change the net profit of the firm." Do you agree or disagree? Explain.

12-5 Define *contribution margin* and *product margin* and indicate the difference in the concepts.

12-6 Identify the benefits and costs relevant to the short-run decisions of (a) adding a new product, and (b) dropping a product.

12-7 Why might management decide to produce a product internally at a higher cost than to buy the same product in the open market? Give some possible examples.

12-8 A number of requirements must be met before linear programming can be used appropriately. List these requirements and explain the importance of each.

12-9 Explain the role of the objective function in linear programming. How is the objective function usually measured?

12-10 Define the term *opportunity cost.* Is contribution margin a valid measure of opportunity cost? Is net income by product a valid measure of opportunity cost? Explain.

EXERCISES

12-11 *(True of False).* Indicate whether the following statements are *true* or *false.*

1. The product margin is best measured by allocating all fixed costs to the product lines.
2. Only future costs that differ between alternatives are relevant to decisions.
3. The opportunity cost is best measured by sales revenue less fixed costs.
4. Fixed costs, since they do not change with production decisions, can *never* be relevant.
5. Joint costs can be directly traced to individual products.
6. Where the decision is to hold production facilities constant and to increase or decrease production output, variable costs are not relevant.
7. A widely used basis for joint cost allocations where products differ widely is the relative sales-value basis.
8. The principal reason for allocating joint costs is to enhance management's ability to make decisions.
9. A product should be processed further only if the net income from the product is increased.
10. The contribution margin per unit serves as the measure of the opportunity cost in objective functions used in linear programming.

12-12 *(Identification of Opportunity and Relevant Costs).* List some of the opportunity costs and the relevant costs associated with the following situations.

1. Continuing your education by working toward a graduate degree or taking your bachelor's degree and going to work.
2. Changing your field of study in your junior year from premedicine to prelaw.
3. Purchasing a scientific-business calculator for $200 or purchasing an inexpensive $20 four-function calculator.
4. Taking a part-time job at $3.50 per hour near your home, as opposed to taking a part-time job that pays $4.00 per hour and is one-half hour travel time from your home.
5. Quitting your present salaried position and starting your own business or maintaining your current job.
6. Depositing a $1,000 gift in a savings and loan institution or investing it in a government savings bond.
7. Going to the mountains for a weekend of skiing or staying home and studying.

8. Developing your film in your own darkroom or having it processed by a commercial developer.

9. Hiring only college graduates or hiring only high school graduates in your office.

10. Using a $1,000 gift to buy a car or using it to buy a new stereo system.

12-13 *(Sell or Modify Obsolete Product).* The Good Buddy Electronics Company produces a line of electronic products including a citizen band radio sold at $125 under the brand name Good Buddy. When the Federal Communication Commission banned the sale of 23-channel citizen band radios, the company had 12,000 23-band units in its inventory and sufficient components parts on hand to produce another 10,000. These components parts have no use in other company products and a maximum market price of $15 each. The standard cost per unit includes the following costs:

Component parts	$ 60
Direct labor	15
Variable overhead	10
Fixed overhead	5
Variable selling	10
	$100

An electronics wholesaler has offered to purchase the 12,000 units at $50 each. On the other hand, the Good Buddy Company can modify the 23-band units to 40-band units at the cost of $34 each. The modified units could then be sold for $100 each.

REQUIRED:

A. What should the company do with the 23-band units on hand?
B. What should the company do with the component parts?

12-14 *(Differential Costs of Automobile).* Heide Nelson is a sales representative for the Silver Spoon Company. She is considering expanding her sales territory to two new towns. The following record shows last year's automobile expenses for traveling 40,000 miles.

Gasoline	$1,600
Oil and lubrication	300
Parking and toll fees	500
Tires (1 set per 40,000 miles)	250
Insurance	300
Licenses and taxes	150
Tune-ups, maintenance, and repairs	550
Depreciation based upon straight-line depreciation	1,500
Total costs	$5,150

If Heide includes the two new towns, she will have to travel an additional 5,000 miles per year.

REQUIRED:

A. Indicate which of these costs are likely to be fixed and which are likely to be variable.
B. Which costs are relevant to her decision to expand the sales territory?
C. Prepare a schedule showing the estimated differential costs between traveling the old territory and the new one.
D. Discuss any nonfinancial factors Heide should consider.

12-15 *(Dropping a Department).* One of the goals of the Tenino General Hospital is to be financially self-sufficient. During the past two fiscal years the hospital has incurred operating losses. The hospital's controller has proposed two possible expense reductions listed below.

Part A.
The Tenino General Hospital currently employs its own janitorial staff, which incurs the following costs per year.

Labor	$100,000
Supplies	40,000
Overhead	130,000
	$270,000

The hospital employees are asking for a 25% wage increase and it appears that an increase of at least 20% will be necessary. An outside contractor has approached the hospital and offered a three-year contract to do the job for $200,000 per year. Overhead includes depreciation of $20,000, allocated administrative and other fixed costs of $100,000, and variable indirect costs of $10,000.

REQUIRED:

A. Should the Tenino General Hospital accept the offer? Show your analysis.
B. If a 25% wage increase is granted to the hospital employees, what is the highest contract price the hospital could pay the outside contractor without increasing total hospital costs? Explain fully.

Part B.
The hospital performs a certain lab test with the following average costs per test.

Lab technician	$1.50
Supplies	1.00
Overhead	2.50
	$5.00

An outside lab has offered to do the tests for $3.00 each. If the center accepts the offer, it will release the appropriate technician and sell the lab equipment at its book value. Lab overhead is composed of depreciation of lab equipment calculated on a straight-line basis, an apportioned share of administrative costs, and variable overhead equal to 50% of the salary of the lab technician.

REQUIRED:
Prepare an analysis to show whether the center should do the test itself or accept the offer.

12-16 *(Decisions Based upon Linear Programming)*. The Marlan Metal Products Company has just established a department for the production of two new products—metal trays and storage devices. This department is ready to begin operations with five metal-forming machines and five metal-cutting machines which have been rented for $300 each per month from a local machine company. Both products require production time on both machines. Each of the machines is capable of 400 hours of production per month. No additional machines can be obtained.

	Machine hrs. per unit		
	Trays	*Storage devices*	*Total available machine hrs./mo.*
Metal-cutting machines	1	2	2,000
Metal-forming machines	2	2	2,000

The controller's department has summarized expected costs and revenues as follows:

	Trays	*Storage devices*
Selling price per unit	$18.00	$27.00
Variable cost per unit	14.00	20.00

Demand for the storage devices is unlimited but Marlan believes that no more than 800 units of the trays can be sold per month.

The following linear programming formulation and accompanying graph represent the facts described above. Marlan must operate within the specified constraints as it tries to maximize the contribution margin from this new operation. Marlan intends to operate at the optimal level, which it has determined to be the point labeled "OP" on the graph below.

Linear Programming Formulation

$$\begin{aligned}
&\text{Maximize } Z = \$4T + \$7S \\
&\text{subject to:} \\
&\qquad T + 2S \leq 2{,}000 \\
&\qquad 2T + 2S \leq 2{,}000 \\
&\qquad T \leq 800 \\
&\qquad T,S \geq 0
\end{aligned}$$

where:
T = number of units of trays produced
S = number of units of storage devices produced
Z = contribution margin

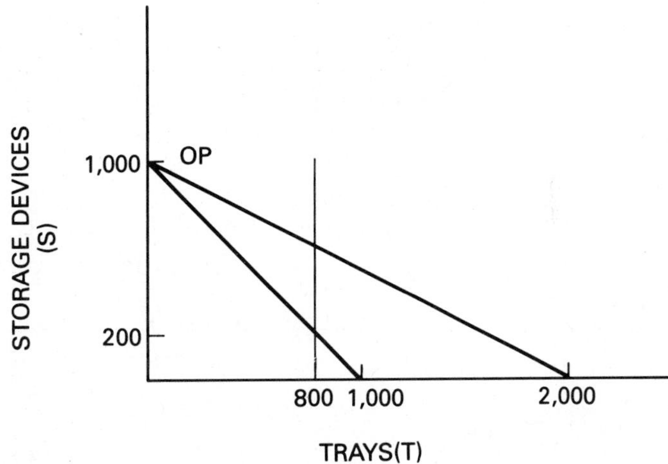

REQUIRED:

Answer the following independent cases. Show your work.

1. If the selling price of storage devices is lowered from \$27 to \$23, the maximum total contribution margin Marlan could earn would
   a. decrease by \$3,800.
   b. decrease by \$4,000.
   c. increase by \$4,000.
   d. decrease by \$3,200.
   e. not be expected to change.

2. The maximum amount Marlan should be willing to spend on advertising in order to increase the demand for trays to 1,000 units per month would be
   a. \$0.
   b. \$600.
   c. \$1,400.
   d. \$5,400.
   e. \$7,000.

3. If one metal-forming machine is returned to the rental agency and the rent can be avoided on the returned machine, Marlan's total profit would
   a. be unaffected.
   b. increase by $300.
   c. decrease by $1,100.
   d. decrease by $1,400.
   e. decrease by $4,300.

4. Marlan has just realized that a material needed for the production of both products is in short supply. The company can obtain enough of this material to produce 1,200 trays. Each tray requires ⅔ as much of this material as the storage devices. Which of the following constraints will incorporate completely and correctly this additional information into the formulation of the problem?
   a. $T \leq 1{,}200$
   b. $\frac{2}{3}S \leq 1{,}200$
   c. $T + \frac{2}{3}S \leq 1{,}200$
   d. $\frac{2}{3}T + 1S \leq 800$
   e. $T - \frac{3}{2}S = 0$

(CMA adapted)

12-17 *(Graphic Linear Programming).* The Tiny People Company manufactures two styles of little dolls for little people. The following cost, revenue, and production data apply to the manufacture of the dolls.

	Production Time Tiny Tina Doll	*Production Time Wee Willie Doll*	*Capacity in Machine Hours*
Molding department	6	4	60
Assembly department	4	2	40

REQUIRED:

A. State the production constraints in algebraic form.
B. Show graphically the production constraints and the feasible region of production.
C. What production output would you recommend to management if the contribution margin of Tiny Tina is $4.00 and of Wee Willie, $6.00?

12-18 *(Expansion of Capacity).* Salmon Sue has just completed a successful fishing season as a part of the salmon fleet off the coast of Alaska. Because of a 20% increase in the price the cannery will pay for salmon next season, she is considering the purchase of a second boat. Salmon Sue believes that she could decrease the time spent fishing by 40% with the use of two boats and still catch 80% of the original amount of fish in each boat.

Revenue from the 19X1 season catch was $80,000. Costs for the past season were:

Diesel fuel	$ 6,000
Crew wages and bonus	28,000
Maintenance	4,500
Depreciation	6,000
Insurance	1,500
Fishing permits	1,000
	$47,000

Diesel fuel and crew wages are the only variable costs. In addition to her crew's wages, Sue pays her crew 20% of the season's revenue as a part of their compensation. Next year diesel fuel can be expected to increase by 25% and the State of Alaska will double the price of fishing permits. The new boat will cost $120,000 and have an estimated useful life of 10 years with no residual value.

REQUIRED:

A. What are the relevant costs that Salmon Sue should consider?

B. What would be the differences in net income for the next fishing season between (1) using only the original boat, and (2) using two boats at 60% of the time spent in 19X1. Support your answers with comparative profit plans.

12-19 *(Make-or-Buy Decision).* Management of the Road Runner Company has asked your assistance in arriving at a decision to continue manufacturing a part or buy it from an outside supplier. The part, Faktron, is a component used in some of the finished goods of the company. The following data are typical of the company's operations.

1. The annual requirement for Faktrons is 6,000 units. The lowest quotation from a supplier was $8.00 per unit.

2. Faktrons have been manufactured in the precision machinery department. If Faktrons are purchased from an outside supplier, certain machinery will be sold and would realize its book value.

3. Following are the total costs of the precision machinery department during the year when 6,000 Faktrons were made.

Materials	$67,500
Direct labor	$50,000
Indirect labor	$20,000
Light and heat	$ 5,500
Power	$ 3,000
Depreciation	$10,000
Property taxes and insurance	$ 8,000
Payroll taxes and other benefits	$ 9,800
Other	$ 5,000

4. The following precision machinery department costs apply to the manufacture of Faktrons: material, $17,500; direct labor, $28,000; indirect labor, $6,000; power, $300; other, $500. The sale of the equipment used for Faktrons would reduce depreciation by $2,000 and property taxes and insurance by $1,000.

6. The following additional precision machinery department costs would be incurred if Faktrons were purchased from an outside supplier: freight, $.50 per unit; indirect labor for receiving, materials handling, inspection, etc., $5,000. The cost of the purchased Faktrons would be considered a precision machinery department cost.

REQUIRED:

A. Prepare a schedule showing a comparison of the total costs of the precision machinery department (1) when Faktrons are made, and (2) when Faktrons are bought from an outside supplier.

B. Discuss the considerations in addition to the cost factors that you would bring to the attention of management in assisting them to arrive at a decision whether to make or buy Faktrons. Include in your discussion the considerations that might be applied to the evaluation of the outside supplier.

(CPA adapted)

12-20 *(Sell or Process Further).* Builders Lumber Company produces 2 × 2s, 2 × 4s, and 4 × 4s from logs in a milling process. Normal capacity of the mill is 10 million board feet, which requires an input of $1,200,000 of timber. Total operating costs for labor and overhead in the milling process are $375,000 per year. After milling, the products may be processed further with all products going through a drying process, where additional costs of production are $75,000. Finally, the 2 × 2s may be processed into decorative spindles in a turning process. The costs of operating the turning process are $150,000. Revenue and production data are:

	2 × 2s	*2 × 4s*	*4 × 4s*
Selling price after milling (per 1,000 board feet)	$140	$200	$230
Selling price after drying (per 1,000 board feet)	$160	$210	$250
Selling price after turning (per 1,000 board feet)	$220		
Normal production (in 1,000 board feet)	2,000	5,000	3,000

REQUIRED:

A. Prepare a schedule that highlights the effects of the possible alternatives. Your schedule should show estimated contribution margins and net incomes.

B. What actions would you recommend to management?

12-21 *(Make-or-Buy Decision with Constraints).* The following costs and other data apply to two component parts used by Excel Electronics.

	Part A	*Part B*
Direct material	$ .40	$ 8.00
Direct labor	1.00	4.70
Overhead	4.00	2.00
Unit cost	$5.40	$14.70
Units needed per year	6,000	8,000
Machine hours per unit	4	2
Unit cost if purchased	$5.00	$15.00

In the past years, Excel has manufactured all its required components. However, in 19X2 only 28,000 hours of otherwise idle machine time can be devoted to the production of components. Accordingly, some of the parts must be purchased from outside suppliers. In producing parts, overhead is applied at $1.00 per machine hour. Fixed capacity costs, which will not be affected by any make-or-buy decision, represent 70% of the applied overhead.

REQUIRED:

A. Assuming that the 28,000 hours of available machine time are to be scheduled so that Excel realizes maximum potential cost savings, determine the relevant production costs that should be considered in the decision to schedule machine time.

B. Compute the number of units that Excel should produce if it allocates the machine time on the basis of the potential cost savings per machine hour.

(CPA adapted)

12-22 *(Linear Programming).* The Shortbranch Company manufactures two products in two departments. It estimates that the following production and cost data are relevant for the coming year.

	Product G	*Product H*	*Available Machine Hours per Week*
Department A	2 hours	4 hours	48 hours
Department B	5 hours	3 hours	60 hours
Contribution margin per unit	$10	$24	

REQUIRED:

A. Summarize the data above with mathematical equations.

B. Solve for the optimum production quantity of each product, using the graphic method.

12-23 *(Sell or Process Further Decision).* From a particular joint process, McCormick Company produces three products: X, Y, and Z. Each product may be sold at the point of split-off or processed further. Additional processing requires no special facilities, and production costs of further processing are entirely variable and traceable to the products involved. In 19X3 all three products were processed beyond split-off. Joint production costs for the year were $60,000. Sales values and costs needed to evaluate McCormick's 19X3 production policy follow.

			Additional Costs and Sales Values if Processed Further	
Product	*Units Produced*	*Sales Values at Split-Off*	*Sales Values*	*Added Cost*
X	6,000	$25,000	$32,000	$9,000
Y	4,000	$41,000	$45,000	$7,000
Z	2,000	$24,000	$42,000	$8,000

Joint costs are allocated to the products in proportion to the relative physical volume of output for income statement purposes.

REQUIRED:

A. Prepare a production schedule that will maximize firm profits.
B. Prepare a profit plan at the maximum profit level.
C. Do you agree with the method chosen for allocating joint costs to the inventory? Why or why not? *(CPA adapted)*

12-24 *(Drop or Replace a Product).* The Frigideze Refrigeration Company produces three types of refrigerated display cases: 30′ chill, 20′ frozen, and 30′ frozen. The following income statement for 19X1 shows profit by product.

REQUIRED:

A. The president of Frigideze was disappointed with the 30′ chill unit during 19X1. He believes that the 30′ chill unit should be dropped. Prepare a recommendation for the president supported with appropriate analysis.
B. The company is operating near capacity. Product engineering has proposed a new walk-in chill unit with estimated sales of $600,000, a contribution margin ratio of 26%, and identifiable fixed costs of $72,000, which include the $30,000 now traced to the 30′ chill plus $42,000 new fixed costs. To produce the new walk-in chill unit the 30′ chill unit would have to be eliminated. Prepare a profit plan for 19X2 showing the product margin for each product including the new walk-in chill unit. Should Frigideze produce the new product?

FRIGIDEZE REFRIGERATION COMPANY
INCOME STATEMENT
Year 19X1

	30′ Chill	*20′ Frozen*	*30′ Frozen*	*Total*
Sales	$300,000	$250,000	$350,000	$900,000
Cost of goods sold	280,000	200,000	240,000	720,000
Gross margin	$ 20,000	$ 50,000	$110,000	$180,000
Selling and administrative costs (allocated on sales basis)	45,000	37,500	52,500	135,000
Net income (loss)	$ (25,000)	$ 12,500	$ 57,500	$ 45,000
Contribution margin ratio	30%	40%	50%	
Portion of fixed production costs specifically identifiable with product	$ 30,000	$ 30,000	$ 50,000	$110,000

12-25 *(Make-or-Buy Decision).* The Clean-Air Restaurant Supply Company produces a range of pollution control and fire protection equipment for restaurants.

Part A.

One product is a disposable grease filter. In a normal year the company produces 20,000 filters. Revenues and costs per unit for the disposable filter are:

Revenue		$15.00
Costs:		
Direct materials	$3.00	
Direct labor	3.00	
Variable overhead	1.50	
Fixed overhead	4.50	
Fixed selling and administrative (10% of sales)	1.50	13.50
Net income		$ 1.50

An outside supplier has offered to supply the filter to the Clean-Air Restaurant Supply Company for $10 per unit.

REQUIRED:
Should management accept the offer? Show your analysis.

Part B.

Assume that if the company purchased the filter from the outside supplier, the productive capacity used for strainers could now be used to produce an automatic fire extinguisher. The new product will have the following revenue and cost characteristics:

Revenue		$10.00
Costs:		
Direct materials	$3.80	
Direct labor	1.20	
Variable overhead	1.80	
Fixed overhead (150% of direct labor)	1.80	
Fixed selling and administrative (10% of sales)	1.00	9.60
Net income		$ .40

REQUIRED:
What would be your recommendation to management? Show your conclusion with comparative profit plans.

PROBLEMS

12-26 *(Multiple Choice on Product Decisions).* The officers of Bradshaw Company are reviewing the profitability of the company's four products and the potential effect of several proposals for varying the product mix. An excerpt from the income statement and other data follow.

	Total	*Product P*	*Product Q*	*Product R*	*Product S*
Sales	$62,600	$10,000	$18,000	$12,600	$22,000
Cost of goods sold	44,274	4,750	7,056	13,968	18,500
Gross profit	$18,326	$ 5,250	$10,944	$ (1,368)	$ 3,500
Operating expenses	12,012	1,990	2,976	2,826	4,220
Income before income taxes	$ 6,314	$ 3,260	$ 7,968	$ (4,194)	$ (720)
Units sold		1,000	1,200	1,800	2,000
Sales price per unit		$ 10.00	$ 15.00	$ 7.00	$ 11.00
Variable cost of goods sold per unit		$ 2.50	$ 3.00	$ 6.50	$ 6.00
Variable operating expenses per unit		$ 1.17	$ 1.25	$ 1.00	$ 1.20

REQUIRED:
Each of the following proposals is to be considered independently of the other proposals. Consider only the product changes stated in each proposal; the activity of other products remains stable. Ignore income taxes.

1. If Product R is discontinued, the effect on income will be
   a. $900 increase
   b. $4,194 increase
   c. $12,600 decrease
   d. $1,368 increase
   e. None of the above

2. If Product R is discontinued and a consequent loss of customers causes a decrease of 200 units in sales of Q, the total effect on income will be
   a. $15,600 decrease
   b. $2,866 increase
   c. $2,044 increase
   d. $1,250 decrease
   e. None of the above

3. If the sales price of R is increased to $8.00, with a decrease in the number of units sold to 1,500, the effect on income will be
   a. $2,199 decrease
   b. $600 decrease
   c. $750 increase
   d. $2,199 increase
   e. None of the above

4. The plant in which R is produced can be utilized to produce a new product, T. The total variable costs and expenses per unit of T are $8.05; 1,600 units can be sold at $9.50 each. If T is introduced and R is discontinued, the total effect on income will be
   a. $2,600 increase
   b. $2,320 increase
   c. $3,220 increase
   d. $1,420 increase
   e. None of the above

5. Part of the plant in which P is produced can easily be adapted to the production of S, but changes in quantities may make changes in sales prices advisable. If production of P is reduced to 500 units (to be sold at $12.00 each) and production of S is increased to 2,500 units (to be sold at $10.50 each), the total effect on income will be
   a. $1,765 decrease
   b. $250 increase
   c. $2,060 decrease
   d. $1,515 decrease
   e. None of the above

6. Production of P can be doubled by adding a second shift, but higher wages must be paid, increasing variable cost of goods sold to $3.50 for each of the additional units. If the 1,000 additional units of P can be sold at $10.00 each, the total effect on income will be

a. $10,000 increase
b. $5,330 increase
c. $6,500 increase
d. $2,260 increase
e. None of the above

(*CPA adapted*)

12-27 (*Optimum Production Decisions with Constraints*). The Jay Kay Company produces two products. The selling prices, costs, and other relevant data follow.

	Product J	*Product K*
Selling price	$34	$50
Direct material	4	24
Direct labor	15	10
Overhead (60% of labor; ⅓ variable)	9	6
Net income	$ 6	$10
Materials used	4 pounds	28 pounds
Labor hours	3 hours	2 hours
Power consumed	12 kwh.	14 kwh.
Demand for products	10,000 units	8,000 units

REQUIRED:

A. How much of each product should be produced if adequate resources are available?

B. How much of each product should be produced if capacity is limited to 40,000 labor hours?

C. How much of each product should be produced if only 101,600 pounds of material are available?

D. How much of each product should be produced if only 126,000 kwh. of power are available?

12-28 (*Linear Programming*). The cost accountant of the Stangren Corporation, your client, wants your opinion of a technique suggested to him by a young accounting graduate he employed as a cost analyst. The following information was furnished you for the corporation's two products, trinkets and gadgets.

EXHIBIT A

	Daily Capacities in Units			
	Cutting Department	*Finishing Department*	*Sales Price per Unit*	*Variable Cost per Unit*
Trinkets	400	240	$50	$30
Gadgets	200	320	$70	$40

1. The daily capacities of each department represent the maximum production for *either* trinkets *or* gadgets. However, any combination of trinkets and gadgets can be produced as long as the maximum capacity of the department is not exceeded. For example, two trinkets can be produced in the cutting department for each gadget not produced, and three trinkets can be produced in the finishing department for every four gadgets not produced.
2. Material shortages prohibit the production of more than 180 gadgets per day.
3. Exhibit B is a graphic expression of simultaneous linear equations developed from the production information above.

EXHIBIT B
GRAPH OF PRODUCTION RELATIONSHIPS

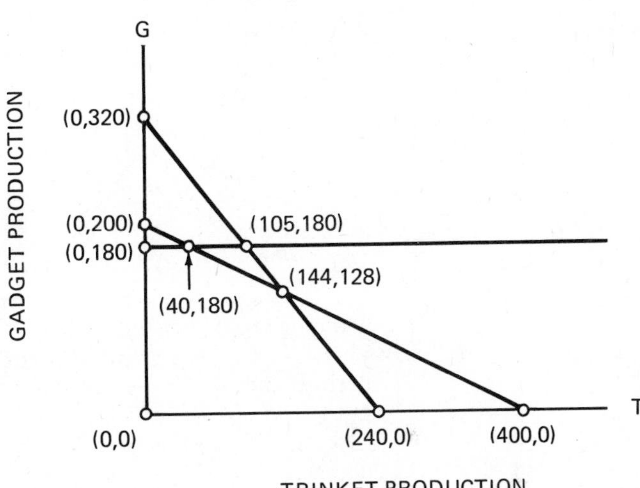

REQUIRED:

A. For what kinds of decisions are contribution margin data (revenue in excess of variable cost) useful?

B. Comparing the information in Exhibit A with the graph in Exhibit B, identify and list the graphic location (coordinates) of the following:
  1. Cutting departments capacity
  2. Production limitation for gadgets because of the materials shortage
  3. Area of feasible (possible) production combinations

C. Compute the contribution margin per unit for trinkets and gadgets.

D. Compute the total contribution margin of each of the points of intersections of lines bounding the feasible (possible) production area.

E. Identify the best production alternative. *(CPA adapted)*

12-29 *(Decisions to Close Plant).* You have been engaged to assist management of the Stenger Corporation in arriving at certain decisions. The Stenger Corporation has its home office in Philadelphia and leases factory buildings in Rhode Island, Georgia, and Illinois. The same single product is manufactured in all three factories. The following information is available regarding 19X4 operations.

	Total	*Rhode Island*	*Illinois*	*Georgia*
Sales	$900,000	$200,000	$400,000	$300,000
Fixed costs:				
Factory	$180,000	$ 50,000	$ 55,000	$ 75,000
Administration	59,000	16,000	21,000	22,000
Variable costs	500,000	100,000	220,000	180,000
Allocated home office expense	63,000	14,000	28,000	21,000
Total	802,000	180,000	324,000	298,000
Net profit from operations	$ 98,000	$ 20,000	$ 76,000	$ 2,000

Home office expense is allocated to the plants on the basis of units sold. The sales price per unit is $10.

The management of Stenger Corporation is displeased with the poor performance of the Georgia factory. The lease on the Georgia factory expires at the end of 19X5. If the lease is renewed, the annual rental will increase by $15,000. If the Georgia factory is shut down, proceeds from the sale of equipment will just cover termination expenses.

If the Georgia factory is shut down, Stenger Corporation will continue to serve the customers of the Georgia factory by one of the following methods:

1. Expand the Rhode Island factory. This would increase fixed expenses of the Rhode Island factory by 15%. In addition, shipping expenses of $2.00 per unit will be incurred on the increased production.

2. Enter into a contract with a competitor who will serve the customers of the Georgia factory. The competitor will pay Stenger Corporation a commission of $1.60 per unit.

REQUIRED:

A. What will the net incomes of Stenger Corporation be under each alternative?

B. Prepare a recommendation to the management of Stenger Corporation.

(CPA adapted)

12-30 *(Linear Programming).* Girth, Inc. makes two kinds of men's suede leather belts, with the following revenue and costs for each product.

	Belt A	*Belt B*
Selling price per unit	$19.50	$5.75
Direct material	$ 5.00	$1.00
Direct labor	6.00	3.00
Variable overhead	1.50	.75
Fixed overhead	2.00	1.00
Allocated general and selling expense	1.00	.30
Net income per belt (loss)	$ 4.00	$ (.30)

Girth, Inc. is able to sell all the belts it can make. Constraints are:

1. Belt A requires a fancy buckle, of which only 400 are available per day.

2. Girth, Inc. has the capacity to make 1,000 units of B per day. Each A belt requires twice as much manufacturing time as a B belt.

3. Belt B requires a plain buckle, of which 700 are available per day.

4. Only enough suede is available to produce 800 belts per day.

REQUIRED:

A. Prepare a graph, labeling each of the constraints by using their corresponding numbers.

B. From the graph determine how many units of Belt A and Belt B should be produced to maximize daily sales.

C. From the graph determine how many units of Belt A and Belt B should be produced to maximize net income.

D. The supplier of fancy buckles (for Belt A) informs Girth, Inc. that it cannot supply more than 100 fancy buckles a day. Other facts remain the same.

1. Reflect this new information on the graph.

2. Determine the number of each of the two belts that should be produced to maximize net income. *(CMA adapted)*

12-31 *(Production with Scarce Resources).* The Exotic Products Company produces a number of products from a rare material in a process requiring highly skilled employees. Because a number of material shortages are possible, planning is difficult.

For the next quarter three products are to be produced with the following *per-unit* revenue, cost, and production characteristics.

	Products		
	Unival	*Doxem*	*Trion*
Selling price	$5,120	$1,780	$1,986
Direct material	$ 200	$ 400	$ 150
Direct labor	2,400	600	720
Variable overhead (30% of labor)	720	180	216
Fixed overhead (50% of labor)	1,200	300	360
Total costs	4,520	1,480	1,446
Net income	$ 600	$ 300	$ 540
Units of material (kilograms)	20	40	15
Hours of labor	200	50	60
Machine hours	30	50	150
Power consumption (kwh)	40	10	18
Projected demand (units)	2,400	800	1,600

REQUIRED:

A. How many units of each product should be produced if there are no shortages of resources?

B. How many units of each product should be produced if only 80,000 kilograms of material are available?

C. How many units of each product should be produced if only 100,000 hours of direct labor are available?

D. How many units of each product should be produced if only 60,000 machine hours are available?

E. How many units of each product should be produced if only 81,600 kwh of power are available?

12-32 *(Decision to Accept Special Order).* George Jackson operates a small machine shop. He manufactures one standard product available from many other similar businesses and he also manufactures products to customer order. His accountant prepared the following annual income statement.

	Custom Sales	*Standard Sales*	*Total*
Sales	$50,000	$25,000	$75,000
Material	$10,000	$ 8,000	$18,000
Labor	20,000	9,000	29,000
Depreciation	6,300	3,600	9,900
Power	700	400	1,100
Rent	6,000	1,000	7,000
Heat and light	600	100	700
Other	400	900	1,300
	44,000	23,000	67,000
	$ 6,000	$ 2,000	$ 8,000

The depreciation charges are for machines used in the respective product lines. The power charge is apportioned on the estimate of power consumed. The rent is for the building space, which has been leased for 10 years at $7,000 per year. The rent and heat and lights are apportioned to the product lines on the basis of the amount of floor space occupied. All other costs are current expenses identified with the product line causing them.

A valued custom parts customer has asked Mr. Jackson to manufacture 5,000 special units for him. Mr. Jackson is working at capacity and would have to give up some other business in order to take this order. He can't renege on customer orders already agreed to, but he could reduce the output of his standard product by about one-half for one year while producing the specially requested custom part. The customer is willing to pay $7.00 for each part. The material cost will be about $2.00 per unit and the labor will be $3.60 per unit. Mr. Jackson will have to spend $2,000 for a special device that will be discarded when the job is done.

REQUIRED:

A. Calculate and present the following costs related to the 5,000-unit custom order:
   1. The incremental cost of the order
   2. The full cost of the order
   3. The opportunity cost of taking the order
   4. The sunk costs related to the order

B. Should Mr. Jackson take the order? Explain your answer.

(CMA adapted)

12-33 *(Make-or-Buy Decisions)*. The Vernom Corporation, which produces and sells to wholesalers a highly successful line of summer lotions and insect repellents, has decided to diversify in order to stabilize sales throughout the year. A natural area for the company to consider is the production of winter lotions and creams to prevent dry and chapped skin.

After considerable research, a winter products line has been developed. However, because of the conservative nature of the company management, Vernom's president has decided to introduce only one of the new products for this coming winter. If the product is a success, further expansion in future years will be initiated.

The product selected (called Chap-off) is a lip balm that will be sold in a lipstick-type tube. The product will be sold to wholesalers in boxes of 24 tubes for $8.00 per box. Because of available capacity, no additional fixed charges will be incurred to produce the product. However, a $100,000 fixed charge will be absorbed by the product to allocate a fair share of the company's present fixed costs to the new product.

Using the estimated sales and production of 100,000 boxes of Chap-off as the standard volume, the accounting department has developed the following costs.

Direct labor	$2.00 per box
Direct materials	3.00 per box
Total overhead	1.50 per box
Total	$6.50 per box

Vernom has approached a cosmetics manufacturer to discuss the possibility of purchasing the tubes for Chap-off. The purchase price of the empty tubes from the cosmetics manufacturer would be $.90 per 24 tubes. If the Vernom Corporation accepts the purchase proposal, it is estimated that direct labor and variable overhead costs would be reduced by 10% and direct material costs would be reduced by 20%.

REQUIRED:

A. Should the Vernom Corporation make or buy the tubes? Show calculations to support your answer.

B. What would be the minimum purchase price acceptable to the Vernom Corporation for the tubes? Support your answer with an appropriate explanation.

C. Instead of sales of 100,000 boxes, revised estimates show sales volume at 125,000 boxes. At this new volume additional equipment, at an annual rental of $10,000, must be acquired to manufacture the tubes. However, this incremental cost would be the only additional fixed cost required even if sales increased to 300,000 boxes. (The 300,000 level is the goal for third year of production.) Under these circumstances, should the Vernom Corporation make or buy the tubes? Show calculations to support your answer.

D. The company has the option of making and buying at the same time. What would be your answer to Part C if this alternative were considered? Show calculations to support your answer.

E. What nonquantifiable factors should the Vernom Corporation consider in determining whether to make or buy the lipstick tubes? *(CMA adapted)*

12-34 *Comprehensive—Dropping and Adding Products).* The Horton Door Company has produced five different products for many years. During 19X0, Mr. Horton, the president, contracted with a computerized accounting service bureau to maintain the accounting records and prepare departmental statements. At the end of 19X0, Mr. Horton received the following income statement by product lines.

HORTON DOOR COMPANY
INCOME STATEMENT
Year 19X0

	Products					
	1	*2*	*3*	*4*	*5*	*Total*
Sales	$100,000	$100,000	$100,000	$100,000	$100,000	$500,000
Expenses	70,000	80,000	85,000	95,000	150,000	480,000*
Net income (loss)	$ 30,000	$ 20,000	$ 15,000	$ 5,000	$ (50,000)	$ 20,000

*Fixed costs of $200,000 are allocated to the products on the basis of sales.

The long-term market for the company's products is limited. The company cannot expect future sales of its products to exceed the sales in year 19X0. In an attempt to improve profits and strengthen the company, Mr. Horton decided to drop Product 5, which showed a loss of $50,000 in 19X0.

Mr. Horton was pleased with the following income statement for 19X1. Profits for the company increased to $30,000 after dropping Product 5 but Product 4 showed a loss of $5,000.

HORTON DOOR COMPANY
INCOME STATEMENT
Year 19X1

	Products				
	1	*2*	*3*	*4*	*Total*
Sales	$100,000	$100,000	$100,000	$100,000	$400,000
Expenses	80,000	90,000	95,000	105,000	370,000*
Net income (loss)	$ 20,000	$ 10,000	$ 5,000	$ (5,000)	$ 30,000

*Fixed costs of $200,000 are allocated to the products on the basis of sales.

At the beginning of 19X2, Mr. Horton decided to drop Product 4. Mr. Horton was surprised to see a $15,000 loss for 19X2 with losses shown for both Products 2 and 3. He was assured by his managers that cost behavior patterns had not changed. The income statement for 19X2 follows.

HORTON DOOR COMPANY
INCOME STATEMENT
Year 19X2

	Products			
	1	*2*	*3*	*Total*
Sales	$100,000	$100,000	$100,000	$300,000
Expenses	96,666	106,667	111,667	315,000
Net income (loss)	$ 3,334	$ (6,667)	$ (11,667)	$ (15,000)

REQUIRED:

A. Explain fully why profits increased when Product 5 was dropped but decrease when Product 4 was dropped.

B. Explain why Products 2 and 3 now show a loss.

C. Three alternatives have been proposed for the Horton Door Company. Only one of the three can be accepted.

  1. Drop Products 2 and 3 and sublease a portion of the facilities for $100,000 per year.

  2. Maintain Products 1, 2 and 3 and add a new Product 6. Sales of the new product will be $200,000, variable costs $100,000, and identifiable fixed costs $30,000.

  3. Maintain Products 2 and 3 and change Product 1 by adding identifiable fixed costs of $20,000 per year. The new Product 1 will have double the current sales and variable costs.

Prepare an income statement by product for each alternative and indicate which alternative should be accepted.

12–35 *(Alternative Uses of Idle Capacity).* Query's Quarry produces a line of building blocks that it markets through building materials stores for $.20 each. Currently, 1,000,000 blocks are produced each year using only 60% of plant capacity. Standard costs per block were:

Direct materials	$.060
Direct labor	.015
Variable overhead	.020
Variable selling	.025
Fixed overhead	.030
Fixed selling	.010
	$.160

Management would like to use the excess capacity and has three possibilities. Only one of the three may be selected.

1. The company could produce additional units of the regular block and ship the additional production out of the present market area, which is saturated. Management estimates that the company could market 600,000 blocks this way. Additional freight charges would be $.025 per block and fixed overhead would increase by $100,000 per year. There would be no other changes in the cost structure.

2. The company could process the regular block further, making it into a decorative block. Management believes the company could sell 300,000 decorative blocks at a price of $.35 each, in addition to current sales of 1,000,000 regular blocks. The following estimates are for the additional costs of processing 300,000 blocks further.

Direct material	$.005
Direct labor	.065
Variable overhead	.030
Variable selling	.010
Fixed overhead	.005
Fixed selling	.015
	$.130

3. The company could produce and market a new product, X-Brick, to cover walls behind wood-burning stoves. The product would be sold in a package of bricks. The capacity could be used to produce 60,000 units (packages) per year at a price of $10 per unit with the following unit cost estimates:

Direct materials	$2.00
Direct labor	2.50
Variable overhead	1.50
Variable selling	1.00
	$7.00

The new X-Brick would require additional fixed overhead of $60,000 and fixed selling cost of $40,000.

REQUIRED:

A. Prepare a profit plan setting forth the contribution margin and net income for current production of 1,000,000 blocks (assuming no changes).

B. Prepare a profit plan for each of the three alternatives. Your profit plan should show *only* the incremental effect of each alternative setting forth the product margin.

C. Which alternative should be selected? What will be the total net income of the company if that alternative is selected? How much does it exceed the next best alternative?

12-36 *(Decisions Concerning Purchase of Raw Materials).* The management of the Southern Cottonseed Company has engaged you to assist in the development of information to be used for management's decisions. The company has the capacity to process 20,000 tons of cottonseed per year. The yield of a ton (2,000 pounds) of cottonseed is as follows:

Product	*Average Yield Per Ton of Cottonseed*	*Average Selling Price Per Trade Unit*
Oil	300 pounds	$ .15 per pound
Meal	600 pounds	$50.00 per ton
Hulls	800 pounds	$20.00 per ton
Lint	100 pounds	$ 3.00 per cwt.

A special marketing study revealed that the company can expect to sell its entire output for the coming year at the listed average selling prices. The study also indicated that cottonseed prices will vary widely in the next few years. At the present time Southern Cottonseed Company is paying $12 per ton.

You have determined the following costs for the company.

Processing costs:
  Variable: $9.00 per ton of cottonseed put into process
  Fixed: $108,000 per year
Marketing costs:
  All variable: $20 per ton sold
Administrative costs:
  All fixed: $90,000 per year

Management would like to know the average maximum amount that the company can afford to pay for a ton of cottonseed. The average maximum amount is the amount that would result in the company's having losses no greater when operating than when closed down, under the existing cost and revenue structure. Assume that the fixed costs will continue unchanged even when the operations are shut down.

REQUIRED:

A. Compute the revenue for the products produced from a ton of cottonseed.
B. What is the breakeven point in tons of cottonseed?
C. Compute the average maximum amount that the company can afford to pay for a ton of cottonseed.
D. Identify and discuss the factors other than costs that the company should consider in deciding whether to shut down a plant.
E. The stockholders consider the minimum satisfactory return on their investment in the business to be 25% before corporate income taxes. The stockholders' equity in the company is $968,000. Compute the maximum average amount that the company can pay for a ton of cottonseed to realize the minimum satisfactory return on the stockholders' investment in the business. *(CPA adapted)*

13 Decisions Concerning Resource Levels

A company cannot undertake the activities necessary to carry out short-range decisions without adequate financial resources. The purpose of decision making is to allocate resources in an optimal manner. The term **resources** encompasses financial resources, such as cash and assets to be converted into cash; human resources; physical resources, such as inventory, land, buildings, and equipment; and intangibles such as patent rights and the position of the firm in the marketplace. All these resources are important to firm management. In this chapter we will examine the resources necessary to support short-range decisions—cash, receivables, and inventories. Then, in Chapters 14 and 15, we will look at long-range resource decisions—buildings and production equipment.

PLANNING FOR SHORT-TERM RESOURCE NEEDS

Short-range resource planning is concerned with liquidity and solvency. **Liquidity** describes the amount and composition of the assets. **Solvency** represents the ability of the firm to pay its debts as they become due. We are primarily concerned with liquidity. By maintaining sufficient cash and other liquid assets, and budgeting the timing and magnitude of the cash inflows and cash outflows, the firm should remain solvent.[1]

How liquid does the firm need to be to finance its operations? Determining the proper amount of cash and other liquid assets involves a trade-off between profitability and risk. With too much liquidity the firm incurs an excessive capital cost and subjects itself to greater risk through mismanagement and embezzlement. Too little liquidity subjects the firm to excessive costs (inability to take quantity and cash discounts, for example), lost sales, and the risk of insolvency.

In planning for liquidity, we are concerned with the circulation of liquid resources, called working capital, during an operating cycle. **Working capital** is the difference between current assets and current liabilities. Current assets include cash and those assets that are expected to be converted into cash or consumed in the normal course of operations within an operating cycle or a year, whichever is longer. Current liabilities are those liabilities that are due within an operating cycle or a year, whichever is longer. The expectations are that current liabilities will be paid out of current assets.

An operating cycle is the period of time required for the cash invested in inventories to be returned to the firm through the collection of cash from the sale of its products. In Exhibit 13–1 the operating cycle is illustrated as a circle that begins and ends with cash. The first step in the cycle is the purchase of raw materials. The next step is production, where labor and overhead costs are incurred to convert the raw materials into a salable product. The third step is the sale of the product and incurrence of selling and administrative expenses. In the final step, cash is collected from the customer and becomes

[1]The term *insolvent* also has a technical meaning. A firm is technically insolvent when its liabilities exceed its assets.

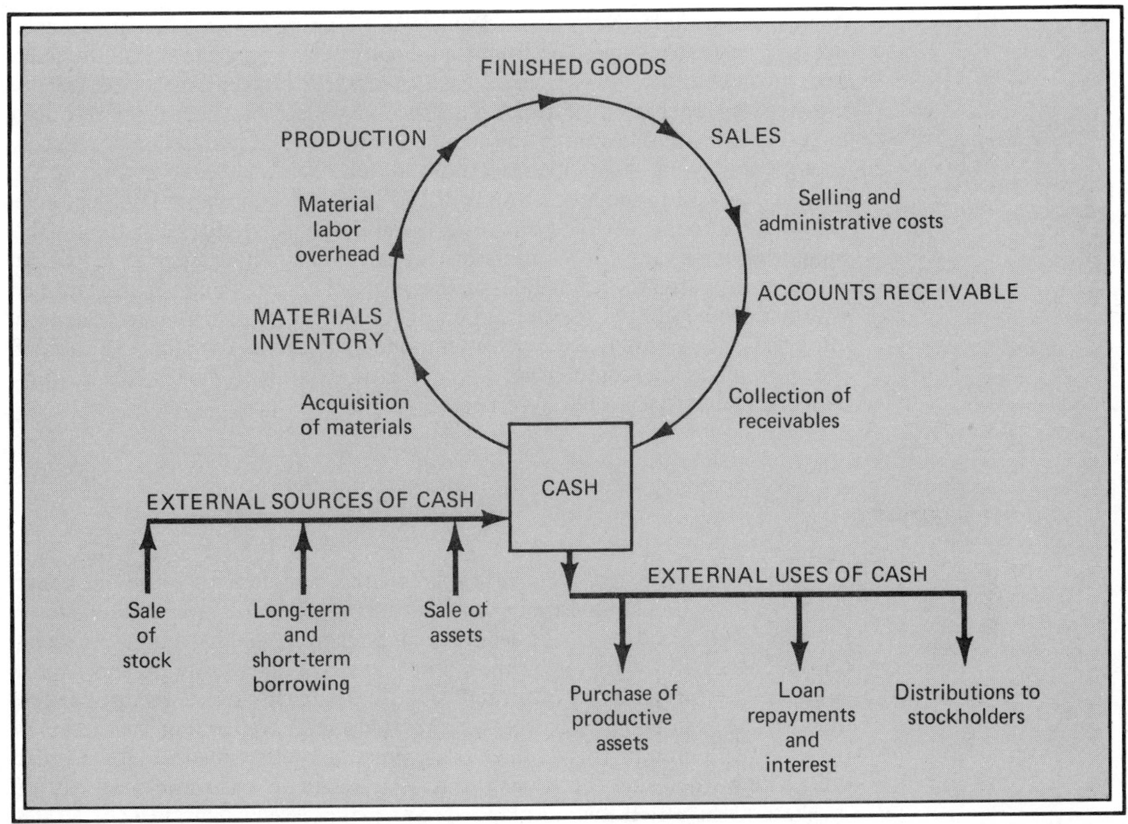

EXHIBIT 13-1
Cash flows—operating cycle

available to start another cycle. In addition to the cash generated from operations, new cash enters working capital through the issuance of capital stock, long-term and short-term borrowing, and the sale of assets. Cash exits in the form of investments in productive assets, repayment of loans and interest, and distributions to stockholders.

The amount of working capital needed depends upon the size of the business (illustrated by the size of the circle) and the length of the operating cycle (illustrated by the speed or velocity of movement around the circle). Changes in the size of the circle may be due to growth of the business or seasonal variation. As sales increase, additional working capital is needed and the circle grows. Velocity may be increased by delaying payments to materials suppliers, shortening the time required in the production process, and speeding up collections from customers.

We are interested in two aspects of planning for short-term resource needs. The first involves the timing of cash flows. To maintain liquidity, the firm must plan for the sources of cash necessary to meet cash requirements during a given period of time. The second aspect of short-term resource planning involves the answer to the questions, "How much working capital is enough and what composition should it have?" An excessive amount of working capital reduces profitability. Too little working capital subjects the firm to additional costs and increases the risk of insolvency. Each step in the operating cycle requires planning of the particular financial resource at that point: cash, accounts receivable, or inventory. The remainder of the chapter will be devoted (1) to an examination of the timing of cash through the cash budget; (2) to a study of the decision models developed for planning each of the working capital components; and (3) to an examination of financial ratios concerning short-term resource needs.

THE CASH BUDGET

Cash is the focal point of short-term resource planning since the operating cycle begins with the investment of cash in the purchase or manufacture of inventories and ends with the recovery of cash from the collection of receivables. The cash budget is the most important tool in managing short-term resources. By projecting a continual "rollover" of cash flows for short periods of time, the cash budget becomes a powerful tool for controlling the timing of cash flows. Through this budget cash flows may be timed so as to meet obligations when due; borrowing and repayment of loans and maturity of marketable securities may be planned so as to increase profitability and, at the same time provide cash when needed. In addition, investment in securities, capital expenditures, and other discretionary payments such as dividends may be timed by the development of the cash budget.

In Chapter 8 (Exhibit 8–19), the cash budget was illustrated and briefly discussed as a part of the master budget. In that illustration the computation of specific cash flows was related to the profit plan and the projected statement of financial position. From an operational standpoint, the cash budget is much more than a subcomponent of the master budget.

The critical use of the cash budget is in the control process, which is implemented *in advance* of the events. There is little value in comparing actual cash flow transactions with planned cash flow transactions after the fact. Cost and revenue control concentrates upon comparing actual performance with planned performance and taking action to prevent future deviations; it is the comparison of actual and past performance that provides the information for action. In cash planning the continual revision of the budget and replanning for short periods of time *before the event* provide control.

In this chapter we illustrate a "rolling" cash budget. When cash budgets are prepared for short periods of time and a new time period added as one passes, the cash budget will reflect a uniform future planning period. For example, at the beginning of the year a cash budget would be prepared by week for the first month, by month for the remainder of the first quarter, and by quarter for the remainder of the year. At the end of the first week, a new week, the fifth week of the year, would be added, and the first week would be dropped. At the end of the month, both a new month and a new week would be added. At the end of the quarter, a new week, a new month, and a new quarter would be added.

Illustration of a Cash Budget

Let us assume that the Carter Company has planned its operations through a profit plan and determined its needs for plant, equipment, and other long-term investments through a capital expenditures budget. The profit plan, capital expenditures budget, and beginning statement of financial position for the Carter Company are presented in Exhibit 13–2. Additional data from the master budget necessary to prepare monthly cash budgets are presented in Exhibit 13–3.

The cash budget for the year 19X1 (Exhibit 13–4) shows that cash collections from customers are adequate to meet cash payments for operations and the nonoperating cash flows such as dividends, the installment on the long-term debt and interest, and acquisition of equipment. For the year as a whole there appears to be no need for new funds. However, when we look at the quarterly projections in Exhibit 13–4, the large collections of cash occur during the middle of the year, and the large payments of cash occur during the first and last quarters of the year. Additional cash will be needed during the first and last quarters of the year. It is unusual for a firm to have a seasonal pattern of receipts that matches the seasonal pattern of payments.

Knowing that a cash deficiency of $27,500 will occur during the first quarter is not sufficient. Carter Company needs to know when the deficiency will occur and whether more than $27,500 will be needed. A cash budget by month will provide a more precise planning tool. In the cash budget for the first three months of the year (Exhibit 13–5), operations will require additional cash of $3,600 in January, $9,100 in February, and $14,800 in March.

The explanation of the cash flows in Exhibit 13–3 should be sufficient to understand and follow the first-quarter column in Exhibits 13–4 and 13–5. It may be helpful however, to explain the computation of collections from customers and payments to suppliers for materials. Fifty percent of a sale is collected in the first month following the sale and the remainder in the second month following the sale. Collections from customers for the Carter Company in January, February, and March were computed as follows:

CARTER COMPANY
ACTUAL STATEMENT OF FINANCIAL POSITION
December 31, 19X0

ASSETS

Current Assets:		
Cash		$10,000
Marketable securities		10,000
Accounts receivable		7,500
Raw materials inventory		6,000
Finished goods inventory		8,000
Total		$41,500
Plant, Property, and Equipment:		
Land	$ 5,000	
Building	20,000	
Equipment	25,000	
Total	$50,000	
Accumulated depr.	10,000	40,000
Total assets		$81,500

LIABILITIES AND STOCKHOLDERS' EQUITY

Current Liabilities:		
Accounts payable		$ 5,400
Accrued expenses		1,500
Current portion of long-term debt		5,000
Total		$11,900
Long-Term Liabilities:		
Note payable		20,000
Total liabilities		$31,900
Stockholders' Equity:		
Common stock	$30,000	
Retained earnings	19,600	49,600
Total liabilities and stockholders' equity		$81,500

CARTER COMPANY
PROFIT PLAN
19X1

Sales		$180,000	$12
Variable costs:			
Production	$90,000		
Selling	15,000	105,000	7
Contribution margin		$ 75,000	$ 5
Fixed costs:			
Salaries	$36,000		
Other	6,000		
Depreciation	6,000	48,000	
Net operating income		$ 27,000	
Interest expense	$ 3,500		
Investment income	500	3,000	
Net income before taxes		$ 24,000	
Income taxes		6,000	
Net income		$ 18,000	

CARTER COMPANY
CAPITAL EXPENDITURES BUDGET
19X1

Project: Replacement of equipment	
Cost:	$20,000
Financing:	
Cash	$ 6,000
Sale of old equipment	2,000
Note payable	12,000
	$20,000

EXHIBIT 13–2
Carter Company financial statements

CARTER COMPANY
BUDGETARY DATA
19X1

Item	Amount: January	February	March	April	Explanation
Units sold	600	1,000	1,400	1,800	
Units produced	1,400	1,800	2,000	2,200	
Ending inventory:					
Finished goods	2,400	3,200	3,800	4,200	Units—Two months sales on hand ($5 per unit)
Materials	3,800	4,200	4,200	3,500	Units—Two months production on hand ($3 per unit)
Sales	$7,200	$12,000	$16,800	$21,600	$12 per unit (November $6,000 December $6,000)
Cash collected	$6,000	$ 6,600	$ 9,600	$14,400	50% collected in month after sale, 50% two months after sale
Purchases	$6,600	$ 6,600	$ 6,000	$ 4,500	$3 per unit (December $5,400)
Cash paid for materials	$5,400	$ 6,600	$ 6,600	$ 6,000	Paid in month following purchase
Direct labor	$2,800	$ 3,600	$ 4,000	$ 4,400	Paid in month of expense ($2 per unit)
Variable overhead	$1,400	$ 1,800	$ 2,000	$ 2,200	Paid in month following expense ($1 per unit) December $1,000
Variable selling	$ 600	$ 1,000	$ 1,400	$ 1,800	Paid in month following expense ($1 per unit sold) December $500
Fixed expenses:					
Salaries	$3,000	$ 3,000	$ 3,000	$ 3,000	Paid in month of expense
Other	$ 500	$ 500	$ 500	$ 500	Paid in month of expense
Interest					Annual rate 8%, paid semi-annually, June & Dec.
Income taxes			$ 1,500		25% of income, paid quarterly, Mar., June, Sep., Dec.
Dividends	$1,500			$ 1,500	Paid quarterly, Jan., Apr., Jul., Oct.

EXHIBIT 13–3
Budgetary data for cash budget of Carter Company

CARTER COMPANY CASH BUDGET 19X1 by Quarter					
	First Quarter	*Second Quarter*	*Third Quarter*	*Fourth Quarter*	*19X1*
Sources of cash:					
From operations:					
Collections	$ 22,200	$56,400	$71,400	$ 31,200	$181,200
Payments:					
Suppliers for material	$ 18,600	$13,500	$ 4,500	$ 9,000	$ 45,600
Direct labor	10,400	11,400	4,200	4,000	30,000
Variable overhead	4,200	6,200	3,100	1,500	15,000
Variable selling	2,100	5,200	5,700	2,100	15,100
Fixed expense—salaries	9,000	9,000	9,000	9,000	36,000
Other fixed expenses	1,500	1,500	1,500	1,500	6,000
Income taxes	1,500	1,500	1,500	1,500	6,000
Total	47,300	48,300	29,500	28,600	153,700
Cash Excess (Deficiency) from operations	$(25,100)	$ 8,100	$41,900	$ 2,600	$ 27,500
Other sources:					
Sale of equipment	$ 2,000				$ 2,000
Long-term debt	12,000				12,000
Investment income	100			$ 300	400
Total	14,100	0	0	300	14,400
Total Sources	$(11,000)	$ 8,100	$41,900	$ 2,900	$ 41,900
Uses of cash:					
Dividends	$ 1,500	$ 1,500	$ 1,500	$ 1,500	$ 6,000
Purchase fixed assets	20,000				20,000
Reduce long-term debt				5,000	5,000
Interest on debt		1,600	300	1,500	3,400
Total	$ 21,500	$ 3,100	$ 1,800	$ 8,000	$ 34,400
Increase (Decrease) in cash	$(32,500)	$ 5,000	$40,100	$ (5,100)	$ 7,500
Beginning cash balance	10,000	5,000	5,000	5,000	10,000
Total	$(22,500)	$10,000	$45,100	$ (100)	$ 17,500
Required ending balance	5,000	5,000	5,000	5,000	5,000
Cash Excess (Deficiency)	$(27,500)	$ 5,000	$40,100	$ (5,100)	$ 12,500

EXHIBIT 13–4
Illustration of annual cash budget for Carter Company

CARTER COMPANY
CASH BUDGET
January, February, March, 19X1

	January	*February*	*March*	*Total for Quarter*
Sources of cash:				
From operations:				
Collections from customers	$ 6,000	$ 6,600	$ 9,600	$ 22,200
Payments:				
Suppliers for material	$ 5,400	$ 6,600	$ 6,600	$ 18,600
Direct labor	2,800	3,600	4,000	10,400
Variable overhead	1,000	1,400	1,800	4,200
Variable selling	500	600	1,000	2,100
Fixed expenses—salaries	3,000	3,000	3,000	9,000
Other fixed expenses	500	500	500	1,500
Income taxes			1,500	1,500
Total payments	13,200	15,700	18,400	47,300
Cash Excess (Deficiency) from operations	$ (7,200)	$ (9,100)	$ (8,800)	$(25,100)
Other sources:				
Sale of equipment			2,000	2,000
Long-term debt			12,000	12,000
Investment income	100			100
Total sources	$ (7,100)	$ (9,100)	$ 5,200	$(11,000)
Uses of cash:				
Dividends	$ 1,500			$ 1,500
Purchase of equipment			$ 20,000	20,000
Total	1,500	0	20,000	21,500
Increase (Decrease) in cash	$ (8,600)	$ (9,100)	$(14,800)	$(32,500)
Beginning cash balance	10,000	5,000	5,000	10,000
Total	$ 1,400	$ (4,100)	$ (9,800)	$(22,500)
Required ending balance	5,000	5,000	5,000	5,000
Cash Excess (Deficiency)	$ (3,600)	$ (9,100)	$(14,800)	$(27,500)

EXHIBIT 13–5
Illustration of monthly cash budget for Carter Company

	January	*February*	*March*	*Balance remaining at end of March*
Sales	$7,200	$12,000	$16,800	
Collection of:				
November sales ($6,000)	$3,000			
December sales ($6,000)	3,000	$ 3,000		
January sales		3,600	$ 3,600	
February sales			6,000	$ 6,000
March sales				16,800
Collections by month	$6,000	$ 6,600	$ 9,600	
Balance remaining in accounts receivable at the end of March				$22,800

For simplicity we have assumed that all payments are made on schedule and that there are no bad-debt losses. In reality most firms have late collections and bad debts. For example, rather than collecting 50% of the sales in the first month and 50% in the second month after the sale, a firm may find an actual collection experience similar to the following:

5%	in month of sale
30%	in month following sale
55%	in second month following sale
8%	collected over next six months
2%	bad debts
100%	

This complexity does not change the theory in Exhibits 13–4 and 13–5; it merely makes the calculations more involved.

Payments to suppliers are made in the month following purchase. Because the Carter Company plans a finished goods inventory level equal to the next two months of sales and a raw materials inventory level equal to the next two months of issuance to production, the purchase and payment for materials will precede the sale of finished goods and collection of cash by several months. This is one of the major factors in the timing of cash flows for operations. Computation of cash payments to suppliers for material follows:

	January	*February*	*March*	*Balance remaining at end of March*
Purchases	$6,600	$6,600	$6,000	
Payment of:				
December purchases	$5,400			
January purchases		$6,600		
February purchases			$6,600	
March purchases				6,000
Payments by month	$5,400	$6,600	$6,600	
Balance remaining in accounts payable at the end of March				$6,000

From the cash budget we can see that the Carter Company may be able to improve the timing of cash flows by paying an annual dividend rather than quarterly dividends and timing the equipment acquisition, if it is not critical to March, later in the year when operations generate more cash.

The "rollover" of a cash budget is illustrated in Exhibit 13–6. At the end of January, a new cash budget is prepared for February, March, and April, and the cash budget for January is dropped. This exhibit assumes that no revisions to the original cash budget are necessary. If conditions had changed, it might have been necessary to revise the cash flows for February and March. In this way the cash budget will always represent management's plans for the next three months. In our illustration the Carter Company must raise $2,900 of additional cash to finance operations and $1,500 to pay the quarterly dividend in April. We are assuming that interest is paid semi-annually and short-term borrowings are repaid with interest as soon as cash is available.

How can the Carter Company generate the cash needed to meet the cash deficiencies during the first several months of the year? Because cash inflows and cash outflows are not timed perfectly, the balance of cash or working capital fluctuates temporarily. As the business generates more cash than needed, short-term loans are repaid and marketable securities are purchased. As the business requires more cash than operations can generate, marketable securities are sold and short-term loans are used. The cash budget for the Carter Company could be expanded to show the financing of the cash deficiency through the sale of marketable securities and use of short-term bank loans. For example, in Exhibit 13–5, the cash deficiency is projected at $3,600 in January, $9,100 in February, and $14,800 in March. The $10,000 of marketable securities in the beginning balance sheet (Exhibit 13–2) would be sold during January and February, and short-term loans totaling $17,500 by the end of March would be used during February and March.

CARTER COMPANY
CASH BUDGET
February, March, April 19X1

	February	*March*	*April*	*Three Month Total*
Sources of cash:				
From operations:				
Collections from customers	$ 6,600	$ 9,600	$ 14,400	$ 30,600
Payments:				
Suppliers for materials	$ 6,600	$ 6,600	$ 6,000	$ 19,200
Direct labor	3,600	4,000	4,400	12,000
Variable O/H	1,400	1,800	2,000	5,200
Variable selling	600	1,000	1,400	3,000
Fixed expenses—salaries	3,000	3,000	3,000	9,000
Other fixed expenses	500	500	500	1,500
Income taxes		1,500		1,500
Total	15,700	18,400	17,300	51,400
Cash Excess (Deficiency) from operations	$ (9,100)	$ (8,800)	$ (2,900)	$(20,800)
Other sources:				
Sale of equipment		2,000		2,000
Long-term debt		12,000		12,000
Total sources	$ (9,100)	$ 5,200	$ (2,900)	$ (6,800)
Uses of cash:				
Dividends			$ 1,500	$ 1,500
Purchase of equipment		$ 20,000		20,000
Total	0	20,000	1,500	21,500
Increase (Decrease) in cash	$ (9,100)	$(14,800)	$ (4,400)	$(28,300)
Beginning balance of cash	5,000	5,000	5,000	5,000
Total	$ (4,100)	$ (9,800)	$ 600	$(23,300)
Required ending balance of cash	5,000	5,000	5,000	5,000
Cash Excess (Deficiency)	$ (9,100)	$(14,800)	$ (4,400)	$(28,300)

EXHIBIT 13-6
Illustration of a "rolled over" cash budget for Carter Company

A firm facing acute cash shortages, particularly one that is approaching bankruptcy, must have weekly or daily projections of cash. The timing period and depth of cash planning must be determined by the company. Detailed cash planning will increase the company's planning costs but should provide many benefits. Some of the benefits are: reducing the amount of cash on hand, thereby reducing interest expense or generating investment income, generating savings by taking cash discounts and avoiding penalties, and reducing borrowing costs by demonstrating good management of resources. Planning of short-term resources, like planning of other resources, should be extended as long as the benefits from planning exceed the cost of planning.

Plotting Cash Balances

A firm holds cash for two reasons: transactions and contingencies.[2] Because there are timing differences between the transactions creating cash inflows and cash outflows, a balance of cash must be maintained to meet the day-to-day needs of normal transactions. This amount must increase as the level of economic activity in the firm increases.

The contingency reason for holding cash is best described by the old adage, "Set a little aside for a rainy day." Because budgeted cash inflows and outflows are projections of the future, a degree of uncertainty exists. There must be some provision for uncertainties and for unplanned or unexpected occurrences such as a major equipment breakdown.

Often the amount of cash needed for transactions may be projected with a high degree of accuracy. For example, if daily cash flows are plotted for past periods, a pattern can develop. In Exhibit 13–7, examples of daily cash inflows and cash outflows are plotted for one month. The weekly payroll caused cash outflows to peak on Wednesday and drop off to minimum flows for the remainder of the week. Normal purchase terms in the example are *n*/10, EOM (payable within 10 days after the end of the month), causing a peak cash outflow on the eighth and ninth days of the month. Cash inflows peaked just prior to the twentieth because the normal sales terms were *n*/20, EOM. With different terms for purchases and sales, the timing of the cash flows varies, and the company must maintain a relatively high cash balance.

Net daily cash flows are shown in Exhibit 13–8. For the first 11 days of the month the cash outflows exceeded cash inflows and the cash balance declined. By the eleventh of the month the cumulative net cash outflow reached $37,000, after which the cash inflows exceeded cash outflows and the cash balance grew. From the twenty-fourth to the end of the month, cash inflows and cash outflows were nearly identical.

By plotting net cash flows for several months, the strength of the cash flow pattern and deviations can be determined. The firm can establish the necessary cash balance for normal transactions and then, by studying the deviations and considering nonroutine payments such as dividends, can establish the balance for contingency purposes.

The contingency balance may be reduced by maintaining short-term borrowing authority, called a *line of credit,* at a bank. Maintenance may cost .5% to 1% of the credit line, but this is considerably below the cost of capital incurred by the firm. Each dollar of cash balance freed means another dollar that may be invested in productive assets.

---

[2]A third reason—speculation—is often advanced for holding resources. The motives behind speculation differ, and a discussion of speculation is beyond the scope of this text.

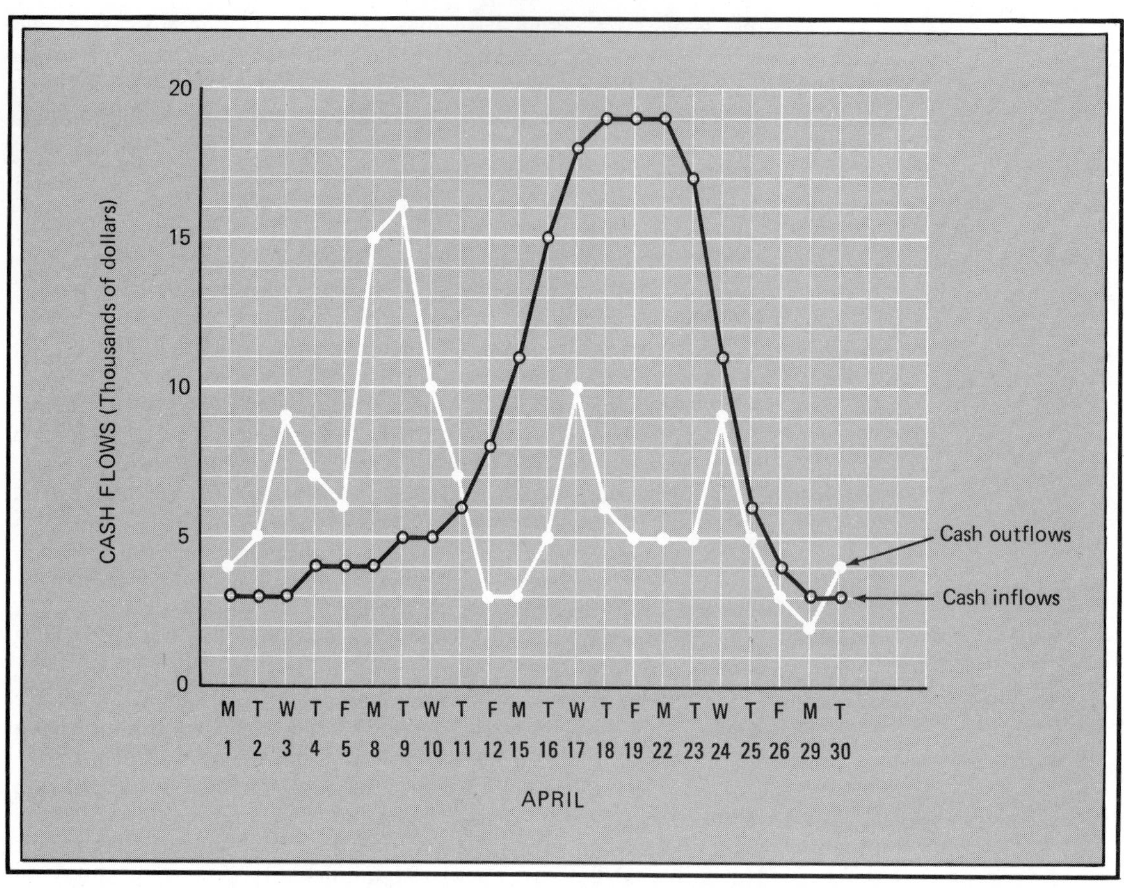

EXHIBIT 13–7
Daily timing of cash flows

PLANNING ACCOUNTS RECEIVABLE

The firm manages its accounts receivable by establishing policies on credit length, cash discounts, credit-granting criteria, and the nature of the collection effort. Establishment of receivables policies, like management of other current assets, involves a trade-off between profitability and risk. A policy that increases sales will increase the total contribution margin and profitability. However, increasing the amount of receivables will increase the total carrying costs of the resources invested in receivables and the risk of bad-debt losses. For resource planning it is necessary to know the timing and magnitude of collections from sales, and it is the firm's credit and collection policies that

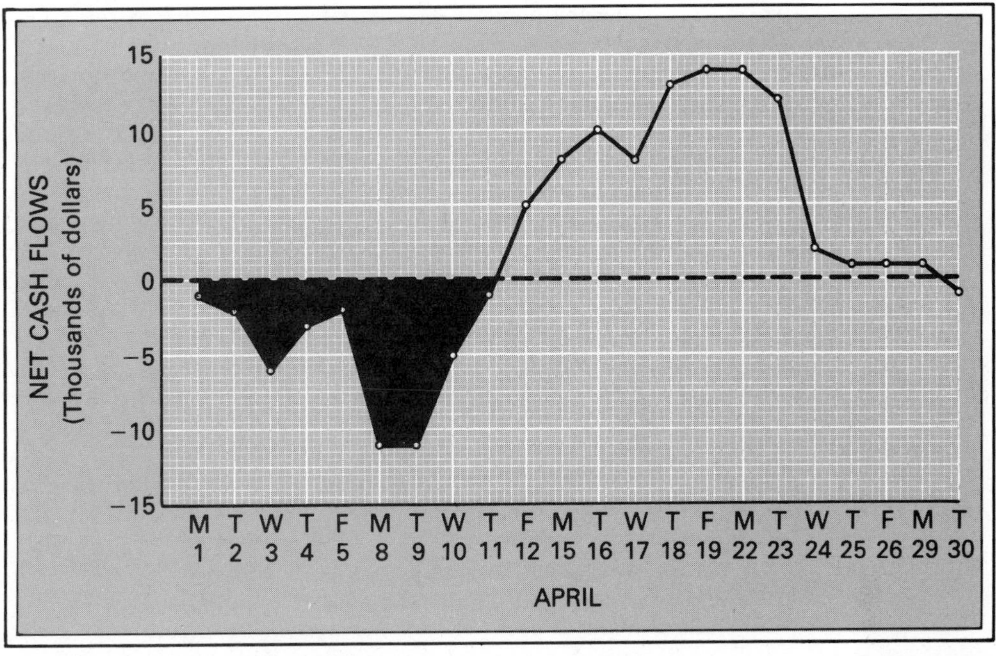

EXHIBIT 13–8
Daily net cash flows

determine the timing and magnitude of cash flows. Any policy that extends credit terms will postpone the collection of cash. The granting of cash discounts or increases in collection expenses will reduce the magnitude of net cash inflows.

In most lines of business there are established trade practices concerning cash discounts and the length of credit. To offer shorter credit periods and smaller cash discounts than competitors may drastically reduce sales. To offer longer credit periods and larger cash discounts could provide a competitive advantage that should increase sales; at the same time it will negatively affect the timing of cash and the magnitude of cash collections. A firm must balance the benefits of added sales with the costs of a decreased cash flow per dollar of sales.

To illustrate the balancing of profitability and risk, let's assume that a company is considering a more liberal extension of credit. The new credit terms are expected to increase sales by 10% and increase the average balance of accounts receivable by $150,000 through an increase in the accounts receivable collection period from 30 to 60 days. Currently, sales are $1,200,000 per year and the contribution margin ratio is 30%. The company has established a policy that any additional investment must have a required rate of return of 15%, the rate required to compensate creditors and owners for the use of their money.

The new policy will increase the contribution margin by $36,000 (sales $1,200,000 × 10% increase × 30% contribution margin ratio). If we assume no change in the rate of bad debt losses, the additional cost of the new policy is the 15% required rate of return amounting to $22,500 (15% × $150,000 additional receivables). The new credit terms should be granted, for the company will be $13,500 better off ($36,000 contribution margin less $22,500 required return).

Any change in credit terms, particularly one that extends time, will probably change the rate of bad-debt losses. Let's assume that, in addition to the other changes, the bad-debt loss is increased from 1% of sales to 2% of sales. Is the decision still favorable? The new policy will increase bad-debt losses by $18,000 per year, computed as follows:

Old level of bad-debt losses	=	1% of current sales levels
	=	1% × $1,200,000
	=	$12,000
New level of bad-debt losses	=	2% of new level of sales
	=	2% × ($1,200,000 × 110%)
	=	$26,400
Change in bad-debt losses	=	$14,400 ($26,400 − $12,000)

The company should not offer the more liberal credit terms, because it will be $900 worse off as a result ($36,000 contribution margin less $22,500 required return and less $14,400 additional bad-debt losses). By liberalizing the credit terms, the company was unable to make enough contribution margin on the additional sales to offset the cost of carrying the additional receivables plus the additional bad-debt losses. Of course, any additional costs in granting credit and collecting the receivables should be included in the analysis, although they are not included in this example.

PLANNING INVENTORIES

Firms hold inventories for the same two basic reasons they hold cash: transactions and contingencies. In some ways, planning for an inventory of cash is much like planning for an inventory of raw materials or finished goods. The firm must hold a minimum amount of inventory to satisfy production and sales demands. If the rate of usage and delivery dates could be predicted with certainty, the firm would need to hold only the minimum inventory level necessary for the known transactions. However, business activity is not certain and provision must be made for contingencies, as well as for expected transactions.

Exhibit 13–9 shows the fluctuations of the level of a raw material inventory item over a period of time. A similar illustration could be prepared for a finished goods inventory item as well. The cycle begins when goods are received at the **replenishment point.** In our example, 200 units are delivered on Day 0, when the inventory balance is 100 units. This brings the inventory level

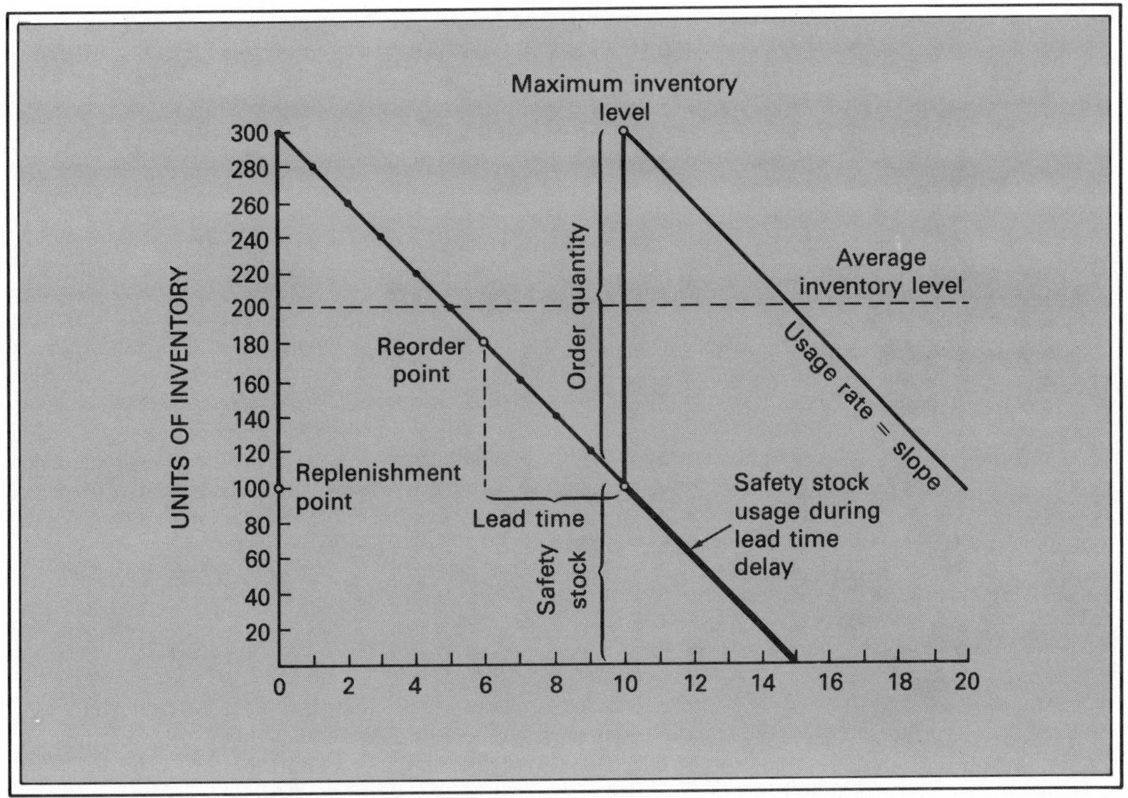

EXHIBIT 13–9
Illustration of inventory model

to 300, the maximum level the inventory will reach. As goods are withdrawn from the inventory, at the rate of 20 units per day, the balance of inventory on hand declines until it reaches 180 units. This level is the **reorder point,** the point at which an order must be placed to provide a **lead time** of 4 days to ensure delivery when needed. If delivery is on time, the next **replenishment point** is reached at Day 10. If delivery is delayed for any reason, the company has 5 days of safety stock. The **safety stock,** or contingency level, makes provisions for uncertainties in usage rate and lead time. If usage rate and lead time are certain, there is no need for a safety stock.

In Exhibit 13–9 the inventory can be viewed as composed of two components—working stock (200 units) and safety stock (100 units). If actual events correspond identically to the planned events, the average inventory balance will be 200 units. Since usage is assumed to be constant each day, the average balance of working stock will be one-half of the working stock. Of course, the safety stock will not be touched if the usage rate and lead time are as planned. Thus, the average balance of safety stock will be 100 units. The average inventory on hand will be the sum of the average working stock and average safety stock, or 200 units.

The important decisions in inventory planning are the quantity to order each time an order is placed and the amount of the safety stock. The objectives of inventory planning should be to ensure that the organization maintains an optimal balance of inventory that will minimize total costs of having an inventory.

Three types of costs are associated with maintaining inventories. The first type results from placing the order and includes clerical and transportation costs. The second type results from carrying inventory and includes storage costs, handling, financing costs, property taxes, insurance, and losses from obsolescence. The third type of costs result from not carrying sufficient inventory and includes contribution margin from lost sales, costs from production disruptions, customer ill will, added transportation costs, and added production costs from inefficient production runs. Ideally, any decision model used will minimize the total of the three costs. The first two types of costs relate to the quantity to be ordered and the third relates to the level of the safety stock.

Inventory Control Decision Models

Inventory control models range from very simple methods, which depend upon visual observation, to mathematical inventory models that determine the most economic order size and safety stock by balancing the costs of carrying too much inventory against the costs of carrying too little inventory.

At one extreme the manager or purchasing officer periodically checks to see what inventory items are in short supply and places orders when he or she believes a minimum level has occurred or when the inventory of a particular item is exhausted. The quantity ordered is usually some standard quantity in the industry or an amount necessary to fill the storage area. Few, if any, inventory records are kept on inventory levels, purchase quantities, and purchase dates. The visual observation method can incur excessive purchasing, carrying, and stockout costs. When the physical count is taken at the annual closing, it often reveals excessive investment in obsolete or slow-moving goods.

A refinement of the visual observation method is to draw a reorder line in the bin or storage area so that additional units will be reordered when a certain level is reached. The reorder line is placed high enough in the bin to cover normal usage until the new order arrives. A variation is to use two bins; one for working stock and one for safety stock. An order is placed when the working stock bin is empty.

Another inventory control approach some firms use is to establish target inventory levels by applying a desired inventory turnover figure to past or expected usage rates for the inventory. However, the target inventory levels used in turnover represent average levels; they do not indicate economic order sizes or minimum safety levels. In theory, turnover should be the residual of decisions based upon economic models, not the decision model itself.

THE ABC METHOD

The inventory in even a moderate-sized firm may consist of several thousand types of inventory items. A complete analysis cannot be justified for each inventory item. The ABC Method classifies inventory items into groups, usually three, according to the annual cost of the item used (annual usage × unit cost). Group A consists of these items with a large dollar volume of usage. Often, only 10% to 15% of the number of inventory units comprises as much as 80% to 85% of the total dollar usage. Group B includes those inventory items with a smaller dollar volume of usage, and Group C includes the number of inventory items that have a small dollar volume of usage. Group C may account for as much as 60% to 70% of the total inventory units, but as little as 5% to 15% of the total annual usage.

A firm should place the majority of its inventory control effort on Group A items, since they account for the bulk of the inventory usage. Economic order quantities and safety stock levels should be developed to control Group A inventory items. On the other hand, this careful planning effort may not be justified for the Group C items. We should expect all Group A and some Group B inventory items to be purchased in economic quantities and closely controlled because of their high usage. Other Group B and Group C inventory items will be purchased and controlled with more informal techniques, such as the two-bin system.

Occasionally there is a Group C item that is so vital to the production function that the firm should not use informal controls. In this case the item would be included with the Group A items. The exceptional item helps highlight the true purposes of ABC analysis. It does not tell you what items are vital or determine the most appropriate control systems. It merely says, "A few items comprise a large portion of the dollar volume, while many items comprise a small portion of the dollar volume." The manager must still decide how to best control each class of items. Stated another way, the ABC analysis is *not* a control system, it is a way to decide which items are most in need of tight control systems.

ECONOMIC PURCHASE ORDER QUANTITIES

Management scientists have developed a decision model to determine the optimum quantity of materials to be purchased on each purchase order. This model will determine the optimum inventory working stock level.

Each time a purchase order is placed, the firm incurs clerical and transportation costs. To minimize the costs of placing purchase orders, the firm could order the firm's entire annual needs at one time, incurring only the cost of one purchase order. However, if they did this, they would have a large average inventory of working stock. Because of the large inventory balance, they would incur increased carrying costs—the incremental costs of storage facilities, insurance, interest on the investment in inventory, salaries of the storeroom personnel, property taxes and losses from spoilage and obsolescence.

The optimum amount to purchase at any one time is the quantity that would minimize the total costs of purchasing and carrying the inventory. The optimum quantity can be determined by the formula:[3]

$$\underset{\text{in dollars}}{EOQ} = \sqrt{\frac{2AB}{I}}$$

Where:

EOQ = Economic order quantity

A = Annual usage in dollars

B = Purchasing cost per purchase order

I = Carrying costs expressed as a percentage of inventory costs.

This formula is based upon the assumption that the goods are withdrawn from the inventory at a constant rate and that the purchasing costs and carrying costs are relatively constant per order.

To illustrate the EOQ formula, let's assume that Part 23 has a total annual usage of 900 units at a cost of \$3.00 per unit. The cost of procuring one order is \$10 and the cost per dollar of inventory for carrying costs is \$.20. The usage is assumed to be uniform throughout the year. The dollar value of each purchase order would be:

$$Q = \sqrt{\frac{2AB}{I}}$$

$$Q = \sqrt{\frac{(2)(\$2,700)(\$10)}{.20}}$$

$$Q = \$520$$

In units, each purchase would be for 173 units (\$520 ÷ \$3.00).

The fact that this formula minimizes inventory costs can be shown as in Exhibit 13–10. In this illustration, dollars or cost are plotted on the vertical axis, and number of purchase orders on the horizontal axis. The procurement costs are incurred only when a purchase is made. This cost increases linearly with each purchase order. Conversely, carrying costs are high when the inventory is procured in a single order and grows smaller with each additional purchase order because three is a smaller average inventory on hand.

[3]See appendix at end of chapter for development of formula.

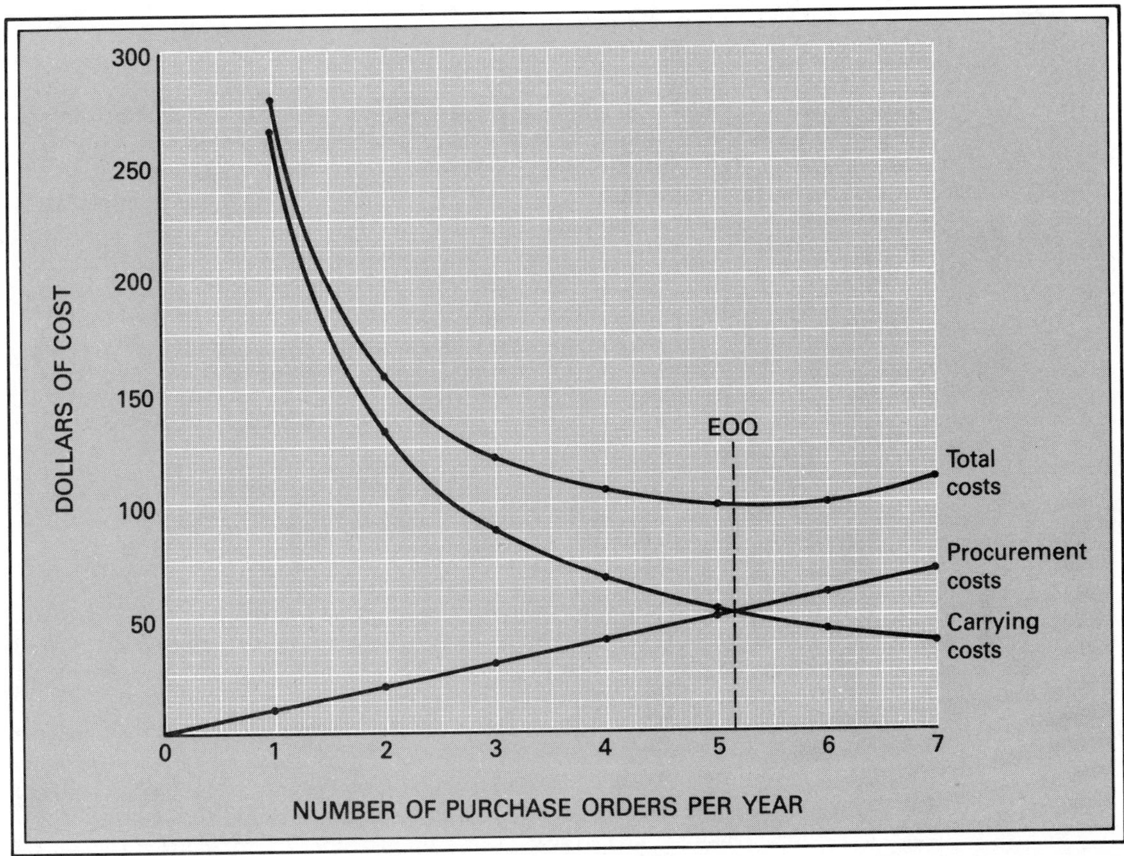

EXHIBIT 13–10
Economic order quantity graph

In Exhibit 13–10 the procurement costs increase at the rate of \$10 per purchase order. With one purchase order per year the purchasing costs are \$10. The carrying costs are \$270, since with one purchase order the average inventory will be \$1,350 (\$2,700 ÷ 2) and the carrying costs are \$.20 per dollar of inventory. The total inventory costs will be \$280. At 6 purchase orders per year the procurement costs will be \$60; the carrying costs are \$45 [\$.20(2,700 ÷ 12)], and the total inventory costs will be \$105. The minimum inventory costs are where the procurement costs equal the carrying costs. In our example this is slightly greater than 5 purchase orders per year. This corresponds to our EOQ amount of \$520 per order, since the \$2,700 annual usage divided by \$520 per order equals 5.2 purchase orders per year.

In the discussion above we have taken the point of view of purchasing either raw materials or finished goods. The same logic would also apply to management decisions in regard to how many units to produce on each production run. Many companies produce items in lots or batches rather than in a continuous, uninterrupted flow. Where products are produced in batches, a firm must incur a setup cost each time a batch is produced. These setup costs include the additional costs of preparing and realigning the machines; installing dies, jigs, and templates; necessary paperwork to prepare the production run; and reorienting the workers to their jobs.

If we substitute setup costs for procurement costs, the formula would provide the optimum quantity that should be produced on each production run. For example, assume that a firm manufactures plastic mirror frames in a molding process. On an annual basis they manufacture 1,000 frames at a cost of $4.00. The firm's differential costs of carrying the item in the finished goods inventory are 20% of the inventory value per year, and the setup cost per production run is $200. The optimum production run is:

$$Q = \sqrt{\frac{2AB}{I}}$$

$$Q = \sqrt{\frac{(2)(\$4{,}000)(\$200)}{.20}}$$

$$Q = \sqrt{8{,}000{,}000}$$

$$Q = \$2{,}828$$

Each production run should be for $2,828 of product, or 707 units ($2,828 ÷ $4).

Four points should be discussed before we leave EOQ formulas. First, the fact that the sum of the differential costs is minimized does not mean that the decisions that incur the costs are optimal. For example, even though we know that procurement costs are $10 per purchase order, this does not mean that we have the most efficient purchasing system. The purchasing procedures, the setup methods, and the warehouse operations may be efficient, grossly inefficient, or (more likely) somewhere in between. However, even in an inefficient system this decision mode offers a means of minimizing costs.

Second, the use of an EOQ formula calls for estimates of annual usage, procurement or setup costs, and carrying costs. The validity of the answer is obviously dependent upon the data gathered. Input errors result in output errors. However, the EOQ formula is somewhat insensitive to error. For example, assume that a forecasting error resulted in an EOQ of 40 ($Q = \sqrt{1{,}600}$); had the firm been able to forecast perfectly, the EOQ would have been 20 ($Q = \sqrt{400}$). There is a 400% input error (1,600 versus 400) but only a 200% output error (40 versus 20).

Third, the EOQ formula above is built upon the assumption of continual, uniform usage. Where this is not true, more sophisticated models are appropriate.

Finally, the EOQ formula deals only with the working stock; it does not facilitate the decision about the safety stock level. Thus the EOQ formula minimized the costs of only one segment of the total inventory. In the following section we will examine some of the decision models for establishing the optimum level of safety stock.

SAFETY STOCK QUANTITIES

In dealing with the economic order quantity, the problem is "how much" to buy. The "how much" creates the working stock, which is one-half of the order quantity, assuming uniform usage. In dealing with safety stock, the problem is "when" to buy. This can be illustrated by the following example. Assume that a firm uses 20 items of Material X per month. A beginning inventory of 100 items is on hand. Further assume that 40 items of X are ordered when the inventory reaches 80 and that the lead time is one month. The total inventory varies between 60 and 100; the average is 80. There are 20 units of working stock and 60 units of safety stock created by "when" it was ordered, not by "how much" was ordered; if the reorder point were changed to 50, the inventory will vary between 30 and 70 with an average of 50. The working stock is 20 units, and the safety stock is 30 units.

The reorder point is directly related to the safety stocks since, as the reorder point is moved forward, the amount of the cushion is increased. The reorder point results from the combination of lead-time requirements plus protection stocks. The safety allowance and the reorder point are interrelated so that by increasing one the other is increased by the same amount. If one is determined, the other is automatically established. The economic order quantity previously discussed is independent of safety stock analysis.

There are many methods of determining safety stock levels. One intuitive rule is to have a large safety stock with a high quantity usage, long lead time, or frequent ordering schedule. Small safety stocks can be maintained when there is low usage, short lead time, or infrequent ordering. Other firms provide a constant safety stock of one month or two months' usage regardless of the item.

The best theoretical approach would be to develop a formula, similar to the EOQ formula, one that would balance the costs of carrying the safety stock inventories with the costs of being out of stock. Such a formula would depend upon the ability to determine usage behavior that fits a known statistical pattern and the assignment of a cost of a stock-out.

Since the need for safety stock is to compensate for fluctuations in demand and usage during the lead time, as well as fluctuations of the lead time, some firms try to assign probability patterns to these fluctuations. By predicting the dispersion of usage around average usage and the dispersion of lead times around the average lead time, statistical analysis of the probability of a stock-out is possible. Even here the acceptable number of stock-outs must be a management decision.

The decision models for safety stock are more complicated than the decision models for working stock. Regardless of their simplicity or complexity, all of these models are based upon underlying assumptions (for example, constant uniform usage), estimates (costs of stock-out, purchasing or setup, carrying costs and annual usage), and each requires judgmental choices by management (acceptable levels of stock-outs). Thus, while these models greatly facilitate management's choices, they do not replace them.

RATIO ANALYSIS

One way to examine the adequacy of working capital is through ratio analysis. The investor or creditor outside the firm may be limited to a set of financial statements and may find the analysis of ratios the best method of assessing strength and profitability of the company. Over the years ratios have been developed and used in an attempt to measure performance and provide a basis for predicting future results by external users of the financial statements. For example, stockholders would be interested in ratios that show earnings per share of stock, return on investment, and other ratios that measure profitability. By studying the trend of earnings per share over time, the stockholder hopes to be able to predict future earnings. Long-term creditors are interested in ratios that relate to the overall strength of the company and therefore compare debt to total assets or stockholders' equity. If the amount of long-term debt is low in relation to total assets, the firm should be in a better position to repay the debt. The long-term creditor is also interested in ratios that relate earnings to the amount of interest the company is committed to pay. Bankers and short-term creditors are interested in the amount of working capital and the composition of working capital.

In this chapter we are interested in planning for short-term resources. Therefore, we will concentrate on the ratios used by bankers and other short-term creditors interested in the management of short-term resources. The most common ratios for analysis of working capital are the current ratio, liquidity ratio, accounts receivable turnover, and inventory turnover. They deal with the major steps in the operating cycle.

The **current ratio** is current assets divided by current liabilities; in a broad sense this ratio shows the ability to meet current obligations. Many long-term debt agreements require some minimum current ratio. An old rule of thumb requires that the minimum acceptable current ratio be 2 to 1, although it can vary by industry. Unfortunately, the current ratio says nothing about composition of the working capital or about timing of payments. There is no assurance that a firm with $150,000 of current assets and $50,000 of current liabilities, and, therefore, a current ratio of 3 to 1, will be able to pay its creditors. For example, most of the $150,000 could be in slow-moving inventories.

The use of **liquid assets** (cash, marketable securities, and receivables), rather than total current assets, provides a better measure of short-run liquidity. If $75,000 of the $150,000 current assets in the previous illustration were in liquid assets, the **liquidity ratio** would be 1.5 to 1 ($75,000 of liquid assets ÷ $50,000 of current liabilities). An old rule of thumb placed the minimum acceptable liquidity ratio at 1 to 1.

The current and liquidity ratios are subject to important limitations. First, they relate to positions at a single point in time. Unless that particular time is representative of the continuing financial position of the firm, the ratios may be misleading. Second, they relate only to current, or liquid, assets and current liabilities as measured under generally accepted accounting principles. Thus, only *existing* assets and liabilities are measured. Yet the projected cash flows may be as important as the items present among the current assets and current liabilities.

The **accounts receivable turnover** relates the balance of accounts receivable to credit sales. It is computed by dividing accounts receivable into credit sales. If a firm has annual credit sales of $120,000 and an accounts receivable balance of $20,000, the accounts receivable turnover is six times. A refinement of the ratio computes the number of days' sales outstanding. A turnover of six times a year would be stated as "60 days of sales outstanding" (360 days ÷ 6 turnovers). In a seasonal business the number of days' sales outstanding will be affected by when the ratio is computed. If the ratio is computed at a time when sales activity is very high and, as a result, accounts receivable are very high, the turnover will be low. If computed when activity is low, the turnover figure will be high. One way to avoid this distribution is the use of average accounts receivable, i.e., beginning and ending balances divided by two.

Finished goods inventory turnover is determined by dividing cost of goods sold by the finished goods inventory. If cost of goods sold is $72,000 and the inventory if $24,000, the finished goods inventory turnover is three times. **Raw materials inventory turnover** is the cost of materials used in production divided by the raw materials inventory. Unfortunately, there is no basis for evaluating whether three, four, or some other number of inventory turns is appropriate. Industry averages offer some guidelines, but we must also consider the lead time required to replace the *inventory* and the risk or cost of running short.

To illustrate the calculation of these ratios, we will compute and discuss the ratios for the Zurfluh Candy Company. The statement of financial position (balance sheet) and the income statement are presented in Exhibit 13–11. Computation of the current ratio, liquidity ratio, accounts receivable turnover, and inventory turnovers are presented in Exhibit 13–12.

By the rules of thumb indicated earlier, the current and liquidity ratios are deficient. The actual current ratio of 1.7 to 1 compares unfavorably with the 2 to 1 rule of thumb. The actual liquidity ratio of .6 is below the desired 1 to 1 level.

Ratios for many types of businesses are computed and available through published sources. The current ratio, days sales in accounts receivable (accounts receivable collection period), and inventory turnover figures are available for the confectionery and related products industry.[4] The most recent industry current ratio is 2.58 to 1, well above the 1.7 to 1 for the Zurfluh Candy Company.

[4]Dun and Bradstreet, Inc., *Key Business Ratios,* 1976, p. 8.

ZURFLUH CANDY COMPANY
STATEMENT OF FINANCIAL POSITION
December 31, 19X1
(000 Omitted)

Assets		*Liabilities and Equities*	
Cash	$ 5	Accounts Payable	$ 17
Accounts Receivable	12	Notes Payable	3
Inventory	33	Other Payables	10
Total Current Assets	$ 50	Total Current Liabilities	$ 30
Property (net)	50	Long Term Debt	5
		Common Stock	10
		Retained Earnings	55
	$100		$100

ZURFLUH CANDY COMPANY
INCOME STATEMENT
For 19X1
(000 omitted)

Sales	$250
Cost of Goods Sold	150
Gross Margin	$100
Operating Expenses	90
Net Income	$ 10

EXHIBIT 13–11
Financial statements for ratio computation

The accounts receivable turnover of 20.8 times per year, or 17 days, for the Zurfluh Candy Company compares favorably with a 21-day collection period for the industry. The days sales in receivables should be compared with the credit terms offered by the Zurfluh Candy Company. For example, if the credit terms are 30 days, customers are not taking full advantage of the credit offered or the company may be missing sales because it is excessively cautious in granting credit.

If we learn that the total inventory of $33,000 is composed of $12,500 finished goods and $20,500 raw materials, there is a turnover of 12.0 and 3.7, respectively. This results in an average days on hand of 30 and 97. We have no basis to judge whether 30 days of finished goods and 97 days of raw materials are excessive or deficient. Inventory models which consider the cost of

CURRENT RATIO:

$$\frac{\text{Current assets}}{\text{Current liabilities}} = \frac{\$50}{\$30} = 1.7 \text{ to } 1$$

LIQUIDITY RATIO:

$$\frac{\text{Cash, marketable securities, and receivables}}{\text{Current liabilities}} = \frac{\$5 + \$12}{\$30} = .6 \text{ to } 1$$

ACCOUNTS RECEIVABLE TURNOVER:

$$\frac{\text{Sales}}{\text{Accounts receivable}} = \frac{\$250}{\$12} = 20.8 \text{ times}$$

Days sales in accounts receivable:

$$\frac{360}{\text{Accounts receivable turnover}} = \frac{360}{20.8} = 17.3 \text{ days}$$

INVENTORY TURNOVER:

Finished Goods Turnover:

$$\frac{\text{Cost of goods sold}}{\text{Finished goods inventory}} = \frac{\$150}{\$12.5} = 12 \text{ times}$$

Days sales in finished goods inventory:

$$\frac{360}{\text{Finished goods turnover}} = \frac{360}{12} = 30 \text{ days}$$

Raw Materials Turnover:

$$\frac{\text{Cost of materials used}}{\text{Raw materials inventory}} = \frac{\$75}{\$20.5} = 3.7 \text{ times}$$

Days of material use in raw materials inventory:

$$\frac{360}{\text{Raw materials turnover}} = \frac{360}{3.7} = 97 \text{ days}$$

EXHIBIT 13–12
Computation of selected ratios

purchasing goods, the cost of holding goods, and the lead time required to replace goods are necessary to evaluate inventory levels in terms of efficiency of cost expenditures. However, published inventory turnover data compute a total inventory turnover for the industry at 7.4 times by relating total inventory to sales. A similar computation for the Zurfluh Candy Company results in a total inventory turnover of 7.6 times (sales \$250 ÷ inventory \$33), very close to the industry figure. These are only average guidelines and must be used with awareness of specific firm conditions.

Ratio analysis is useful to analysts outside the firm and to management for an overall view but it provides very little guidance for specific management decisions. Banks and other lenders consider high current and liquidity ratios and only a small amount of debt as favorable. Although large current and liquidity ratios may impress the bankers, they can result in excessive liquidity. Overall, the ratios for the Zurfluh Candy Company indicate that the company may face liquidity problems. The ratios, however, cannot provide the company's management with guidance for specific management decisions. In order to plan liquidity, management needs information concerning expected resource inflows and outflows. A better method for management decision making is the development of planning models.

SUMMARY

A company cannot undertake the activities necessary to carry out short-range decisions without adequate resources. Determining the proper amount of financial resources involves a trade-off between profitability and risk.

There are two aspects of planning for short-term resource needs. The first involves the timing of cash flows through preparation of a cash budget. The development of a cash budget illustrates the projection of cash flows from the planned transactions for a specific period of time. By "rolling over" the cash budget for short periods of time, the cash budget provides control in advance of the event. The more acute the cash shortage, the shorter the time period that should be used for cash planning.

The second aspect of planning for short-term resource needs involves the development of planning models for each step in the operating cycle to determine optimum resource levels. Most short-term resources are held for two reasons: (1) to provide sufficient resources to service the firm's normal transactions, and (2) to provide for contingencies. The more information the firm has about resource needs, the smaller the contingency balance that may be necessary.

Planning and budgeting for short-term resource needs involves the determination of the proper level of liquidity for the company. With too much liquidity, the firm incurs excessive costs. With too little liquidity, the firm is unable to carry out its objectives. Ratio analysis is used by analysts outside the firm who do not have access to the budgets and other plans of the company. Ratios, however, cannot provide guidance for specific management decisions; more useful are models, such as the EOQ formula, which balance the cost of carrying a quantity of a resource with the costs of obtaining the resource.

APPENDIX

The first step in the development of an economic order quantity (EOQ) formula, for the minimization of procurement or setup costs and carrying costs, is to state the costs in symbol form. The manager has the option of one, two, five, or N purchase orders or production runs per year. Each purchase order or setup incurs a cost, which we will term B. Annual procurement or setup costs will be:

$$N \times B \tag{1}$$

The manager also knows that the fewer purchase orders or setups per year, the larger average quantity he will have on hand. If he chooses one purchase order or setup per year, his average inventory will be:

$$\frac{A}{2} \tag{2}$$

where A is the annual usage in dollars. If the choice of two purchase orders or setups per year is chosen, the average inventory on hand will be:

$$\frac{A}{2 \times 2} \tag{3}$$

and hence the possibility of the average inventory on hand is:

$$\frac{A}{N \times 2} \tag{4}$$

As the inventory increases, the costs of carrying the inventory will increase. As the number of Ns increase, the amount of carrying costs will decrease. If I is the cost of carrying the inventory, the cost of possessing an inventory with N purchase orders or setups will be:

$$\frac{A \times I}{N \times 2} \tag{5}$$

Since the minimum cost is where the carrying costs equal the procurement or setup costs, we can then say that the following will present minimum costs:

$$\frac{A \times I}{N \times 2} = N \times B \tag{6}$$

Then, since the number of purchase orders or setups is:

$$N = \frac{A}{Q} \tag{7}$$

Where Q is the economic order quantity in dollars we can substitute A/Q in formula (6) for each N. This gives:

$$\frac{A \times I}{2\,A/Q} = \frac{A}{Q} \times B \tag{8}$$

and

$$\frac{IQ}{2} = \frac{AB}{Q} \tag{9}$$

$$IQ^2 = 2AB \tag{10}$$

$$Q^2 = \frac{2AB}{I} \tag{11}$$

$$Q = \sqrt{\frac{2AB}{I}} \tag{12}$$

SUPPLEMENTARY READING

Baer, Wilmer. "A Cash Flow Model." *Managerial Planning,* March–April, 1972.

Boyer, Robert. "How to Help Your Client Obtain a Bank Loan." *The Journal of Accountancy,* October, 1977.

Elliott, W. Larry. "Operational Approach to Cash Management." *Management Accounting,* December, 1976.

Kellogg, Martin N. "Analysis and Control of a Cash Flow System." *The Controller,* October, 1957.

National Association of Accountants. *Techniques of Inventory Management.* New York: National Association of Accountants, 1964.

Perry, James E. "Analyzing the Borrower's Situation." *Journal of Accountancy,* October, 1977.

Pillin, Dominic A. "Credit by Exception: A Cash Management Tool." *Management Accounting,* July, 1977.

Prater, George I. "Accounting and Inventory Decisions." *Managerial Planning,* November–December, 1968.

Rinehart, Jack R. "Economic Purchase Quantity Calculations." *Management Accounting,* September, 1970.

Smith, Ephraim P., and Raymond G. Laverdiere. "Cash Management." *Managerial Planning,* July–August, 1973.

QUESTIONS

13-1 Cash is the focal point of short-term resources planning. Explain why this is true.

13-2 Explain and illustrate the operating cycle for a manufacturing company.

13-3 Define the following terms: *short-term resources, liquidity, solvency, working capital, line of credit,* and *turnover.*

13-4 Explain the process of "rolling over" a cash budget. Why is it important to prepare a cash budget on this basis?

13-5 Working capital (and its components) are held for two reasons. Explain the two reasons and indicate briefly how the amount of cash needed for each reason is determined.

13-6 Explain the ABC method of inventory control. For each inventory component (A, B, and C) indicate the models you would use to assist in planning the inventory.

13-7 The equation for the economic order quantity is:

$$EOQ = \sqrt{\frac{2AB}{\mathrm{I}}}$$

Explain each of the terms A, B, and I and indicate how they are measured.

13-8 During the year 19X7, the following changes were noted:

Current ratio increased.
Liquidity ratio decreased.
Working capital remained constant.

What components of working capital changed to produce these changes?

13-9 Indicate how a firm may use ratios in planning and controlling short-term resources. What limitations do you see in their use?

13-10 The president of a retailing firm established an inventory policy: For each store the days sales in inventory should equal the industry average. He believes that if they are not equal to the industry average, the firm has too much or too little inventory. Discuss this policy and indicate any weaknesses you may see.

EXERCISES

13-11 *(Matching).* Match the following terms and definitions.

1. Liquidity
2. Operating cycle
3. Rollover budget
4. Accounts receivable turnover
5. Safety stock
6. Inventory turnover
7. Line of credit
8. Working capital
9. Economic order quantity
10. Reorder point

A. Average total inventory minus average working stock.
B. The period of time covering the investment and recovery of cash in inventory.
C. The difference between safety stock and maximum inventory level.
D. A loan agreement that allows the firm to borrow, when needed, up to a given maximum.
E. Sales divided by accounts receivable.
F. A term referring to the amount and composition of assets.
G. Usage divided by average inventory.
H. Safety stock plus lead-time usage.
I. Continual replanning by dropping projection for an old period and adding projection for a new period.
J. Current assets minus current liabilities.

13-12 *(True or False).* Indicate whether the following statements are *true* or *false*.

1. Liquidity refers to the amount and composition of assets, whereas solvency refers to the ability of a firm to pay its liabilities when due.

2. A favorable current ratio will be decreased by paying a large account payable which is classified as a current liability.

3. Working capital is the difference between liquid assets and current liabilities.

4. An operating cycle runs from the time cash is invested in inventories to the time cash is collected from customers after the product is sold.

5. Cash provided by operations is measured by adding dividends back to net income.

6. An EOQ model is used to determine the optimum level of total inventory the firm should hold.

7. The inventory reorder point would tend to be delayed (extended) by a decrease in the expected usage of material during the lead time.

8. In the ABC method used for inventory control, the A type will probably have the largest safety stock.

9. Accounts receivable turnover are affected by the firm's credit and collection policies.

10. Inventory turnover and receivable turnover are useful tools for the day-to-day management of short-term resources.

13-13 *(Cash Collected from Customers).* All sales by the Wise Vise Company are made on account. The following credit transactions occurred during 19X7.

Credit sales	$360,000
Accounts receivable, Jan. 1, 19X7	$ 64,000
Accounts receivable, December 31, 19X7	$ 80,000
Allowance for uncollectible accounts receivable, Jan. 1, 19X7	$ 6,000
Allowance for uncollectible accounts receivable, Dec. 31, 19X7	$ 4,000
Bad-debt expense	$ 3,600

REQUIRED:

A. How much cash was collected from customers during 19X7?

B. Determine the accounts receivable turnover and the number of days sales outstanding. If the firm has a credit policy of net 30 days, how has it performed in collecting its receivables?

13-14 *(Collections from Customers).* The sales budget for the Corey Wholesale Company for the first quarter of 19X4 is:

January	$40,000
February	$30,000
March	$60,000

All sales are on credit and the company's collection pattern shows:

In month of sale	60%
In following month	37%
Uncollectible	3%

A 2% cash discount is allowed on collections in the month of sale.

REQUIRED:

A. How much cash will be collected from customers in February?

B. How much cash will be collected from customers in March?

C. What is the balance of accounts receivable at the end of March?

13-15 *(Inventory Terms).* From the diagram shown, answer the questions that follow.

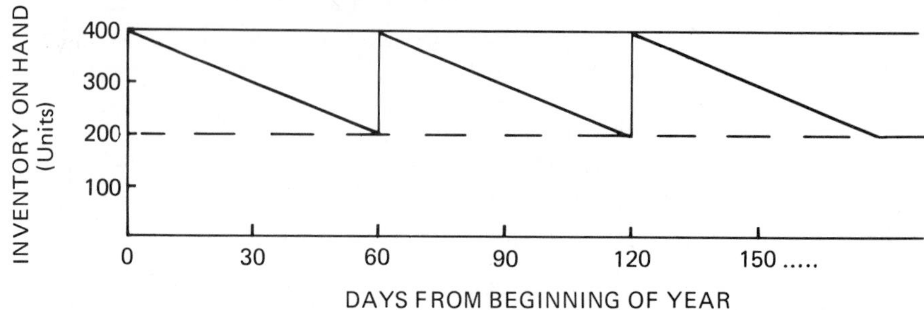

REQUIRED:

A. What is the maximum inventory?
B. What is the safety stock?
C. How long is the turnover cycle?
D. What is the economic order quantity?
E. How many orders will be placed this year?
F. Assuming that an order takes 10 days to receive, at what level of inventory should the order be placed so as to maintain the safety stock?

13-16 *(Economic Order Quantity).* Broketown Industries has revised its procedures to control raw materials and plans to purchase in economic order quantities. The following data relate to inventories.

Annual requirement	1,200,000 pounds
Purchase price	\$3.00 per pound
Ordering cost	\$50 per order
Carrying cost of inventory	10% of cost
Safety stock requirements	20,000 pounds

REQUIRED:

A. Compute the economic order quantity for Broketown Industries.
B. Graph the flow of raw materials for the year, showing number of units on the vertical axis and time on the horizontal axis. Assume that the inventory is at the maximum level on the first day of the year. Assume that the lead time is approximately two days. Label the following on the graph: replenishment point, reorder point, lead time, safety stock, and economic order quantity.

13-17 *(New Credit Policy).* Raging River Electronics believes sales will increase if new credit terms are offered to customers. The profit plan, based on the old credit terms, projected sales for 19X3 at \$720,000, a 40% contribution margin ratio, bad debts of .5% of sales, and an accounts receivable turnover of ten times. The company has established a 20% target rate of return.

The new credit policy should increase sales by 10%. However, the new credit policy can be expected to reduce the accounts receivable turnover to six times per year and increase bad debts to 1.5% of sales.

REQUIRED:
Should the company adopt the new credit policy? Explain.

13-18 *(Cash Balance for Normal Transaction).* The J. A. Jacobs Company has adopted a four-week, 28-day month for internal planning and reporting. The following data on operating cash inflows and outflows may be regarded as normal for one month. (Saturdays and Sundays are omitted.)

Day	*Cash Inflow*	*Cash Outflow*	*Day*	*Cash Inflow*	*Cash Outflow*
1	$ 5,000	$ 3,000	15	$4,000	$ 3,000
2	5,000	10,000	16	4,000	3,000
3	4,000	10,000	17	3,000	10,000
4	4,000	3,000	18	4,000	3,000
5	5,000	2,000	19	5,000	3,000
8	8,000	8,000	22	4,000	3,000
9	15,000	8,000	23	4,000	3,000
10	20,000	10,000	24	3,000	15,000
11	20,000	2,000	25	3,000	4,000
12	8,000	2,000	26	5,000	5,000

REQUIRED:

A. Disregarding cash flows from other than operations (i.e., borrowing, repayment, purchase or sale of assets), what minimum cash balance would you recommend for transaction purposes at the beginning of the month?

B. What is the largest cash payment that could be made on the fifteenth day of the month to maintain an ending cash balance at least equal to the beginning cash balance?

13-19 *(Economic Order Quantities).* The Robney Company is a restaurant supplier that sells a number of products to various restaurants in the area. One of its products is a special meat cutter with a disposable blade.

The blades are sold in packages of 12 for $20 per package. After a number of years, it has been determined that the demand for the replacement blades is at a constant rate of 2,000 packages per month. The packages cost the Robney Company $10 each from the manufacturer and require a three-day lead time from date of order to date of delivery. The ordering cost is $1.20 per order and the carrying cost is 10% per annum.

Robney is going to use the economic order quantity formula:

$$\text{EOQ in units} = \sqrt{\frac{2(\text{Annual requirements})(\text{Cost per order})}{(\text{Price per unit})(\text{Carrying cost})}}$$

REQUIRED:

A. Calculate:
   1. The economic order quantity
   2. The number of orders needed per year
   3. The total cost of buying and carrying blades for the year

B. Assuming there is no reserve (e.g., safety stock) and that the present inventory level is 200 packages, when should the next order be placed? (Use 360 days equals one year.)

C. Discuss the problems that most firms would have in attempting to apply this formula to their inventory problems. *(CMA adapted)*

13–20 *(Liquidate or Salvage a Failing Business).* For many years the Short String Manufacturing Company supplied components for a product produced in the Milford Plant of the Mechanical Equipment Company. Three years ago competitors introduced an electronic product eliminating the market for the product and forcing the Mechanical Equipment Company to close the Milford Plant and consolidate operations in their home plant. The Short String Manufacturing Company has been unsuccessful in entering other markets and has sustained large losses. Recently, the company exhausted its financial resources and turned to the court for protection from creditors.

You have been appointed by the court to determine whether (1) the company should be liquidated, or (2) it can be salvaged. The following statement of financial position shows that if the company is liquidated at this time, the mortgage holders would be paid in full, but the general creditors (those who do not have a mortgage or similar claim on specific assets) would be paid approximately one-third of their claims. (Note: With the exception of the unit cost data, *all* dollar figures in the problem are in thousands.)

Negotiations with creditors have resulted in the general creditors agreeing to reduce their claims to 50% of the June 30, 19X6 balance if they are paid within two years. General creditors will receive the proceeds from accounts receivable and the sale of obsolete inventory immediately. The balance of their reduced claims will be paid as cash is generated from operations with interest at 10%. The mortgage holders will not accept any change in the mortgage terms. Payments of $10 per year plus interest at 10% must be made on the mortgage.

A new customer has been located who will purchase a special component from Short String during the next two years at the rate of 6,000 units during the first year and 12,000 during the second. Components are to be delivered as soon as produced. Existing facilities will be used but will require $20 of repairs in the first year and $15 in the second. Of the $60 *liquidation value* for plant on the June 30 statement of financial position, $15 relates to

SHORT STRING MANUFACTURING COMPANY
STATEMENT OF FINANCIAL POSITION
June 30, 19X6
(000)

	Book Balances	*Liquidation Balances*
ASSETS:		
Cash	$ 0	$ 0
Accounts receivable	100	50
Inventory	80	20
Plant and equipment	100	60
Total	$ 280	$130
EQUITIES:		
General creditors	$ 240	$ 80
Mortgage	50	50
Common stock	200	
Retained earnings	(210)	
Total	$ 280	$130

land and $45 to plant and equipment. Short String will need new production facilities to operate beyond three years. The following data apply to production of the new component.

Unit Revenue and Cost Data in Dollars

Selling price		$70
Material	$10	
Labor	16	
Variable overhead	8	
Variable delivery	10	44
Contribution margin		$26

Fixed costs (excluding interest and depreciation) will amount to $120 per year.

If Short String produces the new component, no finished goods inventory will be maintained, and components will be shipped as soon as they are produced. Raw materials inventory equal to 60 days usage and average collection period for accounts receivable of 30 days will be maintained. Because of the "court protection," short-term funds for working capital are readily available. Purchases of materials are paid in the month following purchase. Assume uniform production within a year.

REQUIRED:

A. Prepare a cash budget for each of the two years indicating the cash available for general creditors.

B. What are the claims of the general creditors and will they be paid if the company produces the component?

C. Should the company be liquidated or allowed to continue operations?

13-21 *(Constructing Data from Ratios).* The Aaby Company has the following ratios and other financial measures.

Current ratio	4 times
Liquidity ratio	2 times
Working capital	$12,000
Inventory turnover	6 times
Sales	$60,000
Days sales in receivables	36

REQUIRED:

Assuming that there are no supplies or prepaid expenses, determine the following:

A. Current assets.

B. Current liabilities.

C. Inventory.

D. Accounts receivable.

E. Total of cash and marketable securities.

F. Gross margin.

13-22 *(Multiple Choice).* The Dilly Company marks up all merchandise at 25% of gross purchase price. All purchases are made on account with terms of 1/10, net/60 (1% discount if paid in 10 days, balance due in 60 days). Purchase discounts are always taken. Normally, 60% of each month's purchases are paid for in the month of purchase; the other 40% are paid during the first 10 days of the first month after purchase. Inventories of merchandise at the end of each month are kept at 30% of the next month's projected cost of goods sold.

Terms for sales on account are 2/10, net/30 (2% discount if paid in 10 days, balance due in 30 days). Cash sales are not subject to discount. Fifty percent of each month's sales on account are collected during the month of sale, 45% are collected in the succeeding month, and the remainder are usually uncollectible. Seventy percent of the collections in the month of sale are subject to discount; 10% of the collections in the succeeding month are subject to discount.

Projected sales data for selected months follow.

	Sales on Account—Gross	Cash Sales
December	$1,900,000	$400,000
January	$1,500,000	$250,000
February	$1,700,000	$350,000
March	$1,600,000	$300,000

1. Projected gross purchases for January are
a. $1,400,000
b. $1,470,000
c. $1,472,000
d. $1,248,000
e. None of the above

2. Projected inventory at the end of December is
a. $420,000
b. $441,600
c. $552,000
d. $393,750
e. None of the above

3. Projected payments to suppliers during February are
a. $1,551,200
b. $1,535,688
c. $1,528,560
d. $1,509,552
e. None of the above

4. Projected sales discounts to be taken by customers making remittances during February are
a. $12,210
b. $15,925
c. $13,250
d. $11,900
e. None of the above

5. Projected total collections from customers during February are
a. $1,875,000
b. $1,861,750
c. $1,511,750
d. $1,188,100
e. None of the above *(CPA adapted)*

13-23 *(Computation of Financial Ratios).* Financial statements for the Blueball Company follow.

BLUEBALL COMPANY
STATEMENT OF FINANCIAL POSITION
December 31, 19X6

Assets		*Equities*	
Cash	$ 50,000	Accounts payable	$ 80,000
Accounts receivable (net)	100,000	Short-term notes payable	50,000
Inventories	300,000	Income tax payable	30,000
Marketable securities	90,000	Long-term note payable	400,000
Prepaid expenses	20,000	Reserve for contingencies	40,000
Investment in subsidiary	50,000	Capital stock	250,000
Land	50,000	Retained earnings	150,000
Building and equipment (net)	300,000		
Patents	40,000		
	$1,000,000		$1,000,000

BLUEBALL COMPANY
INCOME STATEMENT
For the Year Ended December 31, 19X6

Sales	$2,000,000
Cost of goods sold	1,200,000
Gross margin	$ 800,000
Operating expenses	500,000
Net income	$ 300,000

REQUIRED:

A. From the financial statements determine the following:
   1. Current assets
   2. Current liabilities
   3. Fixed assets
   4. Working capital
   5. Stockholders' equity
   6. Total assets

B. The treasurer has acquired the following set of industry ratios with which to compare and evaluate the Blueball Company's working capital position. Compute each of the following ratios for the Blueball Company and comment upon the company's working capital position.
   1. Current ratio—industry 3 to 1
   2. Liquidity ratio—industry 1.75 to 1
   3. Days sales in receivable—industry 25 days
   4. Days in inventory—industry 45 days
   5. Return on stockholders' equity—50%

13-24 *(Financial Ratio Analysis.)* Thorpe Company is a wholesale distributor of professional equipment and supplies. The company's sales have averaged about $900,000 annually for the three-year period 19X3–19X5. The firm's total assets at the end of 19X5 amounted to: $850,000.

The president of Thorpe Company has asked the controller to prepare a report which summarizes the financial aspects of the company's operations for the past three years. This report will be presented to the Board of Directors at their next meeting.

In addition to comparative financial statements, the controller has decided to present a number of relevant financial ratios to assist in the identification and interpretation of trends. At the request of the controller, the accounting staff has calculated the following ratios for the three-year period 19X3–19X5:

	19X3	*19X4*	*19X5*
Current ratio	2.00	2.13	2.18
Acid-test (quick) ratio	1.20	1.10	0.97
Accounts receivable turnover	9.72	8.57	7.13
Inventory turnover	5.25	4.80	3.80
Percent of total debt to total assets	44	41	38
Percent of long-term debt to total assets	25	22	19
Sales to fixed assets (fixed asset turnover)	1.75	1.88	1.99
Sales as a percent of 19X3 sales	1.00	1.03	1.06
Gross margin percentage	40.0	38.6	38.5
Net income to sales	7.8%	7.8%	8.0%
Return on total assets	8.5%	8.6%	8.7%
Return on stockholders' equity	15.1%	14.6%	14.1%

In the preparation of his report, the controller has decided first to examine the financial ratios independently of any other data to determine if the ratios themselves reveal any significant trends over the three-year period.

REQUIRED:

A. The current ratio is increasing while the acid-test (quick) ratio is decreasing. Using the ratios provided, identify and explain the contributing factor(s) for this apparently divergent trend.

B. Analyze the effectiveness of management's decisions regarding the firm's resources. *(CMA adapted)*

13-25 *(Establishment of Borrowing Policies).* Wymon Company has experienced some financial difficulties in the past 18 months and is short of cash. Management estimates that an additional $150,000 will be needed within the next 2 months.

Relations between Wymon Company and its primary commercial bank, American Bank, have been excellent over the years. The bank has lent the company money on a regular basis as needed, and the company has always repaid the loans on the due date. In fact, Wymon currently has a sizable long-term loan from the bank.

Because Wymon has been a good customer, American Bank is willing to lend the $150,000 on a two-year note. Because of the increased financial risk arising from Wymon's financial difficulties, the bank would charge a higher rate of interest and require stronger collateral than in the past. The bank would charge interest at 20% annually and require that the loan be secured by a warehouse receipt. The additional costs incurred by Wymon to maintain a field warehouse arrangement would be $2,400 per year. This loan would enable Wymon to pay for its material purchases within the discount period.

The only other feasible alternative available to Wymon is to make an agreement with its trade creditors "to stretch" its accounts payable beyond the normal credit terms. Wymon currently purchases $75,000 of raw materials every 30 days on terms of 2/10, net 30. Wymon's creditors would allow the company to stretch the accounts payable beyond the due date but would charge a penalty of 2.5% per month for any balance outstanding for more than 30 days.

Wymon's management has prepared a detailed plan of its operations for the next two years. The plan indicates that the company's cash shortage will no longer exist at the end of this two-year period. Therefore, if the loan alternative is selected, Wymon Company will begin to liquidate the loan and discontinue the field warehouse arrangement at the end of the two-year period. If management selects the alternative of stretching the accounts payable, the company will pay its accounts payable within the 30-day credit period at the end of the two-year period and begin working toward taking cash discounts. American Bank and Wymon's creditors have reviewed both of these alternatives and accepted them as reasonable.

REQUIRED:

A. Assuming that the $150,000 can be raised, calculate the monthly cost of:
   1. the warehouse receipt loan with American Bank.
   2. the plan to stretch the accounts payable.
   Which plan would you recommend?

B. What are the disadvantages associated with "stretching" accounts payable?

(CMA adapted)

PROBLEMS

13-26 *(Determine Maximum Line of Credit).* You are a commercial loan officer for the Third Commercial State Bank. The loan committee of the bank has approved a loan to the Dixon Machinery Company, an equipment dealer. The company is to be granted a line of credit on which the company may draw at the beginning of each month as needed but must be repaid as soon as excess cash is generated from operations. However, the entire loan with interest is to be repaid by the end of six months. There is a shortage of money for commercial loans in your bank and the loan committee has asked you to grant the minimum line of credit possible to serve the customer.

The profit plan, sales budget, cash budget, and other budgetary data presented by the customer in support of the loan are presented below. (All dollar amounts in the problem are in thousands of dollars.)

DIXON MACHINERY COMPANY
PROFIT PLAN
First six months of 19X7
(000)

Sales		$1,200
Cost of goods sold		720
Gross margin		$ 480
Variable expenses		120
Contribution margin		$ 360
Fixed expenses:		
Operating expenses	$120	
Depreciation	60	180
Planned income		$ 180

DIXON MACHINERY COMPANY
SALES BUDGET
First six months of 19X7
(000)

Month	*Projected Sales*
1	$ 100
2	200
3	200
4	300
5	300
6	100
Total	$1,200

DIXON MACHINERY COMPANY
CASH BUDGET
First six months of 19X7
(000)

Sources of cash:		
From operation:		
Collections from customers		$1,190
Payments:		
to suppliers	$900	
expenses	240	1,140
Cash provided by operations		$ 50

The beginning balance of accounts receivable is $90. The beginning balance of accounts payable is $100. All sales and purchases are paid in the month following purchase. After running out of inventory two months ago the company installed a new inventory control system. The economic order quantity was determined to be $200, the safety stock of $100, and lead time of 60 days. Orders were placed for one EOQ quantity to be delivered in the first month and one in the second month of 19X7.

The beginning cash balance of $20 is the minimum the loan agreement will allow. The bank will allow the company to draw the amount needed each month at the beginning of the month. Repayments must be made as soon as excess cash is generated by operations. Assume that interest will be paid at the end of the six months or when the loan is repaid if sooner. Interest is computed at 1% of the loan at the beginning of each month (round the interest to the nearest thousand).

REQUIRED:

A. Prepare cash budgets for each of the six months in the period. Ignore income taxes.

B. What is the maximum line of credit your bank should grant to the Dixon Machinery Company? How much excess cash is generated by operations during the six months?

13–27 *(Constructing Statements from Ratios).* Financial ratios are often used to project balances as well as to test the soundness of a balance or its relationship with an industry position. The Rag Tag Mill End Carpet Shop is being formed. There are no similar shops for remnants of quality carpeting, and the promoters predict immediate success. A prospective creditor will loan the shop $10,000 to start, but he insists that by the end of the first year of business the financial statements of the shop must meet or exceed normal ratios and other financial measures for this type of firm. The following are ratios the creditor expects the firm to meet or exceed.

Current ratio	2 to 1
Liquidity ratio	1 to 1
Inventory turnover	3.6 times per year
Accounts receivable turnover	12 times per year
Ratio of long-term debt to working capital	1 to 1
Ratio of total debt to owners' equity	1 to 1
Cash as a percentage of liquid assets	50%
Gross margin on sales	60%
Net income on sales	10%

Other data:

The note will be payable in 2 years. Interest at 10% will be paid annually.

Fixed assets will be depreciated on a straight-line basis over 10 years.

The following accounts should be used.

Statement of financial position:	Income statement:
Cash	Sales
Accounts receivable	Cost of goods sold
Inventory	Operating expenses
Fixed assets	Depreciation expenses
Accounts payable	Interest expense
Long-term note payable	
Owners' equity	

REQUIRED:

A. Using the ratios required by the potential creditor, prepare an income statement for the year and a statement of financial position at the end of the first year of operations for the Rag Tag Mill End Carpet Shop. Assume that any amount required to reach the desired ending balance in owners' equity will be invested by the owners. Ignore taxes.

B. How much will the owners be required to invest in order to achieve the desired financial position at the end of the year?

13-28 *(Cash Budget).* The Wooden Mouse, Inc. is a specialty gift shop in a popular ski area. For the past two years, skiing has been poor and, as a result, several specialty shops have failed. The Wooden Mouse has serious cash flow problems and needs help in planning cash flows for the coming season. Snow for the 19X3 ski season is expected to be normal, so the following sales may be expected:

December	$20,000
January	$50,000
February	$60,000
March	$30,000
April	$20,000
May to November	$10,000 per month

The inventory policy is to maintain an inventory equal to the next two months' sales. The beginning inventory is $12,000, the minimum amount required if a poor season is predicted.

Purchases are subject to 5/10, n/60 terms. (A 5% discount is allowed on payments within 10 days of the purchase; the balance is due within 60 days.) All purchases are made in the first half of the month. No purchases were made during October; purchases during November were $5,000. Because of the cash shortage, no discounts have been taken for two years.

Fifty percent of the sales are for cash; the balance are on credit cards with a 5% service charge. One-half of the credit sales are collected in the month of sale; one-half are collected in the month following the sale. Sales in November were $10,000.

The company has a 60% gross margin rate, operating expenses are $9,000 per month (including $1,000 of depreciation) plus 20% of sales. Seventy-five percent of the expenses are paid in the month the expense is incurred; the balance is paid in the following month.

A line of credit for $30,000 was arranged at the bank; $8,000 was drawn against the line of credit in November. Interest is 1% per month on the unpaid loan balance and is payable on April 1. The loan principle is to be reduced as soon as cash is available but must be paid in full by April. All loan transactions (except interest) must be in even thousand-dollar amounts. The company must maintain a minimum cash balance of $2,000, which is the December 1 balance. Because the shop will operate at a loss for the remainder of the year, the owner wants a cash balance of $15,000 on May 1. Ignore income taxes.

REQUIRED:

A. Prepare a cash budget, by month, for the 19X3 ski season. Assume that discounts will be taken.

B. Will the owner of Wooden Mouse, Inc. be able to accomplish the cash and loan payment objectives during the 19X3 ski season? If cash requirements exceed the line of credit during a particular month, what can the firm do to improve cash inflows or reduce or postpone cash outflows? Explain, but do not recast the cash budget.

13-29 *(Continuation of Problem 13–28; Adjusted Cash Budget for a Failing Firm).* Using the data in Problem 13–28 for the Wooden Mouse, Inc., assume that the long-run weather forecast is for little snow and, therefore, poor skiing. Sales for the company are projected as follows if the weather is bad for skiing:

December	$10,000
January	$20,000
February	$25,000
March	$20,000
April	$10,000
May to November	$10,000 per month

REQUIRED:

A. Assuming that all other facts in Problem 13–28 remain unchanged except for the revised sales forecast, prepare a new cash budget for Wooden Mouse, Inc.

B. What are your recommendations for the owners of Wooden Mouse, Inc.?

13-30 *(Establishment of Receivables and Payables Policies).* Luther Company produces and sells a complete line of infant and toddler toys. Its sales, which are characteristic of the entire toy industry, are very seasonal. The company offers favorable credit to customers who place their Christmas orders early and accept a shipment schedule arranged to fit the production schedules of Luther. The customer must place orders by May 15 and be willing to accept shipments beginning August 15; Luther guarantees shipment no later than October 15. Customers willing to accept these conditions are not required to pay for their Christmas purchases until January 30.

The suppliers of the raw materials used by Luther in the manufacture of toys offer more normal credit terms. The usual terms for the raw materials are 2/10, net/30. Luther Company makes payment within the 10-day discount period during the first six months of the year; however, in the summer and fall, it does not even meet the 30-day terms. The company regularly pays invoices for raw materials 80 to 90 days after the invoice date during this latter period. Suppliers have come to accept this pattern because it has existed for many years. In addition, this payment pattern has not affected Luther's credit rating or ability to acquire the necessary raw materials.

Luther recently hired a new financial vice-president. He feels quite uncomfortable with the unusually large accounts receivable and payable balances in the fall and winter and with the poor payment practice of Luther. He would like to consider alternatives to the present method of financing the accounts receivable.

REQUIRED:

One proposal Luther Company might consider is to establish a line of credit at a local bank. The company could then draw against this line of credit in order to pay the invoices within the 10-day discount period and pay off the debt in February when the accounts receivable were collected. The effective interest rate for this arrangement would be 12%. Would this alternative reduce Luther's costs of doing business? Support your answer with appropriate calculations. *(CMA adapted)*

13-31 *(Estimating EOQ Input Data).* Evans Inc. is a large wholesale distributor which deals exclusively in baby shoes. Because of the substantial costs related to ordering and storing the shoes, the company has decided to employ the economic order quantity method (EOQ) to help determine the optimum quantities of shoes to order from the different manufacturers. The EOQ formula is

$$\underset{\text{in units}}{EOQ} = \sqrt{\frac{2C_O D}{PC_S}}$$

where

EOQ = optimum number of units per purchase order
D = annual demand
P = purchase price per unit
C_O = cost of placing an order
C_S = the annual cost of storage per dollar of investment in inventory

Before Evans Inc. can employ the EOQ model, they need to develop values for two of the cost parameters—ordering costs (C_O) and storage costs (C_S). As a starting point, management has decided to develop the values for the two cost parameters by using cost data from the most recent fiscal year, 19X5.

The company placed 4,000 purchase orders during 19X5. The largest number of orders placed during any one month was 400 orders in June, and the smallest number of orders placed was 250 in December. Selected cost data for these two months and the year for the purchasing, accounts payable, and warehousing operations appear below.

	Costs for High Activity Month (June; 400 orders)	*Costs for Low Activity Month (December; 250 orders)*	*Annual Costs*
Purchasing Department			
Purchasing manager	$ 1,750	$ 1,750	$ 21,000
Buyers	2,500	1,900	28,500
Clerks	2,000	1,100	20,600
Supplies	275	150	2,500
Accounts Payable Dept.			
Clerks	2,000	1,500	21,500
Supplies	125	75	1,100
Data processing	2,600	2,300	30,000
Warehouse			
Foreman	1,250	1,250	15,000
Receiving clerks	2,300	1,800	23,300
Receiving supplies	50	25	500
Shipping clerks	3,800	3,500	44,000
Shipping supplies	1,350	1,200	15,200
Freight out	1,600	1,300	16,800
	$21,600	$17,850	$240,000

The purchasing department is responsible for placing all orders. The costs listed for the accounts payable department relate only to the processing of purchase orders for payment. The warehouse costs reflect two operations—receiving and shipping. The receiving clerks inspect all incoming shipments and place the orders in storage. The shipping clerks are responsible for processing all sales orders to retailers.

The company leases space in a public warehouse. The rental fee is priced according to the square feet occupied during a month. The annual charges during 19X5 totaled $34,500. Annual insurance and property taxes on the shoes stored in the warehouse amounted to $5,700 and $7,300, respectively. The company pays 8% a year for a small amount of short-term, seasonal bank debt. Long-term capital investments are expected to produce a rate of return of 12% after taxes. The effective tax rate is 40%.

The inventory balances tend to fluctuate during the year depending upon the demand for baby shoes. Selected data on inventory balances are shown below.

Inventory, January 1, 19X5	$160,000
Inventory, December 31, 19X5	$120,000
Highest inventory balance (June)	$220,000
Lowest inventory balance (December)	$120,000
Average monthly inventory	$190,000

The boxes in which the baby shoes are stored are all approximately the same size. Consequently, the shoes all occupy about the same amount of storage space in the warehouse.

REQUIRED:

A. Using the 19X5 data, determine estimated values appropriate for

1. C_O—cost of placing an order.
2. C_S—the annual cost of storage per dollar of investment in inventory.

B. Should Evans Inc. use the cost parameters developed solely from the historical data in the employment of the EOQ model? Explain your answer. *(CMA adapted)*

13-32 *(Prepare a Cash Budget).* The Pantex Corporation has gone through a period of rapid expansion to reach its present size of seven divisions. The expansion program has placed strains on its cash resources. Therefore, the need for better cash planning at the corporate level has become very important.

At the present time each division is responsible for the collection of receivables and the disbursement for all operating expenses and approved capital projects. The corporation does exercise control over division activities and has attempted to coordinate the cash needs of the divisions and the corporation. However, it has not yet developed effective division cash reports from which it can determine the needs and availability of cash in the next budgetary year. As a result of inadequate information, the corporation permitted some divisions to make expenditures for goods and services which need not have been made or which could have been postponed until a later time while other divisions had to delay expenditures which should have had a greater priority.

The 19X8 cash receipts and disbursements plan prepared by the Tapon Division for submission to the corporate office is presented below.

Tapon Division
Budgeted Cash Receipts and Disbursements
For the year ended December 31, 19X8
(000 omitted)

Receipts	
Collections on accounts	$9,320
Miscellaneous	36
	$9,356
Disbursements	
Production	
Raw materials	$2,240
Labor and fringe benefits	2,076
Overhead	2,100
Sales	
Commissions	395
Travel & entertainment	600
Other	200
Administrative	
Accounting	80
Personnel	110
General management	350
Capital expenditures	1,240
	9,391
Excess of receipts over (under) disbursements	$ (35)

The following additional information was used by the Tapon Division to develop the cash receipts and disbursements budget.

1. Receipts—Miscellaneous receipts are estimated proceeds from the sales of unneeded equipment.

2. Sales—Travel and entertainment represents the costs required to produce the sales volume projected for the year. The other sales costs consist of $50,000 for training new sales personnel, $25,000 for attendance by sales personnel at association meetings (not sales shows), and $125,000 for sales management salaries.

3. Administration—The personnel costs include $50,000 for salary and department operating costs, $20,000 for training new personnel, and $40,000 for management training courses for current employees. The general management costs include salaries and office costs for the division management, $310,000, plus $10,000 for officials' travel to Pantex Corporation meetings and $30,000 for industry and association conferences.

4. Capital expenditures—Planned expenditures for capital items during 19X8 are as follows:

Capital programs approved by the corporation:

Items ordered for delivery in 19X8	$300,000
Items to be ordered in 19X8 for delivery in 19X8	$700,000
New programs to be submitted to corporation during 19X8	$240,000

REQUIRED:
Present a revised Budgeted Cash Receipts and Disbursement Statement for the Tapon Division. Design the format of the revised statement to include adequate detail so as to improve the ability of the corporation to judge the urgency of the cash needs. Such a statement would be submitted by all divisions to provide the basis for overall corporation cash planning.

(CMA adapted)

13-33 *(Financial Ratios and Changes in Cash Position)*. You have been assigned by the acquisitions committee of Control Group, Inc. to examine a potential acquisition, Retailers, Inc. This company is a merchandising firm which appears to be available owing to the death of its founder and principal shareholder. Recent statements of Retailers, Inc. are shown below:

BALANCE SHEET
As of January 31

	19X0	19X1	19X2
Cash	$ 100,000	$ 120,000	$ 130,000
Accounts Receivable	300,000	370,000	430,000
Inventory	200,000	400,000	400,000
Fixed Assets	700,000	800,000	900,000
Less: Accumulated Depreciation	(200,000)	(250,000)	(325,000)
Total Assets	$1,100,000	$1,440,000	$1,535,000
Accounts Payable	$ 220,000	$ 260,000	$ 300,000
8% Notes payable Due 1/31/Y0	0	280,000	280,000
Common Stock Outstanding	690,000	690,000	690,000
Retained Earnings	190,000	210,000	265,000
Total Equity	$1,100,000	$1,440,000	$1,535,000

INCOME STATEMENTS
For the Years Ended January 31

	19X1	19X2
Sales	$2,629,000	$2,943,000
Cost of Goods Sold	$2,000,000	$2,200,000
Wages	300,000	350,000
Supplies	36,600	42,600
Depreciation	75,000	100,000
Interest Charges	22,400	22,400
Loss on Sale of Fixed Assets	105,000	75,000
Total Deductions	2,539,000	2,790,000
Net Income Before Taxes	$ 90,000	$ 153,000
Income Taxes	40,000	68,000
Net Income	$ 50,000	$ 85,000

CHANGES IN FINANCIAL POSITION
For the Years Ended January 31

	19X1	19X2
Sources:		
Net Income	$ 50,000	$ 85,000
Add back: Depreciation	75,000	100,000
Loss	105,000	75,000
Notes Payable	280,000	0
Total	$ 510,000	$ 260,000
Uses:		
Net Fixed Assets Purchased	$ 230,000	$ 200,000
Dividends Paid	30,000	30,000
Total	260,000	230,000
Increase (Decrease) in Net Working Capital	$ 250,000	$ 30,000

REQUIRED:

A. Calculate the inventory turnover for
   1. 19X1.
   2. 19X2.
   3. Is it better or worse in 19X2 than in 19X1?

B. Calculate the current ratio for 19X2.

C. Calculate a rate of return on the stockholders' equity for 19X2.

D. Describe the cash flow for 19X2 in a schedule that explains the changes in cash position.

(CMA adapted)

13-34 *(Ratios to Decide Credit Policy).* The L. Konrath Company is considering extending credit to the D. Hawk Company. It is estimated that sales to the D. Hawk Company would amount to $2,000,000 each year. The L. Konrath Company is a wholesaler that sells throughout the Midwest. The D. Hawk Company is a retail chain operation that has a number of stores in the Midwest. The L. Konrath Company has had a gross margin of approximately 60% in recent years and expects to have a similar gross margin on the D. Hawk Company order. The D. Hawk Company order is approximately 15% of the L. Konrath Company's present sales. Recent statements of the D. Hawk Company are as follows:

D. HAWK COMPANY
BALANCE SHEET
As of December 31
(000,000 omitted)

Assets	*19X1*	*19X2*	*19X3*
Current Assets:			
Cash	2.6	1.8	1.6
Government Securities (Cost)	.4	.2	—
Accounts and Notes Receivable (Net)	8.0	8.5	8.5
Inventories	2.8	3.2	2.8
Prepaid Assets	.7	.6	.6
Total Current Assets	14.5	14.3	13.5
Property, Plant & Equipment (Net)	4.3	5.4	5.9
Total Assets	18.8	19.7	19.4
Equities			
Current Liabilities:			
Notes Payable	3.2	3.7	4.2
Accounts Payable	2.8	3.7	4.1
Accrued Expenses & Taxes	.9	1.1	1.0
Total Current Liabilities	6.9	8.5	9.3
Long-Term Debt; 6%	3.0	2.0	1.0
Total Liabilities	9.9	10.5	10.3
Stockholders' Equity	8.9	9.2	9.1
Total Equities	18.8	19.7	19.4

INCOME STATEMENT
For the Year Ended
December 31
(000,000 omitted)

	19X1	19X2	19X3
Net Sales	24.2	24.5	24.9
Cost of Goods Sold	16.9	17.2	18.0
Gross Margin	7.3	7.3	6.9
Selling Expenses	4.3	4.4	4.6
Administrative Expenses	2.3	2.4	2.7
Total Expenses	6.6	6.8	7.3
Earnings (loss) Before Taxes	.7	.5	(.4)
Income Taxes	.3	.2	(.2)
Net Income	.4	.3	(.2)

STATEMENT OF CHANGES IN FINANCIAL POSITION
For the Year Ended December 31
(000,000 omitted)

	19X1	19X2	19X3
Sources of Funds:			
Net Income (Loss)	.4	.3	(.2)
Depreciation	.4	.5	.5
Funds from Operations	.8	.8	.3
Sale of Building	.2	—	—
Sales of Treasury Stock	—	.1	.1
Total Sources	1.0	.9	.4
Uses of Funds:			
Purchase of Property, Plant & Equipment	1.2	1.6	1.0
Dividends	.1	.1	—
Retirement of Long-Term Debt	—	1.0	1.0
Total Uses	1.3	2.7	2.0
Net Increase (Decrease) in Net Working Capital	(.3)	(1.8)	(1.6)

REQUIRED:

A. Calculate for the year 19X3 the following ratios:

1. rate of return on total assets.
2. acid-test ratio.
3. return to sales.
4. current ratio.
5. inventory turnover.

B. Would you grant credit to D. Hawk Co.? Support your answer with facts given in the problem.

C. What additional information, if any, would you want before making a final decision?

(CMA adapted)

13-35 *(Complex Cash Budget)*. The Jafa Corporation uses variable costing for managerial purposes and prepared their December 31, 19X3 balance sheet on a variable costing basis as follows:

JAFA CORPORATION
BALANCE SHEET
As of December 31, 19X3

Current Assets			
Cash		$ 10,000	
Marketable Securities		50,000	
Accounts Receivable		80,000	
Inventories			
Finished Goods	$67,500		
Work in Process	45,000		
Raw Materials	9,000	121,500	
Total Current Assets			$ 261,500
Long-term Assets			
Equipment (factory)	$ 300,000		
Less: Accumulated Depreciation	72,000	$228,000	
Plant	$1,000,000		
Less: Accumulated Depreciation	180,000	820,000	
Property		200,000	
Total Long-term Assets			1,248,000
Other Assets			
Intangibles (net)		$ 10,000	
Loan to Officer of Company		10,000	20,000
Total Assets			$1,529,500
Current Liabilities			
Accounts Payable		$ 25,680	
Other Payables		10,000	
Notes Payable (one month note due January 15, 19X4)		50,000	
Current Portion of Long-term Debt (due March 31, 19X4)		50,000	
Total Current Liabilities			$ 135,680
Long-term Debt (8%, 10 years, interest payable December 31, repayment of principal at rate of $50,000 per year beginning in 19X4)			450,000
Total Liabilities			$585,680
Owners' Equity			
Common Stock (issued and outstanding, 70,000 shares, $10 per share)		$700,000	
Retained Earnings		243,820	
Total Owners' Equity			943,820
Total Equities			$1,529,500

Some recent and forecast data are:

	Actual		Forecast			
	Nov.	Dec.	Jan.	Feb.	Mar.	Apr.
Cash Sales (units)	1,200	1,200	1,000	1,000	1,000	2,000
Credit Sales (units)	10,000	10,000	8,000	8,000	8,000	20,000
Selling and Administrative Expenses	\$20,000	\$20,000	\$20,000	\$20,000	\$20,000	\$20,000
Fixed Manufacturing Expenses[1]	\$15,000	\$15,000	\$15,000	\$15,000	\$15,000	\$15,000

[1]Excluding depreciation and amortization.

The company manufactures an automobile safety seat for children which it sells directly to a number of automobile dealers in its four-state region and to retail customers through its own outlet. The selling price through their own outlet is \$30; to the dealers, the price is \$20.

Since all sales through its own outlet are on a cash basis, and sales to dealers, all on account, have been long established, bad debts are negligible. Terms of credit sales are net 30. Sixty percent of the credit sales are paid in the month of the sale and the remaining 40% of the credit sales are paid in the month after the sale.

Raw materials cost \$5.00 per unit. All purchases of raw materials are on account. Accounts payable are on terms of net 30 days; 40% are paid in the month of purchase and 60% are paid in the following month. Direct labor and variable manufacturing overhead costs are \$10 per unit. Direct labor and variable manufacturing overhead costs are incurred in direct proportion to the percentage of completion and paid in cash when incurred.

At the end of each month, desired inventory levels are as follows:

Raw materials—20% of next month's requirements
Work in Process—50% of next month's requirements
Finished goods—50% of next month's requirements

Work in process is assumed to be 50% completed at the end of the month. Raw materials are added at the beginning of production.

Depreciation on the equipment is \$4,000 per month, and depreciation on the plant is \$5,000 per month. Amortization of intangibles is \$500 per month.

Selling and administrative expenses are all fixed and half are paid in the month incurred with the balance paid in the following month.

Fixed manufacturing expenses that require cash payments are paid in the month incurred.

Long-term debt-principal is to be paid each March 31, starting in 19X4 at a rate of $50,000 per year.

The loan to the officer was made on December 31, 19X3 and is due March 31, 19X4. The loan is to be repaid on March 31, 19X4 plus interest at 6% per annum.

The firm requires a minimum cash balance of $10,000 at the end of each month. If the balance is less, marketable securities are sold in multiples of $5,000 at the end of the month. If necessary, cash is borrowed in multiples of $1,000 at the end of the month. Marketable securities earn 6% per annum and the interest is collected at the end of each month. The short-term interest rate on notes payable is 12% per annum and is paid at the time the note is repaid.

Taxes are to be ignored.

REQUIRED:

Prepare a statement forecasting the cash balance including any necessary cash transactions to achieve company cash management objectives for January, 19X4. *(CMA adapted)*

PART 5

THE USE OF DATA IN MAKING CAPACITY DECISIONS

14 Information for Long-Range Decisions

In Chapter 1 management decisions were divided into long-range capacity decisions and short-range operating decisions. Long-range decisions have two unique characteristics. First, they involve *change* in the productive or service potential of the firm. A change in the firm's capacity requires investments of resources, usually large in amount, where each decision is unique and affects the firm's operations over long periods of time. Once a change has been initiated, it may be difficult and costly to reverse.

Second, there is typically a long span of time before benefits from a long-range investment are wholly realized. The use of any resource, including capital or money, has a cost. The cost of obtaining and maintaining this capital must be considered in long-range investment analysis. The purchase of a machine, for example, will usually require several years of operations to recover the investment. During this period of time the company has incurred a cost to its creditors and owners for the use of capital. This cost must be included in the decision to acquire the machine. The same cost of capital is present in the short-run decisions, but its impact is ignored because the decisions affect a short time span and can be reversed quickly; this is not true with long-run decisions.

Because long-run decisions are qualitatively different from short-run decisions, management typically applies different decision rules. In this chapter and the next we concentrate upon these long-run decision rules.

As we have stressed throughout this text, all decisions, both long-run and short-run, derive from the firm goals—the overall guidelines that determine the character and direction of the firm. These broad goals include a statement about the size and type of organization, the lines of products or services to be provided, the markets to be served, the human resources to be employed and their quality of life, the nature of the production facilities, and how the firm is to attain the needed resources. These statements present the firm's overall direction. With these goals clearly established, management can establish the strategies and policies needed to attain them.

As shown in Exhibit 14–1, these goals are the starting point of long-run decisions, decisions that affect the firm's operations for years to come. A decision to build a new production facility commits a firm to a production method, a geographic territory, and a scope of operations for an extended time period. Failure to make satisfactory long-run decisions means that the firm most likely will fail to achieve its goals.

Next the firm must take action to obtain the resources and facilities. As shown in Exhibit 14–1, the decisions to take these actions should be based upon long-range forecasts of the needs of the firm. In this way the goals of the firm are coordinated with the economic environment in which the firm exists. The long-run decisions that commit the firm and require the use of resources now, together with the recovery and earnings on the resources expected over an extended future time period, are:

1. Obtaining new facilities or expanding existing facilities. Here the choice concerns which facilities of those available should be obtained and for what purpose. This decision is based upon estimates as to which facility will give the largest return on the required

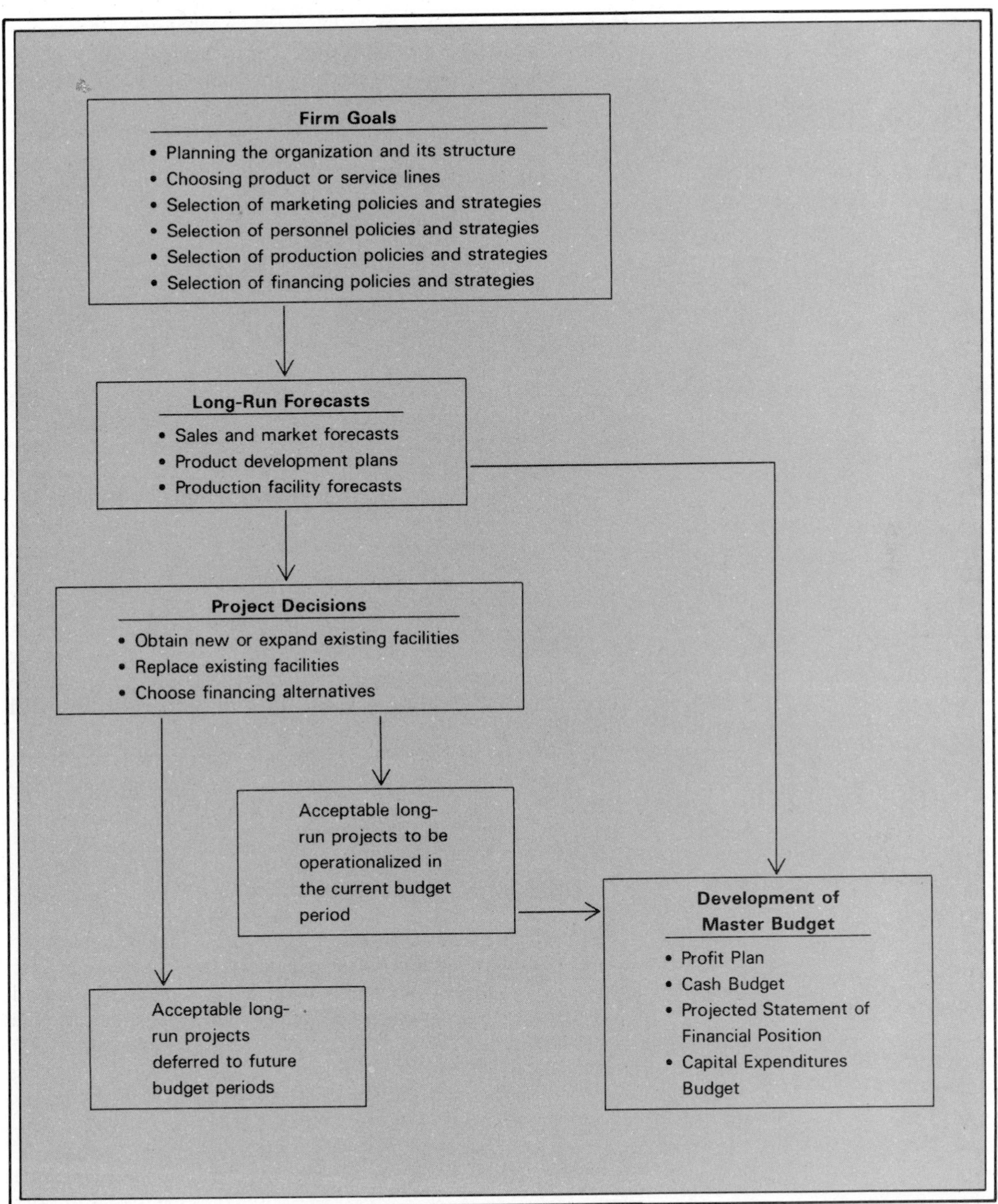

EXHIBIT 14–1
Long range planning flow

investment. Examples include buying new machinery, building a new office building, leasing or purchasing additional salespersons' automobiles, purchasing a subsidiary company, and adding a new production line.

2. Replacing existing facilities. Here the decision concerns substituting new facilities for existing facilities. This decision is based upon estimates that the savings from the new equipment, when compared with the old equipment, will offset the costs of the new equipment. Examples include replacing a manual bookkeeping system with a computer system, buying a new computer model to replace an older model, replacing 2-ton delivery trucks with 5-ton trucks, and replacing an inefficient lathe with one that is numerically controlled.

3. Choosing financial alternatives. This choice involves selecting modes of obtaining resources. One example is whether to lease or purchase an asset. Here the decision is whether or not the resources invested in the purchase alternative will earn an adequate return when contrasted with resources that would be committed in leasing.

Long-range decisions relate to specific projects. The decision rules are applied on a specific case-by-case basis. However, as shown in Exhibit 14–1, in any one budgetary period the acquisitions scheduled for that period will be integrated into the capital expenditures budget. This allows management to coordinate the capital expenditure plans with current operations plans. Once the decision has been implemented and the resources have been acquired, they become a part of the overall firm capacity. At this point they lose their separate identity, and the short-range decisions to maximize the use of the facilities become paramount. Now the revenues and costs traceable to the long-run decisions commingle with the revenues and costs traceable to the short-range decisions.

LONG-RANGE DECISION RULE

The critical factor in a long-range decision is time. The time factor is recognized formally through present-value calculations.[1] In long-range decisions an investment is favorable if the incremental benefits, measured by cash inflows directly attributable to the investment and adjusted for the time value of money, are at least equal to the incremental costs, measured by cash outflows directly attributable to the investment and adjusted for the time value of money. Any investment that provides discounted benefits equal to discounted costs will earn exactly the desired rate of return and will contribute

[1]An explanation of present value will be made later in this chapter. The terms *discounting* or *discounted* wil be used several times prior to that explanation. *Discounting* is the process of adjusting cash flows by an interest rate for the time the money is in use. The interest rate used should relate to the cost the company incurs to obtain capital (cost of capital).

to maintaining the wealth of the enterprise. Any investment that provides greater discounted benefits than discounted costs will contribute to an increase in the wealth of the firm. The basic assumption of any long-range decision is that the firm is trying to maximize its wealth.

MEASUREMENT OF BENEFITS AND COSTS

The conventional accounting measurement of income for a particular period of time involves the matching of revenues, as realized through sale transactions, with the expired costs incurred to produce the revenues. A proper measure of income necessitates the assignment of costs to the period during which revenues are earned. In this way, effort is matched with accomplishment; the resulting income is a measure of the past earning power. The cost of a long-lived asset, such as a building or piece of equipment, enters the matching process by a systematic but arbitrary method of allocating cost over the economic useful life of the asset. For example, consider a firm that purchases a single asset for $12,000. This asset will produce revenues (cash inflows) of $5,000 per year for three years, at which time it will be worn out and have no further value. During the lifetime of the asset, revenues will be $15,000, costs will be $12,000, and income will be $3,000. It is necessary, however, to provide a periodic measurement of income. Assuming that the $12,000 cost will be spread evenly over the economic useful life of the asset, annual cost will be $4,000 and annual income will be $1,000. Income for the three years is presented in Exhibit 14–2. If any other method of depreciation is used the pattern of income will differ. For example, accelerated depreciation, such as sum-of-the-years' digits, will provide an increasing trend of income. *Regardless of the method of depreciation chosen,* the total revenue is $15,000, the total cost is $12,000, and total income is $3,000 over the three-year span.

Year	Revenue	Expired* Cost	Income
1	$5,000	$4,000	$1,000
2	5,000	4,000	1,000
3	5,000	4,000	1,000

*Investment of $12,000 amortized on straight-line basis over three years with no salvage value.

EXHIBIT 14–2
Accounting income for selected investment

For investment analysis, it is necessary to know *when capital is invested,* and therefore not available for other investments, and *when capital is recovered,* and therefore available for reinvestment elsewhere. Invested and recovered capital is determined by *cash flows* directly traceable to the investment. The cash inflows from an investment must be sufficient to provide a satisfactory return to the investor and recover the initial investment. Using our example from Exhibit 14–2, let's assume that the investor desired a return of 12% on the $12,000 investment. Exhibit 14–3 shows that the investor earned at least 12% on the investment balance at the beginning of each year. You will note that income earned over the life of the investment is approximately $3,000, the same amount of income determined in Exhibit 14–2 using conventional accounting measures of income. However, the amount of income in a particular year differs between the two illustrations because the accounting measurements in Exhibit 14–2 *assume* an equal amount of income is earned each year while the measurements in Exhibit 14–3 base the amount of income each year on the investment balance at the beginning of the year.

			Portion of cash inflow that represents		
Year	*Balance of investment— beginning of year*	*Cash inflow (end of year)*	*return (12% × investment at beginning of year)*	*recovery of initial investment*	*Balance of investment— end of year*
1	$12,000	$ 5,000	$1,440	$ 3,560	$8,440
2	8,440	5,000	1,013	3,987	4,453
3	4,453	5,000	534	4,466	(13)
Totals		$15,000	$2,987	$12,013	

[2]The actual return on this investment is slightly more than 12% since $13 more than the $12,000 investment was recovered.

EXHIBIT 14–3
Income and recovery of selected investment

Exhibit 14–3 also shows when the original investment was recovered and the recovered cash was available for investment in other projects. During the first year, the $5,000 cash inflow consisted of income of $1,440 (the 12% return on the $12,000 investment) and $3,560, the partial recovery of the initial investment. During the third year, the $5,000 cash inflow consisted of income of $534 (the 12% return on the $4,453 investment balance at the beginning of the third year) and $4,466, the final recovery of the investment (the extra $13 means that the actual rate was slightly over 12%, actually 12.04%).

The timing of the cash flows, as well as the amount of the cash flows, is important in any long-range decision. For example, if the total cash inflows in our example remained at $15,000 but their timing changed to $6,000 in Year 1, $5,000 in Year 2, and $4,000 in Year 3, the investment would show a higher than 12% rate of return because cash is recovered earlier and may be invested elsewhere. On the other hand, if the timing of the cash inflows were changed to $4,000 in Year 1, $5,000 in Year 2, and $6,000 in Year 3, the investment would earn less than 12%. In all three cases, the accounting measurement of income would show the same cumulative income of $3,000. As the timing of cash flows varies, the accounting measurement of income will vary in individual years, but will not change in total. The rate of return to the investor, however, will vary as cash flows change.

Both the amount of cash flows and the timing of the cash flows must be estimated accurately if a proper investment decision is to be made. Allocations of the cost of long-lived investments are necessary for annual accounting measurements of income, but they are not relevant in investment decisions. The relevant measurements include:

1. A method to recognize the **time value of money.**

2. The amount and timing of cash outflows.

3. The amount and timing of cash inflows.

4. A measure of the time value of money, i.e., a rate of return measure.

We will examine these data needs in detail next.

Present-Value Analysis as a Method of Recognizing the Time Value of Money

The time factor in long-range decisions is formally recognized by consideration of the time value of money. The timing of cash flows, as well as the amount of cash flows, affects value. Because a dollar in hand today can be invested to earn a return, it has a greater value than a dollar to be received one year from today. For example, $100 invested in a savings account at 6% compounded quarterly will grow to $106.13 at the end of one year and will double in slightly under twelve years. The difference between a dollar invested now and the dollar received at some future time is the **time value of money.** This difference is the rate of return you must receive to be indifferent about receiving a dollar today or waiting for a year to receive a dollar.

To make the time value of money concept useful, we must have a way of applying it to a cash flow at any point in time and of comparing the results with a cash flow at any other point in time. This is done through the use of present-value calculations.

Assume that a firm invests a lump sum of $1,000 for a period of three years and that the investment pays a 10% return compounded at the end of each year. The growth of the investment is presented in Exhibit 14–4. The value to which the $1,000 will grow at the end of the three years, at 10% compounded annually, is $1,331. The amount to which a given investment will grow at the end of a given period of time, compounded at a given annual rate of interest, is its **future value.** If you are satisfied with a 10% rate of return on your money, you should be indifferent toward receiving $1,000 now, $1,100 one year from now, $1,210 two years from now, or $1,331 three years from now.

In a long-range decision we want to compare a series of cash inflows and a series of cash outflows at different times over the life of the investment to determine whether a satisfactory rate of return is achieved. To do this, the cash flows must be converted to their discounted values at the *same* point of time. Any point in time could be used. We could state all cash flows in future values at the end of the life of the investment or in present values at the beginning of the life of the investment. However, since the decision is being made now (in the present time period), most firms state the cash flows in the present value of the investment. The **present value** is the amount that must be invested now to reach a given amount at a given point of time in the future, assuming that it is compounded periodically at a specified rate of interest.

In our illustration, $1,000 invested now will accumulate to $1,331 three years from now, when compounded annually at 10%. The present value of $1,331 to be received three years from now is $1,000. It would be useful to develop a set of present-value factors that show the time value of money between given points of time and at given rates of interest. Such a set of values would allow us to determine the present value of any amount at any future date for any rate of interest. Continuing the illustration begun in Exhibit 14–4, we have prepared a portion of a present-value table in Exhibit 14–5 by dividing $1,000 (the present value) by each future value. This computation provides the present value of $1 to be received at the end of one, two, and three years. A similar table could be prepared for any rate and point in time. The present-value factor for $1 to be received one year from now, assuming a 10% rate, is .909; two years from now it is .826; and three years from now it is .751. To illustrate the use of present-value factors, assume that an investment is to be made now in the amount of $2,500 and that it will result in a single cash inflow of $3,000 two years from now. Is it a wise investment if the desired rate of return is 10%? The present value of the initial investment is $2,500 ($2,500 × 1.000). A dollar today is worth one dollar. The present value of the cash inflow is $2,478 ($3,000 × .826). The cash inflow, adjusted for the time value of money, is not equal to or greater than the cost, adjusted for the time value of money; the project should be rejected.

Let's return to the first example in this chapter. A firm had an opportunity to invest $12,000 now in an asset, with the expectation of a $5,000 cash inflow at the end of each of the next three years. Assume that the desired rate of return is 10%. Computation of the present value of cash flows for this investment opportunity is presented in Exhibit 14–6. The present value of the cash outflow (the initial investment) is $12,000. It is not necessary to use a present-value factor of 1.000 for initial payments or receipts ($12,000 ×

Year	Investment at Beginning of Period	Interest at 10% for Period	Investment at End of Period	Formula $I(1+r)^n$
0 (Now)			$1,000	I
1	$1,000	$100	1,100	$I(1+r)$
2	1,100	110	1,210	$I(1+r)(1+r)$
3	1,210	121	1,331	$I(1+r)(1+r)(1+r)$

EXHIBIT 14–4
Future value—$1,000 compounded at 10% annually

Period	Investment* at End of Period (Future Value) at 10%	Present Value / Future Value	General Formula
0 Now)	$1,000	$\frac{\$1,000}{\$1,000} = 1.000$	$\frac{I}{I}$
1	1,100	$\frac{\$1,000}{\$1,100} = .909$	$\frac{I}{I(1+r)}$
2	1,210	$\frac{\$1,000}{\$1,210} = .826$	$\frac{I}{I(1+r)^2}$
3	1,331	$\frac{\$1,000}{\$1,331} = .751$	$\frac{I}{I(1+r)^3}$

**Developed in Exhibit 14–4*

EXHIBIT 14–5
Development of present-value factors

1.000 = $12,000). We do it in this text only for emphasis. The present value of the $5,000 to be received at the end of Year 1 is $4,545 (5,000 × .909); the next $5,000 is $4,130 (5,000 × .826); and the last is $3,755 (5,000 × .751). If we sum the present values of the cash inflows ($4,545 + $4,130 + $3,755) and compare the total ($12,430) with the present value of the cash outflow ($12,000), we find that the incremental benefits adjusted for the time value of money exceed the incremental costs adjusted for the time value of money. The investment should be made because the company will earn more than its desired rate of return of 10%.

	Cash Flow Time Line				PRESENT-VALUE COMPUTATIONS		
Time	0	1	2	3	Amount	x P.V.F.* $S_{\overline{n}\rceil r}$	= Present value
Cash outflow:							
Initial investment	$(12,000)				$(12,000)	x 1.000 $S_{\overline{0}\rceil 10\%}$	= $(12,000)
Cash inflows:							
Cash operating income:							
Year 1		$ 5,000			$ 5,000	x .909 $S_{\overline{1}\rceil 10\%}$	= $ 4,545
Year 2			$ 5,000		$ 5,000	x .826 $S_{\overline{2}\rceil 10\%}$	= $ 4,130
Year 3				$ 5,000	$ 5,000	x .751 $S_{\overline{3}\rceil 10\%}$	= $ 3,755
Total cash inflows							$12,430
Net present value							$ 430

Amount of investment	$12,000
Cash operating income	$ 5,000 per year
Life of investment	3 years
Salvage value	$ 0
Desired rate of return	10%

*P.V.F. – The exhibits in Chapters 14 and 15 identify the present value factor utilized in computation of present value with the following notations: $S_{\overline{n}\rceil r}$ and $A_{\overline{n}\rceil r}$ where: S is a single sum; A is an annuity; n is the number of periods; and r is the discount rate.

EXHIBIT 14–6
Present-value computations for a selected investment

Note that in our illustration the stream of cash inflows is equal and the time intervals are equal. An equal stream of payments made at equal intervals of time is called an **annuity.** The present value of an annuity is equal to the sum of the present values of each of the individual payments in the stream. We could sum the present-value factors (.909 + .826 + .751), apply the sum (2.486) to the amount of a receipt or payment of cash, and determine the present value of the entire stream:

$$2.486 \times \$5{,}000 = \$12{,}430.$$

A table showing the present value of an annuity of $1 may be constructed by adding the present-value factors from the table of present value of $1, as illustrated in Exhibit 14–7. More extensive tables and the general formula for the present value of an annuity of $1 per period are presented in the appendix at the end of the text.

Period	Present Value of $1 (10% Rate)	Cumulative Present Value (Present Value of an Annuity of $1)
1	.909	.909
2	.826	1.735 (.909 + .826)
3	.751	2.486 (1.735 + .751)
4	.683	3.169 (2.486 + .683)
5	.621	3.790 (3.169 + .621)
6	.564	4.354 (3.790 + .564)

EXHIBIT 14–7
Development of table for present value of an annuity at $1.00 at 10% received annually

Availability of present-value tables greatly simplifies the calculation of present values. For most uses the tables in Appendix A, Present value of $1, and Appendix B, Present value of an annuity of $1, provide sufficient accuracy. If a given interest rate is not presented in the table, interpolation between two present-value factors can be made. Interpolation involves the estimation of a present-value factor for a rate or time period between two factors in the table. For example, what is the present-value factor applicable to a sum to be received three years from now with interest computed at 9%? The table in Appendix A shows present-value factors for 8% in three years (.794) and 10% in three years (.751) but does not include the factor for 9%. You want a factor that is approximately halfway between .751 and .794. The amount may be computed as [.751 + ½ × (.794 − .751)], or .7725. This amount differs slightly from the amount calculated by the formula, .7722, because the present-value formula is not linear. However, for most purposes interpolation is sufficiently accurate.

Measurement of Cash Outflows

In any investment decision the relevant cash outflows are the incremental cash outflows that are directly traceable to the investment. In most decisions there are substantial initial cash outflows. An investment in a new building would involve an initial outlay for its purchase or construction. In the case of construction, the initial outlay may be spread over several years. In addition, all cash outflows related to the building subsequent to acquisition must be identified. For a building such outflows would include maintenance, repairs, property taxes, and similar cash outflows directly related to the building over its useful life.

All additional resources required for the higher level of activity must be considered in the decision. In most cases, additional productive facilities also require additional working capital to support the increased level of activity. It will be necessary for the firm to have larger amounts of raw materials, work in process, and finished goods; increased sales will necessitate additional wages and other production costs. The amount of working capital needed to support a plant can often be greater than the cost of the plant facilities. Although the entire amount of working capital should be recovered by the end of the venture, there is a cost associated with the resources invested in the working capital. When the plant is discontinued and the working capital may be used for other purposes, the reduction of working capital should be considered a recovery of cash.

When an investment decision involves any nonmonetary resource currently owned by the firm, such as a building or equipment, the relevant "cost" is the opportunity cost of the asset, not the book value in the accounting records. For example, assume that a division manager is deciding whether to sell an idle plant or use it to produce a new product. If the plant is retained, the investment amount relevant to the decision is the sales price foregone, not the undepreciated cost shown in the accounting records.

Measurement of Cash Inflows

Like cash outflows, the relevant cash inflows are the *incremental cash inflows* to be received in the future and directly related to the decision. In most long-range decisions the cash inflows are spread over the life of the investment. A new plant generates cash inflows in the form of increased contribution margin (increased sales less increased variable costs).

The distinction between revenue, expense, or asset transactions is not carried over into cash flows. A cash inflow directly attributable to the investment, regardless of the reason, should be considered. Therefore, a dollar of cost saved is equivalent to a dollar of revenue received from the sale of a product and should be considered cash inflow. For example, if a new labor-saving machine is installed, the cash inflow should include the savings in expenses, such as labor and fringe benefits, that required cash. There is also no distinction between cash inflow from revenue during the life of an investment and cash inflow from sale or salvage of the productive asset at the end of the project. There may be differential tax effects, but that is a separate issue.

Effect of Income Taxes on Cash Flows

We have stressed that the relevant cash flows in long-range decisions are the incremental cash flows, to be received or paid in the future, that are directly attributable to that decision. The income taxes paid by the company must be considered as a cash outflow. In general, income taxes are assessed as a percentage of the income determined by the conventional accounting system. The amount of taxes to be paid in a particular year is determined by the deduction of depreciation, as well as operating cash inflows and outflows. The tax code is complex; many provisions have been enacted by Congress to encourage or discourage investment in productive assets. Among these provisions are accelerated depreciation (for example, sum-of-the-years' digits method), capital gains taxes on gains from the sale of long-lived assets, and the investment credit. Corporate tax rates[2] and other provisions of the code relating to investments in long-lived productive assets are changed by Congress as governmental fiscal policy changes. We may well see extra deductions and subsidies granted through the tax system to provide solutions to environmental and energy problems.

In this chapter we are dealing with investment in productive assets with long lives. Income taxes have a significant impact on the timing and amount of cash flows from long-lived assets. From the many provisions of the tax code we will examine topics that have the greatest impact on investment decisions. These are:

1. Depreciation for purposes of computing taxable income
2. Carryback and carryforward of operating losses
3. Capital gains tax arising from the sale of long-lived assets
4. The investment credit

DEPRECIATION

When a long-lived asset is acquired, the accounting measurement of income, as well as the Internal Revenue Service (IRS) Tax Code, requires that the cost of the asset be expensed over its useful life in a systematic and rational

[2]Corporate tax rates in 1978 were 20% on the first $25,000 of taxable income, 22% on the next $25,000, and 48% on taxable income over $50,000. For simplicity we will use a rate of 40%.

manner. The cash outflow from purchasing an asset takes place in the year the asset is acquired, but the cost is matched with revenue over the life of the asset to determine income. Therefore, depreciation expense will reduce the taxable income during the lifetime of the asset, not just in the year of acquisition. The cost of an asset to be depreciated is often called a **tax shield.** To the extent that depreciation may be taken, it shields income of future years against tax. The federal tax code allows asset lives for tax purposes that are, in general, shorter than the economic useful lives. For example, a building with an economic useful life of 40 to 50 years may be depreciated over 25 to 30 years. Three methods of computing depreciation are commonly used for tax purposes: *straight-line,* which spreads the cost equally over the life, and *sum-of-the-years'-digits* and *double-declining balance,* which provide for a large amount of depreciation in the first year and declining amounts in each succeeding year.[3] A firm will often use straight-line depreciation in the external financial statements and sum-of-the-years'-digits or double-declining balance depreciation in the tax return. For purposes of investment analysis, we are interested in determining the impact of taxes on cash flows. Therefore, we are concerned with the life and method of depreciation used to determine tax payments, not necessarily net income.

The cash outflow due to taxes can be illustrated by referring to our previous example involving the purchase of an asset for $12,000 with a three-year life and annual cash operating income of $5,000. If we use straight-line depreciation and a three-year life with no salvage value, taxable income for each year would be:

Cash operating income	$5,000
Less: Depreciation ($12,000 ÷ 3)	4,000
Taxable income	$1,000

Assuming a corporate income tax rate for this firm of 40%, the tax payment each year will be $400 ($1,000 × 40%).

The method of depreciation chosen has an impact on cash flows. For example, we may postpone part of the tax payments by adopting the sum-of-the-years'-digits method for tax purposes. To illustrate the impact of sum-of-the-years'-digits depreciation on tax payments, let's assume the facts presented in our previous illustration, but depreciation will be computed by the sum-of-the-years'-digits method rather than by straight-line depreciation. Taxable income and tax payments (or refund) are shown in Exhibit 14–8. Note that the *total* taxable income and taxes paid are the same, regardless of the method of depreciation. Total taxable income for the three years is $3,000, and the taxes paid are $1,200. The timing, however, is different and, thus, affects the cash flows in the investment decision. The differences in cash flows may be illustrated by using a schedule of inflows and outflows for each year,

[3]The sum-of-the-years'-digits method will be used in this text to illustrate accelerated depreication. The declining balance method is more complex and will not be used. It applies a constant percentage to the declining asset balance.

	Year 1	Year 2	Year 3
Cash operating income	$ 5,000	$ 5,000	$ 5,000
Depreciation deduction:			
Year 1 3/6 x $12,000*	6,000		
Year 2 2/6 x $12,000		4,000	
Year 3 1/6 x $12,000			2,000
Taxable income (loss)	$(1,000)	$ 1,000	$ 3,000
Tax payment (refund) assuming 40% rate	$ (400)	$ 400	$ 1,200

Cost of asset	$12,000
Cash operating income	$ 5,000 per year
Life of investment	3 years
Salvage value	$ 0
Depreciation method	Sum-of-the-years' digits
Tax rate	40%

*Sum-of-the-years' digits is 6 (1+2+3); first-year depreciation is 3/6 of cost to be depreciated. Sum-of-the-years' digits for long periods may be computed by the following formula: $S = n\left(\frac{n+1}{2}\right)$ where n is number of years.

EXHIBIT 14–8
Tax payments using sum-of-the-years'-digits depreciation

or cash flow time line, as presented in Exhibit 14–9. In the first year, assuming that the loss produced a tax refund, the cash flow using sum-of-the-years'-digits is $800 higher than with the use of straight-line. Again, it is not depreciation that causes the change in cash flows, it is the *difference in taxes paid* by deducting different amounts of depreciation in particular years.

CARRYBACK AND CARRYFORWARD OF OPERATING LOSSES

The tax code generally allows a corporation with an operating loss to receive a refund for taxes paid in past years or to reduce tax payments in the future. An operating loss may be carried back to each of the previous three years and forward to each of the succeeding seven years as an offset to operating income.

This provision affects cash flows for a particular investment decision because an operating loss may result in a cash inflow from a tax refund. For example, in our illustration involving sum-of-the-years'-digits depreciation, an operating loss of $1,000 was sustained in the first year. If the firm had had taxable operating income of at least $1,000 in the preceding three years and

	Cash Flow Time Line — Years			
	0 (Now)	1	2	3
STRAIGHT-LINE DEPRECIATION				
Cash outflow:				
Initial investment	$(12,000)			
Cash inflow:				
Cash operating income before tax expense		$5,000	$5,000	$5,000
Tax expense on net income		(400)	(400)	(400)
Net annual cash flows	$(12,000)	$4,600	$4,600	$4,600
SUM-OF-THE-YEARS' DIGITS DEPRECIATION				
Cash outflow:				
Initial investment	$(12,000)			
Cash inflow:				
Cash operating income before tax		$5,000	$5,000	$5,000
Tax expense on net income*				
Year 1		400		
Year 2			(400)	
Year 3				(1,200)
Net annual cash flows	$(12,000)	$5,400	$4,600	$3,800

Cost of asset	$12,000
Cash operating income	$ 5,000 per year
Life of investment	3 years
Salvage value	$ 0
Tax rate	40%

See Exhibit 14–8

EXHIBIT 14–9
Comparison of after-tax cash flows between straight-line depreciation and sum-of-the-years'-digits depreciation

had paid taxes of at least \$400, a tax refund of \$400 would be available in Year 1 of the investment project. If this were a new company in its first year of operation, the loss of \$1,000 would be carried forward to offset operating income of \$1,000 in Year 2. In either case, the net tax payment for the three-year period of the investment would be \$1,200. However, the cash flows in individual years would be different. Differences in timing of cash flows may make a significant difference in the attractiveness of the investment.

For a more complete example, assume the following income (loss) and tax payments (refund) for Mad Henry's Pub.

Year	*Income (Loss)*	*Tax Payment (Refund) (40% Rate)*
19X1	\$ 30,000	\$ 12,000
19X2	20,000	8,000
19X3	10,000	4,000
19X4	(100,000)	(24,000)
19X5	10,000	0
19X6	20,000	0
19X7	20,000	4,000
19X8	30,000	12,000
19X9	30,000	12,000
Total	\$ 70,000	\$ 28,000

Income taxes of \$24,000 were paid during 19X1 through 19X3. The loss in 19X4 was first carried back to 19X1, then to 19X2, and finally to 19X3, with \$60,000 of the 19X4 loss offset by income in those three past years. A tax refund of \$24,000 (the taxes paid during 19X1 through 19X3) was collected in 19X4. The remaining loss (\$40,000) was carried forward: \$10,000 to 19X5, \$20,000 to 19X6, and \$10,000 to 19X7. No tax was paid in 19X5 and 19X6, and only \$4,000 [(\$20,000 − \$10,000) × 40%] in 19X7. Note that a total of \$28,000 tax was paid on a total income of \$70,000 during the nine-year period.

CAPITAL GAINS

The capital gains provisions of the tax code, concerning gains and losses from the sale of long-lived assets, are very complex. In general, gains on the sale of long-lived assets not held for resale as inventory may be taxed at approximately half the tax rate on ordinary income if the assets were held at least one year.[4] The tax code requires different treatment for gains and losses from the sale of land and other nondepreciable assets, for depreciable equipment, and for buildings. At one extreme, the entire gain from the sale of land and other

[4]The Tax Reform Act of 1976 increased the holding period for capital gains from six to nine months in 1977, and to one year for 1978 and thereafter.

nondepreciable assets is taxed at the capital gains rate. At the other extreme, a piece of depreciable equipment must be sold for more than its original cost before any of the gain is treated as a capital gain.

The complexity of the tax code limits our discussion to a brief introduction of capital gains. For our purposes, it is sufficient to know that capital gains exist and that they may have a significant impact upon cash flows at the time of the disposition of the assets.

INVESTMENT CREDIT

Congress devised the investment credit as a stimulus for investment in productive assets. The taxpayer is entitled to a credit against his income tax liability in the year of acquisition of 10% of the investment in certain productive assets, excluding land and buildings. (Should this lead to a negative income tax payment, the carryback, carryforward techniques of the tax code generally would apply.) If the assets have a life of less than seven years, or the assets are held less than seven years, only a portion of the investment credit may be taken. To the extent that taxes are reduced, the investment credit represents a subsidy to encourage investment in productive assets.

The combination of the investment credit and accelerated depreciation can have a significant impact on timing of cash flows. Projects that are otherwise unfavorable can become attractive when tax incentives are considered. Any act that speeds up cash inflows or slows down cash outflows of a particular investment will enhance the investment's attractiveness.

Let's return to the illustration used earlier. In this example a firm was considering purchasing an asset for $12,000. The asset is expected to produce cash inflows of $5,000 per year at the end of each of the next three years. In Exhibit 14–6 we found the present value of the before-tax cash outflows for this investment to be $12,000, and the present value of before-tax cash inflows to be $12,430. The positive net present value of $430 ($12,430 − $12,000) indicates the investment is favorable because the actual rate of return exceeds the desired rate of 10%. Taxes, however, are a cash flow and must be considered in any investment analysis. In Exhibit 14–10 the present value of after-tax cash outflows for this investment was $12,000, and the present value of after-tax cash inflows was $11,436. The negative net present value of $564 ($11,436 − $12,000) shows the investment to be unfavorable because the discounted incremental costs exceed the discounted incremental benefits. Therefore, the firm will not earn the desired rate of return on the investment and the project should be rejected. In this illustration, as in many long-range decisions, exclusion of income taxes leads to an incorrect decision.

Suppose the firm elects to use the sum-of-the-years'-digits method of depreciation. Will the delay in tax payments increase the net present value? In Exhibit 14–11 depreciation is computed by the sum-of-the-years'-digits method for tax purposes. The present value of after-tax cash outflows continues to be $12,000. However, the present value of after-tax cash inflows increases to $11,563, leaving a negative net present value of $437. Although the net present value of the investment improved, it is still unfavorable.

	Cash Flow Time Line				Present-Value Computations
Time	0	1	2	3	Amount × P.V.F. $S_{\overline{n}\rvert r}$ = Present value
Cash outflow:					
Initial investment	$(12,000)				$(12,000) × 1.000 $S_{\overline{0}\rvert 10\%}$ = $(12,000)
Cash inflows:					
Cash operating income:*					
Year 1		$ 4,600			$ 4,600 × .909 $S_{\overline{1}\rvert 10\%}$ = $ 4,181
Year 2			$ 4,600		$ 4,600 × .826 $S_{\overline{2}\rvert 10\%}$ = $ 3,800
Year 3				$ 4,600	$ 4,600 × .751 $S_{\overline{3}\rvert 10\%}$ = $ 3,455
Total cash inflows					$11,436
Net present value					$ (564)

Amount of investment	$12,000
Cash operating income	$ 5,000 per year
Life of investment	3 years
Salvage value	$ 0
Depreciation method	Straight-line
Tax rate	40%
Desired rate of return	10%

*Refer to Exhibit 14–9

EXHIBIT 14–10
Present-value computations for a selected investment using after-tax cash flows

As a final illustration of the tax effects on cash flows suppose that, instead of having no salvage value at the end of its useful life to this firm, the asset may be sold for $3,000. The net present value of the investment is computed in Exhibit 14–12, where a salvage value of $3,000 and straight-line depreciation are used. The annual tax payments are greater because the annual depreciation is lower ($12,000 cost − $3,000 salvage = $9,000 to be depreciated in three years). There is no gain on the sale of the asset and

	Cash Flow Time Line				Present-Value Computations
Time	0	1	2	3	Amount x P.V.F. $S_{\overline{n}|r}$ = Present value
Cash outflow:					
Initial investment	$(12,000)				$(12,000) x 1.000 $S_{\overline{0}|10\%}$ = $(12,000)
Cash inflows:					
Before-tax cash operating income		$ 5,000	$ 5,000	$ 5,000	
Income tax*		400	$ (400)	(1,200)	
After-tax cash operating income:					
Year 1		$ 5,400			$ 5,400 x .909 $S_{\overline{1}|10\%}$ = $ 4,909
Year 2			$ 4,600		$ 4,600 x .826 $S_{\overline{2}|10\%}$ = $ 3,800
Year 3				$ 3,800	$ 3,800 x .751 $S_{\overline{3}|10\%}$ = $ 2,854
Total cash inflows					$11,563
Net present value					$ (437)

**Refer to Exhibit 14-9*

EXHIBIT 14-11
After-tax present value of selected investment—Depreciation for tax purposes on sum-of-years'-digits

therefore no tax because the cash received is equal to the book value of the asset (cost less accumulated depreciation) at the date of the sale. The investment is now favorable, showing a net present value of $694.

Measurement of the Rate of Return

In the previous discussion we looked at the technique of discounting to obtain a present value, the measurement of cash inflows, and the measurement of cash outflows. In these discussions we have assumed that the firm had already

	Cash Flow Time Line				Present-Value Computations		
Time	0	1	2	3	Amount	x P.V.F. $S_{\overline{n}\rceil r}$	= Present value
Cash outflow:							
Initial investment	$(12,000)				$(12,000)	x 1.000 $S_{\overline{0}\rceil 10\%}$	= $(12,000)
Cash inflows:							
Cash operating income		$ 5,000	$ 5,000	$ 5,000			
Tax payments*		(800)	(800)	(800)			
Net annual inflow		$ 4,200	$ 4,200	$ 4,200	$ 4,200	x 2.486 $A_{\overline{3}\rceil 10\%}$	= $10,441
Sale of asset at end of life (salvage value)				$ 3,000	$ 3,000	x .751 $S_{\overline{3}\rceil 10\%}$	= $ 2,253
Total cash inflows							$12,694
Net present value							$ 694

Amount of investment	$12,000
Cash operating income	$ 5,000 per year
Life of investment	3 years
Salvage value	$ 3,000
Depreciation method	Straight-line
Tax rate	40%
Desired rate of return	10%

*Cash operating income	$ 5,000
Annual depreciation [($12,000 – $3,000) ÷ 3]	3,000
Annual taxable income	$ 2,000
Annual tax (40%)	$ 800

EXHIBIT 14–12
Net present value of selected investment

selected an appropriate discount rate. In this section we will examine how firms choose a discount rate.

There are many possible rate of return measures that a firm could use as a discount rate. For example, among others they could use the rate of return they could earn if they invested in short-term notes, the return they could receive on long-term bonds, the interest rate they would pay the bank if they borrowed funds, or, if they choose, the interest rate the U.S. Government must pay when it borrows funds. However, most firms make long-term investments in order to maintain or add to the wealth of the firm, so they try to use a rate of return measure that will accomplish this goal. This is why most firms use some measure of the cost of their capital; if they earn the cost of obtaining and maintaining their capital, they will achieve the goal of wealth maintenance. The cost of capital (from the standpoint of the user of the funds) or return on investment (from the standpoint of the provider of the funds) is determined by the general formula:

$$\text{Cost of capital} = \frac{\text{Annual payment to investors}}{\text{Market value of securities}}$$

As shown in the following diagram, a firm usually has more than one source of capital and more than one potential use of this capital.

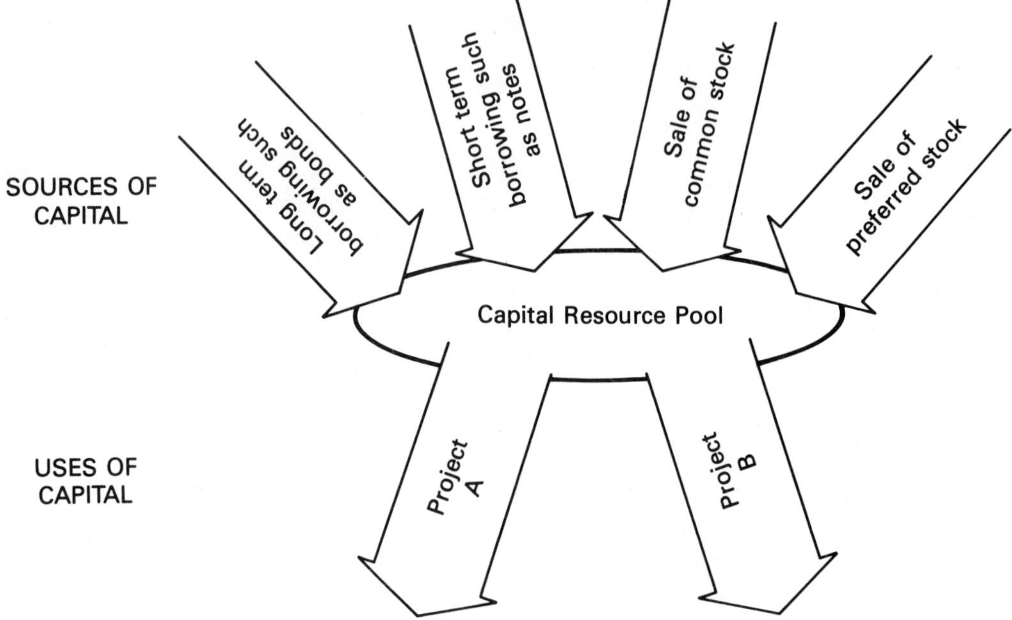

The cost of capital differs depending upon the sources of capital (bonds versus common stock, for example) because each capital source involves a different set of rights and privileges. The bondholder accepts a lower rate of return in exchange for lower risk; he will receive a fixed return over the life of the bond and the face amount of his bond at maturity. The common stockholder has the greatest risk if the enterprise fails and the greatest opportunity for gain if it succeeds. He will receive dividends only if they are earned and declared, and he is last in line to receive assets when the company is liquidated.

A firm has more than one possible measure of the cost of providing its capital. For example, the firm could have the opportunity of investing in

Project B; at the same time, it could have a shortage of resources in their capital resource pool. One approach would be to use the cost of capital from a specific source, say the issuance of bonds, to assess the feasibility of Project B. This approach is misleading. If the cost of a particular source of capital, the **specific cost of capital,** is used to justify a particular investment, the firm may be encouraged to issue excessive amounts of long-term debt because the cost is usually lower than for other sources. As the amount of long-term debt increases, the firm may find themselves in a less favorable borrowing position; the result could be a credit rating change and an increase in the cost of financing.

One approach is to use an overall cost of capital, the **weighted-average cost of capital,** as the minimum acceptable return. A weighted-average cost of capital considers all planned sources of capital simultaneously. A weighted-average cost of capital is computed, first, by determining the specific cost of capital for each source of long-term capital (long-term debt, preferred stock, and common stock equity) and, then, by computing an average rate—weighting the cost of each source of capital by its market value. Current liabilities are usually excluded from the calculation of the weighted-average cost of capital because they are considered as an offset to current assets, rather than a part of invested capital.

To illustrate the computation of the weighted-average cost of capital, let's start with a simple setting of a company with only common stock and then expand the analysis to include long-term debt and, finally, preferred stock. There is no one acceptable method for computing the cost of capital for common stock (equity capital). However, the method we propose has support. We are also assuming that the historical cost of capital is a reasonable forecast of future costs of capital.

COST OF COMMON STOCK

If all earnings are paid out in dividends to common stockholders, the previously shown general formula, where annual payments are divided by the market value of the common stock, can be used to compute the specific cost of capital for common stock. However, very few companies pay out all their earnings in dividends. Some pay none, and the majority pay less than half their earnings in dividends. When earnings are retained, the corporation should grow and be able to pay larger dividends in the future.

We can compute a specific cost of capital for common stock equity by adding a growth factor representing management's objectives for growth in dividends. Thus, $k = d/M + g$, where: k is the specific cost of capital for common stock; d is the current annual dividend; M is the current market value of the common stock; and g is the expected rate of growth in dividends.[5] Assume that the Karl Company has the following capital structure.

---

[5]This model is built upon certain assumptions such as opportunity costs, risk, and constancy of growth rate. For a more complete discussion of this, see Robert G. Higgins, *Financial Management* (Chicago: Science Research Associates, 1977).

Common stock, 10,000 shares, \$10 par value, current annual dividend \$1.00 per share, current market price \$18 per share	\$100,000
Retained earnings	50,000
Total owners' equity	\$150,000

If we assume that a corporate objective is an 8% growth rate in dividends, the specific cost of capital is:

$$
\begin{aligned}
k &= \frac{d}{M} + g \\
&= \frac{\$1}{\$18} + 8\% \\
&= 5.6\% + 8\% \\
&= 13.6\%
\end{aligned}
$$

If this 13.6% cost of capital is accepted as the minimum desired rate of return, we are saying that any new investment must have a minimum rate of return of 13.6% after taxes, to provide for the cost of capital and maintain the value of the company across time.

COST OF LONG-TERM DEBT

Let's assume that the Karl Company has issued long-term debt and now has the following capital structure.

6% long-term debt, 8-year life, market quotation 90, yield to maturity 8%[6]	\$100,000
Common stock	100,000
Retained earnings	50,000
Total long-term debt and owners' equity	\$250,000

Interest on long-term debt is fixed in amount and is deductible for tax purposes. The specific cost of capital for long-term debt is computed as $k = (1 - t)r$, where: k is the specific cost of capital for long-term debt; t is the tax rate; and r is the yield to maturity. In our illustration:

$$
\begin{aligned}
k &= (1 - t)r \\
&= (1 - .40)8\% \\
&= 4.8\%
\end{aligned}
$$

[6] The price of bonds is always quoted as a percentage of the face value of the bond. In this case a \$1,000 bond would sell for \$900 (\$1,000 × 90%). Yield to maturity is the rate the investor will earn on the money if the actual investment is at the market quotation price (\$900 for the \$1,000 bond) and the bond is held to maturity.

COST OF PREFERRED STOCK

The preferred stockholders have given up their right to a share in all earnings for a preference over common stockholders as to dividends and assets in the event of liquidation. Usually the dividends are limited, and the general formula applies in measuring their specific cost of capital.

Assume that the capital structure of the Karl Company includes \$100,000 of preferred stock. The capital structure of the Karl Company now includes:

6% long-term debt, 8-year life, market quotation 90, yield to maturity 8%	\$100,000
Preferred stock, \$100 par, annual dividend \$7.00 per share, current market value \$90 per share	100,000
Common stock	100,000
Retained earnings	50,000
Total long-term debt and owners' equity	\$350,000

The specific cost of capital for preferred stock is:

$$k = \frac{d}{M} = \frac{\$\ 7}{\$90} = 7.8\%$$

WEIGHTED-AVERAGE COST OF CAPITAL

We may now compute the weighted-average cost of capital using the market value of each element in the capital structure as the basis. As shown in the following calculations, long-term debt comprises one-fourth of the total market value, preferred stock comprises one-fourth, and common stock comprises one-half. These proportions are multiplied times the specific cost of capital for each element; the products are summed to arrive at the weighted-average cost of capital.

	Market Value	*Market Value Proportion*		*Specific Cost of Capital*		*Weighted-Average Cost of Capital*
Long-term debt (\$100,000 × 90%)	\$ 90,000	1/4	×	4.8%	=	1.2%
Preferred stock (1,000 shares × \$90)	90,000	1/4	×	7.8%	=	2.0%
Common stock (10,000 shares × \$18)	180,000	1/2	×	13.6%	=	6.8%
Total	\$360,000	4/4				10.0%

The weighted-average cost of capital dropped from 13.6% with only common stock to 10.0% when preferred stock and long-term are added. The use of debt with a lower cost of capital is called **leverage,** or **trading on the equity.** The return to the common stockholder is potentially greater because of the low specific cost of debt capital. To illustrate this point further, let's assume that the amount of long-term debt is doubled. If the interest rate and other terms are not changed, the 4.8% specific cost of capital for long-term debt will continue but will occupy a larger share of the weighted-average cost of capital.

Long-term debt	$180,000	40% × 4.8% =	1.9%
Preferred stock	90,000	20% × 7.8% =	1.6%
Common stock	180,000	40% × 13.6% =	5.4%
	$450,000	100%	8.9%

A TARGET RATE OF RETURN

The weighted-average cost of capital should be the *minimum* rate of return sought across the aggregate of all long-range decisions. However, the use of a single discount rate in investment analysis may not be appropriate for all projects considered, particularly where the projects have different degrees of risk. Some firms deal with risk by ranking the projects by risk classes, such as high-risk projects, moderate-risk projects, and low-risk projects. In a risk/return trade-off, high-risk projects would require a higher return than moderate-risk projects, and moderate-risk projects would require a higher return than low-risk projects. The combination of all projects considered, however, should provide a minimum rate of return equal to the weighted-average cost of capital if the firm is to achieve its goals of capital maintenance plus a growth factor. When we illustrate techniques of investment analysis in this text, we will use only the weighted-average cost of capital. In the next chapter some techniques of dealing with risk and uncertainty will be discussed.

Cash Flow Measures in Industry

In a recent survey Schall and Sundem received responses from 189 firms concerning their methods of cash flow forecasting and cost of capital measures.[7] These were large, stable firms, each with a minimum net plant assets of approximately $200 million, and/or annual capital expenditures of about $20 million. Of the 140 firms that used a discount rate, one-third used more than one cost of capital—46% employed a weighted-average cost of capital, 26% employed a specific cost of capital, 8% used a risk-free rate plus a premium for

[7] Lawrence D. Schall and Gary L. Sundem, "Survey and Analysis of Capital Budget Methods," *The Journal of Finance* (March, 1978).

risk class. Others used a discount rate that depended upon market conditions, or a purely subjective rate based on past experiences.

An after-tax discount rate applied to after-tax cash flow was used by 88% of the firms. The other 12% used pre-tax cash flows and a pre-tax discount rate. The average after-tax discount rate was 11.4%; the average before-tax rate was 14.3%.

Of the firms, 69% predicted cash flow by first predicting net income and then adjusting this by non-cash flow items such as depreciation; 18% predicted cash inflows and outflows directly. The remaining 20% used various other methods.

Application of the Long-Range Decision Rule

The long-range decision rule requires that discounted incremental cash inflows equal or exceed the discounted cash outflows if an investment project is to be accepted. In the next chapter we will see that three techniques satisfy the requirements of the long-range decision rule. They differ only in the way the decision criterion is stated. One of those techniques, net present value, was used in this chapter to present the concept of present value and to demonstrate the effect of differences in timing or amount of cash flows on the long-range decision criterion. Except for the refinements concerning risk, uncertainty, and capital rationing, this chapter has presented the fundamental tools necessary to evaluate most long-range decisions.

SUMMARY

The critical factor in any long-range decision is time. The time factor raises two problems in long-range decisions. First, because all resources have a cost, the time value of money must be reflected when there is a long period of time between investment and a full realization of the benefits. The practice of discounting all benefits and costs to their present value is an adjustment for the time value of money. The weighted-average cost of capital is one method of measuring the discount rate that has been proposed and adopted.

Second, accounting's measurement of net income includes allocations of cost in order to match costs with revenue. For long-range decisions it is important to know when resources are committed and therefore not available for investment elsewhere, and when they are recovered and therefore available for reinvestment. Cash flows provide the relevant measures of costs and benefits for long-range decisions. Allocations of cost, such as those involved in income measurement, should not be allowed to distort the decision information. Income taxes affect the cash flow of the company and, therefore, must be considered in investment decisions.

The most significant practical problem in long-range decision making is the development of estimates of future cash flows relevant to each alternative. Even the most sophisticated model will not yield reliable results if the cash flow estimates are unreliable. The uniqueness of long-range decisions and the fact that these decisions require predictions of future cash flows place most long-range decision data beyond the capacity of the accounting data base.

SUPPLEMENTARY READING

Berezi, Andrew, and Jose Ventura. "A Proposal of Risk Analysis." *The Canadian Chartered Accountant,* August, 1969.

Edwards, James W. *Effects of Federal Income Taxes on Capital Budgeting.* New York: National Association of Accountants, 1969.

Hertz, David B. "Risk Analysis in Capital Investment." *Harvard Business Review,* January–February, 1964.

*Ma, Ronald. "Project Appraisal in a Divisionalized Company." *Abacus,* December, 1969.

*Mehler, Edmund W. "Capital Budgeting: Theory and Practice." *Management Accounting,* September, 1976.

National Association of Accountants. *Return on Capital as a Guide to Managerial Decisions.* New York: National Association of Accountants, 1965.

National Association of Accountants. *Long Range Profit Planning.* New York: National Association of Accountants, 1964.

National Association of Accountants. *Financial Analysis to Guide Capital Expenditure Decisions.* New York: National Association of Accountants, 1967.

*Sihler, William W. "Presenting Capital Expenditure Requests to Management." *Financial Executive,* April, 1973.

QUESTIONS

14–1 List the informational needs of long-range decisions. How do they compare with the informational needs of short-range decisions?

14–2 Why are cash flows, rather than income flows, used in long-range decisions?

14–3 An increase in working capital may be considered to be an investment in long-range decisions. Explain why this is so.

14–4 Define the following terms: *discounting, contribution margin, cash flow, future value of money, present value of money,* and *annuity.*

14–5 Explain: *tax shield, capital gains, investment credit, carryback* and *carryforward,* and *ordinary income.*

14-6 Explain the role of depreciation in long-range decisions.

14-7 Projects that are otherwise marginal or unfavorable may become attractive when tax incentives are considered. Discuss.

14-8 What is the main problem with using a specific cost of capital to justify a particular investment?

14-9 Show how to determine the following, either by formula or example.
A. Specific cost of capital for long-term debt
B. Specific cost of capital for common stock

14-10 A single rate of return should not be utilized for *all* long-range investment decisions. Explain.

EXERCISES

14-11 *(True of False).* Indicate whether the following statements are *true* or *false.*

1. Income taxes may influence the amount of cash flows but will not influence the timing of cash flows.

2. Depreciation is an example of a tax shield.

3. The measurement of the average cost of capital is generally accepted, with little controversy.

4. Straight-line depreciation results in lower incremental cash outflows than sum-of-the-years'-digits depreciation in the earlier year of a particular investment.

5. Income taxes must be considered in measuring the specific cost of capital for long-term debt.

6. Income taxes must be considered in measuring the specific cost of capital for preferred stock.

7. The investment credit affects the amount of cash flows but not the timing of cash flows for a particular investment project.

8. An annuity is any stream of cash flows over time.

9. The present value of any investment that extends over a period of time is always less than its future value.

10. A dollar of cost savings is treated differently than a dollar of revenue in measuring cash flows for a particular investment.

14–12 *(Matching).* Match the following terms and definitions or examples.

1. Incremental cash inflow
2. Tax shield
3. Present value
4. Time value of money
5. Specific cost of capital
6. Rate of return
7. Capital gain
8. Carryback
9. Incremental cash outflow
10. Investment credit

A. Provision of the tax code which allows operating losses to be offset against operating income of previous years.
B. The difference between the value of money at two different points in time due to interest.
C. The after-tax savings in labor due to the purchase of a new piece of equipment.
D. The amount required to satisfy the present and future preferred stockholders in a particular firm.
E. The difference between the cost and selling price for a long-lived asset.
F. Any expense that reduces the amount of tax to be paid.
G. A provision in the tax code that reduces the taxes to be paid when qualified productive assets are purchased.
H. Income from an investment divided by value of the investment.
I. The amount invested now to reach a given amount at a given point of time in the future compounded at a specified rate of interest.
J. The after-tax effect, in terms of cash, of any cost related to a specific investment proposal.

14–13 *(Before- and After-tax Cash Flows).* The Margurita Company is considering an investment proposal that has a three-year life. The owner has asked you to organize the data so that she may make the decision. The company is profitable and pays taxes at a 40% rate.

REQUIRED:
For each of the following transactions determine the before-tax and after-tax cash flows for each of the years. Consider each transaction independently.
A. The investment project will increase revenues by $20,000 per year.
B. Equipment will be leased for three years at an annual rental of $8,000.
C. Repairs of $1,000 must be made to the equipment in Year 2.

D. The investment project will decrease the contribution margin from other products of the company by $4,000 per year.
E. Production for the new project will be carried on in an unused part of the plant that the company has been trying, unsuccessfully, to rent for $2,000 per year.
F. The company paid $6,000 at the beginning of Year 1 for a patent. The cost is expensed immediately for tax purposes but amortized on a straight-line basis over three years for financial accounting purposes.

14-14 *(Present-value Computations).* In each of the following cases you would receive $10,000 of cash. Compute the present value of each set of cash inflows; then rank them according to desirability, using a 12% rate for discounting.
A. $10,000 received in a single sum five years from now.
B. $2,000 received at the end of each of the next five years.
C. $2,000 received at the beginning of each of the next five years.
D. $2,000 received now and $8,000 three years from now.
E. $1,000 now, $1,000 at the end of each of the next four years, and $5,000 at the end of the fifth year.

14-15 *(Present Value—Complex Cash Flows).* In each of the following cases, $5,000 of cash would be received. Compute the present value of the cash flows. Use a 20% rate of interest for discounting.
A. $5,000 paid at the beginning of the 25th year.
B. $1,000 paid at the end of each of the next four years and $1,000 paid at the end of the 10th year.
C. $1,000 paid at the end of each of the next two years and $1,500 paid at the end of each of two years beginning in the third year.
D. $100 at the end of each of the next 50 years.
E. $100 at the end of each of the next 10 years, $400 at the *end* of each of five years beginning with Year 12, and $500 at the *beginning* of each of five years beginning in Year 20.

14-16 *(Specific Cost of Debt Capital).* The Hi-Leverage Company has the following capital structure.

Long-term debt, 8%	$ 80,000
Common stock, $10 par, 2,000 shares authorized, issued, and outstanding	20,000
Retained earnings	40,000
Total	$140,000

The current market price of the bonds is $875 per thousand giving a yield to maturity of 10%. The current tax rate is 48%.

REQUIRED:

A. Compute the specific cost of capital for the long-term debt.

B. Indicate what additional information would be needed to compute the weighted-average cost of capital and how the additional information would be used.

14-17 *(Weighted-Average Cost of Capital).* The most recent balance sheet for the Gulf Coast Container Company contained the following information.

Current liabilities	$ 375,000
8% long-term notes payable	100,000
Common stock, $100 par, 5,000 shares authorized, issued and outstanding	500,000
Retained earnings	25,000
Total	$1,000,000

Other information:

Common stock:	
Current market price of common stock	$80 per share
Current annual dividend	$ 6 per share
Growth rate of dividends	5.5%
Long-term notes payable:	
Current market price	100% of face value
Yield to maturity	8%
Current tax rate	40%

REQUIRED:

A. Calculate the weighted-average cost of capital for the company.

B. Indicate how this rate should be used in long-range decisions.

franchises are available: (1) a franchise in the United States Football League, a strong and profitable league, for $20 million and (2) a franchise in the new International Football League for $2 million. The investors have raised the entire $20 million. If the franchise in the IFL is purchased, the money saved can be utilized to pay bonuses over the next five years to attract stars from the USFL. If this course of action is followed, it is believed that the two leagues

14-18 *(Present Value—Required Annuity).* You are preparing an analysis for a group of investors who wish to purchase a professional football team. Two

would be equal in quality and value by the end of the fifth year. Assume that the funds may be invested at 12% until needed for the bonus.

REQUIRED:
If the bonuses are paid in equal amounts at the end of each of the next five years, what is the maximum annual bonus that may be paid to recruit USFL players? Ignore taxes.

14–19 *(Present Value—Cash Flows).* Consider each of the following cases independently.

A. Hiram Able is about ready to retire. He may take his retirement pay in a single payment of $200,000 or an annuity of $17,436.79 for 20 years. What rate of interest is the pension plan earning during the 20 years?

B. Your aunt has promised to give you a new car when you graduate in three years. The car will cost $5,600. How much must your aunt place in her credit union now, if it earns 6% compounded annually, to pay for the car in three years?

C. On your return to your alma mater for the 20-year reunion of your graduation class, you and several members of your class who have been unusually successful decide to contribute an accounting chair that will provide $20,000 per year for 20 years. With pledges from other members of your class, you go to the trust department of your bank to create a trust that will fund the chair. The bank's trust officer will guarantee an 8% return on the trust. Payments will be made at the end of each of the next 20 years. You may assume that there will be no taxes on the trust or the donors. How much must you and your classmates deposit with your banker to provide for the chair?

14–20 *(Before- and After-tax Cash Flows).* The Jose Company has asked you to develop the data for an investment proposal. The project has a five-year life. The Jose Company is profitable and is subject to a 30% tax rate on additional income.

REQUIRED:
For each of the following transactions determine the before-tax and after-tax cash flows for each of the four years. Consider each transaction independently.

A. A change in the production process resulting in a savings of $10,000 per year for materials.

B. Purchase of a new machine for $40,000 cash. The machine will have a four-year life and no salvage value. Depreciation is computed on a straight-line basis.

C. Use the facts in Part B, except that depreciation is computed on the sum-of-the-years' digits basis.
D. Investment of $50,000 in working capital at the beginning of Year 1.
E. Reduction of working capital by $30,000 in Year 3.
F. Issuance of a $10,000 note payable for cash. Interest at 10% is paid at the end of each year. The note is repaid at the end of the third year.

14-21 *(Ranking of Present-value Alternatives).* Five different cash inflows are listed below.
a. $10,000 now
b. $20,000 in five years
c. $30,000 in ten years
d. $1,000 annually for twenty years
e. $1,000,000 in forty years

REQUIRED:
A. Without reference to the other requirements of this problem, rank the cash inflows listed above as to *your* personal preferences.
B. Rank the proposals in order of desirability, using a zero discount rate.
C. Rank the proposals in order of desirability, using a 10% discount rate.
D. Rank the proposals in order of desirability, using a 20% discount rate.
E. How does your ranking in Part A compare with the subsequent three rankings in Parts B, C, and D?

14-22 *(Cash Flows and Present Value in a Sports Team Setting).* The Leadville Leadfoots, a professional football team that has been in last place for several years, plans to build a team that will be in the playoffs in three years. The team has drafted a Heisman Trophy winner, Steamroller Jones, and is about to begin contract negotiations. The team will play 18 games during the season.

Attendance has been very poor for the past several years. If Steamroller joins the team, ticket sales should increase by at least 20,000 tickets per game. The manager believes that Steamroller will have an impact upon ticket sales for 10 years or less. A study of cost-volume-revenue relationships shows that the contribution margin's effect on cash flow for each additional ticket sold is $8.00.

REQUIRED:
A. Prepare a projection of incremental cash flows that should result if Steamroller signs with the Leadfoots.
B. Assuming a 14% rate of return for all investments, what is the value of Steamroller to the team if he plays for 10 years?

14-23 *(Price of a Bond).* The price an investor pays for a bond is determined by computing the present value of the cash flows the investor will receive during the lifetime of the bond. Assume the following facts about a bond the Oklahoma Instruments Company wants to purchase with some of the company's pension funds.

The bond selected will mature in three years on January 1, 19X4. Interest is paid on January 1 and July 1 of each year. Additional data follow.

Face value of bond (This amount will be paid to the bondholder on January 1, 19X4.)	\$10,000
Coupon rate (Attached to the bond is a page of six coupons. Each coupon is for \$400, the amount of cash the investor will receive every six months when he clips a coupon and sends it to the company.)	8%
Market rate or yield to maturity (On January 1, 19X1, the investment market is insisting that investors earn 12% per year on their investment in bonds of this quality.	12%

REQUIRED:

A. Prepare a schedule showing the cash flows the pension fund will receive from the bond.

B. Compute the price the Oklahoma Instruments Company should pay for the bond on January 1, 19X1.
(Note that the bond pays interest for periods of one-half year. This is the appropriate period for discounting and the rate should be adjusted by using one-half of the annual rate.)

14–24 *(Before- and After-tax Cash Flows).* Continental Parcel Service must acquire a new delivery truck. After careful investigation, it has narrowed the alternatives to three.

1. A light import truck has low operating costs but a short life. The truck costs \$6,000 but must be replaced every two years. Annual operating costs will be \$2,000, and the trade-in allowance will be \$2,000.

2. A heavier truck costs \$8,000 but must be replaced after three years. Annual operating costs will be \$3,000. The trade-in allowance will be \$2,000.

3. A heavy-duty truck has a six-year life. The truck costs \$17,000 and will have a salvage value of \$2,000. Annual operating costs will be \$3,000 with a special overhaul at the end of the fourth year costing \$4,000.

To make the alternatives comparable, the company has selected a six-year life for the investment.

REQUIRED:

A. Prepare a cash flow time line for each alternative, identifying the before-tax cash flows over the six-year period.

B. Prepare a cash flow time line for each alternative, showing after-tax cash flows for the six-year period. Use straight-line depreciation but do not consider the investment credit. Assume a 40% tax rate.

C. What additional difficulties are involved if a life span of less than six years is used?

14-25 *(Present Value of Additional Income).* Marcia received an MBA from Stamvard University and accepted a position in the controller's department at Special Foods. She was pleased to find John, an undergraduate classmate from State U, who had accepted a position with Special Foods immediately upon graduation.

In comparing financial positions, Marcia's starting salary was equal to John's salary, even though he had been with the company for two years. During the two years John had saved $12,000, including the increased equity in the home he had purchased when he started to work for Special Foods. Marcia, on the other hand, was $8,000 in debt. John indicated that although they were in approximately equal positions in the company (in terms of income), he had avoided the $20,000 investment that Marcia had made to graduate from Stamvard. Marcia countered that her MBA should provide her with an annuity in the form of added income that should be worth more than the $20,000 investment. She estimated the annuity to average about $5,000 per year and expected to work for the company at least 30 years.

REQUIRED:

A. Assuming that Marcia has a desired rate of return of 12%, what is the average minimum additional income she would have to earn to be financially equal to John?

B. Assume that Marcia's income will exceed John's income by the following amounts:

Next 5 years	— $0 per year
Following 10 years	— $2,000 per year
Following 10 years	— $7,000 per year
Last 5 years	— $12,000 per year

How does the value of Marcia's annuity compare with John's investment? Explain.

PROBLEMS

14-26 *(Present Value—Rent or Buy a Home).* Frank Furness has accepted a job in the town of Gopher Hollow, and he and his wife are deciding whether they should rent or buy a house. At the end of five years both Frank and Barbara Furness expect to transfer to senior positions in a large city.

The Furnesses have found two similar houses, one for rent and the other for sale. (*Note:* For simplicity all cash flows will be for annual rather than monthly time periods. The concepts remain unchanged, and the computations, particularly present-value computations, are more manageable. Assume that all cash flows take place at the end of the period.) The family's savings amount to $30,000, of which $20,000 will be used as a down payment if a house is purchased, or will be invested in savings certificates earning 8% if a house is rented.

If the Furness family rents, they will pay $5,100 per year, none of which is deductible for income taxes.

A $50,000 house may be purchased with a down payment of $20,000 and annual payments of $4,200, including interest and taxes of $3,700, which are tax-deductible. Repairs and maintenance will amount to about $600 per year. Utilities and other living costs will be the same regardless of whether they purchase or rent. At the end of five years the house can be sold for $63,500, at which time the mortgage should be reduced to $27,900. Because a homeowner may postpone the gain on resale of a home if another house is purchased, Frank does not expect to pay tax on the gain for 25 years. The family will pay tax at the 40% rate on ordinary income; capital gains will be taxed at 30%.

The Furness family wants to know whether it is better to rent or purchase a home for the five years.

REQUIRED:

A. Identify the after-tax cash flows that are relevant to (1) renting, and (2) purchasing a home.

B. Determine the present value of each alternative. Assume an 8% discount rate. What would you recommend?

14-27 *(Selection of Alternatives Using Present Value).* The Popular Publishing Company has a warehouse that is currently being used at 25% of capacity for storage of its inventory. The company has adequate space at other storage sites for the inventory currently stored in the warehouse. It has decided to move the inventory and seek alternative uses for the warehouse. The following possibilities are available.

a. Selling the warehouse now for $50,000.

b. Leasing the warehouse on a 10-year lease for the annual sum of $6,000. At the end of the lease the estimated selling price of the warehouse is $35,000.

c. Leasing the warehouse to an equipment contractor for $15,000 per year for the next two years. After two years it can be sold for only $30,000 because the equipment would heavily damage the floor.

The Popular Publishing Company is a young firm with good growth potential; a 14% return on their investment is one of the major goals of management and the stockholders.

REQUIRED:

A. What are your recommendations to management? Explain fully.

B. What are the opportunity costs of each alternative?

C. What are some of the nonquantifiable costs relevant to the decision?

14-28 *(Present Value Under Different Depreciation Methods).* The Garden Magic Fertilizer Company plans to purchase the following equipment for its production facility.

Purchase cost	$60,000
Annual cost savings generated by the new equipment	$25,000
Repairs at the end of the third year, required because of the corrosive nature of the product	$ 8,000
Salvage value at the end of four years	$ 5,000

The company has established a 12% after-tax rate of return. The tax rate is 40%. Salvage value is not considered in computing depreciation for tax purposes. The equipment qualifies for an investment tax credit of 5%.

REQUIRED:

A. Assuming straight-line depreciation, prepare a schedule showing after-tax cash flows and compute the present value of purchasing the equipment.

B. Assuming sum-of-the-years'-digits depreciation, prepare a schedule showing after-tax cash flows and compute the present value of purchasing the equipment.

14-29 *(Weighted-Average Cost of Capital)*. The Fedore Company has the following capital structure.

Mortgage bonds 6%	$ 20,000,000
Common stock (one million shares)	25,000,000
Retained earnings	55,000,000
	$100,000,000

a. Mortgage bonds of similar quality are selling at 95 (95% of face amount) to yield 6½%.

b. The common stock has been selling for $100 per share. The company has paid 50% of earnings in dividends for several years and intends to continue the policy. The current dividend is $4.00 per share. Earnings are growing at 6% per year.

c. If the company sold a new equity issue, it would expect to net $94 per share after all costs.

d. The tax rate is 50%.

Fedore wants to determine a cost of capital to use in capital budgeting. Additional projects would be financed to maintain the same relationship between debt and equity. Additional debt would consist of mortgage bonds, and additional equity would consist of retained earnings.

REQUIRED:

A. Calculate the firm's weighted-average cost of capital.
B. Explain why you used the weighting system you used.
C. How should the Fedore company use the cost of capital computed in Part A? *(CMA adapted)*

14-30 *(Comprehensive Multiple Choice on Present Value).* Jefferson Jack Company has decided to acquire a new piece of equipment. It may be acquired by any one of three alternatives:

1. Outright cash purchase—purchase price due at the time of purchase.	$28,000
Estimated salvage value.	$ 3,000
2. Outright cash purchase—the full purchase price of $28,000 could be borrowed from the bank with interest at 10% paid annually and the principal paid in one installment at the end of the fifth year.	
Estimated salvage value.	$ 3,000
3. Lease—annual rental of $7,000 paid at the beginning of each year for the life of the equipment.	

Other information:

Assume a 40% tax rate and straight-line depreciation.
A maintenance contract will be acquired with either a lease or purchase at a cost of $600, payable at the beginning of each year.
All cash flows, unless indicated otherwise, are to be made at the end of the year.
The minimum desired rate of return on investment is 10%.
Estimated useful life of the equipment is 5 years.

1. Under the purchase alternative (Alternative 1) the present value of the purchase price of the machine is
a. $20,056
b. $25,000
c. $26,137
d. $28,000
e. None of the above

2. Under the purchase alternative (Alternative 1), the present value of the estimated salvage value is
a. $1,200
b. $1,863
c. $2,000
d. $3,000
e. None of the above

3. Under the purchase alternative (Alternative 1), the annual cash flow related to depreciation is
   a. \$0
   b. \$2,000
   c. \$5,000
   d. \$5,600
   e. None of the above

4. Under the purchase and borrow alternative (Alternative 2), the after-tax cash outflows for interest and maintenance in Year 2 is
   a. \$ 360
   b. \$1,680
   c. \$2,040
   d. \$3,400
   e. None of the above

5. The after-tax effect of *borrowing* the money rather than paying cash is
   a. \$0.
   b. Increase present value by \$4,243.
   c. Decrease present value by \$4,243.
   d. Affect cash flows but not present value.
   e. None of the above.

6. The present value of the payment of the principal on the loan (Alternative 2) is
   a. \$0
   b. \$17,388
   c. \$25,000
   d. \$28,000
   e. None of the above

7. The after-tax present value of the purchase alternative (Alternative 1) is
   a. \$15,813
   b. \$19,015
   c. \$20,056
   d. \$28,000
   e. None of the above

8. The after-tax present value of the purchase and borrow alternative (Alternative 2) is
   a. \$15,813
   b. \$19,015
   c. \$20,056
   d. \$28,000
   e. None of the above

9. The after-tax present value of the leasing alternative (Alternative 3) is
   a. \$15,813
   b. \$19,015
   c. \$20,056

d. $28,000
e. None of the above

10. Which alternative should the company select if the choice is based upon the *lowest* present value?
a. Purchase (Alternative 1)
b. Purchase and borrow (Alternative 2)
c. Lease (Alternative 3)
d. All should be rejected.

14–31 *(Evaluation and Calculation of Cost of Capital).* Shortly after Aron Wheat was appointed president of the Miller Machine Company, he reviewed the long-range decision policy of the company. He was surprised to find proposals rejected that would have been accepted in his previous company, a very successful machine tool company. Aron found that the company had been using a 20% required rate of return. The rate was adopted by the board of directors several years ago, after a president of the company purchased a company airplane. The plane was subsequently sold at a large loss. In spite of limiting investments to those producing the required rate of return, recent earnings and the price of common stock have declined. The company has large amounts of marketable securities earning an average of 6%. The securities will be sold and the funds invested in any project that will earn 20% or better.

The capital structure of the Miller Machine Company follows.

6% long-term debt (current market price $90, yield to maturity 8.5%)	$100,000
7% preferred stock, par $100, 1,000 shares outstanding (current market price per share $95)	100,000
Common stock, par $10, 20,000 shares outstanding, (current market price $12 per share)	200,000
Retained earnings	100,000
Total	$500,000

The company has paid $1.00 per share dividends on common stock for the past few years in addition to the required dividends on preferred stock. The common stockholders of the company expect a long-term growth rate in dividends of 8%. Assume a 40% tax rate.

REQUIRED:

A. On the basis of the limited information available, evaluate the use of the 20% required rate of return by Miller Machine Company.

B. Prepare a recommendation to the new president of the company for a revision of the company's long-range decision policy. Your recommendation should include a suggested rate of return with adequate justification.

14–32 *(Cash Flows and Present Values for Public Transit System).* Thorne Transit, Inc. has decided to inaugurate express bus service between its headquarters city and a nearby suburb (one-way fare $.50) and is considering the purchase of either 32- or 52-passenger buses, on which pertinent estimates are as follows:

	32-Passenger Bus	*52-Passenger Bus*
Number of each to be purchased	6	4
Useful life	8 years	8 years
Purchase price of each (paid on delivery)	$80,000	$110,000
Mileage per gallon	10	7.5
Salvage value per bus	$ 6,000	$ 7,000
Drivers' hourly wage	$ 3.50	$ 4.20
Price per gallon of gasoline	$ .30	$ .30
Other annual cash expenses	$ 4,000	$ 3,000

During the four daily rush hours all buses would be in service and are expected to operate at full capacity (state law prohibits standees) in both directions of the route, each bus covering the route 12 times (six round trips) during that period. During the remainder of the 16-hour day, 500 passengers would be carried and Thorne would operate only four buses on the route. Part-time drivers would be employed to drive the extra hours during the rush hours. A bus traveling the route all day would go 480 miles, and one traveling only during rush hours would go 120 miles a day during the 260-day year.

REQUIRED:

A. Prepare a schedule showing the computation of estimated annual revenue of the new route for both alternatives.

B. Prepare a schedule showing the computation of estimated annual drivers' wages for both alternatives.

C. Prepare a schedule showing the computation of estimated annual cost of gasoline for both alternatives.

D. Assume that your computations in Parts A, B, and C are as follows:

	32-Passenger Bus	*52-Passenger Bus*
Estimated revenues	$365,000	$390,000
Estimated drivers' wages	$ 67,000	$ 68,000
Estimated cost of gasoline	$ 16,000	$ 18,000

Assuming that a minimum rate of return of 12% before income taxes is desired and that all annual cash flows occur at the end of the year, prepare a schedule showing the computation of the present values of net cash flows for the eight-year period. Include the cost of buses and the proceeds from their disposition under both alternatives, but disregard the effect of income taxes.

(CPA adapted)

14-33 *(After-tax Cash Flows and Present Value).* The Baxter Company manufactures toys and other short-lived fad-type items.

The research and development department came up with an item that would make a good promotional gift for office equipment dealers. Aggressive and effective effort by Baxter's sales personnel has resulted in almost firm commitments for this product for the next three years. It is expected that the product's value will be exhausted by that time.

In order to produce the quantity demanded, Baxter will need to buy additional machinery and rent some additional space. It appears that about 25,000 square feet will be needed. 12,500 square feet of currently unused but leased space is available now. (Baxter's present lease with 10 years to run costs $3.00 a foot.) There are another 12,500 square feet adjoining the Baxter facility, which Baxter will rent for three years at $4.00 per square foot per year if it decides to make this product.

The equipment will be purchased for about $900,000. It will require $30,000 in modifications, $60,000 for installation, and $90,000 for testing; all of these activities will be done by a firm of engineers hired by Baxter. All of the expenditures will be paid for on January 1, 19X3.

The equipment should have a salvage value of about $180,000 at the end of the third year. No additional general overhead costs are expected to be incurred.

The following estimates of revenues and expenses for this product for the three years have been developed.

	19X3	*19X4*	*19X5*
Sales	$1,000,000	$1,600,000	$800,000
Material, labor, and overhead	$ 400,000	$ 750,000	$350,000
Allocated general expenses	40,000	75,000	35,000
Rent	87,500	87,500	87,500
Depreciation	450,000	300,000	150,000
Total costs	977,500	1,212,500	622,500
Income before tax	$ 22,500	$ 387,500	$177,500
Income tax (40%)	9,000	155,000	71,000
Income after tax	$ 13,500	$ 232,500	$106,500

REQUIRED:

A. Prepare a schedule that shows the incremental, after-tax, cash flows for this project.

B. Prepare a schedule showing the present value of the cash flows in Part A. Assume a 12% discount rate. *(CMA adapted)*

14-34 *(Complex Cash Flow and Present Value Analysis).* R. Oliver and J. Rand have formed a corporation to franchise a quick food system for shopping malls. They have just completed experiments with the prototype machine which will serve as the basis of the operation. Because the system is new and untried, they have decided to conduct a pilot operation in a nearby mall. When it proves successful, they will aggressively market the franchises.

The income statements below represent their best estimates of income from the mall operation for the next four years. At the end of the four-year period they intend to sell the operation and concentrate on the sale of and supervision of franchises. On the basis of income stream projected, they believe the operation can be sold for $190,000; the income tax liability from the sale will be $40,000.

Projected Income
For Years Ending December 31

	1977	*1978*	*1979*	*1980*
Sales	$120,000	$150,000	$200,000	$230,000
Less: Cost of goods sold	$ 60,000	$ 75,000	$100,000	$110,000
Wages	24,000	30,000	40,000	44,000
Supplies	2,000	2,300	2,400	3,200
Personal property taxes	1,000	1,200	1,600	1,800
Annual rental charge[1]	12,000	12,000	12,000	12,000
Depreciation[2]	11,000	11,000	11,000	11,000
Development costs[3]	20,000	20,000	20,000	20,000
Total expenses	130,000	151,500	187,000	202,000
Net income before taxes	$ (10,000)	$ (1,500)	$ 13,000	$ 28,000
Income taxes @ 40%	—[4]	—[4]	600[4]	11,200
Net income after taxes	$ (10,000)	$ (1,500)	$ 12,400	$ 16,800

[1]The shopping mall requires tenants to sign a 10-year lease. Three years' rental is payable at the beginning of the lease period with annual payments at the end of each of the next seven years.

[2]Construction of an operational machine is estimated to be completed on January 1, 1977. The $130,000 purchase price will be paid at that time. The salvage value at the end of its 10-year life is estimated at $20,000. Straight-line depreciation is to be used for statement purposes and sum-of-the-years'-digits for tax purposes.

[3]The prototype machine cost $200,000 to develop and build in 1975. It is not suitable for commercial use. However, since it was the basis of the system, it is to be amortized at $20,000 per year. The same amount will be deducted for tax purposes.

[4]The losses of the first two years are offset against the $13,000 income in 1979 before income tax charges are calculated.

REQUIRED:

A. Calculate the cash flow for the mall operation for the four-year period beginning January 1, 1977, ignoring income tax implications.

B. Adjust the cash flows for the tax consequences as appropriate.

C. Oliver and Rand plan to employ discounted cash flow techniques to judge whether the mall operation is a sound investment. What arguments are advanced to justify the use of the discounted cash flow technique?

(CMA adapted)

15 Techniques of Investment Analysis

A long-range investment opportunity is favorable if its discounted benefits are at least equal to its discounted costs. This approach to long-range decisions measures benefits and costs as the cash inflow and outflow directly attributable to the investment opportunity. These cash flows are discounted by some acceptable rate of return to reflect the time value of money.

The information needed for long-range decisions was discussed in Chapter 14. Techniques for using this data in investment analyses are examined in this chapter. We have separated the techniques into two types: those which satisfy the long-range decision rule and those which do not. Investment techniques that do not satisfy the long-range decision rule are deficient in theory, although they are often used in practice.

TECHNIQUES THAT SATISFY THE LONG-RANGE DECISION RULE

Three techniques satisfy the long-range decision rule. These three vary only in the way the decision criteria are stated. The first two, net present value and discounted benefit-cost ratio, apply a desired or predefined discount rate to cash flows. This permits a measurement of the alternatives by their net present value or the ratio of discounted benefits to discounted costs. The third method, adjusted rate of return, computes the rate of return actually earned from each investment opportunity. To the extent that funds are available all projects that satisfy the decision criteria should be accepted. Only if there is a shortage of funds is it necessary to compare and rank the proposals.

A summary of the financial data applicable to three investment opportunities follows. Assume the applicable cost of capital is 10% and all cash flows occur at the end of the period.

			Cash Operating Income at End of Year		
Investment	*Initial Investment*	*Productive Life*	*1*	*2*	*3*
A	$20,000	2	$13,000	$15,400	—
B	$ 9,000	3	$ 0	$ 8,000	$8,000
C	$12,000	3	$ 5,000	$ 5,000	$5,000

Investment A has a life of only two years, beginning in year 1. Investment B has no income in the first year of its three-year life. Investment C is the illustration used in Chapter 14. In the remainder of this chapter, various investment techniques will be applied to this data. All illustrations will involve after-tax cash flows. We will assume that the firm has had income during the previous three years and that any loss may be carried back against this income with the result of a tax refund in the year of the loss. Depreciation for tax purposes will be computed on a straight-line basis for simplicity. A tax rate of 40% will be assumed.

The after-tax cash flows of the three investment opportunities are presented in Exhibit 15–1. This data will be used as the relevant cash flows for the remainder of the chapter. There is one unusual cash flow. In the first year, depreciation expense for Investment B produces a loss for tax purposes and generates a tax refund of $1,200.

Net Present Value

The **net present value** of a particular investment, as shown in Chapter 14, is the difference between the present value of future cash inflows and the present value of future cash outflows. All future cash inflows and outflows are discounted to their present values by the use of a predetermined discount rate. When the net present value is zero (discounted cash inflows are equal to discounted cash outflows), the investment will earn a rate of return equal to the minimum predefined rate of return. If the net present value is positive (discounted cash inflows exceed discounted cash outflows), the investment will earn a rate of return greater than the desired rate of return. If the present value is negative (discounted cash inflows are less than discounted cash outflows), the investment's return will be less than the desired rate of return.

Computation of net present value for each of the investment opportunities is presented in Exhibit 15–2. Investments A and B have positive net present values and are therefore acceptable at the desired rate of return of 10%. Investment C has a negative net present value and is unacceptable.

Discounted Benefit-Cost Ratio

The **discounted benefit-cost ratio** is a ratio of discounted benefits (in the form of cash inflows) to discounted costs (in the form of cash outflows). The technique is identical to the net present-value method through the discounting step. However, instead of netting the discounted inflows and discounted outflows and arriving at a net present value, the ratio of discounted benefits to discounted costs is computed.

A ratio of 1.00 indicates that discounted benefits and discounted costs are exactly equal, and that the actual return on the investment is equal to the desired rate of return, and therefore, that the project should be accepted. If the ratio is greater than 1.00, the benefits exceed the costs. If the ratio is less than 1.00, the investment provides less than the desired rate of return and should not be accepted. Exhibit 15–3 shows the calculations of the discounted benefit-cost ratios for the three investment opportunities shown in Exhibit 15–2. Investments A and B show discounted benefit-cost ratios of 1.08 and 1.17, respectively, indicating favorable investment opportunities. Investment C shows a ratio of .95, indicating an unfavorable investment.

COMPUTATION OF TAXES (40% RATE)	YEARS 1	YEARS 2	YEARS 3
INVESTMENT A			
Revenues	$ 13,000	$ 15,400	
Depreciation expense*	10,000	10,000	
Taxable income	$ 3,000	5,400	
Tax (payment) refund	$ (1,200)	$ (2,160)	
INVESTMENT B			
Revenues	$ 0	$ 8,000	$ 8,000
Depreciation expense†	3,000	3,000	3,000
Taxable income (loss)	$ (3,000)	$ 5,000	$ 5,000
Tax (payment) refund	$ 1,200	$ (2,000)	$(2,000)
INVESTMENT C			
Revenues	$ 5,000	$ 5,000	$ 5,000
Depreciation expense §	4,000	4,000	4,000
Taxable income	$ 1,000	$ 1,000	$ 1,000
Tax (payment) refund	$ (400)	(400)	(400)

AFTER-TAX CASH INFLOWS	YEARS 1	YEARS 2	YEARS 3
INVESTMENT A			
Revenues	$ 13,000	$ 15,400	
Tax	(1,200)	(2,160)	
Cash inflows net of tax	$ 11,800	$ 13,240	
INVESTMENT B			
Revenues	$ 0	$ 8,000	$ 8,000
Tax	1,200	(2,000)	(2,000)
Cash inflows net of tax	$ 1,200	$ 6,000	$ 6,000
INVESTMENT C			
Revenues	$ 5,000	$ 5,000	$ 5,000
Tax	(400)	(400)	(400)
Cash inflows net of tax	$ 4,600	$ 4,600	$ 4,600

*$20,000 cost ÷ 2-year life = $10,000 annual depreciation expense
†$ 9,000 cost ÷ 3-year life = $ 3,000 annual depreciation expense
§$12,000 cost ÷ 3-year life = $ 4,000 annual depreciation expense

EXHIBIT 15–1
After tax cash flows for selected investments

	Cash Flow Time Line				Present-Value Computations		
Time	0	1	2	3	Amount	x P.V.F. $S_{\overline{n}\rceil r}$	= Present value
INVESTMENT A							
Cash outflow:							
Initial investment	$(20,000)				$(20,000)	x 1.000 $S_{\overline{0}\rceil}$ 10%	= $(20,000)
Cash inflows:							
Year 1		$11,800			$11,800	x .909 $S_{\overline{1}\rceil}$ 10%	= $10,726
Year 2			$13,240		$13,240	x .826 $S_{\overline{2}\rceil}$ 10%	= $10,936
Total cash inflows							$21,662
Net present value							$ 1,662
INVESTMENT B							
Cash outflow:							
Initial investment	$ (9,000)				$ (9,000)	x 1.000 $S_{\overline{0}\rceil}$ 10%	= $ (9,000)
Cash inflows:							
Year 1		$ 1,200			$ 1,200	x .909 $S_{\overline{1}\rceil}$ 10%	= $ 1,091
Years 2 and 3			$ 6,000	$ 6,000	$ 6,000	x 1.577 $A_{\overline{3}\rceil}$10% − $A_{\overline{1}\rceil}$10%	= $ 9,462
Total cash inflows							$ 10,553
Net present value							$ 1,553
INVESTMENT C							
Cash outflow:							
Initial investment	$(12,000)				$(12,000)	x 1.000 $S_{\overline{0}\rceil}$ 10%	= $(12,000)
Cash inflows:							
Years 1, 2, and 3		$ 4,600	$ 4,600	$ 4,600	$ 4,600	x 2.486 $A_{\overline{3}\rceil}$ 10%	= $ 11,436
Net present value							$ (564)

EXHIBIT 15–2
Net present value of selected investments

Investment	Discounted* Benefits (Discounted Cash Inflows)	Discounted* Costs (Discounted Cash Outflows)	Discounted Benefit-Cost Ratio
A	$21,662	$20,000	1.08
B	10,553	9,000	1.17
C	11,436	12,000	.95

Data from Exhibit 15-2

EXHIBIT 15-3
Discounted benefit-cost ratio for selected investments

A word of caution about the use of ratios: The ratio of two numbers depends, in part, upon the array of data used to arrive at the two numbers. For example, ratios based upon *gross* operating cash flows that show revenues and costs separately would differ from ratios based on *net* operating cash flows that show revenues less costs. Although the use of different data bases may cause a ratio to change, it cannot cause a favorable investment opportunity to appear unfavorable, nor an unfavorable investment opportunity to appear favorable. As a general rule, revenue and costs from operations for each year should be netted to arrive at a single cash inflow from operations. Nonoperating cash flows should be shown separately. These include original investments, additional working capital requirements, invested proceeds from the sale of the asset, and recovery of working capital when the project is terminated.

Adjusted Rate of Return

The net present-value and discounted benefit-cost ratio methods use a preestablished rate of return. The **adjusted rate-of-return** method, or **discounted rate-of-return** method, as it is often called, determines the actual rate of return of an investment opportunity. This method determines the rate necessary to make the discounted cash inflows equal to the discounted cash outflows. Remember that with the net present-value method, if the net present value is zero, the actual rate of return is exactly equal to the predefined rate of return. With the adjusted rate-of-return method, a predefined rate is not used; instead, the actual rate of return is computed.

Unless the cash inflows are equal over the life of the project and begin in the first year of the project, a trial-and-error process is necessary. Initially, the net present value is calculated at an arbitrary rate of return. If the net present value is negative, a lower rate is tested; if the net present value is positive, a higher rate is tested. New rates are tested until a net present value of zero is reached. The actual discounted rate of return for the investment is the rate used where there is a zero net present value.[1]

Because we chose a 10% rate in computing the net present value of each investment, we know that the actual rates of return are higher than 10% for Investments A and B, but less than 10% for Investment C. Let's accept the determination of the net present value at 10% for our first trial. Then, through a process of subsequent trials, we can determine the actual rates of return expected from Investments A and B. For our second trial we will compute the net present value of Investments A and B at 18%. If the net present value is not at or very near zero, we'll try again at higher or lower rates, depending on whether the net present value is positive or negative.

In Exhibit 15–4, using an 18% rate, Investment A shows a negative net present value of \$(499); Investment B shows a very small negative net present value of \$(22). We will accept 18% as the actual rate for Investment B. However, we must make another trial for Investment A at a rate of return less than 18%. The next trial for Investment A, using a 16% rate of return is presented in Exhibit 15–5. The net present value on this last trial is so near zero, \$9, that we can say that the discontinued rate of return for Investment A is 16%.

When cash inflows are equal over the life of the project, as in the case of Investment C, it is not necessary to use a trial-and-error approach. Instead, the actual rate may be determined directly from the present-value tables. The adjusted rate of return for Investment C is easier to compute because the cash inflows are equal and the cash outflows are made at the beginning of the investment. The following formula may be used to find the actual rate of return at which the present value of the cash inflows is equal to the present value of the cash outflows.

$$\text{Cash outflow} \times \text{Present-value factor} = \text{Cash inflow} \times \text{Present-value factor}$$

By inserting the known amounts and solving the equation, we compute the present-value factor to equate the two cash flows.

$$\$12{,}000 \times (1.000) = \$4{,}600 \times (\text{P.V.F.})$$

$$\$12{,}000 = \$4{,}600 \times (\text{P.V.F.})$$

$$\text{P.V.F.} = \$12{,}000 \div \$4{,}600$$

$$\text{P.V.F.} = 2.609$$

[1]Under certain conditions, such as a positive cash flows in time period 0 and negative cash flows in later periods, it is possible to have more than one internal rate of return. Study of this situation is beyond the scope of this book.

	Cash Flow Time Line				Present-Value Computations
Time	0	1	2	3	Amount × P.V.F. $S_{\overline{n}\rvert r}$ = Present value
INVESTMENT A					
Cash outflow:					
Initial investment	\$(20,000)				\$(20,000) × 1.000 $S_{\overline{0}\rvert 18\%}$ = \$(20,000)
Cash inflows:					
Year 1		\$11,800			\$ 11,800 × .847 $S_{\overline{1}\rvert 18\%}$ = \$ 9,995
Year 2			\$ 13,240		\$ 13,240 × .718 $S_{\overline{2}\rvert 18\%}$ = \$ 9,506
Total cash inflows					\$ 19,501
Net present value					\$ (499)
INVESTMENT B					
Cash outflow:					
Initial investment	\$ (9,000)				(9,000) × 1.000 $S_{\overline{0}\rvert 18\%}$ = \$ (9,000)
Cash inflows:					
Year 1		\$ 1,200			\$ 1,200 × .847 $S_{\overline{1}\rvert 18\%}$ = \$ 1,016
Years 2 and 3			\$ 6,000	\$ 6,000	\$ 6,000 × 1.327 $A_{\overline{3}\rvert 18\%} - A_{\overline{3-1}\rvert 18\%}$ = \$ 7,962
Total cash inflows					\$ 8,978
Net present value					\$ (22)

EXHIBIT 15-4
Adjusted rate of return for selected investments—Second trial assuming an 18% rate of return

Referring to the table for the present value of an annutiy of \$1 (Appendix B), we can find the rate to which the 2.609 present-value factor applies. In the three-year row (Investment C has a three-year life), find the present-value factors nearest to 2.609. The nearest factors are those applica-

	Cash Flow Time Line				Present-Value Computations		
Time	0	1	2	3	Amount	× P.V.F. $S_{\overline{n}|}r$	= Present value
INVESTMENT A							
Cash outflow:							
Initial investment	\$(20,000)				\$(20,000)	× 1.000 $S_{\overline{0}|}$ 16%	= \$(20,000)
Cash inflows:							
Year 1		\$11,800			\$ 11,800	× .862 $S_{\overline{1}|}$ 16%	= \$ 10,172
Year 2			\$13,240		\$ 13,240	× .743 $S_{\overline{2}|}$ 16%	= \$ 9,837
Total cash inflows							\$ 20,009
Net present value							\$ 9

EXHIBIT 15–5
Adjusted rate of return for selected investments—Third trial assuming a 16% rate of return

ble to 6% and 8%, 2.673 and 2.577, respectively. Interpolating between these values, we find the discounted rate of return for Investment C to be approximately 7.33%.

$$\begin{aligned}\text{Actual rate of return} &= 6\% + \left(2\% \times \frac{2.673 - 2.609}{2.673 - 2.577}\right)\\ &= 6\% + \left(2\% \times \frac{.064}{.096}\right)\\ &= 6\% + 1.33\%\\ &= 7.33\%\end{aligned}$$

If we assume a cutoff rate equal to a weighted-average cost of capital of 10%, Investments A and B should be accepted and Investment C should be rejected.

Problems of Capital Rationing

The techniques of net present value, discounted benefit-cost ratio, and adjusted rate of return are acceptable methods of deciding whether a specific project is economically feasible. Given the assumptions implicit in the cost of capital, a zero net present value and benefit-cost ratio equal to one will maintain the firm's wealth. When there are excess resources in the capital resource pool, the firm should invest in any project that is economically feasible, as long as the project is consistent with firm goals.

When the resources in the pool are not adequate to invest in all available favorable projects, the decision maker must select a way of ranking the projects. The goal, with capital rationing, is to select those projects that will add the largest value to the firm. To illustrate this problem, let's assume that in addition to Projects A and B illustrated earlier, the firm also has three other projects, D, E, and F, that are acceptable. Each of these projects is independent of the other and *not* mutually exclusive. Mutually exclusive means that when one project is accepted, the other is automatically rejected. Data for the five projects are shown below.

Project	*Initial investment*	*Net present value*	*Benefit-cost ratio*
A	$20,000	$1,662	1.08
B	$ 9,000	$1,553	1.17
D	$10,000	$ 776	1.08
E	$24,000	$1,125	1.05
F	$ 7,000	$1,300	1.19

If the firm has $70,000 to invest, all five projects are feasible and should be accepted. If the firm has only $10,000 to invest, Project B would return the largest net present value. Project B, with a net present value of $1,553, is preferable to Project F with a net present value of $1,300, even though the benefit-cost ratio for Project F is higher. This is true because Project B consumes more of the $10,000 resource pool than does Project F. Thus, while one dollar of investment in Project F yields a higher benefit-cost ratio than one dollar of investment in Project B, there are not as many dollars of investment in Project F. This, of course, assumes that the opportunity cost of the uninvested resource pool is zero.

Now, let's assume that there is $20,000 in the resource pool. By a trial-and-error method, we can determine that in addition to the individual Projects A, B, D, and F, the following combinations of projects are available:

Projects	*Total investment*	*Total net present value*
B and D	$19,000	$2,329
B and F	$16,000	$2,853
D and F	$17,000	$2,076

The combination of Projects B and F returns the highest combined net present value ($2,853) with the lowest investment ($16,000).

If $30,000 were in the pool, there would be the following feasible combinations of projects in addition to those above:

Projects	*Total investment*	*Total net present value*
A and B	$29,000	$3,215
A and D	$30,000	$2,438
A and F	$27,000	$2,962
B, D, and F	$26,000	$3,629

The optimum combination is Projects B, D, and F with a total net present value of $3,629, and an investment of $26,000.

From this example we can see that the net present value is a useful measure in capital rationing situations. If the original investment requirements of each project were identical, we could rank the projects by their individual excess net present value without worrying about possible combinations. Where there is capital rationing, the net present values must be considered in total over the feasible projects. In our illustration, Project A has the highest net present value for any of the five projects; yet under the capital rationing situations illustrated (under $30,000 in the resource pool), it was not among the accepted proposals.

It should also be noted that under each of the capital rationing illustrations, idle resources remained in the investment pool. Firms would not typically leave these dollars idle or consider their opportunity cost zero. As a minimum, the firm should seek secure, short-term investments such as treasury bills. Idle resources result in lower return on the stockholders' equity, an unfavorable situation.

As a final problem in capital rationing, the assumption of independent projects will be modified. Assume that Projects B and F are mutually exclusive; both are production machinery that would occupy the same alcove in the factory. If the firm buys Project B, there would be no space for Project F. The possible combinations for under $20,000 are:

Projects	*Total investment*	*Total net present value*
B and D	$19,000	$2,329
D and F	$17,000	$2,076
A	$20,000	$1,662
B	$ 9,000	$1,553
D	$10,000	$ 776
F	$ 7,000	$1,300

Given that B and F are mutually exclusive, the best available alternative is to select B and D. If Projects B, D, and F are all mutually exclusive, the best alternative is Project A.

Problems of Comparison

Two problems in comparing investment alternatives should be discussed. The first concerns unequal lives; the second, reinvestment of cash as it is recovered. These problems relate only to the methods that use discounted cash flow techniques.

When the productive lives of investment opportunities differ widely, it may be necessary to set a life span common to all investments being considered. One way is to use the shortest life as the time period for analysis. Investment opportunities with longer lives would be treated as if they were terminated early; a salvage value is used to measure the value at termination. A second way assumes replacement of the short-lived assets and uses the longest life as the time period for analysis. For example, a firm is considering which truck to purchase for making deliveries. One truck has a three-year life and the other, six years. Both will provide the necessary service, but the second truck requires a larger initial investment. We may base the investment on a time frame of three years, treating the resale value of the six-year truck as a cash inflow at the end of the first three years. Another method would be to consider the replacement of the three-year truck with another three-year truck, making the lives equal at six years.

Inherent in discounted cash flow analysis is the assumption that as cash is recovered from an investment, it will be reinvested at the rate originally planned. In the net present-value and discounted benefit-cost ratio methods, the assumed rate of reinvestment is the predefined rate of return. Since we will not accept an investment below the predefined rate, this is a reasonable assumption. However, in the adjusted rate-of-return method, when there is capital rationing because of a shortage of funds, it is assumed that cash will be reinvested at the actual rate of return of the project. If a project with a high rate of return returns cash soon and few investment projects are available when the cash is recovered, the project may be less desirable. If the timing of cash flows differs widely among investment projects, the adjusted rate-of-return method may lead to inadequate decisions. The firm may not be able to reinvest at the actual rate achieved by the investment being considered.

TECHNIQUES THAT DO NOT CONSIDER THE TIME VALUE OF MONEY

Discounted cash flow is a rather recent concept. It is only in the last two decades or so that it has been widely taught in business schools and used extensively in practice. Two techniques of investment analysis are widely used in industry that do not satisfy the long-range decision rule requiring adjustment for the time value of money—the payback period and unadjusted rate-of-return methods. A discussion of these methods follows.

Payback Period

Payback period is a simple technique that asks the question, "How long does it take to recover the initial investment?" Investment opportunities are ranked according to the time, in years, required to recover the initial investment. The payback periods for the three investment opportunities considered earlier are presented in Exhibit 15–6. If the cash inflow starts in Year 1 and is equal throughout the life of the investment, the initial investment may be divided by the annual cash inflow to determine the payback period. If the cash inflows are not equal or do not begin in the first year, all inflows must be summed in chronological order until the point is reached where cash inflows equal the initial investment. Payback periods for the three investments, computed in Exhibit 15–6 are: 1.62 years for Investment A, 2.30 years for Investment B, and 2.61 years for Investment C. Investments A, B, and C are ranked in that order.

Although the payback period is very simple to compute, it has serious shortcomings because it does not consider the life or relative profitability beyond the payback period. The following two investments would have the same payback period. Investment Y is clearly the better investment and would be ranked above Investment X by all other techniques of investment analysis.

Investment	*Initial Investment*	*Annual Cash Inflow*	*Productive Life*	*Payback Period*
X	$10,000	$5,000	3 years	2 years
Y	$10,000	$5,000	10 years	2 years

The payback method is a very conservative technique. In a high-risk situation, for example, where threat of nationalization of foreign investments exists, the benefits of the projected long life of the investment might never be enjoyed. In such cases, an investment with a short payback period and low rate of return may be preferable to an investment with a higher rate of return but a longer payback period. Payback period can serve as a supplement to other methods. For example, one way to compensate for risk is to set a maximum payback period and use this period as a constraint in conjunction with the net present-value or adjusted rate-of-return methods.

Unadjusted or Accounting Rate of Return

An **unadjusted or accounting rate of return** (not adjusted for the time value of money) is widely used. It is simple to compute and, because it is consistent with the accounting measurements of income, can be computed from the accounting records. This method divides the average income from the investment, as measured by the accounting concept of income, by the initial

INVESTMENT A

			Amount Recovered
Initial investment	$(20,000)		
Cash inflows:			
Year 1	$ 11,800		$11.800
Year 2	13,240	Year of recovery	8,200
Year 3	0		—
			$20,000
Payback period = 1 + ($8,200 ÷ $13,240)	=	1.62 years	

INVESTMENT B

Initial investment	$ (9,000)		
Cash inflows:			
Year 1	$ 1,200		$ 1,200
Year 2	6,000		6,000
Year 3	6,000	Year of recovery	1,800
			$ 9,000
Payback period = 2 + ($1,800 ÷ $6,000)	=	2.30 years	

INVESTMENT C

Initial investment	$(12,000)		
Cash inflows:			
Year 1	$ 4,600		$ 4,600
Year 2	4,600		4,600
Year 3	4,600	Year of recovery	2,800
			$12,000
Payback period = 2 + ($2,800 ÷ $4,600)	=	2.61 years	

Where annual cash inflows are equal payback may be determined by dividing initial investment by the annual cash inflow.

Payback period = $12,000 ÷ $4,600 = 2.61 years

EXHIBIT 15–6
Payback period of selected investments

investment.[2] The income calculation amortizes the initial investment over the life of the project as depreciation. Because average revenue and average costs are used, depreciation must be computed on a straight-line basis.

[2]The investment figure may be measured in several ways. Two of the most common measures are *initial investment* and *average investment*. We have chosen the initial investment for simplicity of calculation.

	INVESTMENT		
	A	B	C
Average annual revenue:			
A. ($13,000 + $15,400) ÷ 2	$ 14,200		
B. ($0 + $8,000 + $8,000) ÷ 3		$ 5,333	
C. ($5,000 + $5,000 + $5,000) ÷ 3			$ 5,000
Average annual depreciation:			
A. $ 20,000 ÷ 2	$(10,000)		
B. $ 9,000 ÷ 3		$ (3,000)	
C. $ 12,000 ÷ 3			$ (4,000)
Average annual taxes:			
A. ($1,200 + $2,160) ÷ 2	$ (1,680)		
B. (−$1,200 + $2,000 + $2,000) ÷ 3		$ (933)	
C. ($400 + $400 + $400) ÷ 3			$ (400)
Average net income	$ 2,520	$ 1,400	$ 600
Initial investment	$ 20,000	$ 9,000	$ 12,000
Unadjusted rate of return (Average net income ÷ Initial investment)	13%	16%	5%

EXHIBIT 15–7
Unadjusted rate of return for selected investments

Using the after-tax cash flows prepared in Exhibit 15–1, the unadjusted rates of return for the three investments are presented in Exhibit 15–7. Investment B ranks highest with a 16% rate of return, followed by A with 13%, and C with 5%. For consistency, the data for each investment show average annual revenues as the *net* of cash collections from customers and cash payments for operating expenses.

With the unadjusted rate-of-return method, a dollar of revenue received or cost paid late in the life of the investment will have the same impact as a dollar received or paid initially. This effect can lead to improper decisions. For example, assume the following investment alternatives.

	Investment M	*Investment N*
Initial investment	$10,000	$10,000
Net cash inflows:		
Year 1	$ 7,000	$ 1,000
Year 2	$ 4,000	$ 4,000
Year 3	$ 1,000	$ 7,000
Salvage value	$ 0	$ 0
Net present value (10% rate)	$ 418	$ (526)
Adjusted rate of return	13.2%	7.6%
Payback period	1.75 years	2.71 years
Unadjusted rate of return	6.7%	6.7%

Clearly, Investment M is superior to Investment N, using either the net present-value or adjusted rate-of-return method. However, both investments have the same unadjusted rate of return.

RISK AND UNCERTAINTY

The decision maker rarely can project all cash flows with certainty. Actual cash flows seldom occur exactly as projected. To the extent that one lacks information to determine the probability of alternative outcomes, the decision maker faces **uncertainty,** which increases the riskiness of any decision. A lack of information may be brought into manageable proportions by a search for more complete data or by avoiding the alternatives that carry the possibility of large losses.

The search for better information becomes a question of information economics. Information has a cost. Additional data should be sought only to the point where its benefits exceed the cost of obtaining it. Each long-range decision is unique. With the exception of a few recurring long-range decisions, there may be very little relevant information in the accounting data bank. Data must be drawn from sources outside the company, often at a high cost.

Increased **risk** may result from conditions over which the firm has no control. For example, a local service firm that contracts with a professional sports team to provide souvenirs and novelties faces the risk that the team may move. The novelty firm has no control over whether the owners will choose to move the team. Even if the team stays, management will be uncertain about how many T-shirts, baseball caps, or other novelties will be sold.

Research in investment decisions has developed decision models that explicitly consider risk. In a recent survey[3] concerning capital-budgeting practices, two-thirds of the responding firms explicitly considered risk and uncertainty in their investment decisions. The survey respondents indicated

[3] J. M. Fremgen, "Capital Budgeting Practices: A Survey," *Management Accounting* (May, 1973), pp. 19–25.

the following methods of adjusting for risk and uncertainty. (Several firms indicated more than one method.)

Method	*Percentage of Respondents Indicating Use*
Requirement of a higher-than-normal index of profitability	54%
Requirement of a shorter-than-normal payback period	40%
Adjustment of estimated cash flows by use of quantitative probability factors	32%
Purely subjective, nonquantitative adjustment	29%
Other methods	8%

The first method involves the use of a higher desired rate of return for more risky projects. To illustrate, let's assume three classes of risk: high, moderate, and low. By applying higher required rates of return to the moderate- and high-risk classes, the investment decision process places less weight on distant cash inflows as the degree of risk increases. Assume that a 10% rate of return is required for low-risk projects, an 18% rate for moderate-risk projects, and a 24% rate for high-risk projects. Compare the present value of $1 of cash inflows for the three risk classes at points three and five years in the future (from Appendix A).

Year	*Low risk (10%)*	*Moderate risk (18%)*	*High risk (24%)*
3	.75	.61	.52
5	.62	.44	.34

The $1 inflow in Year 5 from a low-risk investment has a greater present value than the $1 inflow received in Year 3 for either a medium- or high-risk project. A high-risk project must allow recovery of the initial investment sooner and must have a larger cash inflow earlier in the life of the project than does a low-risk project.

The second method of compensating for risk, a shorter-than normal payback, considers only the cash flows in the early life of the project. Commonly, the short payback is used in combination with the net present-value method. The net present-value method determines whether an investment will earn at least a desired rate of return; the payback period places a limit on acceptable risk. For example, the novelty firm may be reasonably certain that the professional sports team will remain for two years; it would take at least that long to negotiate and accomplish a move. The firm may choose to accept investment projects with a net present value at the desired rate of return and a maximum payback of two years.

In the third method, the consideration of risk and uncertainty involves estimating the probabilities of different cash flows. One way is to make three estimates of future cash flows for each investment opportunity: an optimistic estimate, a most likely estimate, and a pessimistic estimate. By assigning subjective probabilities to each of these predictions, the decision maker can decide whether the risk of loss is too great to accept the investment, regardless of the most probable favorable return.

For example, assume that the decision maker expects an optimistic outcome two out of ten times and therefore assigns a probability of .2 to the optimistic cash flow projections. He expects the most likely projections to occur five out of ten times and assigns a probability of .5 to the most likely cash flow projections. Finally, he expects the pessimistic outcome to occur three times out of ten and assigns a probability of .3 to the pessimistic projections. Let's assume that the following after-tax cash flows were projected for our earlier example of Investment B.

	Optimistic	*Most Likely*	*Pessimistic*
First year	$ 1,200	$1,200	$1,200
Second year	$ 9,500	$7,000	$2,000
Third year	$13,500	$6,000	$1,000

The cash projections to be used in investment analysis would be computed as follows:

First year (\$1,200 × .2) + (\$1,200 × .5) + (\$1,200 × .3) = \$1,200

Second year (\$9,500 × .2) + (\$7,000 × .5) + (\$2,000 × .3) = \$6,000

Third year (\$13,500 × .2) + (\$6,000 × .5) + (\$1,000 × .3) = \$6,000

By assigning subjective probabilities to the estimates, we have a good picture of the risk facing the company in this investment. Are the probable cash flows worth the risk of a 30% chance that the investment will lose money? Management would pay considerable attention to this question if such a loss would cause the company to fail.

In the survey by Schall and Sundem,[4] quoted in the last chapter, 36% of the responding firms used a quantitative assessment of individual project risk, 4% did not assess risk, and the other 60% assessed risk only subjectively. Only 23% of the respondent firms assigned projects to risk classes; 77% did not assign risk classes. Of the firms, 19% used different capital budgeting techniques for different risk classes; 81% used the same capital budgeting techniques for all projects. Individual project risk was assessed by a probability distribution of cash flows by 25% of the firms.

---

[4]Lawrence D. Schall and Gary L. Sundem, "Survey and Analysis of Capital Budget Methods," *The Journal of Finance* (March, 1978).

Most of the firms (78%) did take risk explicitly into account. Of the responding 143 firms, 90% increased their desired rate of return separately or in combination with a shortened payback period; 10% used a shortened payback period as their only adjustment for risk.

INVESTMENT TECHNIQUES IN PRACTICE

We have presented techniques that will result in wise investment decisions if applied with sound judgment. What methods are actually used? The results of a survey of investment decision practices are presented in Exhibit 15–8. Most of the firms included in the survey were large corporations that would be expected to use sophisticated techniques.

Three methods were most commonly used: adjusted rate of return (indicated by 71% of responding firms); payback (67%); and unadjusted rate of return (49%). Several firms indicated that more than one method was used. The choice of adjusted rate of return over other discounted cash-flow methods can, in part, be explained by the nature of the measurement criteria provided by the three methods. Most managers think in terms of rate of return and find the adjusted rate of return appealing as a profitability criterion.

Each firm that used more than one method was asked to indicate the most important method used. The adjusted rate of return stands out clearly as the first choice of 45% of the responding firms. Payback and unadjusted rate of return occupy a much smaller role (17% and 26%, respectively) as the first choice. However, as the size of the relevant capital budget declined, and probably the size of the firm as well, the use of the payback as the most important method increased.

Another survey,[5] which compared capital budgeting methods used in 1959 with those in 1970, showed the most sophisticated, primary evaluation method to be:

	Percentage of Respondents	
	1970	*1959*
Discounted cash flow methods	57%	19%
Unadjusted rate of return	26%	34%
Payback	12%	34%
Other	5%	13%
	100%	100%

[5]Thomas Klammer, "Empirical Evidence of the Adoption of Sophisticated Capital Budgeting Techniques," *The Journal of Business* (October, 1972), pp. 387–397.

Amount of Annual Capital Budget	Techniques Satisfying the Long-Range Decision Rule			Techniques that do not Consider Time Value of Money		
	Adjusted Rate of Return	Net Present Value	Discounted Benefit-Cost Ratio	Payback Period	Unadjusted Rate of Return	Other Methods
A. METHODS IN ACTUAL USE*						
Over $100 million	78%	34%	9%	72%	60%	14%
$50-$100 million	79	21	10	62	55	3
$10-$50 million	64	14	2	68	44	11
Under $10 million	67	0	5	52	33	0
No size given	67	33	0	67	0	33
All respondents	71%	20%	6%	67%	49%	10%
B. MOST IMPORTANT METHOD†						
Over $100 million	43%	6%	0%	3%	39%	9%
$50-$100 million	56	10	4	10	20	0
$10-$50 million	45	3	0	26	20	6
Under 10 million	47	0	5	24	24	0
No size given	0	0	0	50	0	50
All respondents	45%	5%	1%	17%	26%	6%

Source: J.M. Fremgen, "Capital Budgeting Practices: A Survey," *Management Accounting* (May, 1973), pp. 19-25.

*Several firms indicated more than one method used.

†Not all firms responded to question; data were adjusted to represent percentage of firms answering question.

EXHIBIT 15–8
Investment analysis techniques in practice

In the Schall and Sundem survey, 86% of the firms used more than one capital budgeting technique; 17% used all four methods—net present value, the internal (adjusted) rate of return, the payback period, and the accounting (unadjusted) rate of return. More than 86% of the firms used either the internal rate of return or net present value, but only 16% used present-value techniques without also using the payback or accounting rate of return.

All the surveys cited show similar results when the discounted cash flow techniques in Exhibit 15–8 are combined. It must be kept in mind that the data in the studies represent practices of some of the largest corporations in the country, with annual capital expenditures of millions of dollars. We should expect these firms to use sophisticated techniques. There is no comparable empirical evidence about smaller firms, but we would expect them to favor payback and accounting rate of return over discounted cash flow techniques today, in much the same proportions indicated by the large corporations in the survey of 1959 practices.

With many shortcomings, why do the payback and unadjusted rate-of-return methods continue to be used so widely? Several reasons have been advanced to explain the use of theoretically inferior investment analysis techniques.

First, business managers of small corporations are not aware of the more sophisticated techniques or do not understand them. Only in the past 15 to 20 years have discounted cash flow techniques been widely taught in the undergraduate business curricula.

Second, inertia. When a practice has worked in the past and is easily understood, there is great reluctance to accept new methods. Decision making is guided by intuition and experience in many companies. Conservative business managers use conservative practices such as the payback method. An examination of the mathematical characteristic of the adjusted rate of return has shown that if project lives are at least twice the payback periods, the payback method will provide results similar to those from the adjusted rate-of-return method. Actually, the payback reciprocal is a close approximation of the discounted rate of return under these conditions. Here an intuitive method gained by experience approximates the theoretically better method.

Third, if the company is evaluated by return on investment and earnings per share computed from accounting income, the decision maker can be expected to favor those investments that maximize the unadjusted (accounting) rate of return. The unadjusted rate of return considers time only through averaging the revenues and costs. Investments that provide for a steadily increasing trend of earnings would be favored over those that lead to wide fluctuations but have a higher time-adjusted rate of return over the life of the project. For this reason, we would expect many decision makers to reject Investment B in our earlier illustration of investment techniques. Investment B would show a loss for accounting purposes in Year 1, and equal profits in Years 2 and 3. Investment A would be the most highly favored because it provides a short payback, a good overall return, increasing profit, and no loss year. Investment C, which was inferior by all five investment analysis techniques discussed in this chapter, may be favored over Investment B because it provides a steady income rather than a loss followed by larger profits. When management owes its continuation in office to satisfied stockholders, there is a strong tendency to emphasize earning trends and avoid periods of loss.

SUMMARY

Five investment analysis techniques were introduced in this chapter. Only the first three—net present-value, discounted benefit-cost ratio, and adjusted rate-of-return techniques—consider the time value of money. The net present-value and discounted benefit-cost ratio methods use a predefined rate of return and base the decision criterion on whether the desired rate is achieved. The adjusted rate-of-return method determines the actual rate of return earned by the investment. The result, in an easily understood percentage form, probably explains the preference for its use over other discounted cash-flow techniques.

The payback-period and unadjusted rate-of-return methods do not consider the time value of money. The payback period measures how long it takes to recover the initial investment. The unadjusted rate-of-return method computes the return achieved by dividing the average income from the investment, as measured by the accounting concept of income, by the initial investment.

Empirical evidence indicates that, at least among large firms, the use of payback period and unadjusted rate of return is declining, whereas the adjusted rate-of-return method is increasing.

SUPPLEMENTARY READING

Bierman, H., and C. Smidt. *The Capital Budgeting Decision.* New York: MacMillan and Co., 1971.

Edwards, James B. "Adjusted DCF Rate of Return." *Management Accounting,* January, 1973.

Fremgen, James M. "Capital Budgeting Practices: A Survey." *Management Accounting,* May, 1973.

Hertz, David B. "Investment Policies that Pay Off." *Harvard Business Review,* January–February, 1968.

Klammer, Thomas. "Empirical Evidence of the Adoption of Sophisticated Capital Budgeting Techniques." *The Journal of Business,* October, 1972.

Klammer, Thomas. "The Association of Capital Budgeting Techniques with Firm Performance." *The Accounting Review,* April, 1973.

*Meredith, G. G. "Decision Criteria for Investment Strategies." *The Australian Accountant,* November, 1971.

Myers, Ronald E. "Performance Review of Capital Expenditures." *Management Accounting,* December, 1966.

National Association of Accountants. *Financial Analysis Techniques for Equipment Replacement Decisions.* New York: National Association of Accountants, 1965.

Rowley, C. Stevenson. "Methods of Capital Project Selection." *Managerial Planning,* March–April, 1973.

QUESTIONS

15-1 "If the net present value of an investment is zero, the company will show no profit on the project." Do you agree? Discuss.

15-2 Define and explain the following concepts: *time value of money, discounting, payback, adjusted rate of return, predefined discount rate, net present value, discounted benefit-cost ratio,* and *unadjusted rate of return.*

15-3 Explain how the long-range decision rule may be applied to the selection of a depreciation method for tax purposes.

15-4 How is it possible that the net present-value method and adjusted rate of return may rank acceptable proposals in different orders?

15-5 Payback method has been described as a "conservative" method. Explain why this is true in relation to other methods.

15-6 What are some of the shortcomings of the payback method? Why has it been so widely used for analysis in the past?

15-7 How is it possible that an investment project may have an unacceptable unadjusted or accounting rate of return and yet an acceptable adjusted rate of return? Give an example.

15-8 If a firm is evaluated by the stockholders and investing public on accounting rate of return and earnings per share, what types of investments is the management likely to desire? Explain. Would this necessarily maximize the "wealth" of the firm? Why or why not?

15-9 Describe some of the methods of dealing with risk and uncertainty in investment analysis.

15-10 A firm's search for additional information should continue only until the cost of obtaining that information equals the benefits received. Discuss.

EXERCISES

15-11 *(Matching).* Match the following terms and definitions.

1. Benefit-cost analysis
2. Present-value factor
3. Cash inflows
4. Net present value
5. Adjusted rate of return
6. Unadjusted rate of return
7. Payback period
8. Risk
9. Discounted benefit-cost ratio
10. Uncertainty

A. The time it takes to recover an investment.
B. The condition faced when a decision maker lacks information.
C. A general model for measuring economic efficiency.
D. Return on investment based upon discounted cash flows.
E. The relevant measure of benefits in a decision model that meets the long-range decision rule.
F. A number developed to assist in the computation of discounted cash flows.
G. The condition faced when the decision maker has no control over the outcome of an event.
H. Discounted benefits minus discounted costs.
I. Discounted benefits divided by discounted costs.
J. Return on investment based upon accounting income.

15-12 *(True or False).* Indicate whether the statements are *true* or *false.*

1. A long-range investment opportunity is unfavorable if discounted benefits are equal to or less than discounted costs, and favorable if discounted benefits exceed discounted costs.
2. If the net present value of an investment opportunity is zero, the project should be rejected.
3. When two mutually exclusive investment projects are considered, the one with the lowest net present value should be accepted.
4. The time value of money is ignored in the unadjusted rate-of-return method.
5. If an investment project is acceptable by the net present-value technique, it will also be acceptable by the adjusted rate-of-return technique.
6. If cash flows are unequal, the net present-value method is easier to calculate than the adjusted rate-of-return method.
7. The payback period method ignores the profitability of an investment opportunity.

8. One way to adjust for risk in an investment project is to use a higher required rate of return.
9. In the absence of capital rationing, all investment projects should be selected that have positive net present values.
10. The net present-value method is superior to the adjusted rate-of-return method for choosing among investments of different size.

15-13 *(Computing Discount Rates).* At what discount rate do the following alternatives have approximately the same present value? (Compute or estimate the rate to the nearest whole percent.)

A. \$476 now or \$1,000 five years from now
B. \$51,000 now or \$1,000,000 eight years from now
C. \$100 at the end of each of the next ten years or \$1,199.85 ten years from now

15-14 *(Computing Discount Rates).* At what discount rate do the following alternatives have approximately the same present value? (Compute or estimate the rate to the nearest whole percent.)

A. \$1,000 now or \$1,000 five years from now
B. \$650 now or \$1,300 nine years from now
C. \$14,834.60 now or \$2,200 each year for twenty-two years
D. \$3,500 at the end of each of the next five years or \$28,412.21 eight years from now.

15-15 *(Payback and Discounting Methods).* The Plastic Box Company is considering the following three investments. Assume a 10% required rate of return. Ignore taxes.

Investment	*Cost (now)*	*Annual Cash Savings*	*Life*
A	\$7,200	\$1,800	4 years
B	\$6,000	\$1,500	6 years
C	\$4,800	\$1,200	10 years

REQUIRED:

A. Compute the payback period for each investment.
B. What conclusion may be drawn from this analysis?
C. Present a stronger method of analysis.

15-16 *(Net Present-Value Analysis).* The Gum Rubber Eraser Company is considering a project that requires an investment of \$4,271 and produces the following cash inflows.

Year	*Cash Flow*
1	$1,000
2	$2,000
3	$3,000

Ignore income taxes and assume a 12% required rate of return.

REQUIRED:

A. Compute the net present value of the investment.

B. How much could you pay in addition to the $4,271 and still earn 12% on your investment?

C. What is the approximate adjusted rate of return on the investment?

15-17 *(Present-Value Analysis of Financing Opportunities).* Long, Short, and Easy, three franchised home appliance dealers, have requested short-term financing from Franklin Industries, their distributor. The dealers have agreeed to repay the loans within three years and to pay Franklin Industries 5% of net income for the three-year period for the use of the funds. The following table summarizes, by dealer, the financing requested and the total remittances (principal plus 5% of net income) expected at the end of each year.

	Long	*Short*	*Easy*
Financing requested	$ 80,000	$40,000	$30,000
Remittances expected at end of:			
Year 1	$ 10,000	$25,000	$10,000
Year 2	40,000	30,000	15,000
Year 3	70,000	5,000	15,000
	$120,000	$60,000	$40,000

Management believes these financing requests should be granted only if the annual pre-tax return to the company exceeds the target internal rate of 18% on investment.

REQUIRED:

A. Prepare a schedule to compute the net present value of the investment opportunities of financing Long, Short, and Easy.

B. Should any of the loans be granted? Explain. *(CPA adapted)*

15-18 *(Payback; Adjusted Rate of Return).* The Mill Valley Smelter will be required to reduce the level of pollutants it discharges into the air. Pollution control must take place in two stages, with the first stage requiring a 50% reduction of pollution for the next five years. Equipment that will meet Stage 1 standards is available at a cost of $399,000 with no salvage value. During the first stage, recovered materials may be sold at a contribution margin of $100,000 per year. Ignore taxes.

REQUIRED:

A. Compute the payback period.

B. Compute the adjusted rate of return.

C. Assuming that the company has a target rate of return of 10% and a minimum payback period of 3.5 years, is the investment economically favorable?

D. Assuming that the government wants to provide an incentive to make the investment economically favorable, what kind of incentive may be given and how will it affect your analysis? What amount of subsidy would be required to make the investment economically favorable?

15-19 *(Continuation of 15–18; After-Tax Payback Period, Adjusted Rate of Return).* The Mill Valley Smelter (Problem 15–18) must purchase pollution control equipment with a five-year life costing $399,000. The company will generate a contribution margin of $100,000 per year from the sale of recovered materials. Assume the following additional information:

1. The income tax rate if 40%. Assume that pollution-control equipment qualifies for a 10% investment credit.

2. The equipment will have a salvage value of $24,000. Depreciation will be computed on sum-of-the-years'-digits basis.

3. The target rate of return is 10%.

REQUIRED:

A. Compute the net present value.

B. Compute the adjusted rate of return.

C. Compute the payback period.

D. Assuming that the criteria for investment evaluation are a 10% target rate of return, and a minimum payback period of 3.5 years, is the investment favorable by their criteria?

15-20 *(Determining Degree of Risk).* Indicate whether you think each of the following investments would be high-risk, medium-risk, or low-risk.

1. Replacement of a machine with a new and more efficient machine to produce the company's major product. The life of the machine is six years, and the patents protecting the product have a 10-year life.

2. Purchase of a contract with an All-American basketball player. He was the unanimous choice of every sportswriter as college player of the year, in spite of missing the last four games because of a knee injury.

3. Purchase of a parcel of land in the desert to be developed by a land developer who has sold the parcels throughout the country. The nearest city is 70 miles away.

4. Investment in a first-mortgage bond issue by Florida Power and Light Company.

5. Purchase of pollution-control equipment necessary to comply with state pollution-control laws. The company is profitable but will probably not receive another waiver for pollution-control compliance.
6. Investment in a cattle-feeding venture. The facility will be computer-controlled, utilizing the most advanced decision and control models. The price of feed has been rising, and the price of fattened beef cattle has been very erratic.
7. Investment of $1,000 in a fund that purchases high-yielding, high-quality certificates of deposit issued by the major banks in the country. The fund will receive a return that is 2% above what an individual investment of $1,000 in certificates will earn. The cost of administration of the fund will be minimal.
8. Purchase of the movie rights to the novel that has headed the best-seller list for the past year.
9. An investment by a company in refurbishing an old building for a restaurant in the central area of a major city. The investment will be part of an overall plan to develop an area called Olde City. It will be several years before the development is complete.
10. A master's degree in business for a person with an engineering or liberal arts degree from a good university.

15-21 *(Capital Rationing).* The Titefist Company has budgeted $100,000 for capital expenditures in 19X1. The following investment proposals have been submitted to the investment committee for approval.

Proposal	*Original Investment*	*Life of Project*	*Payback Period*	*Adjusted Rate of Return*
A	$30,000	3	2	20%
B	$10,000	6	3	12%
C	$50,000	8	5	13%
D	$20,000	2	1	25%
E	$20,000	5	4	8%
F	$10,000	4	3	16%
G	$30,000	10	5	14%

The company's cost of capital is 10%.

REQUIRED:
Which proposals should be accepted? Explain.

15-22 *(Discussion of Capital Budgeting Terms).* Capital budgeting has received increased attention in recent years. The quantitative techniques employed for capital-budgeting decisions depend largely upon accounting data.

REQUIRED:

A. Distinguish between capital budgeting and budgeting for operations.

B. Three quantitative methods used in making capital-budgeting decisions are (1) payback period, (2) unadjusted accounting rate of return, and (3) discounted cash flow. Discuss the merits of each of these methods.

C. Two variations of the discounted cash flow method are (1) time-adjusted rate of return, and (2) net present value (sometimes referred to as excess present value). Explain and compare these two variations of the discounted cash flow method.

D. Cost of capital is an important concept in capital budgeting. Define the term *cost of capital* and explain how it is used in capital budgeting.

(CPA adapted)

15-23 *(Before- and After-tax Present Values).*

A. Compute the net present value of each of the following investments and indicate which should be accepted. Assume a 12% cost of capital and no shortage of funds. (Ignore taxes.)

		Cash Inflows by Year		
Investment	*Initial Investment*	*1*	*2*	*3*
F	$15,000	$9,000	$10,600	0
G	$ 9,000	$3,750	$ 3,750	$3,750
H	$ 6,750	$4,500	0	$4,500

B. Assuming a 30% tax rate and straight-line depreciation, compute the net present value of the investments and indicate which should be accepted. What was the impact of income taxes on your decision?

15-24 *(Purchase versus Lease).* Doctor's Clinic has always leased its equipment from the manufacturer. A new piece of X-ray equipment was ordered before the new administrator was hired. When asked to sign the lease contract, she questioned the terms of the lease and asked for purchase terms. The equipment manufacturer provided the following comparative data.

	Purchase	*Lease*
Life of equipment	4 years	4 years
Original cost	$48,000	—
Annual maintenance insurance, property taxes	$ 3,000	
Repairs in second year	$ 5,000	
Annual rental		$32,275
Salvage value	$10,000	

If purchased, the equipment qualifies for a 5% investment credit. The lessor will take the investment credit on the lease. The clinic uses straight-line depreciation, a 14% required rate of return, and is subject to a tax rate of 40%.

REQUIRED:

Evaluate the contract for the administrator and prepare a recommendation, supported by proper analysis, as to whether she should purchase or lease the equipment.

15-25 *(Different Levels of Risk).* Wixon Wax Works, Ltd. is a diversified company that makes a wide range of investments. The corporate investment committee has been presented with the following investments. There is no capital shortage.

	Investment		
	R	*S*	*T*
Original investment	$10,300,000	$6,040,000	$3,603,000
Life of investment	5 years	6 years	3 years
Annual cash inflows	$ 3,000,000	$2,000,000	$1,500,000
Level of risk	Medium	High	Low

Assume a 10% discount rate has been established for long-term investments. The company adds a 6% penalty for medium-risk and a 10% penalty for high-risk ventures. Ignore income taxes.

REQUIRED:

A. Which proposals are acceptable to the firm? Why?
B. How much must annual cash inflows be increased to accept each proposal you rejected in Part A?

PROBLEMS

15-26 *(Discounted Benefit-Cost Ratio in Not-for-Profit Setting).* The state highway commission is attempting to decide whether to prohibit studded tires on the state's highways. The tire have not been permitted and, for safety reasons, pressure has grown for their use. The results of two studies are presented for evidence.

The first study examined traffic deaths in the state during the past five years. The study found that accidents involving 40 deaths per year would probably have been avoided if studded tires had been used. In addition to deaths, personal property damage and medical costs of $200,000 per year would have also been avoided. The damage and medical cost estimates were drawn from police records and insurance claims. The average age of people killed was 30; their average annual income was $10,000.

The second study was conducted in states that allowed studded tires. It is expected that new tires will be developed within 10 years; they will provide all the benefits of studded tires and will not damage road surfaces. Considering the damage to road surfaces, the highway department estimates that annual damage to the streets, highways, and bridges would amount to additional resurfacing costs of $2,000,000 per year for 10 years.

REQUIRED:

A. Assuming that those killed would have earned the average income to age 60, compute the discounted benefit-cost ratio if studded tires are allowed. Is it favorable? Assume a 10% discount rate.

B. Medical researchers at the state university's school of medicine contend that the money should be spent on kidney research. They contend that the cost per death averted in kidney research is about $25,000. How does the cost per death averted in the studded tire program compare?

15-27 *(Make or Buy).* Consolidated Electric Company is an established company with an excellent reputation for electronic products. For several years the company has been purchasing the critical component XL-12 for one of its major products from Wizard Electronics. The purchase price of XL-12 from Wizard is $22. Approximately 10,000 of these components are purchased each year.

During the past year, Wizard has maintained quality but delayed several shipments that resulted in Consolidated's losing orders with a contribution margin of $100,000 and paying penalties on other orders of $30,000. Wizard is producing at capacity, so it is doubtful that their delivery performance will improve.

Consolidated could produce XL-12 by increasing capacity with additional equipment and dropping a product line current generating a contribution margin of $20,000. The variable production costs would be $18 per unit. The equipment will cost $220,000 and have a useful life of 10 years and a salvage value of $20,000 any time after the fourth year. The product using XL-12 will be replaced by a new product in five years. The equipment will be used for other production after production of the component is discontinued.

The company uses a 12% target rate of return and pays taxes at a 40% rate. Straight-line depreciation is used for both tax and financial reports.

REQUIRED:

Should the company produce XL-12 or continue to purchase it from Wizard? Assume that Consolidated cannot recover from Wizard any losses or penalties it incurs and that it cannot delay delivery dates of its major products.

15-28 *(Unadjusted Rate of Return versus Other Techniques).* The Green Eyeshade Company uses return on investment to evaluate the performance of its divisions and also to evaluate potential capital investments. The High Stool Division has two investment opportunities, each with identical investments, lives, and total cash flows. Taxes are ignored.

	Cash Flows	
Year	*Investment X*	*Investment Y*
0	$(48,036)	$(48,036)
1	$10,000	$30,000
2	$20,000	$20,000
3	$30,000	$10,000

The manager of the High Stool Division has computed the unadjusted rate of return for each investment to be 8.3%. Because the return on investment is less than 10–12%, the range of the corporate target rates of return on investment, both projects were rejected.

Although the High Stool Division manager understands and agrees with the calculations, he does not believe the two investments are equal in quality. He assumes that there is a "better way" to analyze the investment proposals.

The capital structure of the Green Eyeshade Company consists of the following:

8% Long-term debt (currently selling at face value yielding 8% to maturity)	$200,000
Common stock ($10 par, 20,000 shares outstanding, $3.20 annual cash dividend, currently selling at $40 per share)	200,000
Retained earnings	150,000
Total	$550,000

The company expects a 6% growth rate and pays taxes at a 50% rate.

REQUIRED:

A. Do you agree that both investments are earning a return on investment (unadjusted rate of return) of 8.3%? Prove the computations.

B. Are the two investments equal in quality? Explain.

C. Assuming that an adjusted rate of return is to be used to analyze investment opportunities, what target rate of return should be used?

D. Compute the net present value for each investment proposal. Should either investment be accepted?

E. What is the actual adjusted rate of return earned by each project? By this criterion, should either investment be accepted?

15-29 *(Purchase versus Leasing).* The Eastside Data Corporation sells computer services to its clients. As a part of a feasibility study to acquire a new computer, the company developed the following data.

1. The purchase price of the computer is $130,000. Maintenance, property taxes, and insurance will be $20,000 per year. Because of technology changes and expected growth of the service, the company expects to replace the computer at the end of three years. The resale value at that time will be about $10,000. The company will use straight-line depreciation for financial reporting and sum-of-the-years'-digits for tax purposes.

2. The equipment supplier will rent the same equipment to Eastside Data for $52,180 per year plus 10% of the annual billings from the use of the equipment. The rental price includes maintenance.

3. The estimated billings for the service bureau will be $100,000 the first year, $200,000 the second year, and $300,000 the third year.

4. Annual operating costs whether leased or purchased will be $60,000 with a programming and start-up cost of $20,000 in the first year.

5. The income tax rate is 30%. If purchased, the equipment will qualify for an investment credit of 5%.

6. The company expects a rate of return of 16% on long-range investments.

REQUIRED:
Determine whether the equipment should be acquired and, if so, whether it should be purchased or rented.

15-30 *(Investment Analysis versus Cash Needs).* Elsa and Elizabeth are searching for a source of income until their social security and other pension plans begin in five years. To continue their respective life styles, Elsa must have at least $9,000 and Elizabeth $14,000 before taxes. The women have been working at jobs they do not like and want challenging work. Many friends have encouraged the women to open a bakery that specializes in strudel, for which they are locally famous. If they open a bakery, they will call it Der Strudel Shop.

The women have found a bakery for sale that is well located and equipped for their style of baking. Purchase of the business will require $30,000 in cash, which would cover the building ($20,000), equipment ($8,000), and working capital ($2,000). Estimated lives for the building and equipment are ten and five years, respectively.

A granddaughter who is about is graduate from a school of business helped the women analyze the bakery's records. Before consideration of income taxes and a salary for the present owner, the bakery generated $15,000 of cash last year. The women are certain that they should be able to double the cash flows.

Der Strudel Shop will pay corporate income taxes of 30% on total net income after salaries. Elsa will draw a salary of $5,000, and Elizabeth will draw a salary of $7,000. Income after taxes will be distributed equally in the form of dividends. Depreciation will be computed on a straight-line basis. Assume that the business can be sold for the book value of the assets at any time.

REQUIRED:
Prepare an analysis of the investment for Elsa and Elizabeth. Assume that a minimum rate of return is 10%. Your analysis should indicate whether the financial requirements for their desired life-styles can be met.

15-31 *(Complex Cash Flows and Net Present Value).* The Baxter Company manufactures toys and other short-lived fad-type items.

The research and development department came up with an item that would make a good promotional gift for office equipment dealers. Aggressive and effective effort by Baxter's sales personnel has resulted in almost firm commitments for this product for the next three years. It is expected that the product's value will be exhausted by that time.

In order to produce the quantity demanded, Baxter will need to buy additional machinery and rent some additional space. It appears that about 25,000 square feet will be needed. 12,500 square feet of currently unused but leased space is available now. (Baxter's present lease, with 10 years to run, costs $3.00 a foot.) There are another 12,500 square feet adjoining the Baxter facility, which Baxter will rent for three years at $4.00 per square foot per year if it decides to make this product.

The equipment will be purchased for about $900,000. It will require $30,000 in modifications, $60,000 for installation, and $90,000 for testing; all of these activities will be done by a firm of engineers hired by Baxter. All of the expenditures will be paid for on January 1, 1973.

The equipment should have a salvage value of about $180,000 at the end of the third year. No additional general overhead costs are expected to be incurred.

The following estimates of revenues and expenses for this product for the three years have been developed.

	1973	*1974*	*1975*
Sales	$1,000,000	$1,600,000	$800,000
Material, labor, and overhead	$ 400,000	$ 750,000	$350,000
Allocated general expenses	40,000	75,000	35,000
Rent	87,500	87,500	87,500
Depreciation	450,000	300,000	150,000
Total costs	977,500	1,212,500	622,500
Income before tax	$ 22,500	$ 387,500	$177,500
Income tax (40%)	9,000	155,000	71,000
Income after tax	$ 13,500	$ 232,500	$106,500

REQUIRED:

A. Prepare a schedule that shows the incremental after-tax cash flows for this project.

B. If the company requires a two-year payback period for its investment, would it undertake this project? Show your supporting calculations clearly.

C. Calculate the after-tax accounting rate of return for the project.

D. A newly hired business school graduate recommends that the company consider the use of net present-value analysis to study this project. If the company sets a required rate of return of 20% after taxes, will this project be accepted? Show your supporting calculations clearly. (Assume that all operating revenues and expenses occur at the end of the year.)

(CMA adapted)

15-32 *(Long-range Planning Policy).* The TST Corporation is a family-controlled corporation that has been in business for many years. Recently, profits and the price of common stock have declined. The 400 stockholders (outside the controlling family) are unhappy because they have not achieved a dividend growth rate of 8%. They have criticized the management for poor long-range planning. At the end of 19X1, the capital structure of TST Company consisted of:

4,584 shares of $100 par value preferred stock. Annual dividends on preferred are $8.00 per share. The market price of preferred has remained at $110 per share, the amount for which the company may repurchase the stock at any time.

12,500 shares of common, par $100. There were 400 shares of common in the treasury (shown at cost) at the end of 19X1 and 2,000 shares in the treasury at the end of 19X2. Market prices at the end of 19X1 were $150 per share, dropping to $130 at the end of 19X2.

Reserve for contingencies of $100,000 was created because of anticipated losses in a foreign contract. The reserve was returned to retained earnings during 19X2.

Reserve for retirement of preferred stock: The treasury stock had a call (repurchase) price of $110. The $10 over par reduced retained earnings when the stock was repurchased in 19X2. The company set up the reserve in 19X1 to segregate the retained earnings equal to the amount paid above par.

Retained earnings:
The following changes occurred during 19X2.

Beginning balance		$1,663,005
Add:		
Net income for 19X2	$370,485	
Reduction of reserve for contingencies	100,000	470,485
Total		$2,133,490
Deduct:		
Preferred dividends	$ 36,672	
Common dividends	100,000	136,672
Retained earnings, December 31, 19X2		$1,996,818

The TST Company is a producer of high-quality equipment for powering manufacturing operations. (In the past its major product was a steam-driven turbine.)

THE TST CORPORATION
STATEMENT OF FINANCIAL POSITION
Assets

	December 31, 19X2	*December 31, 19X1*
Current assets:		
Cash on hand and in banks	$ 391,739	$ 225,551
Accounts receivable—trade	561,689	559,690
Miscellaneous	18,907	13,031
Inventories	831,278	789,224
Marketable securities at cost	1,435,963	2,031,822
Total current assets	$3,239,576	$3,619,318
Plant assets:		
At cost	$1,680,616	$1,675,866
Less: Accumulated depreciation	1,214,999	1,199,699
Net recorded value	465,617	476,167
Total assets	$3,705,193	$4,095,485

Liabilities and Stockholders' Equity

Current liabilities:		
Accounts payable	$ 143,915	$ 134,867
Salaries, wages, and commissions	119,320	119,580
Federal, state, and municipal taxes	390,180	380,754
Pension plan contribution	65,554	3,946
Total current liabilities	$ 718,969	$ 639,147
Stockholders' equity:		
Capital stock—preferred	—	$ 458,400
Capital stock—common	$1,250,000	1,250,000
Reserves	—	145,840
Retained earnings (restricted by cost of stock in treasury)	1,996,818	1,663,005
	$3,246,818	$3,517,245
Less: Common stock in treasury at cost	260,594	60,907
Total stockholders' equity	2,986,224	3,456,338
Total liabilities and stockholders' equity	$3,705,193	$4,095,485

REQUIRED:

A. On the basis of the limited information available, including the financial statements, comment upon the charges by the stockholders that long-range planning has been poor.

B. During 19X2, TST Corporation retired the outstanding preferred stock. Was this a wise long-range decision?

C. Prepare a set of recommendations to the company for long-range planning. Your recommendations should include how the company should set up a long-range plan, how the decision rule should be stated, and what criteria the company should use for evaluating long-range decisions.

15-33 *(Selection of Alternatives Using Net Present Value).* Edwards Corporation is a manufacturing concern that produces and sells a wide range of products. The company not only mass-produces a number of products and equipment components but also produces special-purpose manufacturing equipment to customer specifications.

The firm is considering adding a new stapler to one of its product lines. More equipment will be required to produce the new stapler. There are three alternative ways to acquire the needed equipment: (1) purchase general-purpose equipment, (2) lease general-purpose equipment, (3) build special-purpose equipment. A fourth alternative, purchase of the special-purpose equipment, has been ruled out because it would be prohibitively expensive.

The general-purpose equipment can be purchased for $125,000. The equipment has an estimated salvage of $15,000 at the end of its useful life of ten years. At the end of five years, the equipment can be used elsewhere in the plant or be sold for $40,000.

Alternatively, the general-purpose equipment can be acquired by a five-year lease for $40,000 annual rent. The lessor will assume all responsibility for taxes, insurance, and maintenance.

Special-purpose equipment can be constructed by the Contract Equipment Department of the Edwards Corporation. While the department is opeating at a level that is normal for the time of year, it is below full capacity. The department could produce the equipment without interfering with its regular revenue-producing activities.

The estimated departmental costs for the construction of the special-purpose equipment are

Materials and parts	$ 75,000
Direct labor	60,000
Variable overhead (50% of DL$)	30,000
Fixed overhead (25% of DL$)	15,000
Total	$180,000

Corporation general and administrative costs average 20% of labor dollar content of factory production.

Engineering and management studies provide the following revenue and cost estimates (excluding lease payments and depreciation) for producing the new stapler, depending upon the equipment used:

	General-Purpose Equipment		*Self-Constructed Equipment*
	Purchased	*Leased*	
Unit selling price	$5.00	$5.00	$5.00
Unit production costs:			
Materials	$1.80	$1.80	$1.70
Conversion costs	1.65	1.65	1.40
Total unit production costs	3.45	3.45	3.10
Unit contribution margin	$1.55	$1.55	$1.90
Estimated unit volume	40,000	40,000	40,000
Estimated total contribution margin	$62,000	$62,000	$76,000
Other costs:			
Supervision	$16,000	$16,000	$18,000
Taxes and insurance	3,000	—	5,000
Maintenance	3,000	—	2,000
Total	$22,000	$16,000	$25,000

The company will depreciate the general-purpose machine over ten years on the sum-of-the-year's-digits (S-Y-D) method. At the end of five years, the accumulated depreciation will total $80,000. (The present value of this amount for the first five years is $62,078.) The special-purpose machine will be depreciated over five years on the S-Y-D method. Its salvage value at the end of that time is estimated to be $30,000.

The company uses an after-tax cost of capital of 10%. Its marginal tax rate is 40%.

REQUIRED:

A. Calculate the net present value for each of the three alternatives that Edwards Corporation has at its disposal.

B. Should Edwards Corporation select any of the three options, and if so, which one? Explain your answer. *(CMA adapted)*

15–34 *(Complex Cash Flows and Present-Value Analysis).* The Beta Corporation manufactures office equipment and distributes its products through wholesale distributors.

Beta Corporation recently learned of a patent on the production of a semi-automatic paper collator that can be obtained at a cost of $60,000 cash. The semi-automatic model is vastly superior to the manual model that the corporation now produces. At a cost of $40,000, present equipment could be modified to accommodate the production of the new semi-automatic model. Such modifications would not affect the remaining useful life of four years or the salvage value of $10,000 that the equipment now has. Variable costs, however, would increase by one dollar per unit. Fixed costs, other than relevant amortization charges, would not be affected. If the equipment is modified, the manual model cannot be produced.

The current income statement relative to the manual collator appears as follows:

Sales (100,000 units @ $4)		$400,000
Variable costs	$180,000	
Fixed costs*	120,000	
Total costs		300,000
Net income before income taxes		$100,000
Income taxes (40%)		40,000
Net income after income taxes		$ 60,000

*All fixed costs are directly allocable to the production of the manual collator and include depreciation on equipment of $20,000, calculated on the straight-line basis with a useful life of 10 years.

Market research had disclosed three important findings relative to the new semi-automatic model. First, a particular competitor will certainly purchase the patent if Beta Corporation does not. If this were to happen, Beta Corporation's sales of the manual collator would fall to 70,000 units per year. Second, if no increase in the selling price is made, Beta Corporation could sell approximately 190,000 units per year of the semi-automatic model. Third, because of the advances being made in this area, the patent will be completely worthless at the end of four years.

Because of the uncertainty of the current situation, the raw materials inventory has been almost exhausted. Regardless of the decision reached, substantial and immediate inventory replenishment will be required. The engineering department estimates that if the new model is to be produced, the average monthly raw materials inventory will be $20,000. If the old model is continued, the inventory balance will average $12,000 per month.

REQUIRED:

A. Prepare a schedule that shows the incremental after-tax cash flows for the comparison of the two alternatives. Assume that the corporation will use the sum-of-the-years'-digits method for depreciating the costs of modifying the equipment.

B. Assuming the incremental after-tax cash flows calculated in requirement A, will Beta Corporation, if it has a cost of capital of 18%, decide to manufacture the semi-automatic collator? Use the net present-value decision rule and assume that all operating revenues and expenses occur at the end of the year. *(CMA adapted)*

16 Planning and Control Systems In Not-For-Profit Organizations

Not-for-profit organizations comprise a significant segment of the United States economy. Approximately one-third of the economic activity in the United States is carried out by not-for-profit organizations. At one extreme is a governmental entity created to provide services that private business cannot or will not provide—national defense, parks, legal systems, public safety, and highways, for example. At the other extreme is the publicly owned enterprise, such as a hospital or power company, that operates like its private counterpart. Between these two extremes are a wide range of not-for-profit organizations created to provide a service to the public. Examples include the Red Cross, Boy or Girl Scouts, churches, and art museums.

In this chapter we will look at governmental and similar not-for-profit organizations. Several characteristics make them different from the for-profit entities in the private sector. These characteristics include the following:

1. Organized for the public good. Governments and many voluntary not-for-profit organizations are created to provide specific services for the citizens of an area. In many cases these are services that the competitive marketplace cannot provide. Typically, there is no direct relationship between the provision of the service and the mode of financing the service, particularly when the financing is through taxes. The comparison of revenues and expenses does not have the same meaning as it would have in the private sector.

2. No profit motive exists. In the private sector, profit provides a device for allocating resources and evaluating performance. No such device exists in government. The goal of government should be the provision of needed services at the lowest feasible cost.

3. The legislative process. Legislative approval is required for all actions of government, including operating budgets, borrowing authorization, program goals and objectives, and tax levies.

4. Stewardship of resources. Historically, the accounting systems of not-for-profit entities were designed to provide accountability for the collection and expenditure of funds. Since concepts such as net income and return on investment have no meaning in a not-for-profit entity, the focus was on asset protection. Thus, the planning and budgeting functions were divorced from the accounting system, except as they facilitated asset protection or legal compliance.

These characteristics have resulted in the development of accounting practices that provide accountability; unfortunately, they do not always provide useful tools for management to plan and control operations and make efficient and effective decisions. Only recently have significant strides been made in management planning and decision making for not-for-profit organizations. This is particularly true for those not-for-profit organizations that have many of the characteristics of for-profit organizations, such as health and educational organizations. These organizations have adopted many of the practices discussed earlier in this text. Therefore, our interest in this chapter is in governmental and other not-for-profit entities that differ significantly from for-profit organizations.

First, we will examine the financial accounting practices of not-for-profit organizations. Then, recent innovations in management accounting for not-for-profit organizations, including program budgeting and zero-base budgeting, will be discussed. Finally, long-range decisions in the public sector will be examined.

FINANCIAL ACCOUNTING IN NOT-FOR-PROFIT ORGANIZATIONS

The wide range of not-for-profit organizations makes a summary description of their financial accounting practices difficult. For example, there should be very few differences in the management accounting or financial accounting practices between city-owned power companies and investor-owned power companies. On the other hand, the accounting for local governments has no real counterpart in the private sector. The major accounting differences between governmental accounting and for-profit organizations are:

1. The accounting entity.

2. Recording the budget.

3. Recording expenditures rather than expenses.

The Accounting Entity

In for-profit organizations the entire organization is an accounting entity. Separate financial statements may be prepared for segments but the focal point for financial accounting is the entire entity. There is no similar entity for a particular governmental unit such as a city. Instead, accounting is performed for a number of **funds.** A fund is an independent fiscal and accounting entity organized to carry on specific activities.

Funds may be classified into two groups—expendable and non-expendable. In the **expendable funds,** all resources of the fund may be spent in carrying out the specific purpose of the fund. No fixed assets or long-term liabilities are recorded; the receipt of cash is treated as revenue, regardless of the source; and the payment of cash is an expenditure, regardless of the purpose. A partial accrual system may be used where taxes receivable and accounts payable are recognized but no fixed assets or long-term liabilities are recorded. Expendable funds include:

General Fund. This fund accounts for the activities of the not-for-profit organization for which no special fund has been created.

Special Funds. These funds account for the receipt and disbursement of money for special activities. Examples include: (1) funds for special sources of revenue, such as a tax on hotel and motel rooms to finance a convention center; (2) funds for payment of principal and interest on long-term debt; (3) funds for acquisition of land, buildings, and other capital facilities; and (4) funds for improvements that benefit particular property owners, such as sewers financed by assessments on the property owners.

The purpose of all expendable funds is to account for the receipt and expenditure of cash. There is no accountability for fixed assets and long-term liabilities in the expendable funds. Acquisition of a building is treated no differently than acquisition of a ream of paper or a lunch for a visiting dignitary. In order to maintain some accountability for them, fixed assets are *listed* in an inventory after they are acquired. This inventory does not represent a formal accounting system, however. The same is true for long-term debt. Proceeds from the sale of the debt are recorded as revenue, and a *list* of the debts payable is maintained. The emphasis in expendable funds is on accountability for receipt and disbursement of cash; it is not on efficiency or performance. For this reason, management accounting, as discussed in the first fifteen chapters of this text, was slow to develop in administration of these funds.

Nonexpendable Funds. These funds are used to operate government-owned enterprises, such as the power company, the motor pool, and central stores. These funds are accounted for the same as their counterparts are in the private sector. Generally accepted accounting principles are followed, and the planning process and other management accounting practices are adopted. Typically, provision of service at the lowest cost, rather than maximization of profit, is the major goal.

Recording the Budget

Since no action can be undertaken without legislative approval, the budget is the key element in the control of not-for-profit organizations. Because of this special control function, the budgets are recorded directly into the books of account. For example, assume that the city council of the City of Paradise approved the budget in Exhibit 16–1. For simplicity we will assume the city uses only a general fund and that it lists its fixed assets separately. This budget is a **line-item budget. Appropriations,** that is, permission and commitment to spend funds, are for specific lines on the budget such as salaries, supplies, equipment, and contractual services. The budget may be detailed by type of salary position or even to a specific position, depending upon the amount of budgetary control the city council wants to exercise. Money may not be shifted from one line item to another line item without city council action. This method of budgeting places very tight controls on specific expenditures but pays little attention to the cost of the specific services or products provided

CITY OF PARADISE
BUDGET
For the
Fiscal Year Ending June 30, 19X5

Budgeted Revenues:	
Taxes	$40,000
Fines, licenses, and fees	12,000
Total	$52,000
Appropriations:	
Salaries	$30,000
Supplies	3,000
Equipment	7,000
Contractual Services	10,000
Total	50,000
Budgeted Surplus	$ 2,000

EXHIBIT 16–1
Budget for a city

to the citizens. It is easy to cut spending by reducing or eliminating a specific line item, but, it is seldom apparent what effect that specific cut will have on service.

When the not-for-profit organization records the budget in the books a system is created in which the budget is continuously compared with actual expenditures. Every time an expenditure is posted, there is a comparison which reduces the likelihood of overexpending a particular line item (which would be a violation of the law). In one sense it is a continual budget report.

At anytime a statement can be prepared directly from the books that compares actual revenues with budgeted revenues and compares expenditures with appropriations. Such a statement of revenues and expenses is presented in Exhibit 16–2. The budgeted surplus (excess of estimated revenues over appropriations) of $2,000 projected at the end of the year actually amounted to $400. Revenues were $2,000 below budget, and expenditures were $400 below appropriations. One item of expenditure, equipment, exceeded the budget by $300. As soon as it was known that the expenditure would exceed the appropriation, the city council had to pass a supplementary appropriation. Since a governmental entity cannot spend more than the amount appropriated, a supplemental appropriation must be enacted by the legislative body.

The balance sheet for the City of Paradise is presented in Exhibit 16–3. We have assumed that all transactions were carried on in a general fund. The city could have used other special funds to record transactions for special activities. It is not uncommon for a city of 100,000 population to have 80 to

CITY OF PARADISE
STATEMENT OF REVENUES AND EXPENDITURES
For the Year Ended June 30, 19X5

	Budget	*Actual*	*Over (under) Budget*
Revenues:			
Taxes	$40,000	$41,000	$ 1,000
Fines, licenses, and fees	12,000	9,000	(3,000)
Total	$52,000	$50,000	$(2,000)
Expenditures:			
Salaries	$30,000	$30,000	$ 0
Supplies	3,000	2,800	(200)
Equipment	7,000	7,300	300
Contractual services	10,000	9,500	(500)
Total	$50,000	$49,600	$ (400)
Excess of revenues over expenditures	$ 2,000	$ 400	$(1,600)

EXHIBIT 16–2
Statement of revenues and expenditures for a city

CITY OF PARADISE
BALANCE SHEET
June 30, 19X5

	General Fund	*General Fixed Assets*
ASSETS		
Cash	$ 200	
Taxes receivable	2,000	
Land		$ 5,000
City hall		15,000
Equipment		13,300
Total	$2,200	$33,300
EQUITIES		
Fund balance	$2,200	
Investment in fixed assets		$33,300

EXHIBIT 16–3
Balance sheet for a city

100 different funds. They may be grouped by type on the published balance sheet, but separate records are maintained for each. In addition to the general fund, the City of Paradise lists its fixed assets in a separate record. Technically, the list of fixed assets is not a *fund,* because there are no cash transactions. This group of accounts is no more than an inventory of fixed assets. A total balance sheet is usually not prepared for a governmental unit. The entity is the *fund,* not the *city.*

Recording of Expenditures Rather than Expenses

Because of the emphasis on accountability, rather than operating results, the expendable funds measure expenditures (cash payments) rather than expenses (expired costs). There is no attempt to match earned revenue against cost expirations as in a for-profit entity. As a result, an expenditure for the purchase of equipment with a useful life of 10 years is treated the same as an expenditure for salaries. This becomes a key problem in management accounting where the proper measure of the cost of services is the resources consumed in providing the service (expired cost), not the amount of cash paid in a particular period of time.

Purchase contracts that involve long delays between entering into the contract and the receipt of the goods and payment cause problems in relating actual expenditures to appropriations. Once a contract has been made, the entity has, for all practical purposes, spent the funds. If the supplier complies with the contract, the fund must pay for the goods. Because of this, when there is a delay between the time when the goods are ordered and the subsequent payment, the fund should record an encumbrance. An **encumbrance** is a pseudo-expenditure account which precludes double spending of the appropriation. When the goods are received, the encumbrance is removed and the expenditure is recorded. If the goods are not received by year-end, the encumbrance is included in the statement of revenues and expenditures as an expenditure, and the encumbrance is included on the balance sheet as a liability. The encumbrance accomplishes two purposes. First, it prevents double spending of the funds, since the encumbrance shows that the appropriation was issued for this contract and cannot be used for something else. Second, unexpended and unemcumbered appropriations are automatically cancelled at the end of the fiscal year. The encumbrance allows the contract made in fiscal year 19X5 but actually paid for in 19X6 to be charged against 19X5 appropriations. In this way the contracts remaining incomplete at the end of the year do not require a new appropriation by the city council.

Evaluation of Financial Accounting by Not-for-Profit Organizations

The emphasis on accountability and recording of expenditures makes it difficult to relate costs to the output of goods and services. In the first place, transactions are separated into various funds by recording special transactions in special funds. Because there is no consolidation of all funds, the cost of a particular program may be spread over several funds. For example, assume that a manager wanted to measure the total cost of education. A special revenue fund may have been used to account for the receipt of tax monies for the operation of the schools. The buildings, equipment, and buses will be listed in the general fixed-asset group, and the annual cost of these assets will not be measured through depreciation. A special program, for example, for gifted or disadvantaged children, may be funded by the city council through the general fund while the interest on the debt to build the school building will be recorded in the debt service fund. A number of additional costs, such as adult education and costs of city library, would be recorded either in the general fund or in some other special fund.

In the second place, all funds in a particular year must be spent or they will be lost. The manager of an activity may make certain that the funds are spent whether the activity actually needs the funds.

MANAGEMENT ACCOUNTING IN NOT-FOR-PROFIT ORGANIZATIONS

Recently, changes in budgeting and accounting have taken place, particularly at the state and local level, with the development and implementation of program budgeting and zero-base budgeting. Because the budget is the vehicle through which resources are allocated and expenditures controlled, the budget is the focal point of management accounting for not-for-profit organizations. In this section we will examine budgeting theory and practices for not-for-profit organizations, particularly local governmental units.

Traditional Budgeting

All government acts must be authorized by law. The collection of cash must conform with constitutional and statutory authority, and the expenditure of cash must be specifically authorized through an approved budget. In the public sector the budget is more than an expression of the decision process. Once approved, it is also the legal ceiling on expenditures. In a profit-oriented firm, the budget is a guide, not a law.

The traditional not-for-profit budget and accounting system usually presents information in two dimensions. First, expenditures are accumulated by the object of expenditure, that is, the reason for which the expenditure was made. Personnel, travel, supplies, and contractual services are a few examples of objects of expenditure. The second dimension involves the fund and the organizational units of the government. Examples include the fire, police, and parks department in the general fund and the schools in a special revenue fund.

In the traditional budget there is no attempt to identify output measures with their costs. While some planning may be by program, so as to relate the outputs of the unit with the inputs, typically, budgeting and accounting are focused upon the inputs via the line item.

Program Budgeting

During the 1960s, a new approach to budgeting in the public sector was developed. The new system, called *Planning, Programming, Budgeting System,* or **program budgeting** for short, focuses upon the output of the organization rather than specific inputs.

At the local level, program budgets have enjoyed widespread public acceptance because they focus on services and outputs that are meaningful to the average citizen, rather than on organizations and inputs. Decision makers at the local government level can compare alternative programs and allocate resources to those programs that will produce the greatest return for the funds invested. Before the emergence of program budgeting, budget deliberations often centered upon the number of additional personnel to be added to the payroll or the type of machinery to be purchased. With program budgeting, the discussion has moved to consideration of a service at a cost that can be afforded.

Program budgeting cuts across organizational lines and requires three dimensions of information: information on output (important for decisions); information on organizational activities (important for control through responsibility accounting); and information on inputs (salaries, materials, etc.). Industry has long dealt with these three dimensions. The public sector had not previously addressed itself to the output dimension, and it has been necessary to establish new patterns of thinking about efficiency.

Program budgeting has several distinguishing characteristics:

1. Development of a program structure with a statement of goals and objectives for each program
2. Multi-year costing
3. Evaluation criteria and output measurement
4. Zero-base budgeting

DEVELOPMENT OF THE PROGRAM STRUCTURE

A good program structure may be the only way the private citizen can gain an overview of the benefits and services provided by local government. The development of a program structure starts with an identification of goals and major desired outputs of the organization. A government entity must identify the goods and services it distributes to the citizen it serves. The second step is to group these services into broad categories, called *programs* or *program categories*. Program categories should be few and represent the major goals of the society served.

A typical program structure for a city follows:

I. Personal safety
II. Health
III. Intellectual development
IV. Satisfactory home and community environment

V. Economic satisfaction and satisfactory work opportunities for individuals
VI. Leisure-time opportunities
VII. Transportation and communication

A statement of goals is then prepared, setting out the benefits or outputs for each program category. A goal for category I, *Personal safety,* might be: "To reduce the amount and effects of external harm to individuals and, in general, to maintain an atmosphere of personal security from such external events."

Each program category is then expanded to identify the specific goods and services necessary to achieve its goals. For example, a subprogram of *Personal safety* would be *Law enforcement,* which carries its own set of goals that may be further expanded into program elements.

A. Law enforcement (Goal: To reduce the amount and effects of crime and, in general, to maintain an atmosphere of personal security from criminals.)
1. Crime prevention
2. Crime investigation
3. Judging and assignment of punishment
4. Detention and supervision of offenders
5. Rehabilitation of offenders

In practice, the development of a program structure and statement of goals is the most difficult part of program budgeting. There is neither a prescribed number of program categories nor a "right" way to express the organization's goals. For agencies that have developed a program structure, the process of program development and goal formulation has been a healthy experience and worth the effort, even when the planning process stopped at that point.

EVALUATION CRITERIA AND OUTPUT MEASUREMENT

After the goals of the organization have been identified and the program structure developed, it is necessary to identify a specific set of criteria that can be used to evaluate actual performance. Each of the objectives explicit in the goal statement should have criteria for measurement. To continue with our previous example, under the crime prevention program could be the following criteria for evaluation.

1. Annual number of each category of offense
2. Crime rate per thousand of inhabitants
3. Number and percentage of population committing criminal acts
4. Annual cost to the population by type of crime

For each evaluation criterion a specific target or objective should be set. The objective may state a level or a change expected for the year.

MULTI-YEAR COSTING

A significant contribution of program budgeting is the focus on the total costs of a program, not for just one year but for several years ahead. In addition to showing past costs, program budgeting estimates costs for the current year and for future years. A five-year period has evolved in practice and apparently is a sufficiently long planning horizon for most needs. At times, special analyses require projections of costs and benefits over the entire life of a project. Understandably, when the projections exceed a five-year time frame, they become vaguer and subject to greater error.

With program budgeting, decision makers in the not-for-profit sector are required to take a long-range outlook in their planning. Proposals with relatively low initial expenditures but large operating and maintenance costs may be examined more closely in this system.

ZERO-BASE BUDGETING

Zero-base budgeting starts from an entirely different premise than traditional budgeting and is a natural subcomponent of program budgeting. Under zero-base budgeting every dollar of budgeted expenditure must be justified, including current programs that are to continue. Traditional budgeting usually accepts the current level of expenditures and requires justification of proposed increases. Traditionally, required cuts in spending are made "across the board" so that continuing expenditures for particular programs get little attention.

Zero-base budgeting is essentially a technique for planning and decision-making for the manager operating a program budget. It forces the manager to identify decision packages to be used in carrying out the activities of a particular program, to evaluate the decision packages, and to rank them in order of priority. The amount of funds available will determine how far down the list of decision packages the organization will go. The study and ranking include decision packages for all existing activites, as well as for new projects or activities. Each of the blocks in Exhibit 16–4 constitutes a step in zero-base budgeting and will be examined next. Development of program objectives was discussed earlier in the chapter as a part of the discussion on program budgeting and will not be repeated.

Development of Decision Packages

A decision package identifies a particular activity, function, or operation suitable for evaluation and comparison with other decision packages. In some ways the decision package methodology of zero-base budgeting is comparable to the identification of investment proposals for long-range decision analysis in the for-profit sector. Decision packages may relate to services or goods provided, citizen groups, geographic areas, capital projects, or any other

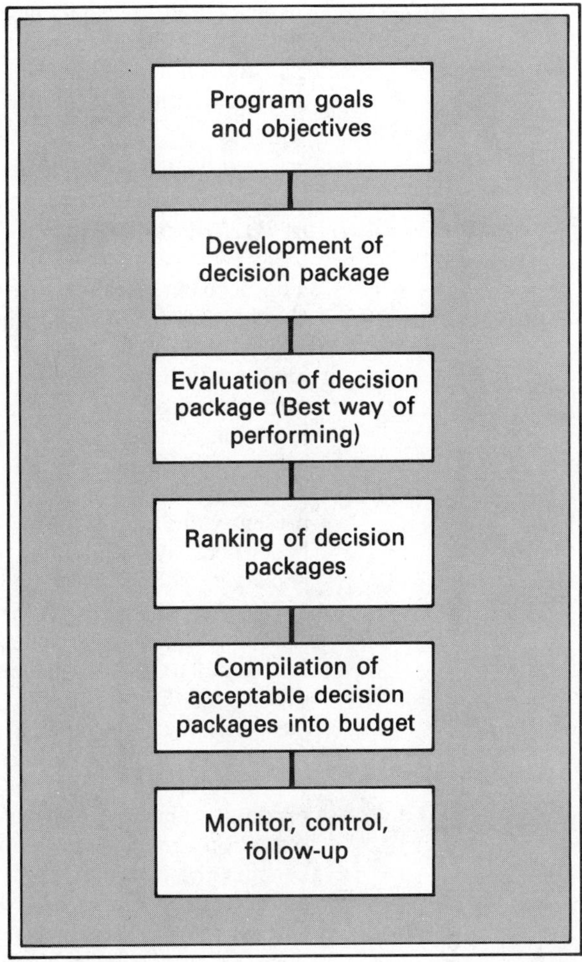

EXHIBIT 16–4
Steps in zero-base budgeting

activity that can be logically tied to the organization's long-range goals and objectives. In the private sector a decision package may relate to products, markets, customer groups, geographic territories, capital projects, or anything else that may be related to the corporate goals and objectives.

Because each decision package should relate to a specific decision, it must be complete and able to stand alone. In addition to all direct costs, the cost of support activities are identified and included in the total cost of the decision package. The minimum size of a decision package is the level of effort required to complete a meaningful activity or job and provide some benefits to the organization. Each decision package should include a presentation of its benefits and costs, its legal necessity, and its technical and operational necessity. Where alternative courses of action are available, the decision package should include information about the alternative courses of action that are available.

Evaluation of Decision Packages

The decision packages are evaluated by systematic analysis. The analysis should answer the question, "What is the organization getting for the expenditure." The analysis should take two forms. First, there should be an identification and analysis of the benefits and costs, or some other relevant quantitative or qualitative measure. Second, the impact of different spending levels on benefits and costs should be determined. It may be possible to achieve significant increases in total benefits by trade-offs in sizes of decision packages. These benefits and costs could be measured and discounted with present-value techniques, as shown in Chapters 14 and 15. The discounted benefit-cost ratio provides one basis for evaluation and ranking of decision packages.

An illustration of benefit-cost analysis is presented in Exhibit 16–5. Discounted benefits are plotted on the vertical axis and discounted costs on the horizontal axis. The diagonal line, labeled *Benefit-cost decision line,* is a plotting of the proposed long-range decision rule. Any plotting of a benefit-cost ratio that falls on or to the left of the line is favorable; any plotting that falls to the right of the line is unfavorable.

Assume that three proposals for combating a major health problem are proposed. The first proposal involves an educational program and is represented on the chart as a dashed line. This proposal provides a high level of benefits at a low level of cost. However, diminishing returns are encountered as the costs are increased; the benefit-cost ratio drops below one quite soon. The second proposal involves preventive medicine and is plotted as a broken line. It shows a favorable benefit-cost ratio over a larger range of spending levels. The third proposal, medical research, is plotted as a solid line. Research requires a high level of costs before any significant benefits are achieved.

The impact of scale is important in this illustration because the relative ranking of alternatives changes at different spending levels. At cost level 1, education ranks highest; at cost levels 2 and 3, the program of preventive medicine ranks highest; at cost level 4 and above, research is the only favorable alternative. A cutback in funds after the project is approved and started, leading to a curtailment of the project from cost level 4 to level 3 or lower; would result in a very inefficient use of funds.

As a part of benefit-cost analysis, the impact of different spending levels on output should be examined. By comparing the incremental effect of additional expenditures on different programs, a significant increase in benefits may be achieved through a modest trade-off of investment among projects.

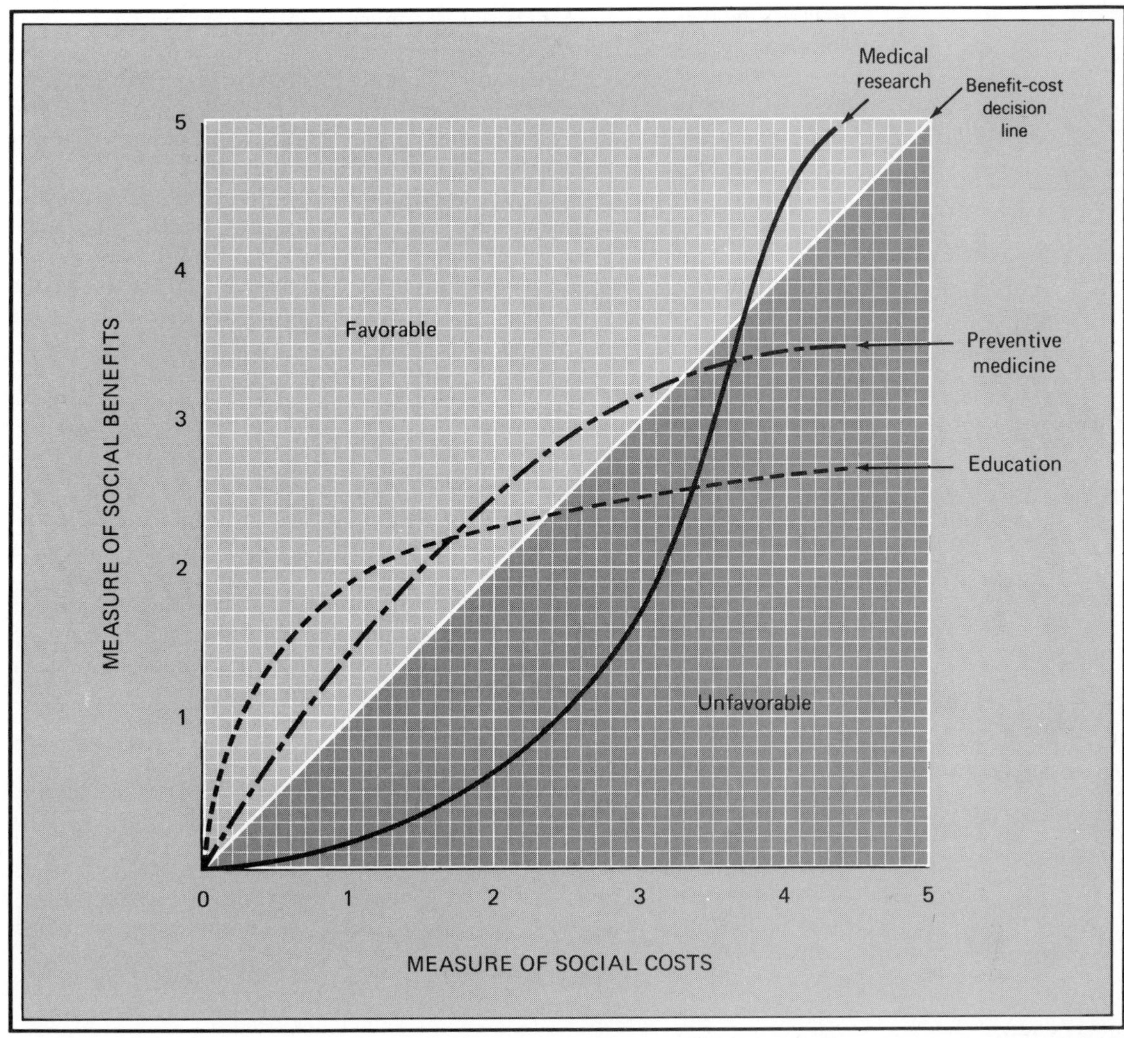

EXHIBIT 16–5
Structure of benefit-cost analysis

Ranking of Decision Packages

The evaluation process provides the data for ranking the decision packages. The ranking of the decision packages by their order of importance or impact is the key step in zero-base budgeting. The ranking step establishes the priorities and makes the selection process easier. Starting with the highest-ranked decision package, the organization continues to select decision packages as long as uncommitted funds exist.

A single criterion, such as net benefits provided or a benefit-cost ratio may be used to rank the decision packages. However, the benefits (and to some extent the costs) may not be measurable in dollars. A number of factors in addition to economic benefits may be used; one example is the number of citizens benefited. One approach to ranking where multi-criteria exist is to have a committee rank the decision packages. A six-point scale is often used. The highest number, six, is used for those projects required by law or considered highly desirable. Successively lower numbers are used as the benefits of the packages decrease. The sum of the committee votes will provide the ranking criterion.

Compilation of Decision Packages into the Budget

The amount of funds available will determine the number of decision packages accepted, since the costs of the acceptable packages are accumulated until the available resources are exhausted. If the decision packages are well stated and the ranking honest, the organization will have selected the decision projects with the highest priority. A subsequent cut in the funds will result in a dropping of only the marginal decision packages. The strength of zero-based budgeting is that it provides a mechanism for comparing decision packages and selecting those with the greatest promise.

Follow-up

Because decision packages are specifically identified, a follow-up control system may be developed that will monitor achievement of objectives, as well as keep expenditures at the budgeted levels. In other budgetary systems there is no similar mechanism for follow-up because of the concentration upon line items.

Evaluation of Zero-Base Budgeting

Like other planning and control systems in the public sector, zero-base budgeting has strong advocates who maintain that it will reduce inefficiency and achieve a high level of effectiveness. The literature records some outstanding results and some failures. Zero-base budgeting is a logical extension of program budgeting. Program budgeting helps in identifying programs and developing goals and objectives for the organization and for particular programs. By adding decision packages and ranking the packages, the analysis is strengthened and priorities are generated.

The greatest strength of zero-base budgeting is that all decision packages are evaluated and ranked. The evaluation process can provide the impact of different spending levels on the decision package. The decision package is compared with other decision packages, and the optimum size of the decision package is also estimated.

Zero-base budgeting has application in many settings. It was developed in an industrial firm and is currently in use in hundreds of private businesses as well as in governmental units. In addition to its use in developing operating budgets, it has been applied to cost-reduction programs, allocating staff overhead, developing long-range goals and objectives, and many other limited projects. In the government sector, zero-base budgeting shows great promise at the state and local level. It is at this level of government that outputs and services can best be identified and improved.

LONG-RANGE DECISIONS IN THE PUBLIC SECTOR

Many enterprises in the public sector face the same long-range decisions as private enterprise. For example, government-owned utilities and transportation systems face the same long-range decisions as investor-owned utilities and transportation companies. The tremendous growth in economic activity by government and other not-for-profit organizations has led to a search for systematic methods of analyzing public expenditures. Decision making in the public sector has been highly qualitative. Often it has been influenced more by funds available than by economic efficiency. Measures of economic efficiency must be used to ensure that decisions are economically sound, as well as politically expedient.

Every decision should have at its core the relationship between benefits and costs of the particular project. In the private sector the primary goal of long-range decisions is the maximization of the wealth of the enterprise. In the public sector the concept is much broader; the goal of **benefit-cost analysis** is to maximize the welfare of society. We are asking, "Will society be better off by engaging in a particular act?" In place of cash inflows to the organization, the public sector is concerned with social benefits. In place of cost, the public sector is concerned with social cost or social value foregone.

Long-range Decision Rule

In the public sector an investment decision is favorable if the discounted social benefits attributable to the decision exceed the discounted social costs attributable to the decision. The welfare of society is increased when the ratio of discounted social benefits to discounted social costs is greater than one.

Measurement of Social Costs

The cost side of benefit-cost analysis should include all unfavorable effects of a decision on society for the entire life of the project. This concept of social costs is a much broader view than the concept of discounted cash flow analysis for the private sector, which we examined earlier. In addition to the incremental cash outflows for a project, any indirect side effects (**externalities**) of a decision that inflict harm on others without compensation must be considered. For example, the construction of a dam for hydroelectric power will flood the river valley above the dam, destroying natural landscape and wildlife refuges and preventing fish from returning to their spawning grounds. A value should be attributed to these externalities to arrive at a comprehensive cost.

The requirement for environmental impact studies, whether for a public or private project, now brings long-range project planning by private enterprise closer to benefit-cost analysis used in the public sector, at least on the cost side of the calculation. Impact on the environment does not enter investment analysis directly in the private sector unless a cash flow is involved. However, the social cost to the environment (much broader than just cash flow) will be a qualitative factor that *must* be considered. Unless environmental quality is maintained, the project cannot be undertaken. In the public sector these social costs are included whether or not cash flow is involved.

Measurement of Social Benefits

The selection and measurement of social benefits constitute an identification of those services we want from government action. Ideally, we want to maximize welfare in the public sector. However, welfare in the broad sense eludes measurement; we often settle for some measure of per capita income as a surrogate for welfare. If a chronically unemployed person or a disabled person is trained and later employed, one measure of the benefits is the added income to society over the lifetime of the individual.

Social benefits may be considered the favorable impacts of a decision, regardless of their recipient. Once the favorable impacts of a project are determined, they should be valued at the prices that a competitive market system would assign to them. This valuation is difficult because in many cases a project is undertaken by the public sector because of market failures in the private sector.

All favorable side effects of a decision should be considered in the calcualations. To continue with our earlier example of a dam, the benefits from its construction should include the value of averting potential flood damage and providing recreation possiblities, as well as the power that will be produced and sold.

In many cases measurement of benefits is very difficult. When a single objective criterion dominates, such as deaths averted, it may be satisfactory to use a nonfinancial measure of benefits. This type of analysis, labeled **cost effectiveness,** relates costs to some nonfinancial measure such as cost per death averted or cost per pupil educated. The analysis may seek to maximize benefits for a given level of costs or to minimize the cost per increment of benefits. In cost effectiveness analysis it is important to identify the correct measure of benefits. Maximizing the teacher/pupil ratio does not necessarily maximize education.

Present Value

With the exception of projects involving water resources, it is only recently that present-value considerations have been utilized in the public sector. Most capital expenditure decisions, to the extent that economic efficiency was even considered, were made on the basis of costs in the first year of the project.

In the private sector we have suggested that the minimum rate of return should be based upon the weighted-average cost of capital. In the few cases where present-value analysis has been used in the public sector, the desired rate of return was based upon the average rate of interest paid on long-term government bonds, usually 3% to 5%. To illustrate the effect of a very low rate, assume that a flood-control project is proposed. The project will cost $50 million at the outset and will provide benefits averaging $4 million per year for 40 years. The present value of benefits and costs at different rates follow.

Benefits		*Costs*
4% rate ($4,000,000 × 19.793) $A_{\overline{40}|\,4\%}$	= $79,172,000	$50,000,000
6% rate ($4,000,000 × 15.046) $A_{\overline{40}|\,6\%}$	= $60,184,000	$50,000,000
8% rate ($4,000,000 × 11.925) $A_{\overline{40}|\,8\%}$	= $47,700,000	$50,000,000
10% rate ($4,000,000 × 9.779) $A_{\overline{40}|\,10\%}$	= $39,116,000	$50,000,000
15% rate ($4,000,000 × 6.642) $A_{\overline{40}|\,15\%}$	= $26,568,000	$50,000,000

By using a rate below 8% (7.57% to be precise), the project will be favorable; by using a higher rate, the costs exceeded the benefits. You can justify a very large dam at a 4% rate, in this case, about $79,000,000 worth of dam.

Most economists now agree that the appropriate rate of return for the public sector is the opportunity cost rate in the private sector from which those funds were removed. The removal of funds from the private sector prevents their investment in the private sector. Unless these funds are better used by the public sector, economicts argue that the funds should remain in the private sector and the project should not be undertaken. An appropriate rate of return in the private sector appears to be somewhere between 10% and 15%. With the exception of some publicly owned enterprises, such as power or water companies, this return has not been achieved in many cases.

Illustration of Benefit-cost Analysis

The benefit-cost analysis chosen for illustration is a study of the Supplemental Food Program (SFP). This study is not offered as an outstanding example of benefit-cost analysis. Rather, it is presented because it includes an interesting measure of economic benefits.

PROGRAM OBJECTIVES

SFP was designed primarily to improve the health of children from low-income families through free food supplements and free professional health care. The real cost associated with malnutrition and lack of medical care is the impaired ability of those who suffered prenatal and infantile brain damage. With medical authorization to secure free food, participating mothers were given an incentive to secure food as well as regular professional health care for themselves and their children.

METHODOLOGY

The study concerns one urban area participating in SFP. Information for the benefit-cost analysis was drawn from medical studies concerning the impact of nutritional deficiencies on mental health, SFP records, and interviews with SFP personnel and residents in the selected neighborhood. A benefit-cost model developed a ratio of discounted benefits to discounted costs for the program.

MEASUREMENT OF ECONOMIC BENEFITS

Significant economic benefits accruing from the program include: (1) the *direct product benefits,* measured by the retail value of the food distributed to the participants ($1,231,465); (2) the *employment opportunities* provided to nonprofessional employees of the program, many of whom had been unemployed ($159,880); and (3) *increased economic contribution* of participants, measured by the present value, in 1970 dollars, of the total additional income expected to be earned over the lifetime of the infants as a result of avoiding permanent brain damage ($237,213).

The number of cases of permanent brain damage avoided was determined by applying the conclusions from other research to this study. On the basis of medical studies concerning the incidence of mental retardation in infants due to insufficient prenatal care and nutrition, it was concluded that 10.68 cases of mental retardation were avoided as a result of SFP. The study assumed that a healthy child would eventually earn the average income of the total population between 18 and 64, whereas the mentally retarded child would eventually earn the average income of those in the age group between 18 and 64 having less than eight years of education. The difference in annual income, based upon census data, is $3,068.26 in 1970 dollars. The following calculation shows the present value of additional lifetime income of each infant (employed during years 18 to 60).[1]

$$\begin{array}{c}\text{Difference} \\ \text{in income}\end{array} \times \text{P.V.F. } A_{\overline{60}|5\%} - A_{\overline{18}|5\%} \times \begin{array}{c}\text{Number} \\ \text{of cases}\end{array} = \begin{array}{c}\text{Present value} \\ \text{of benefits}\end{array}$$

$$\$3{,}068.26 \times 7.2389 \times 10.68 = \$237{,}213$$

MEASUREMENT OF ECONOMIC COSTS

The costs included in the analysis were direct expenditures on the project. No side effects or externalities were identified.

CONCLUSIONS

A summary of the analysis is presented in Exhibit 16–6. The admittedly incomplete benefit-cost analysis indicates that using our criteria, the Supple-

SUMMARY OF BENEFITS:		
Direct product benefits: Value of food		$1,231,465
Employment of nonprofessional people		159,880
Incremental economic contribution of participants		237,213
Total benefits		$1,628,558
SUMMARY OF COSTS:		
Personnel costs:		
Doctors and nurses	$ 48,000	
Other personnel	262,469	$ 310,469
Nonpersonnel costs:		
Travel	$ 17,684	
Space rental	11,200	
Supplies and equipment	6,142	
Other costs	38,505	73,531
Cost of food (60% of retail)		738,879
Total costs		1,122,879
NET BENEFITS		$ 505,679
BENEFIT-COST RATIO		1.45

Source: Terre and Ameiss, "Accounting's Cost/Benefit Analysis for Evaluation of Today's Programs Assisting America's Disadvantage and Low-Income Families," *The National Public Accountant* (May, 1972), pp. 8-18.

EXHIBIT 16–6
Benefit-cost analysis of supplemental food program

[1]The present-value factor was found by subtracting the present-value factor for 18 years at 5% from the present-value factor for 60 years at 5%, or 18.9292 − 11.6896 = 7.2396.

mental Food Program was desirable. The dollar value of the benefits was 45% greater than the costs.

The benefit-cost analysis of SFP did not examine and compare alternative ways of achieving the objective of averting brain damage in infants. In this program it was determined only that the benefits exceeded the costs, not that this program was the best that could have been undertaken.

Political and Other Non-efficiency Considerations

The decision processes in this book have used economic efficiency as *the* appropriate decision criterion. If the costs of a decision are purely economic and can be measured in the marketplace, the analysis works well. In the public sector, however, there are political costs as well as economic costs. In fact, the need for political support may assume primary importance. At any level of government, one may find cases where politicians choose to support inefficient alternatives because they will produce votes. The economically efficient alternatives may result in a very high political cost when the politician seeks reelection.

The social goal of income redistribution is not given weight in the decision criterion given above. One dollar's worth of benefits is equal to any other dollar's worth of benefits. Increments of income to the poor and minorities, for example, are not deemed to be of higher value than increments to the wealthy. In fact, in many political decisions increments of income are weighted differently, depending upon who the recipient is.

RELATIONSHIPS BETWEEN INDUSTRY AND NOT-FOR-PROFIT ORGANIZATIONS

It would be shortsighted to believe that there is no cross-pollination between the profit-oriented and the not-for-profit segments of society. Each has unique problems and answers. Yet the need for data in the planning and control process brings them to some common solutions.

Since the early 1900s, governmental agencies have been actively involved in budgeting their activities. This emphasis upon a formalized budgetary program preceded most business budgeting efforts. Although the benefit of experience has been a positive influence, there have also been negative effects. Because the government has used budgeting as a compliance accounting vehicle rather than for coordinating and planning, severe negative attitudes toward budgeting have developed. In the governmental sphere a budget is an authorization to spend, founded in law. If an unusual occurrence causes activities to increase, the funding may be inadequate. If the activities fall below planned levels, there is an abundance of funds. The not-for-profit budget does not change as activity levels change.

There is another detrimental effect of the static (nonflexible) budgets used by the not-for-profit area. An agency that does not expend all its budgeted funds may receive a smaller appropriation the following year. This practice leads many governmental managers into a spending frenzy at the end of the fiscal year; the result is wasted resources.

A manager's inability to obtain more resources easily as his activities increase also has a negative effect. Because he is funded only once per year and cannot count on obtaining additional resources, he must try to build slack into his budget, often padding his request to anticipate all possible variances. These budgeting games destroy the public's faith in the process and create a situation where the manager may lie to ensure his department's continuing function.

Businesses can learn from these negative experiences of not-for-profit organizations. First, they can strive to maintain flexible budgets where a manager's resources are related directly to his activities. This practice would help avoid the unfavorable results of budget padding, across-the-board cuts, and last-minute expenditures to use the resources before expiration of the budget.

Second, the typical business firm does not attempt to commit its objectives to writing because they are often vague and difficult to specify. The goal orientation implicit in a program-budgeting attitude could bring about a concerted effort to state the organizations' objectives more concretely.

The control of research and development costs and advertising costs are two excellent examples of areas where the program-budgeting approach would be constructive. It is very difficult to plan and control these expenses because the costs are not directly related to a volume measure. Planning and control could be facilitated by the establishment of a program approach where specific objectives are stated and funds are appropriated on the basis of the program outline.

SUMMARY

Not-for-profit organizations comprise a large segment of economic activity in the United States. Not-for-profit organizations are diverse in nature with a governmental unit, such as a city, at one extreme, and a publicly owned enterprise, such as a hospital, at the other. Budgeting, accounting, and decisions in the latter type of not-for-profit organizations are similar to their for-profit counterparts, as described in previous chapters of this text. There are significant differences between budgeting, accounting, and decision practices between some governmental units and the private sector, however.

Financial accounting in not-for-profit organization is strongly influenced by the requirement for accountability. The fund is the accounting entity, and each fund is reported separately, so there is often no overall presentation of operations or financial position.

The budget plays a critical role in not-for-profit accounting. Because it represents approval for expenditure, the budget is the critical tool for management accounting. Traditional budgeting practices have focused on inputs and accountability. Recent advances in management accounting for not-for-profit organizations include the program budget and, more recently, the zero-base budget. The program budget provides a statement of organizational program goals and objectives. Zero-based budgeting develops a framework within program budgets by identifying, evaluating, and ranking decision packages. Management is provided with a structure that establishes priorities and allows allocation of resources based upon these priorities. Zero-base budgeting has application and some acceptance in the private sector as well as the public sector.

In the public sector, investment decisions are often based upon availability of funds rather than economic efficiency. The goal of investments in the public sector should be welfare maximization. This goal requires a broadened definition of costs and benefits to include all social costs and social benefits. The decision approach should reflect all favorable and unfavorable impacts of the action to society, adjusted for the time value of money.

SUPPLEMENTARY READING

Cheek, Logan M. *Zero-Base Budgeting Comes of Age.* New York: AMACOM, 1977.

Estes, Ralph W. *Accounting and Society.* Los Angeles: Melville Publishing Company, 1975.

*Mishan, E. J. "The A B C of Cost-Benefit." *Lloyds Bank Review,* July, 1971.

*Ramanathan, Kavasseri V. "Theory of Corporate Social Accounting." *The Accounting Review,* July, 1976.

Reckers, Philip M. J., and Stagliano, A. J. "Zero-Base Budgeting." *Management Accounting,* November, 1977.

QUESTIONS

16-1 Identify and explain the characteristics of not-for-profit organizations that make them different from for-profit organizations.

16-2 What is a *fund* in accounting for governmental organizations? Explain.

16-3 Distinguish between an expendable fund and a nonexpendable fund. How would their balance sheets differ?

16-4 How does an expenditure in governmental accounting differ from an expense in accounting for a business in the private sector?

16-5 Define the following terms: *appropriation, encumbrance, program, social benefit, social cost,* and *decision package.*

16-6 Contrast traditional not-for-profit budgeting with program budgeting.

16-7 Assume that you have been elected as president of your student government and propose a change from a line-item budget to a program budget. Suggest a program structure for your student government.

16-8 What does the "zero" refer to in zero-base budgeting?

16-9 A key part of zero-base budgeting is the ranking of decision packages. What is a decision package and why is the ranking process so important?

16-10 Describe the difference between the decision criteria of *maximization of wealth* and *maximization of welfare.*

EXERCISES

16-11 *(Matching).* Match the following terms and definitions.

1. Expenditure
2. Benefit-cost analysis
3. Expendable fund
4. Line-item budget
5. Encumbrance
6. Program budget
7. Discounted benefit-cost ratio
8. Social benefit
9. Social cost
10. Net present value

A. An accounting technique to show that some of the authority to spend has been used for an outstanding contract.
B. Discounted benefits minus discounted costs.
C. The total favorable impact of a particular decision.
D. Discounted benefits divided by discounted costs.
E. A general model for measuring economic efficiency.
F. A budget that relates expenditures to inputs.
G. A budget that relates expenditures to outputs.
H. An entity in government accounting that is accountable only for resources that may be spent.
I. The measurement of resources used in governmental accounting.
J. The total unfavorable impact of a particular decision.

16-12 *(True or False).* Indicate whether the following statements are *true* or *false*.

1. A program budget for the not-for-profit sector is intended to serve the same role as the profit plan in the private sector.
2. In accounting for governmental organizations the entity is the entire organization, for example, the entire city.
3. An important difference between accounting for not-for-profit organizations and for-profit organizations is the formal recording of the budget by for-profit organizations.
4. The general fund of a city is an example of an expendable fund.
5. No fixed assets or long-term liabilities are recorded in an expendable fund.
6. In governmental budgeting, expenditures plus encumbrances cannot exceed revenue.
7. Zero-base budgeting refers to a budgetary system where expenditures are such that deviations from the budget will be zero.
8. Under program budgeting, the legislative body authorizes expenditures for several fiscal years rather than for one fiscal year at a time, as under traditional budgeting.
9. All transactions related to a particular program, for example, education, will be recorded in a single fund.
10. The approach used in program budgeting is very similar to the approach used in long-range budgeting in the private sector.

16-13 *(Matching Transactions with Funds).* From the list of funds identify the appropriate fund for each transaction listed below. Use only one fund for each transaction.

Funds operated by Sony City

1. General fund
2. Special revenue fund
3. Capital projects fund
4. Special assessments fund
5. Enterprise fund for government-owned business
6. General fixed-assets group list

Transaction for Sony City

A. A federal grant is received to finance the construction of a theater for the performing arts.
B. The mayor's salary is paid.
C. The city water works purchased and installed a new filter to improve water purity.
D. Cash is received from a special tax on hotel and motel rooms to finance a center to promote tourism.
E. Cash is paid for a new fire truck.

F. The new fire truck purchased in (E) above is added to the list of city-owned assets.

G. Cash is paid to a contractor for work done on a new sewer project. Property owners who are benefited by the new sewer system will be assessed for the cost.

H. A partial payment is made to the contractor when the foundation for the new theater for the performing arts is completed.

I. The city power company sent bills to customers for power used.

J. Cash is received for property taxes to operate the city government.

16–14 *(Development of Program Structure).* The development of a program structure is a critical step in implementation of a program budget. Two different program structures where proposed for the U.S. Post Office.

PROPOSAL I

1. Collection and delivery of mail
   - *a.* Collection
   - *b.* Processing
   - *c.* Transportation
   - *d.* Delivery
   - *e.* Special services
2. Non-mail service
3. Supporting activities

PROPOSAL II

1. First-class mail
2. Second-class mail
3. Third-class mail
4. Fourth-class mail
5. Support programs
6. Construction of facilities
7. Research and development

REQUIRED:

A. Why is the development of a program structure so important to program budgeting?

B. Which of the two proposals do you favor? Why?

C. How will your choice in Part B assist in decision making?

16–15 *(Budget Reduction Policies).* In a not-for-profit setting it is very common to implement budget reductions through an across-the-board budget cut. If projected expenditures are 5% above projected revenues, all agencies are ordered to reduce projected expenditures by 5%.

REQUIRED:

A. Discuss the wisdom of this kind of resource-allocation process.

B. What would you suggest as an alternative to reduce projected expenditures to the desired level?

C. Would a similar across-the-board budget cut work in an industrial setting? Explain.

16–16 *(Long-range Decision).* The Beaver Crossing Town Council has decided to acquire snow-removal equipment and is trying to decide whether to buy or lease. In either case, the equipment will be used for five years. If the town buys, the cost will be $16,000 payable at delivery, with an estimated salvage value of $2,000. If it leases, the rental payments will be made on the first day of each year in the following amounts:

Year 1	$5,000
2	$4,000
3	$3,000
4	$2,000
5	$1,000

Operating and maintenance costs will be the same in either case. The town is currently paying 8% on its long-term debt.

REQUIRED:

A. Prepare a recommendation to the town council. Your recommendation should be well written and supported by a proper analysis of the data.

B. What are some of the nonquantitative factors that may affect the decision?

16–17 *(Present-value Analysis of Alternative Proposals).* You manage the Edsel Foundation, which has a goal of sponsoring research aimed at solving problems in our society. Two research organizations have submitted proposals. Each proposal is to develop certain home appliances in the next four years that will use 50% less power.

Proposal I requires an initial investment of $5,000,000 and annual costs of $1,000,000 for four years.

Proposal II requires an initial investment of $1,000,000 and the following costs during the four years.

Year 1	$2,000,000
Year 2	$5,000,000
Year 3	$1,000,000
Year 4	0

REQUIRED:

Assuming a 10% cost of funds, which proposal is the most attractive? Explain.

16–18 *(Traditional Governmental Budget).* The Town of Crossroads conducts all its activities through a general fund. At the beginning of 19X1 the town's assets consisted of: Cash $800, city hall $12,000, city park $4,000, and equipment $10,000.

At the beginning of the year, the town council approved the following line-item budget: Budgeted revenues: taxes $25,000, other revenue $12,500; appropriations: salaries $16,000, supplies $2,000, equipment $3,000, contractual services $14,000, and miscellaneous $1,000. Actual transactions for the year were: revenues: taxes $20,000, other revenue $15,000; expenditures: salaries $15,500, supplies $1,400, equipment $3,000, contractual services $14,000, and miscellaneous $1,500.

REQUIRED:

A. Prepare a statement of revenues and expenditures for fiscal year 19X1 for the general fund of Crossroads.

B. Prepare a balance sheet for the town. A General Fixed Assets Group is used to list the fixed assets.

C. The treasurer overspent on miscellaneous expenses because he had forgotten about a $500 contract that was made in the summer and spent the entire budgeted amount late in the fall. The treasurer discovered the overexpenditure when the supplier filled the contract and the bill was paid. What should the treasurer have done to prevent the overexpenditure?

D. One citizen group complained that the cut in expenditures (when it was apparent that tax revenues would be low) hurt the town park; another group complained that not enough was spent on streets. In preparing the next budget, what could you do to be more responsive to citizen groups?

PROBLEMS

16-19 *Ranking of Long-Range Decision Alternatives).* The City of Hollyhock Hill must install a new sewer system to meet federal pollution-control requirements. The city covers a large area including several hills. Consultants have proposed two alternatives that will meet all requirements:

a. Build two small treatment plants. *Each* plant would cost $5 million and have current operating costs of $175,000 per year.

b. Build one large treatment plant. The system would cost $12 million but would have annual operating costs of $200,000.

Either system will have a useful life of 25 years. Assume that construction costs must be paid as the plants are completed and that operating costs are paid at the end of each year.

REQUIRED:

A. Prepare a schedule of cash flows for each alternative.

B. Determine the present value of each alternative under each of the following assumptions:

1. A discount rate of 4%, based upon long-term cost of capital, is used.

2. A discount rate of 10%, based upon opportunity cost in the private sector, is used.

C. Are there any other costs or benefits you think should be considered?

D. Which alternative would you recommend if the decision must be placed before the voters?

16-20 *(Long-Range Decisions for Hospital).* The board of trustees of King Memorial Hospital, a not-for-profit hospital, is considering replacement of certain X-ray equipment. Although the old equipment would function for several years, the new equipment will reduce operating costs by $8,000 per year. The new equipment will cost $52,000 and have a 10-year life with no salvage value. The administrator believes that the salvage value of the present equipment will just cover the cost of removal.

The hospital has operated at a small loss for several years with approximately two-thirds of the new facilities financed through issuance of long-term debt and one-third through grants and contributions. Because of the 9% interest rate on the long-term debt, the administration has set a desired rate of return of 10%.

REQUIRED:

A. Should the hospital acquire the new X-ray equipment? Explain.

B. A new clinic, organized to provide limited care to the residents of a low-income neighborhood, has offered to purchase the old X-ray equipment for $3,000. How does this affect your decision in Part A?

C. Assume that it is now three years since the new X-ray equipment was acquired, and a much superior X-ray unit has become available which is smaller and much more efficient. The new equipment will cost $70,000 and will reduce the annual costs by $15,000. Its useful life will be seven years with no salvage value. Because of the advanced technology, the old X-ray equipment has no salvage value. Should the new equipment be acquired? When the proposal was presented to the hospital board, one member of the board thinks it is a mistake to replace good equipment "every three years." He wants to know why the mistake was made and to be sure that the hospital administrator will not make the same mistake again. How would you answer this board member?

D. Another member of the hospital board wants to know why the target rate of return is so high. He computed the cost of capital to be 6%, as follows:

Source of funds	*Specific cost of capital*	*Proportion of financing*	*Weighted-average cost of capital*
Long-term debt	9%	2/3	6%
Grants and contributions	0	1/3	0
Weighted-average cost of capital			6%

Discuss the computation of costs of capital for a not-for-profit organization. What target rate of return should the hospital use?

16-21 *(Present-Value Analysis of Alternative Decision Packages).* The state highway commission is attempting to decide whether to prohibit studded tires on the state's highways. The tires have not been permitted and, for safety reasons, pressure has grown for their use. The results of two studies are presented for evidence.

The first study examined traffic deaths in the state during the past five years. The study found that accidents involving 40 deaths per year would probably have been avoided if studded tires had been used. In addition to deaths, personal property damage and medical costs of $200,000 per year would have also been avoided. The damage and medical cost estimates were drawn from police records and insurance claims. The average age of people killed was 30; their average annual income was $15,000.

The second study was conducted in states that allowed studded tires. Considering the damage to road surfaces, the highway department estimates that annual damage to the streets, highways, and bridges would amount to additional resurfacing costs of $2,000,000 per year, beginning in the fourth year. It is expected that new tires will be developed within 10 years; they will provide all the benefits of studded tires and will not damage road surfaces.

REQUIRED:

A. Assuming that those killed would have earned the average income to age 60, compute the discounted benefit-cost ratio if studded tires are allowed. Is it favorable? Assume a 10% discount rate.

B. Medical researchers at the state university's school of medicine contend that the money should be spent on kidney research. They contend that the cost per death averted in kidney research is about $25,000. How would you rank the two decision packages?

16-22 *(Economic Value of Life).* In evaluating a program to improve the quality of health, one of the major benefits is an estimate of the total annual reduction in the number of premature deaths which results from the particular program. To measure the benefits of the program, it is necessary to estimate the economic value of life. One researcher arrived at the figure of $95,000 for the economic value of human life.

REQUIRED:

A. What are some examples of decisions that, at least implicitly, require placing a value on human life?

B. Explain how you would go about determining a figure for an "economic value of life."

C. Assuming an economic value of life to be $95,000 and a target return on investment of 14%, how much would a foundation have to invest in a program that would save 100 lives per year for ten years if the foundation insisted on a discounted benefit-cost ratio of at least 2 to 1?

16-23 *(Impact of Shopping Center on Municipality).* The town of Horseshoe, located near an urban area, has been asked to grant a permit for a new shopping center. As the only member of the town council with a knowledge of capital budgeting, you have been asked to develop an analysis of the economic impact on the resources of the town.

Your investigation revealed the following direct benefits and costs to the town over a 20-year period.

A. Incremental direct benefits
   1. Sales tax on construction: $20,000 per year for first four years.
   2. Sales tax from shopping center sales: $100,000 per year beginning in Year 5.
   3. Increase in property taxes: $200,000 per year beginning in Year 5.
   4. Business licenses and permits: $20,000 per year beginning in Year 4.
   5. Added taxes to the city from new residents attracted because of the shopping center: $30,000 per year beginning in Year 5.

B. Incremental Direct Costs
   1. Added police protection: $40,000 per year beginning in Year 1 with an additional $40,000 per year beginning in Year 4.
   2. Added street maintenance: $30,000 per year beginning in Year 1.
   3. Fire protection: $20,000 per year beginning in Year 1.
   4. Other city government: $30,000 per year beginning in Year 1.

REQUIRED:

A. Assuming a 6% cost of capital, compute the discounted benefit-cost ratio for this decision. On the basis of this criterion, should the town council approve the permit?

B. Assume that opponents of the shopping center are arguing that 6% is too low and that the appropriate discount rate is 12%. Recompute the discounted benefit-cost ratio using 12%. How does the higher rate affect your recommendation in Part A?

C. Discuss the measures of social costs and social benefits requested by the town council. Explain any changes you would like to see.

16-24 *(Flexible Budgets and Performance Assessment).* The University of Boyne offers an extensive continuing education program in many cities throughout the state. For the convenience of its faculty and administrative staff and also to save costs, the university operates a motor pool. Until February the motor pool operated with 20 vehicles. However, an additional automobile was acquired in February this year, increasing the total to 21 vehicles. The motor pool furnishes gasoline, oil, and other supplies for the cars, and hires one mechanic who does routine maintenance and minor repairs. Major repairs are done at a nearby commercial garage. A supervisor manages the operations.

Each year the supervisor prepares an operating budget for the motor pool. The budget informs university management of the funds needed to operate the pool. Depreciation on the automobiles is recorded in the budget in order to determine the costs per mile.

The schedule below presents the annual budget approved by the university. The actual costs for March are compared to one-twelfth of the annual budget.

UNIVERSITY MOTOR POOL
BUDGET REPORT
For March, 19X6

	Annual Budget	*One-Month Budget*	*March Actual*	*Over* Under*
Gasoline	$24,000	$2,000	$2,800	$800*
Oil, minor repairs, parts, and supplies	3,600	300	380	80*
Outside repairs	2,700	225	50	175
Insurance	6,000	500	525	25*
Salaries and benefits	30,000	2,500	2,500	—
Depreciation	26,400	2,200	2,310	110*
	$92,700	$7,725	$8,565	$840*
Total miles	600,000	50,000	63,000	
Cost per mile	$0.1545	$0.1545	$0.1369	
Number of automobiles	20	20	21	

The annual budget was constructed upon the following assumptions:

a. 20 automobiles in the pool
b. 30,000 miles per year per automobile
c. 15 miles per gallon per automobile
d. $0.60 per gallon of gas
e. $0.006 per mile for oil, minor repairs, parts, and supplies
f. $135 per automobile in outside repairs

The supervisor is unhappy with the monthly report comparing budget and actual costs for March. He claims it presents unfairly his performance for March. His previous employer used flexible budgeting to compare actual costs to budgeted amounts.

REQUIRED:

A. Employing flexible budgeting techniques, prepare a report which shows budgeted amounts, actual costs, and monthly variation for March.
B. Explain briefly the basis of your budget figure for outside repairs.

(CMA adapted)

16-25 *(Development and Evaluation of a Decision Package).* A regional governmental agency serves a nine-county area with small offices located in each of the nine counties. Each office is responsible for the acquisition and storage of operating supplies used in the respective county. Therefore, each office has leased warehouse space and has one employee in charge of purchasing, warehousing, and record keeping for operating supplies.

The services provided by the governmental unit have increased substantially over the past 10 years. Consequently, the use of supplies has increased greatly. Total acquisition cost of supplies reached $5.2 million during fiscal 19X5. Because the activity relating to operating supplies has become so large, the agency management is considering the establishment of a central purchasing and warehousing function for the nine-county area.

Currently the total inventories for all nine county warehouses average $600,000 during a month. The offices pay from $2.10 to $3.25 per square foot for warehouse space. The total expenditures for warehouse facilities for fiscal 19X5 amounted to $275,000. Utilization of warehouse space averaged 60% of leased space for all offices and ranged from 45 to 70% in the individual cases.

The office in the extreme southwest portion of the nine-county region appears to be the most likely choice for the location of the central warehouse and purchasing function at this time. The greatest volume of operating supplies of all offices is used in this county. Warehouse space which should be adequate for the entire nine-county region is available because the present facility for this county, only partially leased at the present time, can be leased in its entirety. In addition, the rental fee would drop from $2.85 per square foot to $2.40 per square foot.

REQUIRED:

A. The agency has recently adopted zero-base budgeting and is developing decision packages. What is a decision package, and should establishment of a central purchasing and warehouse function be treated as a decision package?

B. Assuming that the decision whether to continue with the present system or centralize the purchasing and warehouse function is treated as a decision package, identify and justify the specific economic data that should be included in the decision package.

C. In addition to the economic data, what qualitative factors should the agency include in the decision package?

D. Indicate the criterion that you would use for ranking this decision package among other decision packages. *(CMA adapted)*

16-26 *(Long-range Decision on Sports Stadium).* Voters of King County approved construction of a King County Multipurpose Domed Stadium. Consultants were hired to recommend locations and develop the data for a benefit-cost study. The report of the consultants identified four sites and estimated the following construction costs.

	Estimated Cost		
Location	*Stadium*	*Parking*	*Total*
King Street	$39,234,200	$ 9,417,900	$48,652,100
Longacres	$38,706,600	$12,040,300	$50,746,900
Riverton	$39,436,000	$11,093,000	$50,529,000
Sicks Stadium	$38,101,100	$26,309,500	$64,410,600

Annual cash flows for the stadium were also projected.

Direct cash inflows to the stadium per year:

From sports activities	$1,157,065
All other events	462,690
Office rental and other	475,412
Annual cash inflows	$2,095,167

Direct cash outflows to the stadium per year:

Management	$ 114,000
Payroll (including fringe benefits)	646,600
Contract services	233,450
Materials and supplies	114,300
Other	220,000
Equipment rental	159,145
Contingencies	266,000
Annual cash outflows	$1,753,495

The consultants attempted to estimate the economic impact of the stadium on the county. They estimated that local and out-of-county fans would spend $6,380,000 on tickets, concessions, food, and lodging while attending events at the stadium. Most of the events, including professional sports, would be new to the county. On the basis of other studies, the consultants assumed that for each dollar the sports fan spent on tickets, concessions, food, and lodging, an additional $3.50 of favorable economic impact would be generated in the community.

The county's borrowing cost is 6%, and the opportunity cost of capital in the private sector is 12%. Assume a 30-year life for the stadium.

REQUIRED:

A. For each site, prepare a schedule of cash flows for the stadium project.
B. What is the amount of annual economic benefits the stadium should generate?
C. Compute the discounted benefit-cost ratio for each site.
D. What would you recommend to the King County Council? Are there other factors that should be considered?

16-27 *(Performance Assessment).* In late 19X1 Mr. Sootsman, the official in charge of the State Department of Automobile Regulation, established a system of performance measurement for the department's branch offices. He was convinced that management by objectives could help the department reach its objective of better citizen service at a lower cost. The first step was to define the activities of the branch offices, to assign point values to the services performed, and to establish performance targets. Point values, rather than revenue targets, were employed, because the department was a regulatory agency, not a revenue-producing agency. Further, the specific revenue for a service did not adequately reflect the differences in effort required. The analysis was compiled at the state office, and the results were distributed to the branch offices.

BARRY COUNTY BRANCH PERFORMANCE REPORT

	19X2		19X3		19X4	
	Budget	*Actual*	*Budget*	*Actual*	*Budget*	*Actual*
Population served	38,000		38,500		38,700	
Number of employees						
Administrative	1	1	1	1	1	1
Professional	1	1	1	1	1	1
Clerical	3	3	2	3	1 ½	3
Budgeted Performance Points*						
1. Services	19,500		16,000		15,500	
2. Citizen comments	500		600		700	
	20,000		16,600		16,200	
Actual Performance Points*						
1. Services	14,500		14,600		15,600	
2. Citizen comments	200		900		200	
	14,700		15,500		15,800	
Detail of Actual Performance*						
1. New drivers licenses						
a. Examination & road tests (3 pts.)	3,000		3,150		3,030	
b. Road tests repeat—failed prior test (2 pts.)	600		750		1,650	
2. Renew drivers licenses (1 pt.)	3,000		3,120		3,060	
3. Issue license plates (.5 pts.)	4,200		4,150		4,100	
4. Issue titles						
a. Dealer transactions (.5 pts.)	2,000		1,900		2,100	
b. Individual transaction (1 pt.)	1,700		1,530		1,660	
	14,500		14,600		15,600	
5. Citizen comments						
a. Favorable (+.5 pts.)	300		1,100		800	
b. Unfavorable (−.5 pts.)	100		200		600	
	200		900		200	

*The budget performance points for services are calculated using 3 points per available hour. The administrative employee devotes ½ time to administration and ½ time to regular services. The calculations for the services point budget are as follows:

19X2 4 ½ people × 8 hours × 240 days × 3 pts. × 75% productive time = 19,440 rounded to 19,500
19X3 3 ½ people × 8 hours × 240 days × 3 pts. × 80% productive time = 16,128 rounded to 16,000
19X4 3 people × 8 hours × 240 days × 3 pts. × 90% productive time = 15,552 rounded to 15,500

The comments targets are based upon rough estimates by department officials.

The actual point totals for the branch are calculated by multiplying the weights shown in the report in parentheses by the number of such services performed or comments received.

The system has been in operation since 19X2. The performance targets for the branches have been revised each year by the state office. The revisions were designed to encourage better performance by increasing the target or reducing resources to achieve targets. The revisions incorporated non-controllable events, such as population shifts, new branches, and changes in procedures.

The Barry County branch is typical of many branch offices. A summary displaying the budgeted and actual performance for three years is presented on the facing page.

Mr. Sootsman has been disappointed in the performance of branch offices because they have not met performance targets or budgets. He is especially concerned because the points earned from citizens' comments are declining.

REQUIRED:

A. Does the method of performance measurement properly capture the objectives of this operation? Justify your answer.

B. The Barry County branch office came close to its target for 19X4. Does this constitute an improvement in performance over 19X3? Justify your answer. *(CMA adapted)*

16-28 *(Financial Analysis of Research Institute).* The Breckenridge Institute is a not-for-profit foundation that undertakes scientific research on a contract basis. The institute regularly does research for federal, state, and local governments, as well as for business firms.

The objectives of the institute as established by the board of trustees are to operate a financially sound not-for-profit organization and to provide quality research service at reasonable costs for the government and business community. The board is also committed to operate with a minimum amount of debt.

Pursuant to these objectives, management has endeavored to develop the capability of serving its clients without using outside consultants or subcontracting work to other laboratories. Consequently, the institute has gained an excellent reputation for its research capabilities and for the economical manner in which it is operated.

The Statement of Financial Position for the institute at April 30, 19X6, the Statement of Operations showing the actual results for the year ended April 30, 19X6, and the budgeted amount for the coming year ending April 30, 19X7 appear below. The statement of Cash Receipts and Disbursements presenting actual results and budgeted figures for the years ending April 30, 19X6 and 19X7, respectively, also appear below.

During the construction of the budget the following additional information was developed:

1. Purchases of materials and supplies were budgeted at $610,000.

2. Write-offs of specific accounts receivable are estimated as follows:
   a. $8,000 of the accounts receivable balance at 4/30/X6.
   b. Uncollectible accounts of $12,000 from fiscal 19X7 sales to be written off in fiscal 19X7.

3. The unusually large budgeted expenditure for capital equipment is part of a three-year program begun in 19X6 to enable the institute to enter new areas of scientific research. Similar amounts will be spent in the next two years for additional equipment. Increased revenues from the new capabilities will not be significant until 19X9.

4. The increased level of consultant fees is expected to continue until the capital expansion program is complete.

REQUIRED:

A. In addition to the two budgeted statements already prepared for the coming fiscal year, prepare a budgeted statement of financial position as of April 30, 19X7, for presentation to the board of trustees.

B. Prepare a report which identifies the financial difficulties the institute's management will face in the next several years in fulfilling the objectives established by the board of trustees. *(CMA adapted)*

BRECKENRIDGE INSTITUTE
STATEMENT OF FINANCIAL POSITION
April 30, 19X6
(000 omitted)

Assets			
Current assets			
Cash			$ 110
Marketable securities			80
Accounts receivable			
Government contracts		$230	
Private contracts	$150		
Less: Allowance for uncollectibles	10	140	370
Materials and supplies			64
Prepaid insurance			6
Total current assets			$ 630
Plant and equipment (net of depreciation)			1,200
Total assets			$1,830

Equities		
Current liabilities		
Accounts payable		$ 120
Accrued payroll, payroll taxes, and benefits		46
Due to outside consultants		20
Interest payable		16
Current portion of long-term debt		60
Total current liabilities		$ 262
Long-term debt		240
Total liabilities		$ 502
Original capital	$1,000	
Accumulated excess of revenues over expenditures	328	1,328
Total equities		$1,830

BRECKENRIDGE INSTITUTE
STATEMENT OF OPERATIONS
(000 omitted)

	Actual Results for the Year Ended 4/30/X6	*Budget for the Year Ended 4/30/X7*
Revenues from operations:		
Federal government	$1,500	$1,650
State and local government	224	250
Private (less provision for bad debts of $19 and $25)	1,216	1,335
Interest	4	2
Total revenues	$2,944	$3,237
Operating expenses:		
Personnel:		
Salaries	$1,390	$1,300
Wages	175	200
Employee benefits and payroll taxes	273	300
Consultants	35	250
Employee training	20	35
Material and supplies	548	600
Utilities	60	60
Insurance	20	20
Depreciation	160	165
Other expenses	117	123
Interest charges	16	14
Total operating expenses	2,814	3,067
Excess of revenues over expenses	$ 130	$ 170

BRECKENRIDGE INSTITUTE
CASH RECEIPTS AND DISBURSEMENTS
(000 omitted)

	Actual Results for the Year Ended 4/30/X6	*Budget for the Year Ended 4/30/X7*
Receipts:		
Contracts:		
Federal, state, and local governments	$1,700	$1,820
Private	1,200	1,300
	$2,900	$3,120
Interest	4	2
Sales of marketable securities	—	50
Total receipts	$2,904	$3,172
Disbursements:		
Salaries and wages	$1,560	$1,510
Employee benefits	260	300
Consultant fees	15	230
Employee training programs	20	35
Materials and supplies	540	575
Utilities	55	65
Insurance	20	22
Other expenses	117	123
Interest	18	16
Retirement of debt	60	60
Purchases of capital equipment	80	315
Total disbursements	2,745	3,251
Increase (decrease) in cash	$ 159	$ (79)

Glossary

Absorption Costing A system of measuring inventory costs that assigns the production costs of material, labor, variable overhead, and fixed overhead to the product. Nonproduction costs are treated as period costs. Also called *Full Costing.*

Accountability (A) The responsibility of management to protect and increase the assets of the firm for the stockholders. (B) The assignment of delegated duties to individual managers for the development of responsibility accounting.

Accounting Method (See *Unadjusted Rate of Return.*)

Accounts Receivable Turnover Credit sales divided by average balance of accounts receivable.

Activity Accounting Recording data by a specific organizational segment; (See *Responsibility Accounting.*)

Activity Base A measure of an operating activity within a department, division, plant, or company; used to allocate indirect costs.

Activity Variance A measure of the ability of the firm to meet budgeted sales volume; the difference between the period's planned activity in the master budget and the actual volume attained. The variance may be measured in number of units or in dollars of contribution margin.

Actual Costs (A) Historical costs measured by their cash equivalent value on an after-the-fact, arms-length transaction basis. Also called *Incurred Costs* and *Historical Costs.* (B) Costs measured by consideration given to acquire the resource.

Adjusted Rate of Return The rate of return on a long-term project computed by adjusting cash flows for the time value of money. Also called *Discounted Rate of Return.*

Administrative Costs Costs that are not directly associated with production, selling, or distribution.

Allocation The process of distributing or apportioning costs or revenues to products, departments, divisions, or other organization units on the basis of benefits received or resources used.

Annuity A series of equal payments or receipts to be paid or received at the end of successive periods of equal time.

Appropriation A legislative authorization to spend funds with specific limits as to amount, purpose, or time period.

Asset Turnover Sales divided by total assets available.

Assets The resources currently available to a firm for the benefit of future activities.

Attained Volume The level of production or sales activity actually reached during the accounting period. Also called *Actual Volume.*

Attention Directing The accountant's task of supplying information that focuses upon those activities of a firm needing corrective action.

Attest Function The action of the independent CPA who audits the financial records of a firm to reduce uncertainty regarding the accuracy and fairness of reported financial statements.

Average Cost Fixed costs plus variable costs divided by the units produced.

Average Cost Pricing (See *Cost-based Pricing.*)

Average Costing (See *Weighted-Average Costing.*)

Average Revenue Total revenue earned divided by the total units sold.

Avoidable Costs Costs that would not be incurred if a particular activity were discontinued.

Balance Sheet A formal statement of the resources of a firm and their sources at a particular point in time. Also called *Statement of Financial Position.*

Behavioral Accounting An area of accounting that studies the interactions among individuals, organizations, and the accounting process.

Benefit-Cost Analysis An evaluation of the relationship between the benefits and the costs of a particular project.

Bill of Materials A statement of the quantity of raw materials allowed for manufacturing a specific quantity of units.

Blanket Overhead Rate A method of apportioning overhead to work in process that uses only one rate for the entire factory.

Book Value The carrying value of a resource measured at cost less accumulated depreciation.

Book Value Method (See *Unadjusted Rate of Return.*)

Breakeven Graph A graphic presentation of cost-volume-profit relationships over the relevant range with special emphasis upon the point at which total costs equal total revenue.

Breakeven Point The activity level where total sales equal total costs. Graphically the breakeven point is where the sales line intersects the total cost line.

Budget An integrated plan of action expressed in financial terms.

Budget Rollover Continual revision and projection of a budget by dropping a past period and adding a new period; particularly useful in cash management.

Budget Variance The difference between actual costs incurred and the flexible budget adjusted to actual activity level. Also called the spending variance.

Budgeted Capacity (See *Expected Volume*.)

Budgeted Costs Future costs (predictions, estimates, forecasts) that are formally combined into an integrated plan of action.

C

Capacity Costs (A) Another term for fixed costs. (B) Costs necessary to provide organization and operating facilities to produce and sell at the budgeted volume level.

Capacity Decisions (See *Long-range Decisions*.)

Capacity Variance A variance computed in an absorption costing system showing the overapplication or underapplication of fixed manufacturing costs to products. It is measured as the difference between planned fixed manufacturing costs and applied fixed manufacturing costs. Also called *Volume Variance* or *Fixed Overhead Volume Variance*.

Capital Budgeting (A) The process of long-range planning involved with adding or reducing the productive facilities of a firm. (B) The process of long-range planning for specific projects.

Capital Expenditure Budget A formal plan involving the procurement or disposition of productive resources.

Capital Gains Gains on the sale of assets that are not held for resale as inventory; usually taxed at a lower rate than ordinary income.

Capital Rationing A ranking of investment proposals for a firm with a shortage of capital to invest.

Carryback and Carryforward An IRS tax code provision in which an operating loss may be carried back to each of the previous three years and forward to each of the succeeding seven years as an offset to operating income in those years.

Carrying Costs Costs incurred in maintaining an inventory, including storage and warehousing, insurance, and cost of money invested in inventory.

Cash Budget A formal, integrated plan of cash inflows, outflows, and balances.

Clock Card A record of an employee's work time; used in determining an employee's pay.

Committed Costs (A) Fixed costs incurred by the productive facilities and organization maintained to provide a firm's output capacity. (B) Costs treated as fixed costs because they cannot be separated into their fixed and variable components.

Common Costs (A) In multiple-product firms, costs that are not inherently traceable to individual products or product lines *(Joint Product Costs)*. (B) Costs applicable to more than one costing objective; they cannot be traced to the objective without using an allocation base. Also called *Joint Costs* and *Indirect Costs*.

Comprehensive Budget (See *Master Budget*.)

Comptroller (See *Controller*.)

Conservatism The practice of undervaluing assets and revenues and overvaluing liabilities and expenses so that financial position is never overstated.

Constant Costs (See *Fixed Costs.*)

Constraint A restriction on the production process limiting the amount of resources that can be committed.

Continuous Budget A technique of budget preparation that adds a new period (such as a month) in the future as the period just ended is completed. (See *Budget Rollover.*)

Contribution Center (See *Profit Center.*)

Contribution Margin Selling price per unit less the variable cost per unit. Also called *Marginal Income.* The contribution margin may be expressed on a per-unit basis, as a total, or as a ratio.

Contribution Margin Approach Income statements that separate costs into fixed and variable components and measure the contribution margin by deducting all variable costs from sales.

Contribution Margin from Operations Sales revenue less all variable costs.

Contribution Margin from Production Sales revenue less variable production costs.

Contribution Margin Ratio Sales percentage (100%) minus the variable cost ratio. That portion of each sales dollar that provides the contribution margin. Contribution margin divided by sales.

Control The process of measuring and correcting actual performance to ensure that a firm's objectives and plans are accomplished.

Control Limit An acceptable range within which costs may deviate from standard or budget. Beyond this limit costs are "out of control."

Controllable Cost A cost that can be regulated by a given manager in either the short run or the long run. A cost that is the responsibility of a specific manager.

Controller A firm's principal accounting officer responsible for planning and controlling the firm's financial data base. Also called *Comptroller.*

Conversion Costs The sum of direct labor and manufacturing overhead costs.

Cost (A) The cash or the cash-equivalent value of the resource obtained or the resource committed, whichever can be measured most objectively. (B) Value foregone to achieve an economic benefit.

Cost Accounting Standards Board (CASB) A federal agency established by Congress to assist governmental agencies as buyers of goods and services in understanding and negotiating cost-based prices.

Cost-based Pricing The process of determining a selling price by calculating the cost of a unit of product and adding a markup. An addition for profit is made to some suitable cost base. Also called *Cost-Plus Pricing* and *Average Cost Pricing.*

Cost Centers Organizational units where costs naturally come together. A natural clustering of costs by functional areas.

Cost Effectiveness Analysis The measure of the relationship between the incurrence of costs and a nonfinancial criterion.

Cost of Capital The cost of providing financial resources for the firm.

Cost of Goods Sold Costs released from the inventory and matched with revenue in the period the products are sold.

Cost-Plus-Fixed-Fee Contract A sales contract in which the seller is reimbursed for all reasonable (allowable) costs incurred in fulfilling the contract plus an agreed-upon fee.

Cost-Plus-Percentage Contract A sales contract in which the seller is reimbursed for all reasonable (allowable) costs incurred in fulfilling the contract plus a profit determined as a negotiated percentage of the actual costs.

Cost-Plus Pricing (See *Cost-based Pricing.*)

Cost Reimburseable Contract A sales contract in which the seller is reimbursed for all costs incurred in fulfilling the contract. (See *Cost-Plus-Fixed-Fee, Cost-Plus-Percentage,* and *Cost Renegotiable Contracts.*)

Cost Renegotiable Contracts A sales contract in which the buyer and the seller have opportunities to redefine certain aspects of the contract after production has begun.

Current Assets Cash plus those assets that are expected to be converted into cash or consumed during the coming year or normal operating cycle.

Current Liabilities Liabilities that will mature and require payment within the coming year or operating cycle.

Current Ratio Current assets divided by current liabilities; used as a measure of liquidity.

Currently Attainable Standards Standards of performance that can be attained in the actual operations with skilled, efficient effort. Also called *Normal Standards* and *Average Standards.*

Data Base Information available to management for planning, decision making, and control functions.

Decision Package A funding request for an activity, project, or function in zero-base budgeting; an explicit statement of the benefits and costs is included to facilitate ranking of the request with other funding requests.

Demand Curve A graphic curve showing the product quantity that will be sold at different prices. The curve normally slopes downward and to the right, showing that as the selling price increases, customer demand decreases and that as price decreases, customer demand increases.

Departmental Cost Sheet A basic record for the accumulation of costs in a process-costing system.

Depreciation The allocation of the original cost of plant and equipment to the time periods benefited by the use of the asset.

Differential Benefit The difference in total benefits between any two acceptable alternatives. Also called *Incremental Benefit.*

Differential Cost The difference in total costs between any two acceptable alternatives. Also called *Incremental Cost.*

Differentiality The concept that only costs or benefits that differ between alternatives are relevant to decisions.

Diminishing Returns The economic concept that increased usage of production facilities requires more productive energy per unit to produce one additional unit.

Direct Costing (See *Variable Costing.*)

Direct Costs Costs that are capable of being traced and logically associated with a particular objective such as product, time period, or organizational unit.

Direct Labor Labor that is expended directly on the final product and traced directly to the product by the accounting system.

Direct Materials Materials used in the production of the final product and traced directly to the product by the accounting system.

Discounted Benefit-Cost Ratio A method of capital budgeting project assessment that applies a predetermined discount rate to cash inflows and outflows and ranks the alternatives by their ratio of discounted benefits to discounted costs.

Discounted Cash Flow Any capital investment decision process that adjusts cash flows over the life of the investment for the time value of money. (See *Adjusted Rate of Return, Discounted Benefit-Cost Ratio,* and *Net Present Value.*)

Discounted Rate of Return (See *Adjusted Rate of Return.*)

Discounting The process of adjusting cash flows for the time value of money. Also called *Present-value Analysis.*

Discretionary Costs Fixed costs that arise from specific management decisions to appropriate a specific sum. Also called *Managed Costs* and *Programmed Costs.*

Distribution Costs Nonproduction costs that arise from ensuring that the proper goods are in the proper place, ready to sell. Also called *Order-Filling Costs.*

Division A responsibility center where the manager is held responsible for both production and marketing operating decisions and for decisions involving investments in the resources necessary to implement plans.

Economic Income (A) A concept that no income exists until all who provided resources are paid for the cost of their resources. (B) The maximum amount that can be paid in dividends and leave the firm with the same economic wealth at the end of a period that it had at the beginning of the period.

Economic Order Quantity The amount of purchases (or production) that should be made at any one time to minimize the carrying costs and the procurement (or setup) costs.

Economies of Scale Gains in operating efficiencies due to increases in volume.

Effectiveness The accomplishment of a desired objective, goal, or action.

Efficiency The accomplishment of a desired objective, goal, or action with the minimum resources necessary.

Efficiency Variance (A) A quantity variance for labor determined by the difference between the actual hours worked and the standard hours times the labor wage rate. (B) A variance for overhead determined by the difference between the actual hours worked and the standard hours times the variable overhead rate.

Elasticity of Demand The responsiveness of consumers to price changes. If consumers are sensitive to price changes, demand is elastic. If consumers are unresponsive to price changes, demand is inelastic.

Encumbrance A pseudo-expenditure used to prevent overspending when a delay exists between entering into a contract and payment on the contract. It is removed when the expenditure is recorded.

Engineering Cost Estimates A method of separating costs into their fixed and variable components by direct estimates based upon technical expertise.

Equilibrium Point The intersection point of the supply and demand curves. At this point the amount that producers provide equals the amount that customers demand, and the market is in balance.

Equivalent Production The number of whole units of product for which a department or cost center is accountable during the time period.

Ex Ante A performance assessment measure determined before actual operations.

Ex Post A performance assessment measure determined after actual operations that includes adjustments for actual operating circumstances.

Excess Material Requisition A form used to request needed production materials in excess of the standard amount of materials allowed for the output.

Excess Present Value A technique of discounted cash flow analysis that determines whether the present value of future cash inflows at the desired rate of return is greater or less than the present value of the future cash outflows. Also called *Net Present Value.*

Expected Actual Standard A standard based upon the most likely attainable results; an estimate of what will happen, not what should happen.

Expected Value The sum of all possible outcomes multiplied by the probability of their occurrence.

Expected Volume The anticipated level of activity for the coming year. Also called *Budgeted Capacity* or *Expected Capacity.*

Expendable Fund An independent fiscal and accounting entity in a not-for-profit organization in which all resources may be spent to carry out the specific purpose of the entity. No fixed assets or long-term liabilities are recorded in an expendable fund.

Expenditure A cash payment used as the measure of resources consumed in not-for-profit organizations.

Expense (A) A cost that has been consumed in the production of revenue. (B) An expired cost.

Expired Costs (A) A cost that has no future revenue-producing potential. (B) An expense.

Externalities Indirect side effects of a decision in the public sector.

F

Factory Burden (See *Overhead.*)

Factory Overhead (See *Overhead.*)

Factory Overhead Rate (See *Overhead Rate.*)

Favorable Variance (A) A variance where actual costs are less than budgeted or standard costs. (B) A variance where actual revenue exceeds budgeted revenue.

Feedback The reporting function of accounting concerned with providing information to management so that performance may be evaluated and, if necessary, actions altered.

Financial Accounting Focus of accounting data for interfirm allocations and for the generation and maintenance of the capital structure of a firm.

Financial Accounting Standards Board (F.A.S.B.) An independent group of accountants concerned with establishing policy for external reporting practices.

Financial Costs Costs of obtaining financing for an organization's capital requirements.

Finished Goods Inventory The cost of unsold but completed goods that are held in inventory awaiting sale.

First In, First Out (FIFO) An inventory costing method where the first costs received are the first costs transferred out.

Fixed Budget A plan that expresses only one level of estimated activity or volume. Also called *Static Budget.*

Fixed Costs Costs that in total do not change with changes in output volume. On a per-unit basis, the cost per unit of output will vary inversely with changes in volume.

Fixed Overhead Spending Variance The difference between actual fixed production costs incurred and budgeted fixed production costs shown in the flexible budget.

Fixed Overhead Volume Variance The difference between budgeted fixed costs and fixed costs applied to Work-in-Process Inventory.

Fixed Price Contract Agreement to a price that remains unchanged over the life of a contract.

Flexible Budget A statement of how costs change with changes in the activity level; often expressed as the formula $y_c = a + b(x)$ where a is the total fixed costs, b the variable rate, and x a measure of the activity level. May refer to any specific cost or grouping of costs. Also called *Variable Budget.*

Forecast A projection of variables, both controllable and noncontrollable, that is used in the development of plans and budgets.

Full Costing (See *Absorption Costing.*)

Functional Classification (A) Classification of costs by the department or the responsibility center affected. (B) Allocation of costs to functions performed, such as office expense, warehouse expense, order-filling costs, etc.

Fund An independent fiscal and accounting entity for carrying on specific activities in a not-for-profit organization.

Future Benefits Benefits that are expected to be gained at some future time, based on predictions, estimates, and forecasts.

Future Costs Costs that are expected to be incurred at some future time, based on predictions, estimates, and forecasts.

Future Value of Money The value to which an invested sum will grow by the end of a certain period if compounded at a given annual rate of interest.

Futurity A time or event that is yet to come.

G

General Costs (See *Administrative Costs.*)

Goal The basic plan or direction of a decision maker. The direction toward which all decisions and activities are focused.

Goal Congruence The process of combining the many diverse, separate goals of firm subcomponents into a unified whole.

Heuristic (A) A trial-and-error approach to problem solving. (B) Methods of investigation that lead to further investigation.

High-Low Method A method of determining fixed and variable costs that utilizes the highest and lowest activity levels and their related costs.

Historical Costs (See *Actual Costs.*)

Historical Overhead Rate A method of apportioning overhead costs to work in process after production for the period is completed.

Ideal Volume The maximum plant output (in units) that can be achieved in the short run, with no allowances for repairs, maintenance, or rest periods.

Ideal Standard A standard that can be achieved only if all conditions are perfect.

Identifiable Costs Costs that can be associated with a particular product or department.

Idle Time (A) Labor time not involved in productive effort; usually treated as indirect labor. (B) Unused plant capacity.

Incentive Contract A cost-plus contract where there is a bonus incentive if costs are below the budgeted amount. In some cases a penalty is assessed if costs exceed the budgeted amount.

Income Statement A statement that evaluates operating performance by comparing revenues (accomplishments) with costs (efforts).

Incremental Analysis (A) The process of measuring the additional costs or benefits of one alternative chosen over another. (B) A method of comparing alternative plans of action by calculating the present values of the differences between *net* cash inflows.

Incremental Cost The total additional cost that will be incurred if a particular alternative is chosen. The difference in total costs between two alternatives. (See *Differential Cost.*)

Incurred Costs (See *Actual Costs.*)

Indirect Costs Costs that cannot be logically assigned to an objective without allocation. (See *Common Costs.*)

Indirect Expenses (See *Overhead.*)

Indirect Factory Costs (See *Overhead.*)

Indirect Labor Labor included in overhead because it cannot be traced directly to the units of output or to a department.

Indirect Manufacturing Costs (See *Overhead.*)

Indirect Materials Minor materials included in overhead because they are not directly traceable to the finished products.

Information Economics The study of the costs and benefits of data in the belief that the benefits from using data should exceed the costs of gathering it.

Insolvency The inability of a firm to meet its debts when they are due. In bankruptcy situations insolvency is defined as liabilities exceeding assets.

Inspection of Contracts A method of separating costs into their fixed and variable components by examining existing production activities and contracts.

Interfirm Allocations Allocation of resources among firms in the economy, usually through the capital (stock and bond) markets.

Intrafirm Allocations Allocation of resources within a firm to the various departments or responsibility centers.

Inventory Turnover Cost of goods sold or cost of goods consumed divided by inventory value.

Investment Centers Segments of a firm where resources, revenues, and costs are traced and the rate of return on investment is used as a control measure.

Investment Decisions (See *Long-range Decisions;* also see *Capital Budgeting.*)

Investment Tax Credit A special tax provision that allows direct reductions of income taxes for the acquisition of certain depreciable assets.

Investment Turnover Sales divided by investment in assets. One component of return on investment. A measure of activity that shows if assets have generated revenue.

Invoice A form sent by a supplier billing a firm for materials purchased; serves as a source document for the purchases entry.

Iterative Process An approach to budgeting where the budget is developed through a sequential series of steps.

J

Job Cost Sheet A basic record for the accumulation of product costs in a job-costing system. Also called *Work Order* or *Job Order.*

Job Costing A system of determining production costs that traces the materials, labor, and other factory costs to specific units or batches.

Joint Costs (See *Common Costs.*)

Joint Process A production process in which a single input results in more than one output.

Joint Product Cost (See *Common Costs.*)

L

Labor (See *Direct Labor* and *Indirect Labor.*)

Labor Efficiency (Quantity) Variance The variance that measures the efficient or inefficient use of labor; the difference between standard hours in actual production and actual hours worked priced at the standard wage rate.

Labor Rate (Price) Variance The variance that measures the ability to control wage rates and labor mix; the difference between actual wage rate and standard wage rate multiplied by the actual hours worked.

Last In, First Out (LIFO) An inventory costing method where the last costs received are the first costs transferred out.

Lead Time The interval between the time a purchase order is placed and the time materials are received and available for use.

Learning Curve A mathematical expression of the fact that labor time will decrease at a constant percentage over doubled output quantities.

Least-squares Regression A statistical tool for fitting a straight line to data, providing a systematic and reliable method of estimating fixed and variable costs. Can also be used in projecting sales. Also called *Statistical Regression Analysis* or *Regression Analysis.*

Leverage (See *Trading on the Equity.*)

Liabilities Economic obligations of a firm to outsiders.

Line-item Budget A budget in which accountability for expenditures of money is identified with specific expenditure lines in the budget.

Linear Programming A mathematical method used in a number of business decisions (including optimum product mix problems), where many interacting variables are combined to use limited resources to maximize profits or minimize losses.

Liquidity The amount and composition of a firm's assets with emphasis upon their conversion to cash.

Liquidity Ratio A ratio of liquid assets to current liabilities, computed as: (Cash + Marketable securities + Receivables) ÷ Current liabilities.

Long-range Decisions Decisions adding to or reducing the productive capability of a firm. These decisions affect the cash flows of more than one accounting period so that the time value of money is a significant variable.

Long-range Excess Capacity A measure of capacity held in reserve to meet fluctuations in demand; long-term growth determined in units as the difference between practical capacity and normal capacity.

Loss A cost that has been consumed without providing a benefit or revenue.

Managed Costs Fixed costs whose amounts are determined by management, not by their direct relationship to production output. (See *Discretionary Costs.*)

Management Accounting The focus of accounting data for intrafirm allocations through the planning and control process.

Management by Exception The practice of focusing attention only on those activities where actual performance differs significantly from planned performance.

Manufacturing Expenses (See *Overhead.*)

Manufacturing Overhead (See *Overhead.*)

Margin of Safety The amount (or ratio) by which the current sales volume exceeds the breakeven volume, either in units or dollars.

Margin on Sales Net profit divided by net sales. Also called *Profit Margin.*

Marginal Costing (See *Variable Costing.*)

Marginal Costs The cost of one additional unit of output. The cost incurred to move from output n to output $n + 1$.

Marginal Income (See *Contribution Margin.*)

Marginal Revenue The increment in total revenue obtained when output is increased by one additional unit.

Master Budget An integrated plan of action for a firm as a whole, expressed in financial terms.

Matching The accounting process of comparing costs and revenues for a period in the determination of net income.

Material Price Variance A measure of the ability to control material prices incurred; the difference between the actual material cost and the standard material cost multiplied by the actual quantity purchased. Also called *Material Purchases Variance.*

Material Purchased Price Variance (See *Material Price Variance.*)

Material Quantity Variance (See *Material Usage Variance.*)

Material Requisition A request for release of material held in the storeroom to authorized personnel. The source document to record raw material issues.

Material Usage Variance A measure of the efficient or inefficient use of materials; the difference between the standard quantity in actual production and the actual quantity used priced at the standard cost per unit of material.

Materials Physical commodities consumed to make the final product.

Mixed Cost A cost that has both fixed and variable cost attributes.

Monopolistic Competition An economic marketplace where there is a large number of firms. Each firm has little control over price except to create product differentiation.

Monopoly An economic marketplace characterized by a single firm as the sole producer of a product for which there are no close substitutes.

Motivation The internal and external factors that influence an individual to act.

Multiple Regression Analysis A mathematical method of measuring the change in the dependent variable (cost) with changes in two or more different independent variables (measures of volume).

Natural Classification Classification of overhead costs by the nature of the expense, i.e., utilities, insurance, depreciation, rent, or taxes.

Negotiated Market Price A transfer price negotiated between the buying and selling divisions where no open market price is established.

Net Book Value The unexpired cost of an asset carried on the financial records of the firm. Historical cost of an asset less accumulated depreciation to date.

Net Present Value A method of selecting capital investment projects. Proposals are assessed by the difference between discounted cash inflows and discounted cash outflows using a predetermined desired rate of return. (See *Present Value.*)

Net Working Capital The excess of current assets over current liabilities. Also called *Working Capital.*

Noncontrollable Costs Costs that a given manager cannot affect by his decisions.

Nonexpendable Fund An independent fiscal and accounting entity that is responsible for resources that are not consumed in the accounting period. This type of fund is used to operate publicly owned enterprises.

Nonproduction Costs The costs of selling and distributing the final product and of general administration.

Nonrelevant Benefits Benefits that are not affected by a decision and will not change as a result of the decision.

Nonrelevant Costs Costs that are not affected by a decision and will not change as a result of the decision.

Normal Overhead Rate An overhead rate based upon normal volume.

Normal Standard A standard that can be achieved if activites are efficient. (Also called an *average* or *currently attainable* standard.)

Normal Volume The level of output necessary to meet sales demands over a span of years (usually three to five), encompassing seasonal and cyclical variations.

O

Objective Function A mathematical statement used in linear programming that relates production output to contribution margin.

Objectives Specific quantitative and time-performance targets to achieve a firm's goals.

Oligopoly An economic marketplace where a few firms control a significant share of the market. Firms are mutually interdependent and often follow the dominant firm in pricing and production volume decisions.

Operating Cycle The period involved from the time cash is invested in inventory until the time cash is recovered from sale of the goods.

Operating Decisions (See *Short-range Decisions.*)

Opportunity Cost (A) Benefit that would have been obtained from an alternative if that alternative had been accepted. (B) The cost of foregone revenue by choosing a particular alternative.

Order-Filling Costs (See *Distribution Costs.*)

Order-Getting Costs (See *Selling Costs.*)

Out-of-Pocket Costs Costs that will require an expenditure of cash as a result of a decision.

Overabsorbed Overhead The excess of overhead cost applied to the product over the actual overhead costs incurred. Also called *Overapplied Overhead.*

Overapplied Overhead (See *Overabsorbed Overhead.*)

Overhead All costs of operating the factory except those designated as direct labor and direct material costs. Also called *Factory Burden, Manufacturing Expense, Indirect Factory Costs, Manufacturing Overhead, Indirect Expense, Indirect Manufacturing Costs,* and *Factory Overhead.*

Overhead Efficiency Variance (See *Variable Overhead Efficiency Variance.*)

Overhead Rate A method of allocating the indirect factory costs to the products, creating an average overhead cost per unit of production activity.

P

Payback Period The length of time necessary to recover the initial investment of a project; investment cost divided by annual net cash flow.

Performance Budget An adjusted budget prepared *after* operations to compare actual results with costs that *should* have been incurred at the actual level attained.

Performance Report A report to a manager comparing actual results with planned results in his area of responsibility.

Period Costs Costs that are not inventoried and are treated as an expense in the period in which they are incurred.

Planning The process of selecting goals and objectives and the actions required to attain them.

Planning Budget (See *Master Budget.*)

Plant-wide Overhead Rate (See *Blanket Overhead Rate.*)

Practical Capacity (A) The most efficient operating level if fixed costs remain constant and output levels per unit of effort do not diminish; ideal capacity less allowances for repairs, maintenance, and rest periods. (B) Maximum sustainable long-run capacity.

Predetermined Overhead Rate An overhead rate determined in advance of production by dividing estimated (budgeted) overhead costs by an estimated (budgeted) volume base.

Preferred Stock Capital stock with priority over other shares in the areas of dividends and distribution of assets upon liquidation.

Present Value The concept that a sum invested today will earn interest and be worth more at a later date; a dollar in the hand today is worth more today than a dollar to be received (or spent) in the future.

Present Value of Money The amount that must be invested now to reach a given amount at some future given point of time, assuming it is compounded annually at a given rate of interest.

Price Variance A measure of how well actual prices agreed with planned prices; the difference between the actual prices and the standard (budgeted) prices multiplied by the actual quantity purchased.

Prime Costs The sum of direct material and direct labor.

Procedures Detailed instructions specifying how certain activities are to be accomplished.

Process Costing A method of determining the unit cost of manufacturing where production costs are divided by units produced during a given time period.

Producing Departments Departments or organizational units that contribute directly to the conversion of raw materials into finished products. Departments that come in physical contact with the products.

Product Costs Costs that attach to the unit of product and remain as an asset in the inventory until the goods to which they are attached are sold.

Product Margin The contribution margin of a particular product less directly identifiable fixed costs.

Production Base A common denominator that equates all units produced. The most common measures of production base are units of product, machine hours, labor hours, and labor cost.

Production Budget A component of the master budget that establishes the level of production planned for some future period.

Production Costs Costs that are necessary to produce a finished product. Also called *Manufacturing Costs.*

Productive Assets Assets committed to production, storage, or distribution of a firm's products or services.

Profit Centers Organizational units where both revenue and costs naturally come together and net profit or net contribution margin are used as control measures.

Profit Margin Percentage of profit on sales. One component of the return on investment calculation. Profit divided by sales.

Profit Plan A budgeted income statement.

Profit-Planning Chart (See *Breakeven Graph.*)

Profit-Volume Chart A graphic technique that shows breakeven analysis by plotting only the contribution margin on the chart.

Pro Forma Statements Financial statements prepared before actual occurrence of events. Also called *Budgeted Statements.*

Profitability Accounting (See *Responsibility Accounting.*)

Program Budgeting A budgetary system used in the public sector that focuses upon the output of the organization rather than on specific inputs. Also called *Planning, Programming, Budgeting System.*

Programmed Costs (See *Discretionary Costs.*)

Projected Statement of Financial Position A projected balance sheet prepared to reflect expected financial position at the end of the planning period.

Purchase Order A form sent to a supplier by the purchasing department requesting the shipment of material.

Purchase Requisition A form issued by the storeroom requesting the purchasing department to procure some specific material.

Purchasing Budget A component of the master budget showing planned purchases for some future period.

Pure Competition An economic marketplace where a large number of independent firms produce a standardized product. No single firm can influence the market price; the price equals marginal revenue; a firm's demand schedule is horizontal.

Quantity Variance A measure of how well actual quantities agreed with planned quantities; the difference between the actual quantities used and the standard (budgeted) quantities for actual production, multiplied by the standard price.

R

Rated Capacity Equipment capacity determined by its designers.

Rate Variance (See *Price Variance.*)

Raw Materials Inventory Production materials on hand but not yet processed.

Regression Analysis (See *Least-squares Regression.*)

Regression Method (See *Least-squares Regression.*)

Relevant Benefit A benefit that is cogent to the alternative being considered and will be affected by the decision.

Relevant Cost A cost that is cogent to the alternatives being considered and will be affected by the decision.

Relevant Data for Decision Making Future differential costs or benefits related to a particular decision.

Relevant Range The span of volume over which the cost behavior (or management plans) can be expected to remain valid.

Reorder Point The inventory level where an order must be placed to provide adequate lead time to ensure delivery when needed.

Replenishment Point The point in time when the physical inventory is restocked by deliveries.

Report on Profit Plan A financial report explaining the differences between the profit plan and the actual income statement for a particular time period.

Residual Income A measure of divisional performance; the cost of capital deducted from divisional net income or contribution.

Residual Sum of Squares The sum of the variation of each y value from the corresponding predicted value given by the regression equation.

Responsibility Accounting (A) A system of recording costs and revenues where each manager is assigned only those factors that he can affect by his decisions. (B) A system that attempts to assign and match authority and responsibility.

Responsibility Centers A broad term that implies the development of an organizational structure where there is identifiable responsibility for each cost, revenue, and resource.

Return on Investment (ROI) The most widely used single measure of an operation's performance; (1) profits divided by assets committed or (2) margin on sales times asset turnover.

Revenue The inflow of economic values from company operations. Also called *Sales* or *Sales Revenue.*

Revenue Center Responsibility centers where only revenues are traced directly.

Risk An exposure to loss because of inability to control conditions upon which the firm is dependent.

Rolling or Moving Average A method of calculating an average; the oldest data are dropped and the newest data added each time the average is calculated.

S

Safety Stock The minimum inventory level that provides a cushion against running out of stock because of changes in demand or changes in lead time.

Sales Forecast A projection of sales for a particular future period of time.

Sales Mix The relative combination of the quantities of each type of product sold in a multiproduct firm.

Scattergraph A graphic representation showing the general relationship of cost to some base of activity; used in segregating costs into their fixed and variable components.

Scattergraph Method A method of segregating fixed and variable costs by plotting cost and activity data on a graph and then fitting a line by visual inspection so that half the plots lie above the line and half lie below the line.

Scheduled Production A production plan that identifies the specific quantity and type of goods to be produced in the next period.

Segment A subcomponent of a firm; a responsibility center.

Segment Margin The contribution margin of a subcomponent, segment, or division of a firm less all separable, identifiable fixed costs.

Selling Costs Nonproduction costs that result from marketing activities. Also called *Order-Getting-Costs*.

Semifixed Costs (See *Semi-variable Costs.*)

Semivariable Costs Costs that are neither completely fixed nor completely variable, changing with changes in production volume, but not in direct proportion. They may be stepped, mixed, or curvilinear.

Separable Costs (A) Costs that can be identified with a specific segment of the firm. (B) Costs that would be avoided if a product line or segment of the firm were dropped.

Service Department A department that supports the producing departments in their activities but is not directly in contact with converting the raw materials into finished products.

Setup Costs Costs incurred to prepare a factory for a production run.

Short-range Decisions Decisions involving production output, pricing, and product mix. They are concerned with the optimum use of existing resources and, typically, the time value of money is not considered significant.

Simplex Method A mathematical method of solving simultaneous equations which, because of bulk and size, would be impractical to solve graphically or manually.

Simulation A method—usually computerized—that uses a mathematical statement of the interrelationships of variables to test the effects of changes.

Solvency Ability of a firm to pay its debts when due.

Source Document A form that serves as a basis for an accounting entry; an original record.

Specific Cost of Capital The cost of a specific source of capital.

Spending Variance The difference between actual overhead and budgeted overhead in the performance budget for the actual level of operations. Also called *Budget Variance.*

Split-off Point The point in the production process where products with joint costs are separated and become individual products.

Stairstepped Cost A semivariable cost that increases in discrete intervals.

Standard A precise measure of what should occur if performance is efficient.

Standard Absorption Costing A system of product costing that focuses upon management planning and control; product cost is determined by the sum of the standard costs for materials, labor, and both variable and fixed overhead. The variances between actual and standard are treated as period costs.

Standard Cost A predetermination of what a unit of product *should* cost; a planning and control reference.

Standard Error of the Estimate A measure of how well a regression line fits the actual data when using least-square regression analysis. The further the observations from the regression line, the larger will be the standard error.

Standard Overhead Rate A predetermination of what overhead *should* cost per unit of output.

Standard Variable Costing A system of product costing that focuses upon management planning and control; product cost is determined by the sum of the standard costs for materials, labor, and variable overhead. The fixed overhead costs and the variances between actual and standard costs are treated as period costs.

Statement of Financial Position (See *Balance Sheet.*)

Static Budget (See *Fixed Budget.*)

Statistical Regression Analysis (See *Least-squares Regression.*)

Sunk Cost A cost that has already been incurred and will not require a future expenditure of cash.

Supplementary Fixed Overhead Rate An overhead rate calculated at the end of the accounting period to adjust the inventories from variable costing to absorption costing.

Supply Curve An economic concept that relates market prices to the quantity of product that suppliers or producers are willing to supply.

T

Tax Shield Recognition that a cost shields income of future years against tax to the extent that the cost may be deducted against income. The most common example is a depreciable asset.

Time-adjusted Rate of Return The rate of interest at which the present value of budgeted cash inflows for a project equals the present value of budgeted cash outflows for the project.

Time Ticket A factory record of how the employee spends his time.

Time Value of Money The difference between the value of a dollar today and its value at some future point in time if invested.

Total Contribution Margin The contribution margin per unit times the number of units sold.

Total Cost The sum of all fixed costs and all variable costs.

Total Revenue The quantity sold times the price per unit.

Traceable Cost (See *Controllable Cost.*)

Trading on the Equity Using borrowed money with a fixed interest cost to invest in a project with a higher rate of return so that the return on the stockholders' equity is increased.

Transfer Price The price charged by one segment of an organization when it supplies a product or service to another segment of the same organization.

Unadjusted Rate of Return A rate of return that has not been adjusted for the time value of money.

Uncertainty A lack of information about the probability of alternative results.

Underapplied Overhead The amount by which overhead incurred exceeds overhead applied to the products.

Unexpired Costs Assets; costs carried forward to future periods where they have the potential of contributing to future revenues.

Unfavorable Variance (A) A variance where the actual costs are greater than the budgeted or standard costs. (B) A variance where actual revenue is less than planned or budgeted revenue.

Usage Variance (See *Quantity Variance.*)

Variable Budget (See *Flexible Budget.*)

Variable Costs Costs that vary in total dollar amount in direct proportion to changes in production volume. The cost per unit of output is constant over the relevant range of activity.

Variable Cost Ratio Variable costs divided by sales.

Variable Costing A system of measuring inventory costs that assigns variable production costs of material, labor, and variable overhead to the product unit cost. Fixed overhead costs and nonproduction costs are treated as period costs. Also called *Marginal Costing* and *Direct Costing.*

Variable Overhead Efficiency Variance The variance that measures the effect of inefficient or efficient use of labor on variable overhead costs; the difference between standard hours in actual production and actual hours worked, priced at the variable overhead rate.

Variable Overhead Spending Variance The difference between actual variable costs incurred and the amount that the flexible budget allows for variable costs for the actual volume worked.

Variable Profit Ratio (See *Contribution Margin Ratio.*)

Variance The difference between actual results and planned results.

Volume Variance (See *Fixed Overhead Volume Variance.*)

Weighted-average Inventory A method of inventory costing where total dollars of goods available during the period are summed and divided by the total units available.

Work-in-Process Inventory The cost of uncompleted products still in the factory.

Working Capital The excess of current assets over current liabilities.

Zero-base Budgeting A planning and budgeting process used with program budgeting which requires a manager to justify the total amount requested for each funding request and to rank them in order of importance.

Appendix A

Present Value of \$1 $PV = (1 + r)^{-n} = \frac{1}{(1 + r)^n}$

Period	2%	4%	6%	8%	10%	12%	14%	16%	18%
1	.980	.962	.943	.926	.909	.893	.877	.862	.847
2	.961	.925	.890	.857	.826	.797	.769	.743	.718
3	.942	.889	.840	.794	.751	.712	.675	.641	.609
4	.924	.855	.792	.735	.683	.636	.592	.552	.516
5	.906	.822	.747	.681	.621	.567	.519	.476	.437
6	.888	.790	.705	.630	.564	.507	.456	.410	.370
7	.871	.760	.665	.583	.513	.452	.400	.354	.314
8	.853	.731	.627	.540	.467	.404	.351	.305	.266
9	.837	.703	.592	.500	.424	.361	.308	.263	.225
10	.820	.676	.558	.463	.386	.322	.270	.227	.191
11	.804	.650	.527	.429	.350	.287	.237	.195	.162
12	.788	.625	.497	.397	.319	.257	.208	.168	.137
13	.773	.601	.469	.368	.290	.229	.182	.145	.116
14	.758	.577	.442	.340	.263	.205	.160	.125	.099
15	.743	.555	.417	.315	.239	.183	.140	.108	.084
16	.728	.534	.394	.292	.218	.163	.123	.093	.071
17	.714	.513	.371	.270	.198	.146	.108	.080	.060
18	.700	.494	.350	.250	.180	.130	.095	.069	.051
19	.686	.475	.331	.232	.164	.116	.083	.060	.043
20	.673	.456	.312	.215	.149	.104	.073	.051	.037
21	.660	.439	.294	.199	.135	.093	.064	.044	.031
22	.647	.422	.278	.184	.123	.083	.056	.038	.026
23	.634	.406	.262	.170	.112	.074	.049	.033	.022
24	.622	.390	.247	.158	.102	.066	.043	.028	.019
25	.610	.375	.233	.146	.092	.059	.038	.024	.016
30	.552	.308	.174	.099	.057	.033	.020	.012	.007
35	.500	.253	.130	.068	.036	.019	.010	.006	.003
40	.453	.208	.097	.046	.022	.011	.005	.003	.001
45	.410	.171	.073	.031	.014	.006	.003	.001	.001
50	.372	.141	.054	.021	.009	.003	.001	.001	

20%	22%	24%	26%	28%	30%	35%	40%	45%	50%
.833	.820	.806	.794	.781	.769	.741	.714	.690	.667
.694	.672	.650	.630	.610	.592	.549	.510	.476	.444
.579	.551	.524	.500	.477	.455	.406	.364	.328	.296
.482	.451	.423	.397	.373	.350	.301	.260	.226	.198
.402	.370	.341	.315	.291	.269	.223	.186	.156	.132
.335	.303	.275	.250	.227	.207	.165	.133	.108	.088
.279	.249	.222	.198	.178	.159	.122	.095	.074	.059
.233	.204	.179	.157	.139	.123	.091	.068	.051	.039
.194	.167	.144	.125	.108	.094	.067	.048	.035	.026
.162	.137	.116	.099	.085	.073	.050	.035	.024	.017
.135	.112	.094	.079	.066	.056	.037	.025	.017	.012
.112	.092	.076	.062	.052	.043	.027	.018	.012	.008
.093	.075	.061	.050	.040	.033	.020	.013	.008	.005
.078	.062	.049	.039	.032	.025	.015	.009	.006	.003
.065	.051	.040	.031	.025	.020	.011	.006	.004	.002
.054	.042	.032	.025	.019	.015	.008	.005	.003	.002
.045	.034	.026	.020	.015	.012	.006	.003	.002	.001
.038	.028	.021	.016	.012	.009	.005	.002	.001	.001
.031	.023	.017	.012	.009	.007	.003	.002	.001	
.026	.019	.014	.010	.007	.005	.002	.001	.001	
.022	.015	.011	.008	.006	.004	.002	.001		
.018	.013	.009	.006	.004	.003	.001	.001		
.015	.010	.007	.005	.003	.002	.001			
.013	.008	.006	.004	.003	.002	.001			
.010	.007	.005	.003	.002	.001	.001			
.004	.003	.002	.001	.001					
.002	.001	.001							
.001									

Appendix B

Present Value of an Annuity of $1 $PV = \frac{1 - (1 + r)^{-n}}{r}$

Period	2%	4%	6%	8%	10%	12%	14%	16%	18%
1	0.980	0.962	0.943	0.926	0.909	0.893	0.877	0.862	0.847
2	1.942	1.886	1.833	1.783	1.736	1.690	1.647	1.605	1.566
3	2.884	2.775	2.673	2.577	2.486	2.402	2.322	2.246	2.174
4	3.808	3.630	3.465	3.312	3.170	3.037	2.914	2.798	2.690
5	4.713	4.452	4.212	3.993	3.791	3.605	3.433	3.274	3.127
6	5.601	5.242	4.917	4.623	4.355	4.111	3.889	3.685	3.498
7	6.472	6.002	5.582	5.206	4.868	4.564	4.288	4.039	3.812
8	7.325	6.733	6.210	5.747	5.335	4.968	4.639	4.344	4.078
9	8.162	7.435	6.802	6.247	5.759	5.328	4.946	4.607	4.303
10	8.983	8.111	7.360	6.710	6.145	5.650	5.216	4.833	4.494
11	9.787	8.760	7.887	7.139	6.495	5.938	5.453	5.029	4.656
12	10.575	9.385	8.384	7.536	6.814	6.194	5.660	5.197	4.793
13	11.348	9.986	8.853	7.904	7.103	6.424	5.842	5.342	4.910
14	12.106	10.563	9.295	8.244	7.367	6.628	6.002	5.468	5.008
15	12.849	11.118	9.712	8.559	7.606	6.811	6.142	5.575	5.092
16	13.578	11.652	10.106	8.851	7.824	6.974	6.265	5.668	5.162
17	14.292	12.166	10.477	9.122	8.022	7.120	6.373	5.749	5.222
18	14.992	12.659	10.828	9.372	8.201	7.250	6.467	5.818	5.273
19	15.678	13.134	11.158	9.604	8.365	7.366	6.550	5.877	5.316
20	16.351	13.590	11.470	9.818	8.514	7.469	6.623	5.929	5.353
21	17.011	14.029	11.764	10.017	8.649	7.562	6.687	5.973	5.384
22	17.658	14.451	12.042	10.201	8.772	7.645	6.743	6.011	5.410
23	18.292	14.857	12.303	10.371	8.883	7.718	6.792	6.044	5.432
24	18.914	15.247	12.550	10.529	8.985	7.784	6.835	6.073	5.451
25	19.523	15.622	12.783	10.675	9.077	7.843	6.873	6.097	5.467
30	22.396	17.292	13.765	11.258	9.427	8.055	7.003	6.177	5.517
35	24.999	18.665	14.498	11.655	9.644	8.176	7.070	6.215	5.539
40	27.355	19.793	15.046	11.925	9.779	8.244	7.105	6.233	5.548
45	29.490	20.720	15.456	12.108	9.863	8.283	7.123	6.242	5.552
50	31.424	21.482	15.762	12.233	9.915	8.304	7.133	6.246	5.554

20%	22%	24%	26%	28%	30%	35%	40%	45%	50%
0.833	0.820	0.806	0.794	0.781	0.769	0.741	0.714	0.690	0.667
1.528	1.492	1.457	1.424	1.392	1.361	1.289	1.224	1.165	1.111
2.106	2.042	1.981	1.923	1.868	1.816	1.696	1.589	1.493	1.407
2.589	2.494	2.404	2.320	2.241	2.166	1.997	1.849	1.720	1.605
2.991	2.864	2.745	2.635	2.532	2.436	2.220	2.035	1.876	1.737
3.326	3.167	3.020	2.885	2.759	2.643	2.385	2.168	1.983	1.824
3.605	3.416	3.242	3.083	2.937	2.802	2.508	2.263	2.057	1.883
3.837	3.619	3.421	3.241	3.076	2.925	2.598	2.331	2.109	1.922
4.031	3.786	3.566	3.366	3.184	3.019	2.665	2.379	2.144	1.948
4.192	3.923	3.682	3.465	3.269	3.092	2.715	2.414	2.168	1.965
4.327	4.035	3.776	3.543	3.335	3.147	2.752	2.438	2.185	1.977
4.439	4.127	3.851	3.606	3.387	3.190	2.779	2.456	2.196	1.985
4.533	4.203	3.912	3.656	3.427	3.223	2.799	2.469	2.204	1.990
4.611	4.265	3.962	3.695	3.459	3.249	2.814	2.478	2.210	1.993
4.675	4.315	4.001	3.726	3.483	3.268	2.825	2.484	2.214	1.995
4.730	4.357	4.033	3.751	3.503	3.283	2.834	2.489	2.216	1.997
4.775	4.391	4.059	3.771	3.518	3.295	2.840	2.492	2.218	1.998
4.812	4.419	4.080	3.786	3.529	3.304	2.844	2.494	2.219	1.999
4.843	4.442	4.097	3.799	3.539	3.311	2.848	2.496	2.220	1.999
4.870	4.460	4.110	3.808	3.546	3.316	2.850	2.497	2.221	1.999
4.891	4.476	4.121	3.816	3.551	3.320	2.852	2.498	2.221	2.000
4.909	4.488	4.130	3.822	3.556	3.323	2.853	2.498	2.222	2.000
4.925	4.499	4.137	3.827	3.559	3.325	2.854	2.499	2.222	2.000
4.937	4.507	4.143	3.831	3.562	3.327	2.855	2.499	2.222	2.000
4.948	4.514	4.147	3.834	3.564	3.329	2.856	2.499	2.222	2.000
4.979	4.534	4.160	3.842	3.569	3.332	2.857	2.500	2.222	2.000
4.992	4.541	4.164	3.845	3.571	3.333	2.857	2.500	2.222	2.000
4.997	4.544	4.166	3.846	3.571	3.333	2.857	2.500	2.222	2.000
4.999	4.545	4.166	3.846	3.571	3.333	2.857	2.500	2.222	2.000
4.999	4.545	4.167	3.846	3.571	3.333	2.857	2.500	2.222	2.000

Index